Mastering Mobile Network and Related Security

Protecting telecom networks in a connected world

Tiju Johnson

bpb

www.bpbonline.com

First Edition 2025

Copyright © BPB Publications, India

ISBN: 978-93-65897-746

LIMITS OF LIABILITY AND DISCLAIMER OF WARRANTY

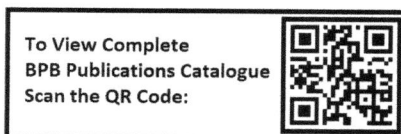

To View Complete
BPB Publications Catalogue
Scan the QR Code:

www.bpbonline.com

Dedicated to

To the two extraordinary women who raised me, thank you for believing in me when I didn't believe in myself. And to my wife and daughter, whose unwavering support and curiosity made this book possible.

About the Author

Tiju Johnson is a seasoned senior security architect with over twenty years of experience in the security field, with nearly a decade in securing telecommunications networks. He has specialized in designing and implementing robust security frameworks for both enterprise and service provider networks and has delivered solutions that address the most complex security challenges while ensuring alignment with industry standards and regulatory requirements. His strength lies in transforming high-level security strategies into actionable implementations that enhance organizational resilience against evolving cyber threats. This book represents the culmination of his hands-on experience and industry insights gained across a decade of securing telecom networks across the globe. He is currently working as a senior security solutions architect and has been part of white paper contributions with 5G Americas.

About the Reviewers

❖ **Balkrishna Patil** is a technology transformation manager with over 20 years of experience in IT infrastructure and cloud services. He assists clients in successfully executing digital transformation initiatives. With a proven ability to design and implement cloud migration strategies, manage complex IT projects, and provide expert technical guidance, he has dedicated himself to delivering cost-effective, innovative solutions that enhance business agility and resilience.

Balkrishna has led multimillion-dollar projects across diverse industries, including life sciences, oil and gas, education, and federal, state, and local public services. His expertise spans enterprise IT infrastructure, specializing in analyzing, designing, deploying, and supporting cloud and on-premises solutions. Additionally, he has provided strategic technical and functional guidance to business and application teams, ensuring seamless alignment with organizational goals.

Committed to continuous learning, Balkrishna holds several industry certifications, including AWS Certified Solutions Architect (professional and associate), Azure Cloud Practitioner, FinOps Practitioner, and VMware Certified Associate. His core competencies include AWS, Azure, hybrid cloud architecture, cybersecurity, and IT governance, enabling him to drive secure, scalable, and efficient cloud solutions for organizations navigating digital evolution.

❖ **Major Sumit Sharma** (*Retd.*) is a seasoned cybersecurity professional and Indian Army veteran, currently serving as Senior Manager - Cybersecurity at one of India's premier international airports. In this strategic role, he serves as deputy to the Chief Information Security Officer (CISO), where he leads governance, risk, and compliance (GRC) initiatives and drives both offensive and defensive cybersecurity strategies to protect critical infrastructure. His work ensures alignment of cyber risk with enterprise-wide frameworks, reinforcing stakeholder trust in the airport's digital resilience.

Previously, Sumit was a Senior Consultant at Deloitte, specializing in AWS architecture and third-party risk management. His distinguished 12-year tenure in the Indian Army saw him spearhead cutting-edge projects in AI/ML-based drone surveillance, cloud security, and automation for mission-critical operations.

Sumit holds an Executive Business Management certificate from IIM Indore, and is certified in ICS Cybersecurity, ISO 27001, AWS and Microsoft Azure certificates.

Acknowledgement

There are a few people I want to thank for the continued and ongoing support they have given me during the writing of this book. First and foremost, I would like to thank the two extraordinary women who raised me and supported me through thick and thin: my wife for keeping me away from easy streaming distractions, and my daughter for her patience during the many hours I spent writing instead of being with her.

I want to express my profound gratitude to the various telecom service provider projects I was fortunate to be part of during my tenure with Cisco Systems. These experiences not only shaped my understanding of the industry but also allowed me to contribute to nation-building efforts and positively impact millions of lives. I am equally indebted to Dr. Nadhem Al-Fardan, whose inspirational mentorship encouraged me to step beyond my comfort zone and make meaningful contributions to the security industry. Your guidance has been invaluable to both this work and my professional journey.

I would like to thank the team at BPB Publications for their support. I am grateful to all technical reviewers and editors for their helpful feedback and for accommodating the changes to chapter structures that differed from our original plan.

Preface

In an age where communication networks form the invisible infrastructure of our daily lives, the security of telecom service providers has never been more critical. From the earliest days of mobile technology to today's sophisticated 5G networks, telecommunications has undergone a remarkable evolution—one that has created unprecedented opportunities alongside complex security challenges.

This book was born from a simple observation: as telecom networks have evolved to be more powerful, they have also become more vulnerable, and there were very few resources covering the security considerations for this evolution. The systems that connect billions of people worldwide now present an expanded attack surface that spans physical hardware, virtualized infrastructure, cloud environments, and an increasingly software-defined ecosystem.

When the first generation of mobile networks emerged, security considerations were often secondary to functionality. The closed, proprietary nature of these early systems offered a form of security through obscurity. Today's networks, by contrast, are built on open standards, utilize commercial off-the-shelf hardware, and rely on software virtualization, creating a fundamentally different security paradigm that demands new approaches and methodologies.

Throughout these pages, we examine the full spectrum of telecom infrastructure, from the **radio access network (RAN)** to the transport networks to the **IP Multimedia Subsystem (IMS)**, from **Mobile Edge Computing (MEC)** to the core virtualization technologies that underpin modern networks. Rather than treating these as discrete components, we approach telecom security holistically, recognizing that vulnerabilities in one area inevitably affect others.

For security professionals, this book offers practical guidance on implementing robust security architectures across diverse telecom environments. Engineers will find detailed technical analyses of vulnerabilities and countermeasures specific to telecom systems. Students and those new to the field will discover a comprehensive introduction to the unique security challenges of telecom environments.

It is my hope that this book serves as both a warning and a guide, illuminating the risks while providing the knowledge needed to mitigate them. The security of telecom service providers is not merely a technical concern but a societal imperative. The networks we secure today will carry the communications, power the innovations, and connect the communities of tomorrow.

The journey through telecom security is complex and continuing. Let us embark on it together.

This book is divided into 17 chapters. They aim to cover the entire telecom components starting with the first generation of mobile networks and concluding with the fifth generation. The details are listed as follows.

Chapter 1: Global Security Standards and Evolution of Security in Mobility – The chapter explores how global security standards have shaped the evolution of mobility security from the earliest days of cellular networks to today's sophisticated 5G environments. The tracing of critical developments from the minimal security provisions in 1G systems to the comprehensive frameworks we now implement. Drawing from experiences working with major telecom providers, examining how standards bodies like 3GPP and GSMA have responded to emerging threats while balancing security with performance and interoperability.

Chapter 2: Generations of Mobile Networks and 1G – This chapter explores the evolution of mobile networks, focusing on the **first generation** (**1G**) that launched the cellular revolution in the 1980s. It examines how the early analog systems, while revolutionary for their time, were designed with minimal security considerations, lacking encryption and authentication mechanisms that we now consider fundamental. Through analyzing 1G's vulnerabilities, including susceptibility to eavesdropping and call interception, we establish a historical baseline that helps us understand how security requirements have evolved alongside network technologies.

Chapter 3: 2G and Enabled Services – This chapter explores the security landscape of 2G networks and their foundational services that continue to impact modern telecommunications. The chapter examines the vulnerabilities inherent in **Signaling System 7** (**SS7**), which, despite its age, remains a critical protocol underlying much of our global communications infrastructure. It also analyzes the security challenges of SMS services, revealing how these seemingly simple text messages created both revolutionary connectivity and persistent security gaps. Through many experiences implementing security measures across multiple carriers, the demonstration shows how these legacy systems continue to present significant risks even as we advance to newer technologies and provide practical approaches to mitigate these vulnerabilities without disrupting essential services.

Chapter 4: IP Multimedia Subsystem – This chapter explores the critical security considerations surrounding the **IP Multimedia Subsystem** (**IMS**), the architectural framework that has revolutionized how we deliver multimedia services across telecom networks. The chapter examines how IMS bridges traditional voice communications with IP-based services, creating both opportunities and vulnerabilities that security professionals must address. It also shares practical approaches to securing the various IMS components—from the session border controllers to the application servers—while maintaining the performance and flexibility that make IMS so valuable to modern telecom operations.

Chapter 5: Third Generation of Mobile Networks – This chapter examines the 3rd **generation of mobile networks** (**3G**), which marks a pivotal shift in telecom security architecture. It explores how the **universal mobile telecommunications system** (**UMTS**) implemented integrity protection for signaling messages, yet still contained security gaps that malicious actors could exploit. Through these experiences securing numerous 3G networks, the chapter also shares some practical approaches to mitigating these risks while maintaining the performance benefits that made 3G so transformative for mobile communications.

Chapter 6: 4G Mobile Networks – This chapter examines the security architecture of 4th Generation mobile networks, where the all-IP nature of LTE introduced both revolutionary capabilities and novel security challenges. It explores how the evolution from circuit-switched to packet-switched core networks fundamentally changed our approach to telecom security. In the implementation of 4G security frameworks across multiple operators, the chapter also analyzes the effectiveness of LTE's mutual authentication mechanisms, the vulnerabilities in inter-technology handovers, and the security implications of diameter signaling.

Chapter 7: 5G Mobile Networks – In this chapter, the readers will explore the revolutionary 5G ecosystem that has fundamentally transformed how we approach telecom security. It examines how 5G's software-defined architecture, network slicing capabilities, and distributed computing model create both unprecedented opportunities and complex security challenges. In the implementation of security frameworks for early 5G deployments, the chapter details the unique threat vectors targeting various 5G core components. It demonstrates why traditional perimeter-based security approaches fail in 5G networks and presents practical zero-trust implementations that have proven effective across multiple service provider environments.

Chapter 8: Private 5G – This chapter explores the rapidly evolving world of Private 5G networks and their unique security implications for enterprises and critical infrastructure. It examines how these dedicated cellular networks provide organizations with unprecedented control over their communications while introducing distinct security challenges compared to public networks. This chapter also presents frameworks for securing Private 5G deployments through specialized authentication protocols, physical security measures, and threat monitoring systems.

Chapter 9: Network Slicing and Related Security – This chapter explores the revolutionary concept of Network Slicing and its profound security implications for telecom providers. It discusses how this core 5G capability allows operators to create multiple virtual networks atop a shared physical infrastructure, each tailored to specific use cases with unique security requirements. It presents a comprehensive security framework addressing authentication, encryption, and monitoring specifically designed for multi-tenant slice environments. The security of network slicing is not merely a technical challenge; it is fundamental to delivering on 5G's promise of supporting critical services from autonomous vehicles to remote surgery.

Chapter 10: RAN and Transport Security – This chapter examines the critical domain of RAN and Transport Security, where the most vulnerable portions of our telecom infrastructure often reside. It will guide you through the evolution of security controls from physical site security to the complex cryptographic protocols protecting today's front haul and backhaul connections.

Chapter 11: Container Adoption in 5G Networks – In this chapter, the readers will know how container technology has revolutionized 5G network deployment, bringing unprecedented flexibility and scalability to telecom infrastructure. Through practical case studies, the chapter lists how secured containers can strengthen network isolation while enabling the agility demanded by modern telecom operations.

Chapter 12: Perimeter and Edge Security – The chapter examines the critical domain of perimeter and edge security—a fundamental yet increasingly complex aspect of telecom infrastructure protection. The traditional network perimeter has evolved dramatically with the advent of cloud computing, virtualization, and distributed architectures. It will also guide you through the essential strategies for securing these network boundaries, from next-generation firewalls to advanced traffic inspection techniques that protect the entry points to your telecom infrastructure.

Chapter 13: Identity and Access Management – This chapter explores the critical domain of Identity and Access Management within telecom environments—a cornerstone of the zero trust security approach. It also examines how proper authentication, authorization, and accounting mechanisms create the foundation for securing complex telecom infrastructure spanning from legacy systems to modern 5G networks. Drawing from my field experience, it demonstrates practical implementations of privileged access management, identity federation, and multi-factor authentication tailored specifically for telecom operators.

Chapter 14: Security Monitoring – This chapter explores the critical domain of Security Monitoring within telecom environments. It demonstrates how continuous surveillance forms the backbone of effective security posture, particularly in complex telecom infrastructures spanning from legacy 2G to modern 5G networks. Drawing from my experience implementing monitoring solutions across various telecom providers, it also presents frameworks for establishing security operations centers tailored to telecom-specific threats.

Chapter 15: Network Security Testing – This chapter explores the critical discipline of Network Security Testing in telecom environments. It has detailed how rigorous testing methodologies can uncover vulnerabilities before malicious actors exploit them. The chapter aims to transform security testing from a periodic compliance exercise into an integrated, continuous process that strengthens your network's resilience against evolving threats.

Chapter 16: Beyond 5G – The chapter explores the emerging security landscape that lies beyond 5G technology. As we venture into the realm of 6G networks and quantum communications. The chapter also explores the security challenges that exist are not merely theoretical—they represent real considerations that security professionals must begin planning for today, even as these technologies remain on the horizon.

Chapter 17: Securing Future Networks – This chapter reflects on the critical security insights gained through decades of telecom evolution. The chapter also discusses how security considerations have transformed from afterthoughts to foundational elements of network design, and shares the hard-won lessons that only come from navigating real-world threats and vulnerabilities. Looking ahead, it also explores the emerging security paradigms that will shape our industry as 6G technologies, quantum communications, and AI-driven defenses converge to create both new opportunities and challenges.

Code Bundle and Coloured Images

Please follow the link to download the
Code Bundle and the *Coloured Images* of the book:

https://rebrand.ly/fedhynh

The code bundle for the book is also hosted on GitHub at
https://github.com/bpbpublications/Mastering-Mobile-Network-and-Related-Security.
In case there's an update to the code, it will be updated on the existing GitHub repository.

We have code bundles from our rich catalogue of books and videos available at
https://github.com/bpbpublications. Check them out!

Errata

We take immense pride in our work at BPB Publications and follow best practices to ensure the accuracy of our content to provide with an indulging reading experience to our subscribers. Our readers are our mirrors, and we use their inputs to reflect and improve upon human errors, if any, that may have occurred during the publishing processes involved. To let us maintain the quality and help us reach out to any readers who might be having difficulties due to any unforeseen errors, please write to us at :

errata@bpbonline.com

Your support, suggestions and feedbacks are highly appreciated by the BPB Publications' Family.

Piracy

If you come across any illegal copies of our works in any form on the internet, we would be grateful if you would provide us with the location address or website name. Please contact us at **business@bpbonline.com** with a link to the material.

If you are interested in becoming an author

If there is a topic that you have expertise in, and you are interested in either writing or contributing to a book, please visit **www.bpbonline.com**. We have worked with thousands of developers and tech professionals, just like you, to help them share their insights with the global tech community. You can make a general application, apply for a specific hot topic that we are recruiting an author for, or submit your own idea.

Reviews

Please leave a review. Once you have read and used this book, why not leave a review on the site that you purchased it from? Potential readers can then see and use your unbiased opinion to make purchase decisions. We at BPB can understand what you think about our products, and our authors can see your feedback on their book. Thank you!

For more information about BPB, please visit **www.bpbonline.com**.

Join our book's Discord space

Join the book's Discord Workspace for Latest updates, Offers, Tech happenings around the world, New Release and Sessions with the Authors:

https://discord.bpbonline.com

Table of Contents

CHAPTER 1

Global Security Standards and Evolution of Security in Mobility

Introduction

This chapter delves into the intricate landscape of global security standards and the evolution of security practices in the mobile domain. We will explore the intricate interplay between technological advancements, regulatory frameworks, and the ongoing efforts to fortify our digital infrastructure against emerging cyber threats.

Firstly, we will examine the pivotal role of international organizations and regulatory bodies in developing and promoting security standards for mobile technologies. These standards serve as essential guidelines, ensuring a baseline level of security and interoperability across different platforms and regions.

Furthermore, we will trace the evolution of security measures in mobile devices, networks, and applications, shedding light on cutting-edge technologies and methodologies employed to safeguard mobile systems. From encryption and authentication protocols to secure communication channels and data protection mechanisms, this chapter will provide a comprehensive overview of the security landscape in mobility.

Structure

This chapter will cover the following topics:

- Global security standards

- 3rd Generation Partnership Project
- European Telecommunications Standards Institute
- International Telecommunication Union
- GSM Association
- National Institute of Standards and Technology
- Evolution of security in mobility
- Evolution of service provider network from 1G to 5G

Objectives

Through this comprehensive detailing of global security standards and the evolution of service provider networks, readers will gain a profound understanding of the challenges, solutions, and ongoing efforts to fortify our digital infrastructure, enabling secure and reliable mobile experiences for individuals, businesses, and societies worldwide.

Global security standards

Imagine a set of rules that everyone in a specific industry agrees on. These rules, called standards, guarantee that whatever products, systems, or services are made, they work well and follow the same guidelines. This ensures compatibility, meaning things fit together seamlessly, with safety, consistency, security, and high quality.

To create a new standard, different groups, such as companies that make things, phone carriers, regular people who use them, special interest groups, and even governments, all have to agree. This process guarantees that the final standard is based on the best practices, everyone involved approves, and experts have tested and verified it.

The standardization mechanisms ensure a baseline of best-practice solutions consensually agreed upon, tested, and verified by industry experts. Mobile network technology, from the early generation to the latest, has always evolved following these globally agreed-upon standards.

In the telecommunications industry, there are several global security standards forums and organizations that play critical roles in establishing and maintaining security standards.

3rd Generation Partnership Project

The **3rd Generation Partnership Project (3GPP)** is a global leader in mobile communications standardization. It is a collaborative effort driven by telecommunication associations (organizational partners) who work together to develop technical specifications for mobile technologies like 3G, 4G, and the ever-evolving 5G. These specifications ensure seamless connectivity and service interoperability between devices and networks from different vendors around the world.

At the heart of 3GPP are the **Technical Specification Groups (TSGs)**. These working groups are responsible for creating, approving, and maintaining the technical specifications and reports that define the blueprint for mobile communication systems.

A few crucial TSGs of 3GPP are listed in the following section, with details on their scope of work.

Technical Specification Group SA2

The **Technical Specification Group SA2 (TSG SA2)** is one of the most crucial groups within the 3GPP standardization organization. SA2 is responsible for the overall system architecture and high-level design of 3GPP-based mobile networks.

The primary focus of SA2 is to specify the core network architecture, defining the functional entities, interfaces, and protocols that enable the seamless operation and integration of the various components within the 3GPP ecosystem. This includes the specification of the **5G system (5GS)** architecture, which introduces a new, more flexible, and modular core network design compared to previous generations.

Some of the key areas that SA2 is responsible for include:

- **5G System architecture**: SA2 defines the core network architecture of the 5G system, including the functional entities such as the **Access and Mobility Management Function (AMF)**, **Session Management Function (SMF)**, and **User Plane Function (UPF)**, as well as the interfaces between them.

- **Network slicing**: SA2 specifies the network slicing concept, which allows for the creation of customized logical networks tailored to specific use cases, such as enhanced mobile broadband, ultra-reliable low-latency communications, and massive machine-type communications.

- **Mobility management**: SA2 defines the mobility management protocols and procedures, enabling seamless **User Equipment (UE)** mobility across different access technologies, such as **5G New Radio (NR)**, **Long Term Evolution (LTE)**, and Wi-Fi.

- **Session management**: SA2 is responsible for specifying the session management functions, including the establishment, modification, and release of user sessions, as well as the associated **quality of service (QoS)** parameters.

- **Policy and charging control**: SA2 oversees the policy and charging control framework, which allows for the enforcement of operator-defined policies and the accurate charging of subscriber services.

- **Security and privacy**: SA2 collaborates with other 3GPP groups, such as SA3, to ensure the security and privacy aspects of the core network architecture, protecting the confidentiality and integrity of user data and signaling.

Technical Specification Group SA3

The **Technical Specification Group SA3 (TSG SA3)** is responsible for defining the security and privacy-related aspects of 3GPP-based mobile networks. As one of the core technical groups within 3GPP, SA3 plays a vital role in ensuring the confidentiality, integrity, and availability of the cellular ecosystem. Their work ensures that mobile communications are protected from unauthorized access and that personal information remains confidential.

Some of the key areas that SA3 is responsible for include:

- **Security architecture and protocols**: SA3 specifies the overall security architecture of the 3GPP system, including the security protocols and mechanisms used for authentication, key agreement, and data protection. This includes the development of the **Authentication and Key Agreement (AKA)** protocols, which are essential for secure UE registration and connectivity.

- **Network access security**: SA3 defines the security measures for controlling access to the 3GPP network, such as the specification of the **Universal Subscriber Identity Module (SIM/USIM)**-based authentication procedures and the protection of the radio interface against eavesdropping and integrity attacks.

- **Application and service security**: SA3 is responsible for ensuring the security of the various applications and services running on top of the 3GPP network, including the specification of secure protocols for communication between the UE and application servers.

- **Privacy protection**: SA3 is tasked with defining the privacy-related aspects of the 3GPP system, ensuring the protection of user information and the minimization of personally identifiable data collected and processed by the network.

- **Security assurance**: SA3 oversees the development of security assurance specifications, which define the security requirements and testing procedures for 3GPP network elements and user equipment to ensure their compliance with the defined security standards.

- **Security management and monitoring**: SA3 specifies the security management and monitoring functions, enabling the detection and mitigation of security threats and attacks within the 3GPP network.

Radio Access Network

The TSG **radio access network (RAN)** is responsible for the development and specification of the radio access technologies that power cellular networks. This includes the 4G LTE and 5G NR standards, as well as the evolution of previous-generation radio access technologies.

The primary focus of the TSG RAN is to ensure the seamless and efficient operation of the radio interface, defining the protocols and mechanisms that enable UEs to connect and communicate with the cellular network.

Core Network and Terminals TSG

The **Core Network and Terminals** (**CT**) TSG is responsible for specifying the protocols and interfaces between the network elements and user equipment, ensuring the seamless integration of different components within the 3GPP architecture. The CT TSG's work includes the definition of signaling protocols for call and session management, as well as the specification of the protocols for user data transport, such as the **GPRS Tunneling Protocol** (**GTP**) and the **Session Initiation Protocol** (**SIP**). Additionally, the CT TSG oversees the standardization of terminal capabilities and features, ensuring that user devices can fully leverage the capabilities of the 3GPP network.

By working collaboratively, these TSGs, along with others within the 3GPP, play a pivotal role in shaping the future of mobile communications, guaranteeing a secure, reliable, and ever-evolving mobile experience for users worldwide. A couple of important 3GPP specifications for LTE and 5G include **TS 33.401** and **TS 33.501**.

ETSI

European Telecommunications Standards Institute (**ETSI**) is a non-profit organization that develops globally applicable standards for information and communication technologies, including telecommunications. It plays a crucial role in the service provider industry by establishing globally applicable **Information and Communication Technologies** (**ICT**) standards. ETSI brings together a diverse range of stakeholders, including service providers, network operators, manufacturers, and research institutions, to collaborate on developing and maintaining common standards. These standards encompass various aspects of telecommunications networks, services, and protocols, enabling interoperability, security, and quality assurance among different systems and technologies. Service providers heavily rely on ETSI standards to ensure seamless connectivity, roaming capabilities, and the delivery of reliable and secure services to their customers. ETSI's work extends across various domains, including mobile networks (2G, 3G, 4G, and 5G), fixed networks, broadcasting, internet protocols, cybersecurity, and emerging technologies like the **Internet of Things** (**IoT**) and **artificial intelligence** (**AI**). By adhering to ETSI's widely adopted standards, service providers can ensure compatibility, efficient resource utilization, and enhanced user experiences while maintaining regulatory compliance across different regions and countries.

It has several working groups dedicated to security-related standards and protocols for telecommunications, of which some are:

- **Security Algorithms Group** (**SAG**): SAG is a specialized group within ETSI that evaluates and recommends cryptographic algorithms for use in telecommunications security standards. They assess the strength and suitability of encryption algorithms for various applications, such as mobile networks, internet protocols, and cybersecurity.

- **Technical Committee on Cybersecurity (TC CYBER)**: This committee is responsible for developing standards and specifications related to cybersecurity, including areas such as network and information security, security algorithms, security protocols, security management, and security testing methodologies. They are also responsible for developing standards and specifications related to cybersecurity, including threat intelligence, incident response, and security management.

- **Network Function Virtualization (NFV) Security (SEC)**: This group addresses security considerations and requirements specific to NFV environments, including virtualized infrastructure and network functions. This group has played a significant role in developing standards for **Network Functions Virtualization (NFV)** and **Multi-access Edge Computing** (MEC), which are crucial for service providers in deploying virtualized network functions and edge computing capabilities.

- **Cybersecurity (CYBER)**: This group focuses on emerging technologies. The CYBER group actively addresses cybersecurity risks associated with emerging technologies like 5G networks and quantum computing. They release standards that ensure the security of these technologies throughout their lifecycles. ETSI fosters collaboration between industry leaders, governments, and academia within its CYBER group. This collaborative approach by the group ensures that the standards they develop are comprehensive, practical, and meet the needs of a globalized digital landscape. While established by the European Telecommunications Standards Institute, ETSI's CYBER standards hold significant weight globally. Many countries outside of Europe adopt these standards as a baseline for their own cybersecurity regulations.

- **LTE/SAE Security Working Group**: This working group addresses security aspects specific to 4G LTE and **System Architecture Evolution (SAE)** networks, such as authentication protocols, key management, and security architectures for LTE systems. Key standards developed by this group include TS 33.401 (security architecture), TS 33.402 (non-access-stratum security), and TS 35.201 (Specification of the 3GPP confidentiality and integrity algorithms).

- **5G Cybersecurity Working Group**: 5G Cybersecurity Working Group plays a critical role in shaping the secure future of 5G networks. This group comprises industry leaders, government representatives, and academic experts who collaboratively develop robust security standards and specifications tailored to the unique characteristics of 5G. Their focus areas include authentication and authorization, encryption, privacy, and security architecture. Authentication and authorization define secure methods for devices and users to gain access to the network, preventing unauthorized entry and ensuring only authorized entities can perform specific actions, while encryption standardizes strong encryption algorithms to protect the confidentiality and integrity of sensitive data transmitted across 5G networks. This includes securing user data, signaling information, and network control traffic. Privacy tasks of this working group involve developing mechanisms to safeguard user privacy by minimizing data collection and ensuring appropriate control over personal information. This aligns with regulations like GDPR and CCPA, while the security architectures part of the workgroup helps to design secure network architectures for 5G that incorporate best practices in network segmentation, access control, and vulnerability management. This includes addressing security considerations for new 5G functionalities like network slicing and edge computing.

These working groups collaborate with various stakeholders, including service providers, network operators, equipment manufacturers, and regulatory bodies, to ensure that security standards and protocols meet the evolving needs of the telecommunications industry.

International Telecommunication Union

The **International Telecommunication Union** (**ITU**), established in 1865 and making it the oldest UN agency, is a specialized body focused on ensuring the smooth operation and continued development of ICTs on a global scale. It acts as the central coordinator for telecommunication regulations and standards, fostering seamless interconnection between different networks and technologies. This includes defining technical specifications for mobile networks (like 5G), internet protocols, and cybersecurity measures to safeguard critical communication infrastructure. The ITU achieves this through a robust structure of working groups and study groups, where member states, industry leaders, and academics collaborate on everything from radio spectrum allocation to next-generation networks. Ultimately, the ITU plays a vital role in bridging the digital divide, promoting ICT development in underserved regions, and shaping the future of global communication. Some of the key ITU working groups and study groups related to security include:

- **ITU-T Study Group 17** (**SG17**): This specialized group addresses a wide range of security areas, encompassing cybersecurity, identity management, and the protection of **personally identifiable information** (**PII**). SG17 works collaboratively to develop international standards and recommendations that safeguard ICTs. These standards are instrumental in ensuring the security of networks, systems, and applications we rely on daily.

- **ITU-T Study Group 2** (**SG2**): This specialized group focuses on the operational aspects that underpin the smooth functioning of telecommunication services, networks, and performance. While not solely dedicated to security, SG2's work encompasses areas that directly impact information security. This includes standards for network management, service provisioning, and performance measurement, all of which play a critical role in building secure and resilient telecommunication infrastructure.

- **ITU-T Focus Group on Security**: The ITU-T Focus Group on Security plays a critical role in fostering international cooperation among governments, industries, and academia to develop globally recognized security standards and recommendations. These standards address emerging security challenges and technologies, ensuring the safety and resilience of ICTs that underpin our global digital infrastructure. The group stays ahead of the curve by identifying and analyzing security threats and vulnerabilities in ICTs. This proactive approach helps to mitigate risks before they become widespread problems. They develop technical reports and specifications that establish best practices for secure ICT deployment and operation. These standards provide a common ground for governments and industries to implement effective security measures. The focus group also keeps pace with the evolving technological landscape by studying the security implications of new technologies like AI and blockchain. Their recommendations ensure these technologies are implemented securely.

- **ITU-D Study Group 1**: This group plays a critical role in cultivating a conducive environment for the advancement of telecommunications and ICTs. This group tackles a broad range of policy and regulatory issues that underpin a healthy digital ecosystem. Promoting robust cybersecurity frameworks to safeguard critical infrastructure, protect consumer data, and build trust in digital services and developing efficient spectrum allocation strategies to ensure sufficient radio frequencies are available for mobile broadband, satellite communications, and other emerging technologies is one of their focus area are some of the focus areas of this group events.

GSM Association

The **Groupe Speciale Mobile Association (GSMA)**, founded in 1995, is a powerful industry association that goes beyond simply representing **mobile network operators (MNOs)** worldwide. It acts as a key driver for innovation and progress in the mobile ecosystem. One crucial area of focus is security. The GSMA boasts several working groups dedicated to mobile telecommunications security. These groups tackle a wide range of challenges, from developing robust authentication protocols to combating emerging threats like mobile fraud and SIM swapping. Their recommendations and security guidelines play a vital role in ensuring the safety and integrity of mobile networks for MNOs and, ultimately, mobile phone users around the globe. Some of these working groups include:

- **Fraud and Security Group (FASG)**: The GSMA's FASG acts as a central hub for the mobile industry to combat fraud and security threats. FASG goes beyond just detection, prevention, and mitigation strategies. They actively assess the evolving threat landscape, analyzing risks to mobile operators and their customers. This allows them to define and prioritize industry-wide solutions. FASG fosters collaboration by providing a platform for secure intelligence and incident sharing amongst its members. They also play a key role in specifying technical safeguards and security protocols, promoting their adoption by network operators and suppliers. This collaborative approach strengthens the entire mobile ecosystem, ensuring a more secure and trusted environment for all.

- **Device Security Group (DSG)**: The GSMA's DSG serves as a central collaborative forum for mobile **operators, device manufacturers (OEMs)**, chipset vendors, and other industry stakeholders to address the evolving security landscape of mobile devices. They tackle issues pertaining to device authentication and authorization, which include initiatives to ensure the legitimacy of devices on mobile networks and prevent unauthorized access and potential fraud. The DSG also focuses on fortifying the device boot process and safeguarding against malware tampering before the operating system even loads. The group works on promoting secure software development lifecycles, timely patching of vulnerabilities, and encouraging longer software update lifespans for mobile devices. The DSG addresses the unique security challenges of IoT devices, promoting baseline security standards and interoperable communication protocols.

- **Identity Management Group (IDM)**: The GSMA IDM plays a critical role in safeguarding user privacy and data integrity within mobile ecosystems by addressing a comprehensive range of topics around secure mobile network identities and authentication. The IDM tackles fortifying SIM card security by defining standards and best practices to prevent unauthorized access and cyberattacks. This includes initiatives like the development of **embedded Universal Integrated Circuit Card (eUICC)** standards, which offer a more secure alternative to traditional SIM cards. They focus on developing robust authentication protocols that ensure secure and reliable user verification for accessing mobile network services. Examples include **two-factor authentication (2FA)** and Mobile Connect, a GSMA standard that allows users to log in to apps and websites with their mobile phone number instead of creating separate accounts and passwords. The IDM explores and implements advanced identity verification mechanisms to combat fraud and enhance user confidence in mobile transactions. This encompasses initiatives like the **Mobile Subscriber Identity Module (MSIM)** for secure and privacy-preserving identification of users on mobile networks.

- **Privacy Working Group**: The GSMA's Privacy Working Group tackles privacy issues head-on, ensuring user data is handled responsibly within mobile networks. Their focus extends beyond just security to encompass the entire lifecycle of user data. The working group establishes guidelines for how mobile operators gather user information, ensuring it is limited to what is necessary for service provision and obtained with transparent consent. The group addresses how user data is used within the mobile ecosystem. They promote anonymization techniques and user control mechanisms, empowering individuals to decide how their data is leveraged.

National Institute of Standards and Technology

The **National Institute of Standards and Technology** (**NIST**), a non-regulatory agency within the *U.S. Department of Commerce*, plays a vital role in telecommunication security by creating non-mandatory standards and best practices. While there is no dedicated NIST working group solely focused on telecom security, several groups working on cybersecurity issues publish resources applicable to the telecommunications industry. These resources can guide telecommunication service providers, equipment manufacturers, and users in implementing appropriate security measures. *NIST's Special Publication (SP) 800 Series*, for instance, covers a range of cybersecurity topics highly relevant to telecommunications, such as secure software development, cryptographic key management, and securing information systems. Some of the prominent working groups of NIST are:

- **Cybersecurity Framework (CSF) Working Group**: The CSF Working Group is a collaborative effort led by NIST to develop and maintain the cybersecurity framework. This voluntary framework provides a set of industry-agnostic best practices for organizations to improve their cybersecurity posture. It helps organizations identify, prioritize, and mitigate cybersecurity risks by offering a prioritized, structured approach. The CSF is not a one-size-fits-all solution but rather a flexible framework that can be customized to fit the specific needs of any organization, regardless of size or industry.

- **IoT Security Working Group**: NIST IoT Cybersecurity Program recognizes the surge in IoT devices and their critical role in telecommunication networks. This program functions as a collaborative effort between NIST, industry leaders, government agencies, academia, and consumer organizations. Their primary focus is on developing robust cybersecurity frameworks, best practices, and implementation guidance to ensure the security of IoT devices, networks, and the data they transmit.

- **Wireless and Mobile Communication Security Working Group**: NIST plays a vital role in ensuring the security of wireless and mobile communication technologies. The **Mobile Communication Security Working Group** (**WMCSWG**), a working group under NIST, is the main group delivering this responsibility. The WMCSWG is a collaborative effort between industry, government, and academia to develop standards and guidelines for securing wireless networks, mobile devices, base stations, and core networks. These standards and guidelines address various security aspects like authentication and authorization, encryption, key management, vulnerability assessment, and mitigation.

- **Identity and Access Management (IAM) Working Group**: IAM is a fundamental cybersecurity pillar for telecommunication networks, ensuring that only authorized users can access sensitive data and functionalities. The IAM Working Group plays a crucial role in bolstering telecommunication security by developing standards and guidelines for managing user identities, access controls, and authentication mechanisms specific to the industry's needs. The IAM working group establishes guidelines for securely adding and removing user accounts within a telecommunication network. This ensures authorized access for legitimate users while preventing unauthorized access attempts. The IAM working group also promotes the adoption of **multi-factor authentication** (**MFA**) to add an extra layer of security beyond traditional passwords. MFA requires users to provide additional verification factors, such as a one-time code from a mobile device, to access sensitive data or functionalities.

- **Secure Voice over Internet Protocol (VoIP) Working Group**: This group comprises VoIP security experts from industry, government, and academia. Their primary focus is on developing a robust framework of security recommendations and best practices specifically tailored to secure VoIP deployments. These recommendations address various security aspects, including encryption protocols, authentication methods, and secure call routing. By implementing these guidelines, organizations can significantly enhance the security of their VoIP infrastructure and mitigate the risks of eavesdropping, call tampering, and unauthorized access.

- **Cloud Computing Security Working Group**: The Cloud Computing Security Working Group tackles the evolving security landscape as telecommunication services shift to cloud-based platforms. By aligning with NIST's guidelines, the Cloud Computing Security Working Group ensures that security measures for data protection, access control, and secure deployment models are up-to-date and address the latest cloud security threats. This collaborative effort fosters a more secure cloud computing environment for telecommunication services. NIST has developed a series of SP focused on cloud computing security, including SP 500-299, which outlines the **NIST Cloud Computing Security Reference Architecture** (**NCC-SRA**). This framework offers guidance on implementing a core set of security components to safeguard cloud ecosystems. NIST also established the **Multi-Cloud Security Public Working Group** (**MCSPWG**) to address the specific security challenges that arise in complex cloud environments involving multiple cloud service providers.

- **Critical Infrastructure Protection (CIP) Working Group**: The CIP Working Group plays a vital role in safeguarding a nation's critical infrastructure. Recognizing telecommunication networks as a cornerstone of this infrastructure, the CIP Working Group dedicates its efforts to developing robust strategies and guidelines. These guidelines aim to shield telecommunication systems from cyberattacks and guarantee their resilience in the face of evolving threats. NIST's CIP Working Group fosters collaboration among industry stakeholders to implement best practices, creates risk management frameworks, and spearheads the development of secure communication protocols. Through these endeavors, the NIST CIP Working Group is instrumental in ensuring the continued reliability and security of our critical telecommunication infrastructure.

The following is a tabular representation of all the above-mentioned global bodies, along with their focus area, roles, and sample activities:

Organization	Focus area	Role	Example activities
3GPP	Mobile telephony standards (GSM, LTE, 5G)	Develops technical specifications for mobile networks	Defines protocols for network access, radio interface, core network
ETSI	ICT standards in Europe	Creates technical standards for a wide range of ICT products and services	Defines standards for mobile networks (competing with 3GPP), radio spectrum usage, broadcasting
ITU	Global telecommunication policy and regulation	Sets international standards for telecommunications and radio spectrum allocation	Develops recommendations for internet protocols, security frameworks
GSMA	Mobile industry interests	Represents the interests of mobile network operators worldwide	Publishes guidelines for network security (NESAS with 3GPP)
NIST (US)	IT standards and guidelines (not global)	Develops cybersecurity frameworks and best practices	Publishes recommendations for 5G network security

Table 1.1: Global security standards

Evolution of security in mobility

Cellular networks have come a long way since their introduction in the 1980s. Initially, their focus was on secure voice communication, enabling the first mobile phones. As adoption exploded globally, functionalities expanded rapidly. Now, cellular networks not only support crystal-clear voice calls but also high-speed data transfer. This has revolutionized mobility, allowing for multiple use cases and further adoptions like:

- **Remote medical procedures**: With secure and reliable data transmission, cellular networks enable real-time consultations and even remote surgeries using advanced robotics.

- **Rise of autonomous vehicles**: The massive data exchange required for autonomous vehicles to navigate, communicate, and react to their environment relies heavily on secure cellular networks.

- **Mobile revolution**: From online banking and shopping to video conferencing and entertainment streaming, cellular networks have become the backbone of a truly mobile and interconnected society.

However, alongside this growth, security concerns have evolved as well. To secure a network, it needs to comply with a few fundamental security requirements that form the basic pillars of a secure network. These are:

- **Data confidentiality**: A cornerstone of modern mobility security, it ensures sensitive information remains encrypted and shielded from unauthorized access during transmission. This principle has become increasingly crucial as connectivity has soared in vehicles and mobile devices. Early mobility security primarily focused on physical security measures like car locks and alarms. However, the rise of connected vehicles and the integration of smartphones with transportation systems introduced a new attack surface for cybersecurity. Data encryption protects much of the information collected by these systems, including location data, financial details used for in-car payments, and even biometric data for driver identification.

- **User and data authentication and integrity**: In the early days, with basic phone lines and telegrams, user authentication relied on simple voice recognition or pre-arranged codes. Data authentication involved checksums and basic error-detection methods. However, the rise of digital communications and the internet introduced a new era of security threats. Interception, data tampering, and impersonation became real possibilities. To address these growing concerns, robust user and data authentication mechanisms emerged. Passwords, MFA with tokens or biometrics, and digital certificates using **public key infrastructure** (**PKI**) became standard practices. These methods ensure that only authorized users can access communication channels and resources. Similarly, encryption techniques like **Secure Sockets Layer** (**SSL**) and its successor, **Transport Layer Security** (**TLS**), became crucial for data integrity and origin authentication. These methods encrypt data during transmission, making it unreadable to anyone who intercepts it. Additionally, digital signatures using cryptography verify the sender's identity and ensure the message has not been altered in transit.

- **Availability**: Throughout the evolution of telecommunications, ensuring resources are accessible and not disrupted by malicious actors has been a paramount concern. Early analog phone systems had limited vulnerabilities, but with the shift to digital networks and the rise of the internet, threats like denial-of-service attacks emerged. To combat this, telecom providers have implemented robust network security measures, including firewalls, intrusion detection systems, and redundancy protocols. These advancements not only protect user access but also safeguard the critical infrastructure that underpins our interconnected world.

- **Non-repudiation**: This security service ensures that neither party involved in a communication can deny sending or receiving a message. This concept has become increasingly important with the rise of digital communications. Early telephony lacked any form of non-repudiation, making it difficult to prove who initiated a call or the content discussed. The evolution of technologies like digital signatures and tamper-evident message logs within secure protocols addressed this gap. These advancements provide a verifiable record of communication, crucial for legal and business purposes in today's digital world.

- **Access control**: Access control has been a cornerstone of telecommunications security since its inception. Early analog systems relied on physical limitations, like locked rooms or designated operators, to restrict access to critical infrastructure. As technology evolved, access control mechanisms became more sophisticated. Digital networks introduced password authentication, a significant leap forward. However, the rise of the internet and mobile communication opened new vulnerabilities. Modern access control leverages a multi-layered approach, including firewalls, encryption protocols, and MFA, to secure networks and user identities. This continuous evolution ensures that only authorized devices, users, and applications can access telecommunications resources, protecting sensitive data and critical infrastructure.

The latest market trends highlight advancements in global security standards and service provider networks. Key developments include the rise of **Zero Trust Architecture** (**ZTA**) to limit network breaches, AI and ML for proactive threat detection, and blockchain to enhance transaction security and IoT integrity. In service provider networks, 5G security focuses on mitigating new threats with advanced encryption, while private 5G networks offer tailored security for critical sectors. **Software-defined networking** (**SDN**) and **network function virtualization** (**NFV**) modernize security management. Challenges include IoT vulnerabilities, evolving ransomware, and cloud security concerns, prompting stricter standards and improved incident responses. Regulatory compliance, cybersecurity education, and innovations like quantum cryptography address global security needs. These efforts aim to build secure, scalable digital ecosystems.

Evolution of service provider network from 1G to 5G

The **first generation** (**1G**) of cellular networks, introduced in the 1980s, laid the foundation for mobile communication. This network generation, designated by the G in xG, relied on analog modulation, limiting their capabilities to basic voice calls at speeds of around 9.5 kbps. Security in 1G was practically non-existent. Calls were transmitted unencrypted, making them susceptible to eavesdropping. Additionally, the analog nature of 1G resulted in inefficient spectrum usage, limiting network capacity and hindering future growth.

2G introduced the concept of digital modulation, which meant that voice was converted into digital code and then into analog (radio) signals to overcome a few of the 1G limitations. 2G, too, was predominantly used only for voice, but in its later stages, data services over 2G were introduced. 2G has multiple security limitations. It uses weak encryption between the subscriber handset and the tower. There is no authentication of the tower to the handset, which allows a malicious user to impersonate a real 2G tower. Subscriber privacy was not considered as part of the design, and hence, multiple agencies are able to intercept mobile data traffic and user locations. In the 2G GSM network architecture, two security procedures, authentication and encryption, are considered in different nodes of the architecture. *Figure 1.1* shows the various components of a 2G network architecture.

For 2G authentication, the **Authentication Center (AuC)** residing in the **Home Location Register (HLR)** plays a major role. The AuC stores a unique 128-bit secret key (Ki) for each subscriber. This Ki key serves as a counterpart to a similar key (Ki') programmed onto the **Subscriber Identity Module (SIM)** card in the user's mobile device. However, it is important to note that 2G security relies on algorithms like A5/1 and A5/2 for encryption, which have been demonstrably vulnerable to cracking by sophisticated attackers in recent years.

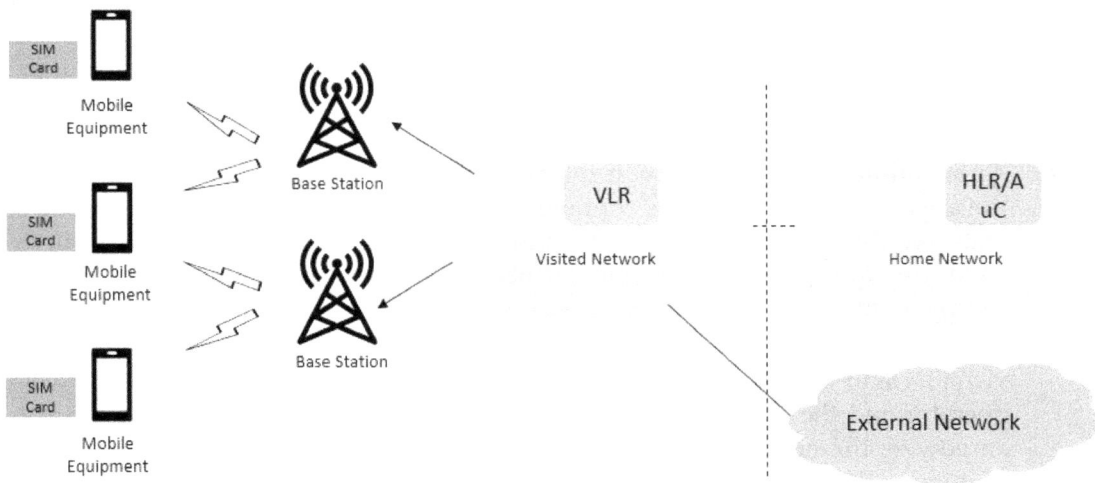

Figure 1.1: *2G GSM security components*

During the development of the 3rd Generation system, ETSI took the opportunity to review security in existing mobile systems and to develop a new security architecture to be used in UMTS. This formed the base of the 3GPP Release 99 deployment of 3G systems. Security in 3G systems revolved around a few basic considerations:

- Integrity protection of signaling messages
- SIM-based authentication
- Data integrity on the air interface
- Confidentiality of user traffic on the air interface
- Confidentiality of user identity on the air interface
- 3G authentication and key agreement

In 3GPP TS 33.102 Release 99, a 3G security architecture (*Figure 1.2*) was defined, in which five security feature groups are defined. Each of these feature groups meets certain threats and accomplishes certain security objectives, as defined in 3GPP:

1. **Network access security**: It refers to the set of security features that provide users with secure access to 3G services and which protect against attacks on the (radio) access link. These security features are implemented through the use of security protocols, algorithms, and mechanisms, such as the AKA protocol, ciphering and integrity protection, and the secure storage and handling of security credentials.

2. **Network domain security**: It refers to the set of security features that enable nodes in the core network to securely exchange signaling data and protect against attacks on the wireline network. Its main goal is to protect the 3G core network infrastructure and the critical signaling communications between network elements, ensuring the overall security and integrity of the 3G system.

3. **User domain security**: It refers to the security features that protect the access to the UE and the storage of sensitive information within the UE. By implementing user domain security features, the 3G security architecture aims to protect the user's device, credentials, and sensitive information from various threats, such as theft, unauthorized access, and malware attacks.

4. **Application domain security**: It refers to the set of security features that protect the applications and services running on top of the 3G network. By using these features, the 3G security architecture aims to provide a secure and trusted environment for the deployment and use of 3G-based applications and services, complementing the security features at the network and user equipment levels.

5. **Visibility and configurability of security**: It refers to the set of features that provide visibility and control over the various security mechanisms to both the network operator and the user. Using these security features, the 3G security architecture empowers the network operator and the user to actively monitor, manage, and customize the security controls to meet their specific security requirements and preferences.

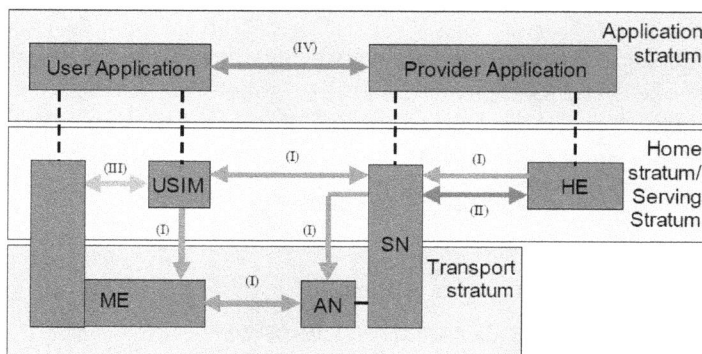

Figure 1.2: *Overview of 3G security architecture*
Source: *3GPP TS 33.102 version 3.6.0 Release 1999*[1]

---

1   https://www.etsi.org/deliver/etsi_ts/133100_133199/133102/03.06.00_60/ts_133102v030600p.pdf

3G networks address the security limitations of their predecessors, 2G, by implementing a layered security architecture. This enhanced protection combats various threats like eavesdropping, impersonation, and data breaches. This layered approach included the introduction of mutual authentication and encryption methods, as detailed in the following:

- **Mutual authentication**: Unlike 2G, 3G utilizes an extension of the GSM AKA protocol to achieve mutual authentication. This ensures both the user's device (UE) and the network verify each other's identities, preventing unauthorized access from rogue base stations.

- **Encryption algorithms**: 3G employs a robust combination of encryption methods to safeguard data during transmission.

- **KASUMI**: This 128-bit block cipher forms the core of 3G security and is also known as the A5/3 algorithm in newer GSM systems. KASUMI utilizes an eight-round Feistel network with subkeys derived from the main key for enhanced protection.

- **SNOW3G**: This stream cipher leverages two components: a **Linear Feedback Shift Register** (**LFSR**) and a **Finite State Machine** (**FSM**). Its 128-bit key and initialization vector create a dynamic encryption stream for continuous data protection.

- **Rijndael Cipher**: The most recent addition, the Rijndael cipher, serves as a block cipher based on the **Advanced Encryption Standard** (**AES**). The set of algorithms utilizes a 128-bit key alongside user data for encryption with Rijndael.

This layered approach with multiple encryption algorithms provides greater security flexibility compared to 2G. Additionally, 3G networks incorporate mechanisms for data integrity verification, ensuring data has not been tampered with during transmission.

4G network works based on TCP/IP network architecture. Since IP is the most favorable option for networking and data communication, 4G is less expensive than the devices of the previous generation. This makes 4G technology available and accessible to all types of network vendors. Thus, this makes 4G susceptible to a lot more security risks and thus also increases the threat landscape. 4G is prone to more security-related problems and threats due to this open environment when compared with earlier wireless technologies, which use a closed environment. An overview of 4G security architecture is shown in *Figure 1.3*.

3GPP TS 33.401 has documented the security requirements of LTE, which revolve around:

- User-to-network security
- Security visibility and configurability
- Security requirements on eNodeB

It also defines the security architecture for 4G, with a minor update to the existing 3G security architecture.

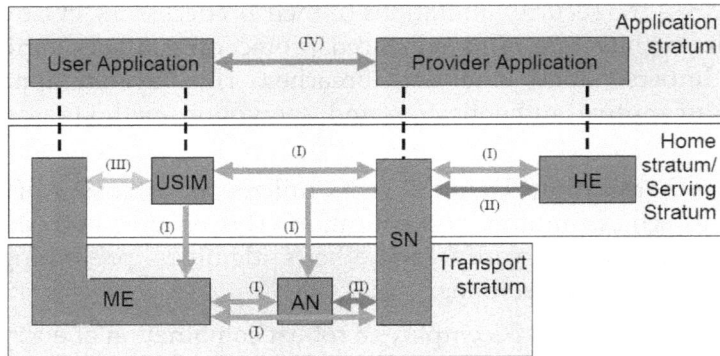

Figure 1.3: *Overview of 4G security architecture*
Source: *3GPP TS 33.401*[2]

4G LTE networks prioritize secure communication through robust authentication and encryption mechanisms. The **Mobility Management Entity (MME)** acts as the gatekeeper, initiating the process when a subscriber first connects. The eNodeB (LTE base transceiver station) relays authentication information between the mobile device and the MME via the secure S1 interface. This information is then verified against the **Home Subscriber Server (HSS)**, which holds subscriber credentials similar to the HLR in older GSM and UMTS networks.

To safeguard data confidentiality and integrity, the HSS dynamically generates unique encryption keys for each session. These keys are securely delivered to the eNodeB to encrypt communication between the device and the network. This multi-layered approach prevents eavesdropping and ensures data remains unaltered during transmission.

4G LTE utilizes a suite of cryptographic algorithms to achieve this secure communication, including the EPS Integrity Algorithm (eia1, eia2, etc.) and the **EPS Encryption Algorithm (EEA)**. While EEA1/EIA1 share similarities with UMTS's SNOW3G algorithm, 4G offers more advanced options for enhanced security. These algorithms are constantly evaluated and improved by industry standards bodies to stay ahead of evolving threats.

In addition to these core functionalities, 4G security extends to other areas like user privacy and network integrity. Measures are in place to prevent unauthorized access to user location data and protect against denial-of-service attacks that could disrupt network operations.

Another addition to the world of telecommunication was the introduction of **embedded SIM (eSIM)** during the 4G era. First commercially deployed in 2012 for automotive applications, eSIM gradually expanded its presence in consumer devices, with a notable milestone being its integration into the Apple Watch Series 3 in 2017. This innovation eliminated the need for physical SIM cards by embedding the SIM functionality directly into the device's hardware, streamlining the process of switching between mobile carriers and managing multiple mobile subscriptions.

---

2   https://www.etsi.org/deliver/etsi_ts/133400_133499/133401/15.07.00_60/ts_133401v150700p.pdf

5G is the fifth generation of mobile technology that brings along with it greater speed, enabling more data capacity; lower latency, which translates to more critical communications and responsiveness; and connectivity to a lot more devices for massive IoT use cases. To achieve this, 5G should be capable of delivering multi-network slicing, multi-level services, and multi-connectivity. To achieve the required flexibility, agility, and scale, 5G solutions will be delivered via virtual and/or containerized environments that may be hosted in private, public, or hybrid cloud environments.

Out of the box, 5G has designed security controls to mitigate a few of the risks and threats that were dominant in the earlier versions, 2G/3G/4G. As most service providers are developing solutions to cater to 5G requirements, support for different access networks, including 2G, 3G, and 4G, is on the cards. This means that 5G will mostly inherit the security challenges of previous generations.

Within 3GPP, the SA3 working group is responsible for security and privacy architectures and protocols. It defines the security architecture:

- The security features and the security mechanisms for the 5G system and the 5G core.

- The security procedures are performed within the 5G system, including the 5G core and the 5G NR.

The SA working group has also updated the security architecture, which is defined for 4G, to cater to 5G requirements. 5G security architecture consists of the transport stratum, serving stratum, home stratum, and application stratum, which are isolated from each other. These are discussed as follows:

- **Transport stratum**: The transport stratum has low-security sensitivity. It consists of some UE functions, all gNodeB functions, and some core network functions, such as the **User Plane Function** (**UPF**). These functions, excluding the UE functions, do not involve sensitive data, such as **Subscription Permanent Identifiers** (**SUPIs**) and user root keys.

- **Serving stratum**: This stratum has relatively high-security sensitivity than the Transport stratum and includes core network functions of the operator's home network such as the **Access and Mobility Management Function** (**AMF**), **Network Repository Function** (**NRF**), **Security Edge Protection Proxy** (**SEPP**), and **Network Exposure Function** (**NEF**). The core network functions of this stratum manage only mid-level derived keys (such as AMF keys) in the key hierarchy.

- **Home stratum**: It has high-security sensitivity and includes the **Authentication Server Function** (**AUSF**) and **Unified Data Management** (**UDM**) of the operator's home network, as well as the USIM in the UE, and therefore it contains sensitive data such as the SUPIs, user root keys, and high-level keys. This stratum does not involve gNodeBs or other functions of the core network.

- **Application stratum**: The application stratum involves 5G applications that need E2E security assurance for services that require high security in addition to transport security.

The following figure gives an overview of the 5G security architecture:

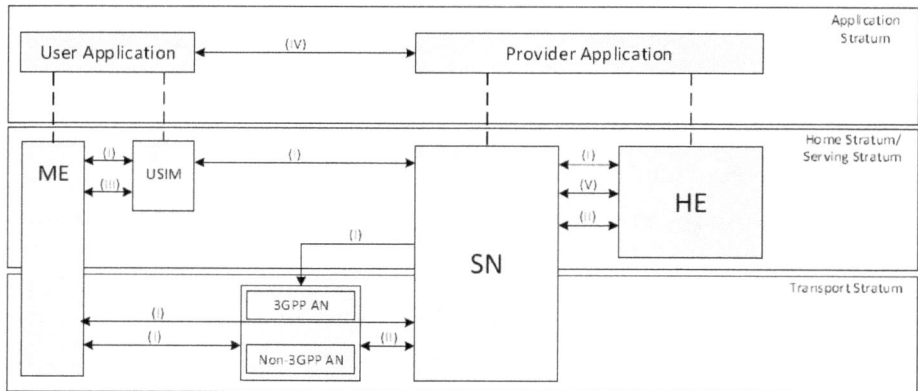

Figure 1.4: Overview of 5G security architecture
Source: 3GPP TS 33.501[3]

The above figure illustrates the following security domains, as defined in 3GPP TS 33.501. The security domains that have been mentioned in the 3GPP TS 33.501 are as follows:

1. **Network access security**: It refers to the set of security features that provide secure access to 5G services and protect against attacks on the radio access link. This feature ensures the secure authentication of the UE to the 5G network, along with establishing a secure context between the UE and the 5G network, including the negotiation of security algorithms and the derivation of cryptographic keys. User identity and location privacy features ensure the privacy of the user's permanent identity (for example, SUPI) by using a temporary identity (GUTI) for signaling over the radio interface.

2. **Network domain security**: It refers to the set of security features that enable network nodes to securely exchange signaling data and user plane data. This feature ensures the secure authentication of the different network elements (for example, gNodeBs, AMF, SMF) before they can communicate and exchange sensitive information. Network domain security also defines the mechanisms for the secure generation, distribution, and management of the cryptographic keys used to protect the signaling interfaces between network elements.

3. **User domain security**: It refers to the set of security features that secure the user access to the UE and the storage of sensitive information within the UE. This feature ensures the secure storage and processing of the user's authentication and encryption keys. By implementing user domain security features, the 5G security architecture aims to protect the user's device, credentials, and sensitive information from various threats, such as theft, unauthorized access, and malware attacks, complementing the network access security and network domain security measures.

---

3   https://www.3gpp.org/dynareport/33501.htm

4. **Application domain security**: It refers to the set of security features that enable applications in the 5G networks to exchange messages securely. These security features aim to provide a secure and trusted environment for the deployment and use of 5G-based applications and services, complementing the security features at the network and user equipment levels.

5. **SBA domain security**: It refers to the set of security features that enable **Network Functions (NFs)** of the Service-based architecture to securely communicate within the serving network domain and with other network domains. Such features include network function registration, discovery, and authorization security aspects, as well as protection for the service-based interfaces. It also involves the use of secure protocols, such as HTTP/2 over TLS, to protect the data exchanged between the NFs. It defines the mechanisms for the secure generation, distribution, and management of the cryptographic keys used to protect the service-based interfaces and interactions.

6. **Visibility and configurability of security**: It refers to the set of features that provide visibility and control over the various security mechanisms to both the network operator and the user. Using these security features, the 3G security architecture empowers the network operator and the user to actively monitor, manage, and customize the security controls to meet their specific security requirements and preferences.

Note: The visibility and configurability of security is not shown in the figure.

The 3GPP addresses the need for robust user authentication in 5G with two primary authentication protocols: 5G-AKA and **Extensible Authentication Protocol (EAP)**-AKA. These protocols establish secure connections between a UE, like your smartphone, and its home network.

5G-AKA builds upon and improves the existing **Evolved Packet System (EPS)**-AKA protocol used in 4G networks. It strengthens authentication and key exchange while introducing **Subscriber Concealed Unique Identity (SUCI)** to shield user privacy. However, 5G-AKA inherits some of the vulnerabilities present in EPS-AKA. To address this and future-proof authentication, 3GPP has defined a **service-based architecture (SBA)** for the 5G core network. This architecture introduces new network entities and services that support a unified authentication framework. This framework allows the 5G-AKA procedure to function seamlessly in both open and access-network agnostic environments, using a wider range of defined authentication methods. This flexibility strengthens overall network security by accommodating diverse future applications and network configurations.

Figure 1.5 shows the various network functions that are relevant for authentication in a 5G network:

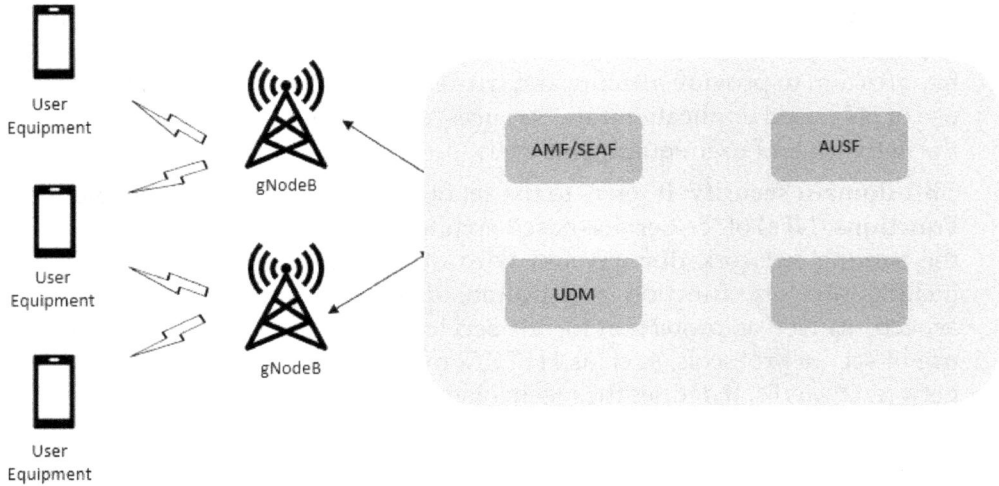

Figure 1.5: *5G core functions relevant for authentication*

So, as we can infer from the above details, there has been a gradual improvement in security considerations, and mobile network security has evolved significantly over the years to address various security challenges and threats. The following figure shows a high-level evolution of security in mobile networks:

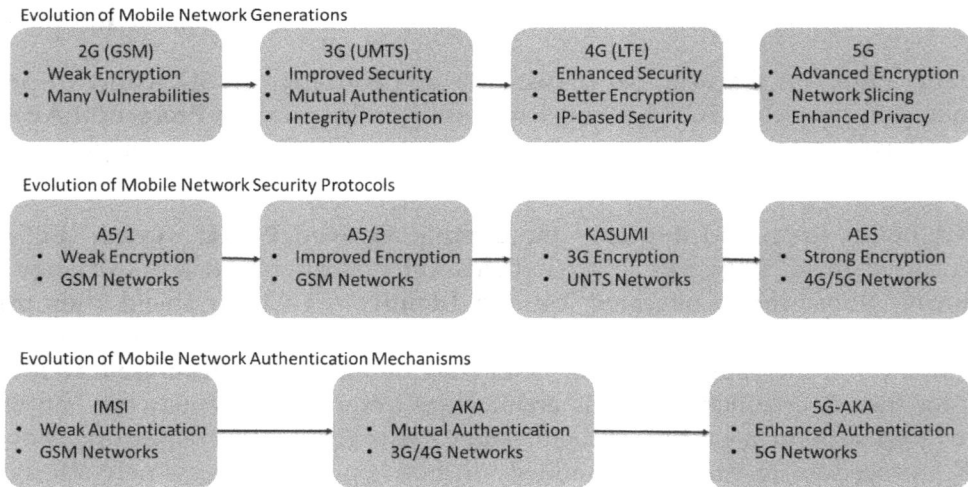

Figure 1.6: *Evolution of security in mobile networks*

The figure illustrates the progression from weaker security measures in early mobile network generations (2G) to stronger encryption algorithms, authentication protocols, and advanced security features in later generations (3G, 4G, and 5G). The evolution aims to address security vulnerabilities, enhance user privacy, and provide more robust protection against various threats.

Each evolution of the mobile network introduced improved data rates, network capacity, and security mechanisms. As shown above, 2G networks like GSM employed weak encryption (A5/1) and lacked robust authentication. 3G (UMTS) networks introduced mutual authentication (AKA) and stronger encryption (KASUMI, AES). 4G LTE networks offered higher speeds, advanced encryption (AES-128/256), and robust authentication (EPS-AKA). The latest 5G networks provide ultra-high data rates, low latency, enhanced encryption (256-bit), new authentication mechanisms (5G-AKA), network slicing for security isolation, and virtualization technologies for improved security. With each generation, security has been a key focus, driving the adoption of stronger encryption algorithms, robust authentication protocols, and advanced privacy-preserving measures to counter emerging threats and vulnerabilities.

The following table shows the various telecommunication generations along with their features and security mechanisms:

Generation	Technology	Feature	Security			
			Client authentication	Network authentication	Signaling integrity	Encryption
1G	AMPS	Voice only	No	No	No	No
2G	CDMA, GSM/ EDGE	Voice, SMS	Yes	No	No	No
3G	UMTS, CDMA, WiMAX	Voice, data and video signals	Yes	in USIM Mode	Yes	KASUMI, SNOW-3G
4G	LTE	Voice, internet speed up to 1 Gbps, video, and streaming capability	Yes	Yes	Yes	SNOW-3G, AES-128 CTR, ZUC
5G	ITU	4x time higher efficiency than 4G with a peak throughput of 20 Gbps	Yes	Yes	Yes	SNOW-3G, AES-128 CTR, ZUC

Table 1.2: Summary of generations of telecommunications

Conclusion

Throughout this chapter, we have discussed the landscape of global security standards and the evolution of security practices in the realm of mobility. We have explored the pivotal role played by international organizations and regulatory bodies in establishing robust guidelines and frameworks, ensuring a baseline level of security and interoperability across platforms and regions.

We also traced the remarkable journey of security measures in mobile devices, networks, and applications, shedding light on cutting-edge technologies and methodologies employed to safeguard our digital infrastructure against cyber threats.

In the next chapter, we will go through the various generations of mobile networks and explore the first generation of mobile networks, concentrating on the 1G network components and the various challenges faced by this initial generation.

Points to remember

As we navigate the complex landscape of global security standards and the evolution of security in mobility, it is crucial to keep several key points in mind:

- **International collaboration**: Effective security measures in the mobile domain require close collaboration among international organizations, regulatory bodies, and stakeholders across various industries and regions. Fostering open dialogue, knowledge sharing, and the establishment of universally accepted standards are paramount to ensuring a cohesive and robust security framework.

- **Proactive approach**: Security in mobility is a continuous journey, not a destination. Staying ahead of emerging threats and anticipating potential vulnerabilities is essential.

- **Encryption and authentication**: Robust encryption techniques and rigorous authentication protocols form the bedrock of secure mobile communications and data protection.

- **Continuous improvement**: The field of mobile security is constantly evolving, and complacency can be detrimental. Embracing a mindset of continuous improvement, monitoring emerging trends, and adapting security strategies to address new challenges is crucial for maintaining a robust and resilient security posture in the ever-changing mobile landscape.

Exercises

1. Define the following organizations and explain their roles in the telecommunications industry:

    a. 3GPP

    b. ETSI

    c. ITU

    d. GSMA

2. Describe the key differences between 1G, 2G, 3G, 4G, and 5G mobile network technologies in terms of data rates, latency, and supported applications.

3. Compare and contrast the security challenges faced in early generations of mobile networks (1G, 2G) with those of modern networks (4G, 5G).

4. Discuss the evolution of encryption algorithms and authentication mechanisms used in mobile networks, highlighting the improvements in security from one generation to the next.

5. Imagine you are tasked with designing a secure mobile application for a financial institution. What security considerations would you need to address, and how would you leverage the capabilities of modern mobile networks?

6. Investigate the role of standardization bodies like 3GPP and ETSI in defining the specifications for mobile network technologies. Explain the process of standardization and its importance in ensuring interoperability and global adoption.

7. Identify and discuss emerging trends or technologies that may shape the future of mobile networks beyond 5G, such as 6G, satellite communications, or advanced virtualization techniques.

Join our book's Discord space

Join the book's Discord Workspace for Latest updates, Offers, Tech happenings around the world, New Release and Sessions with the Authors:

https://discord.bpbonline.com

CHAPTER 2
Generations of Mobile Network and 1G

Introduction

Telecommunication, the cornerstone of modern global connectivity, has evolved through distinct generations, each marked by ground-breaking technological advancements and transformative shifts in our ways of communication. From its humble beginnings of wired telegraphy to the era of 5G networks and beyond, the journey of telecommunication encapsulates a remarkable progression in human ingenuity, innovation, and interconnectedness. From the earliest forms of telegraphy to the high-speed data networks operating today, telecommunication has continuously shaped the way we interact, exchange information, and conduct business on a global scale. This chapter provides an overview of the mobile network generations and delves into the specifics of 1G, exploring its characteristics, limitations, and the challenges it faced.

The focus in this chapter is on 1G, the pioneering technology that laid the foundation for modern mobile communications. 1G networks, based on analog transmission, were primarily designed for voice calls. This technology utilized frequency modulation radio signals and operated on the 800-900 MHz frequency band. The introduction of 1G marked a significant shift from stationary telephony to mobile communication, offering unprecedented freedom and flexibility to users.

However, 1G networks faced numerous limitations and challenges. The analog nature of the technology made it susceptible to interference and noise, often resulting in poor call quality. Security was a major concern, as 1G calls could be easily intercepted with readily available equipment. The networks also suffered from limited capacity, inefficient use of the radio spectrum, and poor handover between cells, leading to frequent call drops. Despite these challenges, 1G played a crucial role in demonstrating the potential and demand for mobile communication. It set the stage for future generations by highlighting the areas that needed improvement, such as digital technology, better security, increased capacity, and data capabilities.

Structure

This chapter will cover the following topics:

- History of mobile generations
- First generation of mobile network
- Components of 1G
- Challenges in 1G

Objectives

This chapter aims to provide a comprehensive overview of the evolution of mobile network technologies, with a particular focus on the **first generation** (**1G**) of mobile networks. The readers should be able to understand the progression of mobile network generations from 1G to 5G, grasping the key technological advancements and features that characterize each generation. They should be able to gain in-depth knowledge about 1G mobile networks, including their historical context, core technologies, and operational principles. Readers will learn about the analog nature of 1G systems and how they revolutionized telecommunications by enabling mobile voice calls for the first time. This chapter will also enable readers to identify and analyze the limitations and challenges associated with 1G networks. This includes understanding the issues of limited capacity, poor voice quality, lack of security, and inefficient spectrum usage that were inherent to first-generation systems.

History of mobile generations

The field of telecommunication witnessed its earliest advancements in the 19th century, with the invention of the telegraph by *Samuel Morse* in 1837. This transformative system enabled the transmission of messages over vast distances using electrical signals and Morse code, laying the groundwork for long-range communication. While *Morse's* ground-breaking telegraph did not officially send its first message until 1844, this was a pivotal year for Morse and his associates, *Alfred Vail* and *Ezra Cornell*, as they perfected their invention and sought to have its revolutionary capabilities recognized.

The year 1876 marked a pivotal moment in human history. It was largely due to the invention of the telephone, pioneered by *Alexander Graham Bell*. Unlike the telegraph, which relied on coded messages, the telephone enabled real-time voice communication, drastically improving the speed and efficiency of interpersonal communication. The iconic words, *Mr. Watson, come here! I want to see you*, uttered during his first successful call in March of that year, resonated far beyond their literal meaning. It marked the advancement to a new era in communication. The ability to transmit one's voice instantaneously across distance seemed almost magical. *Bell*, along with his investors, formed the *Bell Telephone Company* in 1877. By the late 19th century, telephone lines snaked across cities and towns, enabling individuals and businesses to communicate in real-time.

Analog Era

Moving ahead to the 1980s, which marked the advent of the 1G of telecommunications, also known as the **Analog Era**. Representing a ground-breaking shift in the way people communicated, 1G networks introduced the world to mobile telephony on a scale never seen before. Operating primarily on analog technology, 1G networks enabled voice communication over long distances through a network of cell sites equipped with large, bulky transceivers. These early mobile phones, often referred to as **brick phones** due to their size and weight, offered limited functionality compared to modern devices but represented a giant leap forward in connectivity. While 1G networks provided basic voice services, they suffered from poor call quality, limited coverage, and susceptibility to interference. Despite these drawbacks, the introduction of 1G networks laid the foundation for the mobile revolution, heralding a new era of personal communication and paving the way for the rapid evolution of telecommunications technology in the decades to come.

Birth of 2G

The 1990s saw a mobile communication revolution with the arrival of 2G, spearheaded by the **Global System for Mobile Communication (GSM)**. This digital leap brought significant improvements. Earlier, people used an analog static, 2G, which offered crystal-clear calls, but now it is a welcome to the digital signals. However, this was not the end of the discovery. 2G networks were more efficient, squeezing more calls into the same space. This, along with the digital encryption for added security, paved the way for the game-changers. For instance, SMS texting. With 2G, communication became flexible and on-the-go. The affordability and accessibility of 2G phones fueled the mobile phone boom, putting this technology within reach of all. The birth of 2G was a pivotal moment in telecom history, laying the foundation of the ever-evolving mobile world and the interconnected digital age that we experience today.

Mobile internet via 3G

In the 2000s, mobile phones underwent a dramatic shift with the introduction of 3G technology. No longer just for calls, 3G networks were a giant leap forward, offering super-fast data and internet access on mobile devices. Data speeds were much faster than before, completely changing the way people use their phones. With 3G, people could now browse the web, exchange emails, and stream multimedia content on the go, paving the way for a surge of innovative mobile apps and services. 3G meant that the users could stay connected to the internet anywhere, anytime. As the world jumped on board with the mobile internet, 3G networks became the foundation for a constantly connected society, driving massive growth in connectivity and reshaping the digital world for years to come.

Age of mobile broadband

The 2010s ushered in a revolutionary period for mobile communication, which can be referred to as the **age of mobile broadband**, or 4G. This era was not built from scratch. It leveraged the groundwork of the previous generations, but 4G offered a massive jump in mobile connectivity. It was faster, more reliable, and adaptable than ever before. 4G relied on digital technologies like **Long Term Evolution** (**LTE**), which meant information flew quicker and with less delay. This completely changed how people used the internet on their phones and tablets. High-definition video streamed flawlessly, online games ran smoothly, and downloads happened in a flash. 4G also played a key role in bringing the internet to everyone by reaching underserved communities and remote areas. As the foundation of the mobile world, 4G networks also set the stage for the **Internet of Things** (**IoT**) and paved the way for another ground-breaking advancement to the 5G technology.

Gateway to the future

The introduction of 5G in the 2020s marks a pivotal turning point for mobile communication. This powerful technology holds the promise of completely transforming how we connect, collaborate, and experience the world around us. 5G boasts unparalleled speeds, near-instantaneous response times (low latency), and the capacity to connect multiple devices. This paves the way for revolutionary applications such as autonomous vehicles, remote medical procedures, and highly immersive augmented reality. Through innovations like millimeter-wave frequencies and network slicing, 5G offers data transmission speeds that can be up to 100 times faster than 4G. This eliminates delays and enables real-time communication and data exchange at an unprecedented level. 5G networks will also empower the expansive IoT ecosystem by seamlessly integrating and facilitating communication between billions of connected devices, from those used in smart city infrastructure to those deployed in industrial automation.

While 5G networks are still being deployed globally, researchers and telecommunications operators are already exploring the next generation of wireless technology known as 6G. Expected to emerge around 2030, 6G aims to revolutionize connectivity by operating at terahertz frequencies and potentially achieving speeds up to 1 terabit per second, roughly 100 times faster than 5G. This future network is envisioned to enable transformative applications like holographic communications, immersive extended reality, and advanced artificial intelligence integration, while also focusing on sustainability, improved coverage, and lower latency than ever before.

Evolution of mobile networks

The service provider architecture has undergone a significant transformation over the past few decades, driven by the rapid advancements in mobile communication technologies. In general, a **Service Provider Network** (**SPN**) consists of multiple functional zones or parts, namely air interface, access network, transport network, core network, and external network, as shown in *Figure 2.1*:

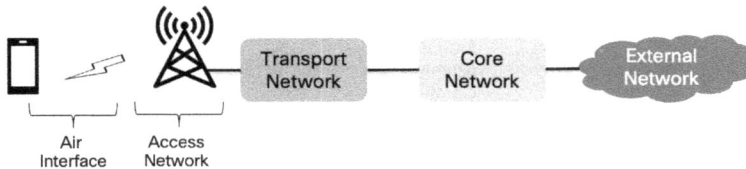

Figure 2.1: *Generic service provider architecture*

In the early days of 1G networks, the architecture was basic, consisting primarily of **Mobile Switching Centers** (**MSCs**) that handled voice calls and provided basic mobility management. The network was designed around circuit-switched technology, with the dedicated voice channels allocated for each call. The general 1G architecture is shown in *Figure 2.2*:

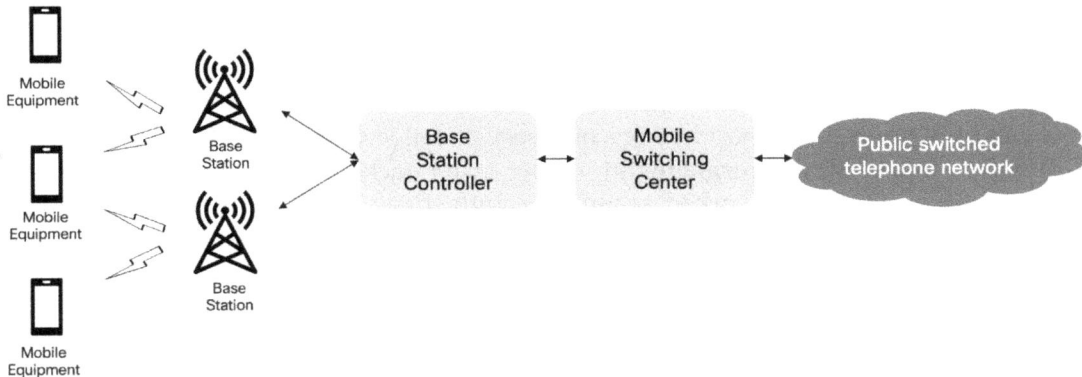

Figure 2.2: *General 1G architecture*

The transition to 2G networks brought the introduction of digital transmission and the integration of packet-switched data services alongside circuit-switched voice. This era witnessed the emergence of additional network elements such as the **Base Station Controller** (**BSC**), which coordinated the radio resources, and the **Home Location Register** (**HLR**), which managed subscriber data and mobility. The 2G architecture was still predominantly circuit-switched, with limited data capabilities. *Figure 2.3* shows the 2G and 2.5G architecture:

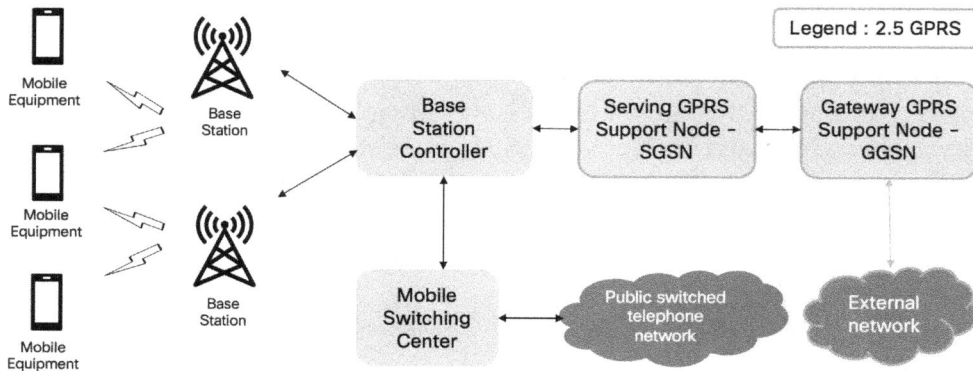

Figure 2.3: 2G and 2.5G architecture

The 2G architecture, like the 1G, is divided into multiple parts. These are as follows:

- The first part of the 2G architecture is the mobile equipment and its SIM card, i.e., the mobile station. It talks directly to the towers, which are the base transceiver stations.

- The second part is the base station subsystem. These towers are managed by the controllers, i.e., the base station controllers, which keep connections smooth.

- The third part is the network or the mobile switching subsystem. It is similar to a control center. It uses databases to handle things like routing calls, checking identities, and keeping track of subscribers.

2.5G was built upon 2G by introducing a new service called **General Packet Radio Service** (**GPRS**). It is like sending information in smaller, faster packages instead of one big stream (like 2G). This innovation worked seamlessly with the existing 2G networks, allowing users to switch between them easily. It was a big improvement in speed without needing a complete network rebuild. Within 2.5G, the **Serving GPRS Support Node** (**SGSN**) is responsible for keeping devices connected, managing data sessions, and ensuring security. It directly communicates with the cellular network to send and receive data to and from the mobile equipment. The **Gateway GPRS Support Node** (**GGSN**) acts as a bridge between the mobile data network and the wider external network or the Internet. It routes data traffic, assigns internet addresses to devices, and even handles billings.

The move to 3G networks marked a significant shift towards a more integrated, all-IP architecture. The 3G network introduced the concept of the **Radio Network Controller** (**RNC**), which replaced the BSC, SGSN, and GGSN, which handled the packet-switched data traffic. This architecture enabled the convergence of voice and data services, laying the foundation for multimedia applications and higher-speed data access. For the reference of the 3G architecture, see *Figure 2.4*:

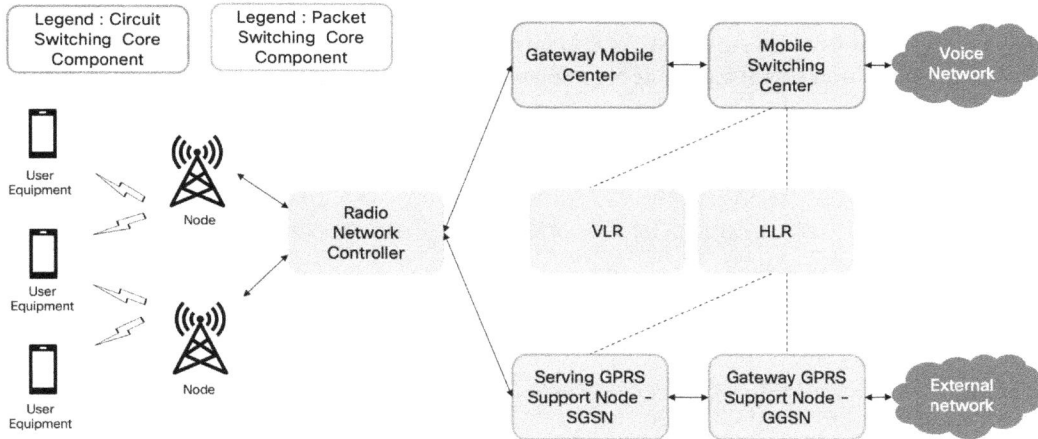

Figure 2.4: *3G architecture*

3G networks introduced a more advanced architecture compared to 2G. The main change is the BSC being replaced by the RNC. The RNC acts as a central hub, managing radio access points, allocating radio resources, and handling **User Equipment** (**UE**) movement within its coverage area. It also connects to the core network, like the BSC, but uses separate **packet switching** (**PS**) and **circuit switching** (**CS**) cores. The PS core, with its SGSN, is responsible for the user location, authentication, and data packet routing. The GGSN acts as a gatekeeper, connecting the cellular network to the Internet or private networks. It functions like a combination of router, firewall, and gateway, ensuring secure and controlled data exchange between different networks.

The 4G, or LTE, witnessed a further evolution of the service provider architecture. The network elements were streamlined with the introduction of the **Evolved Packet Core** (**EPC**), which consolidated the SGSN, GGSN, and other components into a more efficient, all-IP-based system. The LTE radio access network (E-UTRAN) replaced the RNC, simplifying the overall network structure. The architecture of 4G is shown in *Figure 2.5*:

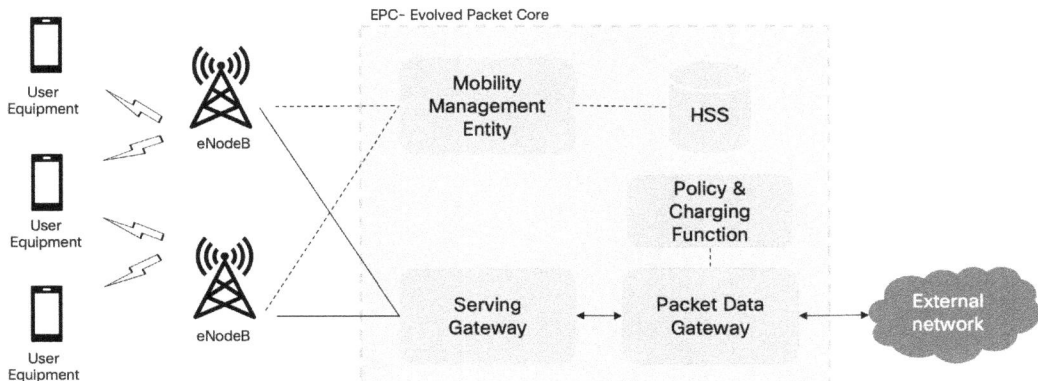

Figure 2.5: *4G architecture*

One of the main components of the 4G architecture is the UE, which can be a smartphone, tablet, or any other mobile device. The UE communicates with the network through the **Evolved UMTS Terrestrial radio access network** (**E-UTRAN**), comprised of the **Evolved Node Bs** (**eNodeBs**). These eNodeBs act as the base stations, transmitting and receiving radio signals to and from the UEs.

EPC is the brain of the 4G network, handling tasks like user authentication, session management, and data routing. EPC is made up of many key components. These are discussed in the following:

- **Mobility Management Entity (MME)**: It acts as the control center, managing connections between UEs and the core network.

- **Serving Gateway (SGW)**: It anchors the user data packets, ensuring seamless handover between eNodeBs as the UE moves.

- **Packet Data Network Gateway (PGW)**: It connects the mobile network to the broader internet, allowing UEs to access the data services.

- **Home Subscriber Server (HSS)**: It is a secure database that stores user identities and subscription information.

Another important change in the 4G as compared to the other mobile generations is the segmentation of traffic between the control plane and the user plane. The control plane handles signaling messages, setting up, and managing data sessions between UEs and the network. The user plane, on the other hand, carries the actual data traffic, like voice calls, video streams, and web browsing. This intricate architecture empowers service providers to manage network resources effectively, identify and resolve bottlenecks, and ultimately, deliver a seamless and high-quality 4G experience to customers. This knowledge also serves as a stepping stone towards future advancement, paving the way for the smooth integration of 5G technology and beyond. The segmentation of the control plane and the user plane is shown in the following figure:

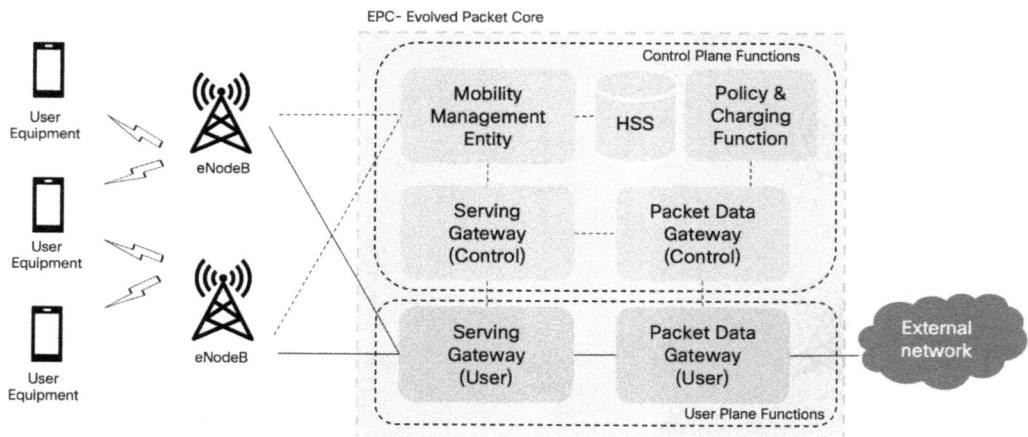

Figure 2.6: Control plane and user plane segmentation

With the shift to 5G, service providers are witnessing a revolution in the network architecture. The **5G Core Network** (**5GC**) ditches the traditional monolithic approach in favor of a modular, cloud-based design. This new architecture utilizes **Network Functions** (**NFs**), which are essentially independent software building blocks. These NFs can be deployed and scaled on-demand, granting service providers unmatched flexibility, agility, and scalability in delivering services to their customers. *Figure 2.7* shows the 5G architecture:

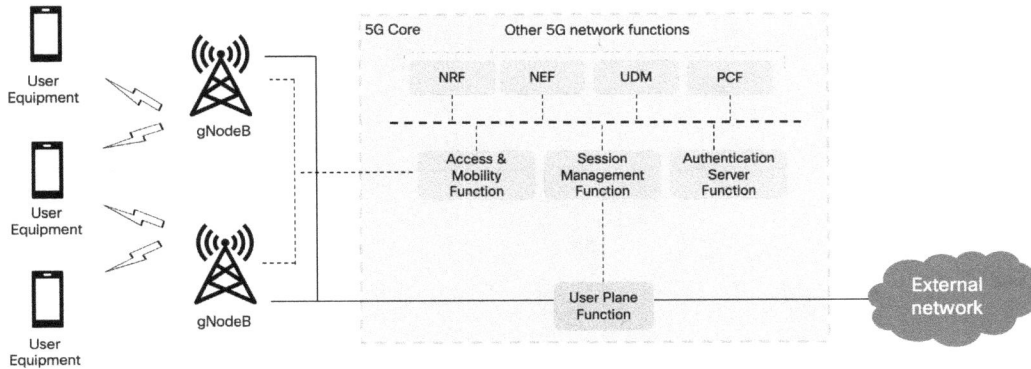

Figure 2.7: 5G architecture

Unlike the previous generations which were designed primarily for a fast mobile data, 5G boasts a comprehensive and an adaptable framework catering to a wider range of services. 5G Core Network, is the center of 5G architecture and is responsible for the network's operations. Unlike traditional core networks, the 5G core is completely software-based and cloud-native. The **service-based architecture** (**SBA**) that 5G core brings along, offers agility and scalability, allowing service providers to easily adapt to the evolving demands. The core network handles critical functions like user authentication, security, session management, and traffic routing. It accomplishes these tasks through a set of NFs, each specializing in a specific task. These NFs are virtualized software components, offering flexibility in deployment and management. Complementing the core network is the 5G **radio access network** (**RAN**), responsible for the actual airwave communication between the network and the user devices. The 5G RAN introduces significant advancements, including massive **Multiple-Input and Multiple-Output** (**MIMO**) technology that utilizes multiple antennas to boost data rates and the network capacity. Additionally, 5G employs higher frequency bands compared to 4G, enabling faster data transmission but with a shorter coverage range. To address this concern, 5G incorporates new techniques like beamforming, which focuses radio signals towards specific user equipment, improving its efficiency.

Figure 2.8 shows a summarized version of all the five generations of mobile networks:

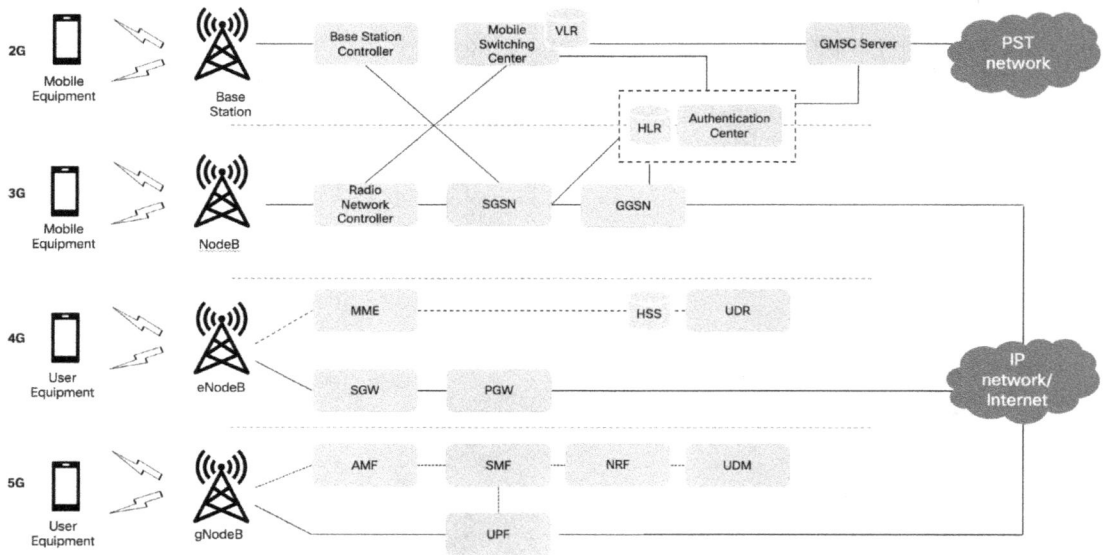

Figure 2.8: *Summarized view of mobile generations*

Moving ahead to the future of the 6G networks, the service provider architecture is expected to continue evolving towards a more distributed, edge-centric model. The integration of artificial intelligence and machine learning into the network will enable advanced automation and intelligent decision-making, allowing for more dynamic and adaptive resource allocation.

Various telecommunications companies and research institutions worldwide have begun early experimental trials for 6G technology. In 2020, China successfully launched what it claimed to be the first 6G satellite to test terahertz signal transmission. Samsung and LG have conducted tests exploring terahertz frequency bands, while *Nokia's Bell Labs* and *Japanese carrier NTT DOCOMO* have made significant strides in sub-terahertz frequency testing. In Europe, the Hexa-X project, LED by Nokia and supported by the European Union, has been conducting foundational research for 6G since 2021, including experiments with advanced antenna technologies and AI-native network architectures. These early trials, though still in preliminary stages, are crucial for understanding the challenges and possibilities of operating wireless networks at such high frequencies.

Throughout these evolutions, the service provider architecture has become increasingly software-defined, with a greater emphasis on programmability, modularity, and cloud-based principles. This has enabled service providers to adapt more quickly to changing market demands, offer more personalized and customized services, and leverage the power of emerging technologies to deliver a more enhanced user experience.

First generation of mobile networks

In 1979, 1G was launched commercially in Tokyo, Japan by *NTT DoCoMo*. 1G of wireless telecommunication technology consists of various standards. In 1981 many Nordic countries like Norway, Sweden, Denmark, Finland, Switzerland, Netherlands, Eastern Europe and Russia got new standards known as **Nordic Mobile Telephone** (**NMT**), similarly, **Advanced Mobile Phone System** (**AMPS**) started to be used in North America and Australia, **Total Access Communications Systems** (**TACS**) in UK and **C-Netz** in Germany.

NMT was developed in two versions: NMT 450 and NMT 900, where the numbers indicate the frequency bands being used in them. This standard specification lacked security as the traffic was not encrypted. It made communication vulnerable to eavesdropping, as this could be achieved by tuning a scanner to the correct frequency. Later versions of NMT specifications went on to define an optional analogue encryption. The cell size, in an NMT network, ranged from 2 km to 30 km.

AMPS was based on the **Frequency Division Multiple Access** (**FDMA**) technology. FDMA allows the number of users to share the available frequency by segmenting the frequency block into smaller subcarriers and allocating those subcarriers on a per-user basis. As the adoption of 1G flourished, analogue channels created capacity issues as each channel could only be allocated to one user at any given time. So, the channel is closed to the other conversations until the initial call is finished and cannot be reused for a different user. As the number of users began to increase, new cells were added. Along with limited capacity concerns, there were security problems as well. For example, if someone were able to get hold of another person's serial code, it would be possible to make illegal calls.

Components of 1G

1G mobile architecture consisted of the following components:

- **Mobile Station (MS)**: It refers to the user's mobile phone or device equipped with a transceiver, antenna, and other necessary components to communicate with the network.

- **Base Station Subsystem (BSS)**: In the 1G cellular network, **radio access network** (**RAN**) was not considered as an independent unit. The RAN in the 1st generation consisted of the **Base Station Sub-systems** (**BSS**) and antennas. The BSS comprises two main components: the **Mobile Switching Center** (**MSC**) and the **Base Station Controller** (**BSC**). The MSC acts as the central hub of the network, handling call routing, switching, and mobility management functions. On the other hand, the BSC is responsible for managing multiple base stations, allocating radio resources, and coordinating handovers between cells.

- **Base station (BS)**: The base station, also known as the **cell site**, consists of the radio transceivers and antennas responsible for transmitting and receiving signals to and from mobile devices within its coverage area.
- **Public Switched Telephone Network (PSTN)**: The PSTN serves as the backbone of the telecommunication network, providing connectivity between mobile users and landline phones.

Figure 2.9 shows the complete architecture of the 1st generation of the mobile network:

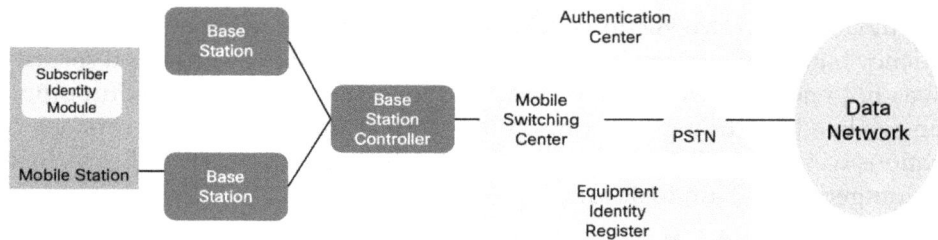

Figure 2.9: *1st generation of mobile network*

Challenges with 1G

As an initial first-generation technology, 1G had many drawbacks and challenges, due to which it is not currently in use. Being an analog technology, the phones had poor battery life, and voice calls were without much security. The top 1G speed was 2.4 Kbps. Analogue signals are more likely to deteriorate over time and place, and so, are more prone to interference problems, which can cause voice data to be of poor quality and occasionally result in dropped calls. Mobile phones used during those days were big and thick in size due to the need to house big antennas. Also, mobile phones had lower battery life because data transmission used to take a lot of energy. Another big drawback was roaming, which was not supported in 1G technology.

Some of the major challenges of 1G were:

- **Size of the user device/phone**: 1G mobile phones were often referred to as brick phones due to their substantial size and weight. These devices were typically large, bulky, and heavy, often weighing around 2-3 pounds (0.9-1.4 kg) and measuring approximately 10-13 inches (25-33 cm) in length. The Motorola DynaTAC 8000X, one of the most iconic 1G phones, was about the size of a brick and weighed close to 2.5 pounds. These devices featured large batteries to support their power-hungry analog operations, contributing significantly to their size.
- **Battery life of the phone was very limited**: Battery life was a significant challenge for mobile phone users in the days of 1G. The analog nature of 1G technology, combined with the large size and power-hungry components of early mobile

phones, resulted in notoriously short battery life. Typical 1G phones could only operate for a few hours of talk time or standby time before requiring a recharge. The poor battery performance of 1G devices was a major driving force behind efforts to improve energy efficiency in subsequent generations of mobile technology.

- **No security for calls as it was very easy to snoop and mishandle**: Due to the analog nature of 1G technology, voice calls were transmitted as continuous radio waves, making them easily interceptable by anyone with the right equipment. This lack of encryption meant that conversations could be easily snooped on using modified scanners or even amateur radio equipment. The ease of intercepting calls leads to numerous privacy concerns, as sensitive personal and business information could be overheard by malicious actors.

- **Analog signals had interference problems leading to coverage issues**: The analog signals in 1G were susceptible to electromagnetic interference from natural phenomena like weather conditions and solar activity, as well as man-made sources such as electrical equipment and other radio transmissions. As a result, call quality often degraded significantly, manifesting as static, cross-talk, and dropped calls. The analog nature of 1G also meant that signals weakened considerably over distance, leading to limited coverage areas, especially in rural or less populated regions.

- **Like in the case of AMPS technology, capacity was a major concern**: The analog nature of the Advanced Mobile Phone System meant that each voice call required a dedicated frequency channel, leading to inefficient spectrum usage. In densely populated urban areas, the available frequency bands became saturated, resulting in call blocking and dropped connections during peak usage times.

- **Speed was extremely slow**: G networks were designed primarily for voice calls and offered data transmission capabilities that were painfully slow by modern standards. These analog systems typically provided data speeds of around 2.4 **kilobits per second (Kbps)**, which is less than 1% of the speed of a basic 2G connection. To put this in perspective, downloading a simple text email could take several minutes, and transferring a small image file might require an hour or more.

Due to all these reasons, we do not use 1G anymore. In the next chapter we will discuss about second generation of mobile networks.

Conclusion

The evolution of mobile network technology from 1G to 5G represents a remarkable journey of innovation and progress in telecommunications. Each generation has brought significant improvements in speed, capacity, and functionality, revolutionizing the way we communicate and interact with the world around us.

The first generation of mobile networks, 1G, marked the beginning of cellular technology in the 1980s. It introduced the concept of wireless voice calls, enabling people to communicate on the move for the first time. Despite its limitations, 1G laid the foundation for future advancements. The subsequent generations, 2G, 3G, and 4G; each brought significant improvements. 2G introduced digital technology, enabling text messaging and improved call quality. 3G ushered in the era of mobile internet and video calling, while 4G dramatically increased data speeds and capacity, paving the way for smartphone applications and mobile streaming services. The latest generation, 5G, promises to be transformative, offering ultra-fast speeds, extremely low latency, and the ability to connect a massive number of devices simultaneously.

Reflecting on the journey from 1G to 5G, we can appreciate the challenges overcome and the rapid pace of technological advancement in mobile communications. Each subsequent generation addressed the issues in previous generations while introducing new capabilities, ultimately leading to the highly connected world we live in today.

In the next chapter, we will explore the **second generation** (**2G**) of mobile networks, which marked a pivotal transition from analog to digital communications in the early 1990s. This revolutionary shift not only enhanced voice quality and security but also introduced text messaging (SMS) and basic data services that would forever change how people communicated. We will examine key 2G technologies and the critical security improvements that addressed many of 1G's vulnerabilities, setting the stage for the mobile revolution that would follow.

Points to remember

- Mobile network technology has evolved through five major generations, starting with analog 1G systems in the early 1980s and progressing through increasingly capable digital generations. Each generational shift brought substantial improvements in speed, capacity, security features, and application support, transforming mobile networks from simple voice communication systems to the foundation of today's digital economy and connected world.

- The first generation of mobile networks represented the pioneering phase of cellular technology, introducing the revolutionary concept of cellular architecture with frequency reuse and handoff capabilities. Prominent 1G standards included AMPS in North America, NMT in Scandinavia, and TACS in the UK, all operating as analog systems primarily designed for voice communications with extremely limited data capabilities of approximately 2.4 Kbps.

- The transition from 1G to 2G marked a fundamental shift from analog to digital technology, bringing significant improvements in capacity, security, and service offerings. 2G introduced text messaging (SMS), basic data services, and improved privacy through digital encryption. This generation laid the groundwork for mobile communications to become a mainstream consumer technology rather than a luxury for business professionals.

- Mobile internet capabilities truly emerged with 3G networks, which delivered substantially higher data rates (up to 2 Mbps under ideal conditions) and supported a wider range of applications, including mobile web browsing, email, video calling, and location-based services. 3G represented the beginning of the transformation of mobile phones into multipurpose devices and data-centric platforms.

- The 4G/**Long Term Evolution** (**LTE**) standard revolutionized mobile communications by providing true broadband speeds to wireless devices, supporting bandwidth-intensive applications like high-definition video streaming, online gaming, and cloud computing. With theoretical speeds of up to 100 Mbps and an all-IP architecture, 4G enabled the smartphone revolution and the app economy.

- Key components of 1G networks included the MTSO, which served as the central coordination center for call routing and management; base stations (cell sites) that provided radio coverage through strategically placed antennas; and FDMA technology that divided available spectrum into channels, allowing multiple simultaneous users.

- 1G networks suffered from numerous security vulnerabilities that made them highly susceptible to fraud and abuse. The lack of encryption meant calls could be easily intercepted using commercially available radio scanners, while the absence of authentication mechanisms allowed phone cloning, through which criminals could capture device identifiers and create duplicate phones that billed to legitimate users' accounts.

- Technical limitations severely constrained 1G performance, including poor spectral efficiency that limited overall system capacity; analog signal degradation that reduced call quality, especially at cell boundaries; substantial power requirements resulting in large, heavy devices with short battery life; and virtually non-existent international roaming capabilities that restricted mobility.

- The handoff process in 1G networks, while revolutionary at the time, was relatively crude compared to modern systems, often resulting in noticeable interruptions during calls as users moved between cells. The analog technology also made 1G networks highly susceptible to interference from environmental factors and competing radio signals.

- Despite its significant limitations, 1G technology represented a crucial first step in mobile communications, demonstrating the viability of cellular architectures and creating consumer demand for mobile services. The lessons learned and challenges encountered during the 1G era directly informed the development of subsequent generations, establishing the evolutionary path that continues with today's 5G deployments and future 6G research.

Exercises

1. Which of the following correctly describes the first generation (1G) of mobile networks?

   a. Digital networks with SMS capabilities

   b. Analog networks for voice communication only

   c. Networks that supported basic internet browsing

   d. Networks that used GSM technology

2. In what decade was 1G technology predominantly deployed?

   a. 1970s

   b. 1980s

   c. 1990s

   d. 2000s

3. Which of the following was NOT a component of 1G mobile networks?

   a. Mobile Telephone Switching Office

   b. Base stations

   c. Packet-switched core network

   d. Radio transceivers

4. AMPS was a 1G standard primarily used in:

   a. Europe

   b. Japan

   c. United States

   d. China

5. Which security concern was most prominent in 1G networks?

   a. SIM card cloning

   b. Lack of encryption

   c. DDoS attacks

   d. Malware infections

6. What was the primary technological advancement that distinguished 2G from 1G?

   a. Transition from analog to digital signals

   b. Introduction of video calling

   c. Higher data transfer speeds

   d. Integration with the internet

7. Which frequency range was typically used by 1G networks?

   a. 800-900 MHz

   b. 1800-1900 MHz

   c. 2100-2200 MHz

   d. 3400-3800 MHz

8. What was a major limitation of 1G mobile networks?

   a. Limited battery life

   b. Poor voice quality and frequent call drops

   c. Incompatibility with landline phones

   d. All of the above

9. Describe the evolution of mobile network generations from 1G to 5G, highlighting the key technological advancements in each generation.

10. Explain the basic architecture of 1G mobile networks and list their primary components.

11. What were the three most significant security vulnerabilities in 1G networks? How were these addressed in subsequent generations?

12. Compare and contrast the analog technology used in 1G with the digital technology introduced in 2G. What specific improvements did this transition bring?

13. Why was frequency reuse an important concept in 1G networks, and how was it implemented?

Join our book's Discord space

CHAPTER 3
2G and Enabled Services

Introduction

Introduced during the 1990s, second-generation wireless technology employs a circuit-switched network structure that segments the radio spectrum into multiple channels. The inception of 2G stemmed from various constraints of capacity, quality, and the restricted scope of the initial analog mobile communication systems, prompting the evolution towards digital cellular mobile communication systems.

2G diverges from 1G primarily in its adoption of digital technology beyond the base station, featuring digital encryption. As voice and data are transmitted in digital format in 2G, it is relatively easy to perform encryption and mitigate a few security threats like eavesdropping. In 2G, the voice quality was also improved due to the possibility of error detection and correction.

Unlike its predecessor, 2G facilitated voice communication, and data functionality was subsequently introduced with 2.5G, known as **General Packet Radio Service (GPRS)**.

The architecture of 2G mobile networks encompasses various integral elements that come together to facilitate voice and data transmission. The principal standards for 2G networks include **Global System for Mobile Communications (GSM)** and **Code Division Multiple Access (CDMA)**.

Structure

The chapter covers the following topics:

- General architecture
- Network interfaces in 2G
- SS7 signaling protocol
- Securing SS7 signaling protocol
- SMS service
- Drawing curtains on 2G

General architecture

The main components of 2G include the **Base Station System** (**BSS**) and the **Mobile Switching Center** (**MSC**) within the Network and Switching Subsystem. Refer to the following figure for a better understanding:

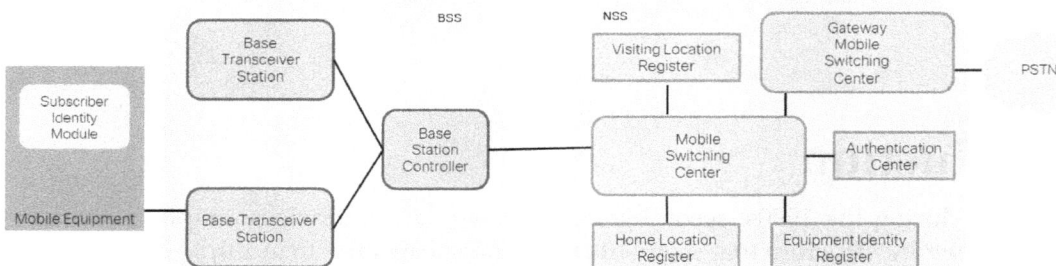

Figure 3.1: *2G architecture*

Mobile Equipment

The end user device is called the **Mobile Equipment** (**ME**), which consists of a radio transceiver, signal processor, and a **Subscriber Identity Module** (**SIM**) card provided by the communication service provider. SIM is an important component as it holds the subscriber number, encryption keys, and operational information.

Base Station Subsystem

Base Station Subsystem (**BSS**) is responsible for managing the radio network resources within the mobile network, essentially serving as the bridge between mobile equipment and the core network. The components within the BSS handle various tasks like carrying signaling between the ME and the network, tracking the locations of phones and seamless handovers, and ensuring good signal quality. BSS is made of the following two main components to perform the mentioned tasks:

- **Base Transceiver Station** (**BTS**): These are the towers with antennas, responsible for transmitting and receiving radio signals to and from the ME.

- **Base Station Controller** (**BSC**): This acts as the brain of the BSS. Multiple BTS can connect to a single BSC. A BSC can control several BTSs and manage radio resources like frequency allocation, handovers (when ME moves between cells), and power control.

Network Switching Subsystem

The **Network Switching Subsystem** (**NSS**) is the integral behind-the-scenes component that handles the complex operations required for everyday mobile communications. It serves as the *brain* that ensures the seamless functionality we experience when making calls, sending messages, or accessing the internet on our mobile devices. The primary responsibilities of the NSS include verifying the authentication and authorized access of mobile equipment to the network and safeguarding the network from unauthorized access attempts. It also plays a crucial role in providing essential information about the user's location, enabling features like emergency calling and location-based services. Crucially, the NSS establishes the necessary connections between mobile devices and other communication networks, including landlines and other mobile users.

In essence, the NSS facilitates the core mobile communication capabilities the 2G network relies on, handling the heavy computational and data management tasks that enable the mobile device to conveniently access voice, messaging, and internet services on the go.

NSS is made up of the following components:

- **Mobile Switching Center** (**MSC**): It is the main component of the 2G mobile network responsible for several functions. It takes care of the routing of voice calls and data sessions between mobile devices within the same network or between different networks, along with the establishment and termination of calls and data, and handling signaling messages between mobile devices and base stations. The MSC collects information related to call duration, data usage, and other relevant parameters for billing and charging purposes, enabling operators to accurately bill subscribers for the services they use. The MSC also serves as an interface point for interconnecting with other MSCs, **Public Switched Telephone Networks** (**PSTN**), and other telecommunications networks, facilitating the exchange of voice and data traffic between different networks.

- **Home Location Register** (**HLR**): The HLR is a central database that stores and manages subscriber information for mobile phone users within a specific network operator's coverage area. It serves as the main repository for essential data related to each subscriber, including their subscriber identity, service profile, location information, and authentication keys. Based on this information, HLR plays a crucial role in call setup. It also facilitates subscriber mobility by keeping track of the current location of subscribers within the network.

- **Visitor Location Register (VLR)**: The VLR is a database that temporarily stores crucial information about mobile subscribers who are currently located within the coverage area served by a specific **Mobile Switching Center (MSC)**. When a mobile device roams into a new geographic region, it registers with the local MSC, prompting the MSC to query the VLR for the relevant subscriber details related to that area. The VLR maintains data such as the subscriber's identity, service profile, and current location area. This information is essential for facilitating the call setup and routing processes within the 2G cellular network.

- **Authentication Center (AuC)**: The AuC is a crucial component responsible for authenticating and authorizing subscribers before granting them access to the cellular network. When a mobile device attempts to connect to the network, the AuC verifies the subscriber's SIM card to ensure that only legitimate and authorized users can gain access. The AuC generates and securely stores the necessary security parameters and encryption keys used for encrypting communications between the mobile device and the network. For each subscriber session, the AuC dynamically generates temporary authentication and encryption keys. These session-specific credentials are used to verify the subscriber's identity and encrypt data transmissions during the active communication session.

- **Gateway Mobile Switching Center (GMSC)**: The GMSC serves as the interface between the mobile network and external communication networks. When a call originates from a mobile device within the network and is directed to an external number, the GMSC is responsible for determining the appropriate routing path for the call and forwarding it to the destination network or subscriber. Conversely, when a call is received from an external network and destined for a mobile subscriber, the GMSC routes the call to the relevant MSC within the mobile network, ensuring the call reaches the intended mobile user.

- **Equipment Identity Register (EIR)**: The EIR is a database that maintains comprehensive records of the unique **International Mobile Equipment Identity (IMEI)** numbers assigned to every mobile device. When a mobile device attempts to connect to the network, the EIR checks the device's IMEI number to verify its legitimacy. If a device's IMEI is listed as stolen, lost, or marked as problematic in the EIR, the network can take appropriate actions, such as blocking the device from accessing network services. By performing this IMEI validation, the EIR plays a crucial role in preventing the unauthorized use of the network and reducing instances of device-related fraud, including identity theft and subscription fraud.

GPRS was a major leap forward for 2G mobile networks. It was designed to bring data capabilities to the 2G network. It introduced a new way to transmit data, in packets, alongside existing voice calls. This was a big improvement over the slow dial-up connections of the time. GPRS offered speeds ranging from 56 to 114 kilobits per second, depending on network conditions. Another change GPRS brought was a new billing system. Instead of paying for how long a device was connected, the subscribers were charged based on the amount of data they used. This meant that the subscriber only paid for what the device transmitted, not just for being online.

GPRS paved the way for a new era of mobile content and services. It allowed users to send and receive text, images, and even some basic multimedia files. This laid the groundwork for the richer multimedia experiences that later mobile technologies would deliver.

The following two new nodes were added to the existing 2G architecture to enable GPRS: Serving **GPRS Support Node (SGSN)** and **Gateway GPRS Support Node (GGSN)**.

- **SGSN**: This acts as the intermediary between the mobile devices and the core GPRS network. Its primary responsibility is routing and forwarding IP packets between mobile devices and external data networks like the Internet. It also helps in tracking the location of mobile devices within the GPRS network and managing their mobility as they move between different geographic areas covered by different SGSNs. It also plays a major role in authenticating mobile devices when they connect to the GPRS network and enforcing security policies to protect the confidentiality and integrity of data transmitted over the network.

- **GGSN**: This acts as a routing agent, routing data packets between the mobile network and the Internet (or other data networks). When the user's phone uses mobile data, the GGSN assigns it a temporary Internet address, so it can connect with websites and apps. It also checks the user's identity to make sure that the user is allowed to use the network and keeps track of how much data the user uses so that his/her bill reflects the usage.

The 2.5G architecture is shown in the following figure:

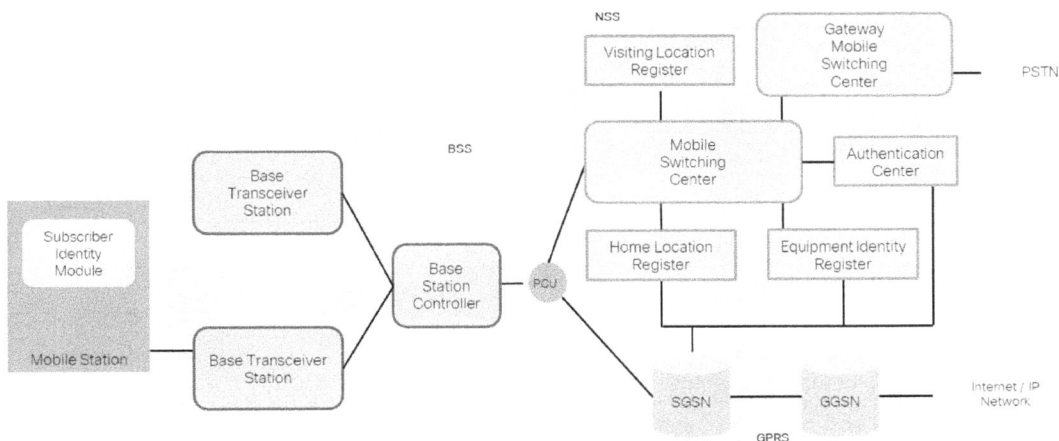

Figure 3.2: 2.5G architecture

Network interfaces in 2G

In order to ensure mobile networks could integrate components from various manufacturers, standard interfaces were established. This ensured uniform communication protocols regardless of the manufacturer, fostering compatibility. This strategy facilitated the entry of numerous equipment manufacturers into the market, bolstering the number of suppliers and intensifying competition. The interfaces varied based on the type of connection between the various network components, as shown in the following figure:

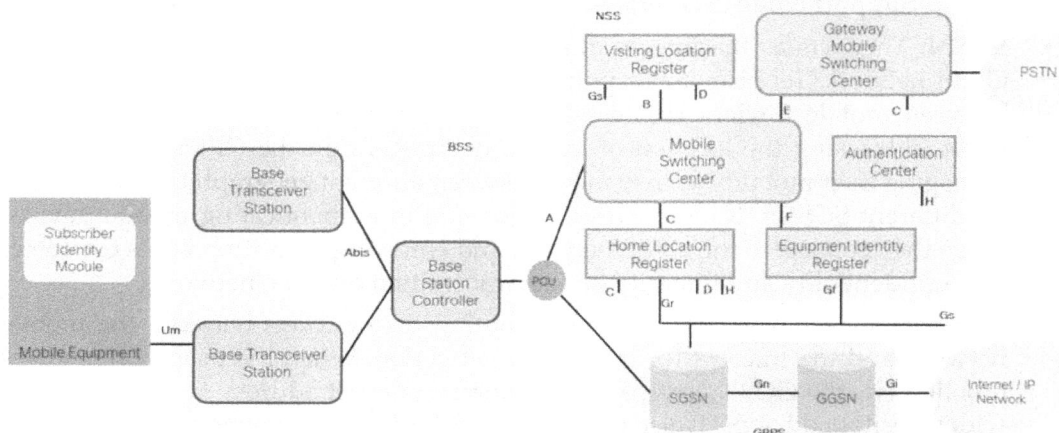

Figure 3.3: Network interfaces in 2G

The following table depicts the various interfaces used in 2G:

Interface	Description
Um	Air interface between ME and BTS
Abis	The interface between BTS and BSC
A	The interface between BSC and MSC
B	The interface between MSC and VLR
C	Interface between HLR and MSC/GMSC
D	The interface between HLR and VLR
E	The interface between multiple MSCs or GMSCs
F	Interface between EIR and MSC or GMSC
G	The interface between multiple VLRs
Gb	The interface between SGSN and BSS for data transfer and mobility

Interface	Description
Gn	The interface between SGSN and GGSN
Gi	The interface between the GGSN and the external data network
Gr	The interface between SGSN and HLR
Gc	The interface between GGSN and HLR
Gs	The interface between SGSN and VLR
Gf	The interface between SGSN and EIR

Table 3.1: Interfaces in 2G

SS7 signaling protocol

In 2G mobile networks that use the **Global System for Mobile Communications (GSM)** standard, **Signaling System 7 (SS7)** acts like a behind-the-scenes conductor. It manages the signals and controls everything from starting and ending calls to sending busy signals and keeping other essential functions running smoothly across the entire network. SS7 essentially allows different parts of the network to talk to each other, making it possible to set up and manage voice and data connections in GSM systems.

In addition to setting up and releasing calls, SS7 is the main protocol behind several telecommunication services, some are mentioned in the following:

- **Local Number Portability (LNP)**
- Telephone marketing numbers such as toll-free
- **Short Message Service (SMS)**
- **Enhanced Messaging Service (EMS)**, Ringtone, logo

One of SS7's key features is the separation of signaling messages from the voice circuits. This means that the control information necessary for establishing and managing calls, such as call setup, routing, billing, and other network functions, is transmitted separately from the actual voice data. By segregating signaling from voice circuits, SS7 enables more efficient and flexible communication within the network. It allows signaling messages to be processed and routed independently of the voice channels carrying the actual conversations. This separation enhances the reliability, security, and scalability of telecommunications networks as it permits the optimization of signaling traffic and the implementation of advanced network features without impacting voice quality or call performance.

The SS7 architecture comprises three signaling components, **Service Switching Points (SSPs)**, **Signal Transfer Points (STPs)**, and **Service Control Points (SCPs)**, as shown in the following figure:

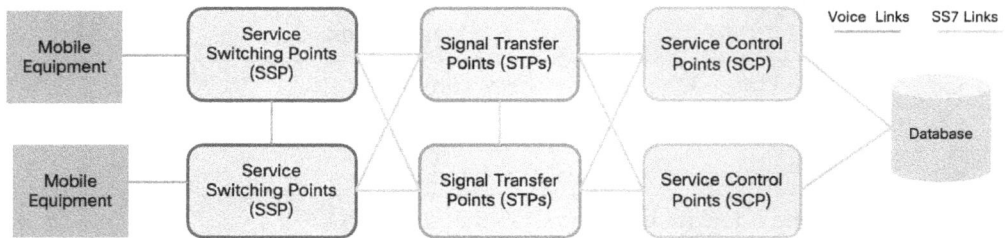

Figure 3.4: SS7 architecture

Refer to the following explanations for a better understanding:

- **SSP**: They are the entry and exit points for SS7 networks. They are responsible for handling call-related signaling functions, such as call setup, call routing, and call teardown. SSPs convert global title digits (i.e., a dialed number) from a subscriber line to SS7 signaling messages. It communicates with other SS7 nodes to exchange signaling messages and route calls through the network.

- **STP**: They are normally a gateway or router within the SS7 network. Gateway STPs work as an interface to other networks. It routes SS7 signaling messages between SSPs, SCPs, and other STPs based on routing information contained in the messages. It also performs message routing, translation, and screening functions to ensure efficient and secure communication within the SS7 network.

- **SCP**: The SCP is a database server within the SS7 network that stores and processes service logic and subscriber data. SCPs also serve as an interface to applications such as databases like the HLR, VLR, etc. When an SSP requires additional information or service logic to complete a call, it queries the SCP via SS7 signaling messages. It is also instrumental in providing intelligent network services such as call forwarding, call screening, and prepaid billing.

The SS7 components are connected via SS7 links or signaling links. These are physical or logical connections between SS7 nodes used to transmit SS7 signaling messages. They can be either direct links between adjacent nodes or links between nodes via intermediate STPs. Signaling Links carry signaling information in the form of SS7 **Protocol Data Units** (**PDUs**), allowing SS7 nodes to exchange control information and coordinate call setup and management.

SS7 Protocol Stack and SIGTRAN

SIGTRAN or signaling transport is used to transport SS7 signaling messages over IP networks, while, as we know, SS7 networks rely on circuit-switched connections for signaling. SIGTRAN enables the transport of SS7 signaling messages over IP networks, including the Internet, using IP-based protocols such as TCP and **Stream Control Transmission Protocol** (**SCTP**). SIGTRAN is also used for VoIP. The **signaling gateway** (**SG**) functions as a signaling point/agent positioned at the periphery of the network, handling the reception and transmission of native signaling. It presents itself as an SS7 Signaling Point to the SS7 network and as an IP node to the IP network. The primary role of the SG is to facilitate the conversion between the circuit-switched and IP domains. The following figure shows the SS7 protocol stack along with the SIGTRAN stack:

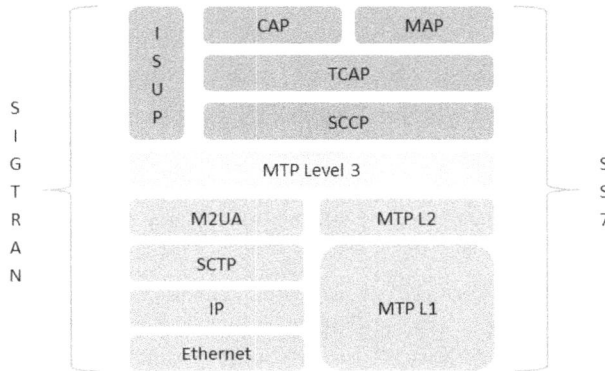

Figure 3.5: *SS7 and SIGTRAN protocol stack*

Listed in the following are the uses and functionalities of the various SS7 protocols, which are depicted in the figure shown above:

- **Integrated Services Digital Network User Part (ISUP)**: It handles the setup, maintenance, and teardown of circuit-switched telephone calls over the **Public Switched Telephone Network (PSTN)** or other telecommunications networks. ISUP is responsible for signaling between switching nodes in the network to establish and control voice and data calls. It provides essential functions such as call setup, call supervision, call release, and call routing within the telecommunications network.

- **CAP**: CAMEL Application Part stands for Customized Applications for Mobile Networks Enhanced Logic. It enables the implementation of advanced services in mobile networks, such as call forwarding, prepaid billing, location-based services, etc., and allows for the customization of services based on subscriber profiles, preferences, and other criteria.

- **Mobile Application Part (MAP)**: It facilitates various functions including mobility management, subscriber authentication, location updating, and SMS delivery.

- **Transaction Capabilities Application Part (TCAP)**: It enables the exchange of non-circuit-related information between nodes in the network. It provides transaction-oriented services, allowing applications to request and receive various types of data from other nodes in the network. TCAP is commonly used for services such as querying databases, invoking remote procedures, and exchanging messages between different network elements.

- **Signaling Connection Control Part (SCCP)**: Its primary function is to manage and control the signaling messages exchanged between signaling points in the telecommunications network. SCCP provides services such as message routing, error correction, and network management functions. It plays a vital role in establishing, maintaining, and releasing connections for various telecommunications services, including voice calls, data transmission, and signaling information exchange between network elements.

- **MTP LEVEL 3**: It transports the user's signaling messages over the IP using SCTP. It handles the routing of signaling messages between signaling points based on the **Destination Point Code** (**DPC**) included in the SS7 message headers. Additionally, it manages congestion control, message sequencing, error checking, and link status monitoring within the SS7 network.

- **MTP LEVEL 2**: It is responsible for the reliable transfer of signaling messages between signaling points in a telecommunications network. MTP Level 2 operates at the data link layer of the OSI model, and provides functions such as message delimitation, error detection, error correction, and flow control.

- **M2UA**: MTP2 User Adaptation Layer allows signaling messages to travel between **Signaling Gateways** (**SGs**) and **Media Gateway Controllers** (**MGCs**) using IP networks instead of the older, specialized system. This provides a dependable and fast way for communication between parts of phone networks that use SS7 signaling and those that rely on IP. In simpler terms, M2UA helps bridge the gap between traditional phone systems and internet-based communication.

- **SCTP**: Stream Control Transmission Protocol is designed to transport signaling messages reliably and efficiently between nodes in telecommunication networks, particularly in IP-based networks. SCTP offers features such as message segmentation, multi-streaming, multi-homing, and support for both reliable and unreliable transport of data.

- **IP**: Internet Protocol is the fundamental protocol that enables the routing and delivery of data packets between network devices. It is used for the transmission of signaling messages over IP networks, such as the Internet.

- **MTP Layer 1**: It is the foundation, handling the physical delivery itself. It deals with the nuts and bolts of getting the messages across, like sending electrical pulses over wires or light pulses through fiber optics. The type of connection used, such as T1/E1 lines or fiber optic cables, determines how these signals are transmitted.

Security threats in SS7 and SIGTRAN networks

SS7 is vulnerable to various security threats due to its design and protocols. Some of the common threats are listed in the following:

- **Man-in-the-middle attacks**: In a man-in-the-middle attack, active eavesdropping occurs where the attacker establishes separate connections with the victims and serves as an intermediary, relaying messages between them. This process deceives the victims into thinking they are communicating directly when the attacker controls the entire conversation. Consequently, the attacker can intercept and manipulate all messages exchanged between the two victims.

- **DDoS attack**: In a DDoS attack, all effort is aimed at rendering a service inaccessible to its designated users, either temporarily or permanently. This is typically achieved by inundating the service with an excessive volume of requests, causing message processing to become unmanageable or significantly delayed, or by disrupting user connections, thereby preventing them from initiating or receiving calls.

- **Replay attacks**: A replay attack in SS7 involves the retransmission or deliberate delay of legitimate data. This can be initiated by the original sender or by an adversary who intercepts the data and resends it, potentially as part of a masquerade attack involving the substitution of IP packets.

- **SMS flooding and spamming**: SMS flooding attacks in SS7 involve the reception of excessive and unsolicited SMS messages directly by the subscriber, which can be either legitimate or fraudulent.

- **SMS interception and spoofing**: SS7 vulnerabilities can be exploited to intercept SMS messages or spoof the sender's identity. Attackers can intercept two-factor authentication codes sent via SMS or send fraudulent messages to users.

- **Call and SMS hijacking**: Attackers can hijack phone calls or SMS messages by exploiting SS7 vulnerabilities. They can reroute calls or intercept SMS messages intended for specific subscribers, facilitating fraud or unauthorized access to sensitive information.

- **Subscriber privacy violations**: SS7 weaknesses can compromise subscriber privacy by exposing sensitive information such as call logs, location data, and subscriber profiles to unauthorized entities. This information can be leveraged for identity theft, blackmail, or other malicious purposes.

- **Location tracking**: SS7 weaknesses allow attackers to track the location of mobile devices by intercepting signaling messages related to location updates. This information can be abused for stalking, espionage, or other malicious purposes.

The following figure explores the mentioned vulnerabilities and other common vulnerabilities in the SS7 protocol:

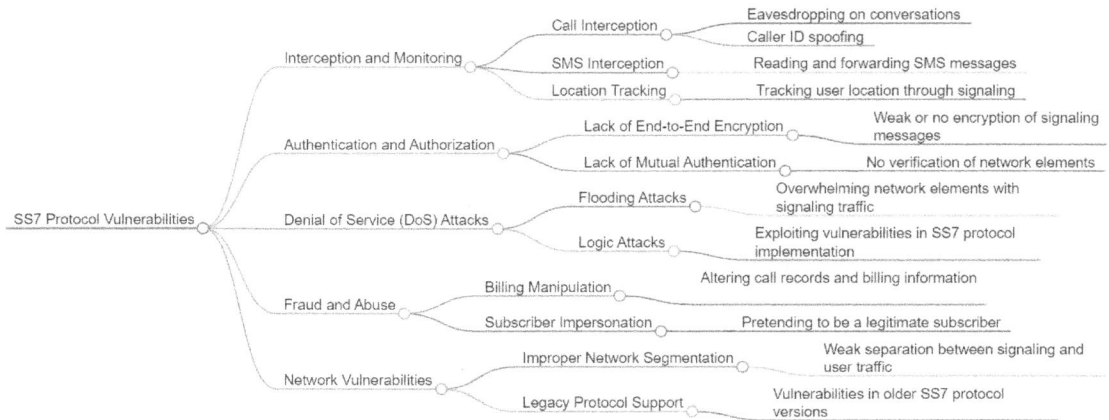

Figure 3.6: Vulnerabilities in SS7

Similarly, SIGTRAN is vulnerable to various security threats. Some of the common threats are listed in the following:

- **Association hijacking**: In this, the attacker attempts to take control of an existing association between two signaling endpoints in a SIGTRAN network. This could be achieved through various means such as exploiting vulnerabilities in the protocol stack, intercepting network traffic, or impersonating one of the endpoints. Once successful, the attack can lead to manipulation of signaling messages, disruption of communication between legitimate endpoints, or gain unauthorized access to sensitive information exchanged between the endpoints.

- **Address camping/stealing**: In this attack, the malicious party monitors or intercepts signaling traffic to identify and camp on (occupy) signaling addresses that are not in active use. By doing so, the attacker can effectively block legitimate signaling traffic or attempt to impersonate legitimate nodes within the network. While stealing attack refers to the unauthorized acquisition of signaling addresses by a malicious entity. This could involve various techniques, including intercepting signaling messages and falsely claiming ownership of specific addresses to divert traffic or disrupt network operations.

- **Amplification attack**: This works by targeting vulnerabilities in protocols like SCTP and M3UA. The attacker sends a small, malicious request to a specific server or device. This server is tricked into responding with a much larger amount of data than it received. This flood of data, much bigger than the original request, overwhelms the target network or system, taking it offline.

The following figure explores the mentioned vulnerabilities and other common vulnerabilities in the SIGTRAN protocol:

SIGTRAN Protocol Vulnerabilities

- Insecure Protocol Design
  - Lack of End-to-End Encryption — Weak or no encryption of signaling messages
  - Weak Authentication Mechanisms — Inadequate verification of network elements
- Denial of Service (DoS) Attacks
  - Flooding Attacks — Overwhelming network elements with signaling traffic
  - Resource Exhaustion — Depleting network resources through malicious requests
- Unauthorized Access
  - Lack of Access Control — Insufficient restrictions on signaling message modifications
  - Signaling Message Tampering — Altering signaling messages for malicious purposes
- Network Topology Exposure
  - Revealing Network Structure — Leaking information about network elements and interconnections
  - Traffic Pattern Analysis — Identifying and exploiting patterns in signaling traffic
- Legacy Protocol Support
  - Vulnerabilities in Older Versions — Security issues in previous SIGTRAN protocol versions
  - Interoperability Challenges — Difficulties in maintaining secure communication across versions
- Insecure Configuration
  - Improper Network Segmentation — Weak separation between signaling and user traffic
  - Inadequate Monitoring and Logging — Lack of visibility into signaling activities

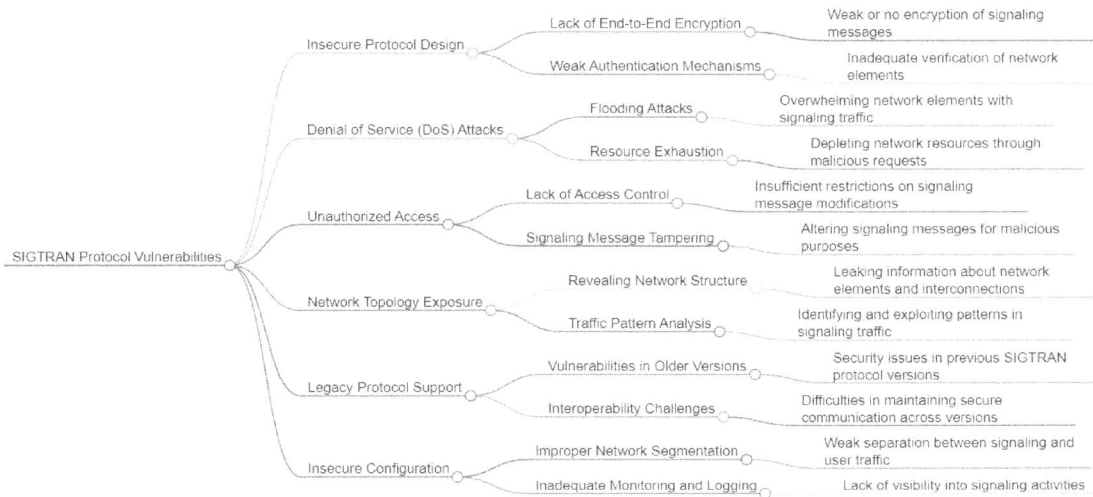

Figure 3.7: *Vulnerabilities in SIGTRAN*

Securing SS7 signaling protocol

SS7 firewalls are deployed by communication service providers to enhance the security posture of telecommunication networks. Due to the above-mentioned vulnerabilities, SS7 firewalls are employed to protect against potential threats and attacks.

An SS7 firewall may exist independently as a dedicated appliance or in a virtual form, be a part of a unified SS7 and Diameter Firewall solution, or have its functions integrated into **Signaling Transfer Points** (**STPs**) and endpoint nodes. SS7 firewall capabilities need to be situated at the network periphery, ensuring that messages undergo optimal processing upon entry into the network.

While deploying an SS7 firewall, the following guiding principles must be considered along with configuring the firewall based on best practices and the communication service provider's environment.

- The defense in layer concept must be adopted to secure signaling traffic. Do not rely only on the SS7 firewall to mitigate all threats. Some of the controls to mitigate relevant threats can be configured on other mobile network components.
- Ensure that all relevant security logs are being sent to a logging server or an SIEM solution in the service provider's security operations center. Custom alerts and dashboards must be created to enable the monitoring team to analyze and act.
- The firewall should be deployed with considerations of network segmentation and security zones. The home network is usually considered the trusted zone, while the zone that carries roaming signalling to other national or international operators is considered an untrusted zone.

- The SS7 firewall itself should be hardened based on the security best practices that may be internally developed by the service provider's information security team or use the guidelines provided by the vendor of the firewall.

- SS7 firewall should be considered based on various parameters like bandwidth, performance, high availability, and placement. The SS7 firewall itself should not be a single point of failure impacting the availability of services.

- While choosing the firewall, ensure its compliance with relevant global security standards.

The following table shows the various components where SS7 filtering can be applied, in addition to applying all controls on the SS7 firewall:

Features	HLR	SMSC	MSC/SGSN	STP	SS7 firewall
MAP Screening (Op, CgGT, IMSI)	Can be applied	NA	Can be applied	Can be applied	Can be applied
Compare the current VLR and Cg SCCP	Can be applied	Can be applied	NA	NA	Can be applied
Compare IMSI and HLR	NA	NA	Can be applied	NA	Can be applied
Compare IMSI and SCP	NA	NA	Can be applied	NA	Can be applied
SMS Home Routing	Can be applied	Can be applied	NA	NA	Can be applied
Check Location	Can be applied	NA	NA	NA	Can be applied
Check CgGT spoofing	NA	NA	NA	Can be applied	NA

Table 3.2: SS7 filtering applicability

SS7 firewall deployment options

SS7 firewall can be deployed in multiple scenarios based on the communication service provider's environments and arrangements with other operators.

Routed mode

In this mode, the SS7 firewall receives traffic that the STP routes towards it. The STP can choose to route all relevant traffic to the firewall or only specific traffic. The following figure depicts the routed mode of the SS7 firewall design:

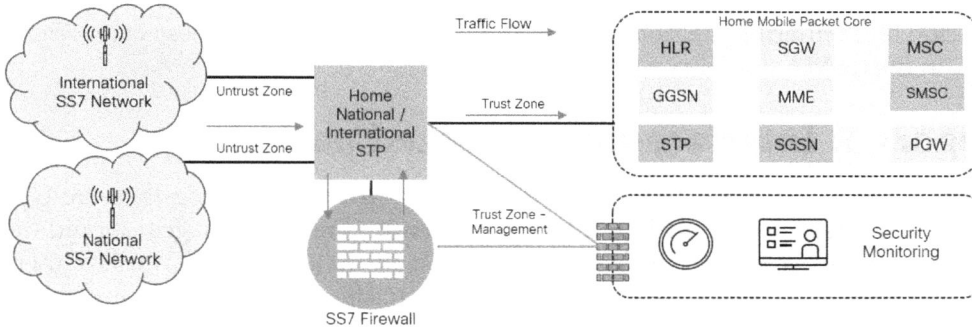

Figure 3.8: SS7 firewall in routed mode of deployment

The home national or international STP can select the traffic it needs the SS7 firewall to inspect, and act based on its configuration. Cleaned traffic is then allowed to pass on to the mobile core components. In this case, the STP too can be configured with basic mitigation configurations and hardening best practices to reduce the risks of common attacks and threats like a DoS attack.

Inline mode

In this mode, the SS7 firewall frontends signal traffic coming from national and international roaming operators, and protect the home STP from external threats. All signaling traffic will flow via the SS7 firewall for inspection, and based on its configuration, relevant actions will be taken on the traffic being inspected. The following figure depicts the inline mode of deployment for the SS7 firewall:

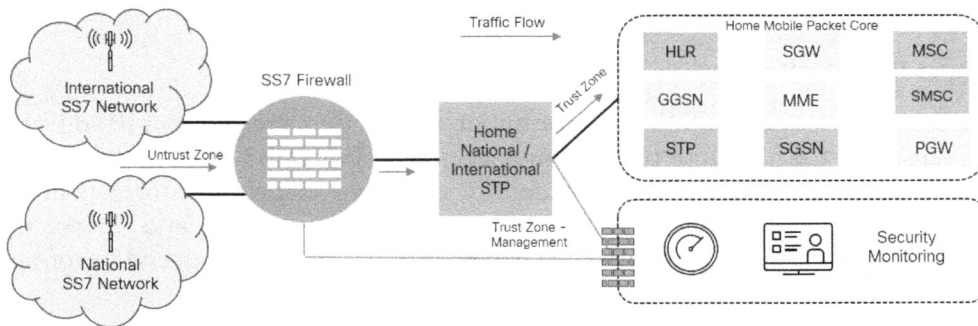

Figure 3.9: SS7 firewall in an inline mode of deployment

Categorization of signaling packets

Rules in an SS7 firewall can be defined based on the categories of the signaling application packets and based on IP layer details like the source IP address and port information.

The application packets can be categorized into three buckets or categories, and non-application layer filtering methods, as mentioned in the following. These categories are as defined in the GSMA guidelines document.

Category 1: Interface-unauthorized packet

Category 1 refers to SS7 messages classified as intra-network, meaning they are typically intended for internal use within a single network. These messages should not be exchanged across **Points of Interconnect** (**POIs**) with other networks unless there is a specific agreement between the operators involved. In simpler terms, *Category 1* messages are not allowed on interfaces connecting to roaming partners unless explicitly authorized through a bilateral agreement.

Category 2: Home-network packet

This refers to checks for signaling application packets that are sent from the *Home* or allocated network of a subscriber. Typically, this is done by screening to see if there are no inconsistencies between the information in the lower layers and the application layer. This also refers to messages that should normally be about subscribers and related to their home networks.

Category 3: Plausible network packet

This refers to checks for application packets which is sent from the current network where the subscriber is present. Typically, checks on these packets are based on inter-message correlation and may involve the plausibility of messages in terms of location, velocity, and time. This refers to packets that should normally only be sent from a visiting subscriber from that subscriber's current visited network.

Low-layer format filtering

This method focuses on scrutinizing information like sender and recipient IP addresses, as well as screening the format of protocol messages. This involves basic filtering operations conducted at lower protocol layers to identify violations of protocol formats and basic spoofing attempts. These filtering tasks rely on protocol screening and do not require comprehensive information about upper-layer applications or the decoding of specific parameters.

Configuring SS7 firewall rules

The GSMA document FS 11—SS7 interconnect security monitoring and firewall guidelines details the rules that can be configured in the SS7 firewall based on the above-mentioned categories.

At a high level, the SS7 firewall should comprise the types of rules mentioned in the following:

- Screen messages for vulnerabilities.
- Enable **Global Title** (**GT**) screening on the SS7 firewall.
- Block inbound MAP messages that are for intra-PLMN use only.
- Block outbound MAP messages that are for intra-PLMN use only.
- Block category 2 MAP message where the IMSI at the MAP layer relates to one of the protected network's customers.
- Block category 2 MAP message where the IMSI relates to an inbound roamer, but the operator ID determined from the IMSI at the MAP layer is not consistent with that derived from the Calling GT at the SCCP layer.
- Check and block MAP *Category 3* messages that are normally only received in relation to an outbound roaming subscriber from the visited network in which the subscriber is currently roaming.
- Where a network does not support handover across network boundaries, MAP packets with information associated with the handover of active calls, received from a VLR, should be blocked.
- Where CUG and GroupCall services are not supported across network boundaries, MAP packets that can be used as part of the CUG and GroupCall service, addressed to a VLR, should be blocked.
- Where a network does not support handover across network boundaries, the MAP packet that can be used to pass information associated with the handover of active calls should be blocked.
- Where GroupCall and CUG functions are not supported across network boundaries, the MAP operations associated with these functions should be blocked.
- Where CCBS is not supported across network boundaries, the MAP operations associated with these functions can be blocked.

SMS service

In 2G networks, SMS messages are transmitted using the MAP protocol, which operates at the network layer and facilitates communication between various network elements.

Three MAP interfaces in 2G support the short message service:

- H interface between the HLR and the SMS C (SMS-GMSC, Gateway Mobile Switching Center).
- E interface between MSC and the SMSC (SMS-GMSC, SMS-IWMSC, Inter Working Mobile Switching Centre).
- Gd interface between SGSN (Service GPRS Support Node) and the SMSC (SMS-GMSC, SMS-IWMSC).

The following figure shows various components of the SMS architecture, with the details of the various interfaces that connect these components:

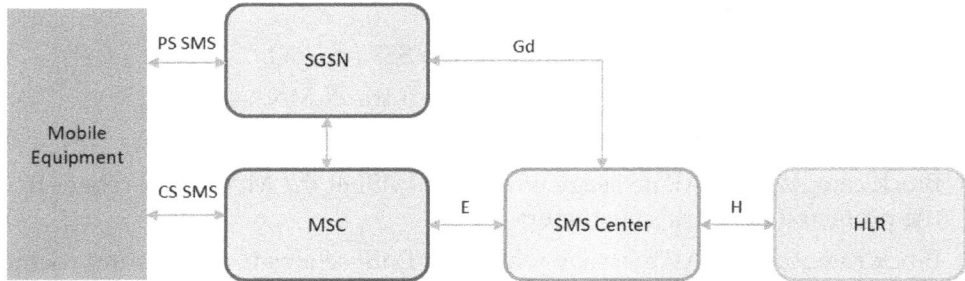

Figure 3.10: *SMS components*

Security threats in SMS service

Abuse of SMS services in SS7 signaling can lead to compromising the integrity, privacy, and security of SMS communications. There are plenty of commercial tools available today that can be used to exploit a service provider's SMS service. Some of the common malicious activities that involve SMS communication are mentioned in the following:

- **SMS spoofing**: Attackers can manipulate SS7 signaling protocols to spoof the sender's identity, making it appear as if the SMS message is originating from a different source than it is. This can be used for phishing attacks, scams, or impersonation.

- **SMS interception**: SS7 vulnerabilities can be exploited to intercept SMS messages in transit between mobile devices and the SMS center. Attackers can eavesdrop on sensitive information contained in SMS messages, such as authentication codes, one-time passwords, or personal conversations.

- **SMS flooding**: Attackers can flood the SS7 network with a high volume of SMS messages, overwhelming network resources and disrupting service for legitimate users. This type of attack can lead to **Denial-of-Service** (**DoS**) situations and degradation of service quality.

- **SMS spamming**: Like email spam, SMS spamming involves the mass distribution of unsolicited SMS messages for advertising, phishing, or other fraudulent purposes. SS7 vulnerabilities can be exploited to send bulk SMS messages to many recipients.

- **SMS relay attacks**: In SMS relay attacks, attackers intercept SMS messages and relay them to unauthorized recipients without the knowledge or consent of the sender or recipient. This can be used for unauthorized access to sensitive information or unauthorized transactions.

- **SMS call forwarding and diversion**: Attackers can exploit SS7 vulnerabilities to manipulate call forwarding and diversion settings associated with SMS messages. This can lead to unauthorized rerouting of SMS messages to attacker-controlled devices or phone numbers.

- **SMS relay for authentication bypass**: Attackers can intercept SMS messages containing authentication tokens or one-time passwords sent during the login process. By relaying these intercepted messages to their own devices, attackers can bypass authentication mechanisms and gain unauthorized access to user accounts.

The following figure explores the vulnerabilities and other common vulnerabilities in the SMS service:

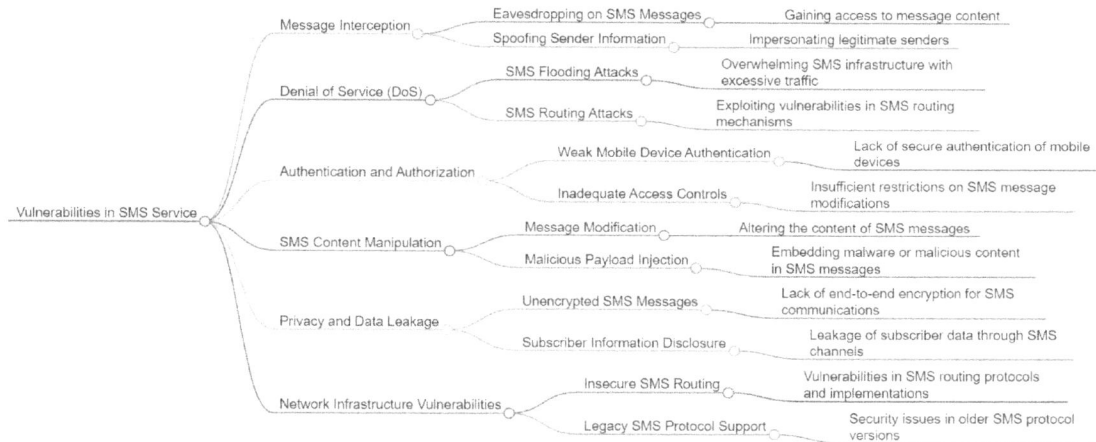

Figure 3.11: Vulnerabilities in SMS service

Securing SMS service

While deploying an SMS firewall, the following guiding principles must be considered, along with configuring the firewall based on best practices in the communication service provider's environment.

- The defense in the layer concept must be adopted to secure signaling traffic. Do not rely only on the SMS firewall to mitigate all threats. Some of the controls to mitigate relevant threats can be configured on other mobile network components, like **Home and Visitor Location Register (HLR/VLR)**, **Short Message Service Center (SMSC)**, **Mobile Switching Center (MSC)**, etc.

- SMS firewall must be configured initially in a learning mode for it to analyze and identify the SMS traffic in the network. This can be for a period of two or three months. Once this phase is complete, the rules should be configured to block malicious traffic.

- Ensure that all relevant security logs are being sent to a logging server or an SIEM solution in the service provider's security operations center. Custom alerts and dashboards must be created to enable the monitoring team to analyze and take action.

- The firewall should be deployed with considerations of network segmentation and security zones.

- The SMS firewall itself should be hardened based on the security best practices that may be internally developed by the service provider's information security team or use the guidelines provided by the vendor of the firewall.

- The SMS firewall should be considered based on various parameters like bandwidth, performance, high availability, and placement. The SMS firewall itself should not be a single point of failure impacting the availability of services.

- When choosing a firewall, ensure its compliance with relevant global security standards.

To secure SMS messages, specific solutions are currently available for service providers to consider and deploy. The basic features required in a node that can secure SMS messages include:

- SMS anti-spamming functions
- SMS content analysis
- SMS volume analysis
- SMS anti-spoofing functions
- IR.71 recommendations set against SMS fraud
- SMS anti-faking functions
- SMS TCAP Handshake
- TCAPsec
- SRI/FSM correlation
- Protection against HLR lookup
- Use of a Dummy IMSI
- SMS Home Routing

Service providers can deploy an SMS firewall to inspect and control malicious traffic as per the general architecture as shown in the following figure:

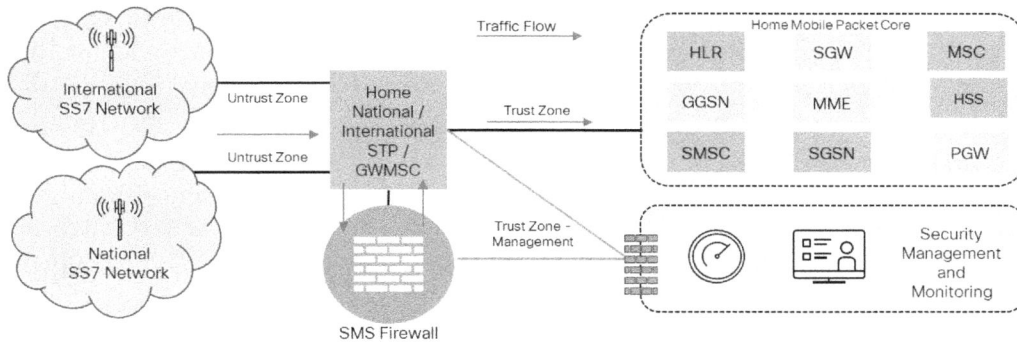

Figure 3.12: *SMS security components*

As documented in GSMA SG 22 SMS security, the SMS firewall should comprise of the following functionalities:

- Filtering mechanism based on attributes of the `MAP_SRI_For_SM`, `MAP_MT_Forward_SM`, and `MAP_MO_Forward_SM` messages.
- Checking the SCCP Calling Party Address against the SC-Address for the `MAP_SRI_For_SM`, and `MAP_MT_Forward_SM` messages.
- Detecting *unusual error* patterns.
- Detecting *flooding* of HLR with requests for subscriber identity and location.
- Detecting `MAP_SRI_For_SM` received without corresponding `MAP_MT_Forward_SM` messages.
- Ability to hide the actual location of the receiving MS (enhanced user privacy).
- Ability to correlate `MAP_SRI_For_SM` with subsequent `MAP_MT_Forward_SM` messages.
- Ability to check on network subscription (A-MSISDN or A-IMSI).
- Comparing the SCCP Calling Party Address of the `MAP_SRI_For_SM` against what is received in the corresponding `MAP_MT_Forward_SM`.
- Ability to protect mobile networks from SMS-based attacks, including those that target inbound roamers.
- Ability to perform a handshake check for **Mobile Originated** (**MO**) and **Mobile Terminated** (**MT**) short message service transfer.
- Reduce spam by performing a content/spam check.
- Ability to perform mobile-originated spoof check

Along with deploying an SMS firewall and configuring it appropriately, it is recommended to configure other components in the SS7 network to prevent SMS fraud as documented in GSMA IR 71. SMS SS7 Fraud Prevention. Listed in the following are the various configurations that can be added to the SMS firewall:

- On HLRs, a screening based on the Calling SCCP Global Title for the MAP Message SRI for SM should be activated. The HLRs will reject the entire SRI for the SM request, in case it is not sent from an implemented SMS-C Global Title.

- On every MSC/VLR, a screening based on the Calling SCCP Global Title for the MAP Forward Short Message should be activated. The MSC/VLRs will reject the entire MAP Forward Short Message request in case it is not sent from a defined SMS-C Global Title.

- To prevent the SMS faking case, the *SMS Home Routing* feature will force the SMS to be routed back to the home network.

- To avoid the spoofing case, a control access based on the MSISDN must be activated on the SMS-C. All SMS MO with an MSISDN different than the operator's own MSISDN range should be rejected.

- In addition to the IMSI check for the SMS MO request, a comparison is made between the VLR location and the calling SCCP address (MSC/VLR) where the subscriber should be located. If the location stored in the HLR is different than the SCCP calling address from which the SM MO is coming, the SM MO will be rejected.

Drawing curtains on 2G

For certain **Internet of Things (IoT)** and **Machine-to-Machine (M2M)** devices that transmit relatively small amounts of data, the high speeds provided by 4G networks may not be necessary. In several markets, 2G technology remains a viable option for applications involving low-volume or infrequent data transfers, especially in countries with large geographical areas where remote locations are only covered by 2G networks. Additionally, there is a cost-benefit consideration in using 2G technology for these types of IoT and M2M devices. The module cost for 2G-enabled devices is significantly lower than the cost of 4G modules, even with the inclusion of 2G or 3G backward compatibility. This cost advantage can be an important factor for IoT deployments where the operational expenses need to be minimized.

In summary, while the overall industry trend is towards the adoption of newer, higher-speed cellular technologies, 2G networks can still serve a purpose for specific IoT and M2M applications that have modest data requirements, particularly in regions where 2G coverage remains the primary option for remote connectivity.

The existing cellular networks, including 2G, have undergone significant improvements to extend their lifespan and maximize the utility of the deployed infrastructure. However, the radio frequency spectrum available to each service provider is finite. In the coming years, the demand for more advanced technologies, 5G, 6G, and NB-IoT, is expected to rise further. Typically, 2G networks based on GSM technology utilize the 850-1800 MHz or 900-1900 MHz frequency bands. These same frequency bands can be repurposed and used by more advanced cellular technologies to deliver higher data throughput and more advanced functionalities. The reallocation of these frequency resources from older networks to newer, more capable technologies is a crucial strategy for service providers to meet the growing demand for high-speed, data-intensive mobile services and applications in the future.

As 2G network technology ages, the cost of maintaining the associated infrastructure and equipment becomes increasingly burdensome for service providers. By shutting down their 2G networks, service providers can significantly reduce the operational and maintenance expenses linked to these older cellular technologies. This cost-saving measure allows them to allocate resources more efficiently towards the deployment and enhancement of newer, more advanced 4G and 5G networks.

In certain regions, regulatory authorities are mandating the discontinuation of 2G network operations to facilitate a swifter transition towards more advanced cellular technologies. By shutting down their 2G networks, service providers can comply with these regulatory directives and requirements imposed by the governing bodies. This regulatory pressure is driving service providers to migrate away from the older 2G infrastructure and focus their efforts on the deployment and enhancement of the next generation 4G and 5G networks.

But shutting down 2G services can also have a higher impact if not planned well in advance. The impact can apply to multiple scenarios, but the most critical impact will be for roaming scenarios where a visiting subscriber will depend on the 2G services of the provider to connect to critical numbers. While roaming, if the device or network lacks support for 4G services, it will typically attempt to connect to a 2G or 3G network instead. This is a common scenario when traveling and roaming internationally. However, many countries, such as the United States, have already decommissioned their 2G and 3G networks as they transition their focus towards faster and more efficient 4G technology. This shift means that users without 4G compatibility may find themselves unable to make or receive calls, send text messages, or even contact emergency services when visiting these countries. Often, travelers may be unaware of this limitation until they arrive at their destination and try to utilize their mobile services.

This situation poses a significant risk, as the inability to access voice services can be more than just an inconvenience; it can potentially put lives in danger, especially in emergencies. While some individuals may view the lack of voice connectivity as a mere nuisance, the grave concern lies in the compromised ability to reach emergency responders when needed.

Several major service providers around the world have already shut down or are in the process of shutting down their 2G networks. Refer to the following list:

- **United States:**
  - AT&T shut down its 2G network in 2017.
  - T-Mobile shut down its 2G network in 2022.
  - Verizon shut down its 2G network in 2021.

- **Europe:**
  - o Vodafone UK shut down its 2G network in 2022.
  - o Orange France shut down its 2G network in 2021.
  - o Deutsche Telekom in Germany shut down its 2G network in 2021.
- **Asia:**
  - o Singtel in Singapore shut down its 2G network in 2017.
  - o Telstra in Australia shut down its 2G network in 2016.
  - o DOCOMO in Japan shut down its 2G network in 2012.
- **Latin America:**
  - o Claro in Brazil shut down its 2G network in 2021.
  - o Movistar in Argentina shut down its 2G network in 2022.

Conclusion

The 2G cellular network architecture has played a pivotal role in shaping modern mobile communications. Its general architecture, comprising the Mobile Equipment, Base Station Subsystem, and Network Switching Subsystem, laid the foundation for efficient and widespread mobile connectivity. At the heart of this system lies the SS7 signaling protocol, which facilitates the exchange of control information between network elements. However, as with any technology, SS7 is not without its vulnerabilities. Security threats to SS7 have emerged over time, necessitating the implementation of protective measures such as SS7 firewalls. Various deployment models for these firewalls have been developed to safeguard network integrity and user privacy.

One of the most widely adopted services enabled by 2G technology is the SMS. This text-based communication system revolutionized how people interact, offering a quick and convenient method of exchanging information. Nevertheless, the popularity of SMS has also made it a target for malicious actors, exposing users to various security threats. As a result, the importance of securing SMS communications has become increasingly apparent, with network operators and service providers implementing various measures to protect user data and maintain the integrity of the messaging system.

As we look at the future of mobile communications, it is clear that the lessons learned from 2G networks and their associated services have significantly influenced subsequent generations of cellular technology. The emphasis on security, scalability, and user experience continues to drive innovation in the field, paving the way for more advanced and secure communication systems.

In the next chapter, we will explore the **IP Multimedia Subsystem (IMS)**, an architectural framework designed to deliver multimedia services over IP networks. As we transition from circuit-switched networks to packet-switched IP-based systems, IMS represents a crucial step in the evolution of mobile communications. This chapter will delve into the core components of IMS, its relationship with existing cellular networks, and how it enables a wide range of rich, interactive services. We will examine the key protocols and interfaces that make IMS possible, as well as the challenges and opportunities it presents for both network operators and end-users. By understanding IMS, we will gain insight into the future of mobile communications and the convergence of voice, video, and data services in an all-IP environment.

Points to remember

- The 2G general architecture is composed of three main components: Mobile Equipment, Base Station Subsystem, and Network Switching Subsystem. These elements work together to provide cellular communication services. The Mobile Equipment, typically a mobile phone, connects to the Base Station Subsystem, which manages radio resources and handles communication between the mobile device and the network. The Network Switching Subsystem is responsible for call routing, subscriber management, and interfacing with other networks.

- **Signaling System No. 7 (SS7)** is a crucial signaling protocol used in 2G networks. It enables communication between different network elements, facilitating services such as call setup, teardown, and roaming. However, SS7 faces several security threats, including eavesdropping, location tracking, and fraudulent activities. These vulnerabilities arise from the protocol's lack of built-in security measures and its trust-based architecture.

- To mitigate SS7 security risks, SS7 firewalls can be deployed using various models. These include centralized deployment at network borders, distributed deployment across multiple network elements, and hybrid approaches combining both centralized and distributed methods. Each model offers different advantages in terms of security coverage, performance, and implementation complexity.

- The SMS is a popular 2G-enabled service that allows users to send and receive text messages. While convenient, SMS faces security threats such as interception, spoofing, and malware distribution. These vulnerabilities stem from the lack of end-to-end encryption and the potential for message manipulation during transmission.

- To enhance SMS security, various measures can be implemented. These include using encryption protocols to protect message content, implementing sender authentication mechanisms to prevent spoofing, and employing filtering systems to detect and block malicious messages. Additionally, user education about potential risks and best practices for secure SMS usage plays a crucial role in overall SMS security.

Exercises

1. Describe the three main components of the 2G general architecture and their primary functions:
    a. Mobile Equipment
    b. Base Station Subsystem
    c. Network Switching Subsystem

2. What is SS7 (Signaling System 7), and why is it important in 2G networks?
3. List and briefly explain three common security threats associated with SS7.
4. Compare and contrast the following SS7 firewall deployment models:
    a. Centralized model
    b. Distributed model

5. Explain the basic concept of the SMS in 2G networks.
6. Identify and describe four potential security threats in SMS services.
7. What measures can be implemented to enhance the security of SMS communications? Provide at least three examples.
8. How does the HLR contribute to the functioning of 2G networks?
9. Explain the role of the MSC in handling SMS messages.
10. What is IMSI, and how is it related to subscriber privacy in 2G networks?
11. Describe the process of SMS delivery in a 2G network, from sender to recipient.
12. What are some limitations of SMS security in 2G networks compared to more modern cellular technologies?
13. Explain the concept of SMS spoofing and its potential impact on users.
14. How does encryption contribute to securing SMS communications in 2G networks? Discuss the challenges of implementing end-to-end encryption for SMS in 2G networks.

Join our book's Discord space

Join the book's Discord Workspace for Latest updates, Offers, Tech happenings around the world, New Release and Sessions with the Authors:

https://discord.bpbonline.com

CHAPTER 4

IP Multimedia Subsystem

Introduction

In the evolving field of modern communication technologies, the **IP Multimedia Subsystem** (**IMS**) has emerged as a revolutionary framework for delivering a wide range of multimedia services over IP networks. Developed by the **3rd Generation Partnership Project** (**3GPP**) and the **European Telecommunications Standards Institute** (**ETSI**), IMS aims to provide a convergent platform that seamlessly integrates voice, video, data, and various multimedia applications.

This chapter explores the details of IMS, exploring its architecture, protocols, interfaces, and security considerations. By understanding these fundamental aspects, service providers, network operators, and developers can harness IMS's full potential to deliver rich and secure multimedia experiences to end-users.

This chapter will start with examining the general architecture of IMS, which follows a layered approach consisting of the service layer, control layer, and transport layer. This modular design enables flexibility and scalability, allowing for the integration of diverse multimedia services and applications. The chapter will also cover the key protocols employed within the IMS ecosystem, including the **Session Initiation Protocol** (**SIP**), Diameter, and **Real-time Transport Protocol** (**RTP**).

Furthermore, the chapter will shed light on the various interfaces and reference points that facilitate communication between the various components of the IMS architecture.

Understanding these interfaces, such as the Gm, Mw, and Mx, is crucial for ensuring interoperability and end-to-end service delivery within the IMS network.

Despite its robust design, IMS is not immune to security threats. This chapter will explore the potential vulnerabilities inherent in IMS deployments, including eavesdropping, denial of service attacks, and identity spoofing. To mitigate these risks, we will understand the role of **Session Border Controllers** (**SBCs**) as a critical security component within the IMS architecture. SBCs provide a range of security functions, such as topology hiding, denial of service protection, and signaling and media encryption, acting as a secure gateway between the IMS network and external networks.

This chapter will also aim to examine the security mechanisms specific to the SIP, a key component of IMS. Techniques like SIP digest authentication, **secure RTP** (**SRTP**), and **Transport Layer Security** (**TLS**) will be discussed in depth, highlighting their roles in ensuring the confidentiality and integrity of SIP signaling and media streams.

As the demand for rich multimedia experiences continues to grow, IMS stands as a comprehensive and robust solution for delivering these services over IP networks. By understanding the complexities of IMS, industry professionals can leverage its capabilities to provide secure, interoperable, and innovative multimedia services to end-users across a wide range of devices and networks.

Structure

This chapter will cover the following topics.

- General architecture
- Protocols used in IMS
- IMS interfaces and reference points
- Vulnerabilities in IMS
- Security functions in IMS

Objectives

The primary objective of this chapter is to provide a comprehensive understanding of the IMS, a standardized architecture designed to deliver a wide range of multimedia services over IP networks. By exploring the various aspects of IMS, readers will gain valuable insights into its architecture, protocols, interfaces, and security considerations.

General architecture

The IMS was introduced in the early 2000s as part of the **3rd Generation Partnership Project (3GPP)** release 5. This release marked the initial standardization of IMS within the framework of the 3GPP. Traditionally, as we have seen in the initial chapters of this book, mobile networks relied on circuit-switched networks for voice calls. However, with the rise of data and the internet, packet-switched IP networks became more efficient for handling diverse multimedia services like voice, video calls, and instant messaging.

3GPP defines IMS as a new subsystem consisting of a new mobile network infrastructure that assists the union of data, speech, and mobile network technology over an IP-based infrastructure. IMS is an architecture and not a mobile network protocol. It offers a standardized architecture for implementing multimedia services over IP networks. This ensures interoperability between different devices and network operators, enabling seamless communication across different platforms.

The IP multimedia subsystem enables communication service providers to offer their subscribers multimedia services. The IM subsystem enables the convergence of, and access to, voice, video, messaging, data, and web-based technologies for the wireless and wireline user. IMS users can mix and match a variety of IP-based services in any way they choose during a single communication session. Users can integrate voice, video, and text, content sharing, and presence as part of their communication and can add or drop services as and when they choose.

IMS allows traditional voice services to coexist and integrate with new internet-based services like VoIP, video calls, and instant messaging, offering a unified communication experience. By utilizing packet-switched IP networks, IMS enables efficient data transmission, handles multimedia content effectively, and potentially reduces operational costs. The modular architecture of IMS allows for easy network expansion and integration of new services as needed, adapting to evolving customer demands.

The following figure, from 3GPP TS 23.228, represents the IMS reference architecture including interfaces towards the CS network and other IP-based multimedia networks:

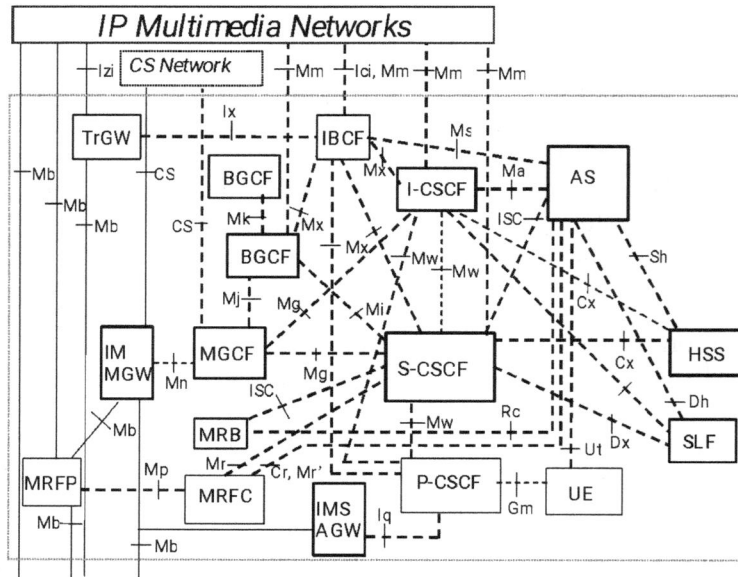

Figure 4.1: *3GPP IMS Architecture*[1]

IMS follows a layered approach to its architectural design, as shown in *Figure 4.2*. This means that transport and bearer services are separated from the IMS signaling network and session management services.

Imagine IMS architecture as a layered cake. On the bottom layer are the transport and bearer services, which handle the nuts and bolts of moving data around the network. These services are separated from the next layer, which is the IMS core or the control layer. The IMS core is responsible for signaling and session management, like setting up calls and keeping them going.

On top of the cake sits the application layer. This layer is crucial because it provides the services that users experience directly, such as presence and group lists. The beauty of the layered approach is that the application layer is designed to work independently of the access network. This means that regardless of whether you are using a mobile phone or a computer to connect to IMS, you will get the same functionality from the application layer. IMS acts as the bridge between the access network and the services, ensuring a consistent experience for users.

---

1   Source: **https://www.3gpp.org/Dynareport/23228.html**

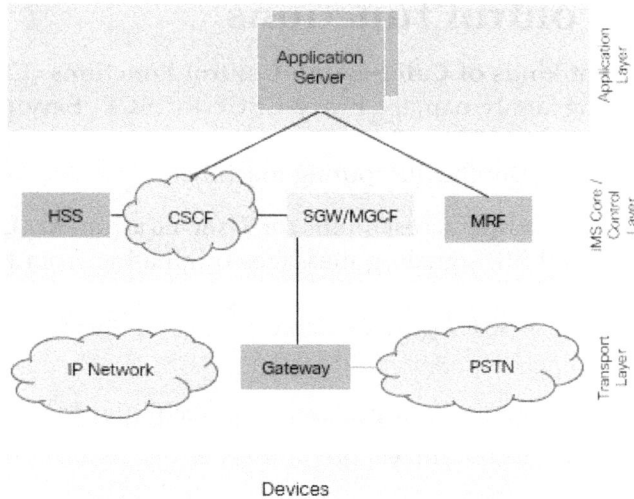

Figure 4.2: IMS Layered Architecture

As IMS is a layered architecture, it is made up of multiple entities with varying functionalities. These can be classified into the following six categories:

- Session management and routing family (CSCFs)
- Databases (HSS, SLF)
- Services (Application server, MRFC, MRFP)
- Interworking functions (BGCF, MGCF, IMS-MGW, SGW)
- Support functions (PCRF, SEG, IBCF)
- Charging

Figure 4.3 shows simplified components of the IMS architecture:

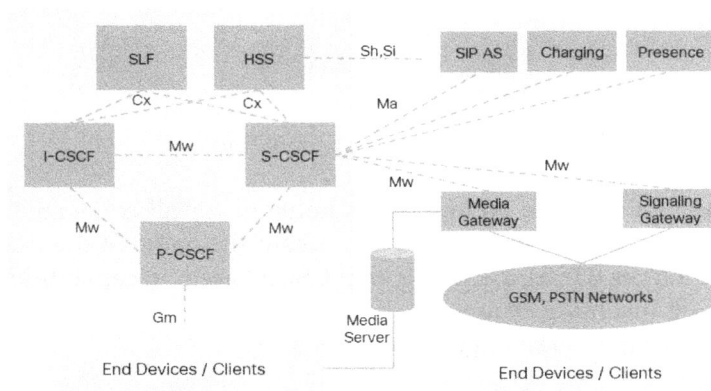

Figure 4.3: IMS Architecture Components

Call session control functions

There are three different kinds of **Call Session Control Functions** (**CSCF**) in the session management and routing family, namely: **Proxy-CSCF(P-CSCF)**, **Serving-CSCF (S-CSCF)**, and **Interrogating-CSCF** (**I-CSCF**). All these entities play a role during registration and session establishment and form the SIP routing machinery.

The P-CSCF serves as the initial access point for **User Equipment** (**UE**) within the IMS network. Consequently, all SIP signaling messages originating from the UE are directed towards the P-CSCF. Conversely, any SIP signaling destined for the UE from the IMS network is routed via the P-CSCF. *Figure 4.4* depicts the components of the IMS call session control functions.

Additionally, the P-CSCF assumes four primary responsibilities:

- **SIP compression**: It optimizes SIP messages to reduce network bandwidth consumption.

- **IPSec security association**: It establishes secure connections using the IPSec protocol.

- **Interaction with the Policy Decision Function (PDF)**: It collaborates with the PDF to enforce network policies and access control rules for the user.

- **Emergency session detection**: It identifies and prioritizes emergency calls (for example, calls to police or ambulance services).

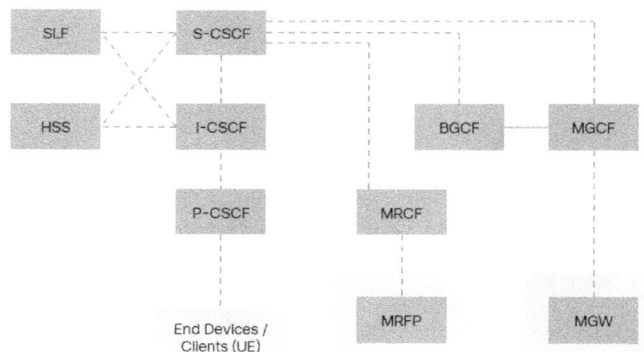

Figure 4.4: *Call Session Control Functions*

I-CSCF is a contact point within an operator's network for all connections destined to a subscriber of that network operator. It helps to obtain the name of the next hop from the **Home Subscriber Server** (**HSS**), assigning an S-CSCF based on capabilities received from the HSS and routing incoming requests to an application server. It also helps to provide Topology Hiding Inter-network Gateway functionality.

The S-CSCF acts as the central control point within the IMS core, orchestrating user registration, routing decisions, session management, and service profile storage.

At a high level, the following is a breakdown of its connection to the IMS core entities:

- **Registration**: When a user registers, the request arrives at the S-CSCF.
- **Authentication**: The S-CSCF retrieves authentication data from the HSS
- **Challenge-response**: The S-CSCF sends a challenge to the UE based on the data from the HSS.
- **Verification**: Upon receiving the UE's response, the S-CSCF verifies it with the HSS.
- **Session management**: If successful, the S-CSCF accepts the registration and manages the user's session state.
- **Service profile**: The S-CSCF stores the user's service profile(s) retrieved from the HSS.

Once the procedures outlined above are completed, the user will be able to initiate and receive IMS services.

Databases

IMS consists of two main databases: HSS and **Subscription Locator Function (SLF)**.

The HSS is the main data storage for all subscribers and service-related information of the IMS. This information includes user identities, registration information, access parameters, and service-triggering information. IMS access parameters are used to set up sessions and include parameters like user authentication, roaming authorization, and allocated S-CSCF names.

The HSS authenticates and authorizes users attempting to access IMS services. It provides authentication information, such as user credentials and security keys, to the CSCF during registration and session establishment. The HSS also maintains subscriber profiles, which include service profiles, service data, and other user-related information. It provides subscriber profile information to the CSCF and Application Server when needed for service delivery. The HSS helps in mobility management by keeping track of the user's current location and registers the user's IP address with the serving CSCF. It supports user mobility by updating the user's location information when the user moves between different access networks. Another important function of HSS is to provide necessary subscriber data to the CSCF during call/session setup and tear-down procedures. It supports various IMS services, such as **Voice over IP (VoIP)**, video conferencing, and instant messaging, by providing the required subscriber information.

The HSS communicates with other IMS entities using standardized interfaces and protocols, such as the Diameter protocol for **authentication, authorization, and accounting (AAA)** functions. It interacts with the CSCF using the Cx and Dx interfaces and with the AS using the Sh interface.

The HSS consists of several logical components, including the **User Data Repository (UDR)**, the **Authentication Center (AUC)**, and the **IP Multimedia Services Identity Module (ISIM)**

Within the IMS database entities, the **Subscriber Location Function (SLF)** acts as a directory service. When the I-CSCF, S-CSCF, or Application Server needs to find the HSS that stores a specific user's data, the SLF helps them locate the appropriate HSS. This is particularly important when a network operator utilizes multiple, independent HSS nodes. When a network element needs to locate a subscriber's specific HSS for tasks like routing calls or data packets, it queries the SLF. The SLF then efficiently directs the request to the appropriate HSS based on the subscriber's identity, ensuring messages and services reach the user seamlessly, even when subscriber data is distributed across multiple servers. This centralized location lookup enhances network efficiency and scalability in scenarios with complex HSS architectures.

Services

Multimedia Resource Function Controller (MRFC), **Multimedia Resource Function Processor (MRFP)**, and **Application Server (AS)** are the three IMS service-related functions. ASs are entities that provide value-added multimedia services in the IMS.

AS has the capability to process and impact an incoming SIP session received from the IMS, along with the capability to originate SIP requests. It also sends accounting information to the charging functions. An SIP AS can be used to provide presence, messaging, push-to-talk, and conferencing services.

The MRFC communicates with the S-CSCF using SIP messages, relaying call setup instructions, and receiving updates. The MRFC then directs the MRFP. The MRFP fulfills the MRFC's instructions by providing and processing the media resources needed for the call, such as mixing audio streams or transcoding video formats.

Interworking functions

In the IMS architecture, there are four interworking functions, which are needed for exchanging signaling and media between IMS and the core network. **Breakout Gateway Control Function (BGCF)**, **Media Gateway Control Function (MGCF)**, IMS-MGW, and **Serving Gateway (SGW)**.

BGCF manages connections between different network types. When an IMS call needs to connect to a traditional phone network (PSTN) or another network entirely, BGCF acts as a bridge, figuring out the most suitable network for the call to be transferred to. BGCF utilizes various routing protocols to determine the optimal network for the call. Once the target network is identified, BGCF seamlessly hands off the call signaling to the appropriate entity in that network. This could be another BGCF, an MGCF, or a soft switch, depending on the specific configuration.

MGCF acts as a traffic director, specifically for voice calls. It bridges the gap between the IMS network (IP-based) and the traditional phone network (PSTN). It essentially translates the signaling languages between these two different worlds, allowing calls to flow smoothly. It manages the setup, maintenance, and teardown of voice calls. It acts like a central switchboard, directing media streams (voice data) between IMS users and PSTN users or between IMS users themselves. MGCF controls one or more IMS-MGWs.

IMS-MGW, as part of the IMS architecture, plays the role of media converter by translating between the media formats used in IMS (like RTP for voice) and the formats used in legacy networks. It also converts the signaling protocols used by IMS to the protocols understood by traditional networks, ensuring calls can be established and managed. It acts as an intermediary, allowing devices on different network protocols to communicate seamlessly.

The signaling Gateway acts as an interface between the IMS core and the traditional **Circuit Switched** (**CS**) network. It translates signaling messages between the two networks. IMS uses SIP for signaling, while the CS network uses protocols like **Message Transfer Part** (**MTP**) and **ISDN User Part** (**ISUP**). The SGW converts between these protocols to ensure communication flows smoothly. It also facilitates connection setup and call control between IMS users and users on the CS network. This enables functionalities like making and receiving calls between IMS and traditional phone lines. The SGW works under the control of the MGCF.

Support functions

Policy and charging rules function (**PCRF**) acts as a policy enforcer and charging rule manager. It receives policy rules from other IMS elements like the P-CSCF. These policies specify how network resources should be allocated and prioritized for different users, services, or situations. PCRF works hand-in-hand with charging systems to define how users are billed for services. It can determine factors like the type of service being used, the amount of data transferred, or the user's subscription plan. This information is then used by charging systems to generate accurate bills.

The SEG has the function of protecting control-plane traffic between security domains. The security domain refers to a network that is managed by a single administrative authority. When the traffic is interdomain, meaning that it originates from a different security domain from the one where it is received, the traffic is routed via a SEG.

The IBCF acts as a gatekeeper between different IMS network domains. It can be used to hide the configuration, capacity, and topology of the network from outside an operator's network. IBCF filters and screens SIP messages, safeguarding the IMS network from unauthorized access or malicious content. IBCF can bridge communication between IMS and non-IMS networks, translating protocols and addressing differences to ensure seamless interaction. It also helps to conceal the internal structure of the IMS network from external parties, enhancing security and manageability.

Protocols used in IMS

The **IP Multimedia Subsystem** (**IMS**) relies on a layered approach, utilizing various protocols at different levels for efficient multimedia communication over IP networks. Each layer has specific protocols for communication.

Protocol in the session control layer

Session Initiation Protocol (**SIP**) is the cornerstone protocol for session management in IMS. It operates at the application layer and is responsible for initiating, managing, and terminating multimedia sessions between users. It plays a crucial role in IMS, enabling multimedia sessions between IMS clients and facilitating services like voice, video, instant messaging, and presence. IP messages travel over reliable transport protocols like TCP. It is a text-based protocol that follows a request-response model.

Protocol in the transport layer

Stream Control Transmission Protocol (**SCTP**) provides a reliable, ordered, and connection-oriented transport mechanism for SIP messages, ensuring message delivery and sequencing, especially important for real-time communication. It is typically used to carry signaling traffic between IMS entities such as the CSCF, HSS, and AS. These signaling messages include SIP signaling for call setup, modification, and termination, Diameter messages for AAA, as well as other control plane messages required for IMS services. By leveraging SCTP for signaling transport, IMS networks can achieve reliable and efficient communication between network elements, ensuring the delivery of high-quality multimedia services to end users. Additionally, SCTP's support for features like multi-homing and multi-stream transmission contributes to the robustness and scalability of IMS deployments, especially in large-scale and geographically distributed networks.

Protocol in the media and transport control layer

RTP resides at the transport layer and is responsible for delivering real-time media streams like audio and video data. It focuses on timely delivery over unreliable protocols like **User Datagram Protocol** (**UDP**), prioritizing data flow over error correction. It provides mechanisms for timestamping, sequence numbering, and payload type identification, which are essential for real-time media applications. RTP is agnostic to the specific media encoding formats (codecs) used for audio, video, or other data types. It acts as a wrapper for the encoded media payload, allowing different codecs to be used without affecting the RTP protocol itself. RTP is typically used in conjunction with other protocols, such as the SIP for session establishment and negotiation, and the **Session Description Protocol** (**SDP**) for describing and negotiating media session parameters.

Real-time Transport Control Protocol (**RTCP**) complements RTP by providing control information for media streams, such as quality reports and synchronization data. It also travels over UDP. RTCP provides feedback on the quality of the media streams transmitted using RTP. It collects and reports statistics, such as packet loss, jitter, round-trip delay, and other quality metrics. This information is used by IMS endpoints and network elements to adapt and optimize the media delivery for better quality. It carries a persistent source identifier, known as the **Canonical Name** (**CNAME**), which allows IMS endpoints to identify and associate multiple media streams from the same source. The RTCP packets are typically sent periodically, alongside the RTP media packets, to provide continuous monitoring and control throughout the duration of the multimedia session.

MGCP or H.248 establishes and manages media channels between **Media Gateways** (**MGWs**) that convert media streams between different formats (for example, PSTN to IP). MGCP is a simpler, text-based protocol, while H.248 offers more advanced features like bandwidth management. H.248 is not used within the core IMS architecture, but it still plays a role in the interworking between IMS and legacy circuit-switched networks. The IP Multimedia Media Gateway acts as a media gateway, translating between IP-based media streams and circuit-switched media streams, but it is controlled by the CSCF using SIP signaling rather than H.248.

Security protocols

The IMS architecture implements robust security measures through various protocols to ensure secure communication and authentication across its network elements. These protocols work in concert to protect both signaling and media traffic, maintaining the confidentiality, integrity, and availability of IMS services. The security protocols in IMS follow a defense-in-depth strategy, where multiple layers of security controls protect against different types of threats and attack vectors. This layered approach ensures that even if one security mechanism is compromised, other protective measures remain in place to maintain the overall security posture of the system. Refer to the following points for a better understanding:

- **Diameter**: This protocol operates at the application layer and is used for AAA functions within the IMS network. It provides a secure and extensible way to exchange subscriber data and control messages between network elements like HSS and MME. Diameter is used to authenticate IMS users during registration and session establishment. The Diameter messages are exchanged between the CSCF and the HSS to verify the user's credentials and authorize their access to IMS services. When an IMS user attempts to register or initiate a session, the CSCF uses Diameter to retrieve the user's subscription profile and service information from the HSS. Diameter is also used to support mobility management in IMS. Diameter can be used for Quality-of-Service management in IMS, enabling the exchange of QoS policies and resource reservation information between network elements, such as the PCRF and the **Application Function** (**AF**).

- **Secure Real-time Transport Protocol (SRTP):** This protocol secures media streams by encrypting them during transmission over RTP. It ensures the privacy and confidentiality of multimedia content exchanged between users. During the session initiation process, using protocols like SIP, devices negotiate and agree on using SRTP for secure communication. Secure key exchange mechanisms are employed to establish shared secret keys between communicating parties. These keys are crucial for the encryption and decryption of the media streams. SRTP encrypts the media payload (audio/video data) of each RTP packet before transmission. The receiving device uses the shared key to decrypt the received packets, recovering the original media content. SRTP provides confidentiality, privacy, and integrity functions to the IMS.

IMS interfaces and reference points

The IMS relies on a complex network of interconnected elements for seamless multimedia communication. To ensure smooth information exchange and signaling between these entities, 3GPP defines a standardized set of interfaces and reference points. These act as the communication highways and connection points within the IMS network.

Interfaces represent the technical specifications that define how two network elements communicate. They dictate the data format, message structure, and communication protocols used for information exchange. Examples of IMS interfaces include SIP for session management and diameter for authentication and authorization.

Reference points refer to the logical connection points between network elements. They identify where interfaces are implemented on specific elements within the IMS architecture. For instance, the Cx reference point might specify the connection between a CSCF and an HSS using the SIP interface.

The IMS architecture depicts some of the critical interfaces and reference points between various IMS components, shown in the following figure:

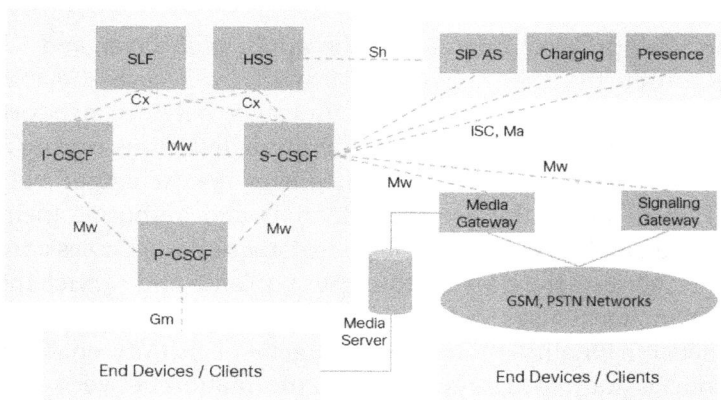

Figure 4.5: *IMS component's interfaces and reference points*

The Gm interface in the IMS architecture is the reference point between the UE and the IMS core network component P-CSCF. It is an IP-based interface that provides access to IMS services and enables communication between the UE and the IMS network elements. The Gm interface uses SIP for signaling purposes, such as session establishment, modification, and termination. Gm interface is also used for IMS user registration and authentication. The UE initiates the registration process by sending a SIP REGISTER message over the Gm interface to the P-CSCF, which then interacts with other IMS elements like the HSS for user authentication and authorization. The interface ensures security and privacy for IMS communications. It supports various security mechanisms, such as IPsec for secure IP transport, and SIP-level security features like digest authentication and encryption.

IMS Service Control (ISC) and **Multimedia Application Server (Ma) Interface** are two related interfaces within the IMS architecture, both facilitating communication between the S-CSCF and AS. The ISC interface, based on SIP, enables standardized connectivity between the S-CSCF and AS residing within the subscriber's home network (Home PLMN) or even a third-party network. ISC leverages a set of SIP methods and responses defined by 3GPP specifications (TS 24.229 and TS 24.880) for message exchange. Ma is an older interface, also based on SIP, that predates ISC. It was primarily used for communication with **Multimedia Application Servers** (**MAS**) within the IMS network. With the evolution of IMS and service offerings, ISC has become the preferred interface for communication between S-CSCF and Application Servers due to its standardized nature and wider industry adoption.

The Sh interface facilitates communication between the AS and the HSS using the diameter protocol. It is a key mechanism for data exchange related to subscriber information and service management. The Sh interface enables the AS to perform various operations on subscriber data stored in the HSS, such as data exchange, data update, and subscription management.

Mw interface refers to the interface between the S-CSCF and the MGCF. The Mw interface provides the communication path between the S-CSCF and the MGCF within the IMS architecture. It allows the S-CSCF to instruct the MGCF on the establishment and release of circuit-switched connections for voice calls between IMS users and users on circuit-switched networks. The Mw interface may also be involved in the management of bearer channels for media streams between the IMS network and the MGW. This includes allocating and releasing resources for voice traffic and ensuring proper synchronization between the packet-switched and circuit-switched domains.

The Cx interface acts as a critical link between the CSCF and the HSS. It operates using the Diameter protocol, which is a secure and extensible protocol for exchanging subscriber data and control messages within the IMS network. The primary function of the Cx interface is to facilitate the exchange of subscriber data between the CSCF (typically the Serving CSCF or S-CSCF) and the HSS. This data is essential for managing and authorizing multimedia sessions for IMS users. Its key functionalities include subscriber registration, authentication, and authorization, and profile updates.

Vulnerabilities in IMS

Due to its reliance on open protocols like SIP and Diameter, distributed architecture, and mobility features, IMS can be susceptible to various attacks. These attacks can be categorized into signaling attacks, media attacks, attacks on service availability, and attacks on the IMS architecture.

Signaling SIP attacks

The SIP acts as the signaling mechanism for establishing, managing, and terminating sessions in IMS. SIP messages, often transmitted in plain text, are vulnerable to several attacks similar to the ones mentioned in the following:

- **Denial of service (DoS) attacks**: Attackers can flood the network with bogus SIP messages, like REGISTER or INVITE requests, overwhelming IMS components (CSCF, HSS) and disrupting legitimate user sessions.

- **Call tampering (Man-in-the-middle)**: If an attacker intercepts the SIP signaling between two users, they can eavesdrop on conversations, redirect calls, or inject malicious content.

- **SIP spoofing (Identity theft)**: By forging SIP messages with a spoofed identity, attackers can impersonate legitimate users to gain unauthorized access to services or launch further attacks.

Media flow RTP attacks

The RTP carries the multimedia content (voice, video) in IMS sessions. The lack of encryption by default in RTP exposes media streams to various attacks, like the ones listed in the following:

- **Eavesdropping**: Attackers can intercept unencrypted RTP streams and listen to ongoing calls without user knowledge.

- **Session hijacking**: By exploiting weaknesses in session establishment protocols, attackers can hijack ongoing sessions and inject malicious content (for example, spam messages) into the media flow.

- **Content modification**: Attackers can tamper with the media stream during transmission, altering the content being delivered to users.

Denial-of-service attacks

Beyond SIP and media flow, IMS is susceptible to broader DoS and DDoS attacks that target critical network components and underlying communication protocols. Listed in the following are a few attacks on the core components of the IMS architecture:

- **Overwhelming IMS Core**: A flood of malicious traffic targeting core elements like the SGW or MGCF can overload these components and render them unavailable to legitimate users.

- **Distributed attacks**: A coordinated DDoS attack, originating from multiple compromised devices, can overwhelm the entire IMS infrastructure, causing widespread service outages.

Figure 4.6 shows a mind map of the various vulnerabilities that exist in the various IMS components and other entities:

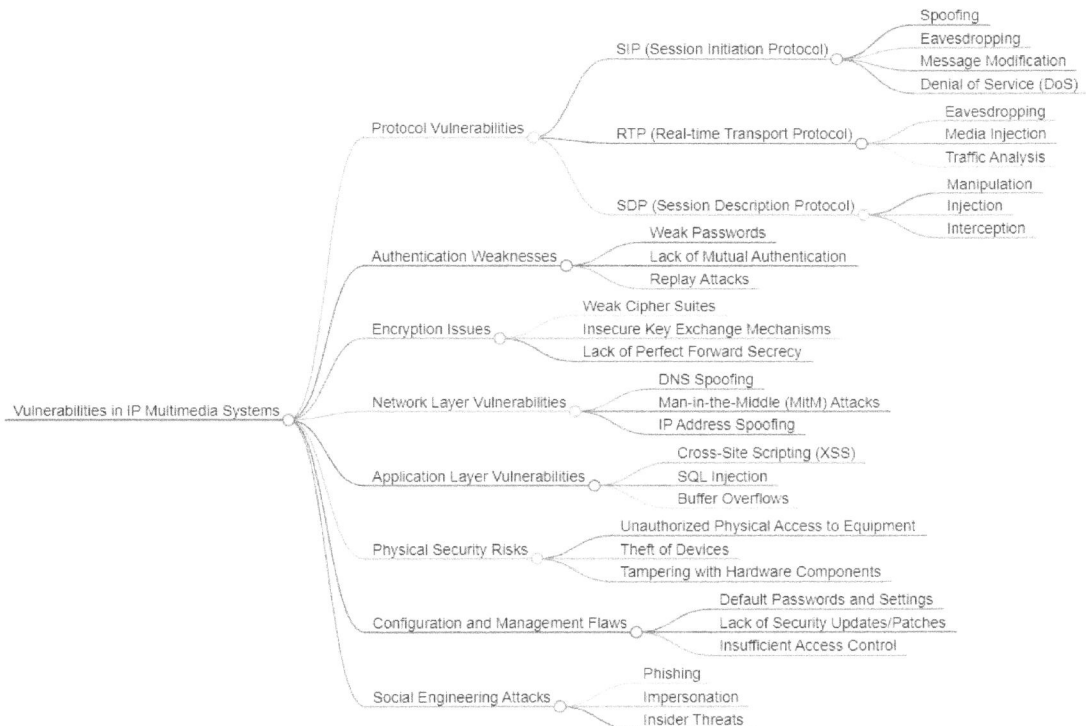

Figure 4.6: *Vulnerabilities in IMS*

Security functions in IMS

As with its layered architecture, IMS employs a multi-layered security approach to protect against various threats and vulnerabilities. At the network level, firewalls, intrusion detection/prevention systems, and inherent components safeguard the IMS core from unauthorized access and malicious traffic. Application-level security mechanisms, such as SIP authentication, encryption (TLS, IPsec, SRTP), and access control policies, ensure secure signaling and media communication, and key management systems facilitate secure key exchange for encryption. Some of these security mechanisms, like authentication, are inherent to the IMS architecture, while others, like security controls at the network layer, depend on additional components to provide the required security functionality. Before we explore each of these security measures, let us review the various security measures in IMS.

Authentication and authorization

Authentication in IMS is accomplished through various methods like 3GPP **Authentication and Key Agreement (AKA)**, **Network Access Subsystem (NASS)**, **NASS-IMS-Bundled Authentication (NBA)**, **GPRS-IMS-bundled Authentication (GIBA)**, and HTTP authentication. Let us understand this in detail:

- **AKA**: The core of IMS security is a secret key that is mutually shared by the ISIM and the AUC of the home network. It relies on a long-term secret key (K) stored securely within the IP Multimedia **Subscriber Identity Module (ISIM)**. This module, typically embedded in a smartcard-based device called the **Universal Integrated Circuit Card (UICC)**, also houses the algorithms used for authentication, AKA. Essentially, ISIM acts as the cornerstone of IMS security by safeguarding the shared secret key. AKA accomplishes mutual authentication of both the ISIM and the AUC and establishes a pair of cipher and integrity keys.

- **NBA**: It is an alternative authentication mechanism for IMS networks. It offers a more streamlined approach compared to the traditional IMS AKA method. NBA streamlines the authentication process, reducing the number of steps required for a UE to access services. By offloading some authentication tasks to the NASS, the NBA can potentially reduce the burden on IMS core elements. NBA facilitates a single sign-on experience for users, eliminating the need for separate logins at different service layers. NBA is typically used in **Telecommunications and Internet Converged Services and Protocols for Advanced Networking (TISPAN)** based access networks, such as those utilizing xDSL technologies. These networks often rely on location-specific authentication, making the NBA a suitable choice.

- **GIBA**: It is another authentication mechanism for IMS networks. Similar to NBA, it aims to streamline the user authentication process compared to traditional IMS AKA. GIBA streamlines the authentication process by leveraging existing GPRS authentication and reusing the secure IP address binding for IMS registration. GIBA, like the NBA, can potentially reduce the burden on IMS core elements as it utilizes information from the GPRS network. However, there are a few limitations with GIBA. Its effectiveness depends on a functional GPRS network, which may not be available in all scenarios. GIBA is primarily suited for scenarios where users connect to IMS services over GPRS connections. With the rise of faster mobile data technologies (for example, LTE, 5G), its relevance might decrease.

Secure signaling

SIP Security (**SIPsec**) encrypts SIP messages, which manage call setup, termination, and other functionalities. Encrypting SIPsec protects call details like caller ID, call forwarding instructions, and other sensitive information from eavesdropping or tampering.

SIPSec can be deployed in two modes: end-to-end SIPsec and hop-by-hop SIPsec. In end-to-end mode, both the sender and receiver of SIP messages implement SIPsec. All communication, including signaling and media, is encrypted throughout the entire path. The hop-by-hop mode encrypts SIP messages between specific points in the network, such as between a user and a service provider or between service providers. This approach can be less resource-intensive but offers a lower level of security compared to end-to-end SIPsec.

Mutual authentication ensures both parties involved in a call are who they claim to be. This prevents attackers from impersonating legitimate users to intercept calls or gain unauthorized access. It is achieved by exchanging digital certificates of the **user agent** (**UA**) and the server. Each party then verifies the validity of the received certificate by checking its authenticity (using a trusted Certificate Authority) and ensuring its revocation status. If both certificates are valid, a secure connection is established with mutual trust. The user and server can now communicate with the assurance that they are interacting with the intended party.

Media encryption

In modern real-time communications, securing media streams is crucial for maintaining privacy and confidentiality. The SRTP has emerged as the standard solution for encrypting media streams in VoIP, WebRTC, and other real-time applications. While SRTP effectively handles media encryption, it requires the secure distribution of encryption keys between communicating parties. Two prominent key management protocols have been developed to address this requirement, as mentioned in the following:

- **SRTP**: It is a cryptographic protocol specifically designed to secure the real-time transport of multimedia content used in applications like VoIP and video conferencing. It builds upon the RTP, adding encryption, message authentication, and replay protection functionalities. SRTP encrypts the media stream (voice, video) during transmission. This safeguards the confidentiality and integrity of the content, preventing unauthorized users from listening in or modifying the media flow.

- **Key management protocols**: These protocols establish secure mechanisms for exchanging encryption and decryption keys used with SRTP. This ensures that only authorized parties can access the media content. Some of the common key management protocols used in SRTP are **key derivation functions** (**KDFs**), **Datagram Transport Layer Security** (**DTLS-SRTP**), the **Multimedia Internet KEYing** (**Mikey**) Framework, and **Encryption Key Transport** (**EKT**).

Network security

The IP-based nature of IMS architectures exposes the services offered by IMS to various security threats common to IP networks. To protect the IMS core infrastructure, user data, and service continuity, several critical network security controls must be implemented. These include the deployment of firewalls, intrusion detection solutions, and access lists, as mentioned in the following:

- **Firewalls**: These act as security barriers, filtering incoming and outgoing traffic. Firewalls control access to IMS components and prevent unauthorized connections from external networks.

- **Intrusion detection/prevention systems (IDS/IPS)**: These continuously monitor network activity for suspicious behavior. IDS can alert administrators of potential attacks, while IPS can take actions to block them.

- **Access control lists (ACLs)**: These define network access permissions, specifying which devices or users are allowed to access specific resources within the IMS network. This helps restrict unauthorized access to sensitive information.

Secure mobility

Secure mobility controls play a crucial role in ensuring authenticated and confidential communication as users move across different access networks. These security mechanisms operate at multiple layers of the network architecture to protect both signaling and media traffic. Refer to the following points for a better understanding:

- **IPsec Tunneling**: This encrypts data traffic between mobile devices and the IMS core network, especially when using potentially insecure wireless connections like cellular data. This protects user data and call information from interception.

- **Universal Subscriber Identity Module (USIM)**: This secure chip on a mobile device stores user credentials and cryptographic keys used for authentication and secure communication within the IMS network.

Secure boot and software updates

Maintaining security and system integrity is paramount in IMS, particularly during critical phases like system boot and software updates. The secure boot provides a foundation of trust by ensuring that only authenticated and verified code executes during the system startup process. This chain of trust begins at the hardware level with a root of trust, typically implemented through specialized **hardware security modules** (**HSMs**) or **Trusted Platform Modules** (**TPMs**), and extends through each stage of the boot process.

- **Secure boot mechanisms**: These ensure only authorized software can boot on devices, preventing malware from compromising the system and potentially bypassing security measures.

- **Digital signing and verification of software updates**: This validates the integrity and authenticity of software updates before installation. This helps prevent attackers from injecting malicious code disguised as legitimate updates.

By implementing these security functions, IMS creates a layered defense that protects user privacy, call integrity, and overall network availability.

Network security capabilities in the IMS architecture can be improved by deploying products and solutions that improve the overall security posture of the IMS deployment. These include the deployment of SBCs, perimeter firewalls, and intrusion detection and prevention solutions.

Role of the perimeter firewall in an IMS architecture

In an IMS architecture, the perimeter firewall plays a crucial role in protecting the IMS core network from external threats and unauthorized access. The IMS architecture is designed to provide multimedia services over IP networks, and the perimeter firewall acts as a security barrier between the IMS core network and external networks, such as the Internet or other service provider networks. The main objective of the perimeter firewall is to ensure that the traffic toward the IMS components is from a trusted source. A diagrammatic representation of the placement of the perimeter firewall, separating the untrusted zone and the trusted zone, is mentioned in the following figure:

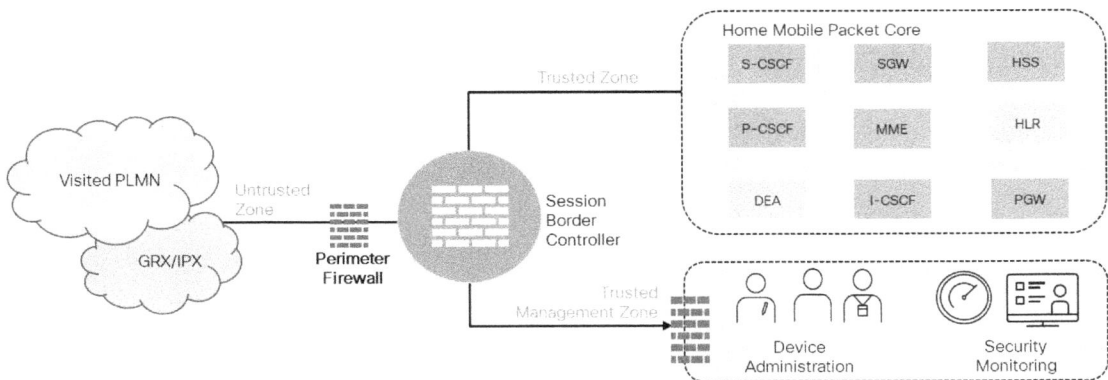

Figure 4.7: Perimeter firewall in IMS architecture

As depicted in the figure, the perimeter firewall separates the trusted IMS core network from untrusted external networks, preventing direct access to the IMS core components from external sources. The firewall also inspects and filters incoming and outgoing traffic based on predefined security rules and policies. It allows only authorized traffic to pass through, blocking any traffic that violates the defined rules or exhibits suspicious behavior. Topology hiding capability can be realized by configuring NAT in this firewall, which helps in hiding the internal IP addresses of the IMS core network components from external networks, enhancing security and preventing direct targeting of internal resources. In addition to traditional packet filtering, modern firewalls can analyze application-level traffic and enforce security rules based on the specific applications or protocols involved, such as SIP used in IMS.

The perimeter firewall can also incorporate intrusion prevention capabilities, detecting and blocking potential attacks or malicious activities targeting the IMS core network. The perimeter firewall can be used to limit the rate of incoming traffic, particularly SIP registrations, to prevent overload situations and ensure smooth operation of the IMS core, thus enforcing basic controls to prevent DoS attacks.

Role of SBC in securing the IMS architecture

SBCs were introduced and deployed in the IMS architecture to enable interoperability and achieve the required SIP functionality. In 2010, the **Internet Engineering Task Force (IETF)** took up the task of defining the requirements of SIP-based SBCs. These requirements are officially documented in RFC 5853.

SBCs are typically deployed at the network edge, serving as transit points for signaling and media traffic. Due to their strategic placement at the network periphery, SBCs provide several essential security services. These include access control mechanisms, detection and prevention of DoS attacks, obfuscation of the internal network topology, and protection of both signaling and media traffic flows. Furthermore, SBCs enable functionalities and services that are not natively supported by endpoints, such as traversal of **Network Address Translation (NAT)** devices, transcoding of media streams, and interworking of **Dual-Tone Multi-Frequency (DTMF)** signaling. Moreover, SBCs offer a wide range of traffic management options, including enforcement of **quality of service (QoS)** policies, facilitation of media recording capabilities, and restriction on the choice of media formats utilized. Refer to the following architecture for clarity:

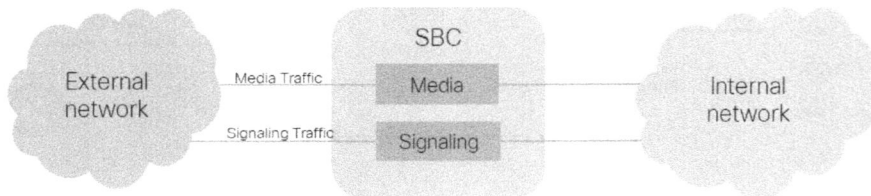

Figure 4.8: High-level SBC Architecture

The architectural design of SBCs comprises two distinct logical components: the signaling plane and the media plane, as shown in *Figure 4.8*. The signaling plane takes care of managing call control protocols, such as SIP and H.323. Its responsibilities encompass modifying protocol headers and bodies, maintaining contextual information for ongoing dialogs, correlating related dialogs, enforcing protocol-specific timers, and determining the freshness or validity of sessions. On the other hand, the media plane is responsible for handling RTP and RTCP traffic. It allocates and deallocates port pairs for media traffic, enables transformation operations on the payloads of media packets, and performs general traffic management functions.

The media and signaling planes within an SBC architecture can either be integrated into a single physical unit or distributed across separate physical devices. In recent times, service providers have deployed SBC as a distributed architecture, where the media plane and signaling plane components reside on distinct physical or virtual nits. This distributed approach allows for scalability, redundancy, and dedicated resource allocation for each plane, enhancing the overall performance and reliability of the SBC solution.

SBCs can be deployed in different roles, depending on their location and functionality within the network. Two common types of SBCs in IMS environments are **Access SBCs (A-SBCs)** and **Interconnect SBCs (I-SBCs)**. An Access SBC, also known as an **Access Border Controller**, is typically deployed at the edge of the service provider's network, acting as the entry and exit point for subscriber traffic. Its primary role is to protect the IMS core network from potential threats originating from the access network or subscriber devices. **Interconnect Border Controller (I-SBC)** is deployed at the interconnection points between the service provider's network and external networks, such as other service provider domains or the public internet. Its primary purpose is to secure and manage the interconnection between different networks and enforce inter-provider policies.

An SBC can be deployed in the IMS architecture as shown in *Figure 4.9*. SBCs are multipurpose devices with a wide span of operations on media, signaling, security, reporting, monitoring, traffic management, and perimeter defense, but all these security functions may not be enabled on the component. As explained in the above section, the perimeter firewall can cater to a few of the security functions that SBC brings along. It is normally left to the service provider to choose the device on which the required security capability is enabled based on various criteria like performance, scale, and use cases.

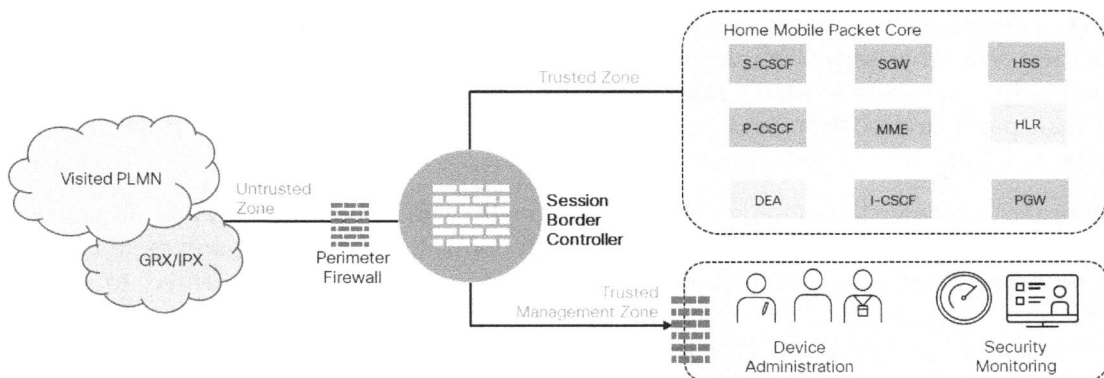

Figure 4.9: SBC in IMS Architecture

Enabling all the features offered by an SBC may not always be essential. In certain scenarios, it is improbable that capabilities like topology abstraction, perimeter defense, and secure media and signaling would be required. The necessity for specific SBC features, as listed in the following, depends on the context and deployment requirements.

Topology hiding in IMS with session border controllers

One of the critical security functions provided by SBCs in an IMS architecture is topology hiding. This feature plays a crucial role in protecting the internal network topology and addressing scheme from external exposure, thereby enhancing the overall security posture of the IMS network.

In an IMS environment, various network elements, such as the CSCF, HSS, and Application Servers, communicate with each other using IP addresses and port numbers. Without topology hiding, these internal IP addresses and port numbers would be exposed to external networks during signaling and media exchange, potentially revealing sensitive information about the network topology and architecture.

Exposing the internal network topology can have severe security implications. Malicious actors could exploit this information to launch targeted attacks, gain unauthorized access, or attempt to bypass security measures.

SBCs deployed at the network edge can effectively conceal the internal network topology by performing **Network Address and Port Translation (NAPT)**. SBCs act as an intermediary between the internal and external networks, performing network address and port translation for both signaling and media traffic. This translation process replaces the internal IP addresses and port numbers with external, public addresses and ports, effectively hiding the internal addressing scheme from external entities.

Topology hiding in SBCs can also be achieved by anchoring signaling and media flows, terminating and re-originating them as necessary. This anchoring process breaks the end-to-end communication path, preventing external entities from directly communicating with internal network elements and obfuscating the internal topology. SBCs can also modify signaling messages, such as SIP messages, to remove or obfuscate any information that could reveal internal network details. This includes stripping or modifying headers, bodies, and other sensitive information that may be present in the signaling messages. Similarly, by acting as a media relay and transcoding point, SBCs can conceal the internal media paths and codecs used within the IMS network, further obscuring the internal topology from an external view.

In order to achieve the topology hiding functionality, SBCs should be strategically placed at the network edge, acting as the entry and exit points for all signaling and media traffic. Redundancy and high availability configurations should be implemented to ensure continuity of service and prevent single points of failure. SBCs should be integrated with other security components in the IMS architecture, such as firewalls, intrusion detection/prevention systems, and **security information and event management (SIEM)** solutions, to provide a comprehensive and cohesive security posture. Robust monitoring and logging mechanisms should be developed to monitor alerts and events from the SBCs to proactively identify and mitigate security issues.

Overload protection with session border controllers

In the evolving field of modern communication networks, ensuring service availability and resilience against malicious attacks and unexpected traffic surges is important. SBCs play a crucial role in protecting IMS architectures from DoS attacks and overload conditions, safeguarding the overall stability and performance of the network.

DoS attacks are malicious attempts to render a network, system, or service unavailable to its intended users. These attacks typically involve overwhelming the target with a massive influx of traffic, consuming its resources, and ultimately causing service disruption or complete denial of access. A flooding attack is a common attack against the IMS architecture. In this attack, the target is flooded with an excessive amount of network traffic, such as IP packets, SIP messages, or RTP media streams, overwhelming its processing capabilities and exhausting resources. Exploiting vulnerabilities or misconfigurations in network protocols, such as SIP or RTP, or targeting specific applications or services with malformed or malicious requests, to cause service disruption or resource exhaustion, are other common attacks that affect the IMS components.

Overload scenarios, on the other hand, can occur due to legitimate but unexpected traffic surges, such as flash crowds or network events that generate excessive signaling or media load. These situations can also lead to service degradation or outages if not properly managed.

SBCs deployed at the edge of the IMS network act as a first line of defense against DoS attacks and overload scenarios. SBCs can filter and rate-limit incoming traffic based on predefined security policies and thresholds. This includes limiting the number of concurrent sessions, controlling the rate of signaling or media packets, and blocking traffic from known malicious sources or addresses. SBCs can be configured to perform protocol validation and anomaly detection of signaling protocols, such as SIP and RTP, to detect and mitigate protocol exploitation attempts. This capability can identify and block malformed or non-compliant messages, preventing potential vulnerabilities from being exploited. SBCs can also be configured to maintain blacklists and whitelists of IP addresses, user agents, or other identifiers to block or allow specific traffic sources. This helps in mitigating DoS attacks originating from known malicious sources and ensuring legitimate traffic is prioritized.

Overload control mechanisms in SBCs can be implemented by enabling overload control algorithms and techniques to manage unexpected traffic surges. These include call gapping, call throttling, and load shedding, which help to regulate the amount of traffic forwarded to the IMS core components, preventing them from becoming overwhelmed.

SIP security

SIP is currently widely deployed within fixed, mobile, and FMC networks. It is used for fixed and mobile access, within fixed and mobile core networks, and for interconnects between core networks. SIP is extremely flexible and can use several message types during session establishment, which can include various optional fields and parameters. *Table 5.1* shows several well-known services that use SIP:

SIP service	Provider platform
Voice over LTE (VoLTE)	IMS
SMS over IP	IMS
Rich Communications Services (RCS)	IMS
Voice over (Vo5G)	IMS
PacketCable	IMS
SIP trunking	IMS and Non-IMS
SIP trunking (business trunking)	IMS
Hosted voice / **Voice over Broadband (VoBB)** for business	IMS and Non-IMS
VoBB for residential	IMS and Non-IMS

Table 4.1: SIP services

As we can infer from the table above, SIP is used in multiple well-known services operationalized by the IMS architecture. This large-scale adoption of the protocol and evolution of service provider use cases and technology has increased the threat landscape of the SIP protocol. As SIP is a crucial component affecting IMS, the vulnerabilities illustrated in *Figure 4.10* for SIP have a direct impact on the security posture of the IMS architecture:

Figure 4.10: Vulnerabilities in the SIP protocol

SIP protocol can be secured using a layered approach that includes security controls and core, access, and border sections service provider network.

Perimeter protection

As part of the border network protection, SBC should be used to protect the core network whenever an SIP-based service is made available to users or when an SIP interconnect between service providers is in place. As mentioned in the above section, the SBC can be either deployed as an A-SBC or an I-SBC, where an A-SBC is deployed on the access (subscriber end) while an I-SBC is deployed on the service provider interconnect end.

As defined in the GSMA FS.38 document, the A-SBC and I-SBC provide the IMS architecture with inherent security capabilities to secure the IMS components. Some of these inherent security capabilities are described in the following:

- **SIP signaling inspection**: SIP signaling inspection refers to the process of examining SIP messages, including headers and payloads as per specification, to enforce security policies, ensure protocol compliance, and detect and mitigate potential threats or vulnerabilities. Any malformed packet should be rejected by the A-SBC and the I-SBC.

- **RTP and RTCP packet inspection**: Like the SIP signaling inspection, the RTP pack inspection ensures that RTP and RTCP packets are as per specifications and are not malformed. Any malformed packet should be rejected by the A-SBC and the I-SBC.

- **Allow packets only from trusted source**: The A-SBC and the I-SBC should discard SIP packets if they do not originate from a valid and trusted endpoint. For example, if the SBC authentication and authorization are based on source IP address rather than SIP registration, and the source IP address of the SIP packet(s) does not match an entry within the SBC, the SIP packets should be considered as coming from non-valid endpoints.

- **Topology hiding**: As detailed in the above section, an A-SBC and I-SBC can be used to implement SIP topology hiding capability before a SIP message is sent outside of the core network. This is done to prevent external parties from finding and understanding the internal (private side) core network addressing.

- **Restrict non-SIP and RTP services and ports**: The public SIP interface offering a relevant IMS service should only allow SIP, RTP, and RTCP. Additional services and ports should not be opened up on the public interface. Scanning these public interfaces should not give away information on the ports that have been allowed or restricted.

- **TLS and IPsec termination**: An A-SBC and I-SBC can be used to implement TLS and IPsec termination to ensure the confidentiality, integrity, and authenticity of data transmitted over VoIP networks. TLS termination on an SBC involves terminating the TLS encryption and decryption process at the SBC itself. When a

TLS-encrypted SIP session arrives at the SBC, the SBC acts as the TLS termination point, decrypting the incoming traffic to its original plaintext form. IPsec termination involves the decryption and encryption of IPsec-protected packets at the SBC. IPsec termination typically occurs when SIP traffic is traversing across untrusted networks, such as the public Internet. The SBC terminates the IPsec tunnel established between two endpoints, decrypts the IPsec-protected packets, and processes the SIP traffic within the decrypted packets.

The perimeter firewall depicted in *Figure 4.7* can be used to apply access control policies for the IMS components. SBC can provide network layer 3 (routing) and network layer 4 (transport) security controls but applying these controls on the SBC can lead to performance impact, if not planned and scoped well. For enhanced security, the I-SBC can be positioned behind the network perimeter firewall. This layered approach allows the firewall to act as a first line of defense against common network attacks, including Layer 3 and Layer 4 attacks. Additionally, the firewall can mitigate network-based volumetric attacks, such as denial-of-service attempts.

Access layer protection

Access layer protection mainly refers to how securely the end users or the subscribers connect and consume the relevant IMS services. For this scenario, the primary initial focus should be on the authentication of the user and the confidentiality and integrity of the SIP signaling traffic. TLS safeguards the integrity and confidentiality of SIP signaling, mitigating privacy breaches and offering protection against external signaling attacks. In real-world VoIP setups, SIP messages are encrypted with TLS only when they travel between a customer's equipment, like a phone or server, and the internet connection point of the service provider's network, like a SBC.

Securing SIP passwords is crucial to defend against financial fraud, unauthorized access to personal information, and certain DoS attacks. SIP credentials, particularly passwords, should never be provided directly to customers or users for endpoint provisioning. Endpoint configuration and credential deployment should be entirely automated, eliminating manual intervention. SIP passwords should be automatically generated using a strong, secure method. These passwords should never be stored or displayed in an unencrypted format. All relevant SIP nodes that store SIP passwords in databases or files should encrypt the password using best-current practice encryption. Similarly, the endpoints that store SIP passwords, should encrypt the password.

Another simple but effective method of securing SIP is to prevent or reduce how malicious actors can gather information about SIP that is available over the internet. Service providers should not use easy-to-guess DNS names for SIP-based services, like `sip.companyname.com`.

It is recommended to change the default standard SIP ports (UDP/5060 and TCP/5061 for TLS) to a custom one to make it harder for SIP ports to be visible to external scans. Similarly, SBC should be configured to block SIP requests that have the SIP fingerprint of known SIP attacks.

At the access interface level, the SIP registrars should be enabled to lock out an account after one or more failed SIP registration attempts. The SIP registrars should also be capable of alerting the security monitoring tool, to take subsequent preventive actions. This helps to prevent SIP password cracking.

As mentioned in the above section, SBC can help analyze the SIP headers and remove confidential information. Several SIP headers exist that contain private user information, and which should be removed when the SIP request or response containing the header is sent outside of a trusted domain of the service provider network. In certain scenarios, IMEI information may be shared during SIP transactions. The IMEI should not be sent to the opposite party or parties involved in the session. The access SBC must be removed from the Contact header before it is sent outside of a trusted domain of the service provider network.

Protection of SIP interconnects

Confidentiality, authentication, and integrity are vital components for securing the SIP interconnects. These are mainly provided by TLS or IPsec.

The IPsec capability for protecting the border between interconnects is mainly provided by **Security Gateways (SecGW)**. The SecGWs are responsible for enforcing the security policy of a security domain towards other SEGs in the destination security domain. All IP traffic shall pass through a SecGW before entering or leaving the security domain, as shown in the figure:

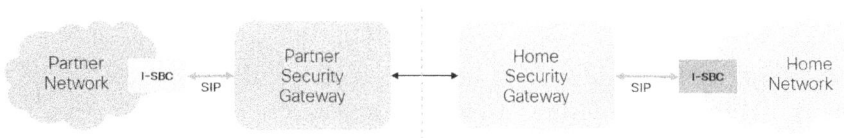

Figure 4.11: Security Gateway for Inter-connect security

For protection of the SP interconnects, 3GPP TS 33.203 states that TLS may also be used between IMS networks on top of IPsec. I-SBCs can be configured to use TLS to secure the SIP between them.

As with protecting the access interface, traditional methods of reconnaissance prevention, and reducing visibility during a port scan can be applied for SIP interconnects. An effective method of securing SIP interconnect is to prevent or reduce how malicious actors can gather information about SIP that is available over the internet. Service providers should not use easy-to-guess DNS names for SIP-based services, like `sip.companyname.com`.

It is recommended to change the default standard SIP ports (UDP/5060 and TCP/5061 for TLS) to a custom one to make it harder for SIP ports to be visible to external scans. Similarly, SBC should be configured to block SIP requests that have the SIP fingerprint of known SIP attacks.

As mentioned in the above section, SBC can help analyze the SIP headers and remove confidential information. Several SIP headers exist that contain private user information, and which should be removed when the SIP request or response containing the header is sent outside of a trusted domain of the service provider network. In certain scenarios, IMEI information may be shared during SIP transactions.

Conclusion

IMS represents a pivotal advancement in delivering multimedia services over IP networks. Its three-tiered architecture, service, control, and transport layers, creates a foundation for integrating diverse multimedia services with flexibility and scalability. This architecture, powered by protocols like SIP, Diameter, and RTP/SRTP, enables seamless communication and comprehensive session management.

The framework's effectiveness stems from clearly defined interfaces and reference points (Gm, Mw, Mx) that facilitate communication between user equipment, call session control functions, and application servers. This sophisticated infrastructure requires robust security measures, with SBCs providing critical protection through topology hiding, DoS prevention, and encryption at network boundaries.

IMS security extends beyond perimeter defense through protocol-specific mechanisms, including SIP digest authentication, SRTP, and TLS, which collectively protect both signaling and media streams throughout the system.

As networks progress toward 5G and beyond, IMS continues enabling increasingly advanced multimedia services. This evolution presents opportunities alongside security challenges that demand vigilant monitoring, proactive security implementation, and adherence to best practices.

The IMS framework demonstrates how complex multimedia services can be delivered securely over IP networks, providing a robust foundation for the future of multimedia communication across diverse devices and networks.

The next chapter examines 3G networks, which represented a significant leap forward in mobile communications. We'll explore its core architectural components and service delivery platforms that enabled the first truly mobile broadband experience. The chapter analyzes inherent vulnerabilities in 3G systems and details the security mechanisms implemented to address these challenges, providing context for understanding how security evolved from 3G through subsequent generations.

Points to remember

- The IMS architecture consists of several key components, including CSCFs, databases (HSS, SLF), application servers for services, interworking functions for legacy network integration, and various support functions. This layered architecture enables fixed-mobile convergence and IP-based multimedia services.
- The three types of Call Session Control Functions serve distinct purposes: **P-CSCF (Proxy-CSCF)** acts as the first point of contact for IMS terminals, S-CSCF handles session control and registration services, and I-CSCF provides routing functionality at domain boundaries.

- IMS implements a comprehensive protocol suite with IPsec and TLS for security, RTP/RTCP for media transport, and SIP as the core session protocol. This protocol stack enables secure, reliable multimedia communications while supporting interoperability between different network elements.

- IMS defines multiple standardized interfaces (reference points) to connect various network elements, including Gm (UE to P-CSCF), Mw (between CSCFs), Cx (CSCF to HSS), and ISC (S-CSCF to application servers). These interfaces ensure proper communication flows and security boundaries within the IMS architecture.

- SBCs serve as critical security elements at network boundaries, providing topology hiding, NAT traversal, protocol normalization, and protection against various attacks, including DoS and malformed message attacks.

- IMS implements multi-layered authentication mechanisms, primarily utilizing IMS-AKA which provides mutual authentication between the user equipment and the network. This prevents unauthorized access and ensures service integrity.

- Protection of SIP signaling is crucial in IMS and is typically handled through IPsec tunnels between UE and P-CSCF as well as TLS between other network elements. This secures call setup, modification, and teardown procedures.

- SRTP protects media streams, providing encryption, message authentication, and replay protection for multimedia content transmitted across the IMS infrastructure.

- The IMS architecture incorporates robust identity management through the HSS, which maintains user profiles, authentication vectors, and service authorization data, enabling proper access control throughout the network.

Exercises

1. Which component in the IMS architecture is responsible for maintaining subscriber information and authentication credentials
   a. P-CSCF
   b. HSS
   c. S-CSCF
   d. I-CSCF

2. Which protocol is primarily used for session management in IMS?
   a. DIAMETER
   b. SIP
   c. RTP
   d. IPsec

3. The Gm reference point in IMS connects:
   a. UE to P-CSCF
   b. P-CSCF to I-CSCF

      c. S-CSCF to HSS

      d. MRFC to MRFP

4. Which security function protects the border between IMS networks and external networks?

      a. SIP Security

      b. Authentication Vector

      c. SBC

      d. Secure Boot

5. In IMS authentication, which mechanism is most commonly used to verify user identity?

      a. HTTP Digest

      b. AKA (Authentication and Key Agreement)

      c. OAuth

      d. Basic Authentication

6. Which protocol is used for media transport in IMS?

      a. SIP

      b. SCTP

      c. RTP/RTCP

      d. DIAMETER

7. The Cx reference point is used for communication between:

      a. UE and P-CSCF

      b. P-CSCF and I-CSCF

      c. I-CSCF/S-CSCF and HSS

      d. BGCF and MGCF

8. Describe the three main CSCF (Call Session Control Function) elements in IMS architecture and their primary responsibilities.

9. Explain how the IMS-Authentication and Key Agreement (IMS-AKA) mechanism works to secure user access to IMS services.

10. What are the security challenges at the SIP signaling layer in IMS, and what mechanisms are used to address them?

11. Explain the role of SBCs in securing an IMS network. What threats do they help mitigate?

12. Describe the security considerations for the interworking functions when connecting IMS to legacy networks.

CHAPTER 5

Third Generation of Mobile Networks

Introduction

The advent of **Third Generation** (**3G**) networks in the early 2000s marked a transformative milestone in mobile telecommunications, introducing enhanced data speeds, superior voice quality, and expanded mobile services. This chapter provides a comprehensive examination of 3G network architecture and its security landscape, with particular emphasis on the **GPRS Tunneling Protocol** (**GTP**).

We begin by exploring the fundamental architecture of 3G networks, examining their components and interconnections to establish a solid understanding of how these systems operate. The discussion then progresses to network interfaces and communication protocols that enable seamless data exchange, followed by an in-depth analysis of inherent security mechanisms and potential vulnerabilities that could compromise network integrity.

A significant focus in this chapter is also placed on the GTP, a crucial element facilitating data transfer and mobility management within 3G networks. We examine GTP's variants, associated vulnerabilities such as tunnel hijacking and signaling weaknesses, and strategies for securing this vital protocol. The chapter concludes with practical guidance on implementing GTP filtering categories and firewall deployment scenarios, providing readers with actionable knowledge for enhancing 3G network security.

Structure

This chapter will cover the following topics.

- General architecture
- Network interfaces in 3G
- Vulnerabilities in 3G network
- Security mechanisms in 3G
- Cryptographic algorithms
- GTP GPRS Tunnelling Protocol
- GTP firewall deployment scenarios

Objectives

The primary objective of this chapter is to provide an in-depth exploration of 3G mobile networks, with a particular emphasis on understanding their architecture, components, and the inherent security risks and vulnerabilities that arise within these complex systems. By exploring the details of 3G networks, a comprehensive understanding of the potential attack vectors and threats that could compromise the confidentiality, integrity, and availability of these critical infrastructures can be identified. Additionally, this chapter will empower the reader with the knowledge and strategies necessary to mitigate these risks effectively, fostering a more secure and resilient 3G mobile network environment. Through a thorough examination of inherent security mechanisms, vulnerabilities, and best practices for securing key protocols like GTP, this chapter attempts to serve as a valuable resource for network administrators, security professionals, and enthusiasts alike, enabling them to navigate the complexities of 3G security with confidence and proactively safeguard these vital communication systems.

General architecture

The need for transitioning from 2G to 3G networks in the early 2000s was driven primarily by the increasing demand for higher data rates, improved network capacity, and the desire to support more advanced multimedia services. As described in the previous chapter, 2G networks were designed primarily for voice communication and offered limited data services with low data rates, typically up to 64 kbps for circuit-switched data and 384 kbps for packet-switched data. With the rise of the internet and expanded adoption, mobile users demanded faster data speeds for activities such as web browsing, email, and file transfers. 3G networks, aimed to cater to this rise in need by promising significantly higher data rates, ranging from 384 kbps to 2 Mbps, allowing for more efficiencies and faster data transfer.

2G networks were not designed to handle the efficient delivery of multimedia services, leading to poor quality and frequent interruptions. The growing popularity of multimedia content, such as streaming audio and video, created a need for networks capable of handling higher bandwidth requirements. With the 3G network's packet-based data transmission, multimedia services were better suited for providing higher data rates and more efficient use of network resources. The advent of 3G networks paved the way for the development of more advanced features and applications, such as video calling, mobile TV, location-based services, and enhanced mobile office applications. 3G networks also offered a more scalable and flexible architecture, allowing for future upgrades and enhancements to meet the ever-increasing demand for data services.

The transition from 2G to 3G networks was a significant step forward in the evolution of mobile communications, enabling faster data speeds, improved multimedia support, global roaming capabilities, and paving the way for more advanced mobile applications and services.

The 3G network architecture was designed to provide a robust and flexible infrastructure for supporting high-speed data services, multimedia applications, and global roaming capabilities. The architecture is based on the **Universal Mobile Telecommunications System (UMTS)** standard, which was developed by the **3rd Generation Partnership Project (3GPP)**.

3G networks can be broadly divided into the following three distinct layers:

- **User or mobile equipment:** This is the 3G phone or modem that houses the UMTS air interface card that facilitates communication with the network.

- **UMTS Terrestrial radio access network (UTRAN):** This handles the air interface between the mobile device and the network, managing signal transmission and reception.

- **Core network (CN):** This is the heart of the network, responsible for service provisioning, user authentication, and call routing.

Figure 5.1 depicts the high-level 3G architecture:

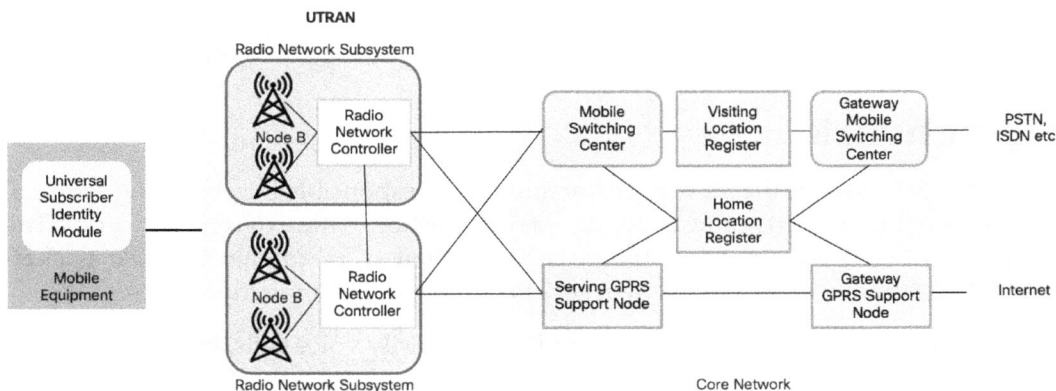

Figure 5.1: *3G Architecture*

User equipment

The UE is a critical component of the 3G network architecture, representing the mobile device used by subscribers to access various services and applications. The UE incorporates a radio interface that enables wireless communication with the UTRAN. This interface supports the air interface protocols and modulation techniques specified in the UMTS standards, such as **Wideband Code Division Multiple Access** (**WCDMA**) and **High-Speed Downlink Packet Access** (**HSDPA**).

The UE contains a SIM card, which is a removable smart card that stores subscriber information, including the **International Mobile Subscriber Identity** (**IMSI**), authentication keys, and subscriber profile data. The SIM card plays a crucial role in identifying and authenticating the subscriber to the network.

UTRAN

The UTRAN is responsible for handling all radio-related functions and providing the air interface between the UE and the core network. The UTRAN plays a vital role in ensuring efficient and reliable communication, managing radio resources, and enabling seamless mobility for subscribers. The UTRAN consists of two main components: *Node B* and the *Radio Network Controller*.

Node B is the base station in the 3G network architecture, similar to the **Base Transceiver Station** (**BTS**) in 2G networks. It handles the physical layer of the air interface, responsible for transmitting and receiving radio signals to and from the UE. It performs functions, such as channel coding, modulation, and demodulation of the air interface signals.

The RNC is the controlling entity in the UTRAN, responsible for managing and controlling one or more Node Bs within its domain. The RNC handles functions such as channel allocation, code management, and power control for the Node Bs under its control. It is responsible for mobility management, including soft and hard handovers, as the UE moves between cells or RNC areas. The RNC also provides encryption and decryption services for user data and signaling between the UE and the core network.

Core network

The CN is the backbone of the 3G network architecture, responsible for providing essential services, managing mobility, and enabling interconnection with external networks. The CN comprises two main domains: the **circuit-switched** (**CS**) domain and the **packet-switched** (**PS**) domain, each with its own set of components and functionalities.

The CS domain handles circuit-switched services, primarily voice calls, but also supports circuit-switched data services. The **Mobile Switching Center (MSC)** is the primary component that handles circuit-switched call control, mobility management, and routing functions for voice services. It coordinates the setup, maintenance, and termination of voice calls.

The Gateway MSC (GMSC) in the 3G CS network acts as the gateway between the 3G network and external circuit-switched networks, such as the **Public Switched Telephone Network** (**PSTN**) or other mobile networks. It facilitates the routing of incoming and outgoing calls to and from external networks.

The Visitor Location Register (VLR) is a temporary database that stores information about subscribers currently located in the area served by a particular MSC. It facilitates efficient call routing and service delivery for roaming subscribers.

The *Packet Switched* domain handles packet-switched data services, such as internet access, multimedia messaging, and streaming. The **Serving GPRS Support Node (SGSN)** within the 3G core network is responsible for routing and delivering data packets to and from the UE within its service area. It manages mobility, authentication, and session management for packet data services.

The Gateway GPRS Support Node (GGSN) acts as the gateway between the 3G network and external packet data networks, such as the Internet or private IP networks. It provides connectivity to these external networks and handles tasks like IP address allocation and billing.

The Home Location Register (HLR) is a central database that stores subscriber information, including subscriber profiles, service details, and location information. It plays a crucial role in managing subscriber mobility and providing consistent services across different networks.

The CN components are interconnected through standardized interfaces and protocols, such as the Iu interface, connecting the UTRAN to the CN, the **Mobile Application Part** (**MAP**) protocol for signaling in the CS domain, and the GTP for packet data transmission and signaling in the PS domain.

Network interfaces in 3G

In 3G telecommunication architecture, several interfaces enable communication between different network elements. The use of interfaces creates distinct modules within the 3G network. One of the major advantages of using the unique interface is that it enables components from different vendors to work together seamlessly. This also helps different network elements to scale independently based on traffic demands. These multiple interfaces create a well-defined communication language within the network. They ensure efficient data flow, modularity, and clear separation of duties between various network components, ultimately leading to a more robust and scalable 3G architecture. The following figure shows various interfaces of the 3G architecture:

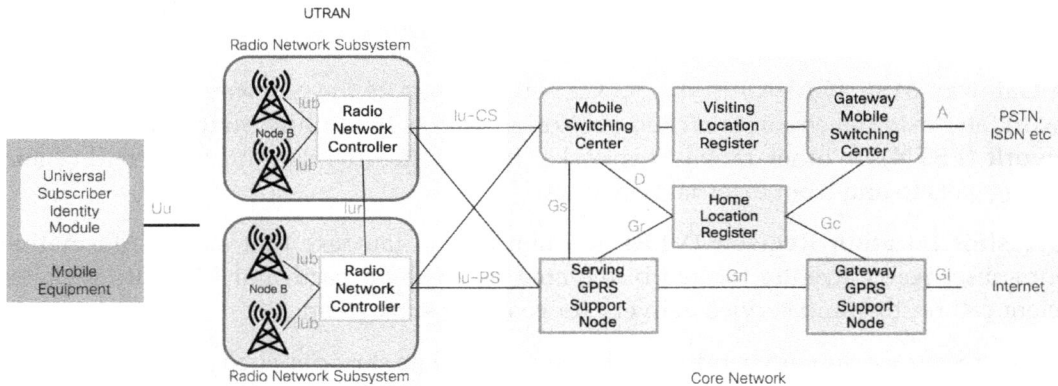

Figure 5.2: *3G Interfaces*

The 3G interfaces and their uses are listed in the following:

- **Uu interface:** The air interface between the UE and the Node B, enabling radio communication for voice and data services.

- **Iub interface:** It connects the RNC to Node B, enabling communication between the radio network controller and the base station for radio resource management and user data transfer.

- **Iur interface:** It enables communication between RNCs for soft handover and seamless mobility support as the user moves between cells managed by different RNCs.

- **Iu interface:**

  o **Circuit-switched (Iu-CS):** It connects the RNC to the MSC in the CS domain, enabling circuit-switched voice and data services.

  o **Packet-switched (Iu-PS):** It connects the RNC to the SGSN in the PS domain, enabling packet-switched data services like internet access.

- **Gn interface:** This connects the SGSN to the GGSN in the PS domain, enabling the transfer of user data packets between these core network elements.

- **Gi interface:** This connects the GGSN to external IP-based networks like the Internet or private IP networks, enabling access to packet data services.

- **Gr interface:** This connects the SGSN to the HLR for subscriber data lookup, enabling authentication and retrieval of subscriber information.

- **Gc interface:** It connects the GGSN to the HLR for certain packet data services, enabling the GGSN to retrieve subscriber information.

- **Gs interface:** It connects the SGSN to the MSC, enabling **Circuit-Switched Fallback (CSFB)** services, which allow voice calls to be handed over from the PS domain to the CS domain.

- **A interface:** This connects the MSC to other MSCs or to the PSTN, enabling circuit-switched voice calls between mobile and fixed-line networks.

Vulnerabilities in 3G network

3G has inherited many of 2G's architectural components and designs. This had also brought in the threats that were prevalent in 2G, into the 3G components. Some of the common 3G vulnerabilities can be termed as weaknesses in its encryption algorithms. Flaws in **Signaling System 7 (SS7)** signaling and other attacks are listed in the following:

- **Encryption weaknesses**:
  o **A5/1 algorithm:** Inherited from 2G, this algorithm has known weaknesses that can be exploited for eavesdropping on calls and data.
  o **Integrity algorithms (UIA1/UIA2):** These algorithms, used to ensure data has not been tampered with, have potential vulnerabilities that could allow attackers to manipulate data.

- **SS7 flaws:** SS7 is a system used for communication between network elements. Vulnerabilities in SS7 can be exploited for:
  o **Interception of calls and SMS:** Attackers can intercept calls and messages sent over the network.
  o **User impersonation:** Attackers can impersonate legitimate users to gain access to accounts or services.
  o **Manipulating billing information:** Attackers can alter billing information for fraudulent purposes.

- **Core network security**:
  o **Reliance on IP protocols:** 3G networks use IP protocols, which are susceptible to traditional IP vulnerabilities, like **Denial-of-Service (DoS)** attacks and unauthorized access.
  o **Increased attack surface:** The introduction of complex services in 3G networks creates more points of entry for attackers to exploit.

A mind-map based representation of the vulnerabilities in the 3G network is shown in the following figure:

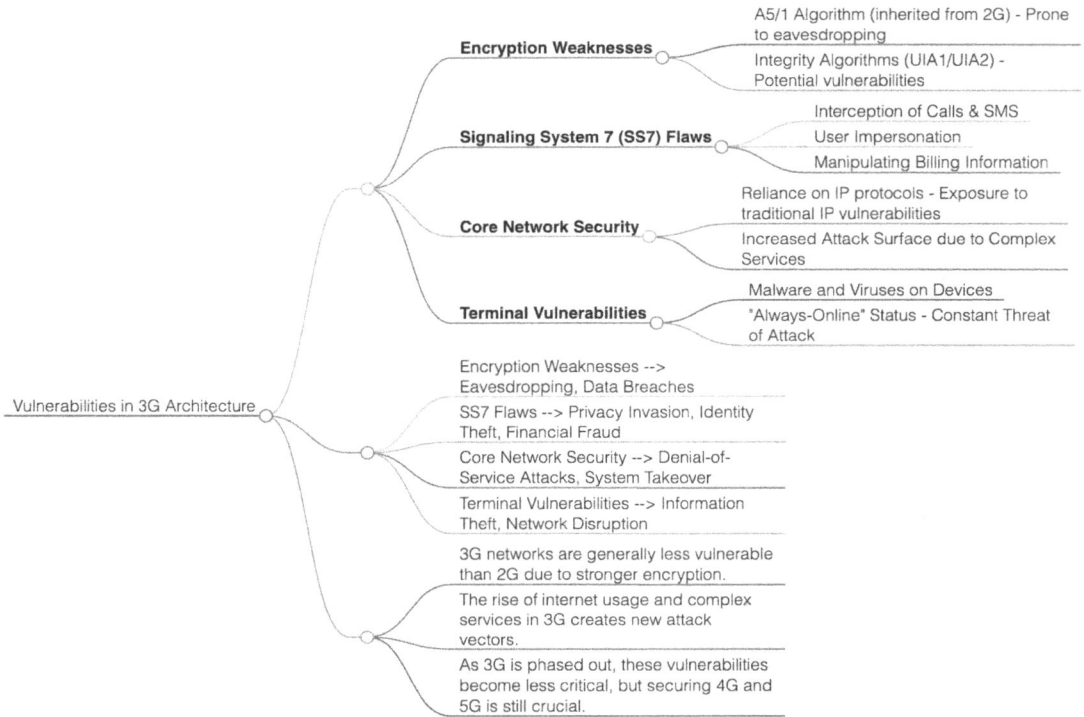

Figure 5.3: Vulnerabilities in 3G architecture

Security mechanisms in 3G

The following figure gives an overview of the 3G security architecture. *(I)* comprises five security feature groups, out of which four are shown in the following figure:

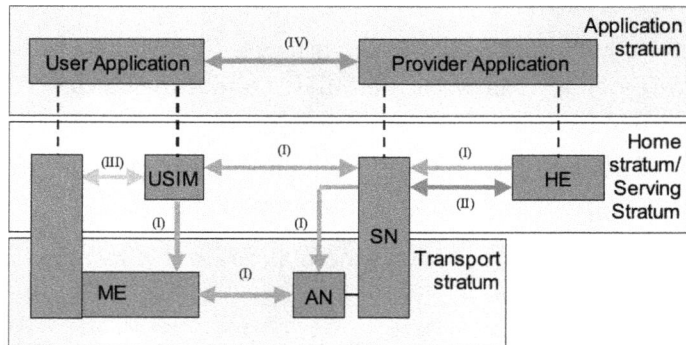

Figure 5.4: Overview of 3G security architecture[1]

---

1   Source: 3GPP TS 33.102

Each of these is aimed at meeting relevant security objectives to mitigate the various 3G threats that are defined in the previous section (refer to *Figure 5.3*).

Let us understand *Figure 5.4* in detail:

- **Network Access Security (NAS)** *[I]*: It acts as the first line of defense in 3G architecture. It safeguards against unauthorized access and protects sensitive user data transmitted over the air interface. NAS employs techniques like mutual authentication, where both the UE and the network verify each other's identities. Additionally, NAS utilizes encryption algorithms to scramble data during transmission, preventing eavesdropping. This robust security layer ensures that only authorized users can access the 3G network and keeps user data confidential during communication.

- **Network Domain Security (NDS)** *[II]*: 3G architecture focuses on protecting the core network, where critical information like user data and signaling messages flow. Unlike 2G, which relied solely on SS7, 3G introduces IP protocols for data transmission. NDS addresses the security challenges of this shift by implementing encryption and authentication techniques. It ensures the confidentiality and integrity of data exchanged between network elements, preventing eavesdropping, data manipulation, and unauthorized access. This safeguards user privacy, protects against fraud, and maintains the overall reliability of 3G services.

- **User domain security** *[III]*: 3G architecture focuses on securing access to mobile devices (user stations) on the network. This is achieved through mechanisms like user authentication and authorization. When a user attempts to connect to the network, their device is verified using credentials like a SIM card and temporary encryption keys. This ensures that only authorized devices can access the network and prevents unauthorized users from impersonating legitimate subscribers. User domain security also plays a role in protecting the confidentiality and integrity of user data transmitted over the air interface. By encrypting data, user domain security safeguards user calls, messages, and other information from eavesdropping or tampering. However, encryption strength can vary depending on the implemented algorithms, with some older options like A5/1 being more susceptible to cracking.

- **Application Domain Security** *[IV]*: It focuses on securing communication between applications running on the user's device and those within the service provider's network. This ensures that data exchanged between applications, like mobile banking or online shopping, is protected from eavesdropping or tampering. While core network security safeguards the infrastructure, *Application Domain Security* acts as an additional layer to guarantee the confidentiality and integrity of user data specifically within the application layer.

- **Visibility and configurability of security** *[V]*: 3G architecture incorporates visibility and configurability of security to ensure that users have some degree of control over the security features employed on their connection. Ideally, users can be informed about which security mechanisms are active (encryption, authentication) and potentially even have the option to enable or disable certain features depending on the level of security desired and the service being used. This allows users to make informed decisions about the trade-off between security and convenience. This depends on the service provider and the type of mobile equipment that the user has.

Cryptographic algorithms

3G mobile networks have significantly improved security mechanisms over their predecessor, 2G (GSM). These advancements rely on a set of cryptographic algorithms that safeguard user privacy, data integrity, and network access. The specific algorithms used for encryption and integrity protection are negotiated between the UE and the network during connection establishment. Both parties must support a common algorithm for secure communication. The security of these algorithms depends heavily on the secrecy of the shared key stored in the USIM card. Strong user authentication and secure handling of USIM cards are crucial for maintaining overall network security. Some of the algorithms that are used in 3G, like A5/1 and UEA0, are considered less secure due to advancements in cryptanalysis. Some of these algorithms are mentioned in the following:

- **Authentication and Key Agreement (AKA)**: This is the core security mechanism in 3G, responsible for user authentication and generating session keys for encryption and integrity protection. AKA employs a challenge-response protocol. The network sends a **random number (RAND)** to the UE. The UE uses this RAND, a secret key shared with the network, stored securely in the USIM card, and a **sequence number (SQN)** to calculate a **response (RES)**. The network performs its calculation using the same values and compares it with the received RES. If they match, authentication is successful, and session keys are derived.

- **UMTS Encryption Algorithm (UEA):** This algorithm encrypts user data traffic using the **cipher key (CK)** generated during AKA. There are two versions of this algorithm. UEA0 (stream cipher) and UEA1 (block cipher). UEA0 is considered less secure and is gradually being phased out by service providers. UEA1 offers stronger encryption and is the preferred choice among service providers within 3G mobile networks.

- **UMTS Integrity Algorithm (UIA):** This algorithm generates a **Message Authentication Code (MAC)** using the **Integrity Key (IK)** from AKA. The MAC is attached to messages to ensure they have not been tampered with during transmission. There are two versions of this algorithm, UIA1 and UIA2. UIA1 is the primary integrity algorithm used in 3G networks. UIA2 is an alternative algorithm, rarely used by service providers nowadays.

- **DECT Standard Cipher (DSC):** Inherited from 2G, it is used for legacy signaling in some 3G networks.

- **DECT Standard Authentication Algorithm (DSAA):** This algorithm is also inherited from 2G and is used in conjunction with DSC for legacy authentication.

GTP GPRS Tunnelling Protocol

The GTP is a fundamental component of the core network architecture in 3G mobile networks. It serves as the backbone for carrying user data traffic and signaling information between various network elements, facilitating seamless connectivity and information exchange. GTP is defined by 3GPP as part of its various publications, like the 3GPP TS 09.60, TS 29.060, TS 29.274, and TS 29.281.

GTP utilizes virtual tunnels to facilitate communication between **GPRS Support Nodes** (**GSNs**) over a dedicated interface. This allows for the efficient separation of network traffic into distinct data streams. GTP manages the entire lifecycle of these tunnels, including creation, modification, and deletion. It ensures the secure transport of IP data payloads between user devices, GSNs within the core network, and the Internet. GTP itself functions across three distinct traffic types: **control plane** (**GTP-C**), **user plane** (**GTP-U**), and charging (GTP' derived from GTP-C).

GTPv1-C and GTPv2-C are both versions of the GTP-C used in mobile networks. GTPv1-C was introduced in 3G networks and is defined in the 3GPP TS 29.060 specification. It is used to establish, modify, and release tunnels for user data traffic between **GPRS Support Nodes** (**GSNs**) within the core network. GTPv1-C itself does not provide encryption; it relies on separate algorithms, like the **UMTS Encryption Algorithm** (**UEA**), for data encryption within the core network. It is also used for control plane signaling between GSNs within a single **Public Land Mobile Network** (**PLMN**) (Gn interface) and across different PLMNs (Gp interface). This enables functionalities like roaming and inter-access mobility. GTPv1-C operates on port 2123 and carries various control messages.

GTPv2-C was introduced in 4G (LTE) networks, in the 3GPP specification 3GPP TS 29.274, and continues to be used in 5G. Similar to GTPv1-C, it manages tunnels for user data traffic but is optimized for the functionalities and addressing schemes of 4G and 5G networks. It is used for control plane signaling messages on EPC interfaces like S5, S8, and S11. GTPv2-C operates on the registered port number 2123. Like GTPv1-C, it relies on separate algorithms for data encryption within the core network.

The 3GPP technical specification 3GPP TS 29.281 defines GTP-U. This protocol encapsulates and routes user data traffic across various signaling interfaces, including S1, S5, and S8. GTP-U messages can be categorized as either user plane data or signaling messages themselves. The standard port number assigned to GTP-U is 2152.

The following figure shows the Gp and Gn interfaces in a 3G mobile network:

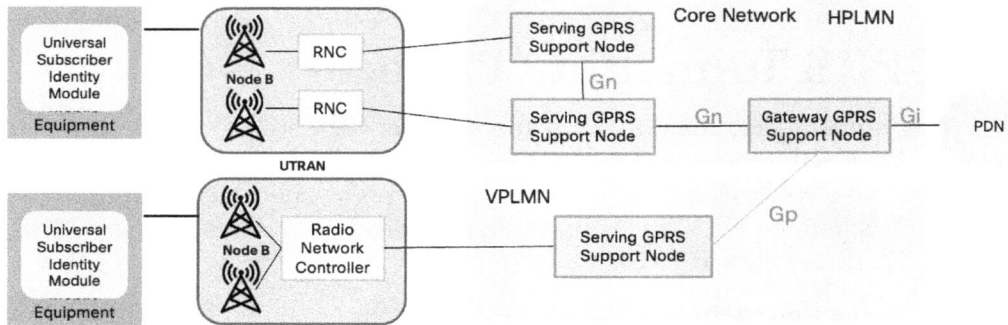

Figure 5.5: GTP interfaces in a 3G Mobile network

Vulnerabilities in GTP

GTP used in 3G mobile networks is susceptible to various vulnerabilities that can potentially compromise the security and integrity of the network. Some common vulnerabilities in GTP include **signaling vulnerabilities**, GTP tunnel hijacking, insecure default configurations, insecure GTP encryption and authentication, and DoS Attacks. A mind-map representation of the GTP-based vulnerabilities is shown in the following figure:

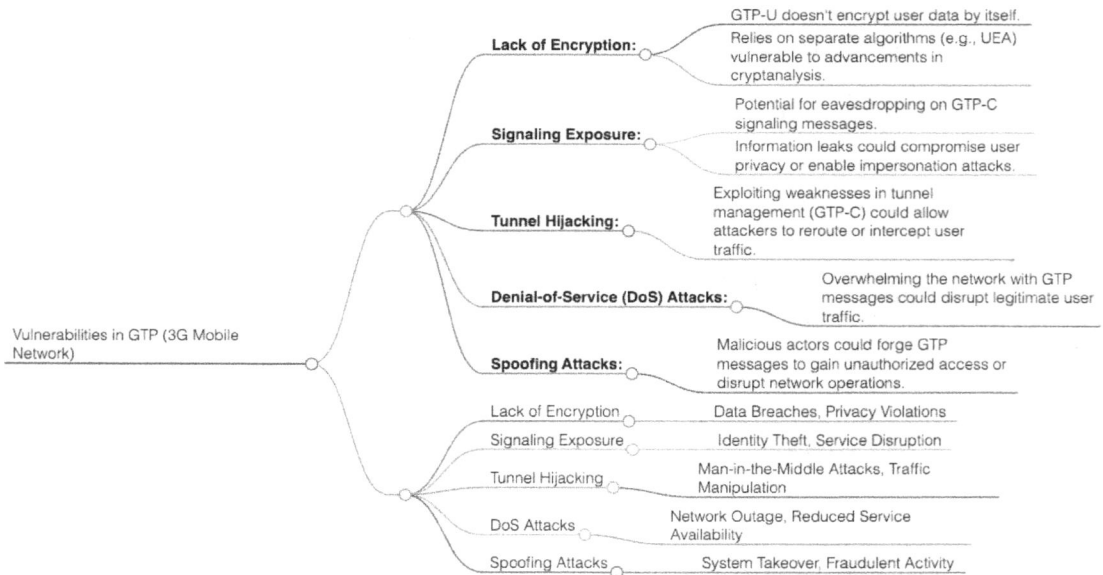

Figure 5.6: Vulnerabilities in GTP

The exposure of 3G network components to vulnerabilities in the GTP enables adversaries to exploit the mobile network by reconfiguring these components for malicious purposes. Once a network component is compromised, attackers can leverage it as a foothold to facilitate lateral movement and gain deeper access to other network components. This compromised access could allow them to decrypt subscribers' packet data sessions, hijack existing internet sessions, and potentially intercept sensitive information or disrupt services. These vulnerabilities pose significant risks to the security, privacy, and integrity of the 3G mobile network and its users.

For an attacker to exploit a vulnerability, the target system must be accessible on the network. In 3G networks, the SGSN and GGSN elements are potential targets as they connect to the external Roaming Exchange and **Internet Protocol (IP) Packet Exchange (GRX/IPX)** network. The Gp interface, used for roaming purposes, needs to be reachable by authorized roaming partners only. Any other interfaces or services not essential for GRX/IPX network functionality should be restricted from exposure to this network. Similarly, for subscribers to access the internet using a specific Internet **Access Point Name (APN)**, the GGSN must connect to the internet itself, typically via the Gi interface. However, there is no requirement for any external entity to directly access GGSN from the public internet. Therefore, the GGSN should not be directly reachable from the Internet to enhance overall security.

Securing GTP

Securing GTP in 3G networks necessitates a layered security approach encompassing various techniques. All service providers should have a set of guiding principles to define the various layers of security that need to be applied to the mobile network components based on their exposure to external entities.

One of the basic forms of network layer-based security is to achieve network segmentation and isolation for relevant network components. Segmenting the network to isolate GTP components and traffic from other parts of the network helps in reducing the attack surface. **Virtual Local Area Network (VLANs)**, virtual routing functions, firewalls, or other network segmentation techniques can be used to separate GTP components and traffic from other network services and components.

The next layer of security control that can be applied is by configuring IP spoofing and DDoS mitigation controls. Anti-spoofing measures, such as ingress/egress filtering or **Unicast Reverse Path Forwarding (uRPF)**, prevent IP spoofing attacks targeting GTP components. For DoS/DDoS mitigation, service providers should consider techniques, such as rate limiting, traffic shaping, or bandwidth management, to protect GTP components from signaling flood attacks or resource exhaustion attacks. Along with the mentioned prevention techniques, service providers should deploy mechanisms to detect and mitigate malformed or invalid GTP signaling messages that could potentially lead to DoS conditions.

Securing network management connectivity and configuration forms another layer of defense against adversaries targeting GTP components. Secure network management practices, including strict access controls, secure protocols (for example, SSH, HTTPS), and secure configuration management processes, should be adopted by the service provider. Network and device configurations should be regularly reviewed and updated to ensure secure settings and eliminate potential misconfigurations.

Application layer-based security controls form another very important method adopted by many service providers to secure GTP. This involves inspecting the GTP traffic and filtering out malicious data. Devices with security capability to inspect GTP should be placed in the GTP traffic path to realize this functionality. *Figure 5.7* depicts the placement of this security capability to inspect GTP:

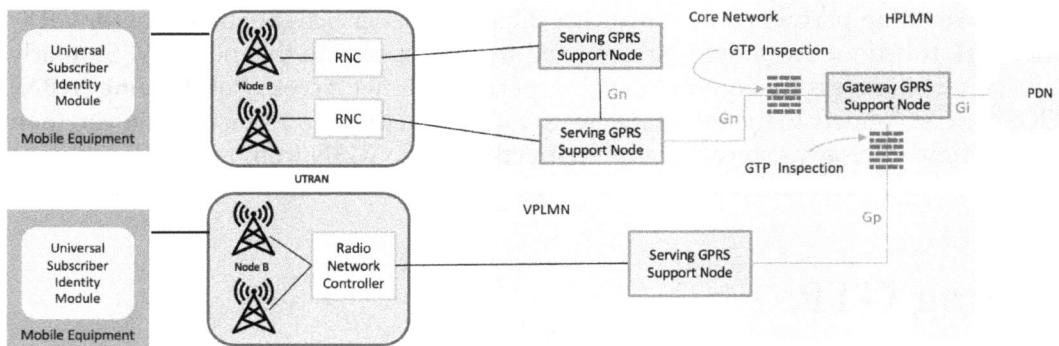

Figure 5.7: GTP Inspection capability placement

GTP inspection

In 3G mobile networks, communication within a service provider's network utilizes the 3GPP Gn interface for GTP traffic. Conversely, communication with roaming partners relies on the 3GPP Gp interface. To ensure network security, the service provider should restrict access at the network edge exposed to the IPX network (external network) to only Gp traffic associated with roaming partners. GTP inspection can then be applied by the service provider at specific locations to filter out various GTP messages.

GTP message filtering categories provide a security mechanism to control access to GTP messages. These categories define specific message types and network entities allowed to send or receive them. By implementing filters based on these categories, network operators can restrict unauthorized access and enhance network security. By restricting access to certain message categories at network borders, operators can also prevent unauthorized entities from manipulating or intercepting sensitive information. Filtering also ensures compliance with roaming agreements between network operators, allowing legitimate roaming traffic while preventing unauthorized access. It also helps to mitigate DoS attacks that attempt to overwhelm the network with GTP messages.

Configuring GTP filtering is not an easy task. Implementing and managing effective filtering policies can be complex, requiring a thorough understanding of GTP message types and network configurations. Overly restrictive filtering might block legitimate traffic, while inadequate filtering could leave vulnerabilities open to be exploited.

There are three primary GTP Message Filtering Categories defined by the **GSM Association** (**GSMA**), as mentioned in the following:

- **Category 1**: This category focuses on message types associated with the specific network interface where the filtering occurs. It primarily regulates control plane messages (GTP-C) exchanged between GSNs within the core network.

- **Category 2**: This category filters messages based on the direction of roaming traffic. It allows inbound roaming subscriber traffic initiated by the home network to enter the visited network. Conversely, it restricts outbound roaming traffic initiated by the visited network from reaching the home network unless authorized.

- **Category 3**: This is the broadest category, encompassing all user plane traffic (GTP-U) and control plane messages (GTP-C) related to outbound roaming subscribers within the visited network. It allows communication between the visited network and the home network for the roaming subscriber.

In the upcoming section, we will read about these categories in detail.

GTP Category 1 filtering

A *GTP Category 1* error indicates that a packet has arrived at a network element, like a GGSN or SGSN, on an interface where it is not authorized. This can occur due to errors in network element configuration, such as incorrect routing rules or interface settings, which can lead to packets being directed to the wrong interface. It can be due to malicious activities by adversaries or a software bug.

A high volume of unauthorized packets on the wrong interface can overwhelm network resources, leading to delays, dropped connections, and overall performance degradation for legitimate users. Unauthorized packets might also contain malicious code or attempt to exploit vulnerabilities in network elements.

Implementing robust configuration management practices helps service providers ensure accurate routing rules and interface settings across all network elements. Deploying a **Network Intrusion Detection System** (**NIDS**) can also help identify suspicious traffic patterns and potential attempts to inject unauthorized packets into the network.

At the 3G network's border where it connects to external networks, it is critical to implement strict control over incoming and outgoing GTP messages. Only messages essential for communication with partnered networks should be allowed.

For international roaming scenarios, a GTP firewall specifically designed for the Gp interface should be deployed between the mobile core network, housing elements like SGSN and GGSN, and the external GRX/IPX network. This firewall acts as a filter, permitting only legitimate Gp messages. All other GTP message types attempting to enter or exit the mobile network will be discarded and logged for further analysis. This filtering mechanism safeguards the network by preventing unwanted or unauthorized GTP traffic.

The firewall should be able to define acceptable GTP message types based on the specific version of the protocol (for example, GTPv1 or GTPv2) and the intended 3GPP interface (for example, Gp or Gs). It should be able to verify if the **Access Point Name** (**APN**) and roaming selection mode specified in the message are valid and expected; along with the capability to check if the **International Mobile Subscriber Identity** (**IMSI**) prefix in the incoming message (derived from **Mobile Country Code** (**MCC**) and **Mobile Network Code** (**MNC**)) matches the roaming partner's network or belongs to a pre-defined group of trusted GGSN/SGSN servers.

All the alerts and logs generated by the firewall for these checks should be logged and monitored to perform proactive monitoring of malicious and fraudulent activities.

The following figure depicts the high-level architecture to achieve *Category 1* filtering:

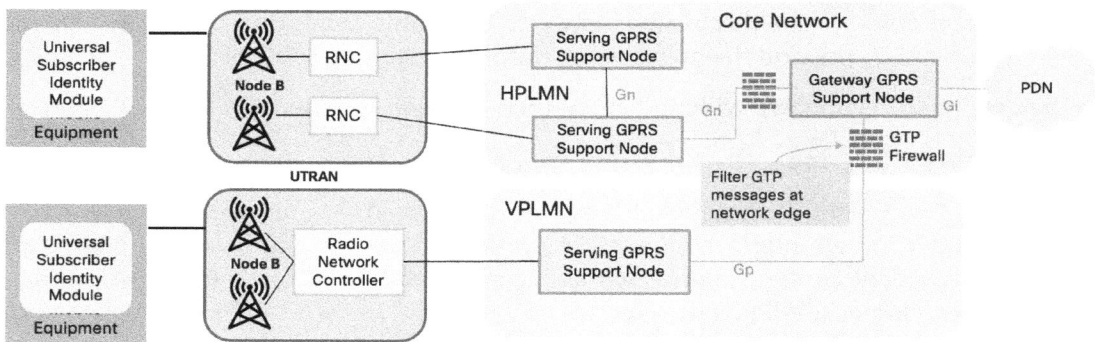

Figure 5.8: GTP Category 1 filtering at edge

GTP Category 2 filtering

Unlike *Category 1 filtering*, which focuses on message type and interface restrictions at the network edge, *Category 2* filtering operates within the mobile core network. It examines GTP messages to ensure they originate from authorized subscribers connected to the home network, the network that issued the SIM card. This filtering helps prevent unauthorized access attempts and potential data breaches. By verifying subscriber identity and access parameters, *Category 2* filtering also helps prevent unauthorized devices from using the network resources.

The firewall deployed to conduct GTP inspection should be capable of validating IMSI information. The firewall filter should verify if the IMSI embedded in the GTP message belongs to a valid subscriber within the home network. Messages with unmatched IMSIs can then be discarded, potentially indicating an attempt from a fraudulent device. The firewall filter can also check if the requested APN and selection mode are valid and consistent with the subscriber's profile; if not, it might indicate unauthorized access attempts or potential misuse.

GTP Category 3 filtering

Category 3 filtering is the most granular level of filtering. It explores message content specific to the message type. It analyzes parameters relevant to specific GTP messages (for example, user data transfer, mobility management) to ensure legitimacy and prevent potential security breaches. By scrutinizing specific message content, *Category 3* filtering can help identify attempts to spoof legitimate user identities or network elements. A deeper inspection of message content can help detect attempts to manipulate user data or control channels within the network. This safeguards the integrity of data transmissions and protects against potential service disruptions.

Service providers should prioritize message plausibility checks whenever possible. These checks aim to verify if incoming GTP messages are valid, contain logical data, and are not corrupted (malformed). Messages failing these checks should be discarded to prevent further processing and potential security risks. As per GSMA FS 20 documentation, some of the useful validity checks are mentioned in the following:

- Useful GTP-C message validity checks are:
    o   Presence of mandatory information elements.
    o   Correct sequence of information elements.
    o   Correct message length.
    o   Correct **Type-Length-Value** (**TLV**) format of information elements.
- Useful GTP-C message plausibility checks are:
    o   Validity of IP addresses in GTP messages.
    o   Cross-layer checks for the validity of the information that appears in multiple layers (e.g., IP addresses in IP header and GTP message information elements).
    o   Validity of information in information elements representing the roaming partner (i.e., IP addresses and IMSIs).
    o   Validity of information in information elements representing a roaming subscriber (i.e., IMSI and MSISDN).
    o   Verification of the occurrence of the information elements.

GTP Firewall deployment scenarios

A Service provider can deploy GTP firewalls in multiple deployment scenarios based on firewall capability and granularity of security controls. Based on the options available the firewall can be deployed in two main deployment scenarios, an IP and GTP-based combined firewall or a dedicated GTP firewall.

In the combined firewall type of deployment, a service provider can make use of an existing edge firewall that is currently doing L3 and L4 filtering, and add GTP filtering capability, if it is supported by the product vendor. While considering this approach, the service provider should consider other factors like the throughput and performance capability of the current box, *Figure 5.9* depicts this approach:

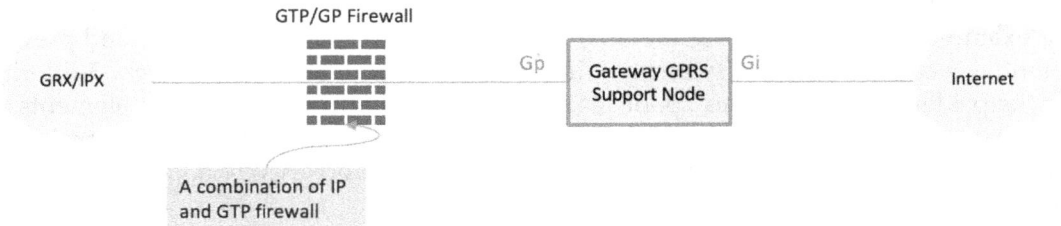

Figure 5.9: GTP Firewall deployment scenario 1

In the dedicated firewall approach, the service provider can choose to deploy separate firewalls to perform specific functions. The edge firewall can perform basic L3 and L4 filtering, while the dedicated GTP firewall, with GTP inspection capability, can perform GTP application-level filtering. *Figure 5.10* depicts the dedicated firewall deployment approach:

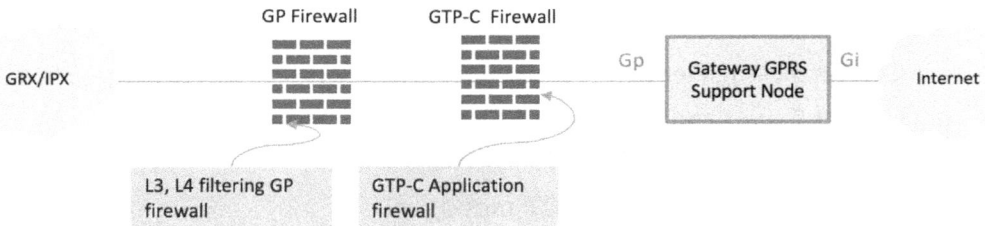

Figure 5.10: GTP Firewall deployment scenario 2

These firewalls can perform GTP-C and GTP-U inspections, but due to the high performance required to conduct terabits of user traffic, in some cases, it is recommended to inspect only control plane traffic.

Conclusion

In conclusion, this chapter has provided a comprehensive exploration of 3G mobile networks, shedding light on their intricate architecture, components, and the inherent security risks and vulnerabilities that plague these critical infrastructures. Through an in-depth examination of the GTP and its associated vulnerabilities, we have gained a deeper understanding of the potential attack vectors that could compromise the confidentiality, integrity, and availability of these networks. However, this knowledge is not merely for academic purposes; it catalyzes action, empowering network administrators, security professionals, and enthusiasts alike to proactively fortify their 3G mobile networks against potential threats. By implementing the security measures and best practices outlined in this chapter, such as secure tunnel establishment, network segmentation, and robust access control mechanisms, we can mitigate the risks and create a more resilient and secure 3G mobile network environment.

As we transition into the next chapter on 4G networks, we will explore how the evolution of mobile technology has addressed many of the security challenges inherent in 3G while introducing new complexities and considerations. The **Long-Term Evolution** (**LTE**) architecture brings fundamental changes, replacing the circuit-switched domain with an all-IP network and introducing key components such as the **evolved NodeB** (**eNodeB**), **Mobility Management Entity** (**MME**), and the **Evolved Packet Core** (**EPC**). These architectural innovations not only enhance network performance and efficiency but also present novel security challenges that demand our attention.

Points to remember

- The 3G architecture consists of three main components: UE, UTRAN, and CN. The UE includes mobile devices and SIM/USIM cards. UTRAN comprises Node Bs (base stations) and RNCs that manage radio resources. The core network contains the CS domain for voice and the PS domain for data services.

- Key interfaces in 3G include Uu (between UE and UTRAN), Iub (between Node B and RNC), Iur (between RNCs), Iu-CS (connecting UTRAN to CS domain), and Iu-PS (connecting UTRAN to PS domain). These interfaces define communication protocols between different network elements and are potential attack vectors if not properly secured.

- Despite improvements over 2G, 3G networks remain vulnerable to several attack vectors, including IMSI catchers, rogue base stations, man-in-the-middle attacks, and signaling attacks. The transition areas between 2G and 3G networks are particularly vulnerable, as attackers can force downgrade attacks to exploit weaker 2G security mechanisms.

- 3G implemented significant security enhancements, including mutual authentication between UE and network, stronger encryption algorithms, integrity protection for signaling messages, and enhanced subscriber identity confidentiality through temporary identities. The AKA protocol represents a major security advancement in 3G systems.

- 3G employs several cryptographic algorithms: KASUMI block cipher for confidentiality (f8) and integrity (f9), MILENAGE for authentication, and a set of key generation functions (f1-f5). These algorithms provide stronger security than their 2G predecessors, but some, particularly KASUMI, have been found to have theoretical vulnerabilities over time.

- GTP is essential for 3G data services, establishing tunnels between SGSN and GGSN for user data transport. However, GTP suffers from vulnerabilities, including a lack of authentication between network elements, susceptibility to DoS attacks, and potential for GTP packet spoofing. Security mechanisms for GTP include implementing GTP firewalls, proper filtering rules, rate limiting, and IPsec for securing GTP tunnels between operators.

Exercises

1. Which component connects the User Equipment to the Core Network in 3G architecture?

   a. SGSN

   b. UTRAN

   c. GGSN

   d. HLR

2. Which interface connects the Radio Network Controller (RNC) to the Mobile Switching Center (MSC)?

   a. Iu-PS

   b. Uu

   c. Iu-CS

   d. Iub

3. What is the primary improvement in authentication for 3G compared to 2G systems?

   a. One-way authentication

   b. Mutual authentication

   c. No authentication

   d. Central authentication

4. Which cryptographic algorithm is used for confidentiality protection in UMTS?

   a. A5/1

   b. KASUMI

   c. DES

   d. RC4

5. What protocol is used to establish tunnels between SGSNs and GGSNs in a 3G network?

   a. TCP/IP

   b. GPRS Tunneling Protocol (GTP)

    c. IPsec

    d. SSL/TLS

6. Which vulnerability was addressed in 3G that was present in 2G systems?

    a. Man-in-the-middle attacks

    b. SIM card cloning

    c. False base station attacks

    d. All of the above

7. Which component generates the cipher and integrity keys in 3G security architecture?

    a. USIM

    b. RNC

    c. MSC

    d. SGSN

8. Describe the main components of the 3G architecture and explain how they interact with each other.

9. Compare and contrast the security mechanisms implemented in 3G versus 2G mobile networks. What specific vulnerabilities were addressed?

10. Explain the concept of mutual authentication in 3G networks. Why is it more secure than the authentication method used in 2G?

11. Describe the role of the **GPRS Tunneling Protocol (GTP)** in 3G networks. What are its main security challenges?

12. What cryptographic algorithms are used in 3G security, and what specific security functions do they serve?

Join our book's Discord space

Join the book's Discord Workspace for Latest updates, Offers, Tech happenings around the world, New Release and Sessions with the Authors:

https://discord.bpbonline.com

CHAPTER 6
4G Mobile Networks

Introduction

4G LTE represents a transformative advancement in mobile communications, delivering high-speed data transmission and enhanced voice services through an all-IP architecture. This evolution from circuit-switched to packet-switched networks brings both improved capabilities and new security challenges that require careful consideration.

The network architecture centers around key components like the EPC and eNodeB, connected through various interfaces that enable seamless communication. LTE implements a multi-layered security approach, encompassing user authentication, encryption, network access security, and privacy protection to safeguard both user data and network integrity.

As networks expand globally, roaming security becomes increasingly important. Critical protocols like **Stream Control Transmission Protocol (SCTP)**, Diameter, and **GPRS Tunneling Protocol (GTP)** facilitate inter-operator communications but can introduce vulnerabilities that need to be addressed through robust security measures.

The integration of voice services through **Voice over LTE (VoLTE)**, **Voice over Wi-Fi (VoWiFi)**, and **Voice over Broadband (VoBB)** represents another significant advancement. Each technology presents its own architecture and security challenges, from signaling attacks to media interception. Understanding these potential threats is crucial for implementing effective countermeasures that ensure service integrity, confidentiality, and availability.

Understanding both the capabilities and vulnerabilities of 4G LTE networks is essential for network operators, security professionals, and technology enthusiasts to maintain secure and efficient mobile communications in our increasingly connected world.

Structure

This chapter will cover the following topics.

- General architecture
- 4G network components and interfaces
- LTE security
- Roaming security
- SCTP Inspection
- Securing VoLTE

Objectives

This chapter aims to provide a comprehensive understanding of 4G LTE mobile networks, focusing on their architecture, security mechanisms, and advanced voice services. By the end of this chapter, readers should be able to grasp the intricacies of LTE architecture, including its key components and all-IP nature. The chapter seeks to equip readers with knowledge of LTE security features, roaming security challenges, and the vulnerabilities associated with protocols like SCTP, Diameter, and GTP. Additionally, it aims to familiarize readers with the architectures, vulnerabilities, and security designs of VoLTE, VoWiFi, and VoBB. Through this exploration, the chapter intends to develop readers' critical understanding of the balance between network functionality and security, preparing them to appreciate the ongoing challenges and future trends in mobile network security. Ultimately, readers should gain a holistic view of 4G LTE networks, enabling them to analyze security implications and understand the complexities of delivering secure voice services over IP-based mobile networks.

General architecture

The world of mobile communication has undergone a dramatic transformation. From the brick phones of the early days to the sleek, multifunctional smartphones of today, the way we connect and consume information has been revolutionized. At the heart of this change lies a series of technological advancements, with the 4G mobile network standing as a pivotal chapter.

4G is the successor to 3G networks. It represents a significant leap forward in terms of data transmission speeds, network capacity, and overall user experience. Compared to its predecessor, 4G offers a noticeable jump, enabling us to download and upload data at blazing-fast speeds. This translates to real-world benefits, streaming high-definition videos without buffering, lag-free online gaming, and lightning-quick file downloads are just a few examples.

The introduction of 4G ushered in a new era of mobile possibilities. With faster connections, users were empowered to explore a richer digital landscape. Video calls became commonplace, social media usage boomed, and mobile applications offering a wider range of functionalities emerged. 4G not only transformed end users' individual experiences but also paved the way for innovative mobile services and applications that are now an integral part of one's daily life.

However, the story of 4G goes beyond just speed. It also introduced advancements in network technology, such as **Multiple-Input, Multiple-Output (MIMO)** and **Orthogonal Frequency-Division Multiplexing (OFDM)**, which enhanced signal quality and efficiency. These improvements allowed for OFDM a greater number of users to connect simultaneously, ensuring a smoother and more reliable network experience.

In this chapter, we will explore the technical aspects of 4G, understand the different standards that make it work, and uncover the impact it has had on the mobile landscape. IT will also cover the limitations of 4G and see how it paved the way for the next generation of mobile technology.

LTE is a wireless communication standard for high-speed data transmission for mobile devices and data terminals. It is the backbone technology that underpins 4G cellular networks. It is the evolutionary path that **Global System for Mobile Communications (GSM)** and **Universal Mobile Telecommunications System (UMTS)** networks have taken to achieve higher data rates, lower latency, and improved spectral efficiency. It defines the protocols, modulation schemes, and transmission techniques used for data communication over the air interface, which provides the wireless connection between mobile devices and the cellular network infrastructure in 4G networks.

Although technically distinct, the terms *LTE* and *4G* are frequently used interchangeably. This is because LTE is the primary and most widely deployed 4G technology globally, and it has become synonymous with 4G networks. LTE has evolved through multiple releases (LTE-Advanced, LTE-Advanced Pro, etc.) to provide even higher data rates, improved capacity, and enhanced features. These advanced versions of LTE continue to be the backbone of 4G networks, offering better performance and capabilities.

The LTE network, also known as **Evolved Packet System (EPS)**, is an all-IP network that operates from start to finish, supporting IPv4 and IPv6. EPS consists of two main components, LTE and EPC. As mentioned above, LTE manages the radio access network (E-UTRAN) and handles the technology for radio communication, while managing the core network and handling data processing and routing. An LTE reference figure depicting these components is shown in the following:

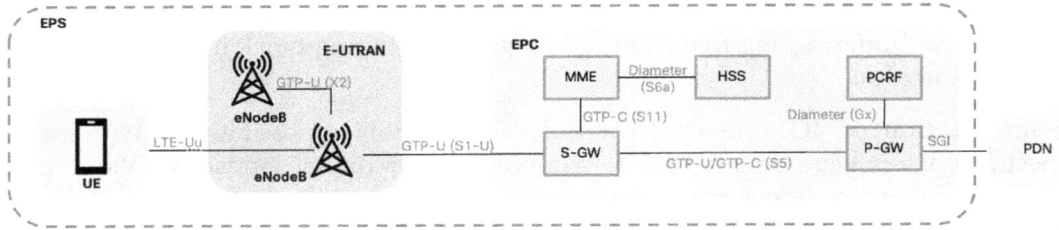

Figure 6.1: LTE reference diagram

4G network components and interfaces

A 4G network is composed of several components that work together to provide high-speed data and communication services. These components play their respective roles in providing connectivity between an end-user device and a service that the user wants to access. This communication occurs through defined interfaces adopted by various telecommunication vendors that produce different 4G network components, as mentioned in the following:

- **User Equipment (UE)**: This is the device that a user uses to connect to the 4G network, such as a smartphone, tablet, or laptop with a 4G modem. The UE is responsible for transmitting and receiving data signals to and from the network.

- **Evolved Node Be (eNodeB)**: These are base stations that transmit and receive radio signals to and from the UEs. They are the evolved version of the NodeB used in 3G networks and are responsible for managing radio resources, scheduling data transmission, and handling handovers between cells. eNodeBs are part of the **Evolved UMTS Terrestrial radio access network** (**E-UTRAN**).

- **Evolved Packet Core (EPC)**: This is the core network part of the 4G system. It is responsible for handling all the data traffic that flows between the UEs and the internet. The EPC consists of several components, like the SGW, PGW, MME, and others mentioned in the following:

  o **Mobility Management Entity (MME)**: It is a control plane component that handles handovers between eNodeBs. This component is also responsible for managing the mobility of UEs, such as attaching them to the network, authenticating them, and tracking their location.

  o **Serving Gateway (SGW)**: It is a data plane element that manages data session states and handles packet forwarding. This is also responsible for routing data packets between the UEs and the **Packet Data Network** (**PDN**).

  o **Packet Data Network Gateway (PGW)**: This connects the EPC to the external PDN, such as the internet. It allocates IP addresses to UEs and performs functions like policy enforcement and charging. It is responsible for routing data packets between the EPC and the PDN.

- o **Home Subscriber Server (HSS)**: This is a central database that stores information about all the subscribers on the network, such as their subscriptions, authentication credentials, and location information. It provides authentication and authorization functions for UEs connecting to the network.

- o **Policy and Charging Rules Function (PCRF)**: The PCRF is responsible for making decisions related to policy control and charging in the 4G network. It determines the appropriate **quality of service (QoS)** and charging rules based on user subscriptions and network policies, as shown in *Figure 6.2*:

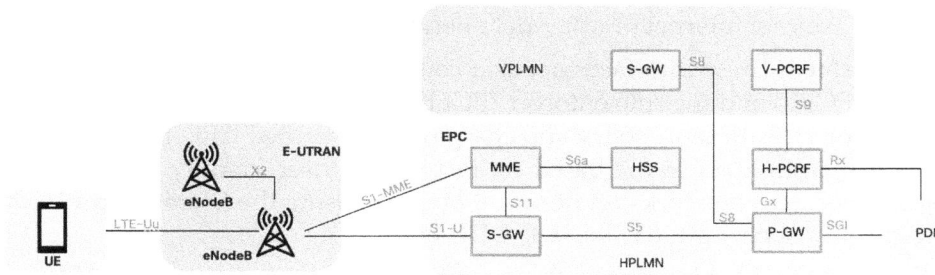

Figure 6.2: *4G architecture and interfaces*

4G network components are connected via specific interfaces, as shown in *Figure 6.3*, and these are named interfaces. These interfaces can be divided into user plane interfaces and control plane interfaces. Control plane interfaces exchange signaling traffic, while the data plane interfaces help in the exchange of user data between the UE and the packet data network.

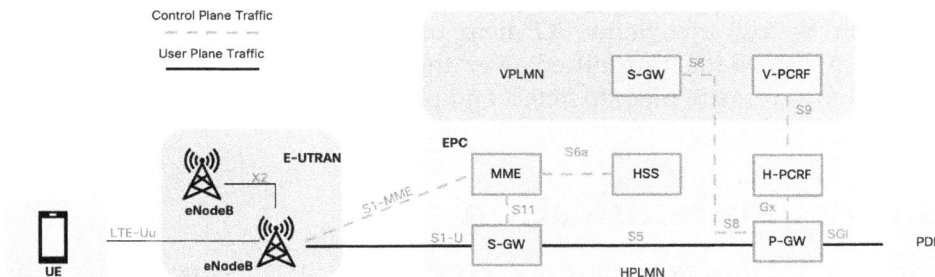

Figure 6.3: *4G control and user plane segregation*

The interfaces that connect the various 4G network components are mentioned in the following:

- **LTE Uu**: This is the air interface between UE and EUTRAN (eNodeB). This interface is an invisible bridge that enables 4G devices to connect and exchange information with the mobile network. The signaling connection is the RRC connection, and the user plane connection is the logical channels represented by Data Radio Bearers.

- **S1-MME interface**: This interface carries control plane signaling between the eNodeB and the MME in the EPC network. It handles tasks like attaching UEs to the network, authentication, and establishing calls.

- **S1-U interface**: This interface carries user plane data traffic between the eNodeB and the SGW in the core network. It is responsible for efficiently routing data packets between UEs and the internet. This interface also facilitates handover (switching between cells) during calls or data sessions.

- **S5/S8 interface**: These interfaces are used for user plane data transfer between the SGW and the PGW. They handle routing data packets between the mobile network and the external internet or other data networks.

- **Gx interface**: These interfaces act as a communication channel between the rule maker (PCRF) and the rule enforcer (PCEF) in the 4G network. The PCRF utilizes the Gx interface to send policy and charging rules to the PCEF. These rules specify how to handle data traffic based on factors like user identity, data type (voice, video, etc.), and network conditions. It operates using the Diameter protocol over various transport options like TCP, UDP, or SCTP.

- **SGi interface**: This interface acts as a reference point between the PGW and the external **Packet Data Network** (**PDN**), like the internet. It defines the protocols used for data exchange between the mobile network and external networks.

LTE security

LTE networks employ various security measures to protect user data and ensure privacy. **Authentication and Key Agreement** (**AKA**) protocols are used to verify the identities of devices and the network and establish secure communication channels. Data encryption algorithms, such as AES and Snow 3G, help prevent eavesdropping and ensure the confidentiality of user data transmitted over the air interface. Additionally, integrity protection mechanisms are in place to detect and prevent data tampering or unauthorized modifications.

LTE mutual authentication

When an end user uses their phone on a mobile network, authentication verifies if the user is allowed to access that network. In LTE networks, a specific method called EPS AKA handles this two-way confirmation process between the user device and the network.

The EPS AKA process in LTE networks ensures secure communication between the user's phone (UE) and the network by verifying each other's identity. It begins this process by generating secret credentials. The HSS, which stores the user information, creates a set of unique codes (RAND, AUTN, XRES, KASME). These act like secret handshakes for this session. The next step is mutual authentication. As part of mutual authentication, the MME in the network picks one of these codes and sends it to the user's phone. The end user's phone uses this code and its secret key to create a response. Both the network and the phone then verify each other's responses using the shared secrets. If everything matches, a secure connection is established with a shared key (KASME) for encrypted communication. EPS AKA also allows the phone to verify the network's identity. This adds an extra layer of security by making sure that the user is connecting to a legitimate network.

To keep the user's conversations secure, the most important key (KASME) is never sent directly over the airwaves (E-UTRAN). Instead, the network (MME) sends a piece of the secret code (authentication vector) to the phone. The end user's phone then uses this piece and its secret information to create the key (KASME) itself, just like the network would. This way, even if someone eavesdrops, they would not be able to steal the key because they would not have all the pieces needed to create it.

NAS security

NAS security secures communication between the phone (UE) and the network (MME) over the air. It performs integrity checks (i.e., integrity protection/verification) and ciphering of NAS signaling messages to ensure secure communication. **Integrity check** makes sure messages are not tampered with during transmission. **Ciphering** (optional encryption) scrambles the messages for confidentiality, making them unreadable even if intercepted. Unlike integrity checks, this is an extra layer of security that can be turned on or off.

For both functions, NAS security uses special keys derived from a shared key (KASME) created during user authentication. There is a separate key for each function: KNASint for integrity check and KNASenc for ciphering (if used).

AS security

AS security safeguards data traveling between the phone (UE) and the cell tower (eNB) on the airwaves. It checks the integrity of control messages (RRC) to ensure they have not been tampered with during transmission. If ciphering is used, it can scramble these messages for extra privacy. Checking message integrity is essential (mandatory), but scrambling data (ciphering) can be turned on or off depending on the situation.

When the phone (UE) connects to a cell tower (eNB) in an LTE network, it creates special keys (KRRCint, KRRCenc, KUPenc) to scramble and verify data. These keys come from a secret shared between them (KeNB). KRRCint and KRRCenc act like a secret code and locks for control messages (like traffic signals between the phone and the tower). KRRCint makes sure messages are not tampered with, and KRRCenc scrambles them for privacy. KUPenc is used to scramble the actual data a user sends and receives (like emails or videos). This scrambling and verification happen at a layer called PDCP within the network. *Figure 6.4* shows the high-level security mechanism in LTE:

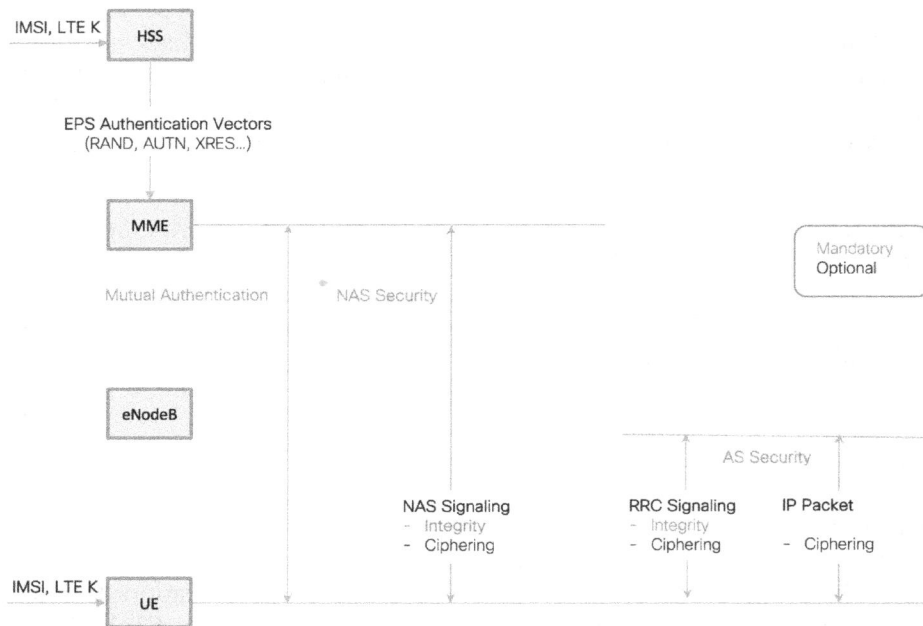

Figure 6.4: *LTE security*

Figure 6.4 shows the overall concept of LTE security.

Roaming security

Roaming security in 4G mobile networks is a critical aspect of telecommunications that addresses the need for protecting users and network resources when subscribers connect to networks outside their home network. This can be scenarios where a user can be connecting to a different service provider within his or her country or connecting to a service provider in a different country. This need arises from the inherent complexities and potential vulnerabilities associated with inter-network communications. *Figure 6.5* shows a high-level roaming architecture of the LTE network.

When users roam onto foreign networks (VPLMN), their data traverses through multiple networks and interfaces, increasing the risk of interception or unauthorized access. Roaming security mechanisms ensure that user data, including voice calls, text messages, and internet traffic, remains confidential and intact throughout its journey. This protection is crucial for maintaining user trust and complying with data protection regulations, especially when users travel internationally and connect to networks in different jurisdictions, thus ensuring the protection of user data and their privacy.

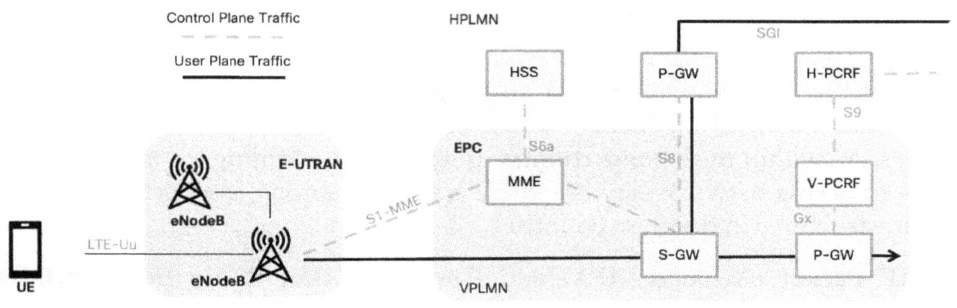

Figure 6.5: *4G roaming architecture*

Enabling roaming security also helps in the prevention of fraud and unauthorized access by malicious adversaries. Strong roaming security measures help prevent impersonation attacks, where an attacker might try to masquerade as a legitimate roaming user to gain free services or access sensitive information. It also protects against billing fraud, ensuring that charges are correctly applied to the appropriate user and preventing exploitation of roaming agreements between operators. Without proper security measures, a compromised device or malicious user from one network could potentially introduce vulnerabilities or launch attacks on the visited network. Robust security protocols ensure that only authenticated and authorized devices can access network resources, maintaining the overall health and reliability of interconnected 4G networks.

4G networks rely heavily on signaling protocols for managing various network functions. Roaming scenarios can expose these signaling interfaces to potential attacks, such as denial of service or location tracking. Robust roaming security measures help protect against these threats by securing signaling channels and implementing proper authentication and authorization mechanisms for inter-network communications. As users move between different networks or network technologies (for example, from 4G to 3G or Wi-Fi), secure handover procedures are crucial. Roaming security mechanisms ensure that these transitions occur smoothly without compromising the confidentiality or integrity of ongoing communications. This is particularly important for maintaining service continuity for applications that require constant connectivity, such as voice calls or real-time data services.

Many countries and regions have specific regulations governing the security and privacy of telecommunications services, including roaming. Implementing strong roaming security measures helps **Mobile Network Operators** (**MNOs**) comply with these regulations, avoiding potential legal issues and fines. It also assists in meeting the requirements for lawful interception and data retention, which may vary across different jurisdictions.

MNOs categorize roaming services into two main types, inbound and outbound. Inbound roaming enables visitors from other networks to utilize the host operator's local infrastructure and offerings. Conversely, outbound roaming allows an operator's customers to connect to and use services on partner networks when away from their home coverage area.

Roaming can also be differentiated based on geographical scope, namely, national and international. National roaming occurs when subscribers use the networks of other domestic operators within their home country. International roaming, on the other hand, permits users to access network services while traveling abroad, connecting to foreign operators' infrastructures in different countries.

Third-party **IP Packet eXchange** (**IPX**) and **General Packet Radio Service** (**GPRS**) **Roaming eXchange** networks pose various security risks, encompassing attacks at the IP layer, unauthorized access to Diameter-layer network paths, data breaches, malicious packet injections, fraudulent signaling activities, and service disruptions through DoS or DDoS attacks. To mitigate these vulnerabilities, it is crucial to implement a range of protective strategies. These include isolating network segments, deploying robust firewalls, concealing network topology details, and implementing thorough signaling screening protocols. Such measures form a multi-layered defense against potential security threats, ensuring the integrity and reliability of the network infrastructure.

Inspecting and securing protocols like Diameter, GTP, and SCTP form a vital process to secure domestic and international roaming connectivity.

SCTP inspection

SCTP was developed as an alternative to TCP and UDP. SCTP offers several features that make it particularly well-suited for signaling transport in telecommunications networks. SCTP was designed to address some of the limitations of TCP while maintaining reliable, in-sequence transport of messages. One of its key features is multi-homing support, which allows a single SCTP association to use multiple IP addresses for increased reliability. This means that if one network path fails, SCTP can seamlessly switch to an alternate path without disrupting the ongoing communication. This feature is particularly valuable in mobile networks where high availability is critical.

SCTP introduces the concept of multi-streaming within a single connection, which is another significant advantage over TCP. This allows for independent delivery of multiple data streams within the same SCTP association. In the context of mobile networks, this means that different types of signaling messages can be sent concurrently, as shown in *Figure 6.6*, without head-of-line blocking, a problem that can occur in TCP when a single lost packet delays the delivery of subsequent packets:

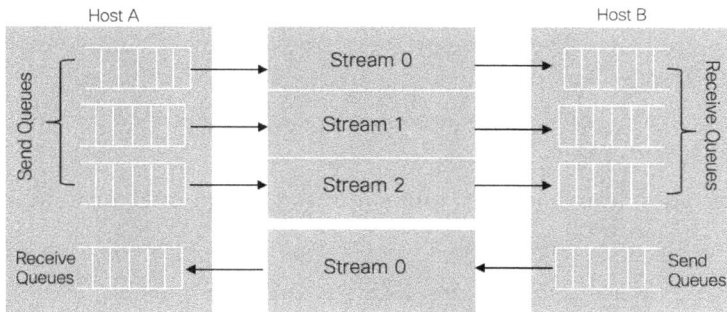

Figure 6.6: SCTP multi-stream association

The SCTP protocol also offers improved security features compared to TCP. SCTP includes a four-way handshake for association establishment, which protects against SYN flooding attacks. It also has built-in mechanisms to prevent blind denial-of-service attacks, making it a more robust choice for signaling in mobile networks where security is paramount.

SCTP is primarily used for transporting signal messages in the core network. It is the preferred transport protocol for interfaces like S1-MME (between eNodeB and MME), S6a (between MME and HSS), and various Diameter interfaces. The reliability and fault tolerance provided by SCTP make it ideal for carrying critical control plane traffic in these networks.

SCTP's message-oriented nature, as opposed to TCP's byte-stream orientation, aligns well with the needs of signaling protocols used in mobile networks. This characteristic allows for easier mapping of signaling messages to SCTP packets, improving efficiency and reducing overhead in message handling. The protocol also includes features like heartbeat mechanisms for continuous monitoring of path availability and unordered delivery options, which can be beneficial in certain mobile network scenarios. These features contribute to SCTP's ability to provide robust and flexible transport for mobile network signaling.

The SCTP protocol stack is a layered architecture that defines how SCTP operates within the broader context of network communications. The following figure depicts a simplified version of the SCTP OSI stack:

Figure 6.7: SCTP OSI stack

- **Application layer**: At the top of the stack is the application layer. In mobile networks, this often includes signaling protocols like Diameter or **S1 Application Protocol (S1-AP)**. These applications use SCTP services for reliable data transport.

- **SCTP layer**: The SCTP layer is located beneath the application layer. This layer implements the core SCTP functionality, like:

  o Association management (establishment, maintenance, and termination)

  o Chunking (breaking application messages into appropriately sized chunks)

  o Sequencing and reassembly of data chunks

  o Stream management for multi-streaming

  o Flow and congestion control

  o Error detection and correction

- **IP layer**: SCTP operates directly on top of the IP layer. It can work with both IPv4 and IPv6. The IP layer is responsible for routing SCTP packets across the network.

- **Data link layer**: IP operates at the data link layer, managing the transmission of data over physical network connections. This layer is not specific to SCTP but is crucial for its operation.

- **Physical layer**: At the bottom of the stack is the physical layer, which deals with the physical transmission medium (for example, fiber optic cables and radio waves for wireless connections).

SCTP inspection and Diameter inspection in mobile networks are different, although they are often related and can be complementary.

Diameter inspection operates at a higher layer in the network stack. Diameter is an application-layer protocol used for **authentication, authorization, and accounting (AAA)** in mobile networks, especially in 4G and 5G systems. Diameter inspection involves examining the content and structure of Diameter messages. This includes verifying the correctness of Diameter headers, checking the validity of **attribute-value pairs (AVPs)**, and analyzing the logic and consistency of Diameter transactions. Diameter inspection is essential for detecting application-level attacks, policy violations, and potential fraud attempts.

MNOs leverage SCTP security to fortify roaming and RAN security. This safeguards communication during user transitions between networks and bolsters the connection between base stations and mobile devices.

In the roaming security case, a firewall can be deployed at the perimeter to secure SCTP traffic. The firewall inspects SCTP traffic that is exchanged between home and visitor networks, as shown in the following figure:

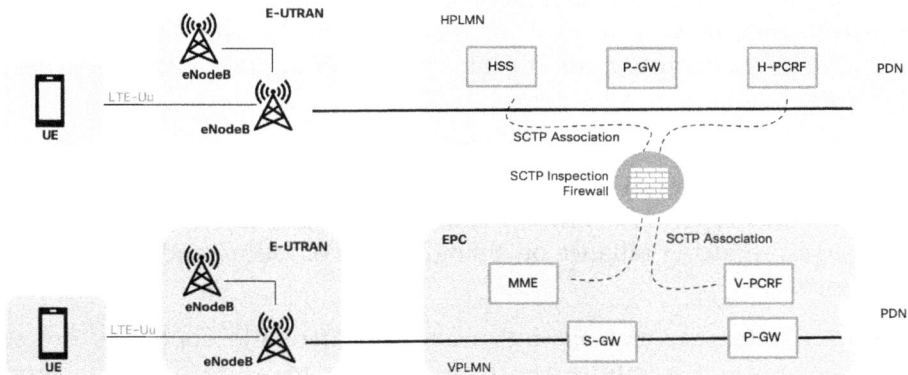

Figure 6.8: *SCTP roaming security*

SCTP Inspection firewall can be configured to check, timeouts, and limit. The types of traffic are mentioned in the following:

- **SCTP timeout**: Maximum length of time that can elapse without SCTP traffic on an association before the firewall closes the association.

- **Discard SCTP timeout**: Maximum length of time that an SCTP association remains open after the firewall denies the session based on Security policy rules.

- **SCTP Shutdown timeout**: Maximum length of time that the firewall waits after a SHUTDOWN chunk to receive a SHUTDOWN-ACK chunk before the firewall disregards the SHUTDOWN chunk.

  o Policy to check if the SCTP node transmits an unknown chunk in an SCTP packet.

  o Policy to respond to chunk flags that do not comply with RFC 4960

  o Policy to respond to the invalid length of an SCTP chunk.

  o Specify the IP address limit for multihoming.

  o Policy to respond to data chunks containing the specified PPID.

The SCTP inspection can be combined with the GTP inspection on firewalls that can inspect both these types of traffic.

Diameter inspection

Diameter serves as the backbone for AAA services in 4G. Diameter messages handle the exchange of information for all AAA functions. When a user's device connects to the network, authentication verifies its identity using credentials stored in a central database. Authorization determines what services and resources the device or the user is allowed to access based on the user's subscription plan. Finally, accounting keeps track of the user's data usage for billing purposes. Diameter can handle a larger number of devices and network elements, making it ideal for the high-density user environments of 4G. Additionally, Diameter encrypts communication and uses digital signatures to ensure the integrity and confidentiality of AAA data.

Diameter is also used by service providers in functionalities like policy enforcement, roaming management, and even location-based services. Diameter operates in a peer-to-peer fashion, thus making 4G network elements like the SGW and HSS directly exchange Diameter messages, reducing reliance on a single point of failure and improving overall network resilience.

Diameter protocol offers several advantages for 4G networks, but it is not without vulnerabilities. Several vulnerabilities need to be mitigated to secure the Diameter protocol. Some of the high-level vulnerabilities are listed in the following, along with a mind map view of the same in *Figure 6.9*:

- **Inheriting legacy issues**: Diameter was designed to address limitations in the older RADIUS protocol used in 2G/3G networks. However, it still relies on some underlying mechanisms from RADIUS, which can introduce vulnerabilities. For instance, Diameter messages themselves are not encrypted by default, making them susceptible to eavesdropping if intercepted on unsecured network connections.

- **Misconfiguration risks**: Like any complex protocol, Diameter's security heavily depends on proper configuration. Weak authentication or authorization settings can leave the network vulnerable to unauthorized access or manipulation. Additionally, if network operators do not leverage all the security features available in Diameter, it can weaken overall network defense.

- **DoS attacks**: Diameter is a critical protocol for core network functions. If attackers exploit vulnerabilities, they could launch DoS attacks by overwhelming Diameter servers with a flood of messages. This can disrupt network operations and potentially lead to service outages for many users.

- **Information exposure**: In some cases, weaknesses in Diameter can allow attackers to intercept sensitive subscriber information transmitted within messages. This could include data like usernames, phone numbers, or even location data, posing privacy concerns for users.

- **Similar threats as SS7**: While Diameter was designed as a more secure alternative to the **Signaling System 7** (**SS7**) protocol used in older networks, it still shares some underlying vulnerabilities. Malicious actors with advanced knowledge could potentially exploit these similarities to gain unauthorized access or intercept information within the 4G network. Refer to the following figure for a better understanding:

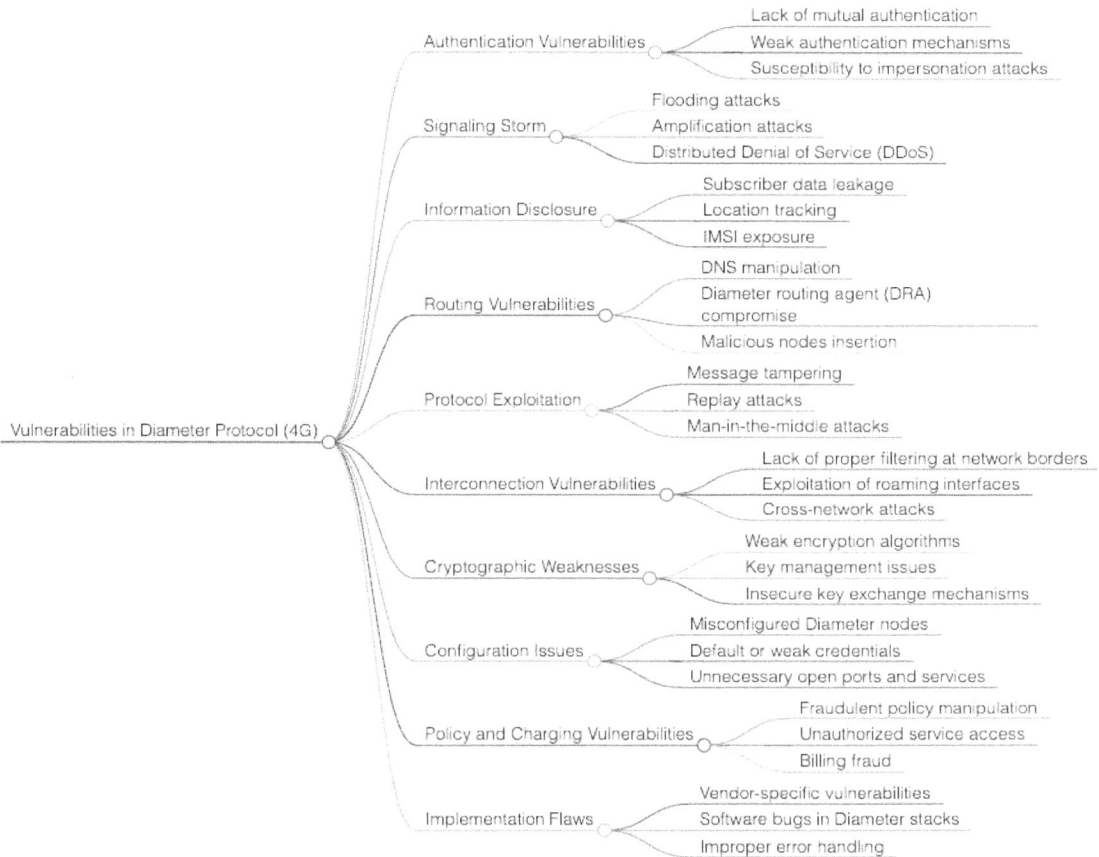

Figure 6.9: Vulnerabilities in the Diameter protocol

Diameter inspection in 4G mobile networks is a critical security measure that plays a vital role in protecting the network infrastructure and ensuring the integrity of communications. Diameter inspection's primary purpose is to examine Diameter signaling messages passing through the network, identifying and filtering out potentially malicious or unauthorized traffic. This inspection helps prevent attacks such as signaling storms, fraud attempts, and unauthorized access to network resources. By scrutinizing Diameter messages, communication service providers can maintain the stability and security of their networks, protect subscriber data, and ensure the proper functioning of critical network elements.

Diameter inspection is typically implemented through specialized network elements or functions, often integrated into **Diameter Edge Agents** (DEAs) or **Diameter Routing Agents (DRAs)**. These inspection points are strategically placed at network borders or key junctions where Diameter traffic flows, as shown in *Figure 6.10*. They analyze incoming and outgoing Diameter messages, checking various parameters such as message format, origin, destination, and content against predefined security policies and rules.

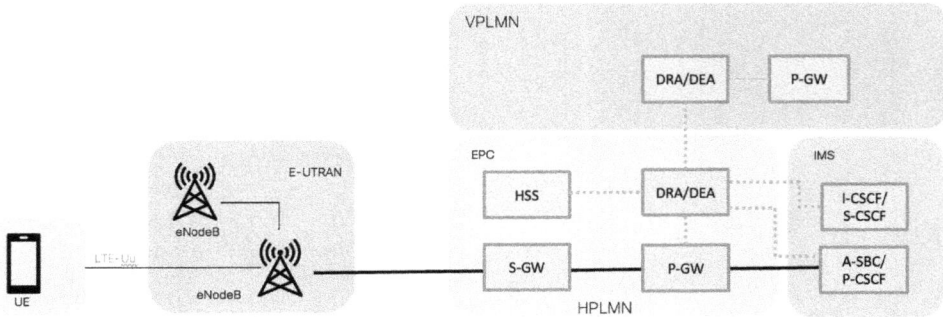

Figure 6.10*: DRA and DEA placement*

In roaming, the Diameter protocol lacks inherent end-to-end security at the application layer. Consequently, it depends on protective measures implemented at lower network layers and necessitates supplementary security protocols. This limitation underscores the importance of deploying a comprehensive, multi-layered security approach to safeguard communications during cross-border mobile network interactions.

Security shall be enforced on each hop of the hop-by-hop architecture of a roaming connectivity. A hop is defined between 2 Diameter-aware nodes, which should provide security functionality like integrity protection, privacy, IP anti-spoofing, and traceability. *Figure 6.11* shows a secure connectivity between two PLMNs:

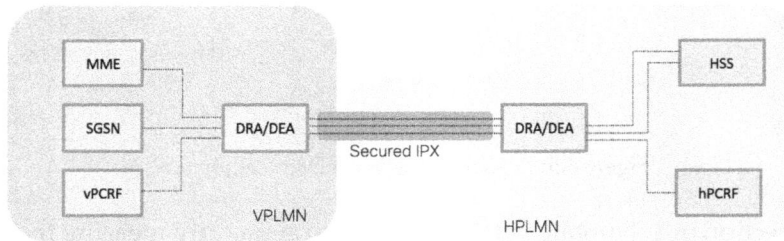

Figure 6.11*: Secured IPX connectivity*

Diameter Firewall and design considerations

As documented in the GSMA Diameter security guideline document, the communication service provider should deploy a Diameter firewall to perform a Diameter inspection. Then Diameter firewall shall enable *Category 1* filtering based on application ID and command code to limit interface misuse. The Diameter firewall shall also enable *Category 2* filtering to deny all Diameter messages except those expressly required for a given interface. Similarly, the firewall shall enable *Category 3* filtering based on Diameter message and location. Logs from this firewall should be forwarded to the service provider's security operations center and monitored proactively.

The firewall should be strategically positioned to monitor and manage all relevant network communications like international data streams routed through IPX providers, domestic network traffic originating within national boundaries, and direct communication links established with other MNOs.

The Diameter firewall should only process the traffic that it needs to, like only the traffic for MNOs who have agreed to the service. The firewall should ideally have access to the original encoding to ensure inspection of all layers. The firewall should be designed and deployed considering a wide range of failure scenarios, including device hardware failures, overload conditions, capacity limitations, misconfigurations, and other such scenarios.

The firewall can be deployed in multiple designs based on its placement in the network.

Overlay model

In this design, as depicted in *Figure 6.12*, relevant traffic destined for the service provider network is routed towards the Diameter firewall, where inspection is performed before the traffic is forwarded to the core network components. It is also possible for the DEA to selectively forward a subset of traffic to the Diameter firewall for inspection. One drawback of this design is the inability to protect the home DEA from DDoS attacks, and there is a threat of the DEA being overloaded with huge traffic volumes.

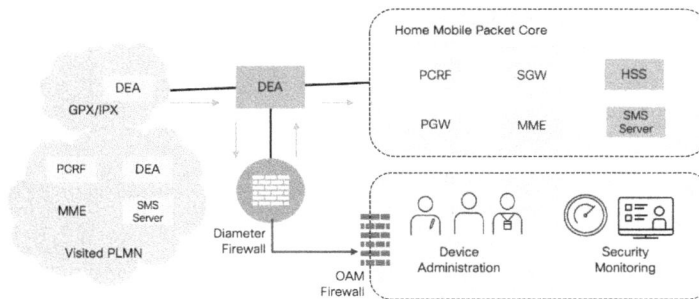

Figure 6.12: Diameter Firewall Overlay Design

Perimeter Diameter Firewall

In this design, the firewall is placed before the DEA. In this case, the Diameter Firewall sits in line with the roaming links and connections. *Figure 6.13* shows that the Diameter Firewall can protect the DEA from DDoS-based attacks:

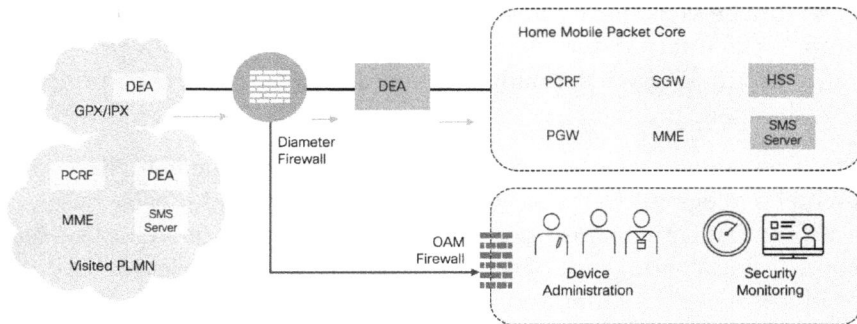

Figure 6.13: Diameter Firewall Perimeter Design

Integrated Firewall Design

In this design, as depicted in *Figure 6.14*, the DEA and the firewall are combined into one. It is like the perimeter design, but for the integration of the DEA and the Diameter Firewall. Due to its integrated model, any DDoS attack on the DEA can impact the availability of service and compromise the security posture of the overall network.

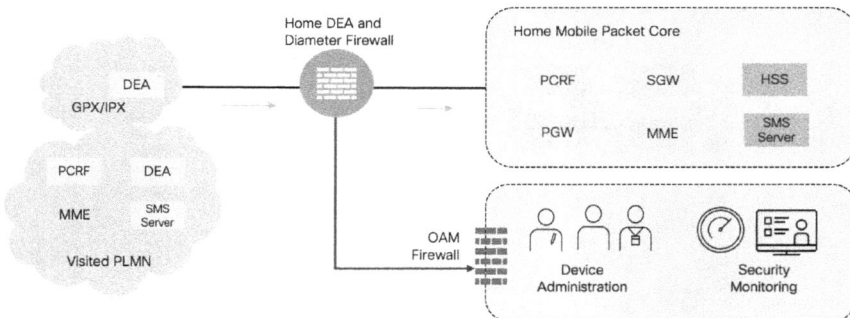

Figure 6.14: Diameter Firewall Integrated design

For most of the service providers, it is a challenge to achieve a balance between service availability and security. Many service providers adopt a hybrid model of firewall deployment and provide a layered approach to secure their network. The following figure, which is commonly adopted by service providers, depicts a high-level view of the Diameter Firewall deployment along with the DRA and DEAs. Here, a GP or perimeter firewall is used at the entry point of the service provider network to restrict access based on a trusted source IP address. The Diameter Firewall then performs the role of Diameter inspection.

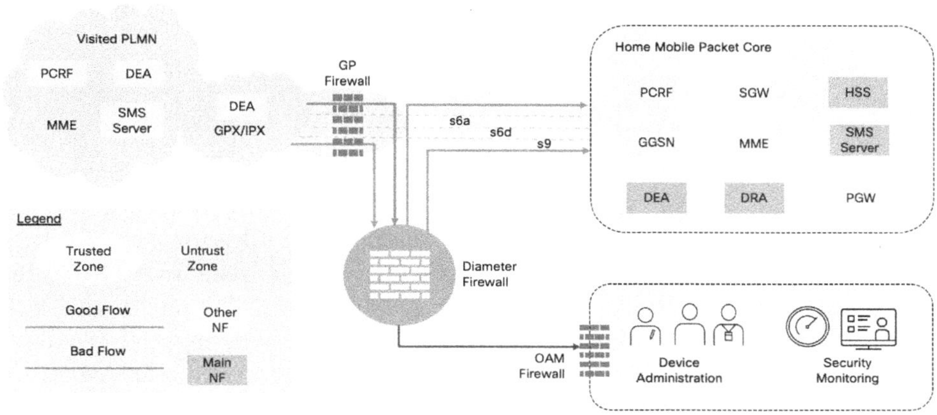

Figure 6.15: *Diameter Firewall Design*

GSMA FS 19 document recommends that the following categories of Diameter should be filtered on the Diameter Firewall.

Diameter Category 1 filtering

Category 1 filtering mechanism serves as the first line of defense against potential threats and malformed messages that could compromise the integrity and security of the core network. *Category 1* filtering is designed to inspect and validate the structure and format of Diameter messages as they enter the network from external or untrusted sources. This filtering is typically implemented at the network edge, often within network elements such as Diameter Firewalls, DEAs, or DRAs, as per the design models discussed in the above section. These elements act as gatekeepers, scrutinizing incoming traffic before it reaches the more sensitive core network components.

The primary focus of *Category 1* filtering is on the syntactical correctness and protocol compliance of Diameter messages. It meticulously examines each message to ensure it adheres to the specifications outlined in the Diameter protocol. This includes checking the overall message structure, validating message headers, and verifying that all mandatory fields are present and correctly formatted. By doing so, it helps prevent protocol-level attacks and protects against malformed messages that could potentially exploit vulnerabilities in the network's Diameter stack implementation.

Category 1 filtering verifies that the header information, such as the message length, command code, and application identifier, is consistent and follows the expected format. This is crucial because malformed headers could lead to processing errors or even crashes in network elements if left unchecked. When a message fails to meet the criteria set by *Category 1* filtering, the system can take various actions. Depending on the configuration, it may discard the message outright, preventing it from progressing further into the network. Alternatively, it might modify the message to correct minor issues or log the incident for further analysis. In some cases, if the message passes the initial checks, it is allowed to proceed to the next stages of processing or filtering.

Diameter Category 2 filtering

Diameter *Category 2* filtering is a more advanced security measure implemented in 4G mobile networks that use the Diameter protocol. While *Category 1* filtering focuses on the basic structure and syntax of Diameter messages, *Category 2* filtering explores the content and context of these messages. *Category 2* filtering primarily deals with the validation of the actual information contained within Diameter messages. This includes checking the consistency and plausibility of the data fields, as well as verifying that the message content aligns with the expected behavior of the network elements involved. For instance, it might examine whether the subscriber information in a message matches what is expected for that particular user or whether the requested service is appropriate for the subscriber's profile.

Category 2 filtering can detect and prevent various types of fraud and abuse. By analyzing the content of Diameter messages, it can identify suspicious patterns or anomalies that might indicate attempts at unauthorized access, service theft, or other malicious activities. This could include detecting unusually high volumes of requests from a single source, identifying requests for services that a user is not entitled to, or spotting inconsistencies in location data that might suggest location spoofing.

Category 2 filtering also plays a crucial role in maintaining the integrity of the network's operations. It can prevent scenarios where misconfigured or compromised network elements might send inappropriate or potentially harmful requests. For example, it could block requests that would result in incorrect billing, unauthorized changes to subscriber profiles, or disruptions to normal network services.

Category 2 filtering often incorporates more complex rule sets and decision-making processes compared to *Category 1* filtering. It may use databases of known good and bad behaviors, apply machine learning algorithms to detect anomalies, or implement sophisticated policy engines to make decisions about whether to allow, modify, or block specific messages.

Implementing *Category 2* filtering requires a deeper understanding of the mobile network's architecture, services, and normal operational patterns.

Diameter Category 3 filtering

Diameter Category 3 filtering represents the most comprehensive level of filtering in Diameter-based systems, building upon the foundational checks performed by *Category 1* and *Category 2 filtering*. *Category 3* filtering involves in-depth analysis and validation of the actual content within Diameter messages. This level of filtering goes beyond simple syntax checks and header validations, discussing the payload and examining the specific information being transmitted. It requires a deep understanding of the Diameter protocol, its various applications, and the expected behavior of different network elements.

One of the primary functions of *Category 3* filtering is to detect and prevent sophisticated attacks that might exploit legitimate-looking messages. For instance, it can identify inconsistencies between different fields within a message or across multiple related messages. This could include checking if the subscriber information in one part of the message matches the expected data based on other parameters or historical data. *Category 3* filtering keeps track of the context and state of Diameter sessions and transactions. This allows it to detect anomalies that might only become apparent when examining a series of messages over time. For example, it can identify unusual patterns in authentication requests or suspicious changes in subscriber location that could indicate a potential security breach.

Category 3 filtering can enforce complex policy rules. These rules can be based on a wide range of criteria, including subscriber profiles, time of day, network conditions, and more. This level of filtering can make dynamic decisions about whether to allow, modify, or block messages based on these sophisticated policies, providing granular control over network traffic and resource allocation.

Category 3 filtering also plays a vital role in preventing fraud and protecting subscriber privacy. It can detect attempts to manipulate charging systems, unauthorized access to premium services, or efforts to track subscriber locations. By thoroughly examining message content, it can identify and block attempts to extract sensitive subscriber information or perform unauthorized operations.

Implementing *Category 3* filtering requires significant computational resources and expertise. It often involves advanced technologies such as ML algorithms to detect complex patterns and anomalies. While it provides the highest level of security, it also needs to be carefully tuned to avoid false positives that could disrupt legitimate network operations.

GTP inspection

The GTP is a fundamental component of the core network architecture in 3G mobile networks. It serves as the backbone for carrying user data traffic and signaling information between various network elements, facilitating seamless connectivity and information exchange. GTP is defined by 3GPP as part of its various publications, like the 3GPP TS 09.60, TS 29.060, TS 29.274, and TS 29.281.

GTP utilizes virtual tunnels to facilitate communication between **GPRS Support Nodes (GSNs)** over a dedicated interface. This allows for the efficient separation of network traffic into distinct data streams. GTP manages the entire lifecycle of these tunnels, including creation, modification, and deletion. It ensures the secure transport of IP data payloads between user devices, GSNs within the core network, and the Internet. GTP itself functions across three distinct traffic types: **control plane (GTP-C)**, **user plane (GTP-U)**, and charging (GTP' derived from GTP-C). Vulnerabilities in GTP and ways to secure it are detailed in *Chapter 5, Third Generation of Mobile Networks*.

Securing VoLTE

Voice over LTE 9 (VoLTE) is a technology that enables high-quality voice calls to be made directly over a 4G LTE network, instead of falling back on older 2G or 3G networks for voice calls as was traditionally done. Traditional voice calls rely on a circuit-switched network, which dedicates a specific channel for the entire duration of the call. In contrast, VoLTE utilizes a packet-switched network, the same technology used for data transmission on 4G LTE. Data is broken down into packets, sent over the network, and then reassembled at the receiving end. VoLTE leverages the **IP Multimedia Subsystem** (**IMS**) framework, which enables voice and multimedia services over data networks.

VoLTE calls offer wider bandwidth compared to traditional calls, resulting in crisper and more natural-sounding audio. Unlike traditional calls, which often interrupt data connection (like internet browsing), VoLTE allows the user to use both voice and data services concurrently. This means the user can browse the web, stream music, or download files while on a call without disruption.

To use the VoLTE service, the end user's phone must be equipped with the necessary hardware and software to support VoLTE functionality. The service providers that the end user is a subscriber of must have VoLTE enabled on their network, and for the user's specific plan.

VoLTE has brought significant improvements to voice communications in 4G networks, but it also introduces various security vulnerabilities. Signaling attacks are a major concern in VoLTE. The **Session Initiation Protocol** (**SIP**) used for call setup and management can be manipulated by attackers. This can lead to registration hijacking, where an attacker takes over a user's VoLTE registration, or call spoofing, where the attacker can initiate calls appearing to come from a different number. These attacks can compromise user privacy and enable fraud. Media-related vulnerabilities pose another significant threat. The **Real-time Transport Protocol** (**RTP**) used for voice transmission can be hijacked, allowing attackers to intercept or manipulate voice traffic. If the media stream is not properly encrypted, it becomes vulnerable to eavesdropping.

Inadequate mutual authentication between the device and the network can allow impersonation attacks. SIM swapping, where an attacker transfers a victim's phone number to a SIM card they control, can be particularly dangerous in the context of VoLTE, potentially leading to unauthorized access to voice calls and associated services.

Privacy issues are a significant concern in VoLTE implementations. The protocol can leak information about user location and identity. Call metadata, which can reveal sensitive information about communication patterns, may not be adequately protected. This data can be exploited for surveillance or tracking purposes, compromising user privacy.

DoS attacks are another vulnerability in VoLTE systems. Attackers can flood the network with signaling messages or media packets, exhausting resources and disrupting service for legitimate users. These attacks can target individual users or entire sections of the network, causing widespread service outages.

A mind map of the mentioned vulnerabilities in VoLTE is shown in the following figure:

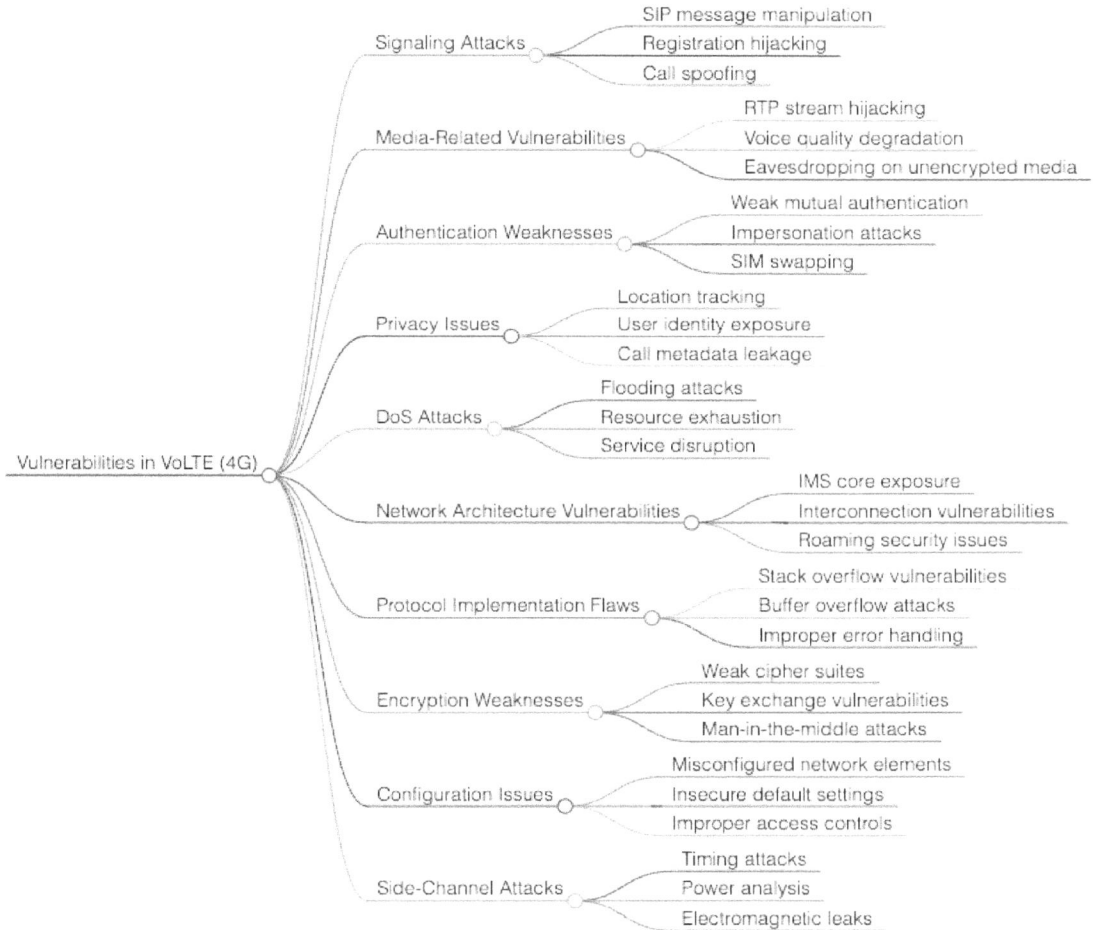

Figure 6.16: *Vulnerabilities in VoLTE*

VoLTE architecture

The component in the 4G mobile network that primarily enables VoLTE functionality is the IMS. While the entire LTE network infrastructure supports VoLTE, the IMS is the key architectural framework that makes VoLTE possible. IMS serves as the core system that enables voice calls over the LTE packet-switched network. IMS and its various components are explained in detail in *Chapter 4, IP Multimedia Systems,* of this book.

While the IMS is the primary enabler of VoLTE, the VoLTE functionality relies on the entire LTE ecosystem. This includes elements like the eNodeB for radio access, the EPC for data transport and mobility management, and various other components that work together to deliver high-quality voice services over the LTE network. The overall architecture of VoLTE depicts the various components, as shown in the following figure:

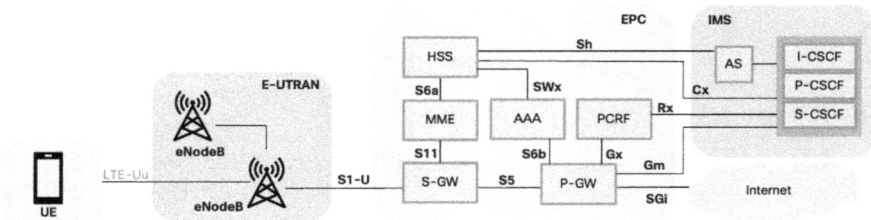

Figure 6.17: *VoLTE architecture*

As mentioned, the VoLTE architecture integrates several key components of the 4G LTE network with additional elements specific to IP-based voice services. The functionalities of these components are detailed in the following:

- **Evolved Node B (eNodeB)**: The eNodeB is the base station in LTE networks. For VoLTE, it handles radio communications between the UE and the core network. It manages radio resources, performs encryption of the radio interface, and routes data to and from the core network. In VoLTE, the eNodeB plays a crucial role in ensuring QoS for voice traffic.

- **MME**: The MME is responsible for mobility management, user authentication, and signaling. In VoLTE, it handles the control plane functions, including tracking the location of mobile devices, managing bearer sessions, and coordinating handovers between different eNodeBs. The MME also plays a role in the initial authentication process for VoLTE services.

- **SGW**: The SGW acts as a router, forwarding data between the eNodeB and the PGW. For VoLTE, it manages user plane mobility and serves as an anchor point during inter-eNodeB handovers. It also collects information for charging and lawful interception.

- **PGW**: The PGW is the interface between the LTE network and external IP networks. In VoLTE, it allocates IP addresses to UEs, enforces QoS policies, and acts as the anchor point for mobility between 3GPP and non-3GPP technologies. It also performs charging functions and acts as a **Policy and Charging Enforcement Function** (**PCEF**).

- **IMS**: The IMS is a key component specific to VoLTE. It is an architectural framework for delivering IP multimedia services. The IMS core includes several sub-components:

- o **Call Session Control Function (CSCF)**: It manages SIP signaling for setting up and controlling VoLTE calls.

- o **Application servers**: It hosts various services including voice mail, call forwarding, and other supplementary services.

- **PCRF**: The PCRF determines policy rules in the network and provides QoS authorization. For VoLTE, it ensures that voice traffic receives appropriate prioritization and resources.

- **Session Border Controller (SBC)**: The SBC sits at the border of the IMS network and provides security, interoperability, and routing functions. It protects against attacks, manages sessions, and facilitates interconnection with other networks.

Securing a VoLTE network requires a multi-layered approach that addresses vulnerabilities at various points in the architecture. Key measures include robust authentication mechanisms like AKA for user equipment, encryption of air interface traffic, and securing the IMS core through protocols such as IPsec and SRTP. Protection of Diameter signaling is crucial, often implemented via DEAs. At network borders, **Interconnection Border Control Functions** (**IBCF**) and security gateways play vital roles in maintaining security. Additionally, comprehensive monitoring through intrusion detection systems, fraud management tools, and SIEM solutions helps detect and respond to threats promptly. Implementing these measures, along with regular security audits and updates, is essential for maintaining the integrity and confidentiality of voice communications in a VoLTE environment.

Figure 6.18 depicts a security design adopted by service providers, which incorporates the layered security approach mentioned above. The GP firewall does the initial filtering of traffic coming into the trusted zone of the service provider from the untrusted zone. The IMS firewall can be used to inspect application traffic to deny and block malicious application traffic. The SBC that sits at the border of the IMS core can also be used to protect against malicious traffic from other interconnects.

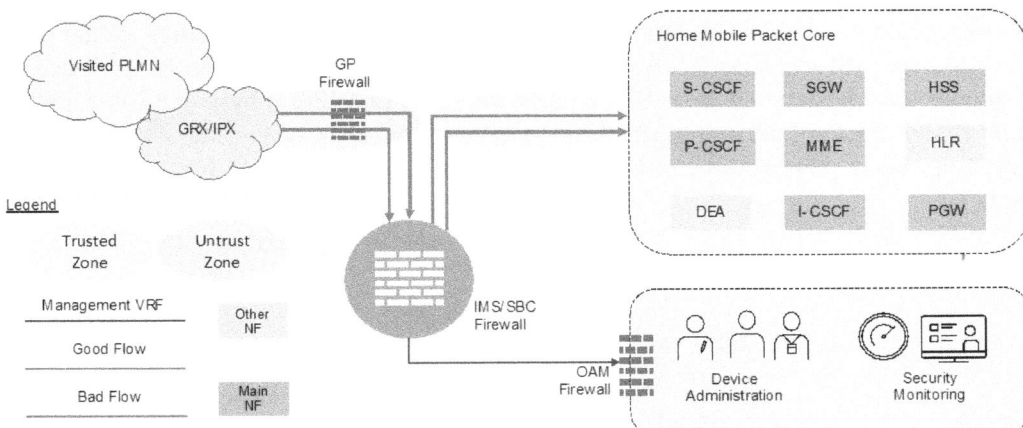

Figure 6.18: VoLTE security architecture

Securing VoWiFi

VoWiFi, also known as **Wi-Fi calling**, is a service that enables mobile devices to route voice calls and text messages over a Wi-Fi network. This technology is particularly useful in areas with poor cellular coverage but accessible Wi-Fi, such as inside buildings, underground locations, or rural areas. VoWiFi utilizes the same IMS infrastructure as VoLTE, allowing for seamless integration with existing mobile network services.

The primary advantage of VoWiFi is its ability to extend voice service coverage without requiring additional cellular infrastructure. Users can make and receive calls using their regular phone number, even in locations where cellular signals are weak or non-existent. This not only improves user experience but also helps mobile operators offload traffic from their cellular networks, potentially reducing congestion and improving overall network performance.

VoWiFi works by establishing a secure tunnel between the user's device and the mobile communication service provider's core network over the internet. This tunnel is typically created using IPsec (Internet Protocol Security) to ensure the privacy and integrity of the voice traffic. Once connected, the device can use standard **Voice over Internet Protocol (VoIP)** technologies to transmit voice data.

VoWiFi networks, while providing voice services over Wi-Fi, are subject to several vulnerabilities that can compromise security and privacy. These vulnerabilities stem from both the Wi-Fi infrastructure and the VoIP technologies used in VoWiFi implementations.

One of the primary vulnerabilities in VoWiFi networks relates to the Wi-Fi access points themselves. Attackers can set up rogue access points or launch evil twin attacks, where they create fake Wi-Fi networks that mimic legitimate ones. Unsuspecting users might connect to these malicious networks, allowing attackers to intercept voice calls and potentially steal sensitive information. This vulnerability is particularly concerning in public spaces where users frequently connect to open Wi-Fi networks.

The encryption used in Wi-Fi networks can also be a point of vulnerability. While modern Wi-Fi security protocols like WPA3 offer strong protection, many networks still use older, less secure standards such as WEP or early versions of WPA. These outdated protocols can be easily cracked, allowing attackers to eavesdrop on VoWiFi calls. Even with strong encryption, weak passwords can undermine security, making brute-force attacks a viable threat.

Signaling protocols used in VoWiFi, particularly SIP, introduce another layer of potential vulnerabilities. SIP is susceptible to various attacks, including registration hijacking, where an attacker can impersonate a legitimate user, and call hijacking, where ongoing calls can be redirected or intercepted. Message tampering in SIP can also lead to the injection of malicious content or the modification of call parameters.

The media streams in VoWiFi calls, typically protected by **Secure Real-time Transport Protocol** (**SRTP**), can be vulnerable if the key exchange process is compromised. Weaknesses in SRTP implementation or key management can potentially allow attackers to intercept and decrypt voice conversations, severely compromising user privacy.

Device-level vulnerabilities also pose significant risks to VoWiFi security. Malware-infected smartphones or tablets can compromise the entire VoWiFi communication process. Such malware might capture voice data before encryption or exploit vulnerabilities in the VoWiFi application itself. Additionally, outdated operating systems or VoWiFi apps with known security flaws can provide entry points for attackers.

The integration points between Wi-Fi and cellular networks in VoWiFi systems can be another area of vulnerability. During handovers between Wi-Fi and cellular networks, there may be brief windows where calls are susceptible to interception or dropping. Attackers might exploit these transition points to disrupt services or gain unauthorized access to calls.

VoWiFi usage can potentially expose users to location tracking, as Wi-Fi access points can be used to triangulate a user's position with considerable accuracy. Moreover, the metadata associated with VoWiFi calls, including call duration, frequency, and parties involved, can be valuable to attackers for profiling and social engineering purposes.

Shown in the following figure is a mind map of the vulnerabilities in VoWiFi:

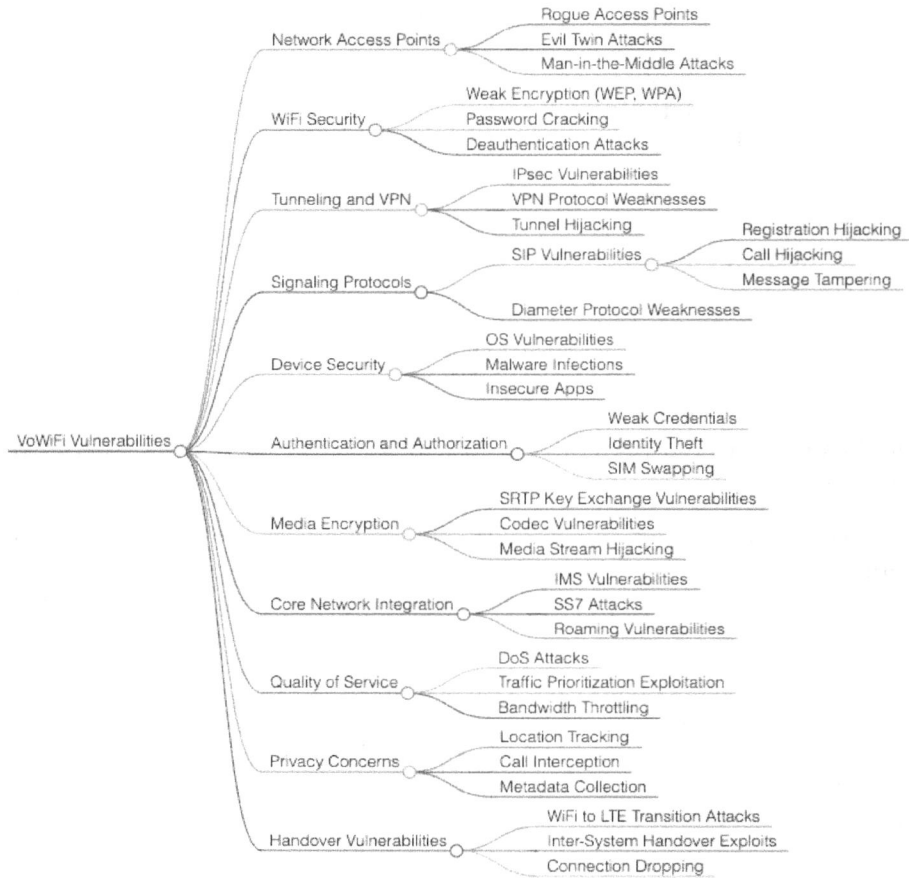

Figure 6.19: Vulnerabilities in the VoWiFi network

Addressing these vulnerabilities requires a multi-faceted approach involving robust encryption, secure authentication methods, regular software updates, and comprehensive network monitoring. User education about safe Wi-Fi practices and the risks associated with public Wi-Fi usage is also crucial in maintaining the overall security of VoWiFi services.

VoWiFi architecture

VoWiFi service provider network is a complex ecosystem of interconnected components that work together to deliver voice services over Wi-Fi networks. This system integrates with existing mobile network infrastructure to provide seamless voice communication services. The various components of this network are listed in the following:

- **ePDG**: A critical component in the VoWiFi architecture is the ePDG. This serves as the entry point for Wi-Fi traffic into the mobile core network. The ePDG manages

IPsec tunnels between user equipment and the core network, ensuring secure communication over potentially unsecured Wi-Fi networks. It acts as a bridge between the Wi-Fi world and the mobile operator's core network.

- **AAA**: These servers play a vital role in user management. These servers handle user authentication and authorization for network access, often working in conjunction with the HSS. The HSS is a centralized database containing user-related and subscription-related information, providing user profiles and authentication data across both Wi-Fi and cellular networks.

- **IMS**: The heart of the VoWiFi service lies in the IMS core. This includes several key functions: the **Proxy Call Session Control Function** (**P-CSCF**) acts as the first point of contact for user equipment in the IMS network. The **Serving Call Session Control Function** (**S-CSCF**) performs session control and registration services, while the **Interrogating Call Session Control Function** (**I-CSCF**) queries the HSS to find the appropriate S-CSCF for a user. Additionally, the **Telephony Application Server** (**TAS**) within the IMS core provides supplementary services for VoWiFi calls.

Security and border control are managed by SBCs. These provide security, NAT traversal, and interoperability functions at the edge of the IMS network, managing SIP signaling and media streams. For interconnection with other networks, the architecture includes components like the IBCF and **Transition Gateway** (**TrGW**). These manage interconnections and handle media-related aspects of interconnecting with other service providers' networks.

Components of the EPC, such as the MME, SGW, and PGW, handle mobility aspects and data traffic, providing connectivity to external networks. The following figure depicts the overall architecture of VoWiFi, along with the security component, ePDG:

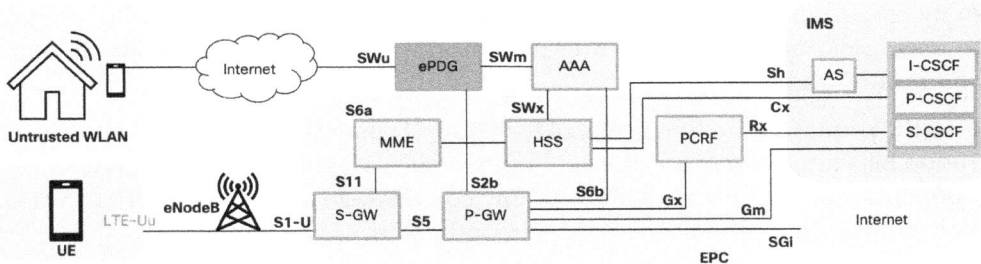

Figure 6.20: *VoWiFi architecture*

Securing VoBB

VoBB in mobile networks refers to a technology that enables voice calls to be carried over broadband internet connections rather than traditional circuit-switched voice networks. This approach leverages IP-based technologies to deliver voice services, like VoIP used in fixed-line communications. In the context of mobile networks, VoBB represents a transition from legacy voice systems to more flexible, IP-based solutions.

VoBB can be implemented using various broadband technologies, including fiber, cable, or DSL connections. In mobile networks, it often refers to voice services delivered over high-speed mobile data networks, such as 3G or 4G LTE, when not specifically using the VoLTE standard. VoBB solutions can be provided by mobile operators or by **Over-The-Top** (**OTT**) service providers, offering users an alternative to traditional cellular voice services.

The key difference between VoBB and VoLTE lies in their implementation and integration with the mobile network. VoLTE is a standardized technology specifically designed for 4G LTE networks and is deeply integrated into the mobile operator's infrastructure. It uses the IMS core and is optimized for the LTE radio access network, offering features like guaranteed QoS, seamless handovers, and integration with other operator services.

VoBB, on the other hand, is a more general term that can encompass various implementations of voice-over IP technologies in a broadband context. It may not be as tightly integrated with the mobile network as VoLTE. It might rely more on the data channel of the mobile network without the specific optimizations that VoLTE provides. VoBB solutions can be more flexible and potentially work across different types of broadband connections, not just LTE.

VoBB networks are susceptible to various vulnerabilities that can compromise their security, reliability, and performance. These vulnerabilities span various aspects of the network architecture and can be exploited by malicious actors.

One of the primary areas of concern in VoBB networks is network access security. Unauthorized access to the network can occur through weak authentication mechanisms or credential theft. Attackers may exploit vulnerabilities in the authentication process to gain illegal entry into the network. Additionally, the use of rogue access points or evil twin attacks, where attackers set up malicious access points mimicking legitimate ones, can lead to users unknowingly connecting to compromised networks, potentially exposing their communication data.

SIP, being the primary signaling protocol for VoBB, is susceptible to various attacks such as registration hijacking, where an attacker impersonates a legitimate user, and call hijacking, where ongoing calls are intercepted or redirected. Message tampering in SIP can also lead to the injection of malicious content or the modification of call parameters.

RTP and **RTP Control Protocol** (**RTCP**), used for carrying voice data, can be vulnerable to stream hijacking and eavesdropping if not properly secured. Weaknesses in the implementation of SRTP key management can potentially allow attackers to intercept and decrypt voice conversations.

Core network components, such as the IMS, are also potential targets. Vulnerabilities in the S-CSCF or breaches in the HSS can lead to widespread service disruptions and exposure of sensitive subscriber data. SBCs, crucial for network edge security, can be vulnerable to DoS attacks or may have configuration errors that compromise their effectiveness.

Interconnection points between different service providers' networks present another set of vulnerabilities. Weaknesses in the IBCF or gaps in inter-carrier security agreements can be exploited to launch attacks or illicitly access services across network boundaries.

Device-level vulnerabilities are also a significant concern. Softphones and mobile VoBB applications can be susceptible to malware infections, insecure storage of credentials, or weaknesses that allow reverse engineering and code injection. These vulnerabilities can lead to individual user accounts being compromised or used as entry points for larger network attacks.

A mind-map of the various vulnerabilities in the VoBB architecture is shown in the following figure:

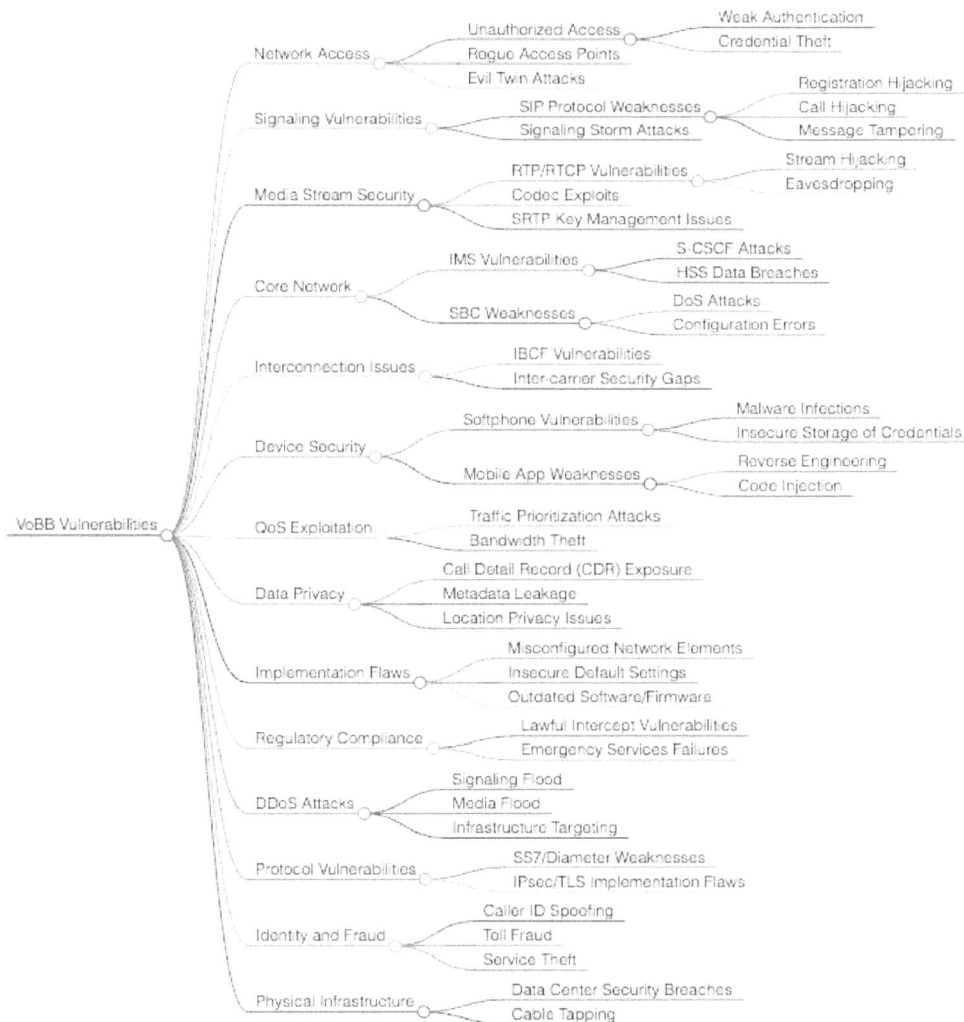

Figure 6.21: Vulnerabilities in VoBB

Addressing these vulnerabilities requires a comprehensive and multi-layered security approach, involving regular security assessments, timely patching and updates, robust encryption, strong authentication mechanisms, and continuous monitoring of network traffic and behavior.

VoBB architecture

The foundation of a VoBB network starts with the Access Network. This includes the mobile broadband infrastructure, such as 3G, 4G LTE, or 5G RAN (covered in the next chapter). These provide the initial connectivity for mobile devices. In some scenarios, Wi Fi access points may also be part of the access network, allowing VoBB services to be delivered over Wi Fi connections. This hybrid approach enables service providers to offer voice services across various types of broadband connections.

At the core of the network are several key components. The PGW serves as the point of interconnect between the mobile network and external packet data networks. It manages IP address allocation for user equipment and enforces QoS policies. Working alongside the PGW is the SGW, which manages user plane mobility and acts as an anchor point for intra-network handovers, ensuring continuity of voice services as users move between different base stations.

The IMS Core is central to the VoBB architecture. It consists of several critical functions. The P-CSCF acts as the first point of contact for SIP signaling from user devices. The S-CSCF is the central node for SIP processing, handling session control, and registration. The I-CSCF serves as a query point to find the appropriate S-CSCF for a user. Additionally, the TAS within the IMS core provides supplementary services such as call waiting, call forwarding, and other advanced telephony features.

SBCs play a crucial role in managing the network borders. They handle SIP signaling and media flows, providing essential functions such as security, NAT traversal, and protocol interworking. SBCs are vital in protecting the core network from potential threats and ensuring smooth communication between different network domains.

The HSS serves as the central database for subscriber information. It stores user profiles, authentication data, and location information, playing a crucial role in user management and service delivery. Working in conjunction with the HSS, the AAA Server manages user authentication and authorization, ensuring that only valid users can access the VoBB services.

Policy control and charging are managed by the PCRF. This component determines policy rules in real-time, managing QoS for VoBB calls and ensuring that services are delivered according to user subscriptions and network policies.

Perimeter Firewalls and security capabilities in SBC, IDS/IPS protect the VoBB network from external threats. Dedicated DDoS protection systems may also be employed to safeguard against large-scale attacks that could disrupt voice services.

The following figure depicts the various components of the VoBB network along with security components like the perimeter GP firewall, which will incorporate access control to detect and mitigate malicious traffic coming from broadband connectivity. The security capabilities of the SBC should be used to detect and mitigate application-layer malicious traffic in the IMS core.

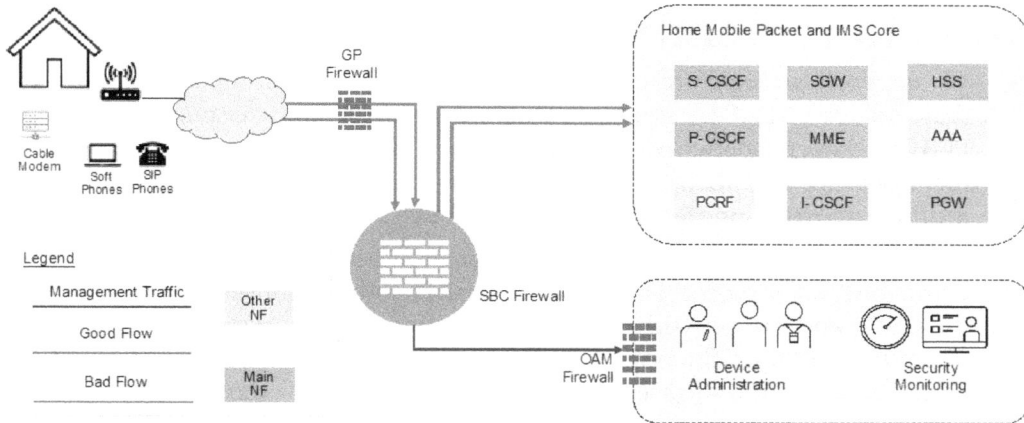

Figure 6.22: *VoBB architecture with security components*

Conclusion

The transition to 4G LTE mobile networks marked a significant leap in telecommunications, offering enhanced speed and capabilities while presenting new security challenges. The network's all-IP architecture introduced sophisticated components designed for high-speed data and voice communications, supported by multi-layered security features including encryption, mutual authentication, and integrity protection.

Roaming security emerged as a crucial concern due to global network interconnectivity. The vulnerabilities in SCTP, Diameter, and GTP protocols highlighted risks in inter-operator communications, prompting the industry to develop robust security measures. The integration of voice services through VoLTE, VoWiFi, and VoBB technologies brought additional security considerations, from signaling attacks to Wi-Fi and broadband-specific threats.

The complexity of modern mobile networks demands comprehensive security approaches covering all architectural layers. The shift to all-IP networks expanded potential attack surfaces, requiring more sophisticated protection mechanisms. Additionally, interoperability and roaming introduced unique challenges necessitating industry-wide collaboration.

While 4G LTE has revolutionized mobile communications, maintaining security remains paramount. The ongoing challenge lies in balancing enhanced functionality with robust security measures to ensure these networks remain trustworthy and essential in our connected world.

In the next chapter we will go through the 5G mobile network, along with its architectural components, vulnerabilities and possible security solutions.

Points to remember

- 4G network architecture encompasses key components, including the eNodeB (base station), MME for signaling and mobility, SGW for user plane traffic routing, PGW for external network connectivity, HSS for subscriber data, and PCRF for QoS management. This distributed architecture improves performance but introduces multiple security interfaces that must be protected.

- LTE security is built on mutual authentication between the UE and the network using the AKA protocol. This protocol verifies both the subscriber identity through the USIM and the network identity, preventing unauthorized access and man-in-the-middle attacks. Encryption and integrity protection are implemented across multiple network interfaces with specific security algorithms for different traffic types.

- Roaming Security requires protection for signaling protocols including SCTP, Diameter, and GTP. SCTP inspection monitors SCTP traffic between networks, detecting malformed packets and preventing DoS attacks. Diameter inspection examines authentication, authorization, and accounting messages, filtering unauthorized commands. GTP inspection monitors GTP traffic, preventing tunnel hijacking and subscriber impersonation attacks.

- VoLTE architecture implements voice calls over LTE packet networks using IMS. It includes session control via P-CSCF, S-CSCF, and I-CSCF components, and a media plane for actual voice transmission. Securing VoLTE requires SIP inspection, media encryption with SRTP, IMS border control functions, and strong authentication mechanisms to prevent eavesdropping, voice data manipulation, and fraudulent call establishment.

- VoWiFi architecture enables voice calls over Wi-Fi networks and consists of untrusted Wi-Fi access points, **evolved Packet Data Gateway (ePDG)** for secure tunneling and integration with the IMS core. Security measures include IPsec tunneling between user devices and the ePDG, EAP-AKA/EAP-SIM authentication, Wi-Fi network validation, and monitoring for anomalous behavior to prevent unauthorized access through compromised Wi-Fi networks.

- VoBB architecture provides fixed voice services over broadband networks with components including residential gateways, access networks, and IMS integration. Securing VoBB requires endpoint authentication, signaling, and media encryption, SBCs at network edges, and DDoS protection mechanisms to safeguard customer premises equipment from being exploited for network-wide attacks.

- Cross-technology vulnerabilities exist where these voice technologies intersect, particularly in handovers between VoLTE, VoWiFi, and VoBB. Security architectures must implement consistent policy enforcement across all three domains, maintain secure session continuity during transitions, and implement inspection points to detect attacks that attempt to exploit differences in security implementations between technologies.

- Diameter Signaling Security is critical for 4G networks as Diameter replaces SS7 for core network signaling. Comprehensive security requires implementing DEAs at network boundaries, filtering messages based on origin or destination validity, performing syntactic and semantic verification of Diameter AVPs, and monitoring for unusual patterns that might indicate reconnaissance or attacks.

- Regulatory compliance for 4G voice services involves meeting lawful intercept requirements while maintaining customer privacy, implementing data retention policies that comply with regional regulations, and ensuring emergency services connectivity across all voice platforms. Security architectures must balance these requirements with overall system security.

Exercises

1. Which component serves as the main control element in the 4G LTE architecture?
    a. PGW
    b. MME
    c. HSS
    d. SGW

2. What protocol is primarily used for signaling in Diameter-based roaming interfaces?
    a. GTP
    b. SCTP
    c. IPsec
    d. SS7

3. Which of the following is NOT a key security feature in 4G LTE?
    a. Mutual authentication between UE and network
    b. End-to-end encryption for all services
    c. Strong key derivation mechanisms
    d. Integrity protection for signaling

4. In the VoLTE architecture, which network element is responsible for session control?
    a. P-CSCF
    b. IMS-AGW
    c. IBCF
    d. TAS

5. What is the primary security vulnerability in VoWiFi deployments?
   a. Unencrypted media streams
   b. Lack of mutual authentication
   c. Untrusted access networks
   d. Weak key generation

6. Which protocol is typically inspected to prevent signaling-based attacks in 4G roaming scenarios?
   a. HTTP
   b. Diameter
   c. SIP
   d. SMTP

7. What component provides subscriber information to the MME during authentication in a 4G network?
   a. SGW
   b. PGW
   c. HSS
   d. PCRF

8. Which security mechanism is used for mutual authentication in 4G LTE networks?
   a. AKA
   b. **Wi-Fi Protected Access 2 (WPA2)**
   c. **Transport Layer Security (TLS)**
   d. OAuth

9. Describe the key differences between SCTP inspection and GTP inspection in securing 4G roaming traffic.

10. Explain the mutual authentication process in LTE and why it is more secure than previous generations.

11. What are the main security challenges when implementing VoLTE in a service provider network?

12. Compare and contrast the security architectures of VoWiFi and VoBB.

13. What are three critical security controls that should be implemented at the interconnect border for 4G networks?

14. Explain how the EPS-AKA protocol contributes to 4G security.

15. Describe the potential threat vectors in a VoLTE to VoWiFi handover scenario.

16. What role does the ePDG play in securing VoWiFi traffic?

CHAPTER 7
5G Mobile Networks

Introduction

The advent of 5G technology marks a transformative milestone in mobile communications, building upon and significantly surpassing its predecessors. This chapter explores the multifaceted landscape of 5G networks, from their foundational standards to their revolutionary capabilities and security implications.

At its core, 5G is governed by comprehensive standards established by the 3GPP, encompassing both the 5G New Radio specifications and core network protocols. The architecture represents a paradigm shift, embracing a service-based approach that leverages **network function virtualization** (**NFV**) and **software-defined networking** (**SDN**) to achieve unprecedented flexibility and scalability.

While 5G introduces enhanced security measures, including robust encryption and improved subscriber privacy mechanisms, it also presents novel challenges. The chapter examines potential vulnerabilities in protocol implementations and network configurations, alongside solutions like the **Security Edge Protection Proxy** (**SEPP**) for secure global roaming.

What truly distinguishes 5G is its trio of game-changing capabilities: **Massive Machine-Type Communications** (**mMTC**), **Ultra-Reliable Low-Latency Communications** (**URLLC**), and **enhanced mobile broadband** (**eMBB**). These features enable revolutionary applications across industries, from autonomous vehicles to smart cities. This chapter provides readers with a comprehensive foundation in 5G technology, preparing them for deeper exploration in subsequent chapters.

Structure

This chapter covers the following topics:

- Introduction to 5G
- 3GPP specifications series
- 5G use cases
- 5G network architecture
- 5G network interfaces
- 5G differentiators
- 5G deployment models
- Virtualization deployment models
- Vulnerabilities in 5G
- Inherent security mechanisms in 5G
- Security trust model for 5G
- Securing service-based architecture
- Roaming security

Objectives

This chapter provides a comprehensive examination of 5G technology, encompassing its foundational elements and transformative capabilities. Our exploration begins with the fundamental standards that govern 5G networks, tracing their evolution and the key organizations that shape these specifications. We then examine the architectural framework of 5G, particularly its innovative service-based approach and the revolutionary concept of network slicing.

Security stands as a central theme throughout the chapter, as we analyze both inherent vulnerabilities and built-in protective measures. This includes an in-depth look at enhanced encryption protocols, improved subscriber privacy mechanisms, and strengthened authentication systems. Special attention is given to roaming security, highlighting how 5G advances inter-operator protection and subscriber identity management beyond previous generations.

The chapter culminates in an examination of 5G's distinguishing characteristics, such as ultra-low latency and massive device connectivity. We explore how these features enable unprecedented applications across various industries while introducing new security and management considerations. Through this comprehensive coverage, readers will develop a thorough understanding of 5G technology, its security landscape, and its potential to reshape telecommunications. This knowledge will enable critical evaluation of both the opportunities and challenges presented by this transformative technology.

An introduction to 5G

5G, short for fifth-generation wireless technology, represents a significant leap forward in mobile network capabilities. It is designed to provide faster data speeds, lower latency, and increased connectivity compared to its predecessor, 4G LTE. 5G networks are built to support the growing demands of our increasingly connected world, from smartphones and tablets to smart cities and the **Internet of Things (IoT)**.

The transition from 4G to 5G networks represents a paradigm shift in telecommunications architecture and capabilities. At its core, 5G adopts a cloud-native architecture, leveraging containerization, microservices, and SDN to enable greater flexibility, scalability, and efficiency. This approach allows for NFV, where network components are software-based and can be dynamically allocated and managed. A crucial aspect of 5G is **radio access network (RAN)** disaggregation, which separates the RAN into three main components: the **Radio Unit (RU)**, **Distributed Unit (DU)**, and **Centralized Unit (CU)**. This disaggregation enables more efficient resource allocation, reduces vendor lock-in, and allows for implementing Open RAN standards, promoting interoperability and innovation. **Multi-access Edge Computing (MEC)** is another pivotal feature, bringing computing and storage resources closer to the network edge. This reduces latency and enables real-time applications, crucial for IoT, autonomous vehicles, and augmented reality. 5G also introduces network slicing, allowing operators to create virtual, isolated network segments tailored to specific use cases or customers, each with its own performance characteristics. This comprehensive overhaul of network architecture (as shown in *Figure 7.1*) and capabilities positions 5G as not just an incremental improvement over 4G, but as a transformative force enabling a wide array of new services and applications across various industries.

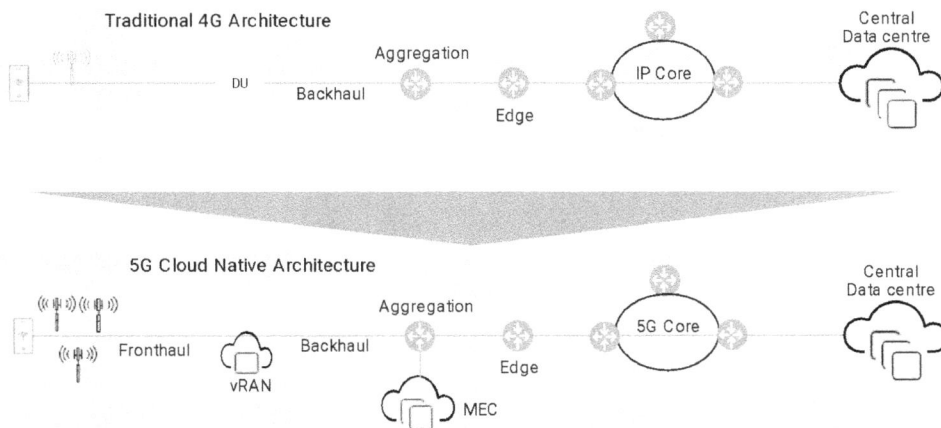

Figure 7.1: *4G to 5G transition*

At its core, 5G technology utilizes higher frequency radio waves than previous generations, allowing for greater data capacity and faster transmission speeds. These higher frequencies, particularly in the **millimeter Wave (mmWave)** spectrum, can deliver multi-gigabit speeds in dense urban areas. However, they also face challenges in terms of signal penetration and range, necessitating a more extensive network of small cells and advanced antenna technologies.

One of the key features of 5G is its dramatically reduced latency, which refers to the time it takes for data to travel from its source to its destination. While 4G networks typically have latencies of around 20-30 milliseconds, 5G aims to reduce this to as low as one millisecond. This near-instantaneous responsiveness is crucial for applications, such as autonomous vehicles, remote surgery, and augmented reality, where even small delays can have significant consequences.

5G networks are also designed to support a massive increase in connected devices. The technology can theoretically handle up to one million devices per square kilometer, enabling the widespread adoption of IoT devices in various sectors. This capability is particularly important for smart city initiatives, industrial automation, and the development of large-scale sensor networks for environmental monitoring and resource management.

The architecture of 5G networks incorporates several advanced technologies to achieve its performance goals. These include massive **Multiple Input, Multiple Output (MIMO)** antenna arrays, beamforming techniques to focus signals more efficiently, and network slicing, which allows operators to create virtual networks tailored to specific use cases within the same physical infrastructure.

While 5G promises transformative capabilities, its rollout has been gradual and faces several challenges. These include the need for significant infrastructure investments, regulatory hurdles in different countries, and concerns about the potential health effects of increased exposure to radiofrequency radiation. Despite these challenges, the technology continues to evolve and expand, with ongoing research into even more advanced iterations, such as 6G, already underway.

3GPP specifications series

The **3rd Generation Partnership Project (3GPP)** is responsible for developing and maintaining global telecommunications standards. They release specifications in a series of *releases*, each building upon the previous one and introducing new features and improvements. Here is a summary of the major 3GPP releases:

- **Release 99** (1999) marked the beginning of the 3G era, introducing the first **Universal Mobile Telecommunications System (UMTS)** specifications. This release laid the foundation for 3G networks and services, offering significantly improved data rates compared to 2G systems.

- In between release 99 and release 15, 3GPP published multiple specifications for 3G, 4G, LTE-Advanced, enhanced machine-type communication, and Vehicle-to-everything. **Release 15** (2018) marked the beginning of the 5G era, introducing the first set of 5G **New Radio** (**NR**) specifications. It defined the basic 5G architecture and introduced features like network slicing and support for the mmWave spectrum.

- **Release 16** (2020) further enhanced 5G capabilities, introducing features like 5G NR in unlicensed spectrum, enhanced **vehicle-to-everything** (**eV2X**) communications, and industrial IoT enhancements.

- **Release 17** (2022) continued to evolve 5G, focusing on areas like enhanced MIMO capabilities, improved positioning accuracy, and further enhancements to IoT and V2X technologies.

- **Release 18** (ongoing) is set to introduce *5G Advanced*, focusing on areas like **artificial intelligence** (**AI**)/**machine learning** (**ML**) integration. This will result in further advancements in IoT and V2X, enhancing network energy efficiency.

3GPP uses a system of parallel *Releases*. It provides developers with a stable platform for the implementation of features at a given point and then allows for the addition of new functionality in subsequent Releases. 3GPP has represented a timeline of the various specifications that are planned to be released in the coming years. The diagrammatic representation from their site as of July 2024 is shown in the following figure:

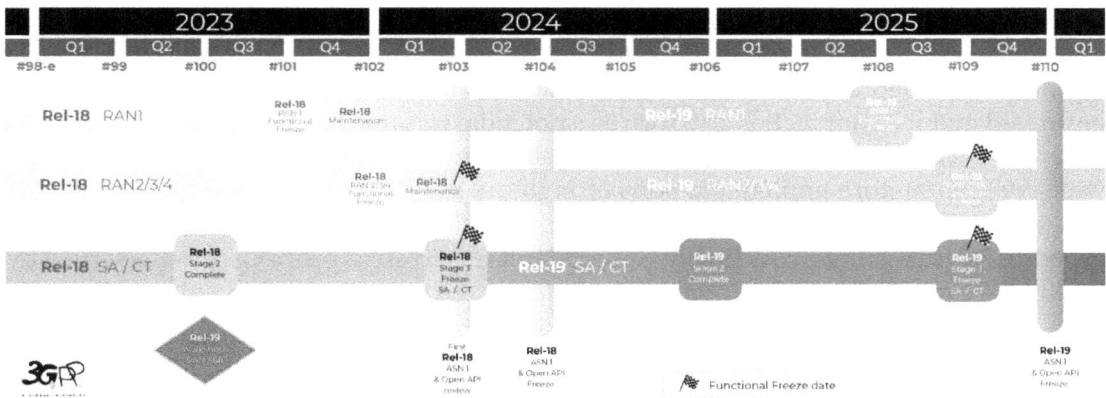

Figure 7.2: 3GPP release timeline[1]

5G use cases

In the early days of 5G, the telecommunications industry and various stakeholders identified several key use cases for 5G technology. These use cases were designed to showcase the potential of 5G and drive its adoption across different sectors. A diagrammatic representation of these use cases is shown in the following figure:

---

1   Source: **https://www.3gpp.org/specifications-technologies/releases**

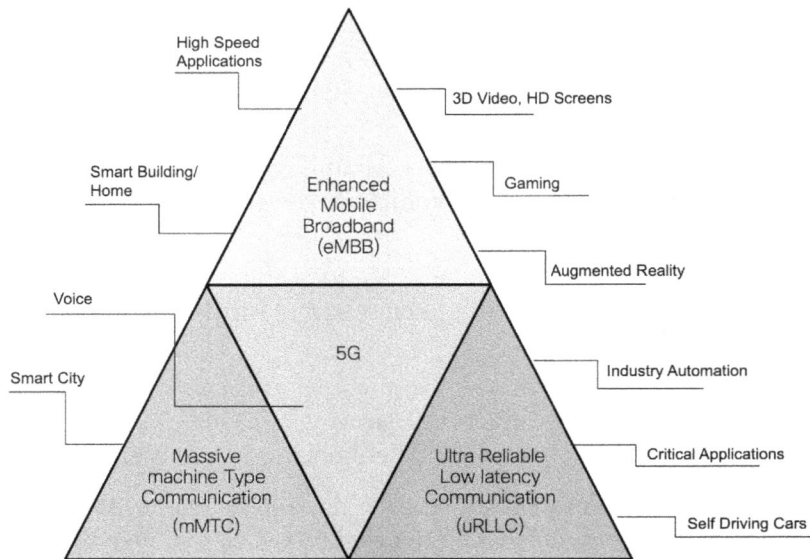

Figure 7.3: 5G use cases

Enhanced Mobile Broadband (eMBB) is one of the primary use cases for 5G. This focused on delivering significantly faster data speeds, lower latency, and increased capacity compared to 4G networks. eMBB is expected to enable seamless streaming of high-quality video content, immersive virtual and augmented reality experiences, and improved mobile gaming. It is also seen as a potential solution for providing fixed wireless access in areas where fiber deployment is challenging or cost-prohibitive. In recent days, we have seen mature implementations of high-quality streaming services, including 8K video and advanced AR/VR applications. **Fixed Wireless Access (FWA)** using 5G has expanded significantly, providing high-speed internet to areas previously underserved by traditional broadband.

URLLC is another critical use case for 5G. This aims to provide extremely low latency (as low as one millisecond) and high reliability, making it suitable for applications that require real-time responsiveness and cannot tolerate delays. Use cases under URLLC included autonomous vehicles, remote surgery, industrial automation, and mission-critical applications like public safety communications. We are witnessing early commercial deployments of autonomous vehicles in controlled environments, and more extensive use of 5G in industrial automation. Remote surgery and other critical healthcare applications are being tested more extensively in real-world scenarios.

mMTC is identified as a key enabler for the IoT. This use case focuses on supporting a vast number of connected devices in a small area, with an emphasis on low-power, low-cost devices. The mMTC is expected to drive smart city applications, agricultural IoT, large-scale sensor networks, and industrial IoT deployments. Its use cases have seen explosive growth with the proliferation of IoT devices. Smart city implementations are more common, with large-scale sensor networks providing real-time data for urban management. Agricultural IoT has expanded, with more farms using connected devices for precision agriculture.

Industry 4.0 and smart manufacturing are significant beneficiaries of 5G technology. The combination of high bandwidth, low latency, and support for a large number of connected devices enables fully automated and flexible production systems, real-time monitoring and control of industrial processes, and improved supply chain management. The 5G technology is well-positioned to enable **vehicle-to-everything** (**V2X**) communications, supporting advanced driver assistance systems, platooning of trucks, and eventually, fully autonomous driving. The low latency of 5G is crucial for real-time decision-making in these scenarios. Telemedicine and e-health applications are important use cases of 5G, especially considering the global pandemic. 5G can enable remote patient monitoring, telesurgery, and improved emergency response services. The high-quality video capabilities and low latency of 5G are crucial for these applications.

5G network architecture

The 5G architecture is designed to be a service-based, cloud-native network that enables the use cases explained in the above section, like enhanced mobile broadband, URLLCs, and mMTC use cases. It is built on a flexible, scalable framework that can adapt to various use cases and service requirements.

The **service-based architecture** (**SBA**) is a fundamental aspect of the 5G core network design. It represents a significant shift from the traditional point-to-point architecture used in previous generations of mobile networks. In SBA, network functions are implemented as a set of interconnected services that can be reused, making the network more flexible, scalable, and efficient.

In the 5G SBA, each network function is modeled as a service that can be accessed by other authorized network functions. These services communicate with each other using a common framework based on HTTP/2 and RESTful **application programming interfaces** (**APIs**). This approach allows for loose coupling between services, making it easier to add, modify, or upgrade individual components without affecting the entire system. One of the key components of the 5G SBA is the **service-based interface** (**SBI**). The SBI provides a standardized way for network functions to communicate, enabling seamless interaction between different services. This interface supports service registration, discovery, and communication, allowing for dynamic and flexible network configuration.

The **Network Repository Function** (**NRF**) plays a crucial role in the SBA. It acts as a central repository and discovery mechanism for all available network function services. When a network function is instantiated, it registers its services with the NRF. Other network functions can then discover and communicate with these services by querying the NRF.

In the 5G SBA, the interaction between network functions is based on a producer-consumer model. As an example, let us consider the role of NRE in producer-consumer interaction. A producer is a network function that offers one or more services to other network functions. The producer exposes its capabilities as services that can be accessed by authorized consumers. When a producer network function in 5G is instantiated, it registers its services with the NRF, making it discoverable to potential consumers. The producer is responsible for implementing the service logic and responding to service requests from consumers. A consumer, on the other hand, is a network function that uses services provided by producers. Consumers discover available services by querying the NRF and then invoke these services as needed. This allows consumers to access functionalities they require without having to implement them directly, promoting modularity and reusability within the network. A diagrammatic representation of the same is shown in the following figure:

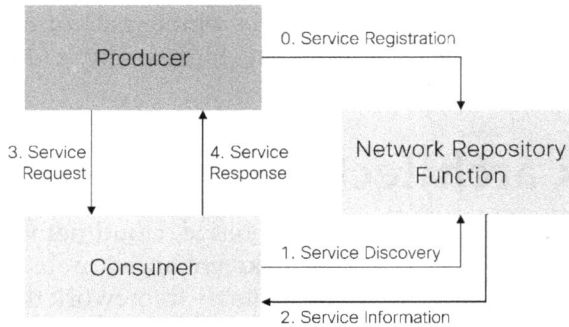

Figure 7.4: *SBA producer-consumer interaction*

At the heart of the 5G architecture is the **5G core network** (**5GC**), which is a significant departure from previous generations. The 5GC adopts an SBA where network functions are modularized and can communicate with each other through standard interfaces, as detailed in the above section. The following figure shows the main network functions that make up the 5G core and the access network elements:

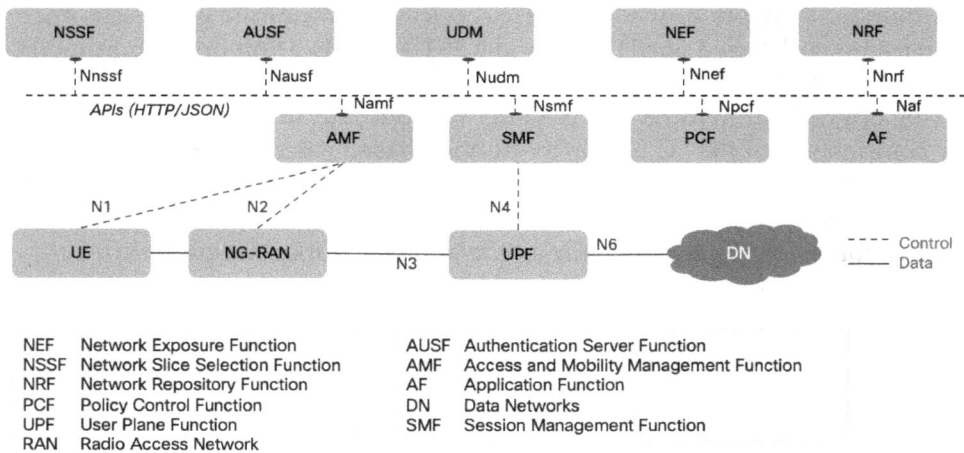

NEF	Network Exposure Function	AUSF	Authentication Server Function
NSSF	Network Slice Selection Function	AMF	Access and Mobility Management Function
NRF	Network Repository Function	AF	Application Function
PCF	Policy Control Function	DN	Data Networks
UPF	User Plane Function	SMF	Session Management Function
RAN	Radio Access Network		

Figure 7.5: *5G architecture*

The following list explains in detail the use of the network functions shown in the above 5G architecture:

- **User Equipment (UE)**: It refers to any device used directly by an end-user to communicate on the 5G network. This includes smartphones, tablets, IoT devices, and other connected gadgets. UEs are responsible for initiating connection requests, maintaining communication with the network, and running applications that utilize network services. They implement the protocols necessary to communicate with the NG-RAN and, through it, with the core network.

- **Next Generation Radio Access Network (NG-RAN)**: The NG-RAN, also known as 5G RAN, is part of the 5G network that handles wireless communications between the UE and the core network. It is mainly made up of **Next Generation NodeB (gNBs)**. They are the 5G base stations that communicate directly with UEs using the new 5G **New Radio (NR)** interface. gNBs handle radio resource management, mobility management, and initial access to the network. They support advanced features like massive MIMO, beamforming, and operation in both sub-6 GHz and mmWave frequency bands.

- **Access and Mobility Management Function (AMF)**: The AMF is responsible for handling connection and mobility management tasks. It manages user authentication, authorization, and registration to the network. AMF also handles mobility-related functions, such as handovers and tracking area updates. It is a key component in the control plane, interfacing between the **radio access network (RAN)** and the core network.

- **Session Management Function (SMF)**: The SMF manages user sessions in the 5G network. It is responsible for establishing, modifying, and releasing sessions for UE. The SMF also handles IP address allocation and management for UEs, as well as policy enforcement for user plane traffic. It works closely with the **User Plane Function (UPF)** to manage data flows.

- **UPF**: The UPF is responsible for packet routing and forwarding, serving as the anchor point for intra- and inter-RAT mobility. It handles policy enforcement, lawful interception, and traffic usage reporting. The UPF is a critical component in providing **quality of service (QoS)** and acts as the interface between the 5G core network and external data networks.

- **Policy Control Function (PCF)**: The PCF provides a unified policy framework for the network. It determines policy rules for other network functions, including session management policies for the SMF and access and mobility policies for the AMF. The PCF ensures that network resources are used efficiently and services are delivered according to defined policies.

- **Unified Data Management (UDM)**: The UDM stores and manages subscriber data and profiles. It handles user identification, access authorization, and subscription management. The UDM also generates security credentials for user authentication and supports the **Authentication Server Function (AUSF)** in the authentication process.

- **AUSF**: The AUSF is responsible for authenticating UEs accessing the 5G network. It works in conjunction with the UDM to perform authentication procedures and provides authentication information to the AMF.

- **Network Slice Selection Function (NSSF)**: The NSSF assists in selecting the appropriate network slice for a UE based on its subscription information and service requirements. It plays a crucial role in implementing network slicing, a key feature of 5G networks that allows multiple virtual networks to be created on top of a shared physical infrastructure.

- **NRF**: The NRF acts as a central repository for discovering and registering available network function services. It facilitates service-based interactions between network functions, supporting the service-based architecture of 5G. The NRF enables dynamic discovery of services, enhancing the flexibility and scalability of the network.

- **Network Exposure Function (NEF)**: The NEF provides a means to securely expose network capabilities and services to external applications. It enables third-party services to access network functions through standardized APIs, supporting innovative use cases and applications.

- **Application Function (AF)**: The AF interacts with the 5G core network to influence traffic routing, access network information, and request specific QoS for applications. It serves as a bridge between external applications and the core network functions.

5G network interfaces

The 5G core network interfaces, also known as **reference points**, are standardized communication channels between various network functions in the 5G architecture. These interfaces enable the modular and flexible nature of the 5G core, allowing different network functions to interact seamlessly. The 5G core uses SBIs for communication between network functions within the control plane, while some critical interfaces, particularly those involving the user plane, remain point-to-point. These include interfaces like N1, N2, and N3. The SBI uses HTTP/2 as the application layer protocol and is designed to support a cloud-native, microservices-based architecture. The following table shows a list of various interfaces, along with their reference point and use:

Name	Reference point	Description
N1	UE-AMF	NAS signaling between UE and AMF
N2	RAN-AMF	Signaling between RAN and AMF
N3	RAN-UPF	User plane interface between RAN and UPF
N4	SMF-UPF	Control plane interface between SMF and UPF
N5	PCF-AF	Policy authorization between PCF and AF

Name	Reference point	Description
N6	UPF-DN	User plane interface between UPF and Data Network
N7	SMF-PCF	Policy control interface between SMF and PCF
N8	UDM-AMF	Interface for subscription, authentication, and mobility management
N9	UPF-UPF	User plane interface between UPFs
N10	UDM-SMF	Interface for subscription management
N11	AMF-SMF	Interface for session management
N12	AMF-AUSF	Authentication interface
N13	UDM-AUSF	Interface for authentication credential information
N14	AMF-AMF	The interface between AMFs for mobility
N15	PCF-AMF	Policy control interface for mobility and access
N16	SMF-SMF	Interface between SMFs
N17	AMF-5G-EIR	Equipment identity check
N18	UDM-5G-EIR	Equipment identity check
N22	AMF-NSSF	Network slice selection
N23	PCF-NSSF	Provides network slice selection policy
N24	PCF-UDR	Access to subscription and policy data stored in UDR
N25	UDM-UDR	Access to subscription data stored in UDR
N26	UE-AMF	Interworking with EPS
N27	NRF-NSSF	NSSF services registration and discovery

Table 7.1: *5G interfaces*

5G differentiators

5G is the next generation of wireless technology, which differs significantly from earlier generations of wireless networks. The 5G network is based on decomposed, virtualized, and distributed network functions. These functions rely on containerized applications, open interfaces, and orchestration platforms to coordinate service delivery. 5G represents a transformational shift in the way the network is built and operated. Collectively, these abstractions expose attack surfaces and lead to challenges in implementing and managing security controls.

Virtualization

Virtualization within mobile network operators is still rapidly evolving, which has the potential to increase operational overhead and network complexity in the short term as vendors and operators look to converge their 4G and 5G cores. In the future, there will be a need for platform(s) to support a mix of containerized and VM-based network functions. Most operators will look to maximize the performance of CNFs by deploying containers on bare metal.

Virtualization is a fundamental enabler of 5G networks. Unlike previous generations, 5G extensively leverages NFV and SDN to create a more flexible and scalable infrastructure. This allows network operators to deploy services more rapidly, optimize resource utilization, and reduce costs. Virtualization also enables network slicing, a key 5G feature that allows multiple logical networks to run on a shared physical infrastructure, each tailored to specific use cases or customers.

One of the primary advantages of virtualization in 5G is increased flexibility and agility. Mobile network operators can quickly deploy, scale, and modify network services without the need for physical hardware changes. This capability dramatically reduces the time-to-market for new services and allows operators to respond more rapidly to changing network demands. For instance, during peak usage periods, additional virtual network functions can be spun up to handle increased traffic and then scaled down when no longer needed, optimizing resource utilization.

Cost reduction is another significant benefit of virtualization in 5G. By using standard hardware instead of proprietary equipment, operators can reduce capital expenditures. Additionally, operational costs are lowered through simplified network management and reduced energy consumption. Virtualization also enables more efficient use of network resources through dynamic allocation, further contributing to cost savings.

Virtualization plays a crucial role in enabling network slicing, a key feature of 5G. Network slicing allows operators to create multiple logical networks on a shared physical infrastructure, each tailored to specific use cases or customers. This capability is essential for supporting the diverse requirements of different 5G applications, from high-bandwidth consumer services to low-latency industrial applications.

Another advantage is improved reliability and fault tolerance. In a virtualized environment, network functions can be easily moved or replicated across different physical hardware, enhancing resilience against hardware failures. This capability also facilitates easier maintenance and upgrades, as services can be migrated to different hardware without interruption.

However, virtualization in 5G also comes with some challenges and limitations. One of the primary concerns is security. The increased software complexity and the use of standard hardware can potentially introduce new vulnerabilities. Ensuring the security of virtualized network functions and the underlying infrastructure requires robust security measures and constant vigilance.

Performance is another area of concern. While virtualization generally improves resource utilization, there can be instances where virtualized network functions may not match the performance of dedicated hardware, especially for tasks requiring high processing power or low latency. This limitation is particularly relevant for certain parts of the RAN where timing requirements are extremely stringent.

Red Hat **OpenShift Container Platform (OCP)** is based on Kubernetes and is the most common container orchestration system used in **Telco** environments today. Ultimately, it is envisioned that most operators will further simplify the NFVI architecture by adopting a container orchestration system to support a mix of VMs and containers. The following figure shows the various options that a mobile network provider can adopt to deploy various network functions:

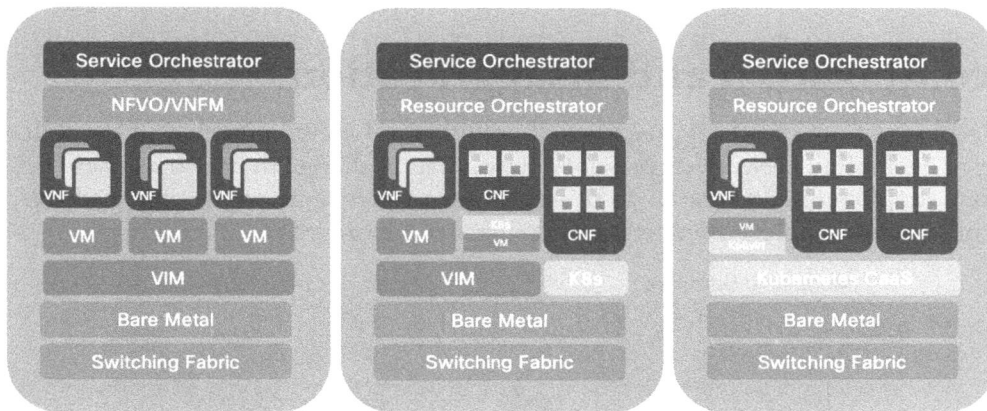

Figure 7.6: *VNF and CNF deployment options*

The following section details the various options that a mobile network provider can adopt to deploy various network functions:

- **Deployment with only VNFs**: This approach represents the first step in network virtualization. In this scenario, all network functions are implemented as VNFs running on a virtualization layer, typically using **virtual machines** (**VMs**) on bare metal compute hardware. In this deployment, traditional network functions are converted into software that runs on standard x86 servers. Each VNF typically runs in its own VM, providing isolation and dedicated resources. This approach offers significant advantages over traditional purpose-built hardware, including improved flexibility, easier scaling, and more efficient resource utilization.

- **Deployment with mostly VNFs and some CNFs**: This hybrid approach represents a transition state for many mobile network operators. While most network functions are still implemented as VNFs, certain functions, particularly newer ones or those being actively developed, are implemented as CNFs. In this scenario, VNFs continue to run in VMs on the bare metal compute, while CNFs run in containers. The containers might be managed by a container orchestration platform like Kubernetes, but this platform would coexist with the traditional virtualization environment used for VNFs. This approach allows mobile network operators to gradually introduce cloud-native principles and technologies into their networks.

- **Deployment with all CNFs and Kubernetes as Container-as-a-Service (CaaS)**: This represents the most modern and cloud-native approach to 5G network deployment. In this scenario, all network functions are implemented as CNFs, running in containers orchestrated by Kubernetes on bare metal compute hardware. Kubernetes serves as the CaaS platform, providing a consistent environment for deploying, scaling, and managing all network functions. This approach fully embraces cloud-native principles, namely, faster scaling and deployment, better resilience, improved resource efficiency, and simplified updates and upgrades.

Decomposition and disaggregation

The decomposition and disaggregation of architectural shifts, depicted in the following figure, in 5G mobile networks represent a fundamental change in how these networks are designed, deployed, and operated. This shift aims to create more flexible, scalable, and efficient networks capable of meeting the diverse requirements of 5G use cases.

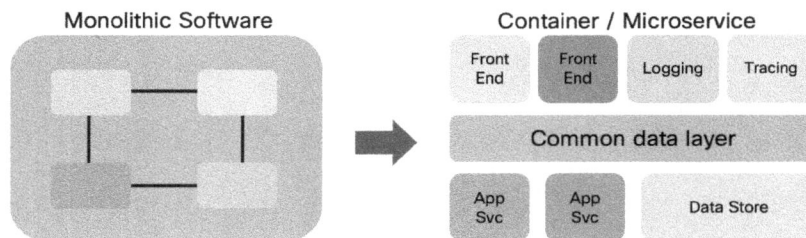

Figure 7.7: 5G decomposition and disaggregation

Functional decomposition

Functional decomposition in 5G refers to the breaking down of monolithic network functions into smaller, more specialized components. Functional decomposition allows operators to disaggregate software from hardware and obtain software capabilities from different vendors. This approach is applied across both the RAN and the core network.

The split RAN architecture exemplifies functional decomposition in the RAN. Traditional RANs had all functions tightly integrated within a single base station. In 5G, these functions are separated into three main components: the RU, DU, and CU. The RU handles **radio frequency (RF)** processing, the DU manages real-time baseband processing, and the CU handles non-real-time processing and control functions. This split allows for more flexible deployment options and enables edge computing scenarios.

Functional decomposition is realized through the SBA in the core network. Unlike previous generations that used point-to-point interfaces, 5G core functions are modeled as a set of interconnected services. Each service, like the access and mobility management function, session management function, etc., can be independently deployed, scaled, and updated. This decomposition enhances flexibility, allows for easier integration of new services, and improves overall network efficiency.

Functional decomposition also enables network slicing, a key feature of 5G. By breaking down network functions into smaller components, operators can more easily create and manage multiple logical networks tailored to specific use cases or customers, all running on the same physical infrastructure.

Network disaggregation

Network disaggregation in 5G refers to the separation of hardware and software components that were traditionally tightly coupled. This concept is closely related to, but distinct from, functional decomposition.

In the RAN, disaggregation is evident in the move towards Open RAN. Traditional RAN equipment was proprietary, with hardware and software tightly integrated and vendor-specific. Open RAN disaggregates these components, allowing operators to mix and match hardware and software from different vendors. This approach promotes innovation, reduces vendor lock-in, and potentially lowers costs.

In the core network, disaggregation is realized through the adoption of cloud-native principles. Network functions that were once tied to proprietary hardware are now implemented as software running on standard, **Commercial Off-The-Shelf** (**COTS**) hardware. This disaggregation allows for more efficient resource utilization and greater deployment flexibility.

Network disaggregation also extends to the transport network. SDN disaggregates the control and data planes of network devices, allowing for more programmable and flexible network management. This is particularly important in 5G, where dynamic resource allocation and network slicing require a high degree of network programmability.

Service-based architecture

SBA for core 5G networks is defined in 3GPP **Technical Specification** (**TS**) 23.501, *System architecture for the 5G System*. It uses SBIs between control-plane functions, while user-plane functions connect over point-to-point links.

SBA is a fundamental design principle in 5G networks, representing a significant shift from the point-to-point interfaces used in previous generations. In SBA, network functions are modeled as a set of interconnected services that can register, discover, and communicate with each other through a common framework. This approach aligns 5G networks with modern cloud-native principles and microservices architecture.

The 5G SBA leverages a **service-oriented architecture** (**SOA**) paradigm, which has been common within the IT application space for many years. 3GPP borrows the SOA vernacular, calling the requesting NF entity the Consumer and the entity providing the service the Producer, as shown in the following figure. The 5G core network functions that are attached to the service bus use RESTful API interfaces to consume and produce services. Further, the SBIs, as defined in the earlier section of this chapter, use the HTTP/2 protocol with JSON serialization format. Refer to the following figure for a better understanding:

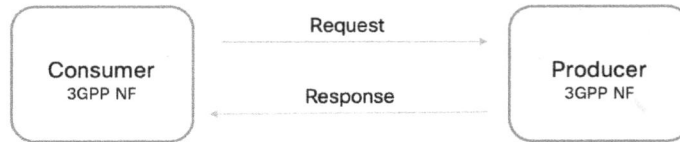

Figure 7.8: Consumer and producer in SBA

The decomposed 5G network function services expose their functionality through well-defined APIs, typically using HTTP/2 as the application layer protocol and a RESTful design. This design allows for a more flexible and modular network composition, where services can be easily added, removed, or updated without affecting the entire network.

SBA, shown in *Figure 7.9*, greatly enhances network flexibility and scalability. Services can be scaled independently based on demand, allowing for more efficient resource utilization. New services can be introduced more easily, fostering innovation and faster time-to-market for new features. With loosely coupled services, failures can be more easily isolated and contained. If a service instance fails, requests can be redirected to other instances, improving overall network reliability.

SBA facilitates multi-vendor deployments. The standardized service interfaces make it easier to integrate network functions from different vendors, promoting competition and innovation in the ecosystem. Refer to the following figure for a better understanding:

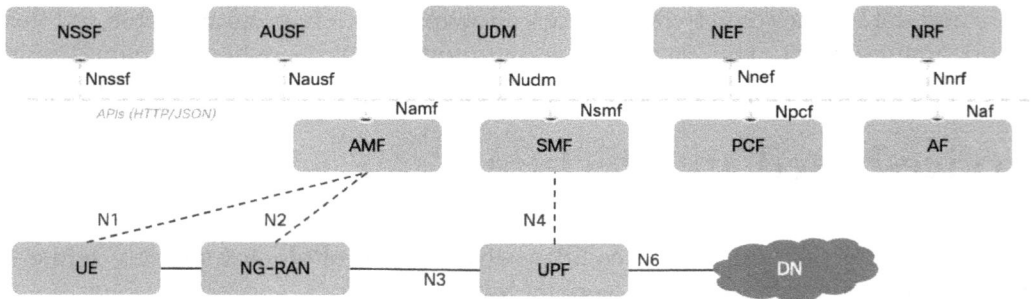

Figure 7.9: 5G service-based architecture

However, SBA also comes with certain limitations and challenges. The increased number of network interfaces and the distributed nature of services can lead to higher complexity in network management and troubleshooting. Ensuring consistent performance across distributed services can also be challenging, especially for latency-sensitive applications.

Every service-to-service interaction requires mutual authentication to ensure that both the service consumer and provider are legitimate and authorized. OAuth 2.0, an open standard for access delegation, is commonly used for this purpose. OAuth 2.0 provides a framework for obtaining and using access tokens to authenticate and authorize API requests.

Implementation of mutual authentication and authorization adds complexity to the network, but it is essential for maintaining the security and integrity of 5G networks.

Network slicing

Network slicing is a key feature of 5G technology that allows mobile operators to create multiple virtual networks (slices) on top of a single physical infrastructure. Each slice can be tailored to meet the specific requirements of different use cases, services, or customer segments. This enables more efficient use of network resources and the ability to support a diverse range of applications with varying performance needs. To enable end-to-end slicing, slice requirements need to be considered for the main sections of a mobile network, like the RAN, transport, and core components, as shown in the following figure:

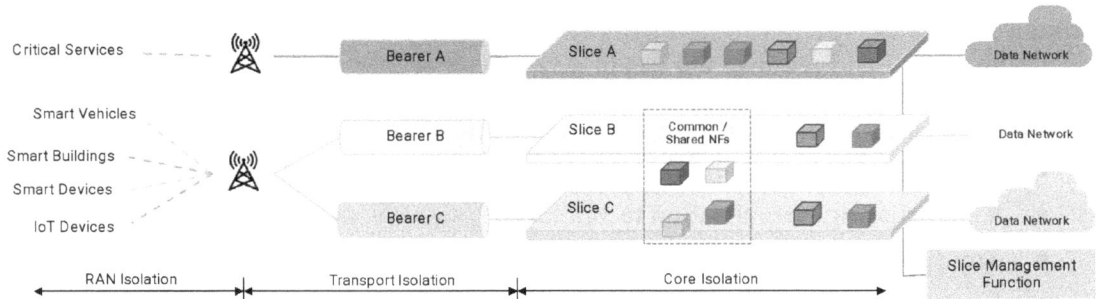

Figure 7.10: End-to-end slice isolation

RAN slicing involves partitioning the radio resources to create multiple virtual networks at the air interface level. This includes allocating spectrum, scheduling resources, and managing QoS for different slices. In 5G, RAN slicing is implemented through techniques, like dynamic spectrum sharing, flexible numerology, and NFV. For instance, a slice dedicated to eMBB might prioritize high data rates and capacity, while an URLLC slice would focus on minimizing latency and ensuring high reliability. RAN slicing allows for fine-grained control over radio resources, enabling operators to guarantee specific performance characteristics for each slice.

Transport slicing refers to the segmentation of the backhaul and fronthaul networks that connect the RAN to the core network. This involves creating isolated, virtual transport networks with dedicated capacity and performance guarantees. Technologies, like SDN and NFV play a crucial role in implementing transport slicing. They allow for dynamic allocation of bandwidth, traffic prioritization, and path selection based on the requirements of each slice. For example, a slice supporting autonomous vehicles might require deterministic latency and high reliability in the transport network, while a slice for IoT devices might prioritize energy efficiency and support for a massive number of connections.

Core network slicing involves creating separate, virtual instances of core network functions for different services or customer groups. This is achieved through the cloud-native architecture of the 5G core, which allows for the deployment of containerized network functions. Each core slice can have its own set of network functions, policies, and configurations optimized for specific use cases. For instance, a core slice for a **Mobile Virtual Network Operator** (**MVNO**) might have its own AAA functions, while a slice for industrial IoT applications could have dedicated network exposure functions and edge computing capabilities. Core slicing enables mobile operators to offer customized services, implement differentiated charging models, and ensure isolation between different customer segments or applications.

The combination of RAN, transport, and core slicing allows for end-to-end network slicing in 5G networks. This holistic approach enables operators to create differentiated services that can meet the diverse requirements of various industries and applications, from consumer-oriented enhanced mobile broadband to mission-critical communications for public safety or industrial automation.

From a security perspective, the security of slices poses a significant challenge. Securing a slice from end-to-end requires the use of a variety of segmentation, resource reservation, and isolation mechanisms at different layers (platform, network, application) across multiple domains (access, transport, core, data network), as listed in the following:

- RAN, considering air interfaces.
- CN, including virtualization technologies.
- Transport network, including segment routing or VPN techniques.
- Gi-access to different service providers.

Network slicing is most frequently discussed in reference to horizontal slicing. Horizontal slicing divides a network according to the SLAs of each application or application function. This allows URLLC, mMTC, eMBB, and other use cases to be delivered separately, which enables operators to customize latency, energy efficiency, and other KPIs for each service. At the same time, vertical slicing allows various entities to control slice attributes or services offered within a slice. For example, this could allow enterprises more autonomy to monitor or actively manage a slice and dedicated slice services.

Edge compute

Edge computing in Telco is often referred to as mobile edge computing, or MEC. MEC is essentially a distributed cloud that brings the execution environment much closer to the UE, enabling new mobile use cases for consumers and industries that need low latency, high bandwidth, device density, data offload, and trusted computing and storage. A general diagrammatic representation of an MEC in the overall mobile network is shown in the following figure:

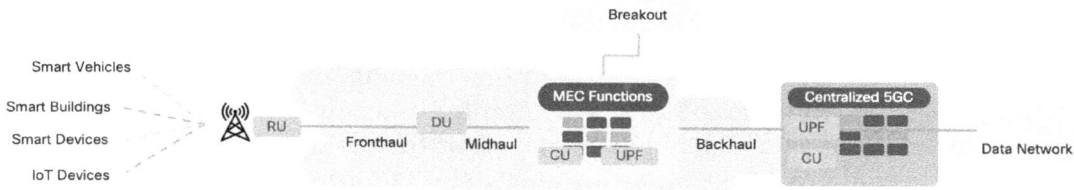

Figure 7.11: *Multi-access edge compute in 5G*

The MEC architecture consists of several key components. At its core is the MEC host, which is the physical server or cluster of servers that provides the computing, storage, and network resources required to run MEC applications. Sitting atop the MEC host is the MEC platform, a software layer that manages the MEC applications and provides them with a set of services. This platform includes the virtualization infrastructure, MEC platform manager, and various MEC services.

MEC functions are the software programs that run on the MEC platform, providing various services to end-users or other network functions. The MEC orchestrator plays a crucial role in maintaining an overall view of the MEC system, including available resources, services, and topology. Finally, the UE represents the end-user devices that connect to the network and utilize MEC services.

Security is a critical aspect of MEC implementations, given the sensitive nature of edge computing and its proximity to end-users. MEC can be implemented as a private cloud, public cloud, or hybrid cloud, and each model comes with its own security implications. MEC systems must ensure the confidentiality and integrity of data processed and stored at the edge through strong encryption mechanisms and secure storage solutions. Secure communication channels between MEC components, as well as between MEC and other network elements, must be established using protocols like **transport layer security and secure sockets layer** (**TLS/SSL**).

MEC enables a wide range of innovative use cases that leverage its low-latency and high-bandwidth capabilities. In the field of AR/VR, MEC can process complex computations closer to the user, reducing latency and improving the user experience for applications, like interactive gaming or industrial maintenance. For connected and autonomous vehicles, MEC can process real-time traffic data and V2X communications, enabling safer and more efficient transportation systems. In industrial settings, MEC facilitates industrial IoT and smart factories by processing data from numerous IoT sensors at the edge, enabling real-time monitoring, predictive maintenance, and process optimization. The healthcare sector can leverage MEC to enable real-time processing of medical data for applications, like remote patient monitoring or emergency response systems.

5G deployment models

5G networks can be deployed in two main architectures: **Standalone (SA)** and **non-standalone (NSA)**. Each of these architectures has different deployment options, providing operators with flexibility to transition from existing 4G networks to full 5G implementations. A diagrammatic representation of the various deployment scenarios that a mobile operator can choose from is shown in the following figure:

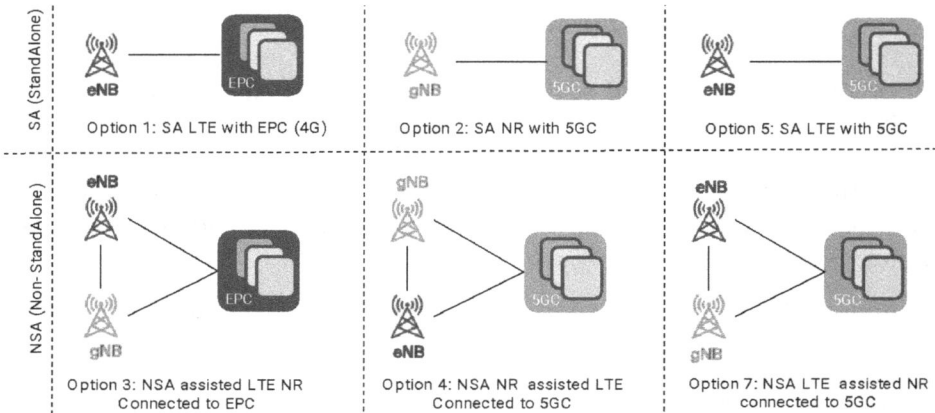

Figure 7.12: 5G deployment scenarios

Standalone 5G represents a complete 5G system, including both 5G **New Radio (NR)** and a **5G Core Network (5GC)**. This architecture provides the full set of 5G capabilities, including eMBB, URLLC, and mMTC. SA deployments are considered the goal for 5G networks, offering improved network slicing, edge computing capabilities, and support for advanced use cases.

Non-standalone 5G refers to a network architecture where 5G NR is integrated with existing 4G LTE infrastructure. In NSA, the 5G RAN relies on the 4G core network **Evolved Packet Core (EPC)** for control functions. This approach allows operators to leverage their existing 4G investments while introducing 5G capabilities, particularly eMBB services. The various deployment options that a service provider can consider are listed in the following.

- **Option 1**: This represents the basic setup for an LTE (4G) network. An eNodeB connects to the 4G core network to form the foundation for high-speed data services and other typical 4G applications.

- **Option 2**: This is a pure 5G standalone deployment. It uses only NR for radio access and the **5G Core (5GC)** for the core network. This option provides the full benefits of 5G, including network slicing, edge computing, and support for all 5G use cases. However, it requires significant infrastructure investment and may take longer to deploy compared to NSA options.

- **Option 3**: This is the most common initial 5G deployment scenario. In this, the 4G LTE network acts as the anchor, handling control plane functions, while 5G

NR provides additional user plane capacity. This option is further divided into Options 3a and 3x, depending on how the user plane is split between LTE and NR.

- o **Option 3a**: In this, the LTE network serves as the anchor for both control and user plane functions. Here, the LTE eNodeB acts as the **master node** (**MN**), while the 5G NR gNodeB functions as the **secondary node** (**SN**). The control plane is handled entirely by the LTE network, including both the eNodeB and the EPC. For the user plane, LTE traffic flows directly between the eNodeB and the SGW, while 5G NR traffic is routed from the S-GW to the eNodeB and then to the gNodeB.

- o **Option 3x**: This uses LTE as the MN and NR as the SN, but with a crucial difference in user plane handling. Option 3x allows for bearer split between LTE and NR, meaning that data can flow from the SGW to the eNodeB and then be split between the eNodeB and gNodeB. This key feature enables the simultaneous use of both LTE and NR for a single bearer, potentially offering higher throughput and more efficient use of radio resources.

- **Option 4**: In this scenario, 5G NR acts as the anchor network, with 4G LTE providing supplementary capacity. The 5GC is used, allowing for some 5G features to be implemented. This option is less common than *Option 3* but can be useful in specific deployment scenarios.

- **Option 5**: This option involves using LTE as the anchor network connected to the 5GC, without any 5G NR deployment. It allows operators to begin transitioning to a 5G core while still using their LTE RAN.

- **Option 6**: This option is like *Option 3* but uses the 5GC instead of the 4G EPC. It allows operators to introduce the 5GC while still leveraging existing LTE RANs. This can be seen as a stepping stone towards full SA deployment.

Virtualization deployment models

Deploying 5G **standalone** (**SA**) gives the telecom operators a golden opportunity to introduce a new operating model and architecture that is modern, agile, and efficient. By modernizing the network infrastructure, operators can achieve 5G specific scaling and resiliency requirements and develop new methods of network and service orchestration and zero-touch based automation.

5G brings on board novel use cases and benefits of URLLC, eMBB, and mMTC connections. These use cases expand the end user subscriber base from just mobile phones to IoT devices, hospitals, and autonomous vehicles-based customers, to name a few. Catering to these high connectivity demands, higher throughput, and lower latencies can be extremely difficult with traditional mobile architecture. Traditional monolithic mobile infrastructure is based on proprietary hardware and closed interfaces. These do not provide the 5G use case required automation, flexibility, or scalability. So, the path ahead for the mobile operator is to embrace a disaggregated architecture through virtualization and various architectural concepts involving multiple cloud-native deployment models, as depicted in the in the following figure:

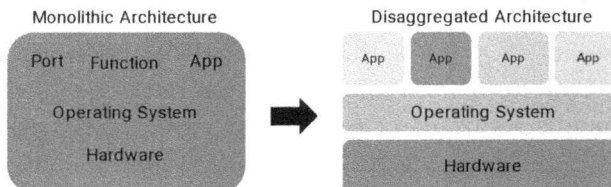

Figure 7.13: Monolithic and disaggregated architecture

As mentioned in this chapter, 5G introduces a specific architecture and related standardized interfaces. Due to this predefined standardization, the best approach is for 5G to be deployed on software-defined infrastructure, which correlates to cloud-native based deployments. Traditionally, for 4G deployment, many of the service providers have deployed their core components on virtualized environments. These virtualized environments are different from the common virtualization done in enterprise data centers. The virtualization needs of a telecom service provider combine multiple requirements to cater to latency-sensitive, jitter-sensitive, high packet rate throughputs or aggregate bandwidth, which must be tuned at various levels and multiple components of the virtualization stack.

Figure 7.14 depicts the basic NFV reference architecture as defined by *ETSI*, excluding the NFV orchestration components. As the telecommunication industry moved from 3G to 4G, one major change was the adoption of telecom-specific COTS software that could be deployed on virtual infrastructure.

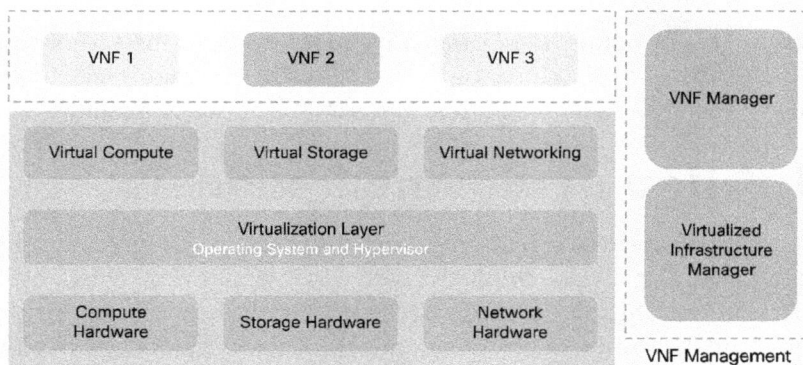

Figure 7.14: ETSI NFV reference architecture

The 4G virtual components are mainly deployed as an on-premise deployment, wherein the service provider buys the compute, storage, and network hardware, along with the virtualization solution to spin up the virtual machines needed to host the 4G components. Amongst these, there can also be instances where a specific telecommunication solution is on its own proprietary hardware. The following figure shows the cloud deployment scenario in 4G days:

Typical 4G deployment

| APP 1 | APP 2 | APP 3 | APP 4 | Telco Application |

| Private On-Prem Cloud | Private On-Prem Cloud | Proprietary Hardware |

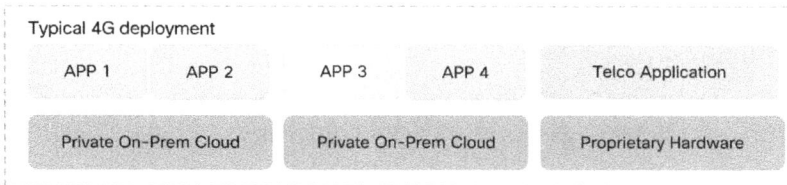

Figure 7.15: *Cloud deployment scenario in 4G days*

The service provider is responsible for the security of all these privately deployed telecommunication components. As in 4G, the service-based architecture was not adopted, the security requirements are different from those of a 5G deployment. The fact that the deployment model in 4G differs to a great extent from that of a 5G deployment, the security requirement and considerations also differs.

In the case of 5G, virtualization that drives centrally managed, software-controlled network functions across various technologies helps to allocate network resources to specific use cases, its users, applications, and services, without dedicated hardware and time-consuming deployment timeframes. Most of the 5G service providers are eyeing use cases, such as cloud gaming, connected vehicles, virtual reality, and the explosion of smart devices. These applications consume a lot of data, need more bandwidth, and are latency-sensitive. This means that service providers cannot just continue to use the deployment models used during the 4G days to meet the 5G requirement. Telecommunication service providers will now need to look at public cloud models and/or hybrid cloud models to deploy their solutions quickly and securely. To solve the latency concerns, communication service providers will need to partner with data center providers or set up edge datacenters to deploy solutions at the edge, closer to end users.

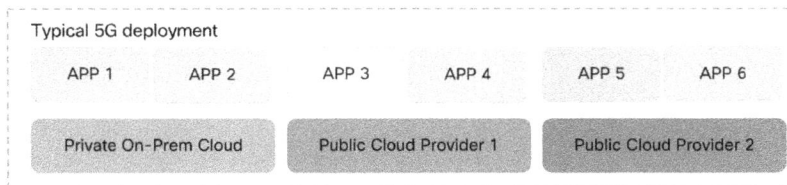

Typical 5G deployment

| APP 1 | APP 2 | APP 3 | APP 4 | APP 5 | APP 6 |

| Private On-Prem Cloud | Public Cloud Provider 1 | Public Cloud Provider 2 |

Figure 7.16: *Cloud deployment scenario in 5G days*

In the new deployment models adopted by 5G service providers, it is evident that native on-premise cloud solutions are not going to meet the various 5G requirements. Telecom service providers need to deploy some applications in their private on-prem data centers while partnering with public cloud providers 1 and 2 to deploy other applications.

These new deployment models not only help a communication service provider to reduce the cost of setting up a full-fledged 5G datacenter on their own, but also help to delegate a few other responsibilities to the cloud provider, like performance, fault tolerance, availability, scalability, and security. This deployment model also helps to create alignment between different network software vendors in terms of data management, observability, and security.

Adopting one of the following deployment models can help the communication service provider in multiple ways:

- Take advantage of the cloud service provider's security features, like anomaly detection, perimeter, and cloud security controls
- Take advantage of the cloud service provider's features, like scale UP or Down based on user traffic, pricing benefits, and analytics
- Reduction in Capex and Opex expenditures

Vulnerabilities in 5G

5G networks, while offering significant advancements in speed, capacity, and connectivity, also introduce new vulnerabilities across various layers of the network architecture. At the network architecture level, the adoption of virtualization technologies and network slicing presents risks, such as hypervisor vulnerabilities and potential breaches in inter-slice isolation. Edge computing, while bringing computation closer to users, expands the attack surface and raises data privacy concerns. A mind-map of the general 5G vulnerabilities is shown in the following figure:

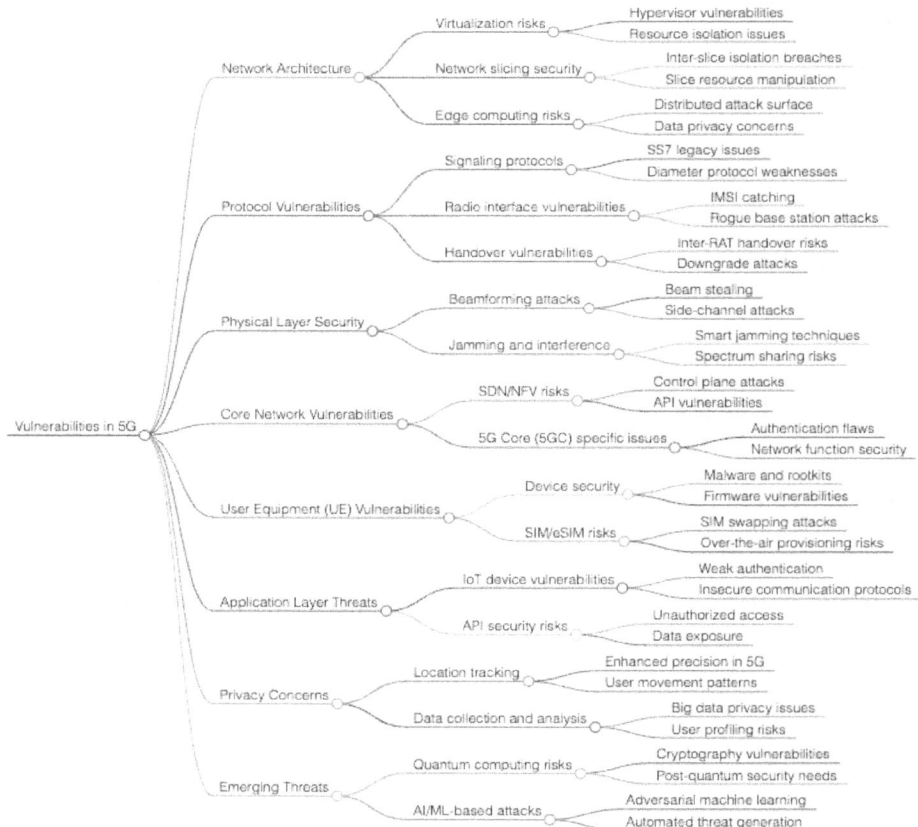

Figure 7.17: *Vulnerabilities in 5G*

Protocol vulnerabilities in 5G stem from both new and legacy systems. Signaling protocols like SS7 and Diameter continue to pose risks, while the radio interface remains susceptible to attacks, such as IMSI catching and rogue base station operations. Handover processes, especially between different radio access technologies, can be exploited for downgrade attacks.

The physical layer of 5G introduces new security challenges related to beamforming technology, which can be vulnerable to beam stealing and side-channel attacks. Additionally, the increased complexity of 5G networks makes them potentially more susceptible to sophisticated jamming and interference techniques.

In the core network, the shift towards SDN and NFV introduces vulnerabilities in the control plane and APIs. The 5GC itself may have specific issues related to authentication and the security of individual network functions.

UE in 5G networks faces threats from malware, rootkits, and firmware vulnerabilities. The use of SIM and eSIM technology also presents risks, including SIM swapping attacks and vulnerabilities in over-the-air provisioning processes.

At the application layer, the massive proliferation of IoT devices in 5G networks introduces concerns about weak authentication and insecure communication protocols. API security becomes crucial, with risks of unauthorized access and data exposure.

Privacy concerns in 5G are amplified due to the enhanced location tracking capabilities and the vast amount of data collected and analyzed. The precision of location data in 5G networks could lead to more accurate user movement pattern analysis, raising significant privacy issues.

Inherent security mechanisms in 5G

The main purpose of the 3GPP specifications is to define standards, procedures, and protocols that are used in the 5G system to enable services. It does not define a holistic architecture for distributed, disaggregated, and virtualization cloud-native environments like those found in 5G.

3GPP's 5G system defines standards, which when fully implemented, provide a good level of protection, however, this does not encompass the full stack. There are many examples of optionality within the 3GPP standards where controls are mandatory for the manufacturers to support but optional for the operator to implement.

3GPP, with its multiple releases, has added inherent security capability for the 5G network.

Security mechanism in release 15

Let us understand primary and secondary authentication. Network and device mutual authentication in 5G is based on primary authentication. This is usually performed during initial registration (when a device is turned on) of an end device. The authentication mechanism has in-built home control allowing the home operator to know whether the device is authenticated in each network. Session keys are established during the successful execution of this process. These keys are in turn used to protect the communication between the device and the network.

Primary authentication is radio access technology agnostic so it can run over non-3GPP technology, such as IEEE 802.11 WLANs. 5G supports three authentication options:

- **5G Authentication and Key Agreement (5G-AKA)**
- **Extensible Authentication Protocol (EAP-AKA)**
- EAP-TLS

EAP allows the use of different types of credentials, like username/password, certificates, and pre-shared keys, besides the ones commonly stored in the SIM card. This flexibility enables many 5G use cases outside of the telecommunications industry.

The support of EAP also applies to secondary authentication procedures. This procedure is executed during the setup of user plane connections for authorization purposes. This helps to determine if the user can perform certain actions, like surfing the internet or making a call. This allows the communication operator to delegate the authorization process to a third party, where existing third-party credentials can be used to authenticate the user and authorize the connection.

Several security issues exist in the inter-operator interface arising from SS7 or Diameter in the earlier generations of mobile communication systems. To counter these issues, 5G release 15 provides inter-operator security from the very beginning. Interconnect security between different operator networks is achieved by introducing a new network function in the 5G architecture called SEPP, as shown in the following figure:

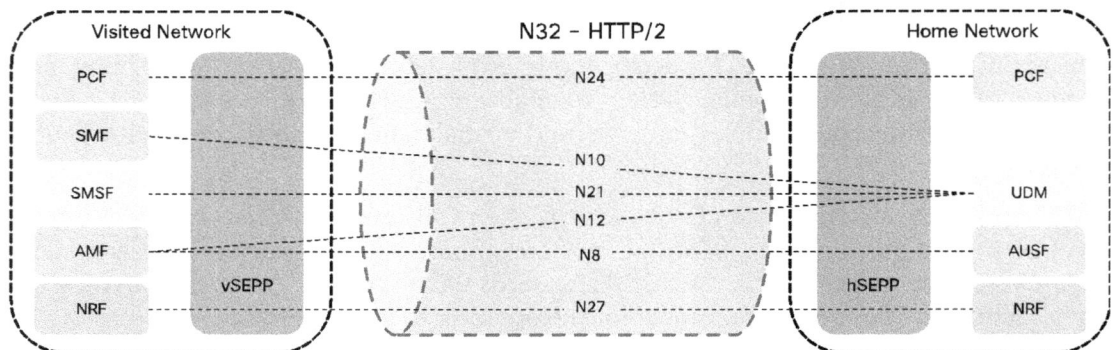

Figure 7.18: SEPP in roaming security

All signaling traffic across visited and home operator networks should transit through these security edge protection proxies. Like the mutual authentication requirement in the service-based architecture, the SEPPs are also required to authenticate, thus enabling filtering capabilities for the traffic originating from the interconnects.

Subscriber identity-related issues have been known since 4G and earlier generations of mobile systems. In 5G, a privacy solution is developed that protects the user's subscription permanent identifier against active attacks originating from false base stations, popularly known as IMSI catchers or Stingrays. Using IMSI catchers or Stingrays, attackers can get hold of the end user's IMSI information and consequently retrieve a user's private information, such as the location, SMS sent by the user, or even data being transferred.

5G makes use of the successor of IMSI, the **Subscriber Permanent Identifier** (**SUPI**). SUPI can be encrypted and transmitted over the air as a **Subscriber Concealed Identifier** (**SUCI**).

All 5G core subscribers are allocated a globally unique 5G SUPI. This is allocated to each SIM card that is inserted into the UE. SUPI is never sent in clear text across the RAN. In order to identify the UE over the radio link, a **Globally Unique Temporary Identifier** (**GUTI**) is assigned to the UE.

As SUPI cannot be transmitted in clear text, it is concealed inside the privacy-preserving SUCI. At the UE side, the encryption key stored within the 5G SIM/eSIM is used to conceal the Mobile Subscriber Identification Number part of the IMSI, for IMSI-based SUPI, and on the 5G operator side, the **Subscription Identifier De-concealing Function** (**SIDF**) of the unified data management network function is responsible for de-concealment of the SUCI and resolves the SUPI from the SUCI based on the protection scheme used to generate the SUCI.

The 5G core network is based on an SBA, which did not exist in 4G and earlier generations. 4G makes use of point-to-point interfaces between network functions, which is now enhanced in 5G to support SBI.

SBA is centered around services that can register themselves and subscribe to other services. This paves the way for the development of new services, which can be connected to other components without introducing specific interfaces. The service-based architecture is specified in 3GPP technical specification 23.501(1). Refer to the following figure for a better understanding:

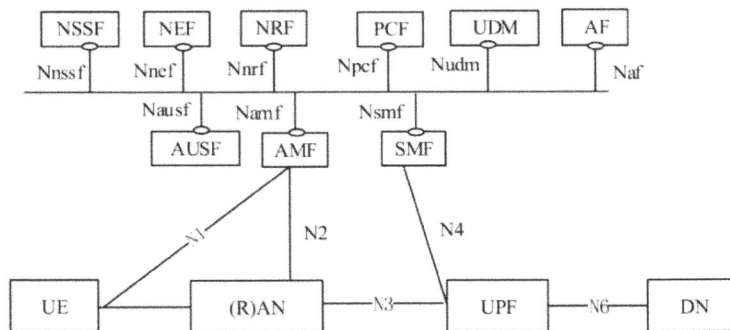

Figure 7.19: 5G service-based architecture[2]

2   Source: **https://www.etsi.org/deliver/etsi_ts/123500_123599/123501/17.05.00_60/ts_123501v170500p. pdf**

The communications with the SBA are request/response or subscribe/notify interactions between service consumers and service producers. These are mainly API based communications and thus require secure communication between the network functions, and service APIs of each NF must be protected and properly authorized. So, in the service-based architecture, the following security mechanisms need to be in place to secure communication between different network functions:

- Mutual authentication and transport security between network functions, based on TLS 1.2 and 1.3.

- Using OAuth 2.0, token-based authorization for access of service consumers to the services offered by service producers.

With the introduction of **network slicing** in 5G, Release 15 also brought in security mechanisms specific to this new architecture, which include slice-specific authentication and authorization, inter-slice and intra-slice protection based on slice isolations, and access control mechanisms for slice selection.

The 5G hierarchy reflects the changes in the overall architecture and the trust model using the security principle of key separation. %G introduces integrity protection of the **User Plane** (**UP**) between the device and the gNB. The support of the integrity protection feature is mandatory on both the devices and the gNB, while its use is optional and under the control of the communication operator.

Security mechanisms in release 16

3GPP release 16 was focused on additional use cases and many features were either added or enhanced, from the earlier release 15. Additions and enhancements were made for non-public networks, edge computing, positioning services, cellular IoT, and URLLC, among others, as mentioned in the following:

- **Enhancement to user plane integrity protection**: Integrity protection acts as a safeguard, ensuring the authenticity and unaltered state of communications within the 5G network. This crucial security measure enables the recipient to verify that the messages they receive have not been altered or manipulated by malicious actors during transmission.

  Beginning from *Release 16*, a new standard has been set for cellular devices, and they must now support full-rate *User Plane* integrity protection as a mandatory feature. This requirement means that all cellular devices are expected to have the capability to apply integrity protection measures to *User Plane* messages, irrespective of the data transfer speed being utilized.

- **Enhancement to IoT security**: *3GPP Release 16* introduced significant enhancements to cellular IoT data security, addressing the unique challenges posed by the massive deployment of IoT devices in cellular networks. These improvements were designed to strengthen the security of IoT communications while considering the resource constraints of many IoT devices. One key enhancement was the introduction of a lightweight authentication procedure for IoT devices. This new mechanism allows for faster, more efficient authentication, reducing signaling overhead and power consumption.

Release 16 also improved the handling of the long-term evolution of security keys for IoT devices. This is particularly important for devices expected to operate in the field for extended periods, sometimes up to a decade or more. The enhanced key evolution mechanisms help maintain the security of these devices over their entire operational lifespan, reducing vulnerabilities that could arise from long-term use of the same security keys.

Enhanced privacy protection measures for IoT devices, were also introduced as part of *Release 16*. These measures help prevent tracking and identification of devices based on their network communications, an important consideration given the often-sensitive nature of IoT data and the potential for IoT devices to reveal information about user behaviors or industrial processes.

- **Enhancement to URLLC security**: *Release 16* introduced streamlined authentication mechanisms specifically designed for URLLC scenarios. These optimizations reduce the time required for security-related handshakes and verifications, helping to meet the strict latency requirements of URLLC applications without compromising on security. *Release 16* implemented improved integrity protection mechanisms for URLLC traffic. These enhancements ensure that URLLC data remains tamper-proof and authentic, even under the constraints of low-latency transmission. The improvements allow for faster verification of data integrity, crucial for time-sensitive applications.

Release 16 enhanced the security of handover procedures for high-mobility scenarios, like connected vehicles. These improvements ensure that the transition between cells or network slices remains secure without introducing delays that could compromise the low-latency requirements of URLLC.

Security mechanisms in release 17

3GPP Release 17, finalized in 2022, focused on enhancing and expanding 5G capabilities across various domains. The primary emphasis was on improving 5G system efficiency, expanding its applicability to new verticals, and introducing advanced features. Key focus areas included enhancing URLLC for industrial IoT and vehicular communications, improving support for non-terrestrial networks (satellite integration), and introducing capabilities for new use cases, such as **extended reality** (**XR**) and unmanned aerial systems. The release also concentrated on advancing network automation and intelligence, enhancing IoT capabilities with features, like **Reduced Capability** (**RedCap**) devices, and improving energy efficiency. It also looked at enhancing security capabilities across multiple use cases like the ones mentioned in the following:

- **Enhanced SUCI protection**: Enhancement to SUCI provides more options for operators and device manufacturers to choose from, based on their specific security requirements and computational capabilities. The main enhancement is the introduction of post-quantum cryptographic algorithms for SUCI protection. This forward-looking approach aims to maintain privacy even in the face of potential future quantum computing threats. This includes more efficient **elliptic curve cryptography** (**ECC**), which provides a balance between strong security and lower computational overhead, which is particularly beneficial for resource-constrained IoT devices.

- **Enhances SUPI protection**: *Release 17* enhanced the key derivation mechanisms for SUPI protection. It focuses on increasing the robustness of the derived keys while maintaining efficiency. *Release 17* also implemented context-aware key derivation mechanisms. These consider factors such as network slice information and device type, resulting in more specialized and secure keys for SUPI protection.

- **Improved interworking with legacy systems while maintaining privacy**: *Release 17* brought about improvements in privacy-preserving identifiers that can be used when interacting with legacy networks. These identifiers maintain user privacy while still allowing for necessary operations in older network environments. Enhanced identity mapping mechanisms introduced in *Release 17* allow for secure translation between the new privacy-enhanced identifiers and legacy identifiers, ensuring smooth operation across different network generations.

- **Improved network slicing security**: *Release 17* introduced more granular and flexible access control mechanisms for network slices. These improvements allow network operators to define and enforce access policies that are tailored to the specific requirements of each network slice. For instance, a slice dedicated to critical IoT devices might require multi-factor authentication, while a slice for massive IoT might use lightweight authentication methods. Slice-specific credentials were introduced, which allow users or devices to have different security credentials for different slices, enhancing overall security by limiting the impact of potential credential compromises.

  Release 17 significantly enhanced the isolation between network slices. One major improvement is the introduction of enhanced resource partitioning mechanisms. These ensure that the resources allocated to one slice, such as computing power, memory, or network capacity, cannot be accessed or impacted by other slices, even in cases of high demand or potential attacks.

  Slice-aware security policy introduced in *Release 17* enables the application of different security protocols and algorithms to different slices based on their specific requirements. For example, a slice dedicated to financial transactions might use stronger encryption algorithms compared to a slice for environmental sensors. Similarly, slice-aware key management was introduced, which allows for the use of different key hierarchies and key rotation policies for different slices, enhancing overall network security.

- **Sidelink security mechanisms**: *Release 17* introduced direct authentication mechanisms for device-to-device communications, reducing reliance on network infrastructure for security in sidelink connections. This is crucial for scenarios where network coverage may be limited or unavailable. To ensure the confidentiality of sidelink communications, *Release 17* implemented robust encryption mechanisms. These use symmetric key cryptography with keys derived during the authentication process, ensuring that only authenticated devices can decrypt the transmitted data.

One key mechanism for privacy protection is the use of temporary identifiers for sidelink communications, like the concept of SUCI used in cellular communications. These temporary identifiers change periodically, making it difficult for unauthorized parties to track specific devices over time. This is particularly important in scenarios like V2X communications, where location privacy is a significant concern.

- **Security for non-public networks (NPN)**: *Release 17* introduced robust isolation mechanisms to ensure clear separation between public networks and NPNs. This isolation is implemented at both the control plane and user plane levels. It prevents unauthorized access from public networks to NPN resources and vice versa, maintaining the integrity and confidentiality of NPN operations. The isolation techniques include dedicated network functions for NPNs, separate subscriber databases, and stringent access controls at network boundaries. This ensures that even if a breach occurs in the public network, it does not compromise the security of the NPN. End-to-end encryption is mandated for NPN-to-NPN communication, ensuring that data remains confidential even when traversing intermediate networks. Additionally, integrity protection mechanisms are in place to prevent tampering with inter-NPN traffic. The standard also defines secure roaming procedures for users moving between different NPNs, ensuring continuity of service without compromising security.

Security trust model for 5G

3GPP technical specification 33.501 captures the security architecture and procedures for a 5G. 3GPP has also defined a 5G security architecture that has evolved from the days of 4G. The security architecture consists of the following domains:

- **(I) Network access security**: This domain includes a set of security features that enable **mobile equipment** (**ME**) to authenticate and access services via the network securely, including 3GPP access and non-3GPP access.
- **(II) Network domain security**: This domain includes features that enable network nodes to securely exchange signaling data and user plane data.
- **(III) User domain security**: This domain includes features that secure the user's access to ME.
- **(IV) Application domain security**: This domain includes features that enable applications in the user domain and in the provider domain to exchange messages securely.

- **(V) SBA domain security**: This domain includes features that enable network functions of the service-based architecture to securely communicate within the serving network domain and with other network domains.

Refer to the following figure for a better understanding:

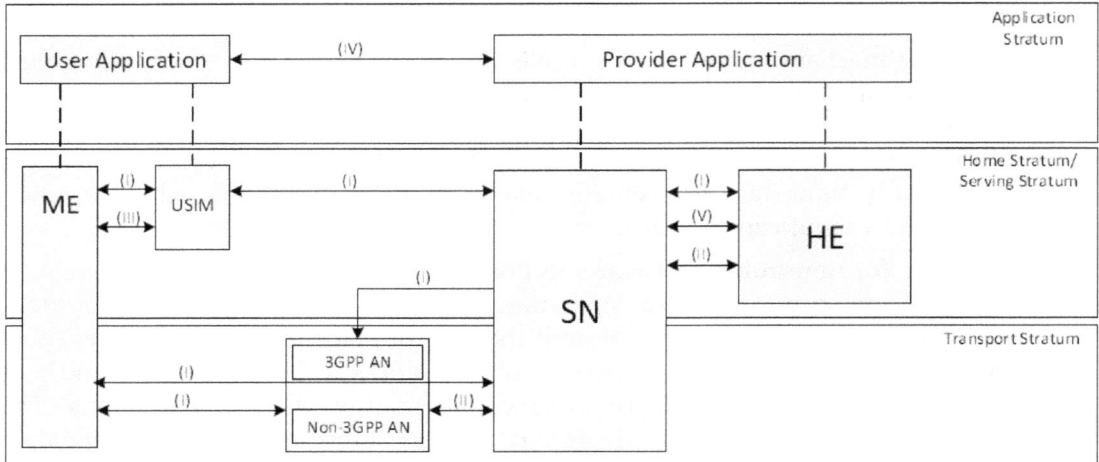

Figure 7.20: Overview of 5G security architecture[3]

In the 5G systems, trust within the network decreases the further one moves away from the core. The idea is that, at the center of the 5G system, is where the crown jewel of the 5G system resides, which requires to be secured from any unwanted access; thus, making it the trust layer or zone that can be trusted due to the level of security controls that might be applied to secure the network functions within it. **Unified data management (UDM) is** at the heart of the 5G systems. UDM supports the **Authentication Credential Repository and Processing Function (ARPF)** and stores the long-term security credentials used in authentication for AKA. It also stores subscriber information.

Authentication Server Function (AUSF) supports authentication for 3GPP and non-3GPP access. AUSF also interacts with UDM and provides UE authentication service to the requester network function. So, as part of the innermost trust layer, we can consider UDM and AUSF network functions, or any other critical network function based on the type of data it handles.

---

3   Source: 3GPP TS 33.501

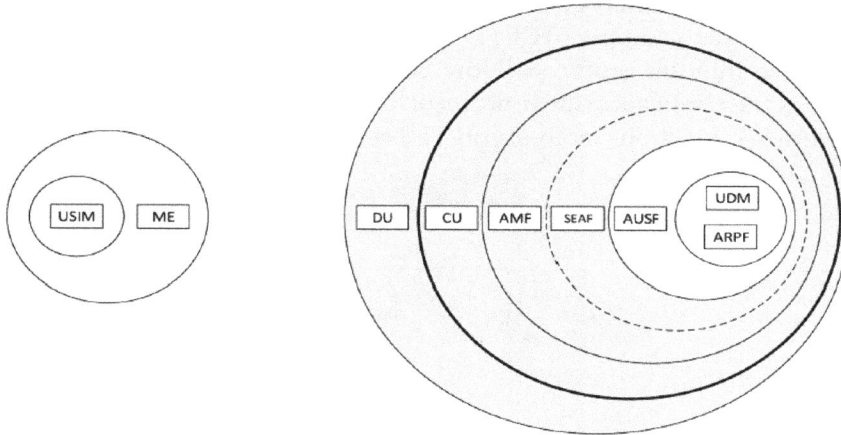

Figure 7.21: Trust model for non-roaming scenario[4]

The following figure shows the trust model for a roaming scenario where the home and the visited network are connected through the **Security Protection Proxy (SEPP)** for the control plane of the internetwork interconnect:

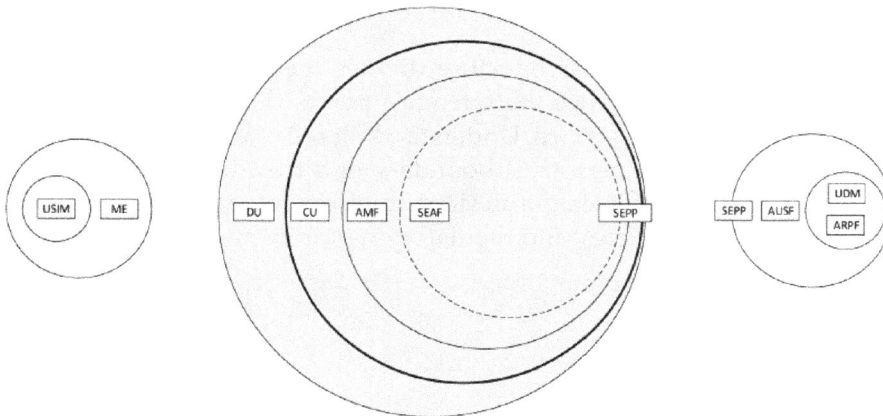

Figure 7.22: Trust model for roaming scenario[5]

Figure 7.23 depicts the main network functions of a 5G core. The 5G core network is made up of an SBA, which provides a modular framework from which 5G applications can be deployed using components from various sources and suppliers. SBA divides the 5G functionalities into different network functions and provides a standard communication infrastructure based on API calls, which are also referred to as SBI. 5G's SBA is an evolution from **Control and User Plane Separation (CUPS)**, with a complete redesign and grouping of 4G functionalities and mapping them into service-oriented network functions.

---

4   Source: 3GPP
5   Source: 3GPP

With SBA, the communication between any two network functions is through standard Internet protocols, for example, TCP/IP and HTTP/2.0. 5G systems benefit from the adoption of these Internet protocols. Now 5G can seamlessly integrate other protocols, such as JSON as the application layer protocol, OAuth2.0 as the authorization protocol for controlling network functions' access, and TLS as the network layer security protection.

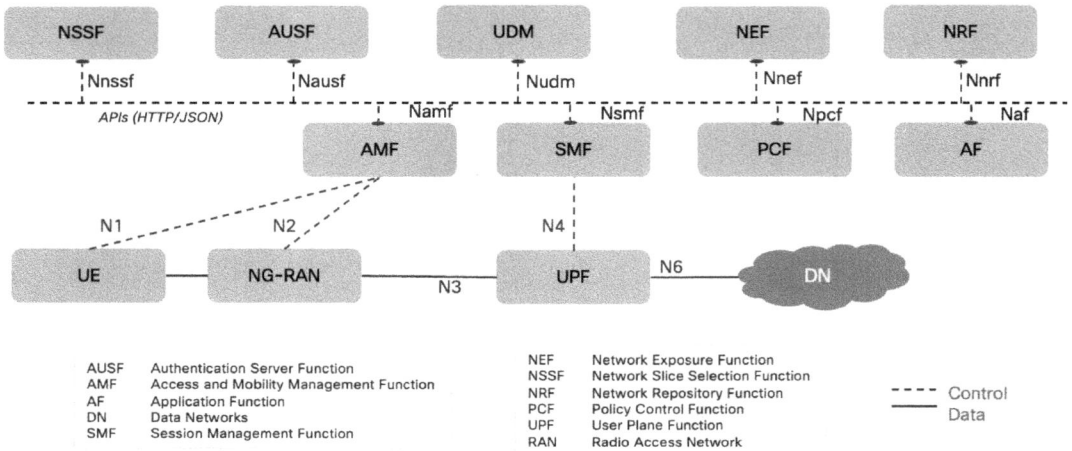

Figure 7.23: 5G core and its reference points

As mentioned, the service-based architecture divides the 5G core into a control plane and a data plane. *Figure 7.23* shows the reference points that lie between two network functions that deliver a specific service. Understanding the roles of some of these network functions will help us in creating a trust boundary or a trust-based grouping, shown in *Figure 7.24*, which can further create a desired trust model, as per the communication service providers' process, policies, and regulatory requirements.

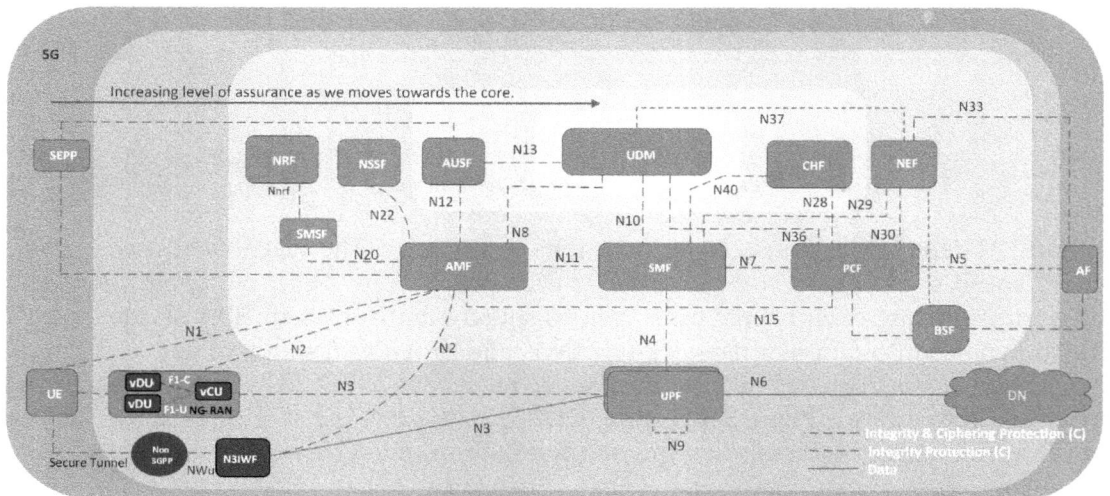

Figure 7.24: 5G trust layers

As shown in *Figure 7.24*, the main crown jewels of 5G components are the center of the trust layer. These components need to be well protected to ensure that critical and super confidential customer data is not impacted for any reason. The trust level assurance increases as we move from the outer layers to the internal layers containing the crown jewels. These can be protected by deploying layered, defense-in-depth-based security controls. In the world of 5G, these controls mainly depend on security around containers and Kubernetes. Use of inherent security controls like the use of dedicated namespaces, network policies and resource limits, and user limits. More of these are discussed in the container security section of this book.

Securing service-based architecture

The 5G SBA is a fundamental redesign of the core network architecture, moving away from the traditional point-to-point network function model to a more flexible, scalable, and efficient design. In SBA, network functions are implemented as a set of interconnected services that can be reused, updated, and scaled independently. These services communicate with each other using standard APIs, typically based on HTTP/2 and RESTful principles. This approach allows for greater modularity, enabling easier introduction of new services, improved network slicing capabilities, and more efficient resource utilization. Key components of the SBA include various network functions like the AUSF, **Access and Mobility Management Function** (**AMF**), and **Session Management Function** (**SMF**), all orchestrated and discovered through the **NRF**. This architecture supports the diverse requirements of 5G use cases, from enhanced mobile broadband to massive IoT and URLLCs, while providing a more agile and programmable network infrastructure. Refer to the following figure for a better understanding:

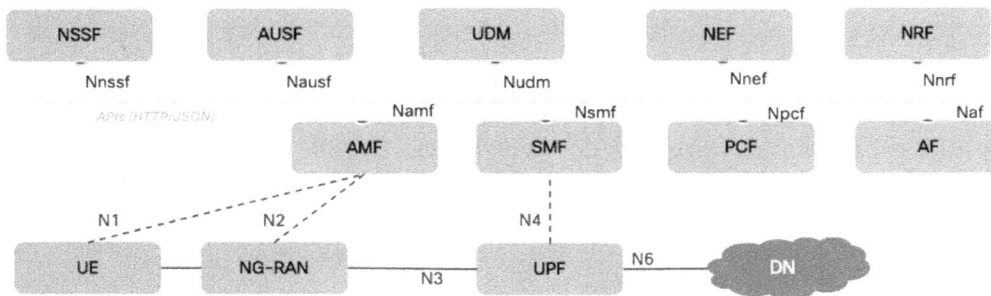

Figure 7.25: 5G service-based architecture

As the SBA relies heavily on open APIs and distributed network functions, it presents a broader attack surface compared to traditional network architectures. Securing the SBA is crucial to protect against threats, such as unauthorized access, data breaches, service disruptions, and API exploitation. Robust security measures for the SBA are essential not only to maintain the integrity, confidentiality, and availability of network services but also to ensure compliance with stringent data protection regulations and to build trust among users and enterprises adopting 5G technologies. The following section goes into details of how the SBA can be secured.

Mutual authentication and authorization

In 5G SBA security, robust measures need to be implemented to ensure the integrity and confidentiality of communications. These include rigorous authentication mechanisms between communicating endpoints, which effectively mitigate the risk of message spoofing. Simultaneously, comprehensive transport protection needs to be enforced, encompassing confidentiality, integrity, and replay protection. Release 15 of 3GPP details the security for direct communication based on mutual authentication between 5G network functions and TLS 1.2 and 1.3-based transport security.

3GPP release 16 introduced indirect communication via a network function called the **Service Communication Proxy (SCP)**. Here, the network function consuming a service invokes a service request to the SCP rather than sending the request directly to a network function that is providing the service.

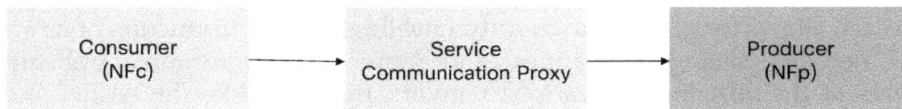

Figure 7.26: Service request process via SCP

In the indirect mode of communication, SCP can be tasked by the **Network Function consumer (NFc)** to locate the **Network Function producer (NFp)**, streamlining service discovery. It facilitates communication between different trust domains within an SBA deployment and can mediate interactions between NF consumers and producers from diverse vendors, enhancing interoperability. The SCP also plays a crucial role in facilitating mutual authentication within the SBA of 5G networks.

SCP acts as a centralized point for authentication in the SBA. When network functions communicate, they often do so through the SCP, which can enforce authentication policies consistently across all interactions. The SCP can validate the digital certificates of both the consumer NF (NFc) and the producer NF (NFp). It checks the validity, expiration, and revocation status of these certificates, ensuring that only legitimate NFs participate in the communication.

The SCP often terminates mTLS connections from both the NFc and NFp. This means it authenticates both parties, ensuring that not only is the server (NFp) authenticated to the client (NFc), but also that the client is authenticated to the server. Thus, ensuring mutual TLS termination (mTLS) based authentication.

SCP helps to enable Zero Trust principles by requiring authentication and authorization for every interaction, regardless of the network location or previous authentications.

Token based authentication and authorization

5G networks implement the OAuth 2.0 framework for a more dynamic and flexible approach to authentication and authorization. This implementation aims to provide a standardized, token-based authorization mechanism for NF-to-NF communications within the SBA. The following figure shows the token-based authentication and authorization:

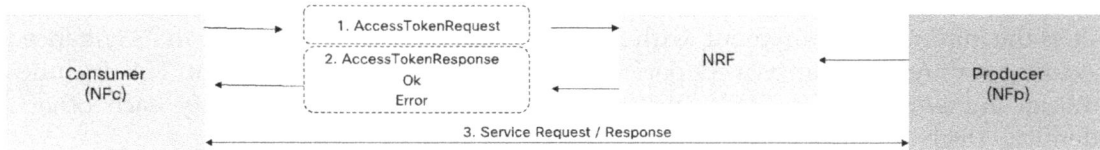

Figure 7.27: *Token-based authentication and authorization*

OAuth 2.0 token-based authorization revolves around a central authorization server, which serves as the cornerstone of the security infrastructure. The process begins when a **Network Function** (**NF**) service consumer undergoes authentication with this central server. Upon successful verification, the authorization server issues an access token to the authenticated client. This access token then becomes the client's credential for accessing services. When the NF service consumer needs to invoke a service from an NF service producer, it presents this token as proof of its authorization. The NF service producer, acting as a gatekeeper, does not immediately grant access upon receiving this token. Instead, it first validates the token's authenticity and permissions. Only after confirming the token's validity does the NF service producer allow the NF service consumer to access its services. In the SBA, the NRF takes the role of the authorization server.

Client Credentials Assertion for OAuth enhancement

Client Credentials Assertion is a method introduced in Release 16 to enhance the security of the OAuth 2.0 client credentials grant type. It provides a more secure way for **network functions** (**NFs**) to authenticate themselves to the **NRF** when requesting access tokens.

In scenarios where the SCP acts as an intermediary for access token requests, it leverages the **Client Credentials Assertion** (**CCA**) mechanism to establish its authority. The CCA, a cryptographically signed, time-limited token generated by the NFc, serves as a digital mandate. This mandate empowers the SCP to represent the NFc in interactions with the NRF, which functions as the authorization server.

In cases where end-to-end TLS security is not feasible due to the SCP's presence, the CCA acts as a bridge of trust. It provides the NRF with cryptographic proof that the SCP is acting with the explicit consent of the NFc when requesting access tokens. This mechanism extends to the SCP's interactions with **Network Function producers** (**NFp**), ensuring that the SCP's role as a trusted intermediary is recognized and accepted throughout the token acquisition and service access processes.

Transport layer security

All communication between NFs in the SBA is protected using **Transport Layer Security** (**TLS**). TLS ensures the confidentiality and integrity of data in transit between NFs. It prevents eavesdropping, tampering, and message forgery. The use of TLS is mandatory in 5G SBA. The 3GPP specifications stipulate stringent requirements regarding both the version of TLS and the specific cipher suites to be employed. Typically, TLS version 1.2 is set as the minimum requirement, with a strong preference for TLS 1.3 due to its enhanced security features and improved performance. SBA's implementation of TLS includes mutual authentication (mTLS), where both the client and server verify each other's identity, which is crucial in the context of NF-to-NF communications.

API security

In the SBA model, all interactions between NFs occur via RESTful APIs, exponentially increasing the attack surface compared to traditional network architectures. This shift necessitates robust API security measures to protect against a myriad of threats, including unauthorized access, data breaches, man-in-the-middle attacks, and API abuse. Securing these APIs is critical not only for maintaining the confidentiality, integrity, and availability of network services but also for ensuring compliance with stringent data protection regulations. Effective API security in 5G SBA encompasses multiple layers, including strong authentication mechanisms (such as OAuth 2.0 and mutual TLS), fine-grained authorization controls, input validation to prevent injection attacks, rate limiting to mitigate DDoS attempts, and comprehensive logging and monitoring for detecting anomalies.

Secure service mesh

A service mesh provides a dedicated infrastructure layer for facilitating service-to-service communications, offering a more robust and flexible approach to securing the multitude of microservices-based NFs within the 5G core. Abstracting security mechanisms from individual NFs and centralizing them within the mesh enables consistent policy enforcement, end-to-end encryption, and granular access control across all service interactions. This approach addresses several key challenges in 5G SBA security, including the need for dynamic security policy updates, enhanced visibility into service communications, and the ability to implement zero-trust principles at scale. The service mesh can provide advanced features such as **mutual TLS** (**mTLS**) for all inter-service communications, automated certificate rotation, fine-grained traffic management, and real-time monitoring of security metrics.

Roaming security

Roaming in 5G, like in previous generations, allows users to access mobile services when traveling outside their home network's coverage area. It enables seamless connectivity across different mobile network operators, both domestically and internationally. 5G introduces a new roaming architecture based on the SBI. This architecture supports both home-routed roaming (where traffic is routed back to the home network) and local breakout (where traffic is routed directly from the visited network to the internet).

The SEPP has been introduced in 3GPP TS 33.501 5GS security architecture. The SEPP is a crucial component in 5G roaming implementation. It acts as a security gateway at the edge of the operator's network. SEPP can be deployed on 5G networks to provide topology hiding, message filtering, TLS channels, and application-layer security protection for roaming messages through the IPX networks. This prevents data breaches and unauthorized tampering at the transport and application layers.

The SEPP is a non-transparent proxy to allow secure communication between service-consuming and service-producing NFs in different PLMNs. The SEPPs are deployed at the perimeter of each network and enforce via N32 interface various protection policies ensuring integrity and confidentiality protection for those elements to be protected and defining which parts are allowed to be changed by an IPX provider sitting between the SEPPs.

Roaming interfaces

The following table shows the various interfaces that play various roles in inter-PLMN roaming scenarios, where LBO is local breakout and **Home Routing** (**HR**). The services will all traverse over the N32 interface between SEPP functions, except for N9.

Network function	Ref ID	Use
AMF – UDM	N8	LBO and HR
SMF - UDM	N10	LBO
AMF-AMF	N14	LBO, HR and Intern-PLMN
AMF-AUSF	N12	LBO, HR
vSMF-hSMF	N16	HR
SMSF – UDM	N21	LBO, HR
vPCF – hPCF	N24	LBO, HR
vNRF – hNRF	N27	LBO, HR
vNSSF – hNSSF	N31	LBO, HR
SEPP – SEPP	N32-c, N32-f	LBO, HR
vUPF – hUPF	N9	HR

Table 7.2: Roaming Interfaces

The N32 interface is key to 5G roaming. N32-c is used for capability negotiation and security policy exchange between SEPPs. *Figure 7.28* depicts the various services that make use of the N32 interface:

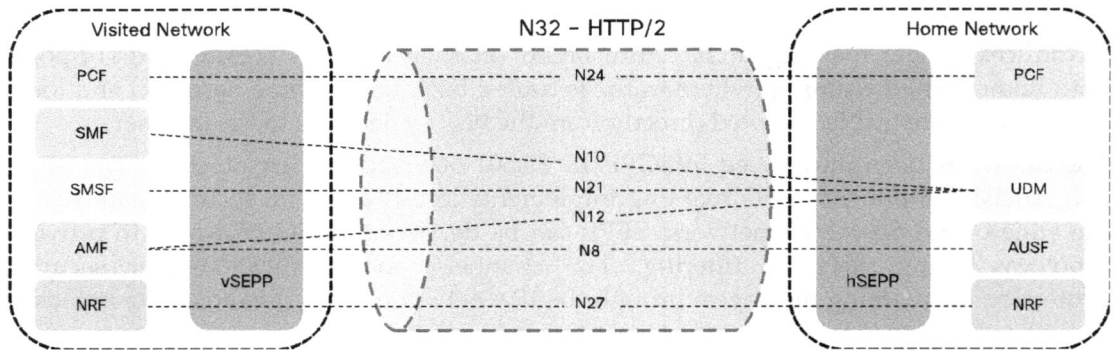

Figure 7.28: SEPP and N32 interface

Roaming Control Plane Security

The SEPP applies its functionality to every Control Plane message in inter-PLMN signaling, acting as a service relay between the actual Service Producer and the actual Service Consumer. For both the Service Producer and Consumer, the result of the service relaying is equivalent to a direct service interaction.

5G inter-PLMN roaming security requires cryptographic keys to achieve peer authentication, message integrity, and confidential communication. These cryptographic keys need to be managed and exchanged between stakeholders involved in roaming. The key aspects of 5G roaming control plane security are HTTP/2 security, JSON security, API security, and authorization mechanisms.

HTTP/2 security

In 5G roaming, HTTP/2 is used as the transport protocol for control plane messages between networks. All HTTP/2 connections in 5G roaming are mandated to use **Transport Layer Security** (**TLS**) 1.2 or higher. This ensures that all communications between the home and visited networks are encrypted, providing confidentiality and integrity protection. In addition to TLS, 5G roaming requires mTLS authentication. Both the client and server must present X.509 certificates to each other, ensuring that only authorized network entities can establish connections.

JSON security

JavaScript Object Notation (JSON) is the primary data format for exchanging information in 5G roaming control plane messages. Securing JSON data is crucial for maintaining the integrity and confidentiality of roaming information. 5G networks use **JSON Web Encryption (JWE)** to encrypt sensitive JSON payloads. This ensures that even if an attacker intercepts the messages, they cannot read the contents without the proper decryption keys. Along with JWE, **JSON Web Signature (JWS)** is used to ensure the integrity and authenticity of JSON messages. This allows the receiver to verify that the message has not been tampered with and comes from a legitimate source. The SEPP receives the payload and proceeds to check the integrity and authenticity of the message.

API security

Application programming interfaces form the backbone of communication in 5G roaming. SEPP is used to manage and secure all incoming and outgoing API traffic for roaming. To prevent **Denial of Service (DoS)** attacks, 5G roaming APIs implement strict rate limiting. This ensures that a single entity cannot overwhelm the system with excessive requests. All API inputs are validated to prevent injection attacks, buffer overflows, and other security vulnerabilities that could arise from malicious input.

In addition, the 5G roaming filter and control actions validate that 5G roaming control information received via the N32 interface in one or more JSON objects is allowed and plausible for this end-user, home network, or visiting network. SEPP may also perform supplementary actions like throttling and traffic policies to control HTTP/2 messages. Comprehensive monitoring and logging of API activities are implemented to detect and respond to potential security threats in real-time.

Authorization

Authorization in 5G roaming ensures that only legitimate entities can access specific resources and perform certain actions. 5G roaming leverages the OAuth 2.0 framework for authorization. This allows for fine-grained access control and the use of short-lived access tokens, reducing the risk of unauthorized access. Access tokens are used in 5G roaming to grant temporary, limited access to resources. These tokens are cryptographically signed and contain claims about the token's scope and validity period. As mentioned earlier in the chapter, before any network function can participate in roaming, it must register with the NRF. This registration process includes authentication and authorization checks.

Roaming User Plane Security

In 5G roaming, the user plane refers to the path through which user data travels between the visitor network and the home network. When a user's device connects to a visited network in a foreign country, the data needs to be securely transported back to the home network. This is where GTP tunnels play a crucial role.

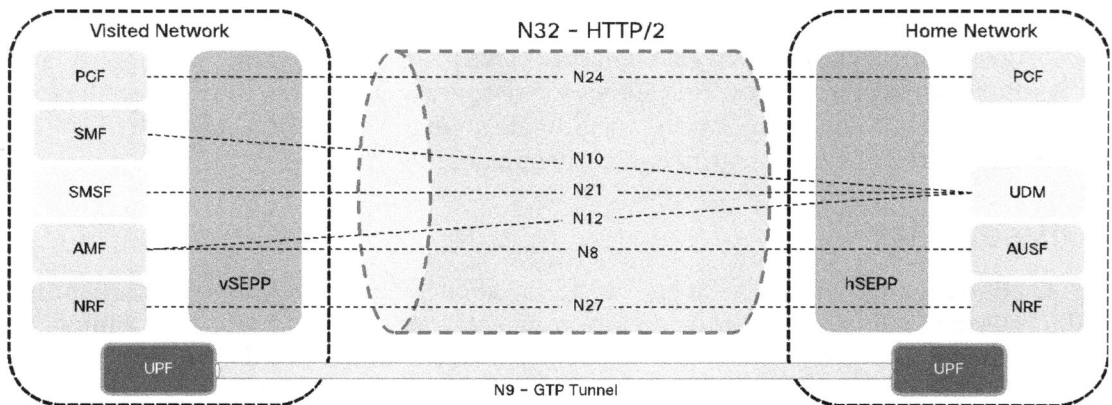

Figure 7.29: *User Plane Security in 5G roaming*

In a roaming scenario, user plane traffic is encapsulated within GTP tunnels between the visited network and the home network, as shown in *Figure 7.29*. These tunnels are established between the **User Plane Function** (**UPF**) in the visited network and the UPF in the home network. GTP tunneling provides a level of isolation for the user traffic, making it more difficult for potential attackers to intercept or manipulate the data in transit.

However, GTP tunneling alone does not provide security to the user plane traffic. To enhance the security of inter-network connections, 3GPP has introduced IPUPS (Inter PLMN User Plane Security). This security measure can be implemented either on existing UPFs at the edge of the 5G core network or on dedicated UPFs specifically designed for IPUPS support.

The security process begins during the establishment of a PDU Session. In home routing scenarios, this triggers the creation of a GTP tunnel between two UPFs. Each end of this connection is assigned a unique TEID, which, combined with the IP address of the corresponding UPF, uniquely identifies the specific PDU Session.

In the IPUPS framework, the two **Session Management Functions** (**SMFs**) responsible for establishing the PDU Session also configure both uplink and downlink **Packet Data Rules** (**PDRs**) at the UPF, using the N4 interface. These rules ensure that any traffic that is either malformed or not associated with a valid TEID is automatically dropped by the relevant UPF. This filtering mechanism guarantees that only legitimate traffic corresponding to active PDU Sessions is transmitted between the visited and home networks, significantly enhancing the overall security of inter-PLMN communications.

Key management

Key management plays a pivotal role in maintaining the security of 5G roaming connections. The 5G system introduces a more dynamic and flexible key hierarchy compared to its predecessors. At the heart of this hierarchy is the master key, from which various other keys are derived for specific security functions. This hierarchical approach allows for better compartmentalization of security, ensuring that a compromise in one area does not necessarily lead to a breach of the entire system.

The **root certificate authority (Root CA)** serves as the trusted anchor in the **public key infrastructure (PKI)** used for authenticating network elements involved in roaming scenarios. By establishing a chain of trust, the Root CA enables secure communication between home and visited networks, ensuring that only legitimate entities can participate in the roaming process. The Root CA issues digital certificates to SEPPs and other network functions involved in inter-operator communications. These certificates are used for mutual authentication and to establish secure connections between network elements. The use of a common Root CA across multiple operators facilitates seamless and secure roaming experiences for users while maintaining the integrity of the overall system.

Conclusion

This chapter explored the comprehensive landscape of 5G technology, from its foundational 3GPP standards to its revolutionary applications and security considerations. The standards ensure interoperability and global adoption while enabling the three key capabilities of 5G: eMBB, URLLC, and mMTC. These capabilities power transformative use cases across sectors, including autonomous vehicles, smart cities, telemedicine, and augmented reality.

5G's service-based architecture represents a paradigm shift from previous generations, offering unprecedented agility and efficiency. Technologies like network slicing and edge computing enable customization of network resources for diverse applications, while interfaces facilitate seamless communication between network functions for dynamic resource allocation and enhanced performance.

The differentiators of 5G- improved speed, capacity, and latency are transformative changes enabling new connectivity paradigms, from massive IoT deployments to real-time control of critical infrastructure.

Security remains a central focus within 5G's complex ecosystem. The expanded attack surface created by numerous network functions and interfaces necessitates comprehensive security measures. The industry has responded with advanced encryption, authentication mechanisms, and NFV security. Roaming security has seen significant enhancements through security edge protection proxies and improved key management systems, crucial for maintaining user trust in cross-border communications.

As 5G continues to evolve, it serves as a foundation for innovation that will shape our digital landscape for years to come, with ongoing research pushing the boundaries of what is possible in network efficiency and application development.

The next chapter explores Private 5G networks, dedicated cellular networks deployed for specific organizations or locations. The chapter analyzes specialized use cases, unique security vulnerabilities, and protection strategies for these closed ecosystems. We will also address the challenges of implementation, integration with existing systems, spectrum allocation, and the balance between customization and standardization that organizations must navigate when deploying Private 5G solutions.

Points to remember

- 5G Use Cases, the fifth generation of mobile networks introduces three main service categories: eMBB for high-speed data services, URLLC for critical applications requiring minimal delay, and mMTC for connecting vast numbers of IoT devices. These capabilities enable transformative applications across various sectors, including automotive, healthcare, smart cities, and industrial automation. Network slicing technology allows operators to create virtual networks optimized for each specific use case.

- The 5G architecture represents a significant departure from previous generations, adopting a service-based approach that replaces traditional point-to-point connections. It consists of key network functions, including AMF, SMF, UPF, PCF, UDM, AUSF, NSSF, and NRF, each serving specific roles in the network. The architecture implements CUPS, supports both 5G New Radio and evolved LTE, and integrates MEC. The design follows cloud-native principles, with network functions implemented as containerized microservices.

- The SBA forms the foundation of 5G core networks, where network functions operate as services that can be discovered and consumed by other functions. This model follows a producer-consumer paradigm, with the NRF serving as a central service registry. Communication between services uses HTTP/2 and REST-based interfaces, enabling dynamic service registration and discovery. This approach provides unprecedented flexibility and scalability in network deployment and operation.

- The 5G system defines various interfaces (reference points) for communication between network functions. Key interfaces include N1 for UE-AMF signaling, N2 for RAN-AMF control plane, N3 for RAN-UPF user plane, N4 for SMF-UPF control, and N6 for UPF-Data Network connectivity. Service-based interfaces (Nx) enable communication between core network functions, while N32 handles inter-PLMN roaming. These standardized interfaces ensure seamless interaction between network components.

- Network virtualization in 5G embraces both NFV and SDN principles. NFV allows network functions to run as software on standard hardware, while SDN enables programmable network control. This virtualization approach provides flexibility, scalability, and efficient resource utilization, enabling operators to deploy and manage network services more effectively. The combination of NFV and SDN supports the dynamic nature of 5G services and network slicing capabilities.

- 5G incorporates enhanced security features compared to previous generations. These include improved user privacy through concealed subscriber identifiers, stronger encryption algorithms, and more robust authentication mechanisms. The architecture supports end-to-end security, network slice isolation, and enhanced protection against various threats. Security functions are integrated across all layers of the network, from radio access to the core network and service layer.

- Roaming security in 5G is significantly enhanced through the SEPP, which provides secure interconnection between home and visited networks. The architecture supports both home-routed and local breakout scenarios, with improved security for signaling traffic and user plane data. Additional features include enhanced authentication procedures and better protection against fraud and security threats in roaming scenarios.

Exercises

1. Which of the following is NOT a key use case for 5G?

   a. eMBB

   b. URLLC

   c. **Massive Machine Type Communications (mMTC)**

   d. **High Power Wide Area Networks (HPWAN)**

2. In 5G service-based architecture, which function acts as a central repository for service discovery?

   a. AMF

   b. SMF

   c. NRF

   d. UPF

3. What protocol is primarily used for communication between network functions in 5G SBA?

   a. HTTPS/1.1

   b. HTTP/2

   c. TCP/IP

   d. SMTP

4. Which security feature is introduced in 5G to protect subscriber identity?

   a. SUPI

   b. SUCI

   c. GUTI

   d. IMSI

5. Which interface connects the RAN to the User Plane Function?

   a. N1

   b. N2

   c. N3

   d. N4

6. Explain three key differences between 4G and 5G network architectures.

7. What is network slicing in 5G? Describe two potential security concerns related to it.

8. Describe the producer-consumer model in 5G service-based architecture with an example.

9. List and briefly explain three main security features introduced in 5G roaming architecture.

10. What role does the SEPP play in 5G networks?

Join our book's Discord space

Join the book's Discord Workspace for Latest updates, Offers, Tech happenings around the world, New Release and Sessions with the Authors:

https://discord.bpbonline.com

CHAPTER 8
Private 5G

Introduction

The advent of 5G technology has ushered in a new era of wireless communication, promising unprecedented speeds, ultra-low latency, and massive device connectivity. While public 5G networks garner much attention, **private 5G (P5G)** networks are emerging as a game-changing solution for enterprises and organizations seeking dedicated, secure, and tailored wireless infrastructure.

This chapter explores the world of private 5G, exploring its unique characteristics, applications, and challenges. We begin by examining the frequency bands utilized in 5G technology, with a particular focus on the spectrum allocations specific to private networks. Understanding these foundational elements is crucial for grasping the capabilities and limitations of P5G deployments.

Next, we will explore the diverse use cases for private 5G networks across various industries, from manufacturing and logistics to healthcare and education. By comparing P5G with established technologies like Wi-Fi, we will highlight the distinct advantages that make it an attractive option for certain applications.

As with any technology, security is important. We will discuss the potential vulnerabilities in private 5G networks and the measures necessary to safeguard sensitive data and operations. This section will provide insights into the unique security considerations that arise when implementing a dedicated cellular network within an organization.

Finally, we will examine the different deployment models available for private 5G networks and the challenges associated with each approach. From fully owned and operated systems to hybrid models involving mobile network operators, organizations have several options to consider when implementing P5G.

By the end of this chapter, readers will have a comprehensive understanding of private 5G technology, its potential impact on various sectors, and the key factors to consider when exploring its implementation. As we navigate through these topics, we will equip you with the knowledge needed to evaluate whether private 5G could be a transformative solution for your organization's wireless networking needs.

Structure

This chapter will cover the following topics.

- Introduction to P5G
- 5G frequency bands
- 5G bands in P5G
- P5G use cases
- P5G vs. Wi-Fi
- Vulnerabilities in P5G
- P5G deployment models
- Securing P5G
- Current challenges in deploying P5G

Objectives

This chapter aims to provide a comprehensive overview of P5G networks, exploring their key aspects and implications for modern telecommunications. We will discuss the frequency bands utilized by 5G technology, with a particular focus on the specific bands employed in private 5G implementations. The chapter will illustrate various use cases for private 5G, highlighting its potential applications across different industries and sectors.

A comparative analysis between private 5G and Wi-Fi will be presented, examining the strengths and limitations of each technology to help readers understand when and where P5G might be preferable. As with any emerging technology, security is a critical concern, therefore, we will discuss potential vulnerabilities in private 5G networks and explore strategies for mitigating these risks.

Finally, the chapter will outline different deployment models for private 5G networks, addressing the challenges associated with each approach. This discussion will provide insights into the practical considerations and obstacles that organizations may face when implementing P5G solutions. By covering these essential topics, readers will gain a well-rounded understanding of private 5G technology, its capabilities, and its role in shaping the future of wireless communications.

An introduction to P5G

Private 5G networks, also known as P5G, are dedicated cellular networks designed for exclusive use by a specific organization or enterprise. Unlike public 5G networks operated by telecom providers, P5G networks are owned and managed by the organization itself, offering enhanced control, security, and customization. These networks leverage 5G technology to provide high-speed, low-latency connectivity within a defined geographical area, such as a factory, campus, or office building.

P5G networks offer several advantages over traditional Wi-Fi or public cellular networks. They provide superior reliability and performance, crucial for supporting mission-critical applications and **Internet of Things (IoT)** devices. The increased bandwidth and reduced latency of 5G technology enable real-time data processing and communication, essential for applications like industrial automation, remote operations, and augmented reality.

Security is a primary benefit of P5G networks. By operating on a closed, private infrastructure, organizations can implement stringent security measures and maintain full control over their data. This is particularly important for industries handling sensitive information or operating in highly regulated environments.

P5G networks also offer greater flexibility and scalability compared to traditional networking solutions. They can be tailored to meet specific organizational needs, supporting a wide range of devices and use cases. This customization extends to network slicing, allowing organizations to allocate resources dynamically based on different application requirements.

The implementation of P5G networks is driving digital transformation across various industries. In manufacturing, these networks enable smart factories with interconnected machinery and real-time monitoring. In healthcare, they support telemedicine and remote patient monitoring. For large campuses or venues, P5G networks provide seamless connectivity for thousands of users and devices.

While P5G networks offer numerous benefits, they also present challenges. The initial investment can be significant, involving spectrum acquisition, infrastructure deployment, and ongoing management. Organizations must also navigate regulatory requirements and ensure compliance with local telecommunications laws.

5G frequency bands

5G networks operate across a range of frequency bands, broadly categorized into low-band, mid-band, and high-band (or mmWave) spectrum. Low-band frequencies (below 1 GHz) offer wide coverage and good penetration but lower speeds. Mid-band frequencies

(1-6 GHz) provide a balance between coverage and capacity, offering improved speeds and moderate range. High-band frequencies (24-100 GHz) deliver extremely high speeds and capacity but have limited range and poor penetration through obstacles. Each band serves different purposes: low-band for widespread coverage, mid-band for urban and suburban areas, and high-band for dense urban environments and specific high-capacity applications. The combination of these bands allows 5G networks to offer a mix of coverage, speed, and capacity to meet diverse needs. *Figure 8.1* shows the relation between various bands concerning capacity, coverage, and latency:

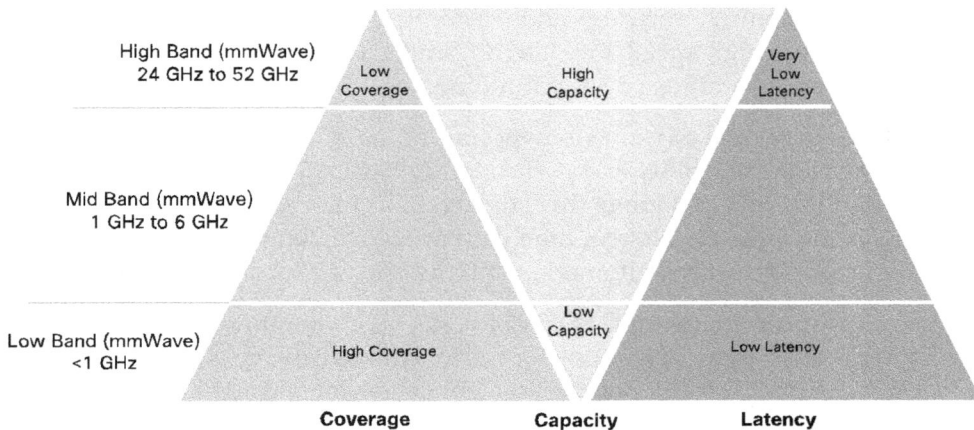

Figure 8.1: 5G spectrums

Coverage-based spectrum

Coverage-based spectrum in 5G primarily refers to the low-band frequencies, which are crucial for providing wide-area coverage. These frequencies, typically below 1 GHz, are often called **coverage layers** due to their ability to travel long distances and penetrate buildings effectively.

The low-band spectrum for 5G includes frequencies such as 600 MHz, 700 MHz, and 800 MHz. These frequencies have wavelengths that can extend for several kilometers, making them ideal for covering large geographic areas with fewer cell sites. This characteristic is particularly valuable in rural and suburban areas where population density is lower, and the cost of deploying numerous cell sites would be prohibitive. Radio waves at these lower frequencies can travel further and more easily penetrate obstacles like walls, vegetation, and buildings. This makes low-band frequencies excellent for providing consistent indoor coverage, which is crucial for residential and commercial users who rely on mobile networks inside structures.

While coverage-based spectrum excels in reach, it comes with a trade-off in capacity. The bandwidth available in these lower frequencies is typically more limited compared to mid-band or high-band spectrum. This means that while coverage is excellent, the peak data rates and overall network capacity are lower than what can be achieved with higher frequency bands.

Capacity-based spectrum

Capacity-based spectrum, often associated with mid-band and high-band (mmWave) frequencies in 5G networks, refers to frequency ranges that are optimized to handle large amounts of data traffic in areas with high user density. These bands are crucial for delivering on the promise of 5G's **enhanced Mobile Broadband (eMBB)** use case, which aims to provide significantly faster data speeds and greater network capacity compared to previous generations. Mid-band spectrum, typically ranging from 1 GHz to 6 GHz, is often considered the *sweet spot* for 5G capacity. These frequencies offer a balanced mix of coverage and capacity, making them ideal for urban and suburban deployments. The most commonly used mid-band frequencies for 5G include the 3.5 GHz band, also known as the **C-band** in some regions, and the 2.5 GHz band. These bands can support channel bandwidths of up to 100 MHz, allowing for data speeds that can reach several hundred megabits per second under optimal conditions.

High-band or mmWave spectrum, which includes frequencies above 24 GHz, represents the pinnacle of capacity-based spectrum in 5G. These extremely high frequencies allow for very wide channel bandwidths, often 400 MHz or more, enabling theoretical peak data rates of multiple gigabits per second. Common mmWave bands for 5G include 26 GHz, 28 GHz, and 39 GHz. The massive capacity of mmWave is particularly suited for extremely dense urban areas, stadiums, convention centers, and other locations where many users require high-bandwidth connections in a small area.

Listed in the following are a few silent features of the Mid-Band Spectrum (1-6 GHz):

- **Frequency range**: Typically, between 1 GHz and 6 GHz
- **Key bands**: 3.5 GHz (C-band), 2.5 GHz
- **Channel bandwidth**: Up to 100 MHz
- **Typical speeds**: Several hundred Mbps under optimal conditions
- **Use cases**: Urban and suburban deployments, balancing coverage and capacity
- **Advantages**: Good balance of coverage and capacity, suitable for wide-area 5G deployment

Listed in the following are a few silent features of the high-band (mmWave) spectrum (24+ GHz):

- **Frequency range**: Above 24 GHz
- **Key bands**: 26 GHz, 28 GHz, 39 GHz
- **Channel bandwidth**: 400 MHz or more
- **Typical speeds**: Multiple Gbps under optimal conditions
- **Use cases**: Dense urban areas, stadiums, convention centers

- **Advantages**: Extremely high capacity and speed
- **Challenges**: Limited range, poor penetration through obstacles

Latency-based spectrum

Latency, in the context of 5G networks, refers to the time delay between sending and receiving data. In 5G, different frequency bands offer varying levels of latency, which is crucial for different applications and use cases. The concept of *latency-based spectrum* involves selecting and utilizing specific frequency bands to achieve the desired latency performance for various services.

Low-band spectrum, typically below 1 GHz, offers wide coverage but generally higher latency compared to other 5G bands. While these frequencies can penetrate buildings and cover large areas, they do not provide the ultra-low latency that some 5G applications require. However, they still offer improved latency compared to 4G networks, making them suitable for applications that need broad coverage and moderate responsiveness.

Mid-band spectrum, ranging from 1 to 6 GHz, provides a balance between coverage and latency. These frequencies offer significantly lower latency than low-band spectrum, making them suitable for many advanced 5G applications. The improved latency in mid-band helps support applications, like augmented reality, virtual reality, and some IoT use cases that require quick response times but do not demand the absolute lowest latency.

High-band spectrum, also known as **millimeter wave (mmWave)**, operates at frequencies above 24 GHz. This band offers the potential for ultra-low latency, often in the range of one millisecond or less. The extremely high frequencies allow for rapid data transmission, making mmWave ideal for applications requiring near-instantaneous response times. Use cases include industrial automation, remote surgery, autonomous vehicles, and real-time gaming.

While high-frequency bands offer lower latency, they come with challenges. mmWave signals have limited range and poor penetration through obstacles, requiring dense network infrastructure. Balancing coverage, capacity, and latency across different spectrum bands is a key challenge for 5G network planning and optimization.

5G bands in P5G

Private 5G networks operate across various frequency bands, each selected to address specific operational demands of enterprise deployments. Low-band frequencies provide extensive coverage and better penetration through buildings, while mid-band frequencies offer a balanced combination of coverage and capacity suitable for most industrial applications. High-band frequencies, including millimeter wave spectrum, deliver exceptional bandwidth and ultra-low latency, though with limited range, making them ideal for dense, localized deployments in facilities like automated warehouses or smart factories. This strategic use of different frequency bands allows organizations to tailor their private 5G networks to achieve optimal performance based on their unique requirements for coverage area, data throughput, device density, and response times.

Low band spectrum in P5G networks

Private networks often use low-band spectrum (below 1 GHz) when wide coverage is a priority. This is particularly useful for large campuses, extensive industrial sites, or agricultural applications. While low-band frequencies offer excellent coverage and penetration through buildings and obstacles, they provide limited capacity and higher latency compared to other bands. In private networks, low-band spectrum is ideal for IoT applications that require connectivity over large areas but do not demand high data rates or ultra-low latency. For instance, a private network in a large manufacturing facility might use low-band frequencies to maintain consistent connectivity with mobile equipment or for basic monitoring systems across the entire premises.

Mid-band spectrum for balanced performance

Mid-band spectrum (1-6 GHz) is often the sweet spot for many private 5G networks due to its balance of coverage, capacity, and latency. These frequencies offer significantly better capacity than low-band and lower latency, making them suitable for a wide range of industrial and enterprise applications. In a private network setting, mid-band spectrum can support advanced IoT deployments, augmented reality applications for maintenance and training, and high-definition video surveillance. The improved latency of mid-band frequencies enables more responsive control systems and real-time data analytics, crucial for modern smart factories and automated warehouses.

High-band spectrum for ultra-high capacity and low latency

High-band or mmWave spectrum (above 24 GHz) is used in private 5G networks where ultra-high capacity and extremely low latency are critical. Despite its limited coverage and poor penetration, mmWave spectrum excels in specific use cases within controlled environments. In private networks, mmWave bands are ideal for applications like robotic control in manufacturing, where microsecond-level responsiveness is essential. They are also used for high-density environments that require massive data throughput, such as large-scale event venues or densely populated office buildings. The ultra-low latency of mmWave enables cutting-edge applications like real-time machine vision for quality control or virtual reality-based design and prototyping in engineering firms.

Many private 5G networks employ a combination of these bands to optimize performance across different areas and use cases. For example, a large industrial complex might use low-band for site-wide connectivity, mid-band operational areas requiring higher performance, and mmWave in specific locations for ultra-high-speed, low-latency applications. This multi-band approach allows organizations to tailor their network to specific operational needs, ensuring optimal coverage, capacity, and latency where it is most needed. The ability to use different spectrum bands gives private 5G networks a high degree of customization and flexibility. Organizations can design their network architecture to meet specific operational requirements, whether it is prioritizing wide coverage for logistics tracking, high capacity for data-intensive applications, or ultra-low latency for critical control systems. This flexibility is a key advantage of private 5G networks over traditional enterprise networking solutions, allowing businesses to create a truly tailored connectivity environment.

P5G use cases

P5G networks are being adopted across various industries, each leveraging the technology to address specific challenges and unlock new opportunities. Mentioned in the following section are a few examples where P5G can be used in multiple industries.

Manufacturing and industry 4.0

P5G networks are at the heart of smart factory initiatives, enabling a new level of connectivity and automation. These P5G networks provide the high-bandwidth, low-latency communication necessary for real-time monitoring and control of production lines. With P5G, manufacturers can implement advanced process control systems that adjust operations on the fly based on real-time data, optimizing production efficiency and quality.

The **Ultra-Reliable Low-Latency Communication** (**URLLC**) capabilities of P5G support time-critical applications such as robotic control and synchronization. This allows for more precise and complex automated manufacturing processes, including collaborative robotics where humans and machines work together seamlessly. P5G networks enable the deployment of a vast array of sensors throughout the manufacturing facility, creating a dense IoT ecosystem. These sensors continuously monitor equipment performance, temperature, vibration, and other critical parameters. The high capacity of P5G networks allows for the collection and analysis of this data in real-time. By leveraging advanced analytics and ML algorithms, manufacturers can predict equipment failures before they occur, scheduling maintenance proactively. This predictive maintenance approach significantly reduces downtime, extends equipment life, and optimizes maintenance costs.

The high-bandwidth capabilities of P5G support **augmented reality** (**AR**) applications in manufacturing. Technicians can use AR headsets to overlay digital information onto their physical workspace, providing step-by-step guidance for complex assembly or maintenance tasks. This not only improves efficiency but also reduces errors and enhances worker training.

P5G networks provide the reliable, low-latency connectivity required for the efficient operation of **automated guided vehicles** (**AVGs**) within manufacturing facilities. These vehicles can navigate complex factory floors, transporting materials and products autonomously. The high-precision indoor positioning enabled by P5G allows for optimized route planning and collision avoidance.

Furthermore, P5G supports the coordination of entire fleets of AGVs, enabling dynamic task allocation and traffic management. This level of automation in intralogistics significantly improves material flow efficiency and reduces labor costs.

P5G networks facilitate the implementation of digital twin technology in manufacturing. A digital twin is a virtual replica of physical assets, processes, or systems. The high-speed, low-latency connectivity of P5G allows for real-time synchronization between the physical manufacturing environment and its digital counterpart. This enables advanced simulation and scenario planning, where manufacturers can test changes to production processes in the digital field before implementing them physically. It also supports ongoing optimization, as the digital twin continuously learns, and updates based on real-world data collected through the P5G network.

P5G networks also support comprehensive environmental monitoring systems in manufacturing facilities. Sensors can track air quality, temperature, noise levels, and the presence of hazardous materials. The low latency of P5G ensures that any safety issues are detected and addressed immediately. Additionally, P5G enables advanced worker safety systems. For instance, wearable devices connected to the P5G network can monitor worker vital signs and environmental conditions, alerting supervisors to potential health or safety risks in real-time.

Healthcare and telemedicine

P5G networks enable high-quality, real-time video consultations between patients and healthcare providers. The high bandwidth and low latency of 5G support crystal-clear video and audio, allowing for more accurate remote diagnoses. This is particularly beneficial for patients in rural or underserved areas, providing access to specialists who might be located far away. The reliability of P5G also ensures that these critical communications are not interrupted, which is crucial for maintaining the quality of care. With P5G, healthcare providers can monitor patients' vital signs and health metrics in real-time, even when they are at home. Wearable devices and IoT sensors can continuously transmit data over the 5G network, allowing for early detection of health issues and timely interventions. This is especially valuable for managing chronic conditions and post-operative care, reducing the need for hospital readmissions.

P5G can significantly enhance emergency medical services. Ambulances equipped with 5G connectivity can transmit real-time patient data to hospitals while en-route. This allows emergency room staff to prepare in advance and make informed decisions even before the patient arrives. The high-speed, low-latency connection also enables video consultations with specialists during transit, potentially saving crucial time in critical situations. The ultra-low latency of P5G networks is crucial for advancing robotic surgery capabilities. Surgeons can potentially perform operations remotely with minimal delay between their actions and the robot's response. This opens possibilities for expert surgeons to operate on patients in different geographical locations, bringing specialized care to areas where it might not otherwise be available.

P5G supports the use of AR and VR for medical training and surgical planning. Medical students and residents can practice complex procedures in virtual environments without risk to patients. Surgeons can use AR overlays during operations to visualize critical anatomical structures in real-time. The high bandwidth of P5G ensures that these data-intensive applications run smoothly without lag or interruption.

Energy and utilities

P5G networks are transforming the energy and utilities sector, offering unprecedented capabilities for grid management, operational efficiency, and the integration of renewable energy sources. In the field of smart grids, P5G enables real-time monitoring and control of power distribution systems, allowing utilities to respond swiftly to fluctuations in demand and supply. This enhanced responsiveness is crucial for maintaining grid stability, especially as the penetration of intermittent renewable energy sources like solar and wind increases. P5G networks support the deployment of **Advanced Metering Infrastructure** (**AMI**), facilitating two-way communication between smart meters and utility companies. This enables more accurate billing, demand forecasting, and the implementation of dynamic pricing models to incentivize off-peak consumption.

In the field of power generation, P5G networks can be used to enhance the efficiency and safety of both traditional and renewable energy plants. For wind farms, these networks enable real-time monitoring of turbine performance and weather conditions, allowing for optimized energy production and predictive maintenance. In solar installations, P5G supports the coordination of large arrays of photovoltaic panels, maximizing energy capture based on sun position and weather patterns. For conventional power plants, P5G networks facilitate enhanced monitoring of critical equipment, reducing downtime through predictive maintenance and enabling remote diagnostics.

The oil and gas industry can leverage P5G to improve operations in challenging and often remote environments. These networks support the concept of digital oilfields, where real-time data from wellheads, pipelines, and processing facilities is continuously analyzed to optimize production and ensure safety. P5G's low latency and high reliability enable remote control of drilling operations, reducing the need for on-site personnel in hazardous areas. In refineries and processing plants, P5G networks support the deployment of IoT sensors for equipment monitoring, environmental compliance, and worker safety applications.

P5G can also play a crucial role in modernizing the distribution and transmission infrastructure of utilities. These networks enable more efficient management of substations through remote monitoring and control, reducing the need for on-site visits and improving response times to outages. For power line inspections, P5G supports the use of drones equipped with high-resolution cameras and sensors, allowing utilities to detect potential issues before they lead to failures. In urban environments, P5G can facilitate the integration of electric vehicle charging infrastructure with the grid, enabling smart charging solutions that balance vehicle needs with grid capacity.

Water utilities can benefit from P5G through improved management of distribution networks. These networks support the deployment of sensors throughout water infrastructure to detect leaks, monitor water quality, and optimize pressure management. In wastewater treatment facilities, P5G enables real-time monitoring of treatment processes, ensuring regulatory compliance and optimizing energy consumption. The high bandwidth of P5G also supports the use of video analytics for security and operational oversight of critical infrastructure.

Transportation and logistics

In ports and large-scale warehouses, P5G can be used to enable the seamless operation of AGVs and drones for inventory management and cargo handling. These high-speed, low-latency networks allow for real-time tracking and routing of AGVs, optimizing warehouse operations and reducing human error. For shipping companies, P5G can support advanced asset tracking, providing real-time visibility of containers and goods throughout the supply chain. This enhanced tracking capability extends to last-mile delivery, where P5G-enabled vehicles can provide accurate, up-to-the-minute delivery status updates to customers.

In the age of public transportation, P5G networks can be used to enhance the efficiency and safety of railway systems. These networks enable improved train control systems, allowing for more precise and responsive management of rail traffic. This results in increased line capacity and reduced delays. For passengers, P5G supports high-quality, uninterrupted internet connectivity during journeys, enhancing the travel experience and enabling new infotainment services. In bus networks, P5G facilitates real-time route optimization based on traffic conditions and passenger demand, improving service reliability and reducing fuel consumption.

P5G networks are crucial for the development and testing of autonomous vehicles, providing the ultra-reliable, low-latency communication necessary for **vehicle-to-vehicle (V2V)** and **vehicle-to-infrastructure (V2I)** systems. P5G enables cars to communicate with each other and with smart city infrastructure in real-time, enhancing road safety and traffic management. For electric vehicles, P5G networks support advanced charging infrastructure, enabling smart grid integration and efficient energy management. In airports, P5G networks can be used in streamlining operations and enhancing passenger experiences. These networks support automated baggage handling systems, improve runway management, and enable more efficient aircraft turnaround times. For passengers, P5G facilitates seamless check-in processes, biometric security systems, and personalized wayfinding services throughout the airport.

Education and research

In educational institutions, P5G can be used to create truly smart campuses where connectivity is seamless and ubiquitous. This high-speed, low-latency network infrastructure supports many applications that are transforming traditional teaching methods. For instance, **virtual and augmented reality (VR/AR)** technologies, powered by P5G, are allowing students to engage in immersive learning experiences, such as virtual field trips to historical sites or interactive 3D models in science classes. These networks also facilitate more effective distance learning programs, ensuring high-quality video streaming for remote lectures and enabling real-time collaboration among students and educators across different locations.

For higher education and research, P5G networks can be used to enable the rapid transfer of massive datasets, crucial for fields like genomics, climate science, and particle physics. Researchers can collaborate on complex simulations and data analysis in real-time, regardless of their physical location. P5G also supports the deployment of advanced IoT sensors across campuses and research facilities, allowing for comprehensive environmental monitoring and energy management. In scientific laboratories, the ultra-low latency of P5G networks can be used to enable precise control of sensitive equipment remotely, opening up new possibilities for experimentation and data collection.

Agriculture and farming

In the vast expanses of farmland, P5G networks can be used to provide robust, high-speed connectivity needed to support a wide array of smart farming technologies. These networks enable farmers to deploy and manage extensive sensor networks across their fields, monitoring crucial factors, such as soil moisture, nutrient levels, and crop health in real-time. This constant stream of data, facilitated by P5G's high bandwidth and low latency, allows for more precise and timely decision-making in crop management.

Drones equipped with high-resolution cameras and multispectral sensors, connected via P5G, can conduct regular aerial surveys of crops, identifying issues, such as pest infestations, disease outbreaks, or irrigation problems before they become visible to the naked eye. The ability to transmit large amounts of visual data quickly enables rapid response and targeted interventions. P5G networks also support the operation of autonomous farm equipment, such as self-driving tractors and robotic harvesters. These machines can work around the clock, guided by GPS and real-time data, optimizing planting, fertilizing, and harvesting processes with unprecedented precision.

In livestock management, P5G can be used to enable advanced tracking and monitoring systems. Smart collars on animals can transmit health and location data in real-time, allowing farmers to monitor their herds remotely and detect issues early. Automated feeding systems and climate-controlled barns can be managed more efficiently through the reliable, low-latency connections provided by P5G. The technology also facilitates the implementation of smart irrigation systems that can adjust water distribution based on real-time soil moisture data and weather forecasts, significantly improving water use efficiency.

Mining and construction

In mining operations, P5G networks aim to provide robust, low-latency connectivity in challenging underground environments where traditional communication systems often fail. This enhanced connectivity supports real-time monitoring of air quality, seismic activity, and equipment performance, significantly improving worker safety. Remote-controlled machinery, enabled by P5G's URLLC, allows operators to manage excavation and drilling from safe distances, reducing the risk of accidents in hazardous areas. The high bandwidth of P5G supports the transmission of high-definition video feeds from multiple cameras throughout the mine, enabling comprehensive surveillance and rapid response to potential issues.

In the construction sector, P5G networks can be used to enable the creation of **connected construction sites** where all assets, from heavy machinery to handheld tools, are constantly monitored and tracked. This level of connectivity facilitates real-time project tracking, allowing managers to optimize resource allocation and identify bottlenecks quickly. Augmented reality applications, powered by P5G's high-speed, low-latency connections, allow workers to visualize complex architectural plans overlaid on the physical site, reducing errors and improving precision in construction. The networks also support the use of drones for site surveying and progress monitoring, providing accurate, up-to-date information to project stakeholders.

Both mining and construction can benefit from P5G's ability to support **massive Machine-Type Communications** (**mMTC**), allowing for the deployment of thousands of IoT sensors across sites. In mining, these sensors can help monitor structural integrity, detect early signs of cave-ins, and track the movement of materials. In construction, they can monitor concrete curing, track material usage, and ensure compliance with safety regulations. The data collected from these sensors, when analyzed in real-time, due to P5G's high-speed connectivity, provides valuable insights for predictive maintenance, resource optimization, and risk management.

P5G vs. Wi-Fi

As enterprises seek to modernize their wireless infrastructure, the choice between P5G and Wi-Fi has become increasingly relevant. Both technologies offer wireless connectivity, but they differ significantly in terms of security, coverage, and performance. Understanding these differences is crucial for organizations looking to implement the most suitable solution for their specific needs.

Security is an important concern for enterprise networks, and both P5G and Wi-Fi have evolved to address this challenge, albeit through different approaches. P5G inherits the robust security features of public 5G networks, which were designed with a security-first mindset. It utilizes advanced encryption methods and mutual authentication between devices and the network, making it highly resistant to eavesdropping and man-in-the-middle attacks. P5G also supports network slicing, allowing organizations to create isolated, virtual networks for different applications or departments, enhancing overall security.

Wi-Fi, on the other hand, has made significant strides in security with the introduction of **Wi-Fi Protected Access 3 (WPA3).** This protocol offers improved encryption and protection against password-guessing attacks. However, Wi-Fi networks are generally more susceptible to interference and unauthorized access attempts due to their widespread use and the ease of detecting Wi-Fi signals. P5G networks, operating on licensed or locally allocated spectrum, are inherently more difficult to detect and interfere with, providing an additional layer of security through obscurity.

When it comes to coverage, P5G and Wi-Fi exhibit markedly different characteristics. P5G networks, particularly those utilizing low-band and mid-band spectrum, offer superior range and penetration compared to Wi-Fi. This makes P5G particularly suitable for large industrial spaces, sprawling campuses, or multi-building facilities where maintaining consistent coverage with Wi-Fi would require a dense and potentially complex network of access points.

Wi-Fi, while limited in range, excels in providing high-bandwidth coverage in smaller, confined spaces. It is particularly effective for indoor environments like offices, homes, and small to medium-sized facilities. The latest Wi-Fi 6 and Wi-Fi 6E standards have improved coverage and capacity in dense environments, but they still fall short of P5G in terms of large-area coverage and outdoor applications.

P5G's ability to maintain connectivity over larger areas with fewer base stations can lead to simplified network management and potentially lower infrastructure costs for large-scale deployments. However, for smaller spaces or organizations with existing Wi-Fi infrastructure, the cost-benefit analysis may favor sticking with or upgrading Wi-Fi systems.

Figure 8.2 depicts the instances where Wi-Fi, private 5G, and public 5G can be used:

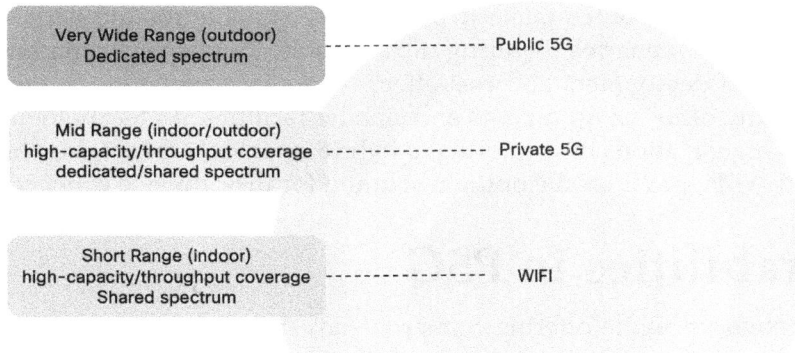

Figure 8.2: *5G vs. Wi-Fi*

In terms of performance, both P5G and Wi-Fi have their strengths, but P5G generally offers superior capabilities in several key areas. P5G networks are designed to handle a much higher number of connected devices per unit area compared to Wi-Fi. This makes P5G particularly suitable for IoT-intensive environments where thousands of sensors and devices need to communicate simultaneously.

Latency is another area where P5G shines. With URLLC, P5G can achieve latencies as low as one millisecond, crucial for applications like industrial automation, augmented reality, and autonomous vehicles. While Wi-Fi 6 has improved latency over its predecessors, it still cannot match the consistent, ultra-low latency performance of P5G.

Bandwidth and data rates are areas of intense competition between the two technologies. Wi-Fi 6E can theoretically achieve multi-gigabit speeds in ideal conditions. However, P5G, when utilizing mmWave spectrum, can potentially offer even higher data rates. Moreover, P5G maintains more consistent performance under heavy network load and over larger areas, whereas Wi-Fi performance can degrade more noticeably in congested environments.

One significant advantage of P5G over Wi-Fi is its superior handling of mobility and handoff between cells or access points. P5G is designed for seamless transitions, even at high speeds, making it ideal for applications involving moving vehicles or roaming users across large areas. Wi-Fi, while improved in recent standards, still struggles with seamless handoffs, particularly at higher speeds or between different networks.

P5G networks typically operate on licensed or locally allocated spectrum, which provides a significant advantage in terms of interference management. This controlled spectrum environment allows for more predictable performance and easier troubleshooting. Wi-Fi, operating in unlicensed bands, is more susceptible to interference from other nearby Wi-Fi networks and devices using the same frequency bands, which can impact performance and reliability.

While both Private 5G and Wi-Fi have their place in enterprise networking, P5G offers distinct advantages in security, large-area coverage, device density, mobility, and consistent performance. These attributes make it particularly suitable for industrial applications, large campuses, and scenarios requiring ultra-reliable, low-latency communications. Wi-Fi, with its ease of deployment and cost-effectiveness for smaller areas, remains a viable solution for many office environments and smaller facilities. As technologies continue to evolve, many organizations may find that a hybrid approach, leveraging the strengths of both P5G and Wi-Fi, provides the optimal solution for their diverse connectivity needs.

Vulnerabilities in P5G

Private 5G networks, while offering numerous advantages, are not immune to security threats and these vulnerabilities span various aspects of the network architecture and operations, each requiring careful consideration and mitigation strategies.

The network infrastructure of private 5G systems presents several potential weak points. Base stations, being the primary point of radio access, are susceptible to physical tampering, which could lead to service disruption or unauthorized access. These stations may also be vulnerable to firmware exploits if not regularly updated, allowing attackers to gain control over network operations. Misconfiguration of base stations is another common issue, potentially exposing the network to external threats or performance degradation.

In the core network, vulnerabilities manifest in both the control plane and the user plane. Control plane attacks could manipulate network signaling, leading to service disruptions or unauthorized access to network resources. User plane attacks might intercept or alter data traffic, compromising user privacy and data integrity. Signaling storms, where a flood of signaling messages overwhelms the network, can also be exploited to cause widespread service outages.

The **radio access network (RAN)** faces unique challenges due to its wireless nature. Jamming attacks can disrupt communication by flooding the radio spectrum with interference, rendering the network unusable. Spoofing attacks involve impersonating legitimate network elements to intercept traffic or inject malicious data. Man-in-the-middle attacks in the RAN can allow attackers to eavesdrop on communications or alter data in transit, compromising the confidentiality and integrity of user data.

Authentication and access control mechanisms are critical security components, but they have their vulnerabilities. SIM card cloning, where attackers duplicate legitimate SIM credentials, can lead to unauthorized network access and potential identity theft. **International Mobile Subscriber Identity (IMSI)** catching attacks can compromise user privacy by intercepting unique subscriber identifiers. Successful unauthorized access attempts can breach network security, potentially leading to data theft or service disruption.

User equipment, such as smartphones and IoT devices, represents a significant attack surface. Malware infections on these devices can lead to data breaches or use the devices as entry points into the broader network. Rogue devices, intentionally introduced into the network, can act as insider threats, potentially exfiltrating data or disrupting services. Firmware vulnerabilities in the UE can also be exploited to gain unauthorized control over devices or access sensitive information.

The backhaul and transport layers of private 5G networks are not immune to attacks. DDoS attacks targeting these layers can overwhelm network resources, causing widespread outages. Traffic interception in the backhaul can compromise data confidentiality, while routing attacks may disrupt network operations or redirect traffic to malicious endpoints.

As private 5G networks increasingly adopt virtualization and network-slicing technologies, new vulnerabilities emerge. Slice isolation breaches could allow attacks to spread between logically separated network segments. Hypervisor vulnerabilities in the virtualized infrastructure could be exploited to gain control over multiple network functions. Resource allocation attacks might manipulate the distribution of network resources, leading to service degradation or denial of service for specific slices.

The increasing use of APIs and service interfaces in Private 5G networks introduces potential vulnerabilities. API exploitation could allow unauthorized access to network functions or data. Insecure interfaces might be leveraged to bypass authentication mechanisms or gain elevated privileges. Service-specific vulnerabilities could arise from poorly implemented or outdated services, providing attackers with entry points into the network.

Protecting data privacy and confidentiality is important in Private 5G networks. Data leakage, whether through misconfigured access controls or intentional exfiltration, poses a significant risk to user privacy and corporate data security. If encryption weaknesses are present, they could be exploited to decrypt sensitive communications. Side-channel attacks might extract sensitive information by analyzing patterns in power consumption, electromagnetic emissions, or timing information of network components.

The human element in network management introduces its own set of risks. Insider threats from disgruntled or compromised employees can lead to intentional data breaches or service disruptions. Misconfiguration risks arise from the complexity of 5G systems, where a simple error could expose critical network components. Inadequate monitoring of network activities may result in delayed detection of security incidents, allowing attackers to maintain prolonged access to the network.

As private 5G networks increasingly incorporate edge computing, new vulnerabilities emerge at the network edge. Edge node compromises could provide attackers with a foothold in the network, potentially allowing lateral movement to more critical systems. Data integrity attacks at the edge could manipulate local data processing, leading to incorrect decisions or actions. Resource exhaustion attacks targeting edge nodes might disrupt local services or propagate to affect broader network operations. A mind-map view of the various vulnerabilities in P5G is shown in the following figure:

Figure 8.3: Vulnerabilities in P5G

P5G deployment models

Private 5G networks can be deployed through several architectural models, each offering distinct advantages and trade-offs to meet diverse enterprise requirements. In the enterprise-built model, organizations maintain complete control over their network infrastructure and data, deploying and managing all network components independently. This approach offers maximum customization and security but requires significant technical expertise and resource investment.

Mobile operator-built deployments leverage the carrier's existing infrastructure and expertise, where operators design, implement, and often manage the private network on behalf of enterprises. This model reduces technical complexity for organizations while ensuring professional network management, though it may offer less direct control over network policies and configurations.

The RAN sharing model introduces a hybrid approach where enterprises share radio access network infrastructure with public networks while maintaining dedicated core network functions. This arrangement optimizes spectrum efficiency and reduces deployment costs, particularly beneficial in areas with existing mobile coverage.

In the RAN and control plane sharing model, enterprises share both radio access and control plane elements with mobile operators while maintaining separate user plane functions. This architecture balances network independence with cost efficiency, particularly suitable for enterprises requiring moderate customization while leveraging operator expertise.

The end-to-end network slicing based model represents an advanced approach where operators create virtually isolated network segments within their public infrastructure. Each slice provides dedicated resources and capabilities tailored to specific enterprise requirements, offering the benefits of private networking while utilizing public network infrastructure. This model enables flexible resource allocation and service customization while minimizing infrastructure duplication. The following section explains these in detail.

P5G deployment built by enterprises

The most common deployment method for P5G is on-premises installation. It is also referred to as the *isolated 5G LAN deployment model*, also known as the **full private**, **no-sharing** model, which represents the most autonomous and secure approach to implementing private 5G networks. The model depicted in *Figure 8.4*, shows enterprises build and operate their own 5G network infrastructure using locally allocated 5G frequencies, maintaining complete control and isolation from public networks or other private networks.

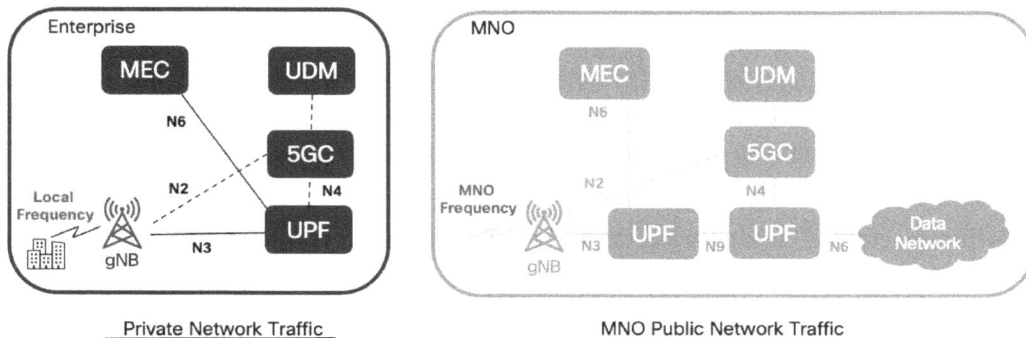

Figure 8.4: P5G deployment — Independent network

This model relies on regulatory bodies allocating specific 5G frequency bands for local, private use. These local frequency allocations vary by country but typically include mid-band (for example, 3.7-3.8 GHz) or mmWave (for example, 26 GHz, 28 GHz) frequencies.

The use of dedicated local frequencies ensures that the private network does not interfere with public cellular networks and provides a guaranteed spectrum for the enterprise's exclusive use. The enterprise takes full responsibility for designing, deploying, and operating the 5G network. This includes owning and managing all network components such as the RAN, core network, and associated management systems. The organization may choose to work with system integrators or equipment vendors for implementation, but ultimately retains complete control over the network. This model ensures that all network resources are dedicated solely to the owning enterprise. This absence of sharing extends to both physical infrastructure and logical network resources. This deployment is aimed at complete network isolation. The network operates entirely independently of public cellular networks. There is typically no interconnection with public networks unless explicitly configured for specific purposes, providing an extremely high level of security and data privacy.

With no sharing of infrastructure or spectrum and complete isolation from external networks, this model offers the highest level of security and data privacy. It is particularly suitable for industries handling sensitive data or critical operations, such as defense, finance, or certain manufacturing sectors. Another advantage of this model is that the enterprises have unlimited freedom to tailor the network to their specific needs. This includes customizing coverage areas, capacity allocation, **quality of service (QoS)** parameters, and security protocols without any external constraints. With dedicated spectrum and infrastructure, organizations can fine-tune network performance to meet specific operational requirements, potentially achieving lower latency and higher reliability than shared or public network options. This model makes compliance easier to achieve and demonstrate.

This model requires significant upfront capital expenditure for spectrum licensing, equipment procurement, and network deployment. Organizations need to carefully evaluate the return on investment. Enterprises deploying this P5G model need resources and technical expertise to run and manage the setup. Managing a private 5G network demands specialized skills. Enterprises need to either develop in-house expertise or maintain ongoing relationships with external experts. As the sole owner and operator, the enterprise is responsible for all future upgrades and expansions. This requires long-term planning and ongoing investment to keep the network up to date with evolving 5G standards and technologies.

The on-premises P5G model is particularly well-suited for military and defense, where network security and control are important. It is also useful for critical infrastructure, such as power plants or water treatment facilities, that require highly secure and reliable communications. For industries dealing with sensitive intellectual property or processes and financial institutions, particularly for high-frequency trading or data centers requiring ultra-low latency and high security, P5G can play a vital role.

P5G deployment built by mobile operators

The isolated 5G LAN deployment model, constructed and managed by **mobile network operators** (**MNOs**) for an enterprise, represents one of the most secure and controlled approaches to private 5G network implementation. This model is characterized by its use of licensed 5G frequencies, complete privacy, and absence of resource sharing with external networks. It is designed to meet the stringent requirements of organizations that demand the highest levels of security, performance, and control over their wireless communications infrastructure. The major difference between this and the previous mode of deployment is that the MNOs build and operate the 5G setup in the enterprise, with their own licensed 5G spectrum, as shown in the following figure:

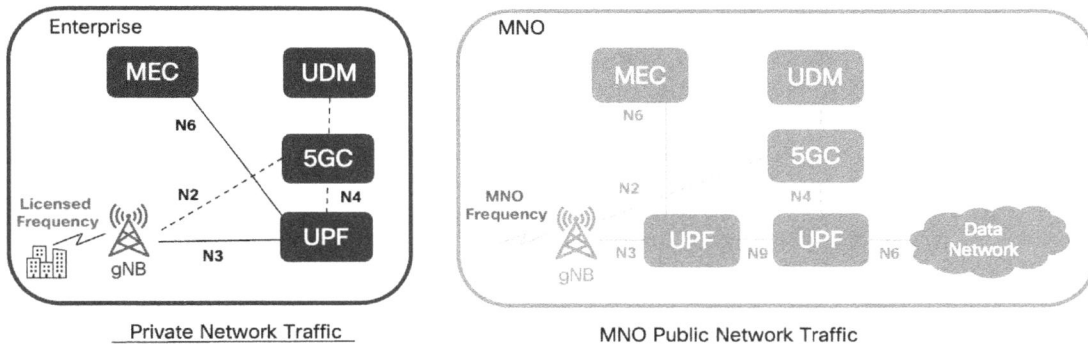

Figure 8.5: P5G deployment., independent network built by MNOs

In this deployment model, the MNO builds a completely isolated 5G network within the customer's premises. The architecture includes all essential components of a 5G network: the **radio access network** (**RAN**), the **5G core** (**5GC**), and the **management and orchestration** (**MANO**) systems. Unlike other models where some components might be shared or cloud-based, every element in this setup is dedicated solely to the organization's use and is physically located on-site.

The RAN consists of 5G base stations (gNodeBs) strategically placed throughout the facility to provide comprehensive coverage. These base stations connect to a locally deployed 5G core network, which handles all the control and user plane functions. This local core ensures that all data processing and routing occur within the organization's premises, never leaving the secure perimeter.

A key feature of this model is the use of licensed 5G frequencies. The MNO, leveraging its spectrum assets, allocates a portion of its licensed spectrum exclusively for the private network. This approach offers several advantages. Licensed spectrum protects against interference from other wireless networks, ensuring consistent and reliable performance. The dedicated spectrum allows for precise capacity planning and guarantees quality of service, which are critical for many industrial and enterprise applications. Additionally, using licensed spectrum through an MNO ensures full compliance with local regulatory requirements, simplifying the legal aspects of network deployment.

The isolated nature of this deployment model offers unparalleled security and privacy benefits. With all network components on the premises, the risk of external breaches is significantly reduced. All data remains within the organization's physical boundaries, addressing data residency and sovereignty concerns. The organization can implement tailored security protocols, including advanced encryption, access controls, and monitoring systems. Unlike hybrid models, there is no connection to public networks, eliminating associated vulnerabilities. The dedicated nature of this deployment also allows for extensive performance optimization. With all processing occurring on-site, ultra-low latency can be achieved, which is crucial for time-sensitive applications like industrial automation or augmented reality. The network can be designed with redundancy and failover mechanisms to ensure continuous operation, which is critical for mission-critical applications. The RAN can be precisely tailored to the specific layout and requirements of the facility, ensuring seamless coverage even in challenging radio environments like factories or warehouses.

Despite its isolated nature, this model offers considerable scalability and flexibility. Additional spectrum or network resources can be allocated as the organization's needs grow, without impacting other networks. The MNO can roll out new 5G features and capabilities to the private network, ensuring it remains at the cutting edge of technology. While isolated, the network can still be integrated with the organization's IT systems, IoT platforms, and edge computing resources as needed.

This deployment model comes with specific operational considerations. Typically, the MNO not only deploys but also operates the network, providing 24/7 monitoring and support. This reduces the need for in-house cellular expertise but may reduce some aspects of direct control. This model often involves significant upfront costs for dedicated equipment and spectrum allocation, usually structured as a long-term managed service contract. The MNO handles spectrum licensing and regulatory compliance, simplifying these aspects for the organization. The isolated nature means that devices on this network typically cannot roam onto public networks without additional configurations or agreements.

RAN sharing model

RAN sharing between private and public networks represents an innovative approach to 5G deployment that bridges the gap between dedicated private networks and the expansive coverage of public cellular infrastructure. This model leverages the concept of network sharing to create a symbiotic relationship between private enterprise networks and public MNOs.

In the deployment model shown in *Figure 8.6*, the RAN infrastructure is shared between a private 5G network and a public cellular network. The shared RAN typically includes components such as antennas, base stations, and other radio equipment. This infrastructure can be owned and operated by either the enterprise, the MNO, or a third-party neutral host provider.

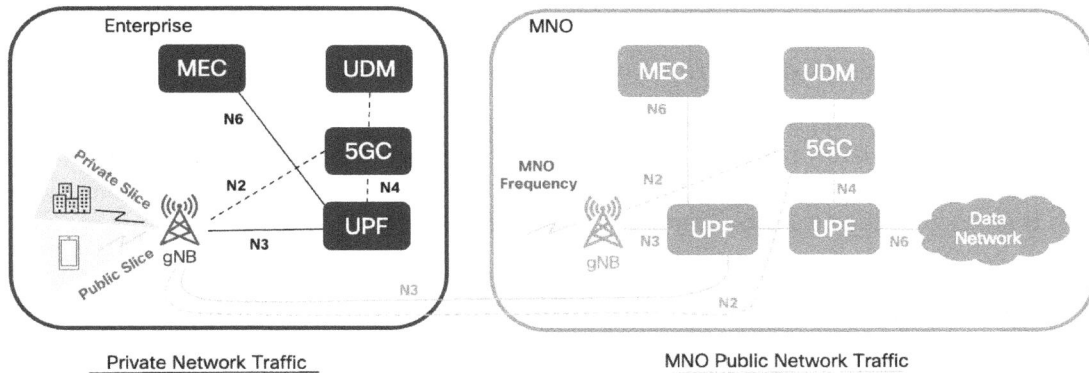

Figure 8.6: *RAN sharing mode of P5G deployment*

The key to this model is the use of advanced network slicing capabilities inherent in 5G technology. Network slicing allows the creation of multiple virtual networks over a single physical infrastructure, each with its specific characteristics and QoS parameters. In the context of RAN sharing, one or more slices are dedicated to the private network, while others serve the public network.

RAN sharing between private and public networks offers several significant benefits. One of the primary advantages is cost efficiency. By sharing the RAN infrastructure, both the enterprise and the MNO can substantially reduce their capital and operational expenditures. Enterprises gain access to high-quality 5G infrastructure without bearing the full burden of deployment and maintenance costs, while MNOs can more effectively monetize their infrastructure investments.

Another key benefit is expanded coverage. This model provides MNOs with an opportunity to extend network coverage into areas that might otherwise be challenging or uneconomical to serve, such as indoor spaces in large buildings or remote industrial sites. This expansion of coverage benefits both the private network users and the MNO's public subscribers.

Spectrum efficiency is another crucial advantage of this deployment model. RAN sharing allows for more efficient use of available spectrum resources. In some cases, enterprises hold their spectrum licenses, which can be utilized more effectively when integrated with an MNO's network, maximizing the value of this limited resource.

While RAN sharing between private and public networks offers numerous benefits, it also presents several challenges that need careful consideration. Security and data privacy are important concerns in this deployment model. Maintaining the security and privacy of the private network while sharing infrastructure with a public network is crucial.

Implementation of robust isolation mechanisms and encryption protocols is essential to prevent data leakage or unauthorized access. Ensuring consistent quality of service can be challenging in a shared infrastructure environment. It is critical to maintain the required performance levels for the private network, especially during peak public network usage. This necessitates careful planning and implementation of sophisticated quality-of-service mechanisms to meet the often-stringent requirements of enterprise applications.

Regulatory compliance is another area that requires attention. Depending on the region, there may be regulatory challenges related to spectrum usage, data sovereignty, and network-sharing agreements that need to be navigated. Staying abreast of and complying with these regulations is crucial for successful implementation.

The operational complexity of managing a shared RAN infrastructure cannot be overlooked. It requires sophisticated orchestration and management systems to ensure smooth operations. Clear delineation of responsibilities between the enterprise and the MNO is crucial, as is the establishment of effective communication channels and processes for issue resolution and network optimization.

RAN sharing between private and public networks is particularly well-suited for certain scenarios like large enterprises with expansive campuses or multiple locations, smart cities where municipal governments can partner with MNOs to deploy shared infrastructure that serves both city operations and the general public, transportation hubs like airports, train stations, and ports can implement private networks for operations while ensuring public connectivity for travelers, lastly, manufacturing facilities or mining operations in remote locations can ensure robust private connectivity for critical operations while providing public access for non-critical communications.

RAN and control plane share a model

The RAN and control plane sharing model represents an innovative approach to private 5G deployment that blurs the lines between private and public networks. This model leverages the concept of network sharing to create a symbiotic relationship between private enterprise networks and public MNOs. In this deployment scenario, the RAN infrastructure and certain control plane functions are shared between the private network and the public network, as depicted in the following figure, offering a unique set of advantages and considerations for both parties involved.

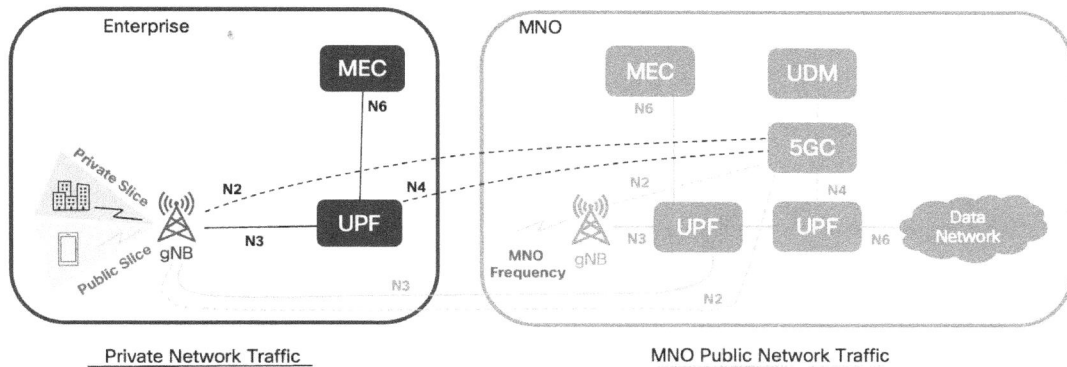

Figure 8.7: *RAN and core sharing mode of P5G deployment*

At its core, this deployment model involves the co-utilization of physical network infrastructure. The RAN, which includes elements such as base stations, antennas, and radio units, is shared between the enterprise and the public MNO. This shared infrastructure can be owned by either party or by a neutral host provider. The key distinction lies in how the network resources are allocated and managed to serve both private and public users.

The control plane, which manages the overall operation of the network, is also partially shared in this model. This includes functions such as authentication, mobility management, and session management. By sharing these control plane elements, the model allows for seamless integration between the private and public networks, enabling features like smooth handovers for users moving between the two domains.

One of the primary benefits of this deployment model is cost efficiency. By sharing the RAN infrastructure, both the enterprise and the MNO can significantly reduce their **capital expenditure** (**CapEX**) on network equipment. This is particularly advantageous for enterprises that might otherwise find the cost of deploying a fully private 5G network prohibitive. For MNOs, it offers an opportunity to expand their network coverage and capacity in specific areas without bearing the full cost of deployment.

The shared model also presents opportunities for improved spectrum utilization. In many cases, the enterprise may have access to a dedicated spectrum for its private network operations. By sharing the RAN, this spectrum can be dynamically allocated between private and public users based on demand, ensuring optimal use of this valuable resource. During periods of low private network usage, excess capacity can be utilized by the public network, and vice versa.

From an operational perspective, the RAN and control plane sharing model can lead to enhanced network performance and coverage. Enterprises benefit from the expertise and resources of the MNO in managing complex network infrastructure, potentially resulting in better service quality. Simultaneously, public network users may experience improved coverage in areas where shared infrastructure is deployed, such as inside large buildings or across expansive industrial campuses.

However, this deployment model also introduces certain challenges and considerations. Security and data privacy are important concerns, as the shared infrastructure must maintain strict separation between private and public network traffic. Sophisticated network slicing techniques and advanced security protocols are typically employed to ensure that enterprise data remains protected and isolated from the public network.

The governance and management of shared networks also require careful consideration. Clear agreements must be established regarding network maintenance, upgrades, and resource allocation. **Service level agreements** (**SLAs**) need to be meticulously defined to ensure that both private and public network requirements are met consistently.

Regulatory compliance is another critical aspect of this deployment model. Depending on the jurisdiction, there may be specific regulations governing the sharing of network infrastructure between private and public entities. Enterprises and MNOs must navigate these regulatory landscapes carefully to ensure compliance while maximizing the benefits of the shared model.

RAN and control plane sharing model is likely to evolve further as 5G technology matures. We may see more sophisticated sharing arrangements, potentially involving multiple enterprises and MNOs in complex ecosystems. As edge computing becomes more prevalent, there might also be opportunities to extend the sharing model to include compute resources, further enhancing the capabilities and efficiency of these hybrid networks.

End-to-end network slicing based model

End-to-end network slicing between private and public networks represents a sophisticated deployment model in the field of P5G. This approach leverages the concept of network slicing to its fullest extent, allowing for the seamless integration of private and public network resources. In this model, both the RAN and the core network are shared between the private enterprise network and the public MNO infrastructure, creating a symbiotic relationship that maximizes efficiency and flexibility.

At the heart of this deployment model is the principle of end-to-end network slicing. Network slicing allows for the creation of multiple virtual networks on a single physical infrastructure, each tailored to specific performance requirements. In the context of RAN and core sharing, this means that specific *slices* of the network can be allocated to private enterprise use, while other slices serve public users. These slices are logically separated, ensuring security and performance isolation, despite sharing the same physical hardware.

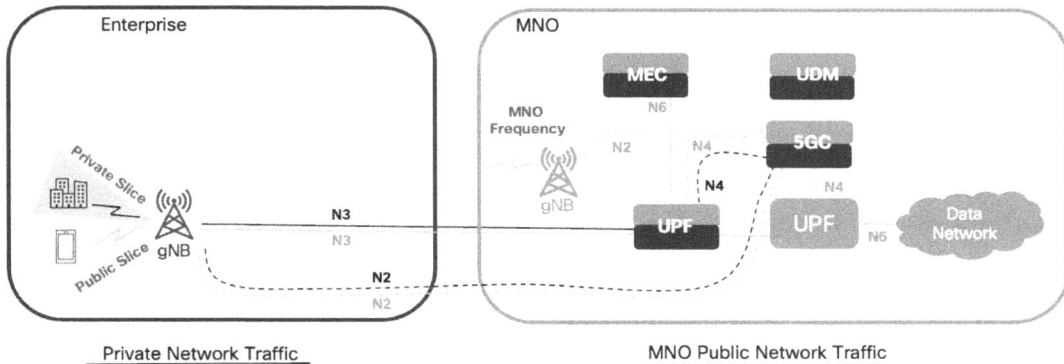

Figure 8.8: End-to-end slicing mode of P5G deployment

The RAN-sharing aspect of this model involves the joint utilization of radio resources. This can include shared antennas, base stations, and spectrum. For the enterprise, this means access to high-quality radio coverage without the need to build and maintain a separate radio network. The MNO benefits from increased utilization of its radio assets and potential cost-sharing for infrastructure deployment. Sophisticated radio resource management algorithms ensure that private network traffic receives priority when needed, maintaining the quality of service expected from a dedicated private network.

Core network sharing in this model extends the concept of resource pooling to the central nervous system of the 5G network. The core network, responsible for critical functions like authentication, session management, and routing, is virtualized and segmented to serve both private and public users. For the enterprise, this provides access to advanced core network features without the complexity and cost of operating a standalone core. It also allows for seamless integration with the wider public network when needed, facilitating scenarios like extended coverage for enterprise users when they leave the primary private network area.

One of the key advantages of this deployment model is its flexibility and scalability. As enterprise needs evolve, network resources can be dynamically reallocated between private and public use. This adaptability is particularly valuable for businesses with fluctuating demand or those undergoing digital transformation. Additionally, the shared infrastructure model can significantly reduce the total cost of ownership for both the enterprise and the MNO, making advanced 5G capabilities more accessible.

Security and data privacy, often primary concerns in shared network models, are addressed through advanced network slicing techniques. Each network slice operates as an isolated environment with its own security policies and data paths. For enterprises dealing with sensitive information, dedicated slices can be configured with enhanced security measures, including end-to-end encryption and restricted access points. This ensures that private network traffic remains separate and secure from public network data, even when traversing shared physical infrastructure.

The implementation of RAN and core sharing requires close collaboration between the enterprise and the MNO. SLAs play a crucial role in defining the allocation of resources, performance guarantees, and operational responsibilities. These agreements ensure that the enterprise retains the control and customization capabilities expected from a private network while benefiting from the expertise and scale of the MNO's operations.

From a regulatory perspective, this model presents interesting challenges and opportunities. It necessitates clear frameworks for spectrum sharing and network operation responsibilities. In some regions, regulators are exploring new licensing models to facilitate this type of shared infrastructure, recognizing its potential to accelerate 5G adoption and improve spectrum efficiency.

Securing P5G

Network security in private 5G deployments requires a comprehensive, multi-layered approach that combines proven security mechanisms with 5G-specific protections. At the foundation lies network segmentation, which isolates critical network functions and user planes while establishing clear security boundaries between different network zones. Encryption and IPSec tunneling protect data both in transit and at rest, ensuring confidentiality across the radio access network and core infrastructure. Sophisticated next-generation firewalls and **intrusion detection/prevention systems (IDS/IPS)** provide real-time threat detection and automated response capabilities, defending against both known and emerging attack vectors. **Mutual TLS (mTLS)** authentication strengthens service-to-service communications by ensuring both endpoints verify each other's identity through digital certificates. Granular access control and robust authentication mechanisms, including integration with enterprise identity systems, ensure that only authorized users and devices can connect to network resources. Continuous security monitoring through advanced analytics and logging provides visibility into network behavior, enabling rapid detection of anomalies and potential security incidents. Together, these security controls create a robust defense-in-depth strategy essential for protecting sensitive enterprise communications and data in private 5G environments.

Network segmentation

One of the fundamental security measures for P5G networks is proper network segmentation and isolation. This involves dividing the network into distinct segments or zones, each with its own security policies and access controls. By implementing network slicing, a key feature of 5G technology, different services or applications can be isolated from one another, reducing the potential impact of a security breach.

Control plane, user plane, and management plane segmentation are other aspects of overall P5G security. P5G networks separate the control plane, which handles signaling and control functions, from the user plane, which carries actual user data. This separation allows for more granular security controls and isolation between network management functions and user traffic.

Micro-segmentation based on 5G trust layers defined in the 5G chapter should also be adopted. Beyond broad network slices, micro-segmentation involves creating even smaller network segments, potentially down to individual devices or applications. This granular approach allows for highly specific security policies and access controls, limiting the potential damage from a security breach.

Virtual LANs (VLANs) and **Virtual Routing and Forwarding (VRF)**, which are traditional networking technologies, should be applied within a P5G network to create logical separations between different network segments or services.

Encryption and IPSec

Encryption is crucial for protecting data in transit within a P5G network. **Internet Protocol (Security IPSec)** is a widely used protocol suite for securing IP communications by encrypting and authenticating each IP packet. In a P5G setup, IPSec can be implemented at various points, such as between the RAN and the core network or between the core network and external networks.

IPSec typically operates in tunnel mode for site-to-site VPNs, encapsulating entire IP packets within a new IP packet. This not only encrypts the data but also hides the original IP header, providing an additional layer of privacy. IPSec provides data confidentiality by encrypting the data to prevent eavesdropping, data integrity by ensuring the data has not been tampered with during transmission, and anti-replay protection by preventing replay attacks where valid data transmission is maliciously repeated.

A **security gateway (SecGW)** can be used to provide this IPSec and encryption capability. SecGW is a crucial component in P5G networks, acting as a secure entry and exit point for traffic between different network segments. It is particularly important in scenarios where the RAN needs to communicate securely with the core network or when the P5G network needs to interface with external networks.

Firewalls, intrusion detection, and prevention systems

Next-generation firewalls play a critical role in P5G security by controlling traffic flow based on application-aware policies. These firewalls can be deployed at the edge of the P5G network to filter incoming and outgoing traffic, as well as between different network segments.

Intrusion detection systems (IDS) and **intrusion prevention systems (IPS)** complement firewalls by monitoring network traffic for suspicious activities and known attack patterns. In a P5G environment, these systems can be particularly useful for detecting and preventing attacks targeting the RAN or core network components.

Mutual TLS

Mutual TLS (**mTLS**) is another important security control for authenticating and encrypting communications between different components of a P5G network. Unlike standard TLS, where only the server authenticates itself to the client, mTLS requires both parties to present certificates, ensuring bidirectional trust.

In a P5G setup, mTLS should be implemented between various network elements, such as:

- Between gNBs (5G base stations) and the core network
- Between different core network functions
- For secure communication with external services or partner networks

mTLS helps prevent man-in-the-middle attacks and ensures that only authorized devices and services can communicate within the P5G network.

Access control and authentication

Robust access control mechanisms are essential for P5G security. This includes implementing strong authentication methods for both users and devices connecting to the network. Some key aspects include:

- **Multi-factor authentication** (**MFA**) for user access
- Device authentication using certificates or SIM-based authentication
- **Role-based access control** (**RBAC**) to limit user privileges
- Continuous authentication and behavioral analysis to detect anomalies

Security information and event management

Implementing a **security information and event management** (**SIEM**) system in a P5G network provides centralized logging, monitoring, and analysis of security events across the entire infrastructure. This helps in detecting and responding to security incidents in real time, as well as conducting post-incident forensics.

A high-level P5G deployment with RAN and core sharing model with security controls, that can be adopted by enterprises and MNOs, is shown in the following figure:

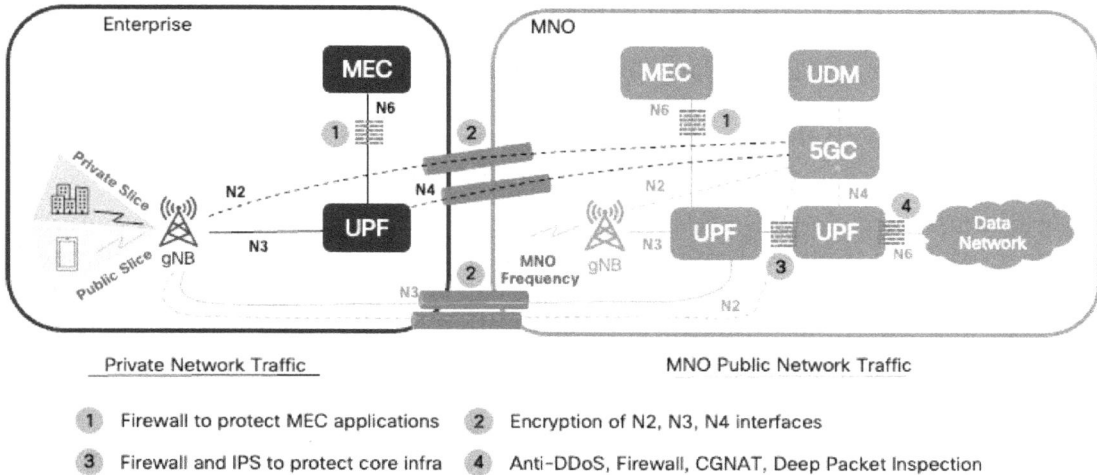

Figure 8.9: *Example of security controls in RAN and core sharing model*

Current challenges in deploying P5G

The deployment of P5G networks represents a significant leap forward in enterprise connectivity, offering unprecedented speed, reliability, and customization. However, this cutting-edge technology comes with its own set of challenges that organizations must navigate. Understanding these hurdles is crucial for successful implementation and maximizing the benefits of P5G.

Spectrum allocation and licensing

One of the primary challenges in P5G deployment is securing the appropriate spectrum. Unlike public 5G networks operated by MNOs, which typically have licensed spectrum, enterprises seeking to deploy P5G must navigate a complex landscape of spectrum options. In many countries, regulators are still in the process of defining frameworks for enterprise spectrum use. This can lead to uncertainty and potential delays in network deployment.

Some countries have allocated specific bands for private industrial use, such as the *CBRS band* in the United States or the *n78 band* in Germany. However, the availability and conditions of use vary significantly across regions. In some cases, enterprises may need to work with MNOs to access licensed spectrum, which can impact the level of control and customization available. Alternatively, they may need to rely on unlicensed or shared spectrum, which can introduce potential interference issues and capacity limitations.

Technical complexity and expertise

Deploying and managing a P5G network requires a high level of technical expertise that many organizations may lack in-house. 5G technology is complex, involving advanced concepts like network slicing, edge computing, and software-defined networking. This complexity extends to both the RAN and the core network components.

Organizations often find themselves facing a steep learning curve, needing to rapidly upskill existing IT staff or hire new specialists with 5G expertise. This challenge is particularly acute for smaller enterprises or those in non-tech industries. The shortage of skilled professionals in the 5G domain further exacerbates this issue, potentially leading to increased costs and deployment delays.

Integration with existing systems

For many organizations, P5G networks need to coexist and integrate with existing IT and **operational technology** (**OT**) systems. This integration can be challenging, particularly in industrial settings where legacy equipment and protocols are common. Ensuring seamless interoperability between P5G networks and existing Wi-Fi, Ethernet, or proprietary industrial communication systems requires careful planning and potentially complex system integration work.

Moreover, organizations need to consider how P5G will fit into their broader digital transformation strategies. This may involve rethinking existing workflows, updating security policies, and modifying application architectures to fully leverage the capabilities of 5G technology.

Security, privacy, and regulatory concerns

While P5G networks offer enhanced security features compared to public networks, they also introduce new security challenges. The increased number of connected devices and the generation of vast amounts of potentially sensitive data create new attack surfaces and privacy concerns.

Organizations need to implement robust security measures, including end-to-end encryption, network slicing for isolation, and advanced authentication mechanisms. They must also ensure compliance with data protection regulations, which can be particularly challenging when dealing with cross-border data flows or industry-specific compliance requirements.

The regulatory landscape for P5G is complex and varies significantly across different countries and industries. Organizations must navigate a range of regulatory requirements, from spectrum licensing to data protection and industry-specific compliance standards.

In some sectors, such as healthcare or finance, additional regulations around data handling and privacy can add layers of complexity to P5G deployments. Staying compliant while maximizing the benefits of P5G technology requires ongoing attention to regulatory developments and potentially significant resources for compliance management.

Cost and ROI justification

Deploying a P5G network represents a significant investment for most organizations. The costs include not only the initial hardware and software but also ongoing maintenance, upgrades, and potentially, spectrum fees. For many enterprises, justifying this investment can be challenging, particularly when existing wireless solutions, like Wi-Fi or 4G LTE, may seem adequate for current needs.

Building a compelling business case often requires a thorough understanding of the long-term benefits and potential new use cases enabled by P5G. This may involve quantifying improvements in productivity, efficiency, or new revenue streams enabled by 5G capabilities like ultra-low latency or massive machine-type communications.

Evolving standards and technology

The 5G ecosystem is still evolving, with ongoing developments in standards, hardware, and software. This dynamic environment can create challenges for organizations deploying P5G networks. There is a risk that current investments may become outdated as new features or more efficient technologies emerge.

Organizations need to balance the desire for cutting-edge capabilities with the need for stability and long-term support. This often requires careful vendor selection and a strategic approach to network architecture that allows for future upgrades and expansions.

While P5G networks offer transformative potential for enterprises across various sectors, their deployment comes with a unique set of challenges. Addressing these hurdles requires a combination of technical expertise, strategic planning, and often, collaboration with experienced partners. As the P5G ecosystem matures and more organizations gain experience with these deployments, many of these challenges are likely to become more manageable, paving the way for wider adoption of this powerful technology.

Conclusion

In conclusion, this chapter has provided a comprehensive overview of P5G networks, exploring various aspects that make this technology a game-changer for enterprise connectivity. We began by examining the frequency bands utilized in 5G technology, which form the foundation for the advanced capabilities of P5G networks. The specific bands employed in P5G implementations were discussed, highlighting how these allocations enable the high-speed, low-latency communications that are critical for many industrial and enterprise applications.

The diverse use cases for P5G were explored, demonstrating its potential to revolutionize industries ranging from manufacturing and healthcare to logistics and smart cities. By comparing P5G with Wi-Fi, we illustrated the unique advantages that private 5G networks offer, particularly in terms of reliability, security, and coverage. However, we also addressed the potential vulnerabilities in P5G systems, emphasizing the importance of robust security measures to protect sensitive enterprise data and operations.

Finally, we explored the various deployment models available for P5G networks and the challenges associated with each. This analysis revealed that while P5G offers significant benefits, its implementation requires careful planning and consideration of factors, such as spectrum availability, infrastructure costs, and integration with existing systems.

As we look to the future, private 5G networks will play a pivotal role in shaping the next generation of enterprise connectivity. While challenges remain, the potential benefits of P5G in terms of performance, customization, and security make it an attractive option for organizations seeking to gain a competitive edge in an increasingly digital world. As the technology continues to mature and more spectrum becomes available, we can expect to see wider adoption of P5G across various sectors, driving innovation and enabling new possibilities in the era of intelligent connectivity.

Looking ahead, the next chapter explores the critical concept of network slicing and its associated security implications in 5G networks. Network slicing transforms how network resources are allocated and managed by creating multiple virtual networks atop a shared physical infrastructure, each optimized for specific use cases and service requirements. As organizations increasingly rely on these customized network segments for different applications, from IoT deployments to mission-critical communications, understanding the security challenges and mitigation strategies becomes paramount. The chapter will examine how network slicing can be secured while maintaining the performance and isolation guarantees that make this technology so valuable for modern telecommunications infrastructure.

Points to remember

- 5G frequency bands operate across distinct ranges, each serving specific needs. Low-band (sub-1 GHz) provides extensive coverage, mid-band (1-6 GHz) balances coverage and capacity, while high-band (mmWave) delivers extreme capacity and ultra-low latency. Understanding these characteristics is crucial for network planning and deployment strategies.

- Private 5G implementations typically leverage mid-band and high-band frequencies to support industrial IoT, automation, and ultra-reliable communications. These bands enable the high performance and reliability required in enterprise environments, with spectrum allocation varying by country and regulatory framework.

- Use cases for private 5G span manufacturing, logistics, healthcare, and critical infrastructure. These deployments enable advanced applications like automated guided vehicles, real-time process control, augmented reality maintenance, and mission-critical communications that demand deterministic performance.

- Compared to Wi-Fi, private 5G offers superior reliability, mobility support, and quality of service guarantees. While Wi-Fi excels in cost-effectiveness and ease of deployment, private 5G provides enhanced security, predictable performance, and extensive coverage necessary for industrial applications.

- Security vulnerabilities in private 5G networks include risks related to radio interface protection, network slice isolation, edge computing security, and unauthorized access. These risks are amplified by the expanded attack surface created by industrial IoT devices and edge deployments.

- Deployment models vary from fully enterprise-owned networks to operator-managed solutions. Options include self-built networks, telecom operator-managed services, hybrid approaches using RAN sharing, and network slicing. Each model offers different levels of control, complexity, and cost considerations.

- Securing private 5G requires a comprehensive approach encompassing physical security, network segmentation, encryption, access control, and continuous monitoring. Zero Trust architectures and AI-based threat detection are becoming essential components of Private 5G security frameworks.

- Current challenges include spectrum availability, deployment costs, ecosystem maturity, and integration with existing industrial systems. Standards evolution, skill gaps, and the need for specialized expertise in both IT and OT domains remain significant considerations for organizations adopting private 5G.

Exercises

1. Which frequency band in private 5G networks provides the best indoor penetration?

   a. mmWave (24-100 GHz)

   b. Mid-band (1-6 GHz)

   c. Low-band (below 1 GHz)

   d. Ultra-high band (above 100 GHz)

2. In a hybrid private 5G deployment model, which component is typically managed by the enterprise?

   a. Core network only

   b. RAN only

   c. Both core and RAN

   d. Neither core nor RAN

3. When comparing private 5G to Wi-Fi 6, which characteristic is NOT an advantage of private 5G?

   a. Lower latency

   b. Better mobility support

   c. Lower deployment cost

   d. Enhanced security features

4. Which private 5G deployment approach offers the highest level of network control and customization?

   a. Fully managed by a telecom operator

   b. Network slicing-based deployment

   c. Fully owned and operated by the enterprise

   d. RAN sharing model

5. Explain three key differences between standalone and non-standalone private 5G deployments, including their advantages and limitations.

6. A manufacturing facility is considering implementing a private 5G network for their AGVs and real-time process monitoring. Discuss which frequency band(s) would be most appropriate and why.

7. Describe two potential security vulnerabilities specific to private 5G networks and suggest appropriate mitigation strategies for each.

8. Compare and contrast the RAN sharing model with network slicing in private 5G deployments. Include considerations for cost, control, and complexity.

Join our book's Discord space

Join the book's Discord Workspace for Latest updates, Offers, Tech happenings around the world, New Release and Sessions with the Authors:

https://discord.bpbonline.com

CHAPTER 9

Network Slicing and Related Security

Introduction

Network slicing has emerged as a pivotal technology in the era of 5G and beyond, offering unprecedented flexibility and customization in network resource allocation. This chapter delves into the multifaceted world of network slicing, exploring its standardization efforts led by organizations such as 3GPP and ETSI, and the critical network functions that enable its implementation, including the **Network Slice Selection Function** (**NSSF**) and **Network Slice Subnet Management Function** (**NSSMF**). We examine the industry frameworks that guide the development and deployment of network slices, such as GSMA's **Generic Slice Template** (**GST**) and **Network Slice Type** (**NEST**), which provide a common language for describing slice requirements across diverse use cases.

As network slicing introduces new paradigms in network architecture, it also brings forth unique security challenges. This chapter provides an in-depth analysis of the security threats specific to network slicing environments, including isolation breaches, resource manipulation, and unauthorized slice access. Furthermore, we explore the robust security controls and design principles essential for safeguarding slice-based networks, encompassing encryption, access control mechanisms, and continuous monitoring strategies. By understanding these fundamental aspects of network slicing and its associated security implications, readers will gain comprehensive insights into this transformative technology and its role in shaping the future of telecommunications.

Structure

This chapter will cover the following topics.

- Standardization of slices
- Network functions enabling slices
- Cross-domain slice orchestration
- Industry framework for slicing
- Soft and hard slicing
- Slice architecture
- Slice threats
- Security concerns in slice
- Security controls for slice
- Slice security design

Objectives

The objective of this chapter is to provide a comprehensive overview of network slicing and its associated security considerations. We will explore the standardization efforts for network slices, examining how industry bodies are working to create uniform definitions and protocols. The chapter will explore the network functions that enable the creation and management of slices, focusing on their roles in slice implementation. We will investigate cross-domain slice orchestration, addressing the challenges and solutions for managing slices across multiple network domains. The industry framework for slices will be discussed, highlighting how different sectors are leveraging this technology. We will differentiate between *soft* and *hard slicing*, explaining their characteristics and use cases. The chapter will also present *general slice architectures*, providing insight into the fundamental designs that underpin network slicing. Finally, we will conduct an in-depth analysis of security threats specific to network slices and explore the essential security controls that should be incorporated into slice designs to mitigate these risks. By the end of this chapter, readers will have a solid understanding of network slicing technology, its implementation, and the critical security considerations that must be addressed in its deployment.

Introduction to network slices

Private network slicing is a revolutionary concept in modern telecommunications, particularly in the context of 5G and beyond. It allows service providers to create multiple virtual networks on top of a shared physical infrastructure, each tailored to meet specific performance, security, and functional requirements of diverse use cases and applications. This approach enables operators to efficiently allocate resources and provide customized services to different customer segments, all while maintaining a single, unified physical network.

In order to better understand the significance of network slicing, consider these common real-world scenarios:

- **Streaming a live sports event**: Imagine millions of fans streaming a major football championship on their smartphones. Network slicing can create a dedicated high-bandwidth slice to ensure smooth, high-quality video for all viewers, even during peak usage times.

- **Smart traffic management**: In a bustling city center, thousands of traffic lights, cameras, and sensors are needed to communicate instantly to manage traffic flow. A low-latency network slice can be dedicated to this critical infrastructure, ensuring rapid response times and preventing gridlock.

- **Remote work revolution**: With more people working from home, a slice can be optimized for secure, high-quality video conferencing and cloud application access, providing a seamless office experience from anywhere.

- **Emergency services communication**: During a natural disaster, first responders require uninterrupted, priority access to the network. A dedicated slice ensures their critical communications remain operational, even if commercial networks are congested or damaged.

- **Massive Internet of Things (IoT) deployment**: In a smart agriculture setting, thousands of soil sensors, weather stations, and automated irrigation systems need to transmit data regularly. A slice designed for massive machine-type communications can efficiently handle these numerous, low-bandwidth connections.

These examples, as illustrated in the following figure, show how network slicing can address vastly different needs simultaneously on the same physical network, from high-bandwidth video streaming to low-latency traffic management and large-scale IoT deployments.

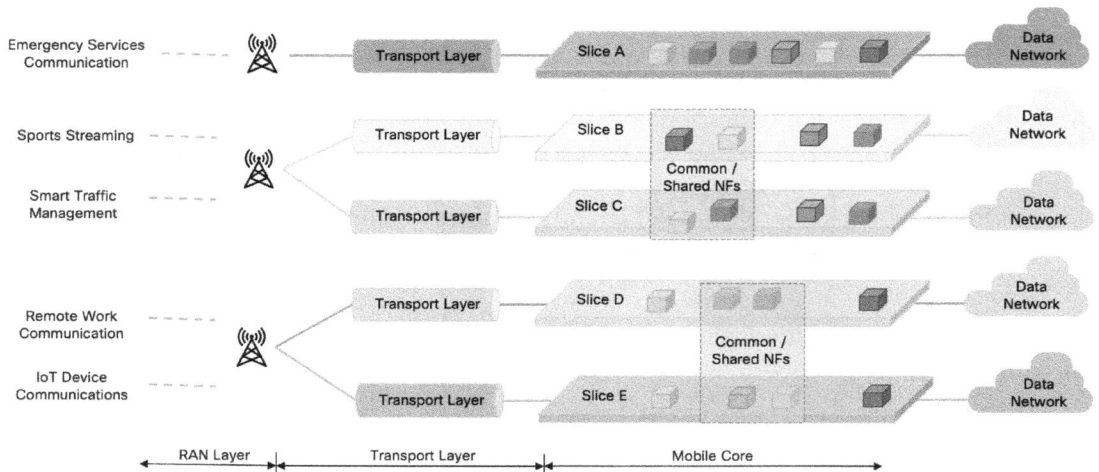

Figure 9.1: *Network slicing examples*

Network slicing in a service provider network can be further explained by using an analogy of highways. Imagine a large, multi-lane highway that connects two cities. This highway represents the entire network infrastructure of the service provider.

Now, picture this highway being divided into several smaller, parallel roads, each separated by barriers. These smaller roads are the *network slices*. Each slice is like a dedicated lane or set of lanes on the highway, designed for specific types of traffic. The following are a few anecdotes that can help in understanding slicing and its features, in simpler terms.

- **Dedicated lanes**: Just as you might have lanes for cars, buses, and emergency vehicles, network slices are dedicated to different types of network traffic or services.

- **Traffic optimization**: Each lane can have its speed limit and rules, optimized for its specific type of traffic. Similarly, network slices can be optimized for different service requirements, like speed, latency, or bandwidth.

- **Isolation**: The barriers between lanes prevent different types of traffic from interfering with each other. In network slicing, this isolation ensures that heavy traffic in one slice does not affect the performance of other slices.

- **Flexible allocation**: During rush hour, you might convert some regular lanes into carpool lanes. Similarly, network resources can be dynamically allocated between slices based on demand.

- **Quality of service**: An ambulance on the emergency lane gets priority and a clear path. In network slicing, critical services can get prioritized resources and guaranteed performance.

- **Efficiency**: This system allows for more efficient use of the overall highway capacity, just as network slicing allows for more efficient use of network resources.

At its core, network slicing leverages virtualization and **software-defined networking** (**SDN**) technologies to partition a physical network into multiple logical networks. Each *slice* functions as an independent, end-to-end network, complete with its resources, topology, and security policies. This level of customization and isolation ensures that the varied demands of different services and applications can be met without compromising the performance or security of others.

Standardization of slices

Network slice standardization is crucial for ensuring interoperability, scalability, and efficiency in 5G and beyond networks. It provides a common framework for operators, vendors, and service providers to design, implement, and manage network slices consistently across different domains and technologies. Standardization enables seamless end-to-end service delivery, facilitates multi-vendor deployments, and promotes innovation by creating a level playing field for all stakeholders. It also ensures that network slices can be orchestrated and managed uniformly, regardless of the underlying infrastructure or service requirements. Moreover, standardization helps in defining clear security protocols, performance metrics, and quality of service parameters, which are essential for meeting diverse use case requirements and regulatory compliance. Slice standardization accelerates the adoption of network slicing technology, reduces deployment costs, and enhances the overall reliability and effectiveness of next-generation mobile networks.

Several standards organizations and industry bodies have developed guidelines, frameworks, and best practices for network slicing. The **3rd Generation Partnership Project** (**3GPP**) has been at the forefront of defining network slicing standards. In its *Release 15* and subsequent releases, as listed in the following, 3GPP has outlined the core concepts, architecture, and management aspects of network slicing. These specifications, as listed in the following cover the end-to-end system, including the RAN, **core network** (**CN**), and **management and orchestration** (**MANO**) domains.

- **Release 15**: This introduced the basic concepts and architecture for network slicing.
- **Release 16**: This enhanced the management and orchestration capabilities.
- **Release 17**: This further refined slice management and introduced enhancements for slice-specific authentication and authorization.

The key 3GPP specifications listed in the following define slice lifecycle management, slice performance, and fault management, slice templates and instance management, and slice subnet management.

- **TS 28.530**: This specification focuses on management and orchestration, outlining key concepts, exploring various use cases, and establishing requirements for these systems.
- **TS 28.531**: Network slicing provisioning is defined in this technical specification. This specification outlines the procedures and requirements for implementing network slicing capabilities.

- **TS 28.541**: This technical specification addresses the management and orchestration aspects of 5G networks. Specifically, it defines the **Network Resource Model (NRM)** for 5G systems.

- **TR 28.801**: This technical report examines the management and orchestration aspects of network slicing technology. This study focuses specifically on how these concepts apply to next-generation networks.

European Telecommunications Standards Institute (ETSI) has contributed significantly to the orchestration and management aspects of network slicing through its work on **network functions virtualization (NFV)** and MANO. ETSI's work, like the ones listed in the following focuses on the virtualization and orchestration aspects of network slicing, ensuring that slicing concepts can be effectively implemented in software-defined networking environments.

- **ETSI NFV-EVE 012** (Report on network slicing support with ETSI NFV architecture framework) specifically addresses the challenges of network slicing in NFV environments, providing guidelines for the realization of network slicing in the NFV architectural framework.

- **ETSI GS NFV-IFA 028** (Report on architecture options to support multiple administrative domains), while not exclusively about network slicing, this specification is relevant for multi-tenant and multi-domain network slice deployments.

As listed in the following the **Global System for Mobile Communications Association (GSMA)** has published several documents on network slicing, which provide industry perspectives on use cases, deployment scenarios, and operational requirements for network slicing. The GSMA's work is particularly valuable in bridging the gap between technical standards and business requirements, providing practical guidance for mobile network operators.

- **Network slicing use case requirements**: This document outlines various use cases for network slicing and their specific requirements.

- **An introduction to network slicing**: This document provides a comprehensive overview of network slicing concepts, benefits, and challenges.

- **Generic network slice template**: This document defines a standardized template for describing network slice characteristics, facilitating interoperability between operators and vendors.

International Telecommunication Union Telecommunication Standardization Sector (ITU-T) work provides a global perspective on network slicing, ensuring alignment with broader telecommunications standards and frameworks. ITU-T has contributed to network slicing standards through its focus on network softwarization and orchestration, mainly through its **ITU-T Y.3100 series of recommendations**. These recommendations cover various aspects of network slicing in IMT-2020 (5G) networks, including:

- **Y.3101**: This series covers the requirements of the IMT-2020 network. It defines the standards and specifications for the fifth-generation mobile network technology.

- **Y.3112**: Y.3112 provides a framework that defines how network slicing can be supported in IMT-2020 networks. This framework specifies the necessary mechanisms and requirements for implementing network slicing capabilities within the IMT-2020 network architecture.

- **Y.3150**: Network softwarization for IMT-2020 is outlined in recommendation Y.3150. This document describes the essential technical aspects of implementing software-defined networking capabilities within IMT-2020 systems.

The **Internet Engineering Task Force (IETF)** has been working on network slicing from the perspective of transport networks and network virtualization. While not specific to mobile networks, their work on **segment routing (SR)** and **Resource Reservation Protocol (RSVP)** extensions, as listed in the following provides valuable insights into the realization of end-to-end network slicing.

- **RFC 8453**, a framework for **Abstraction and Control of TE Networks (ACTN)**, applies to network slicing in transport networks.

- Ongoing work in the **Traffic Engineering Architecture and Signaling (TEAS)** working group on network slicing in IP/MPLS networks.

Network functions enabling slices

In a 5G network setup, several network functions play crucial roles in implementing and managing network slices. These functions are part of the 5G **service-based architecture (SBA)** and work together to enable end-to-end network slicing. Various 5G network functions are detailed and explained in the 5G chapter of this book. This section details the 5G network functions that play a vital role in enabling slices in a 5G network.

Access and mobility management function

Access and mobility management function (AMF) is a cornerstone of the 5G core network, playing a pivotal role in network slicing by managing access control and mobility. In network slicing, the AMF is responsible for slice-aware access control, authenticating and authorizing **User Equipment (UE)** based on their subscription information and the slices they are permitted to access. It enforces slice-specific access policies, ensuring that only authorized devices can connect to slices.

The AMF's role extends to slice-aware mobility management, where it manages UE mobility across different cells and areas while maintaining the UE's connection to the appropriate network slice. This includes handling slice-specific handover procedures to ensure service continuity as UEs move between different parts of the network. Working with the **Network Slice Selection Function (NSSF)**, the AMF is involved in selecting the appropriate slice for a UE during initial attach and handover procedures, maintaining awareness of available **Network Slice Instances (NSIs)** and their capabilities.

The AMF also manages UE registration to the network, including slice-specific registration procedures, as well as deregistration and periodic registration update procedures. It establishes and maintains the control plane connection between the UE and the appropriate network slice and manages idle mode procedures for UEs connected to different slices. This comprehensive management ensures that UEs are always connected to the most appropriate slice based on their subscription, service requirements, and network conditions.

Session management function

Session Management Function (SMF) is crucial in managing user sessions within the 5G core network, and it has significant responsibilities in the context of network slicing. The SMF sets up and manages Protocol Data Unit (PDU) sessions for UEs within specific network slices, applying slice-specific session policies, such as QoS parameters, traffic steering rules, and charging policies. This ensures that each slice can provide its intended service characteristics.

In its role, the SMF allocates and manages IP addresses for UEs within each slice, potentially using slice-specific address pools to maintain proper isolation between slices. It also selects and controls the appropriate User Plane Function (UPF) instances for each slice based on slice requirements and network conditions, configuring UPF behavior for slice-specific traffic handling. This close interaction with the UPF is crucial for implementing the data plane aspects of network slicing.

The SMF works in tandem with the Policy Control Function (PCF) to enforce slice-specific policies for session management, implementing slice-specific QoS control, including QoS flow establishment and modification. It also handles slice-aware roaming scenarios, ensuring appropriate session management when UEs roam between networks. Additionally, the SMF supports slice-specific lawful interception requirements where applicable, adding another layer of customization to the network slicing capabilities.

User plane function

The UPF is at the heart of handling user data traffic in the 5G core network, with critical responsibilities in a sliced network environment. The UPF applies traffic policies specific to each slice, such as QoS enforcement, traffic shaping, and packet filtering. It implements slice-specific packet routing and forwarding rules, ensuring that traffic within a slice receives the appropriate treatment and remains isolated from other slices.

QoS enforcement is a key responsibility of the UPF in network slicing. It enforces QoS parameters for each slice, implementing mechanisms like traffic prioritization and rate limiting based on slice requirements. This ensures that each slice can meet its performance guarantees. The UPF also handles traffic steering, directing traffic to appropriate network or application functions based on slice-specific rules and supporting service chaining within slices, allowing traffic to pass through multiple network functions as required by the slice's service characteristics.

Packet inspection and processing are other important functions of the UPF in network slicing. It may perform slice-specific deep packet inspection if required and apply slice-specific packet processing rules, such as header compression or encryption. The UPF also supports charging and lawful interception functions, potentially with slice-specific requirements, adding to the comprehensive traffic management capabilities it provides in a sliced network environment.

Network repository function

The NRF serves as a central repository for information about available network function services, playing a crucial role in the service-based architecture of 5G networks, particularly in a sliced network environment. The NRF maintains a registry of available network functions and their supported services, including slice-specific functions. This enables other network functions to discover and select appropriate slice-specific services, facilitating the dynamic and flexible nature of network slicing.

In addition to service registration and discovery, the NRF provides information about the load and status of network functions, enabling load balancing across slice-specific function instances. It stores and manages profiles of network functions, including their slice support capabilities, which are crucial for the proper functioning of a sliced network. The NRF also assists in authorizing service access requests between network functions, potentially enforcing slice-specific access rules.

The NRF manages NF Set IDs, which can be used to group network function instances serving the same slice, facilitating efficient management of slice-specific resources. It also provides data to the **Network Data Analytics Function** (**NWDAF**) about service usage patterns across different slices, contributing to the overall analytics and optimization capabilities of the sliced network.

Policy control function

The PCF provides a unified policy framework for the 5G network, with significant implications for network slicing. The PCF defines and manages policies specific to each network slice, covering aspects such as access control, mobility management, session management, and QoS policies. This allows for fine-grained control over the behavior and characteristics of each network slice.

In its role, the PCF coordinates with other network functions (for example, AMF, SMF) to ensure enforcement of slice-specific policies. It makes real-time policy decisions based on network conditions, potentially adjusting policies dynamically to optimize slice performance. The PCF is also responsible for defining and managing QoS parameters for different slices, ensuring that each slice meets its performance requirements.

The PCF manages charging policies for different slices, potentially implementing slice-specific charging models. It provides access and mobility policies to the AMF, which may include slice-specific rules. The PCF also provides UE route selection policies, which may be slice-specific, further contributing to the customized behavior of each network slice.

Network Exposure Function

The **Network Exposure Function (NEF)** plays a crucial role in exposing network capabilities and events to external applications, with significant implications for network slicing. In a sliced network, the NEF exposes slice-specific capabilities to authorized external applications or partners, implementing slice-specific API access policies to control what capabilities are exposed for each slice. This allows for the creation of innovative services that can leverage the unique characteristics of different network slices.

The NEF allows external applications to subscribe to and receive notifications about slice-specific network events, providing a window into the operation of different slices. It provides a secure way for external applications to exchange data with the network, potentially with slice-specific security policies. The NEF may also expose slice-specific analytics data to authorized external parties, potentially in collaboration with the NWDAF.

Furthermore, the NEF enables negotiation of network policies with external applications, potentially on a per-slice basis. This facilitates the creation of new services that leverage slice-specific network capabilities, allowing for a rich ecosystem of applications that can take full advantage of network slicing.

Authentication Server Function

The **Authentication Server Function (AUSF)** is responsible for handling authentication for UEs in the 5G network, with important considerations in a sliced network environment. The AUSF performs authentication procedures that may be specific to network slices, supporting different authentication methods that might be required for different types of slices. For example, high-security slices might require more stringent authentication procedures.

In its role, the AUSF manages authentication credentials, potentially with slice-specific credential sets. It generates and manages security contexts that may be slice-specific and generates authentication vectors for use in slice-specific authentication procedures. The AUSF shares authentication results with other network functions (for example, AMF) in a slice-aware manner, ensuring that slice-specific authentication requirements are met.

The AUSF also supports **Network Slice Specific Authentication and Authorization (NSSAA)**, implementing additional authentication and authorization procedures that may be required for accessing specific network slices. This adds an extra layer of security and access control to the network slicing framework, ensuring that only authorized users can access specific slices.

Unified Data Management

The **Unified Data Management (UDM)** function is responsible for storing and managing subscriber data and profiles, with significant implications for network slicing. In a sliced network, the UDM stores and manages subscription information related to network slices, including which slices a user is allowed to access. It maintains subscribed **Single Network Slice Selection Assistance Information (S-NSSAIs)** for each user, which is crucial for the slice selection process.

The UDM manages user profiles that may contain slice-specific information or preferences. It stores authentication data that may be slice-specific, working in conjunction with the AUSF to support slice-aware authentication procedures. The UDM provides data to support slice-specific access authorization decisions, ensuring that users only access slices they are entitled to.

In addition, the UDM handles updates to slice-related subscription information and performs serving network authorization in roaming scenarios, which may involve slice-specific checks. It also manages SMS services, potentially with slice-specific configurations. This comprehensive management of subscriber data ensures that the network slicing framework has access to all the necessary information to make appropriate slice selection and management decisions.

Network data analytics function

The NWDAF plays a crucial role in collecting and analyzing data from various network functions to provide insights and predictions about network behavior, with significant implications for network slicing. In a sliced network, the NWDAF collects and analyzes data specific to individual network slices, providing insights into slice performance, usage patterns, and potential issues.

The NWDAF monitors the load and performance of different network slices, providing analytics to support dynamic resource allocation between slices. It detects anomalies or unusual behavior within specific network slices, providing early warning of potential issues that could affect slice performance. This capability is crucial for maintaining the quality of service for each slice.

Predictive analytics is another key feature of the NWDAF in network slicing. It predicts future resource requirements for different slices based on historical data and trends, supporting proactive resource allocation and slice scaling. The NWDAF also analyzes **Quality of Experience (QoE)** metrics for services running on different slices, providing insights to support QoE optimization for slice-specific services.

The NWDAF provides analytics to support the optimization of slice-specific policies and performs security-related analytics, potentially identifying slice-specific security threats or vulnerabilities. These comprehensive analytics capabilities make the NWDAF a crucial component in the ongoing management and optimization of network slices.

Network slice selection function

The **Network Slice Selection Function** (**NSSF**) plays a pivotal role in the network slicing ecosystem, being primarily responsible for the slice selection process. The NSSF determines the most appropriate **Network Slice Instance** (**NSI**) for a UE based on a variety of factors, including the UE's subscription information, the type of service requested, network policies, and current network load and slice availability. This ensures that each UE is connected to the slice that best meets its service requirements and entitlements.

In addition to slice selection, the NSSF maintains up-to-date information about available Network Slice Instances and their capabilities, tracking the status and capacity of different slices. This information is crucial for making informed slice selection decisions. The NSSF provides slice selection assistance to the AMF during UE registration and handover procedures and helps in selecting the appropriate AMF instance for a given slice if multiple AMF instances are available.

The NSSF is also responsible for mapping requested NSSAI to specific NSI. In roaming scenarios, it assists in slice selection, potentially interacting with NSSF in other networks. Furthermore, the NSSF implements network slice-specific access control based on network policies and subscription information, adding another layer of control to the slice selection process.

Network slice specific authentication and authorization function

The NSSAAF is a crucial component in the 5G network slicing architecture, specifically designed to handle authentication and authorization for access to individual network slices. This function adds an extra layer of security and access control to the network slicing framework, ensuring that only authorized users can access specific slices, even if they have already been authenticated to the 5G network.

The NSSAAF works in conjunction with other network functions, particularly the AMF and AUSF, to perform slice-specific authentication and authorization procedures. When a UE requests access to a specific network slice, the NSSAAF is invoked to verify whether the UE is authorized to use that slice. This process is known as NSSAA.

In its operation, the NSSAAF interacts with external **authentication, authorization, and accounting** (**AAA**) servers that may be associated with specific network slices. This allows for the implementation of diverse and potentially more stringent authentication methods for different slices, catering to varying security requirements. For instance, a slice dedicated to critical IoT applications might require additional authentication steps or different credentials compared to a slice for enhanced mobile broadband.

The NSSAAF plays a key role in maintaining the security and isolation of network slices. By performing slice-specific authentication and authorization, it ensures that users cannot access slices they are not entitled to, even if they have general access to the 5G network. This is particularly important in scenarios where different slices are used by different tenants or for services with varying levels of sensitivity.

Moreover, the NSSAAF supports the concept of re-authentication and re-authorization for network slices. This means that even after initial access is granted, the NSSAAF can periodically verify the UE's continued authorization to use a specific slice. This feature adds a layer of security, allowing for dynamic access control that can respond to changes in user entitlements or network policies.

The NSSAAF also plays a crucial role in roaming scenarios. When a user is roaming and requests access to a specific slice, the NSSAAF in the visited network can communicate with its counterpart in the home network to verify the user's entitlements. This ensures that slice-specific access policies are enforced consistently across network boundaries.

In the broader context of network slicing, the NSSAAF's functions are essential for realizing the full potential of network slicing in terms of service differentiation and security. By enabling fine-grained, slice-specific access control, the NSSAAF allows network operators to offer highly customized and secure services to different user groups or for different applications, all within the same physical network infrastructure.

Network Slice Admission Control Function

The **Network Slice Admission Control Function** (**NSACF**) is a crucial component in the 5G network slicing architecture, responsible for managing and controlling the admission of UE to specific network slices. This function plays a vital role in maintaining the performance, integrity, and resource allocation of individual network slices by ensuring that each slice operates within its designed capacity and SLAs.

The primary responsibility of the NSACF is to make decisions on whether to accept or reject requests for access to a particular network slice. These decisions are based on various factors, including the current load and capacity of the slice, the priority of the request, the subscriber's profile, and the overall network policies. By carefully controlling admission to each slice, the NSACF helps prevent the overloading of network slices, which could lead to degraded performance or failure to meet SLAs.

The NSACF works closely with other network functions, particularly the NSSF and the AMF. When a UE requests access to a specific slice, or when the NSSF selects a slice for a UE, the NSACF is consulted to determine if the slice can accommodate the new connection without compromising its performance or the experience of existing users.

The NSACF implements various admission control algorithms and policies that can be tailored to the specific requirements of each network slice. For instance, a slice dedicated to critical IoT applications might have very strict admission controls to ensure consistent low-latency performance, while a slice for enhanced mobile broadband might have more flexible policies that allow for some degree of overbooking.

Moreover, the NSACF plays a crucial role in implementing dynamic resource allocation across network slices. It can work in conjunction with analytics functions like the NWDAF to predict upcoming demands on different slices and adjust admission policies accordingly. This allows for more efficient use of network resources while still maintaining the performance guarantees of each slice. The NSACF also supports the concept of slice quota management. Network operators can define quotas for each slice, such as the maximum number of concurrent users or the maximum bandwidth utilization. The NSACF enforces these quotas, ensuring that each slice operates within its allocated resources and does not impinge on the performance of other slices.

In scenarios involving network congestion or high demand, the NSACF can implement prioritization policies. It can ensure that high-priority users or critical services are given preferential admission to their respective slices, even when resources are scarce. This capability is particularly important for slices dedicated to emergency services or other critical applications. The NSACF also contributes to the overall QoE management in a sliced network. By carefully controlling admission to each slice, it helps maintain consistent performance and prevents scenarios where oversubscription leads to a poor user experience. This is especially important in a multi-tenant environment where different slices may be leased to different service providers, each with its own QoE requirements.

The NSACF also plays a role in network slice scaling operations. When a slice is nearing capacity, the NSACF can trigger scaling operations, working with other management functions to allocate additional resources to the slice or to instantiate new slice subnets. Conversely, when a slice is underutilized, the NSACF can signal that resources can be deallocated, contributing to overall network efficiency.

In essence, the NSACF is essential for realizing the full potential of network slicing in terms of resource efficiency, performance isolation, and service differentiation. By enabling fine-grained control over slice admission, the NSACF allows network operators to offer truly differentiated services with varying performance characteristics and resource allocations, all within the same physical network infrastructure.

Network Slice Subnet Gateway

The **Network Slice Subnet Gateway** (**NSSG**) is a crucial component in the 5G network slicing architecture that facilitates communication between different network slice subnets. In a complex network slicing environment, a single end-to-end network slice may be composed of multiple slice subnets, each potentially managed by different administrative domains or implemented across different network segments (for example, RAN, core, transport). The primary role of the NSSG is to act as a bridge between these slice subnets, enabling seamless communication and ensuring that the end-to-end slice functions as a cohesive unit. It handles the routing and forwarding of traffic between slice subnets, applying appropriate policies and maintaining the isolation and performance characteristics of each subnet.

The NSSG implements mechanisms to translate between different addressing schemes or protocols that might be used in different slice subnets. This is particularly important when slice subnets are implemented using different technologies or are managed by different operators. The NSSG ensures that these differences are abstracted away from the perspective of the services running on the end-to-end slice.

The NSSG plays a crucial role in maintaining the security and isolation of network slices. It implements firewalling and access control policies at the boundaries between slice subnets, ensuring that traffic is only allowed to flow between subnets as defined by the overall slice configuration. This helps prevent unauthorized access and maintains the integrity of each slice subnet.

The NSSG also contributes to the QoS management of the end-to-end slice. It can implement QoS policies at the subnet boundaries, ensuring that traffic between subnets adheres to the performance requirements of the overall slice. This might involve traffic shaping, prioritization, or other QoS mechanisms.

In scenarios involving multi-operator or multi-domain slices, the NSSG becomes even more critical. It can be a demarcation point between different administrative domains, implementing agreed-upon interfaces and protocols for inter-domain slice connectivity. This enables the creation of slices that span multiple operators or domains while maintaining clear boundaries and responsibilities. The NSSG also plays a role in slice subnet scaling and resource management. It can monitor traffic flows between subnets and provide this information to management and orchestration systems. This data can be used to trigger scaling operations or to optimize resource allocation across the end-to-end slice.

Communication Service Management Function

The **Communication Service Management Function (CSMF)** is a high-level management function in the 5G network slicing architecture that bridges the gap between communication service requirements and network slice capabilities. It acts as an intermediary between the service layer and the network slice management layer, translating service-level requirements into network slice requirements.

The CSMF's primary responsibility is to take customer or service provider communication service requirements and transform them into network slice requirements that can be used to create or modify network slices. This involves understanding each communication service's specific needs in terms of performance, capacity, functionality, and other parameters and mapping these to the capabilities offered by network slices.

The CSMF interacts with various other management functions and systems. It communicates with service management systems to receive and interpret service requirements. Based on these requirements, it then interacts with the **Network Slice Management Function (NSMF)** to request the creation, modification, or deletion of network slices.

The CSMF plays a crucial role in service differentiation and customization in a network-slicing environment. It enables the network to offer tailored services by ensuring that each service is mapped to a network slice (or slices) that can meet its specific requirements. This might involve selecting existing slice templates, requesting modifications to existing slices, or triggering the creation of entirely new slices.

Moreover, the CSMF contributes to the overall lifecycle management of communication services in relation to network slices. It monitors the performance of services and their associated slices and can initiate changes if the service requirements change or if the current slice allocation is not meeting the service needs. This might involve requesting changes to slice configurations, triggering scaling operations, or migrating services between slices.

The CSMF also plays a role in multi-domain or multi-operator scenarios. It can coordinate with CSMFs in other domains or operators to enable end-to-end service delivery across multiple networks. This is particularly important for services that require consistent performance and functionality across different geographical areas or network boundaries.

In network slicing automation, the CSMF is a key enabler of intent-based networking. It can interpret high-level, intent-based service descriptions and translate these into concrete network slice requirements. This abstraction allows service providers to focus on defining their service needs without having to understand the intricacies of network slice implementation.

Network Slice Subnet Management Function

While the NSMF deals with end-to-end network slices, the NSSMF is responsible for managing individual network slice subnets, which are parts of an end-to-end slice that may correspond to specific network domains (for example, RAN, core, transport) or administrative boundaries.

The primary role of the NSSMF is to manage the lifecycle of network slice subnets. This includes the creation, activation, deactivation, modification, and termination of slice subnets based on requests from the NSMF. The NSSMF translates the requirements for a network slice subnet into a set of network functions and resources needed to implement that subnet.

The NSSMF interacts closely with domain-specific management systems and network functions. It communicates with RAN, core, and transport domain managers to allocate and configure the necessary resources for each slice subnet. This might involve provisioning **virtual network functions** (**VNFs**), configuring **physical network functions** (**PNFs**), setting up connectivity, and applying appropriate policies and parameters.

The NSSMF plays a crucial role in maintaining the performance and isolation of network slice subnets. It monitors the performance of each subnet and can initiate corrective actions if the subnet is not meeting its defined requirements. This might involve scaling resources, modifying configurations, or triggering healing procedures in case of failures.

Moreover, the NSSMF contributes to the efficient use of network resources across slice subnets. It can implement resource-sharing policies, allowing multiple slice subnets to share underlying network resources where appropriate, while still maintaining the required level of isolation and performance for each subnet. The NSSMF also plays a key role in the dynamic adaptation of network slice subnets. It can respond to changing demands or network conditions by modifying subnet configurations or reallocating resources. This might involve scaling subnet resources up or down, modifying QoS parameters, or adjusting the capacity allocated to different services within the subnet.

In multi-domain or multi-operator scenarios, multiple NSSMFs may need to coordinate to manage an end-to-end network slice. Each NSSMF would be responsible for its own domain or operator's portion of the slice, with coordination facilitated by the overarching NSMF. The NSSMF also contributes to the overall visibility and management of network slices. It collects and provides detailed information about the status, performance, and resource usage of each slice subnet. This information is crucial for network operators to understand the behavior of their sliced network and to make informed decisions about slice management and resource allocation.

Cross-domain slice orchestration

3GPP has published a comprehensive high-level network slice management framework that delineates four crucial management functions, defined in the above section, for network slicing. These functions, as detailed in the following section are designed to facilitate the creation, deployment, and management of network slices in a 5G ecosystem.

The **Communications Service Management Function (CSMF)** operates at the highest layer of the **Operations Support System/Business Support System (OSS/BSS)** architecture. Its primary role is to handle customer order management, acting as the interface between the service provider and the customer. This function translates customer requirements into network slice requirements, ensuring that the requested services can be properly implemented and managed.

The NSMF is responsible for orchestrating network slices across multiple domains like the RAN, transport, and core. It acts as the central coordinator, managing the end-to-end lifecycle of network slices. This includes slice creation, modification, and termination based on the requirements received from the CSMF. The NSMF interacts with domain-specific (RAN, transport, core) NSMFs to ensure cohesive management of network slices across different network segments.

Each network domain, such as radio access network, core network, or transport network, has its own NSSMF. This function manages network slice subnets within its specific domain, controlling the resources and configuration of network functions within that subnet. The NSSMF translates the high-level requirements from the NSMF into domain-specific configurations and resource allocations.

The NFMF operates at the application level, managing individual network functions. It handles the lifecycle management of VNFs, PNFs, and **cloud-native network functions** (**CNFs**). This includes tasks such as instantiation, scaling, updating, and termination of these functions as required by the network slices.

The architecture of this framework allows for a hierarchical and modular approach to network slice management. The NSMF acts as the overarching orchestrator, coordinating with domain-specific NSMFs to implement end-to-end network slices. This structure enables the instantiation and configuration of network slice resources tailored to specific use case types defined in 5G, like *eMBB*, *mMTC*, and *uRLLC*. Each of these use case types can be implemented in different domains, with the resources and configurations dictated by the end-to-end network slice intent. This intent is defined at the NSMF level and cascaded down to the relevant NSMFs and NFMFs.

The end-to-end slice orchestrator (part of the NSMF) governs the overall process, ensuring that the slice requirements are met across all domains and that the network slice performs as intended. This orchestrator manages the dynamic allocation of resources, monitors slice performance, and makes adjustments as necessary to maintain the required QoS for each network slice.

This framework, as depicted in the following figure, provides the flexibility and scalability needed to support the diverse requirements of 5G services, allowing network operators to efficiently manage and optimize their network resources while delivering tailored services to their customers.

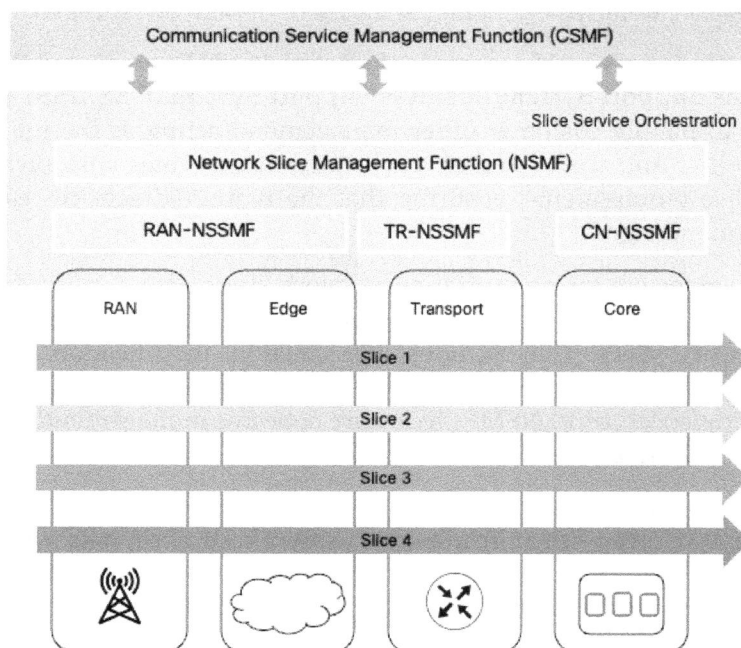

Figure 9.2: 3GPP reference architecture for end to end slicing

Industry frameworks for slicing

Network slicing relies on a complex ecosystem of standards and industry frameworks to ensure interoperability, efficiency, and widespread adoption. These frameworks, developed by various international organizations and industry consortia, provide the necessary guidelines, specifications, and best practices for implementing network slicing across diverse networks and use cases. From technical specifications to operational procedures and business models, these standards form the backbone of network-slicing deployments worldwide. The following paragraphs explore the major contributors to network slicing standardization and their key frameworks, offering insights into how these collaborative efforts are shaping the future of flexible, customized network services.

3rd generation partnership project

3GPP has been at the forefront of defining network slicing for 5G networks. In *Release 15* and subsequent releases, they have established the foundational architecture and specifications for network slicing. Their work includes defining the NSSF, which plays a crucial role in selecting the appropriate network slice for a given service. 3GPP has also specified the management aspects of network slicing, including the NSMF and NSSMF. These specifications cover how slices are created, modified, and terminated across the RAN, core network, and transport network. 3GPP's framework ensures that network slices can be dynamically allocated and managed to meet diverse service requirements.

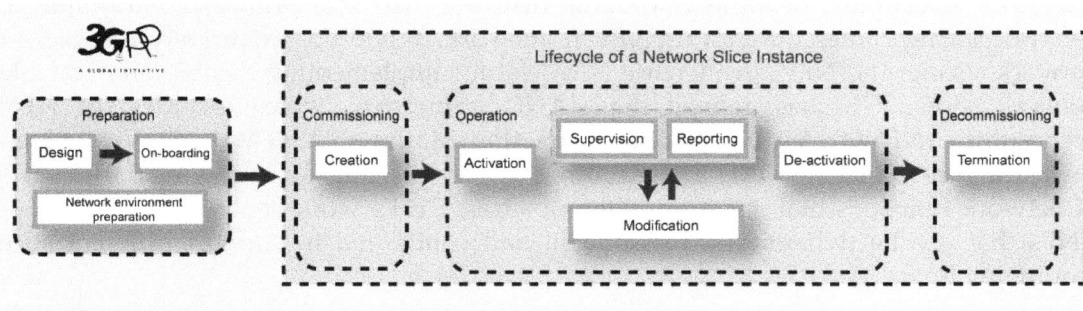

Figure 9.3: *3GPP slice lifecycle*[1]

3GPP has released multiple documents through its multiple 3GPP releases (15, 16, 17, and ongoing work in *Release 18*) to refine and expand network slicing capabilities. The exact version numbers may vary depending on the specific release and update cycle, as listed in the following:

- **TS 28.530**: Management and orchestration, concepts, use cases, and requirements. It provides an overview of network slicing management and orchestration.

---

1   Source: **https://www.3gpp.org/news-events/3gpp-news/sa5-5g**

- **TS 28.531**: Management and orchestration and provisioning. It specifies provisioning procedures for network slicing.

- **TS 28.532**: (Management and orchestration and generic management services.) It defines generic management services applicable to network slicing.

- **TS 28.533**: (Management and orchestration and architecture framework.) It outlines the architectural framework for managing and orchestrating network slices.

- **TS 28.541**: (Management and orchestration, 5G **Network Resource Model** (**NRM**).) It specifies the NRM for 5G networks, including slice-related information models.

- **TS 23.502**: (Procedures for the 5G system.) It describes procedures related to network slice selection and management.

- **TS 38.300**: (NR, overall description, and Stage-2.) It provides an overall description of the 5G **New Radio** (**NR**) access technology, including aspects related to network slicing.

- **TR 28.801**: (Study on management and orchestration of network slicing for next-generation network.) A technical report studying various aspects of network slicing management and orchestration.

European Telecommunications Standards Institute

European Telecommunications Standards Institute's (ETSI's) primary contribution to network slicing comes through its NFV framework. While not exclusively focused on network slicing, the NFV architecture is crucial for implementing flexible and scalable network slices. ETSI has defined the MANO framework, which includes the **NFV orchestrator** (**NFVO**), **Virtual Network Function Manager** (**VNFM**), and **Virtualized Infrastructure Manager** (VIM). These components are essential for managing the lifecycle of network functions that make up network slices. ETSI's work enables the creation of VNFs that can be dynamically instantiated and configured to support different slice requirements.

A list of ETSI's NFV specifications is fundamental to implementing slicing in virtualized networks, as mentioned in the following:

- **ETSI GS NFV-MAN 001 V1.1.1 (2014-12)**: Management and orchestration. This specifies the MANO (Management and Orchestration) framework

- **ETSI GS NFV-IFA 014 V3.6.1 (2022-01)**: Published in January 2022, this document outlines the Network Service Templates Specification. This framework defines templates for describing network services, which can be used to represent network slices

- **ETSI GS NFV-IFA 013 V3.6.1 (2022-01)**: Published in January 2022, it defines Os-Ma-Nfvo Reference Point Interface and Information Model Specification. This framework specifies the interface between the OSS/BSS and the NFV Orchestrator, crucial for slice management

- **ETSI GS NFV-IFA 005 V3.6.1 (2022-01)**: This document describes the Or-Vi reference point interface and information model specification. This framework defines the interface between the NFVO and VIM, important for resource allocation in slices.

- **ETSI GS NFV-IFA 007 V3.6.1 (2022-01)**: It defines the Or-Vnfm reference point. This framework specifies the interface between the NFVO and VNFM, relevant for managing VNFs within slices.

- **ETSI GS NFV-IFA 008 V3.6.1 (2022-01)**: It defines the Ve-Vnfm reference point. This document defines the interface between the VNFM and VNFs, important for configuring VNFs in slices.

- **ETSI GR NFV 001 V1.3.1 (2021-02)**: Released in February 2021, this document outlines NFV use cases, with a particular focus on scenarios involving network slicing.

Next Generation Mobile Networks

Next Generation Mobile Networks (**NGMN**) has been instrumental in developing the conceptual framework for network slicing. They have published several influential white papers that outline the vision, requirements, and architecture for end-to-end network slicing. NGMN's work emphasizes the importance of slicing across different network domains, including RAN, core, and transport. They have defined key concepts such as slice blueprints, which serve as templates for creating and managing slices. NGMN has also focused on the business aspects of network slicing, exploring how it can enable new service models and revenue streams for operators.

International Telecommunication Union

The **International Telecommunication Union** (**ITU-T**) has developed recommendations for network slicing as part of its work on IMT-2020 (5G) networks. Their framework, listed in the following, addresses various aspects of network slicing, including slice management, orchestration, and security. ITU-T has defined a logical architecture for network slicing that includes components like the **slice management function** (**SMF**) and **slice orchestration function** (**SOF**). They have also worked on standardizing the interfaces between these components to ensure interoperability. ITU-T's recommendations guide how to implement network slicing in a way that meets the diverse requirements of different vertical industries.

- **ITU-T Y.3100 (2017)**: Terms and definitions for IMT-2020 network. This document provides foundational terminology for 5G networks, including network slicing concepts.

- **ITU-T Y.3011 (2018)**: Framework of network virtualization for future networks. While not exclusively about network slicing, it provides important context for the virtualization technologies underlying slicing.

- **ITU-T Y.3111 (2017)**: IMT-2020 network management and orchestration framework. This recommendation describes the management and orchestration framework for IMT-2020 networks, including aspects of network slicing.

- **ITU-T Y.3112 (2018)**: Framework for the support of network slicing in the IMT-2020 network. This is a key document that specifically addresses network slicing, providing a comprehensive framework for its implementation in 5G networks.

- **ITU-T Y.3150 (2020)**: High-level technical characteristics of network softwarization for IMT-2020. This recommendation includes network slicing as a key aspect of network softwarization in 5G.

- **ITU-T Y.3170 (2018)**: Requirements for network slicing with cloud-native architecture in IMT-2020 networks. This document focuses on the requirements for implementing network slicing using cloud-native architectures.

- **ITU-T Y.3172 (2019)**: Architectural framework for ML in future networks including IMT-2020. While this document is primarily about ML, this recommendation includes considerations for applying ML to network slicing.

- **ITU-T Y.3174 (2020)**: Framework for data handling to enable ML in future networks including IMT-2020. This document includes aspects of data handling for network slicing in the context of ML applications.

GSM Association

GSM Association (GSMA) has focused on developing practical guidelines for implementing network slicing in commercial networks. They have published several documents, like the ones listed in the following, that address both the technical and operational aspects of network slicing. GSMA's work includes defining slice types, such as eMBB, uRLLC, and mMTC. They have also developed guidelines for slice management, including how to handle roaming scenarios with network slices. GSMA's framework emphasizes the importance of standardized APIs and interfaces to enable interoperability between different vendors and operators.

- **GSMA NG.116 (Generic Network Slice Template)**: This document defines a standard template for describing network slices.

- **GSMA PRD NG.127 (E2E Network Slicing Architecture)**: This outlines the end-to-end architecture for network slicing.

- **GSMA NG.132 (5G Network Slicing Roaming Guidelines)**: This provides guidelines for implementing network slicing in roaming scenarios.

- **GSMA PRD IR.42 (Definition of QoS parameters and their computation)**: While not exclusively about network slicing, this document is relevant as it defines QoS parameters that are important in slice design.

- **GSMA NG.114 (5G Roaming Guidelines)**: This document includes information on how network slicing impacts roaming.

- **GSMA PRD NG.113 (5G Roaming Security)**: This covers security aspects of 5G networks, including considerations for network slicing.

- **GSMA NG.123 (Network Slicing Charging)**: This document provides guidelines on charging mechanisms for network slices.

GSMA has developed the **Generic Network Slice Template (GST)**, which is a set of attributes that can characterize a type of network slice/service. GST is generic and is not tied to any specific network deployment. The **Network Slice Type (NEST)** is a GST filled with values. The values are assigned to express a given set of requirements to support a network slice customer use case. The NEST is an input to the network slice preparation performed by the NSP; the following figure depicts this:

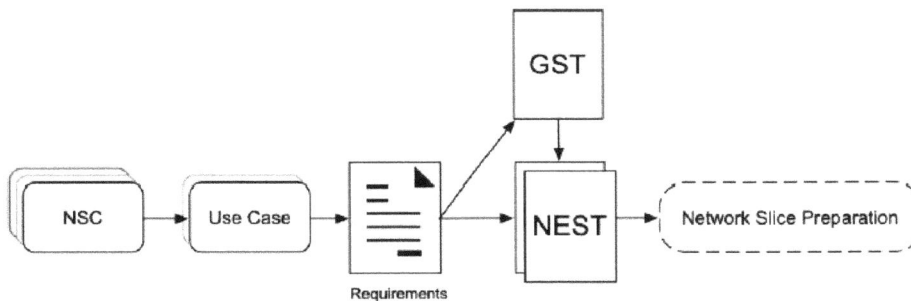

Figure 9.4: *GSMA network slice template*[2]

Open Network Automation Platform

Open Network Automation Platform (ONAP) has made significant contributions to network slicing, particularly in the areas of orchestration, automation, and management. ONAP provides a comprehensive framework for designing, creating, and managing network slices. Its architecture includes key components that are crucial for network slicing implementation. The design-time framework allows for the creation of slice templates and models, while the Runtime Framework handles the instantiation and lifecycle management of network slices. ONAP's approach enables operators to define, deploy, and manage end-to-end network slices across multi-domain and multi-technology environments.

One of ONAP's primary contributions is its sophisticated orchestration capabilities. The platform includes a **service orchestrator (SO)** that can coordinate the deployment of network services across different domains, which is essential for end-to-end network slicing. ONAP's network slicing use case demonstrates how the platform can be used to create and manage network slices, including the ability to design slice templates, instantiate slices, and monitor their performance. This orchestration extends from the core network to RAN, ensuring comprehensive slice management.

2   Source: **https://www.gsma.com/newsroom/wp-content/uploads/NG.116-v4.0-2.pdf**

ONAP incorporates a Policy Framework that is particularly valuable for network slicing. This framework allows operators to define and enforce policies for slice creation, modification, and termination. These policies can be based on various factors such as SLAs, resource utilization, and network conditions. The policy-driven approach enables dynamic and automated management of network slices, ensuring that each slice meets its specific requirements while optimizing overall network resource usage.

ONAP works in conjunction with other industry standards and technologies to enhance network slicing capabilities. For instance, it integrates with 3GPP specifications for network slicing and supports ETSI NFV standards. ONAP also incorporates SDN controllers, allowing for dynamic control of network resources across slices. This integration ensures that ONAP-based network slicing solutions are interoperable and align with broader industry efforts.

The ONAP end-to-end network slicing architecture and interfaces are shown in the following figure:

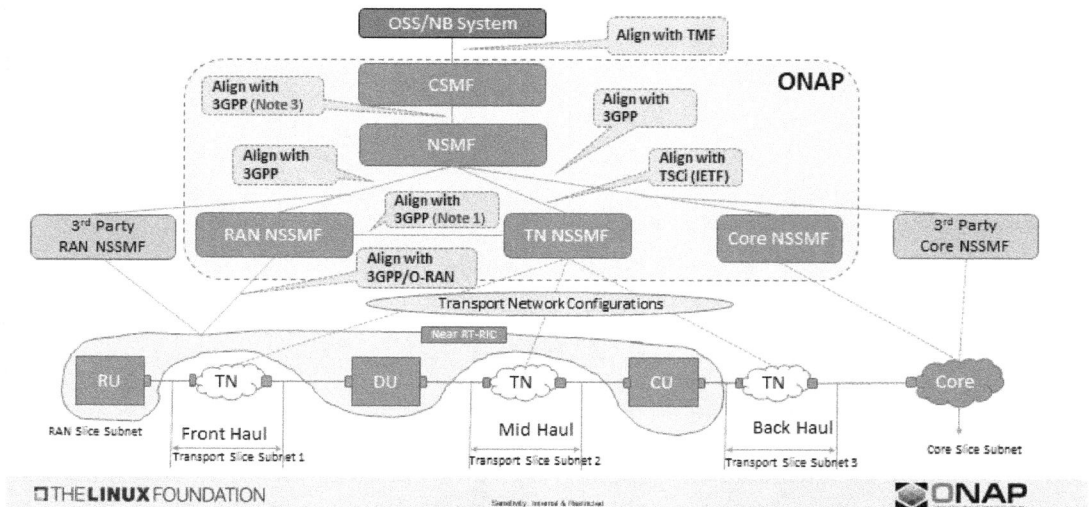

Figure 9.5: ONAP E2E Network Slicing Architecture[3]

Soft and hard slicing

Soft and hard slicing are two approaches to implementing network slicing in a 5G environment. These concepts apply across the different components of a 5G network like RAN, transport network, and core network.

Soft slicing, also known as virtual slicing or resource partitioning, involves the logical separation of network resources without strict physical isolation. In this approach, resources are shared dynamically among different slices based on their requirements and

---

3   Source: **https://docs.onap.org/projects/onap-so/en/as_orchestration/developer_info/E2E_Net-work_Slicing_Understanding.html**

priorities. Soft slicing offers flexibility and efficient resource utilization but may provide less guaranteed performance isolation between slices. Hard slicing, also called physical slicing or **resource dedication**, involves the allocation of dedicated physical resources to each network slice. This approach provides strong isolation between slices, ensuring guaranteed performance and security. However, it can be less flexible and potentially less efficient in terms of resource utilization compared to soft slicing.

RAN slicing considerations

In the RAN, soft slicing is implemented through the dynamic allocation of radio resources. This approach leverages techniques such as **dynamic spectrum sharing** (**DSS**), which allows multiple slices to share the same spectrum based on their real-time needs. Flexible numerology is another key aspect, where subcarrier spacing, and slot duration are adjusted to accommodate varying service requirements across different slices. Additionally, QoS class identifiers are employed to prioritize traffic based on service types, ensuring that critical slices receive necessary resources even during network congestion. This soft slicing approach in RAN enables efficient use of the limited radio spectrum but may not guarantee absolute performance isolation between slices during periods of high network load.

Conversely, hard slicing in the RAN involves dedicating specific physical resources to each slice. This can be achieved through spectrum splitting, where dedicated frequency bands are allocated to different slices, ensuring they have exclusive access to those frequencies. Another method is the use of beamforming technology, where dedicated antenna beams are assigned to specific slices, providing them with isolated spatial resources. Cell splitting is also employed, dedicating small cells or specific sectors to slices. While this hard slicing approach in RAN provides guaranteed performance and strong isolation between slices, it may lead to underutilization of resources if traffic demands fluctuate significantly across different slices.

A diagrammatic representation of RAN slicing is shown in the following figure:

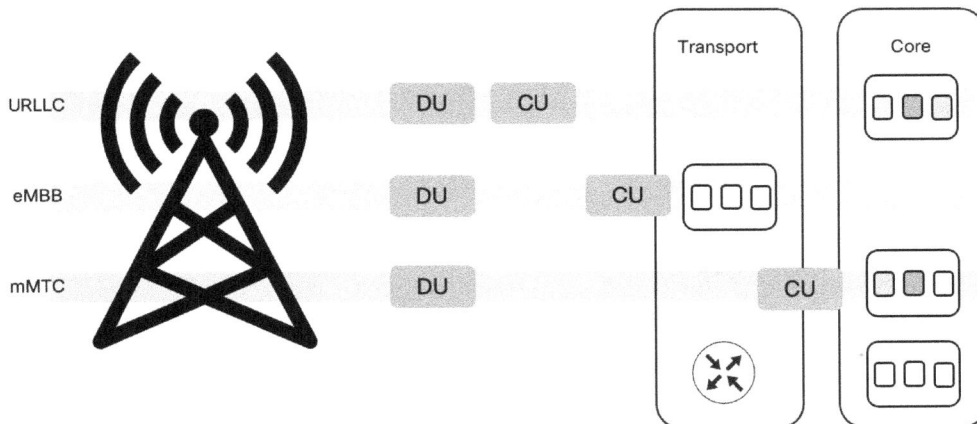

Figure 9.6: *RAN slicing*

Transport slicing considerations

In the transport network, soft slicing often leverages technologies that allow for logical separation and prioritization of traffic. **Virtual LANs (VLANs)** are commonly used to logically separate traffic for different slices within the same physical infrastructure. QoS mechanisms are implemented to prioritize traffic based on slice requirements, ensuring that high-priority slices receive preferential treatment in terms of bandwidth and latency. SDN plays a crucial role in the soft slicing of the transport network, allowing for dynamic adjustment of network paths and bandwidth allocation based on real-time demands of different slices. This approach provides flexibility in resource allocation but may not guarantee strict bandwidth or latency requirements during periods of network congestion.

Hard slicing in the transport network involves physical separation or dedicated allocation of resources. This can be achieved using dedicated fiber links, where separate physical links are allocated to different slices, ensuring complete isolation and guaranteed bandwidth. In optical networks, **Wavelength Division Multiplexing (WDM)** technology can be used to assign dedicated wavelengths to specific slices, providing them with isolated high-capacity channels. For slices with stringent timing requirements, **Time-Sensitive Networking (TSN)** techniques can be employed to provide time-guaranteed transmission. While this hard slicing approach ensures guaranteed performance for each slice, it may result in inefficient resource usage if traffic patterns vary significantly across slices or over time.

A diagrammatic representation of transport slicing is shown in the following figure:

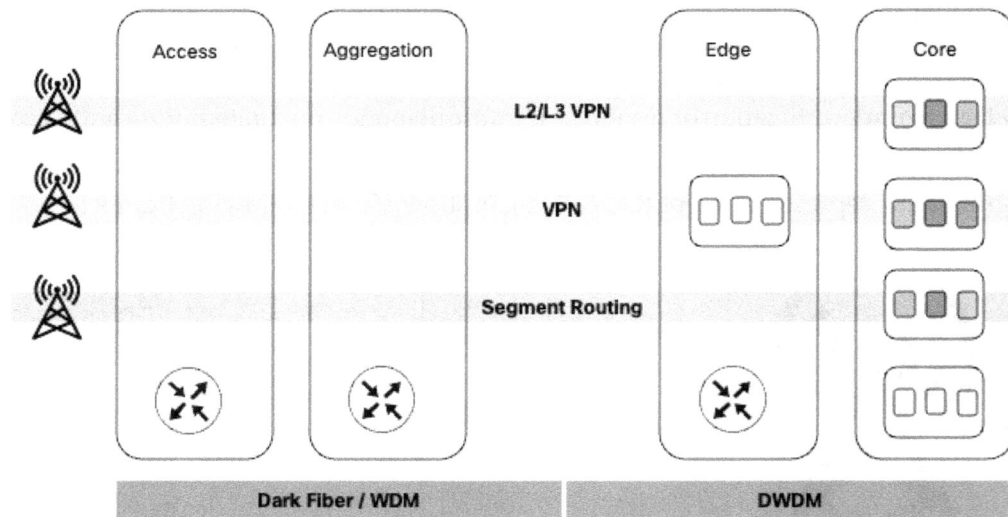

Figure 9.7: Transport slicing

Core slicing considerations

In the core network, soft slicing often revolves around the concept of virtualization and flexible resource allocation. NFV is a key enabler, allowing multiple slices to share virtualized instances of core network functions. These virtualized functions can be dynamically scaled and allocated based on the needs of each slice. The **Control and User Plane Separation (CUPS)** architecture facilitates flexible allocation of control and user plane resources, allowing for more efficient use of network resources across slices. **Service Function Chaining (SFC)** is another important aspect of soft slicing in the core, enabling the dynamic composition of service chains tailored to the specific requirements of each slice. While this approach provides significant flexibility in resource allocation, it may lead to performance variability under high load conditions, as slices compete for shared resources.

Hard slicing in the core network involves the dedication of separate physical or heavily isolated virtual resources to each slice. This can be implemented through the allocation of dedicated instances of core network functions, such as separate **Access and Mobility Management Function (AMF)**, **Session Management Function (SMF)**, and **User Plane Function (UPF)** for each slice. Physical resource dedication goes a step further, assigning separate compute, storage, and networking resources to slice-specific functions. In some cases, completely isolated network segments may be created for different slices, providing the highest level of separation. This hard slicing approach in the core network ensures strong isolation and guaranteed performance for each slice, but it comes at the cost of potentially higher infrastructure requirements and the risk of resource underutilization if slice demands are not consistently high.

The following figure depicts the use of dedicated core network functions in a core slicing scenario:

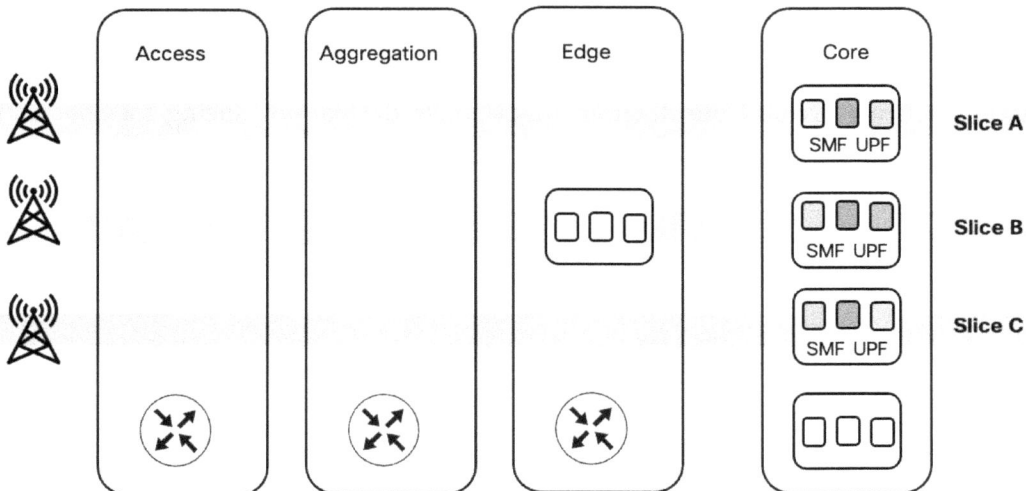

Figure 9.8: Core slicing

Slice architectures

5G network slice architectures are designed to cater to diverse use cases by providing tailored end-to-end connectivity across the RAN, transport network, and core network. These architectures leverage a combination of RAN, transport, and core slicing methods, as mentioned in the above section, to meet the specific requirements of URLLC, eMBB, and mMTC.

In the RAN, slicing can be implemented through techniques such as dynamic spectrum sharing, flexible numerology, and dedicated radio resource pools. For URLLC slices, the RAN may employ mini-slots and grant free access to minimize latency, while eMBB slices might utilize larger bandwidths and higher-order modulation schemes. mMTC slices could leverage narrowband allocations and power-saving modes to support a massive number of devices.

The transport network slicing often involves technologies like **Flexible Ethernet (FlexE)** or segment routing to provide deterministic latency for URLLC, high bandwidth for eMBB, and efficient routing for mMTC traffic. SDN and NFV play crucial roles in creating logical network slices across the transport layer.

In the core network, slicing architectures typically employ an SBA with modular network functions that can be instantiated and scaled independently for each slice. URLLC slices might have dedicated UPFs placed closer to the edge for reduced latency, while eMBB slices could utilize centralized UPFs for efficient high-bandwidth processing. For mMTC, the core might implement specialized functions for efficient handling of small, infrequent data transmissions from a vast number of devices.

The overall slice architecture is orchestrated by an NSMF that coordinates with domain-specific management functions to ensure end-to-end slice performance and isolation. This comprehensive approach to slice architecture enables network operators to efficiently support a wide range of 5G use cases on a single physical infrastructure, dynamically allocating resources and optimizing network behavior for each specific service type. A high-level slicing architecture diagram that depicts the various slicing for specific use cases is shown in the following figure:

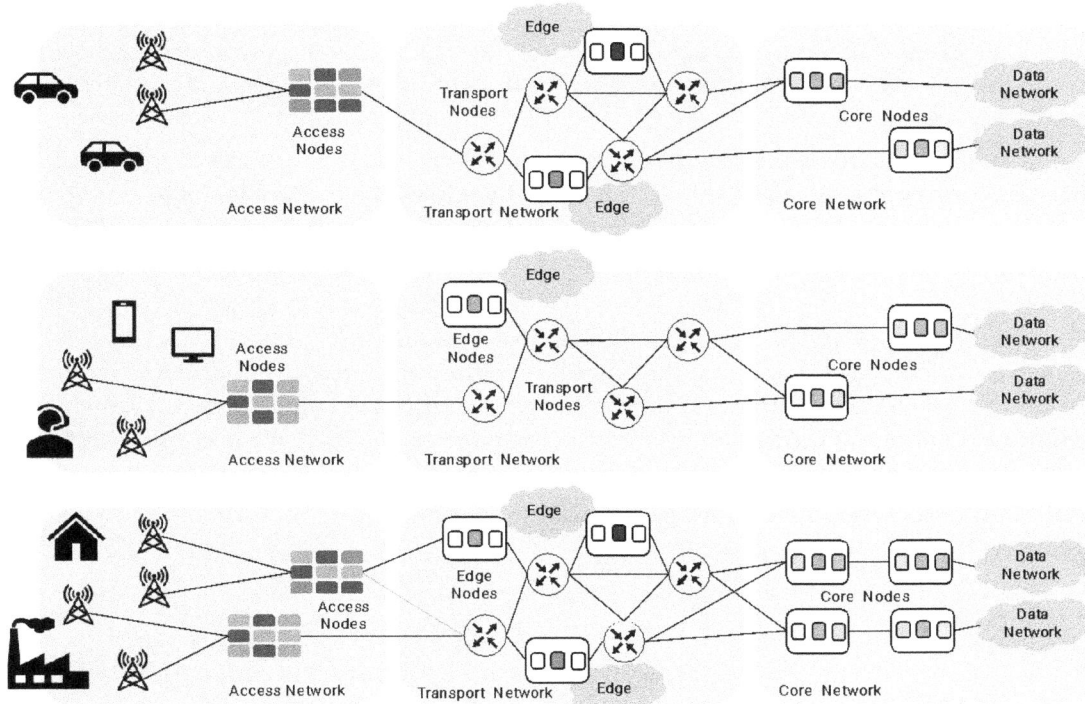

Figure 9.9: Slice architectures

Slice threats

5G network slicing introduces a complex landscape of potential vulnerabilities and threats that span various aspects of the network architecture. At the core of these concerns is the challenge of maintaining robust network slice isolation, where issues such as inter-slice interference, resource leakage, and side-channel attacks can compromise the integrity of individual slices.

The orchestration and management layer presents its own set of risks, including misconfigurations, unauthorized slice manipulations, and potential compromises of the orchestrator itself. Resource allocation mechanisms are vulnerable to attacks that could lead to unfair distribution or exhaustion of resources, impacting the QoS across slices.

Virtualization technologies, fundamental to network slicing, bring forth risks associated with hypervisor vulnerabilities, container escapes, and compromises of virtual network functions. Throughout the slice lifecycle, from instantiation to termination, there are opportunities for malicious actors to interfere with proper management processes.

Authentication and access control mechanisms must be robust to prevent identity spoofing, privilege escalation, and unauthorized cross-slice access. Data privacy and confidentiality are paramount concerns, with risks of data leakage, insufficient isolation, and eavesdropping on inter-slice communications.

The network functions themselves can be targeted, with the potential for compromise, malicious insertions, or manipulation of function chains. As edge computing becomes increasingly integrated with network slicing, it introduces additional attack surfaces at the network edge.

The signaling and control plane faces threats of overload, storms, and manipulation of slice selection processes. Even the underlying physical infrastructure is not immune, with risks ranging from hardware trojans to physical tampering. **Distributed Denial of Service (DDoS)** attacks tailored to exploit slice architectures pose significant threats to network stability.

Monitoring and analytics systems, crucial for maintaining network health, can be subverted through false data injection or exploitation of monitoring blind spots. Finally, the complex regulatory landscape surrounding 5G introduces compliance risks, including potential violations of data sovereignty and challenges in maintaining accurate audit trails across diverse slice environments.

A mind-map representation of the vulnerabilities and threats in 5G slicing is shown in the following figure:

Figure 9.10: Slicing vulnerabilities

Security concerns in slices

Securing 5G network slices is a multi-faceted challenge that requires a comprehensive approach addressing various layers of the network architecture. The dynamic and virtualized nature of 5G slicing introduces new security considerations beyond those of traditional mobile networks. 5G network slicing, with its promise of providing tailored, virtualized network segments for specific use cases, introduces a new paradigm of flexibility and efficiency in network resource utilization. However, this very flexibility also brings forth unprecedented security challenges that must be addressed comprehensively. The criticality of 5G slicing security stems from the fact that these network slices will support a wide array of services, ranging from mission-critical applications in healthcare and autonomous vehicles to massive IoT deployments and enhanced mobile broadband for consumers.

Each of these use cases has unique security requirements and potential vulnerabilities that must be safeguarded against. Moreover, the shared nature of the underlying physical infrastructure among multiple logical slices creates potential attack vectors that could compromise the isolation between slices, leading to data breaches, service disruptions, or unauthorized access to sensitive resources. The interconnected nature of 5G networks also means that a security breach in one slice could have cascading effects on others, potentially impacting critical national infrastructure or essential services. Additionally, the increased reliance on SDN and NFV in 5G slicing architectures introduces new attack surfaces that malicious actors could exploit.

These factors, combined with the evolving regulatory landscape surrounding data protection and privacy, underscore the critical need for robust, adaptive, and comprehensive security measures tailored specifically to the unique challenges posed by 5G network slicing. Failure to adequately secure these network slices could not only undermine the trust in and adoption of 5G technologies but also have far-reaching consequences for businesses, individuals, and national security. Therefore, investing in and implementing strong security frameworks, encompassing the need for confidentiality, integrity, and availability, for 5G slicing is not just a technical necessity but a fundamental requirement for realizing the full potential of 5G technology while ensuring the resilience and trustworthiness of our increasingly connected world. 5G network slices present several vulnerable areas, mentioned in the following section that require careful attention to ensure overall security and integrity.

Slice lifecycle

The 5G network slice lifecycle presents numerous opportunities for security vulnerabilities and threats to emerge, potentially compromising the integrity and safety of the entire 5G ecosystem. This lifecycle, which encompasses the design, instantiation, operation, modification, and termination of network slices, introduces complex security challenges at each stage.

During the design phase, misconfiguration of slice templates or inadequate security policies can lay the groundwork for future exploits. The instantiation process, where VNFs are deployed and resources are allocated, is vulnerable to attacks that could lead to unauthorized slice creation or resource hijacking. Attackers might exploit API vulnerabilities or weaknesses in the orchestration layer to inject malicious VNFs or manipulate slice parameters.

Once operational, slices face ongoing threats such as unauthorized modifications, where adversaries might attempt to alter slice configurations to degrade performance or redirect traffic. The dynamic nature of slice scaling and optimization introduces risks of resource exhaustion attacks, where malicious actors could trigger unnecessary scaling events, leading to service disruptions or increased operational costs. During slice modifications, which are common to adapt to changing service requirements, there is a risk of introducing new vulnerabilities or breaking existing security measures if changes are not properly vetted and implemented. The slice termination phase presents risks of data leakage or incomplete resource cleanup, potentially leaving residual data or access points that could be exploited in future attacks.

Throughout the entire lifecycle, the complex interactions between network slices and shared physical infrastructure create opportunities for side-channel attacks and cross-slice interference. Moreover, the automated nature of many lifecycle management processes in 5G networks means that a compromise in the management and orchestration systems could have far-reaching consequences, potentially affecting multiple slices simultaneously.

The ephemeral nature of some network slices, particularly those created for short-lived events or services, complicates security monitoring and incident response, as evidence of attacks might disappear with the termination of the slice.

Underlying technologies enabling slicing

The underlying technologies that power 5G networks, while innovative and transformative, inherently introduce a range of security vulnerabilities and threats in a 5G setup.

At the core of these concerns is the shift towards SDN and NFV, which fundamentally alter the network architecture. This software-centric approach, while offering unprecedented flexibility and efficiency, expands the attack surface significantly. VNFs can be compromised through software vulnerabilities, potentially allowing attackers to manipulate or hijack critical network components. The centralized control plane in SDN architectures presents a high-value target, if breached, it could lead to widespread network disruption or unauthorized access across multiple network slices.

The disaggregation of network functions in 5G also introduces new inter-function communication channels, each a potential vector for man-in-the-middle attacks or data interception. The extensive use of open-source software in 5G implementations, while fostering innovation, also brings the risk of inheriting vulnerabilities from the broader software ecosystem. Additionally, the massive increase in connected devices enabled by

5G, particularly in IoT scenarios, dramatically expands the potential for distributed DDoS attacks or the creation of large-scale botnets.

The introduction of edge computing in 5G architectures pushes processing and data storage closer to the network edge, potentially exposing sensitive information to less secure environments. The dynamic nature of 5G network slicing, while a key feature, introduces complexities in maintaining consistent security policies across rapidly changing network configurations. Furthermore, the increased bandwidth and lower latency of 5G networks can accelerate the spread of malware or the exfiltration of large datasets before detection systems can respond.

The use of mmWave frequencies in 5G, while offering high data rates, is more susceptible to physical interruption and could be exploited for localized denial of service. Lastly, the complex interplay between legacy systems and new 5G components in **Non-Standalone (NSA)** deployments creates potential security gaps at the points of integration.

Orchestration and management of slices

The orchestration and management layer of 5G networks, while crucial for the dynamic and flexible operation of network slices, introduces a complex landscape of potential security vulnerabilities and threats. This layer, typically comprising components like the MANO framework, NSMF, and various domain-specific management functions, presents an attractive target for malicious actors due to its centralized control over network resources and configurations.

One primary vulnerability stems from the extensive use of APIs for automating slice lifecycle management, resource allocation, and inter-component communication. These APIs, if inadequately secured or improperly implemented, can become entry points for attackers to inject malicious commands, manipulate slice configurations, or gain unauthorized access to sensitive network data. The dynamic nature of slice creation and modification processes also introduces risks of misconfigurations, which can be exploited to breach slice isolation or circumvent security policies. Furthermore, the orchestration layer's privileged access to various network domains makes it a prime target for privilege escalation attacks, where an attacker could potentially gain control over multiple network slices or even the entire infrastructure.

The complexity of managing multiple slices with varying security requirements increases the likelihood of human errors in configuration, potentially leading to security gaps. Additionally, the centralized nature of orchestration systems makes them attractive targets for DDoS attacks, which could disrupt the management of multiple slices simultaneously.

The use of virtualization technologies in the management plane also introduces risks associated with hypervisor vulnerabilities, where a compromise could lead to unauthorized access across multiple virtualized management functions.

Another significant concern is the potential for insider threats, as the orchestration layer typically requires high-level access privileges, making it susceptible to abuse by malicious insiders. The integration of third-party management and orchestration tools further expands the attack surface, potentially introducing vulnerabilities from external software components.

Lastly, the complex interactions between different management functions across the RAN, transport, and core network domains create opportunities for attackers to exploit inconsistencies or gaps in security policies across these boundaries. Addressing these vulnerabilities requires a comprehensive security approach that includes robust authentication and authorization mechanisms, secure API design, continuous monitoring and auditing of management operations, implementation of least privilege principles, and regular security assessments of the entire orchestration and management ecosystem.

Communication channels

The communication channels in 5G networks, while designed for high-speed and low-latency data transmission, can inadvertently introduce several security vulnerabilities and threats in a 5G setup. These channels, which span from the RAN to the core network, are susceptible to various forms of attacks and exploits.

In the RAN, the use of higher frequency bands and beamforming technology, while enhancing data rates, also increases the risk of eavesdropping and man-in-the-middle attacks due to the directional nature of transmissions. The increased use of small cells in 5G deployments expands the network's physical attack surface, making it more challenging to secure all access points against unauthorized physical access or tampering. The adoption of new radio protocols and signaling mechanisms in 5G introduces potential vulnerabilities that attackers could exploit to disrupt communications or inject malicious traffic.

In the transport network, the reliance on SDN and NFV for flexible routing and resource allocation creates new attack vectors. Malicious actors could potentially exploit vulnerabilities in SDN controllers or NFV management systems to redirect traffic, launch DoS attacks, or gain unauthorized access to network resources. The increased use of open interfaces and disaggregated network components in 5G architectures, while promoting innovation and interoperability, also expands the attack surface and introduces potential vulnerabilities at integration points.

In the core network, the SBA and the use of HTTP/2 for inter-function communication introduce web-based vulnerabilities that are not typically associated with traditional telecom networks. These could be exploited to launch API-based attacks or manipulate network functions. The end-to-end encryption mechanisms in 5G, while enhancing overall security, can also make it more challenging for network operators to detect and mitigate threats, as they have limited visibility into encrypted traffic.

Furthermore, the dynamic nature of 5G network slicing introduces complexities in maintaining secure isolation between slices, potentially allowing attacks to propagate across different logical networks if not properly managed. The integration of edge computing in 5G networks also extends the trust boundary to the network edge, introducing new points of vulnerability closer to the end-users.

These diverse and complex communication channels in 5G networks necessitate a comprehensive and adaptive security approach that addresses vulnerabilities at multiple layers of the network architecture, from the physical infrastructure to the application layer, to ensure the overall integrity and security of 5G communications.

End devices

In a 5G network setup, end devices play a crucial role in the overall security landscape, potentially introducing numerous vulnerabilities and threats that can compromise the integrity of the entire system. The sheer diversity and volume of devices connecting to 5G networks, ranging from smartphones and IoT sensors to industrial control systems and autonomous vehicles, create a vast and complex attack surface.

Each device type brings its own set of security challenges, often with varying levels of built-in security measures. For instance, many IoT devices are designed with minimal security features to keep costs low and battery life long, making them prime targets for exploitation. These devices can be compromised and used as entry points into the network or as part of botnets for launching DDoS attacks. The increased connectivity and low-latency capabilities of 5G also enable more sophisticated **Machine-to-Machine (M2M)** communications, which, if not properly secured, can lead to cascading security breaches across interconnected systems. Moreover, the proliferation of edge computing in 5G architectures pushes more processing and data storage closer to end devices, potentially exposing sensitive information to local attacks.

The dynamic nature of 5G network slicing introduces additional complexities, as end devices may connect to different network slices with varying security requirements, necessitating adaptive security measures. Malware specifically designed to exploit 5G features, such as NFV and SDN, could be deployed through compromised end devices, potentially affecting multiple network slices. Additionally, the use of mmWave frequencies in 5G, while offering higher bandwidth, also introduces new possibilities for eavesdropping and man-in-the-middle attacks due to the shorter range and increased number of small cells required.

The integration of AI and ML capabilities in many 5G-enabled devices also presents new attack vectors, as adversaries could potentially manipulate AI algorithms to make devices behave maliciously or leak sensitive data. The rapid evolution of 5G technology and the rush to market may lead to firmware and software vulnerabilities in end devices that could be exploited before patches are developed and applied. This situation is exacerbated by the fact that many IoT devices lack efficient update mechanisms, leaving them perpetually vulnerable. As 5G networks support critical infrastructure and services, compromised end devices could have far-reaching consequences, potentially impacting public safety, economic stability, and national security.

Security controls for slices

In a 5G slice environment, a multi-layered approach to security controls is essential to protect against diverse threats and vulnerabilities. Network isolation mechanisms, strong authentication and access control systems, encryption, IDS/IPS, **Security Orchestration and Automated Response** (**SOAR**) tools continuous monitoring and logging, and other security controls, when implemented cohesively, create a robust defense-in-depth strategy for 5G network slices.

Defense in depth

Defense in depth plays a crucial role in securing a 5G slice setup by providing multiple, overlapping layers of security controls throughout the network architecture. This approach recognizes that no single security measure is infallible and that a comprehensive security strategy must address vulnerabilities at every level of the network stack. In a 5G slice environment, this layered defense begins at the physical layer and moves up the network layer, virtualization layer, and application layer.

Physical layer security leverages the inherent characteristics of the wireless channel and advanced signal processing techniques to enhance the confidentiality, integrity, and availability of network slices. One key aspect is the use of beamforming and massive **Multiple-Input Multiple-Output** (**MIMO**) technologies, which allow for highly directional and focused transmission of signals. This spatial selectivity not only improves signal quality and capacity but also significantly reduces the risk of eavesdropping by limiting the physical area where the signal can be intercepted. Additionally, physical layer authentication techniques can be employed to verify the authenticity of devices connecting to specific network slices based on their unique channel characteristics or RF fingerprints, providing an extra layer of security against impersonation attacks.

At the infrastructure level, employing electromagnetic shielding and implementing strict access controls to physical network components, such as base stations, edge computing nodes, and core network hardware, adds an essential layer of protection against physical tampering and side-channel attacks that could compromise slice integrity.

Security controls like firewalls play a crucial and multifaceted role in securing a 5G slice setup, adapting traditional network security concepts to the unique challenges of the 5G slicing environment. **Next-generation firewalls** (**NGFWs**) can be deployed as VNFs that can be dynamically instantiated and configured for each network slice, providing tailored security policies based on the specific requirements and threat landscape of the slice. These slice-specific firewalls operate at multiple OSI layers, offering deep packet inspection, application-level filtering, and advanced threat prevention capabilities. They are particularly crucial at the boundaries between network slices, enforcing strict traffic segregation and preventing unauthorized inter-slice communication. In the control plane, firewalls protect critical network functions and management interfaces from potential attacks, filtering and monitoring signaling traffic to detect and prevent malicious activities such as slice configuration tampering or unauthorized slice creation. At the user plane level, firewalls can be strategically placed near edge computing nodes or at key aggregation points to provide localized security enforcement, reducing latency for time-sensitive applications while still maintaining robust security postures. The centralized management capabilities of these next-generation firewalls allow for coordinated security policy enforcement across the entire sliced network, ensuring consistent protection from the RAN through the transport network to the core. This centralized yet distributed approach to firewall deployment in 5G slicing not only enhances security but also contributes to the overall network performance by optimizing traffic flow and reducing unnecessary backhaul of traffic for security processing.

Security controls such as IPS, IDS, **web application firewalls (WAF)**, and API security play crucial roles in providing comprehensive protection across various layers of the network architecture. These controls work in concert to create a robust defense mechanism tailored to the unique challenges of 5G slicing. IPS and IDS systems, when adapted for 5G environments, can monitor network traffic patterns specific to each slice, leveraging machine learning algorithms to detect anomalies that might indicate potential security breaches or attacks. These systems can be configured to understand the normal behavior of different slice types (for example, URLLC, mMTC, eMBB) and quickly identify deviations that could signify unauthorized access attempts, data exfiltration, or slice isolation breaches. WAF become particularly important in protecting the management interfaces and APIs associated with slice orchestration and control. As 5G networks rely heavily on software-defined networking and virtualization, WAFs can safeguard these critical components against web-based attacks, including SQL injection, cross-site scripting, and application layer DDoS attempts. API security measures are essential in protecting the numerous interfaces between different network functions, management systems, and even between slices. By implementing strong authentication, rate limiting, and input validation for APIs, operators can prevent unauthorized access to slice resources and protect against API abuse that could lead to service disruptions or data breaches. These security controls can be dynamically instantiated and scaled for each network slice, ensuring that security measures are tailored to the specific requirements and threat landscape of each use case. For instance, a slice dedicated to financial transactions might have more stringent IPS rules and API security measures compared to a slice handling IoT sensor data. Moreover, these security controls can be integrated with the network's SIEM system, providing a holistic view of the security posture across all slices and enabling rapid incident response.

Security controls such as visibility, logging, and monitoring play a crucial role in securing a 5G slice setup by providing comprehensive oversight and enabling rapid detection and response to potential threats. Enhanced visibility across the entire slice architecture is fundamental, allowing network operators to maintain a clear, real-time understanding of the slice topology, resource allocation, and traffic patterns. This visibility extends from the RAN through the transport network and into the core, encompassing both physical and virtualized components. Advanced logging mechanisms are essential for capturing detailed records of all activities within and between slices, including user authentication attempts, resource allocation changes, inter-slice communications, and management operations. These logs serve as a critical source of information for forensic analysis in the event of a security incident and help in maintaining regulatory compliance. Continuous monitoring forms the backbone of proactive security in 5G slicing, leveraging artificial intelligence and machine learning algorithms to analyze vast amounts of data in real time. This includes monitoring for anomalies in traffic patterns, unusual resource utilization, unexpected changes in slice configurations, and potential indicators of compromise across the slice ecosystem. These security controls enable the implementation of automated response mechanisms, allowing for swift mitigation actions such as isolating compromised slice components, adjusting resource allocations to counter DoS attempts, or revoking access credentials in response to detected threats.

Encryption

Security gateway encryption plays a pivotal role in safeguarding 5G slice setups by providing robust protection at critical network junctures. In a 5G sliced architecture, security gateways (devices capable of performing encryption, like a firewall) act as fortified checkpoints, implementing strong encryption mechanisms to secure the boundaries between different network domains and slices. These gateways utilize advanced encryption algorithms, such as **Advanced Encryption Standard (AES)** with 256-bit keys, to encrypt all traffic passing through them, ensuring the confidentiality and integrity of data as it traverses potentially untrusted or shared network segments. For instance, at the interface between the RAN and the core network, security gateways encrypt the control plane and user plane traffic, protecting sensitive signaling information and user data from eavesdropping or tampering attempts. These gateways can be configured to apply slice-specific encryption policies, allowing for tailored security measures that align with the unique requirements of each slice. For example, a slice dedicated to URLLC might employ lightweight encryption algorithms to minimize latency, while a slice handling sensitive enterprise data could use more robust, albeit computationally intensive, encryption methods. Furthermore, security gateways often incorporate key management functions, facilitating the secure distribution and rotation of encryption keys across the slice infrastructure. This dynamic key management helps maintain the long-term security of the encrypted channels, mitigating the risk of key compromise. Additionally, these gateways can integrate with the network's authentication and authorization frameworks, ensuring that only authorized entities can establish encrypted connections within or between slices. As 5G networks evolve to support more diverse and critical applications, the role of security gateways and encryption in maintaining the integrity, confidentiality, and isolation of network slices becomes increasingly important, forming a cornerstone of the overall 5G security architecture.

Inter and intra-slice controls

Inter-slice security controls focus on maintaining strict isolation and preventing unauthorized interactions between different network slices, while intra-slice controls ensure the integrity and security of components within a single slice.

In the inter-slice domain, advanced virtualization techniques, such as hardware-assisted virtualization and secure enclaves are employed to create robust logical boundaries between slices. SDN controllers implement granular traffic segregation policies, ensuring that data from one slice cannot leak into or interfere with another. Secure gateways and firewalls are strategically placed at slice boundaries to monitor and control inter-slice communications, applying strict access control lists and traffic filtering rules. Encryption of inter-slice communication channels using robust cryptographic protocols adds an extra layer of protection against eavesdropping and man-in-the-middle attacks.

Within each slice (intra-slice), security controls are tailored to the specific requirements and use case of that slice. This includes implementing slice-specific authentication and authorization mechanisms, such as lightweight protocols for IoT-focused slices or multi-factor authentication for slices handling sensitive enterprise data. NFV security measures, including secure boot processes for VNFs and continuous integrity monitoring, protect against malicious modifications or compromises of slice components. IDS/IPS is deployed within each slice, configured to recognize and respond to anomalies specific to the slice's expected traffic patterns and behavior. Data protection measures such as encryption at rest and in transit, access logging, and auditing are implemented to safeguard sensitive information processed within the slice. Additionally, slice-aware security orchestration and automated incident response mechanisms enable rapid detection and mitigation of security threats, containing potential breaches within a slice before they can impact the broader network.

The synergy between inter-slice and intra-slice security controls creates a comprehensive defense-in-depth strategy, where multiple layers of security work in concert to protect the 5G slice setup against a wide range of potential threats and vulnerabilities, ensuring the confidentiality, integrity, and availability of services across all slices.

Slice security designs

5G network slicing enables operators to create multiple virtual networks tailored to specific use cases. The lifecycle of a network slice involves three key processes: activation, where a slice is initialized and resources are allocated; updating, which allows for dynamic modification of slice parameters to meet changing demands; and termination, when a slice is decommissioned, and its resources are released. Securing these flows is crucial, as each stage presents potential vulnerabilities. Robust authentication, encryption, and access control mechanisms must be implemented to prevent unauthorized slice creation, modification, or termination. The various controls that can be implemented into a slice activation and update workflow can be seen in the following diagram:

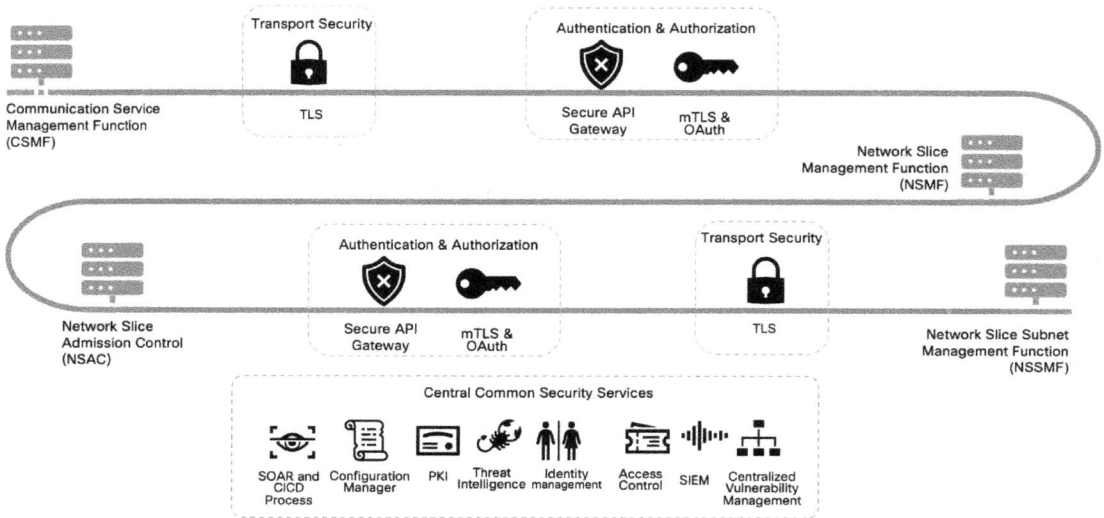

Figure 9.11: Security controls in a slice activation and update

The various controls that can be implemented into a slice termination workflow are mentioned in the following figure:

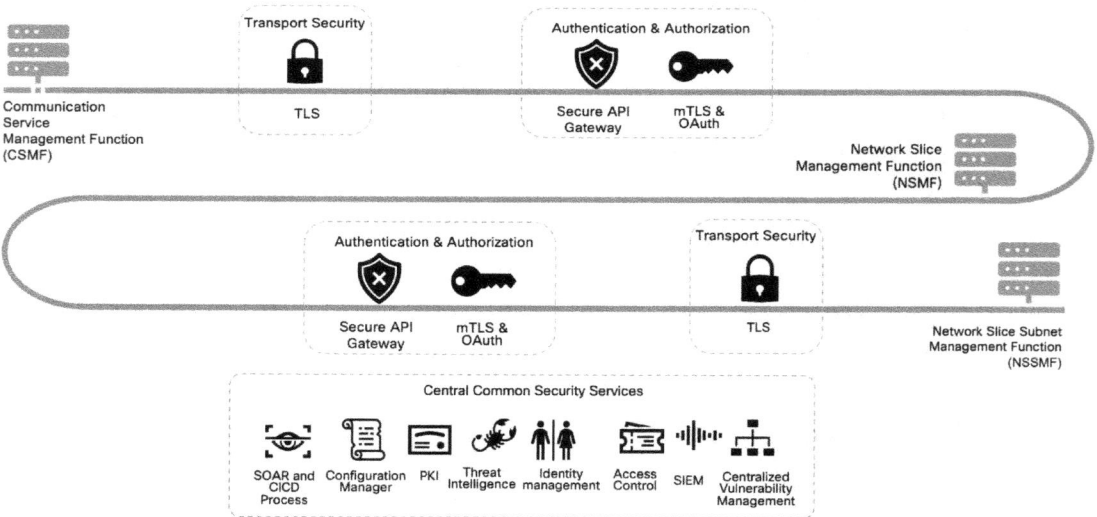

Figure 9.12: Security controls in a slice activation and update

5G network slicing requires comprehensive security measures across all network segments, as mentioned in this chapter. Key security controls include isolation between slices to prevent unauthorized access, robust authentication, and encryption for data protection, and NFV security to safeguard virtualized network components. Additionally, security orchestration and automation are crucial for managing slice-specific security policies. Continuous monitoring and anomaly detection help identify potential threats, while secure APIs ensure protected communication between network functions. Implementing these controls end-to-end from RAN to the core network and edge computing nodes is essential to maintain the integrity and confidentiality of each network slice. Based on the various security controls that can be implemented across the end-to-end 5G network, the following table depicts an overall view of security architecture for slices, and the table depicts the notations of the controls in the figure:

1	Firewall to secure connections from RAN and transport
2	DDoS mitigation solution to secure attacks from end devices
3	API security, mutual-authentications, and authorization controls
4	Data isolation, segmentation, mutual authentications, and authorization controls
5	Segmentation, mutual-authentications, and authorization controls
6	Segmentation between slices
7	Communications security

Table 9.1: Notations of the controls

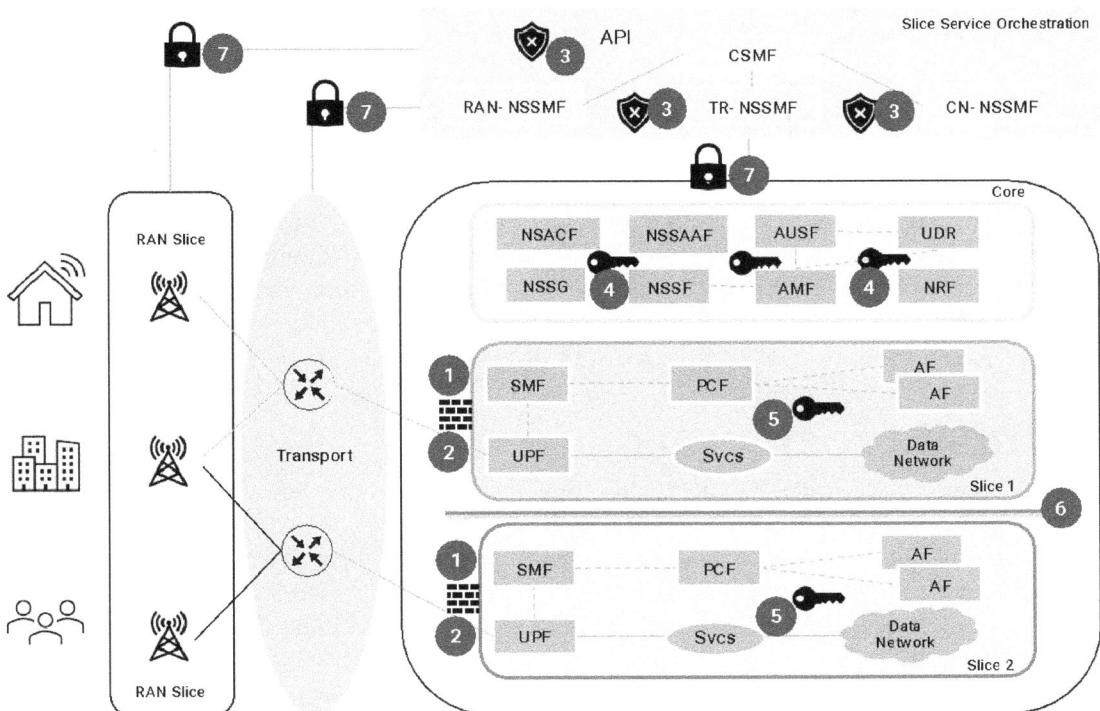

Figure 9.13: Slice security design

Conclusion

The network slicing has emerged as a pivotal technology in the evolving landscape of telecommunications, offering unprecedented flexibility and efficiency. The standardization efforts by organizations such as 3GPP and ETSI have laid the groundwork for interoperable and consistent implementation of network slices across different domains and vendors. Key network functions, including the NSSF and NSSMF, play crucial roles in enabling and managing these slices. The concept of cross-domain slice orchestration has opened up new possibilities for end-to-end service delivery, while industry frameworks like GSMA's GST have provided a common language for defining slice requirements. The distinction between soft and hard slicing approaches offers varying degrees of isolation and resource allocation, catering to diverse use cases and performance needs. General slice architectures have established blueprints for designing and implementing network slices across different network domains. However, as with any transformative technology, network slicing introduces new security challenges. Potential threats such as slice isolation breaches, unauthorized access, and resource exhaustion must be carefully considered and mitigated. To address these concerns, robust security controls must be integrated into slice designs, including strong authentication mechanisms, encryption protocols, and continuous monitoring systems. As network slicing continues to evolve, balancing the benefits of customization and resource efficiency with the imperative of maintaining a secure and resilient network infrastructure will remain a critical focus for the industry.

The next chapter explores the **radio access network (RAN)** and transport infrastructure that forms the backbone of telecommunications service providers. We will examine the evolution toward RAN decomposition and virtualization, detailing the Open RAN architecture that is revolutionizing network deployment through standardized, interoperable interfaces. The chapter will analyze critical RAN interfaces, their security requirements, and implementation challenges. Additionally, we will investigate transport network technologies that interconnect network elements, their inherent vulnerabilities and protocol exploitation, and comprehensive security strategies including encryption, network segmentation, and continuous monitoring that protect this essential infrastructure.

Points to remember

- Network slicing is a key technology in modern telecommunications, enabling the creation of multiple virtual networks on a shared physical infrastructure. Remember that standardization efforts, particularly by 3GPP, have been crucial in defining slice types and their characteristics. The network functions that enable slicing, including the NSSF and NSSMF, play vital roles in slice management and orchestration.

- Cross-domain slice orchestration is essential for end-to-end service delivery, requiring coordination across different network domains and operators. Industry frameworks, such as GSMA's GST and NEST, provide standardized ways to define and implement slices.

- The concepts of soft slicing (logical separation) and hard slicing (physical isolation) offer different levels of resource isolation and security. General slice architectures typically involve three layers: service instances, network slice instances, and network slice subnet instances, each serving specific purposes in the overall slice hierarchy.

- Security threats in network slicing environments include inter-slice isolation breaches, unauthorized access to slice resources, and potential DoS attacks on shared infrastructure. To mitigate these risks, security controls such as strong authentication mechanisms, encrypted communications, robust access control policies, and continuous monitoring of slice behavior are crucial. Additionally, implementing secure slice lifecycle management processes and ensuring proper resource isolation between slices is fundamental to maintaining the integrity and confidentiality of network slices.

Exercises

1. Discuss the role of standardization bodies in the development of network slicing. How do their efforts contribute to interoperability and widespread adoption of slicing technologies?

2. Identify and explain three key network functions that enable network slicing. How do these functions work together to create and manage network slices?

3. Cross-domain slice orchestration presents unique challenges. Describe a scenario where cross-domain orchestration would be necessary and outline the potential difficulties that might arise.

4. Compare and contrast the industry frameworks for network slicing proposed by different organizations. What are the similarities and differences in their approaches?

5. Explain the concepts of soft and hard slicing. In what scenarios would you recommend using one approach over the other?

6. Draw and explain a general slice architecture, highlighting the key components and their interactions. How does this architecture support the isolation and customization of network resources?

7. Identify three potential security threats specific to network slicing. For each threat, propose a corresponding security control that could be implemented to mitigate the risk.

8. How does the implementation of network slicing impact the overall security posture of a network? Discuss both potential benefits and challenges from a security perspective.

9. Evaluate the trade-offs between slice isolation and resource efficiency. How can network operators balance these competing demands when designing and implementing network slices?

10. Describe the process of slice lifecycle management. What security considerations should be considered at each stage of a slice's lifecycle?

11. How might the adoption of network slicing affect regulatory compliance in telecommunications? Consider aspects such as data privacy, quality of service guarantees, and network neutrality.

12. Analyze the potential impact of emerging technologies (for example, AI, edge computing) on the future of network slicing and its security implications.

13. Propose a framework for auditing the security of network slices. What key areas would you focus on, and what metrics would you use to assess the effectiveness of security controls?

14. Discuss the challenges of securing network slices in a multi-tenant environment. How can slice isolation be maintained while still allowing for efficient resource utilization?

Join our book's Discord space

Join the book's Discord Workspace for Latest updates, Offers, Tech happenings around the world, New Release and Sessions with the Authors:

https://discord.bpbonline.com

CHAPTER 10
RAN and Transport Security

Introduction

The **radio access network (RAN)** and its associated transport infrastructure form the critical foundation of modern mobile communication networks, serving as the first point of contact for user devices and facilitating the transmission of vast amounts of data. As these networks evolve to meet the increasing demands of 5G and beyond, they face a complex landscape of security challenges that must be addressed comprehensively. This chapter explores the multifaceted world of RAN and transport security, exploring the intricate interplay between network architecture, emerging technologies, and security imperatives. We begin by examining various RAN deployment models, from traditional centralized approaches to more distributed configurations, and how these choices impact the overall security posture. The concept of RAN decomposition is then explored, highlighting how the disaggregation of RAN functions creates new security considerations and opportunities. A thorough analysis of RAN threats follows, encompassing both traditional vulnerabilities and emerging risks specific to advanced RAN architectures. The chapter then focuses on the critical task of securing RAN interfaces and non-SBA reference points, emphasizing the importance of robust encryption, authentication, and access control mechanisms. Special attention is given to the **Open RAN (O-RAN)** initiative and its security implications, discussing how this open architecture paradigm introduces both new security challenges and innovative solutions. Transitioning to the transport network, we examine its inherent vulnerabilities, considering how the increased reliance on shared infrastructure and software-defined networking amplifies certain risks. The chapter concludes with a comprehensive overview of methods to secure the transport network, including encryption protocols, segmentation strategies, and advanced monitoring techniques. Throughout this exploration, we emphasize the interconnected nature of RAN and transport security, highlighting how vulnerabilities in one domain can have cascading effects on the other, and underscoring the need for a holistic, end-to-end approach to security in modern mobile networks. By providing this comprehensive perspective, the chapter aims to equip network architects, security professionals, and decision-makers with the knowledge and insights necessary to build and maintain secure, resilient, and high-performing mobile network infrastructures in an increasingly complex and threat-laden environment.

Structure

This chapter will cover the following topics:

- Introduction to RAN
- RAN decomposition
- RAN security
- RAN interfaces
- Open Radio Access Network
- ORAN architecture and interfaces
- ORAN security considerations
- Transport network
- Vulnerabilities in transport network
- Securing transport network

Objectives

This chapter aims to provide a comprehensive understanding of RAN and transport security in modern mobile networks. By the end of this chapter, readers will be able to identify and explain various RAN deployment models, including traditional macro cell deployments, small cell configurations, and cloud RAN architectures. They will gain insight into the concept of RAN decomposition and understand how the disaggregation of RAN functions impacts network flexibility and security considerations. The chapter will equip readers with knowledge of potential threats to RAN infrastructure, covering both physical and cyber threats, and how these evolve with changing network architectures. Readers will learn about the critical interfaces within the RAN and non-SBA reference points, understanding their vulnerabilities and the methods to secure them effectively.

The chapter will discuss the ORAN concept, exploring its implications for network security, including both potential vulnerabilities introduced by increased openness and the opportunities for enhanced security through greater visibility and control. Transitioning to transport network security, readers will develop a thorough understanding of the transport network's role in connecting RAN elements and its inherent vulnerabilities. They will explore various methods to secure the transport network, including encryption techniques, segmentation strategies, and the use of security gateways. By covering these topics, the chapter aims to provide a holistic view of security challenges and solutions in the RAN and transport domains of mobile networks, enabling readers to critically assess security architectures and implement robust security measures in diverse network environments.

Introduction to RAN

The RAN is a critical component of modern mobile telecommunications infrastructure, serving as the vital link between end-user devices and the core network. In essence, RAN encompasses all the technology and equipment responsible for connecting mobile devices wirelessly to the broader cellular network. This includes base stations, antennas, and the associated software that manages radio communications. In a typical mobile network, when a user makes a call or accesses data services, their device communicates with the nearest cell tower, which is part of the RAN. The RAN then processes this signal and routes it to the core network for further handling. As mobile networks have evolved from 2G to 5G, the RAN has undergone significant transformations to support increasing data speeds, lower latency, and a growing number of connected devices. Modern RANs are designed to handle complex tasks such as resource allocation, interference management, and seamless handovers between cells, ensuring that users experience consistent and high-quality mobile services. The efficiency and capability of the RAN directly impact the overall performance of mobile networks, making it a crucial focus area for network operators and equipment manufacturers alike as they strive to meet the ever-growing demands of mobile communications in our increasingly connected world.

Deployment of RAN (also called **access**) infrastructure in 5G is different from what is seen in earlier generations of mobile networks. The functions performed by base stations and other devices have been distributed using cloud technologies. The base station has been decomposed with the choice of distributing functions across locations.

The 5G NR network is composed of the next-generation radio access network and the 5G core network. 5G can run in both **Non-Standalone (NSA)** and **Standalone (SA)** modes. As such, the architecture can be composed of gNBs (like 5G base stations) and ng-eNBs (like LTE base stations, as shown in the following figure:

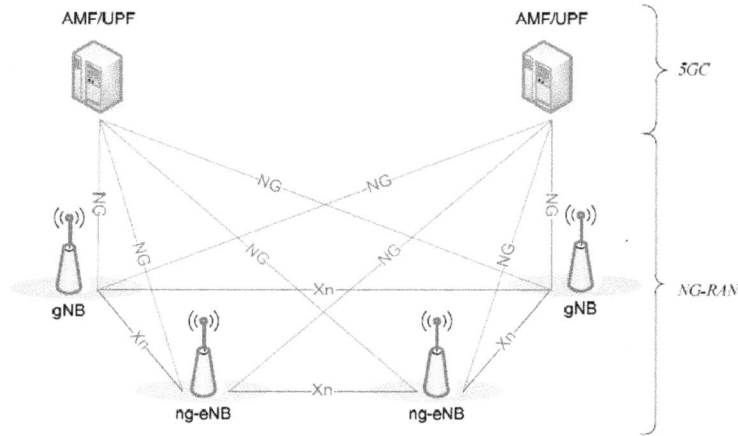

Figure 10.1: *General RAN deployment[1]*

As mentioned above, the RAN has undergone significant transformations since its inception. This evolution has seen various deployment models, each with its unique characteristics, advantages, and challenges, as shown in the following figure:

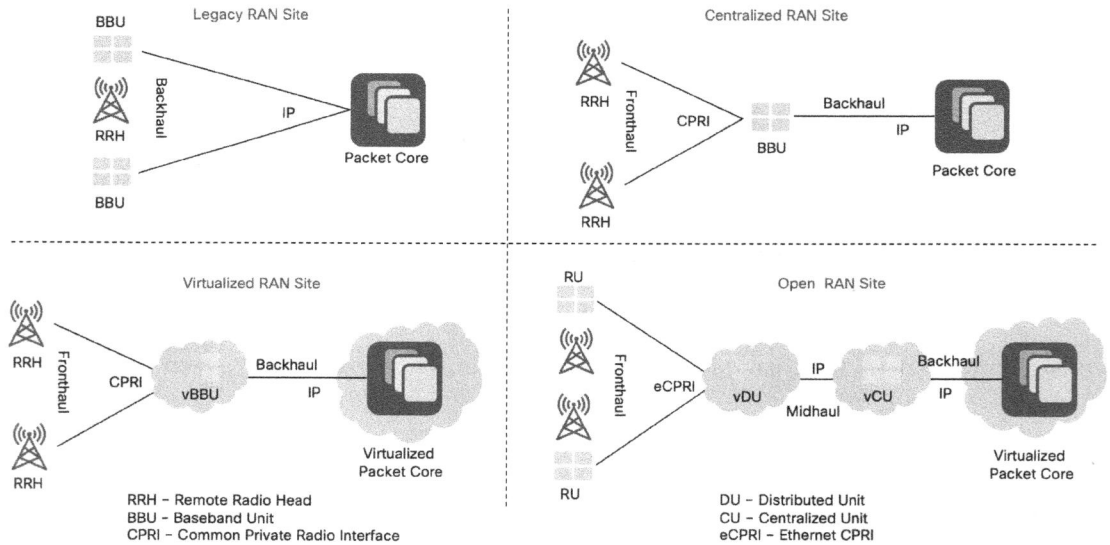

Figure 10.2: *Evolution of radio access network*

---

1   Source: 3GPP

Legacy RAN deployment

Legacy RAN deployments, also known as **traditional** or **distributed RAN**, have been the backbone of cellular networks for decades. In this model, radio equipment and baseband processing units are co-located at cell sites. Each site operates independently, with dedicated hardware and software from a single vendor. Legacy RAN deployments, also known as **distributed RAN** (**D-RAN**), represent the traditional approach to mobile network infrastructure. In this model, the **Radio Unit** (**RU**), **Baseband Unit** (**BBU**), and control functions are co-located at the cell site. This architecture typically utilizes proprietary hardware and software from a single vendor, creating a tightly integrated system.

In legacy RAN, the backhaul connection links the cell site directly to the core network. This connection is usually implemented using fiber optics or microwave links, depending on the geographical constraints and available infrastructure. The backhaul carries both user data and control signaling between the RAN and the core network.

While legacy RAN deployments have served the industry well for many years, they face several security challenges. The proprietary nature of the equipment can lead to vendor lock-in, making it difficult to implement uniform security measures across multi-vendor networks. Additionally, the distributed nature of the architecture means that sensitive baseband processing occurs at potentially vulnerable cell sites, increasing the attack surface for malicious actors.

Centralized RAN deployment

Centralized RAN (**C-RAN**) represents a significant shift from the legacy model by separating the baseband processing functions from the radio units. In this architecture, the BBUs are relocated from individual cell sites to a centralized location, often referred to as a BBU hotel or **Centralized Unit** (**CU**). The radio units remain at the cell sites, connected to the centralized BBU through high-speed, low-latency links.

C-RAN introduces the concept of fronthaul, which is the connection between the **Remote Radio Units** (**RRUs**) at the cell sites and the centralized BBUs. This fronthaul link typically uses **Common Public Radio Interface** (**CPRI**) or enhanced **CPRI** (**eCPRI**) protocols over fiber optic connections to transport the digitized radio signals. The traditional backhaul connection still exists between the centralized BBU location and the core network.

The centralization of baseband processing in C-RAN offers several security advantages, such as reducing the number of vulnerable sites and allowing for more robust physical security measures at centralized locations. However, it also introduces new challenges, particularly in securing the fronthaul links, which carry sensitive radio data. The high bandwidth and low latency requirements of fronthaul connections can make encryption and other security measures more challenging to implement without impacting network performance.

Virtualized RAN deployment

Virtualized RAN (vRAN) takes the concept of centralization a step further by implementing the baseband and other RAN functions as software running on general-purpose hardware. This approach leverages **network function virtualization (NFV)** techniques to create a more flexible and scalable RAN infrastructure.

In vRAN deployments, the connectivity model becomes more complex. The fronthaul connection between the RRUs and the virtualized BBUs remains like C-RAN. However, the backhaul connection now typically interfaces with a cloud-based or edge computing infrastructure where the virtualized RAN functions are hosted. Additionally, vRAN introduces the concept of midhaul, which is the connection between different virtualized network functions, such as the CU and the **Distributed Unit (DU)**, when these functions are split across different locations.

The virtualization of RAN functions brings both security benefits and challenges. On the positive side, vRAN allows for more rapid deployment of security patches and updates across the network. It also enables more sophisticated security monitoring and analytics using virtualized security functions. However, the increased use of **commercial off-the-shelf (COTS)** hardware and the complex nature of virtualized environments introduce new attack vectors, such as hypervisor vulnerabilities and inter-VM attacks.

Open RAN deployment

As detailed in the above sections, legacy D-RAN co-locates radio and baseband units at individual cell sites, relying on proprietary hardware. C-RAN improves resource efficiency by centralizing baseband processing while keeping remote radio units. vRAN takes this concept further by implementing RAN functions as software on general-purpose hardware, leveraging NFV for greater scalability. O-RAN promotes interoperability by introducing open interfaces, software-driven components, and intelligent network control through the **RAN Intelligent Controller (RIC)**, allowing operators to integrate solutions from multiple vendors for optimized performance.

O-RAN represents the latest evolution in RAN architecture, focusing on open interfaces, virtualization, and intelligent RAN control. O-RAN aims to create a more vendor-neutral ecosystem, allowing operators to mix and match components from different suppliers while ensuring interoperability.

The connectivity model in O-RAN builds upon the concepts introduced in vRAN. It maintains the fronthaul, midhaul, and backhaul connections but defines open interfaces for each. The fronthaul interface, based on the O-RAN Alliance's 7.2x split, allows for a more flexible allocation of functions between the RU and DU. The midhaul interface, often referred to as the F1 interface, connects the DU to the CU. The backhaul connection links the CU to the core network.

O-RAN introduces several new security challenges due to its open nature. The use of open interfaces and multi-vendor deployments increases the complexity of ensuring end-to-end security. The disaggregation of RAN functions also expands the attack surface, potentially exposing new vulnerabilities at the interface points between different components. Additionally, the introduction of artificial intelligence and machine learning capabilities in the RIC brings new security considerations related to the integrity and confidentiality of training data and AI models.

RAN decomposition

RAN decomposition, also known as **RAN functional split** or **disaggregation**, is a fundamental concept in the evolution of radio access network architectures. It involves breaking down the traditional monolithic RAN structure into smaller, more flexible functional units. This decomposition allows for the separation of hardware and software components, enabling network operators to distribute RAN functions across different physical or virtual locations based on specific performance, cost, and deployment requirements.

The **higher layer split** (**HLS**), using 3GPP terminology, refers to the RAN option two architecture where a typical base station is *disaggregated* into two units. A CU, housing **Radio Resource Control** (**RRC**), **Packet Data Convergence Protocol** (**PDCP**), and **Service Data Adaptation Protocol** (**SDAP**) functions, and a **Distributed Unit** (**DU**) housing **Radio Link Control** (**RLC**), **Medium Access Control** (**MAC**), and physical layer functions. The **Low Layer Split** (**LLS**), using 3GPP terminology, refers to RAN functional split options from option 6 (MAC/PHY split) down to option 7 (PHY split). These splits offer network operators greater flexibility, efficiency, and scalability by disaggregating RAN functions and distributing them across different network locations.

IEEE 1914 has defined a model for functional splits by introducing three logical block functions: RU, DU, and CU. The placement of the building block defines different networks, namely fronthaul, midhaul, and backhaul. The split and placement of functions are primarily driven by latency, throughput, and maximum distance thresholds. *Figure 10.3* shows a high-level diagrammatic representation of this split.

3GPP defines a further split in control and user plane, where the elements in the CU are split into control plane signaling (CU-CP) and one or more user plane (CU-UP) logical entities. The F1 interface was split into control and user planes, F1-C and F1-U.

With the separation of control and **User Plane Functions** (**UPFs**) within the CU, the different instances of the PDCP function are also split to allow the control plane (PDCP-C) and user plane (PDCP-U) to flow independently over F1-C and F1-U.

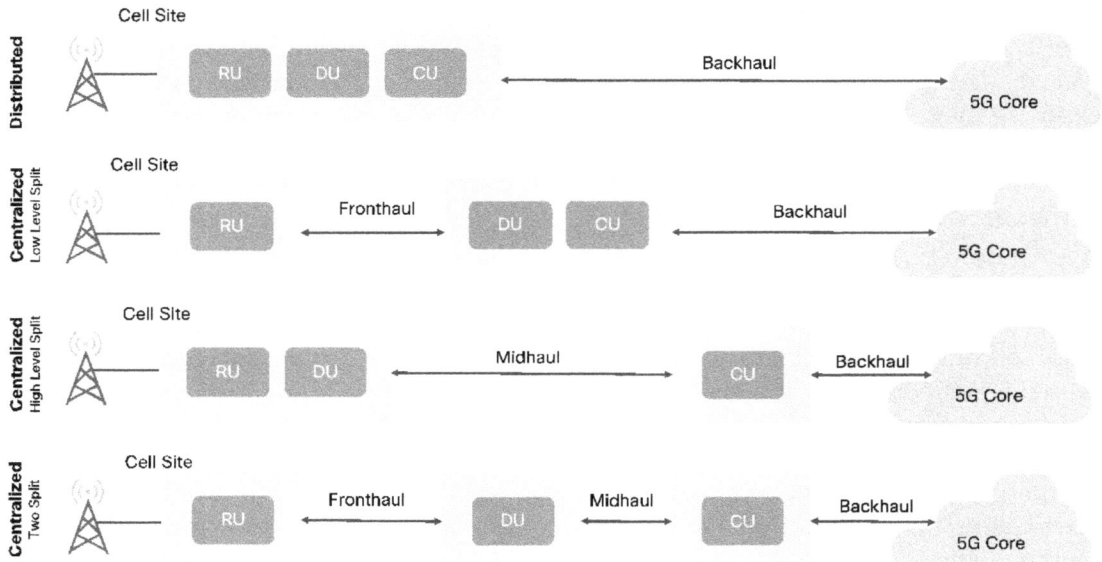

Figure 10.3: RAN decomposition

The 3GPP and O-RAN Alliance have defined several split options, each with its own characteristics and trade-offs, as explained in the following:

- **Split 8 (PHY-RF Split)**: This is the lowest layer split, separating the **radio frequency (RF)** functions from the **physical layer (PHY)** processing. In this configuration, only the RF components, such as power amplifiers and low-noise amplifiers, remain at the radio site, while all baseband processing is centralized. This split offers the highest degree of centralization but requires an extremely high-capacity, low-latency fronthaul link to transport the raw I/Q samples between the DU and the RU. The fronthaul requirements for this split are typically in the range of 10-25 Gbps per antenna, making it challenging to implement in many scenarios, especially with higher-order MIMO systems.

- **Split 7.2 (Lower PHY Split)**: This split, popularized by the O-RAN Alliance, places the lower PHY functions in the RU while moving the upper PHY and higher layer functions to the DU. The lower PHY typically includes functions like **Fast Fourier Transform/Inverse Fast Fourier Transform (FFT/IFFT)**, cyclic prefix addition/removal, and resource element mapping/demapping. This split significantly reduces fronthaul bandwidth requirements compared to Split 8, typically to around 4-10 Gbps per antenna, depending on the configuration. It offers a good balance between centralization benefits and fronthaul constraints, making it a popular choice for many 5G deployments.

- **Split 6 (MAC-PHY Split)**: In this configuration, the entire PHY layer remains at the radio site, while the MAC layer and above are centralized. This split further reduces fronthaul capacity requirements, typically to less than four Gbps per antenna. It allows for some coordination between cells but limits the potential for advanced joint processing techniques. The Split 6 option can be particularly useful in scenarios where fronthaul capacity is constrained but some level of centralized processing is still desired.

- **Split 2 (PDCP-RLC Split)**: This higher-layer split separates the **Packet Data Convergence Protocol** (PDCP) layer from the **Radio Link Control** (RLC) layer. The PDCP layer and above are centralized in the CU, while the RLC, MAC, and PHY layers remain in the DU. This split significantly reduces the bandwidth requirements on the midhaul link between the CU and DU, typically to less than one Gbps per cell. It allows for efficient implementation of dual connectivity and multi-RAT integration but offers limited benefits in terms of baseband pooling and joint processing.

- **Split 1 (RRC-PDCP Split)**: The highest layer split separates the **Radio Resource Control** (RRC) functions from the PDCP layer. This split is particularly useful for multi-RAT scenarios and allows for centralized control of radio resources across different access technologies. The bandwidth requirements for this split are very low, typically in the range of 100-150 Mbps per cell. However, it offers limited opportunities for resource pooling and coordination compared to lower-layer splits.

RAN security

RAN security is a critical aspect of modern telecommunications infrastructure, encompassing a wide range of requirements and use cases designed to protect network integrity, user privacy, and service availability. The security requirements for RAN systems are multifaceted, addressing various layers of the network architecture and potential threat vectors. At the physical layer, requirements include securing the radio interface against eavesdropping and jamming attacks, implementing robust authentication mechanisms for base stations and user equipment, and ensuring the integrity of over-the-air transmissions. Moving up the protocol stack, security measures must protect the control plane signaling, safeguarding critical network functions such as handovers, radio resource management, and access control. Data plane security requirements focus on encrypting user traffic, preventing unauthorized access to sensitive information, and maintaining end-to-end confidentiality. In virtualized and cloud-native RAN deployments, additional security considerations come into play, such as isolating network slices, securing virtualized network functions, and protecting the orchestration and management interfaces.

These security requirements translate into various use cases across different deployment scenarios. For instance, in critical infrastructure environments like smart grids or industrial IoT, RAN security must ensure the reliability and integrity of machine-to-machine communications, often with stringent latency and availability requirements. In public safety networks, secure group communications and prioritized access for first responders are essential use cases. For consumer-facing mobile networks, protecting user privacy, preventing identity theft, and securing mobile financial transactions are important. In the context of private 5G networks for enterprises, use cases include securing sensitive corporate data, protecting intellectual property, and ensuring the integrity of industrial control systems. As networks evolve towards Open RAN architectures, new security use cases emerge, such as securing the open interfaces between disaggregated RAN components, verifying the authenticity and integrity of software and firmware updates from multiple vendors, and implementing zero-trust security models across the distributed RAN infrastructure.

Multiple methods on RAN security articulated in the chapter employ a multi-layered approach to protect data, authenticate users, and prevent unauthorized access. Encryption mechanisms such as IPsec and TLS safeguard transmitted information, while PKI authentication protocols ensure both device and user verification. Access control strategies like RBAC restrict network resource access to authorized entities. Integrity protection via protocols like PDCP prevents data manipulation, and secure key management guarantees that cryptographic materials are regularly rotated and stored safely. Mutual authentication enhances security by verifying both ends of a communication link, while selective security policies provide targeted protection for critical network traffic. Lastly, security gateways improve overall protection by managing IPsec tunnels and securing traffic across network domains.

RAN threats

RANs face a diverse array of threats that span multiple layers of network architecture and exploit various vulnerabilities. At the physical layer, threats like jamming can disrupt radio communications, while eavesdropping and radio link spoofing compromise the confidentiality and integrity of transmissions. Physical tampering of base stations or user equipment poses risks to hardware integrity. Moving up to the protocol layer, attackers may launch signaling storms to overwhelm network resources, execute control plane attacks like rogue base station operations or IMSI catching, or perform man-in-the-middle attacks to intercept and potentially alter communications. Network infrastructure faces threats such as DDoS attacks, which can target both signaling and data planes, as well as DNS attacks and assaults on backhaul/fronthaul links. The increasing adoption of virtualization and cloud technologies in RAN introduces new vulnerabilities, including hypervisor exploits, compromises of VNFs, and attacks on orchestration systems and APIs.

Software-related threats encompass malware injection, firmware tampering, and unauthorized software updates, while supply chain attacks target the integrity of network components before deployment. User-related threats like social engineering, malicious apps, and SIM swapping exploit human factors and end-user vulnerabilities. The emergence of Open RAN architectures brings specific threats related to the **RAN Intelligent Controller** (**RIC**), open interface exploitation, and vulnerabilities arising from multi-vendor integration. **advanced persistent threats** (**APTs**) represent a category of sophisticated, often state-sponsored attacks aimed at long-term network infiltration and espionage. As networks evolve, emerging technology threats such as AI/ML model poisoning, quantum computing threats to cryptography, and IoT device exploitation in 5G networks are becoming increasingly relevant. Lastly, regulatory and compliance threats, including non-compliance with security standards and data privacy violations, can lead to legal and reputational risks for network operators. This diverse threat landscape necessitates a comprehensive and adaptive security approach that addresses vulnerabilities across all network layers and components, balancing robust protection with operational efficiency and user experience.

The mid-map model of the RAN threats affecting the mobile network is shown in the following figure:

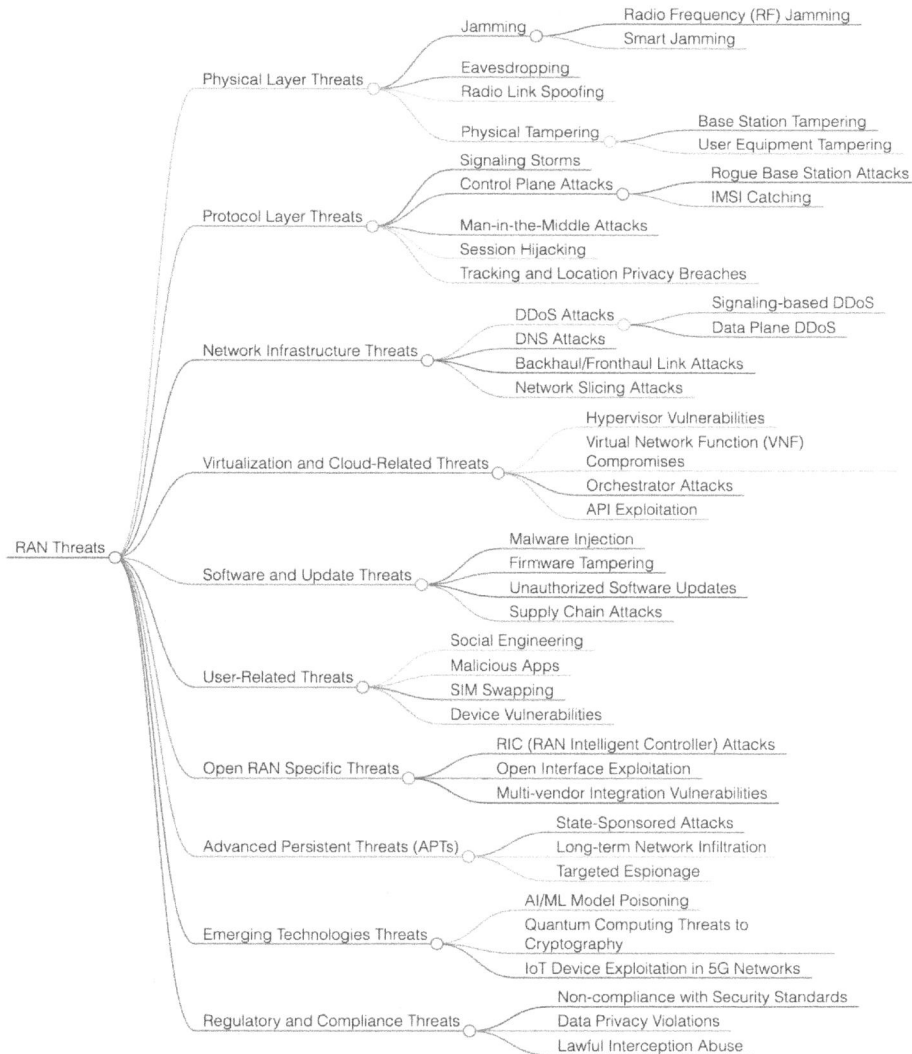

Figure 10.4: RAN threats

RAN interfaces

The evolution of cellular networks from LTE to 5G and the introduction of RAN split architectures have brought about a complex ecosystem of interfaces, each serving specific purposes in the network's operation. In LTE networks, the Uu interface serves as the primary connection between **UE** and the **eNodeB** (**eNB**), carrying both user data and control signaling. eNodeBs communicate with each other via the X2 interface, facilitating handovers and load balancing. The S1 interface, split into S1-MME for the control plane and S1-U for the user plane, connects the RAN to the core network, linking eNBs to the **Mobility Management Entity** (**MME**) and **Serving Gateway** (**SGW**) respectively.

As we move to 5G, the interface landscape evolves to support the new network architecture and enhanced capabilities, as shown in *Figure 10.5*. The NR-Uu interface replaces LTE's Uu, connecting UEs to the 5G base stations (gNBs). The X2 interface evolves into the Xn interface, maintaining similar functionality between gNBs. The S1 interface is replaced by the NG interface, again split into NG-C for the control plane, connecting to the **Access and Mobility Management Function** (**AMF**), and NG-U for the user plane, connecting to the UPF. New interfaces like N1, N2, and N3 are introduced to support the service-based architecture of 5G, facilitating communication between various network functions.

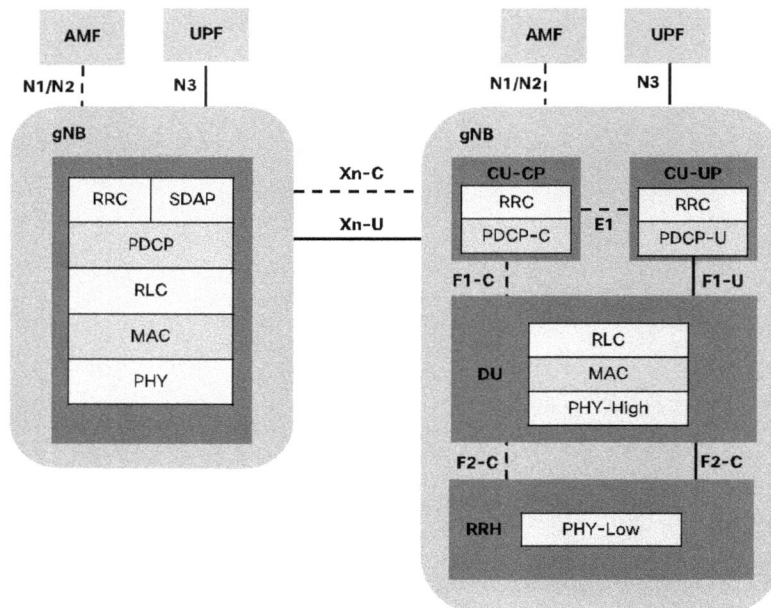

Figure 10.5: RAN interface types

The concept of RAN splitting introduces additional interfaces to support more flexible and open network deployments. The F1 interface connects the CU to the DU in a split RAN architecture, with F1-C handling the control plane and F1-U managing user plane traffic. When the CU is further split into control plane (CU-CP) and user plane (CU-UP) components, the E1 interface facilitates communication between these elements. In Open RAN architectures, additional interfaces come into play. The Open Fronthaul interface, based on an **enhanced Common Public Radio Interface (eCPRI)** or **Radio over Ethernet (RoE)**, connects the DU to the RU. The Open Midhaul interface, typically based on the F1 specification, links the CU to the DU, while the Open Backhaul interface connects the CU to the core network.

Security of gNB internal interfaces

The security of internal interfaces within the gNB (next-generation Node B) architecture plays a crucial role in maintaining the integrity and confidentiality of both control plane and user plane communications in 5G networks. Of particular importance are the F1 and Xn interfaces, which facilitate essential interactions between different components of the network. The F1 interface, split into **F1-C (control plane)** and **F1-U (user plane)**, enables communication between the **gNB Central Unit (CU)** and **Distributed Units (DUs)**. Similarly, the Xn interface, comprising **Xn-C (control plane)** and **Xn-U (user plane)**, supports inter-gNB communications necessary for functions such as handover and load management. Understanding the security requirements and potential vulnerabilities of these interfaces is fundamental to maintaining the overall security posture of the 5G network infrastructure.

F1-C and F1-U reference points

The F1 interface, which connects the CU to the DU in a split RAN architecture, is a critical component of 5G networks. It is divided into two parts: F1-C for control plane traffic and F1-U for user plane traffic. Securing these reference points is crucial to maintaining the integrity, confidentiality, and availability of the network. Protection of RRC signaling is provided by the PDCP protocol, which extends from the UE and CU and includes the F1-C interface. According to 3GPP TS 33.501, integrity protection for RRC signaling on F1-C, over PDCP-C, is mandatory, and the use of encryption for RRC signaling on F1-C, over PDCP-C, is optional.

While PDCP security provides protection, not all signaling messages are protected; it does not protect F1 management and UE context management. It is necessary to establish a new security channel between DU and CU. Options include protection over the network layer via IPsec and key exchange IKEv2 protocols, or by using DTLS over SCTP transport layer security.

3GPP standards outline that both encryption and integrity protection of UP on F1-U, over PDCP-U, are optional. For the F1-U interface, it is important to consider that PDCP-based integrity protection creates significant overhead, particularly on the air interface.

Enabling PDCP-U confidentiality and integrity protection for the F1-U interface needs close consideration. Not all PDU sessions or network slices require integrity protection. The 5G system is designed with the flexibility to enable selective protection of user plane traffic, as shown in *Figure 10.6*. A security policy is used to activate UP confidentiality and/or UP integrity for all DRBs belonging to the PDU session. For example, Integrity protection could be enforced for all PDU sessions associated with a network slice (NSSAI). The RAN vendor may also support conditional attributes (for example, max data rate of 64kb/s) for integrity protection.

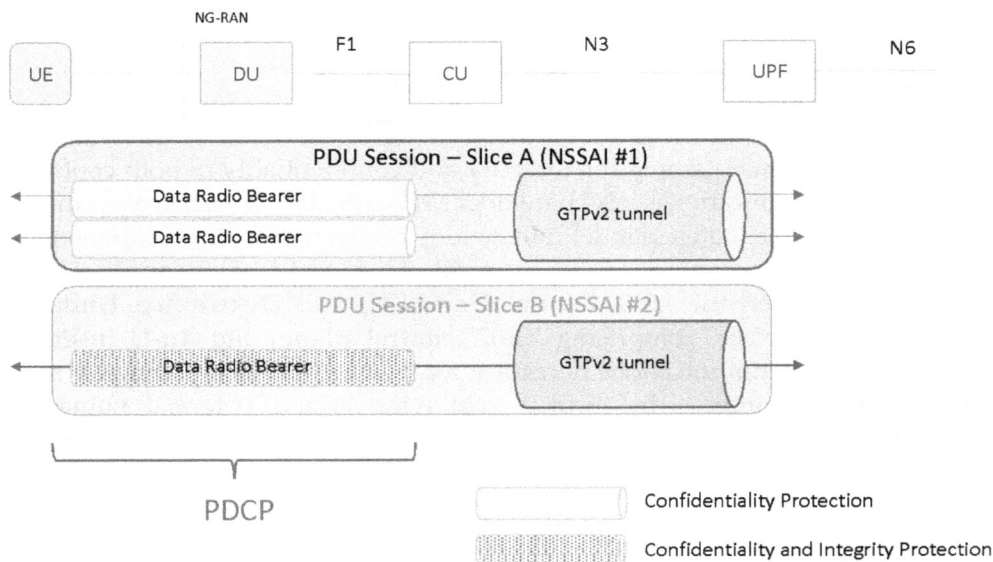

Figure 10.6: Selective security control for F1 interface

Xn-C and Xn-U reference points

The **Xn user plane (Xn-U)** and the **Xn control plane (Xn-C)** interfaces are defined between two NG-RAN nodes. The Xn-C interface supports UE mobility, which is known as Xn handover, which does not involve the AMF. Xn handover is only supported for intra-AMF mobility, where the UE transitions from one NG-RAN node to another NG-RAN node that is associated with the same AMF. Xn-U user plane interface provides non-guaranteed delivery of user plane PDUs.

The NG RAN may use SCTP to negotiate sets of source and destination addresses that may be used in a single association. The NG RAN may dynamically add/remove SCTP associations between the NG RAN node pair. The NG RAN may use SCTP multi-homing to support transport network redundancy between two endpoints, of which one or both are assigned multiple IP addresses.

As such, support for IPSec **transport mode** on Xn interfaces will be challenging for RAN vendors due to the complexities associated with supporting dynamic SCTP associations. An SCTP add/remove requires IPsec to establish new **security associations** (**SA**) and negotiate a new **Internet Key Exchange** (**IKE**).

At the time of writing, there was no broad vendor support for DTLS over SCTP. DTLS over SCTP only applies to Xn-C interfaces and is not mandatory for RAN vendors to support. The 3GPP RAN3 working group has raised concerns over the DTLS maximum user message limit of 16k bytes, as several RAN application messages can exceed this limit. Shown in the following figure is a high-level representation of securing the Xn interface:

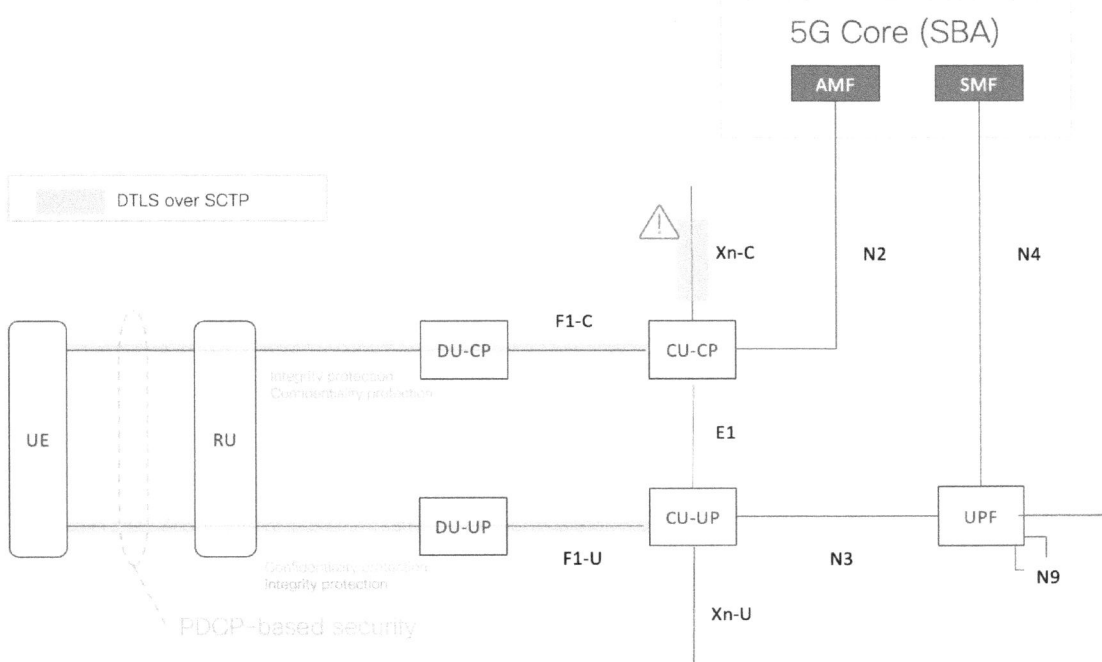

Figure 10.7: Security control for Xn interface

E1 reference point

E1 interface was introduced as part of the 3GPP Release 15 specifications, which laid the groundwork for 5G systems. The primary purpose of the E1 interface is to facilitate communication between two sub-components of the CU in a split RAN architecture: the CU-CP and the CU-UP.

The E1 interface carries several types of information between the CU-CP and CU-UP. This includes signaling for bearer management, which is crucial for establishing, modifying, and releasing data bearers for user equipment. It also facilitates the exchange of information related to QoS management, allowing the control plane to instruct the user plane on how to handle different traffic flows. Additionally, the E1 interface supports the transfer of user plane configuration data and assists in coordinating handover procedures when a user moves between different cells or network areas.

Security is a critical consideration for the E1 interface, given its important role in the network architecture. IPsec is mandatory for RAN vendors to support, but the use of cryptographic solutions to protect E1 is an operator's decision. Given that the IPSec **transport mode** does not require any additional investment, it is recommended to implement it. However, an operator may decide that cryptographic solutions may not be a requirement where the CU-UP and CU-CP have been placed in the same physically secure environment. Shown in the following figure is a high-level representation of IPSec control over the E1 interface:

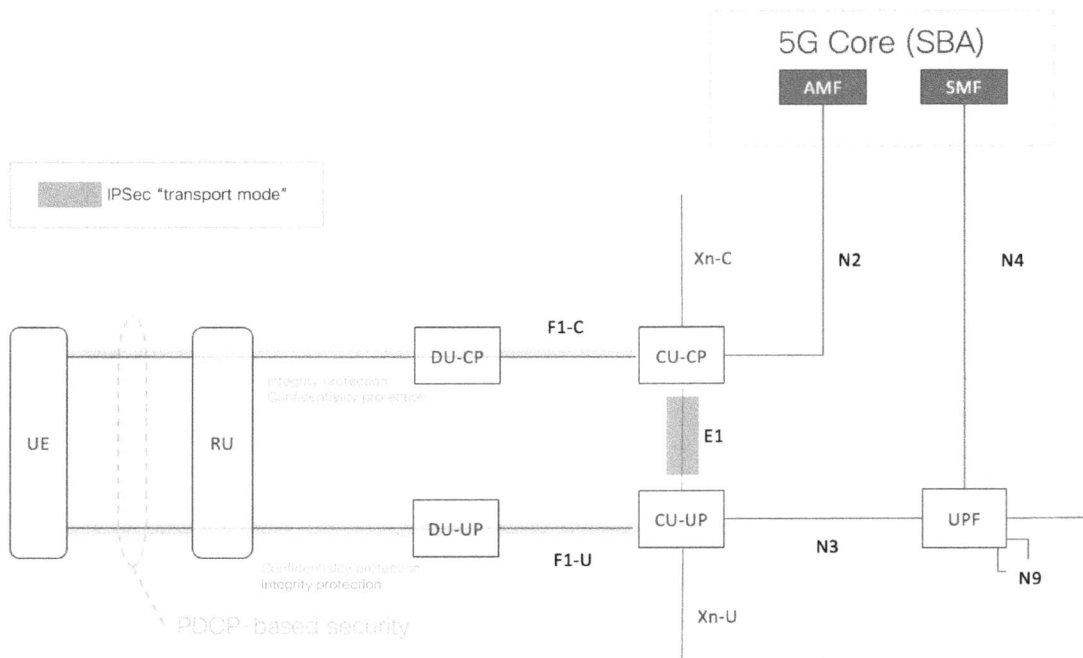

Figure 10.8: Security control for E1 interface

Security of non-service-based interfaces

The 5G network architecture introduces several key interfaces, known as reference points, that play crucial roles in connecting various network functions. Among these, the N1, N2, N3, and N4 interfaces are particularly important for the proper functioning of the 5G system. The N1 interface connects the UE to the AMF, carrying **Non-Access Stratum (NAS)** signaling. This interface is responsible for functions such as registration, authentication, and mobility management. It extends from the UE through the RAN to the AMF, ensuring that the UE can communicate with the core network for essential control plane operations. In the N1 interface, a NAS encryption key (KNASenc) and a NAS integrity key (KNASint) are used for NAS encryption and integrity protection of the interface.

The N2 interface links the RAN to the AMF, facilitating the exchange of signaling information between these two crucial components of the 5G network. It supports functions such as session management, handover procedures, and paging. The N2 interface plays a vital role in ensuring seamless mobility and efficient resource allocation within the network. Due to the criticality of the 5G system, 3GPP TS 33.501 standards mandate that the transport of control plane data over N2 shall be integrity, confidentiality, and replay protected. The use of cryptographic solutions to protect N2 is an operator's decision. For example, protection may not be needed where a gNB CU-CP is placed in a physically secure and co-located environment with the AMF. The N2-AP uses SCTP transport, which provides no protection. Therefore, an added protection mechanism is required. Protection options include IPSec and DTLS over SCTP. For IPSec, a **Security Gateway** (**SEG**) may be used to aggregate many IPSec tunnels on the 5G core network side. For DTLS over SCTP, a compatible gateway is needed to terminate DTLS.

Moving to the user plane, the N3 interface connects the RAN to the UPF. This interface is responsible for carrying user data traffic between the RAN and the core network. It supports high-bandwidth communications and is crucial for delivering the enhanced data rates promised by 5G technology. Integrity and confidentiality threats exist for user applications that do not implement a transport layer or other forms of application layer security. This can lead to data tampering, impacting the integrity of user applications and services such as DNS, and eavesdropping, which may result in information disclosure of user data. When selecting an UPF, operators should favor vendors that support features such as **deep packet inspection** (**DPI**), traffic optimization, and inline services (Firewall, DNS snooping).

The N4 interface, unlike the others mentioned, is entirely within the core network. It connects the **Session Management Function** (**SMF**) to the UPF. This interface is used by the SMF to control and manage the behavior of the UPF, including tasks such as session establishment, modification, and termination. The N4 interface is essential for implementing advanced 5G features like network slicing and edge computing, as it allows for the dynamic configuration of user plane behavior based on service requirements. The N4 reference point uses the PFCP protocol in the establishment, modification, and deletion of GTP-U tunnels on the N3 reference points between the UPF and SMF. By default, the PFCP protocol does not protect from DoS attacks, which can be caused by sending a *Session Deletion Request* or *Modification Request* to the UPF. The use of cryptographic solutions to protect N4 is an operator's decision. For example, protection may not be required where an SMF is placed in a physically secured location and co-located with the UPF. Protection options for N4 follow NDS/IP. For IPSec, a SEG may be used to aggregate many IPSec tunnels on the 5G core network side.

Security is a paramount concern for these interfaces, given their critical roles in the 5G network. To protect these interfaces, network operators typically employ SEGs and **Internet Protocol Security** (**IPSec**). Security gateways are network elements that act as secure entry and exit points for traffic flowing between different security domains. They are often deployed at the edge of the network to protect the interfaces that extend beyond the trusted core network environment, such as N2 and N3.

IPSec is a protocol suite used to secure IP communications by authenticating and encrypting each IP packet in a data stream. It operates at the network layer, providing end-to-end security for IP-based communications. For the N1, N2, N3, and N4 interfaces, IPSec is typically implemented in tunnel mode, which encrypts the entire IP packet and encapsulates it within a new IP packet. This approach not only protects the data payload but also hides the internal network structure, providing an additional layer of security.

The implementation of SEGs and IPSec for these interfaces typically involves establishing IPSec tunnels between the SEGs at the edges of different network domains. For example, an IPSec tunnel might be established between a SEG at the RAN edge and another at the core network edge to protect N2 and N3 traffic. Similarly, for the N4 interface within the core network, IPSec tunnels may be established between the network functions or their hosting environments.

Figure 10.9 depicts the security mechanisms that can be applied to these non-service-based reference points:

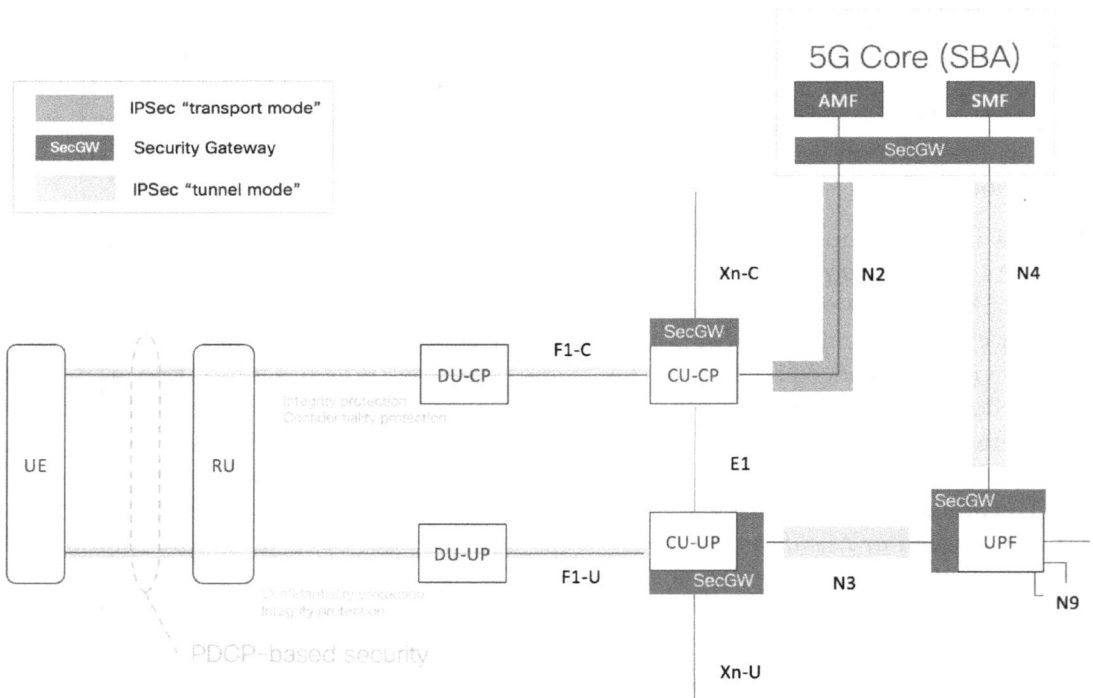

Figure 10.9: *Security control for non-SBA interfaces*

Open Radio Access Network

Open Radio Access Network (ORAN) is an innovative approach to mobile network architecture that aims to make RANs more open, intelligent, and flexible. It represents a significant shift from traditional, proprietary RAN solutions toward a more open and interoperable ecosystem.

At its core, ORAN promotes the disaggregation of RAN components, allowing for the separation of hardware and software elements. This disaggregation enables network operators to mix and match components from different vendors, fostering competition, innovation, and cost reduction in the telecommunications industry. The ORAN Alliance, a consortium of major telecom operators and vendors, is driving the development of open standards and interfaces to ensure interoperability between various RAN components.

One of the key features of ORAN is its focus on network intelligence and automation. ORAN incorporates AI and ML capabilities to optimize network performance, automate operations, and enhance overall efficiency. This intelligence is particularly crucial in managing the complexity of modern networks, especially with the advent of 5G and beyond.

ORAN has several compelling use cases across various sectors. In urban environments, it enables more efficient deployment and management of dense small cell networks, crucial for 5G coverage. For rural areas, ORAN's flexibility and cost-effectiveness make it easier to extend coverage to underserved regions. In industrial settings, ORAN facilitates the implementation of private 5G networks, allowing businesses to tailor their wireless infrastructure to specific needs. Additionally, ORAN's openness and programmability make it well-suited for supporting emerging technologies like edge computing and network slicing, which are critical for applications such as autonomous vehicles, smart cities, and Industry 4.0.

ORAN architecture and interfaces

The ORAN architecture, shown in *Figure 10.10*, represents a significant departure from traditional, proprietary RAN systems. It introduces a disaggregated and virtualized approach to radio access networks, emphasizing openness, intelligence, and flexibility. At its core, the ORAN architecture separates the RAN into three main components: the RU, DU, and CU. This separation allows for greater flexibility in network deployment and management.

The RU is responsible for digital-to-analog conversion, power amplification, and other RF functions. It is typically located at or near the antenna. The DU handles real-time, lower-layer functions of the protocol stack, such as parts of the physical layer and the radio link control. The CU manages higher-layer, non-real-time functions, including the radio resource control and packet data convergence protocol.

One of the key innovations in ORAN architecture is the introduction of the RIC. The RIC is further divided into two components: the **Near-Real-Time RIC** (**Near-RT RIC**) and the **Non-Real-Time RIC** (**Non-RT RIC**). The Near-RT RIC operates on a time scale of ten ms to one second and is responsible for fine-grained radio resource management, load balancing, and mobility management. The Non-RT RIC operates on longer time scales (>1 second) and handles tasks such as policy management, AI/ML model training, and long-term network optimization.

ORAN introduces several key interfaces to enable interoperability and openness. The fronthaul interface, often referred to as the *Open Fronthaul*, connects the RU to the DU. This interface is based on the **enhanced Common Public Radio Interface (eCPRI)** protocol and allows for the use of RUs and DUs from different vendors. The midhaul interface connects the DU to the CU, while the backhaul interface links the CU to the core network. Refer to the following figure for a better understanding:

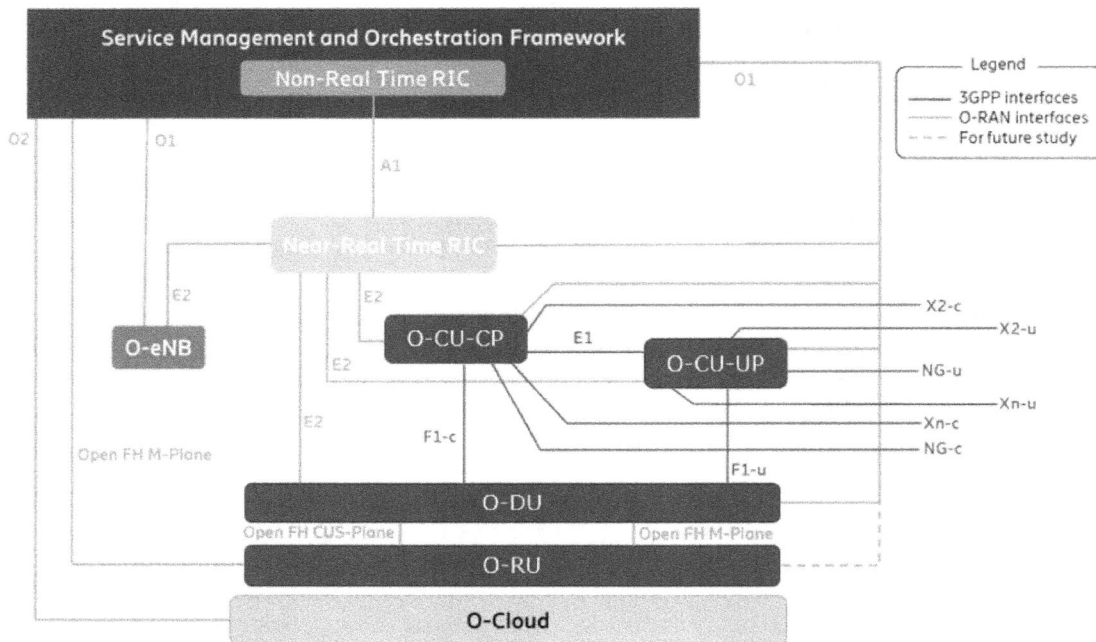

Figure 10.10: *ORAN architecture*[2]

The E2 interface is a crucial part of the ORAN architecture, connecting the Near-RT RIC to the DU/CU. This interface enables the RIC to collect real-time data from the network and implement control decisions. The A1 interface connects the Non-RT RIC to the Near-RT RIC, allowing for the exchange of policy information and AI/ML models.

ORAN also introduces the O1 interface for management and orchestration functions. This interface allows for configuration, fault management, and performance monitoring across all ORAN components. Additionally, the **Open Test and Integration Interface (OTI)** facilitates testing and integration of multi-vendor ORAN deployments.

---

2   Source: **https://docs.o-ran-sc.org/en/latest/architecture/architecture.html**

ORAN security considerations

The ORAN Alliance recognizes the critical importance of security in open radio access networks and has developed comprehensive security recommendations for the various interfaces within the ORAN architecture. These security controls are designed to protect the integrity, confidentiality, and availability of network communications and resources. Let us explore the key security controls recommended for ORAN interfaces in detail.

For the Open Fronthaul interface, which connects the RU to the DU, the ORAN Alliance recommends implementing strong encryption mechanisms. This typically involves the use of IPsec or other standardized protocols to ensure that the sensitive control and user plane data transmitted over this interface remains confidential and protected from tampering. Additionally, mutual authentication between the RU and DU is crucial to prevent unauthorized devices from connecting to the network. The alliance suggests using digital certificates and a **public key infrastructure** (**PKI**) to establish trust between these components.

The midhaul interface, connecting the DU to the CU, and the backhaul interface, linking the CU to the core network, also require robust security measures. The ORAN Alliance recommends implementing **Transport Layer Security** (**TLS**) or **Datagram TLS** (**DTLS**) to provide encryption and integrity protection for these interfaces. These protocols ensure that data in transit is secure from eavesdropping and manipulation. Furthermore, the alliance emphasizes the importance of secure key management practices, including regular key rotation and secure storage of cryptographic materials.

For the E2 interface, which facilitates communication between the Near-RT RIC and the DU/CU, the ORAN Alliance advocates for a comprehensive security approach. This includes not only encryption and authentication but also access control mechanisms. The alliance recommends implementing RBAC to ensure that only authorized entities can issue control commands or access sensitive network data. Additionally, the use of secure APIs and input validation is crucial to prevent potential injection attacks or other security vulnerabilities.

The A1 interface, connecting the Non-Real-Time RIC to the Near-RT RIC, handles policy information and AI/ML models. Given the sensitive nature of this data, the ORAN Alliance recommends implementing strong access controls and encryption. They also suggest using integrity verification mechanisms to ensure that policies and AI/ML models have not been tampered with during transmission or storage. This could involve the use of digital signatures or secure hash functions to validate the authenticity and integrity of the data.

For the O1 interface, which is responsible for management and orchestration functions, the ORAN Alliance emphasizes the importance of secure management protocols. They recommend using protocols like SNMPv3 or NETCONF over SSH to ensure that management traffic is encrypted and authenticated. Additionally, the alliance suggests implementing strong password policies, multi-factor authentication for administrative access, and comprehensive logging and auditing mechanisms to detect and respond to potential security incidents.

The following figure is a snapshot of the mandatory interface security controls enforcing authenticity, confidentiality, integrity, authorization, data origination, and replay prevention, as mentioned in the ORAN Alliance documentation:

Security Control	A1	O1	O2	E2	Open Fronthaul			
					C-plane	U-plane	S-plane	M-plane
Authenticity	TLS	TLS	TLS	IPsec				TLS/SSH
Confidentiality	TLS	TLS	TLS	IPsec		PDCP		TLS/SSH
Integrity	TLS	TLS	TLS	IPsec		PDCP		TLS/SSH
Authorization	OAuth	NACM	OAuth					NACM
Data Origination	TLS	TLS	TLS	IPsec				TLS/SSH
Replay Prevention	TLS	TLS	TLS	IPsec		PDCP		TLS/SSH

Figure 10.11: Interface security controls

Transport network

The transport network in a mobile service provider environment is a critical component that forms the backbone of cellular communications, connecting various elements of the mobile network infrastructure. This network is responsible for carrying voice, data, and signaling traffic between different parts of the mobile network, ensuring seamless connectivity and efficient service delivery to end-users. The following figure shows the overview of the transport network:

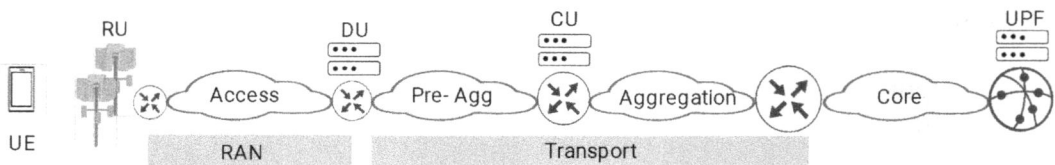

Figure 10.12: Transport network overview

At its core, the transport network in a mobile environment consists of a hierarchical structure that connects cell sites to the core network. This hierarchy typically includes access, aggregation, and core layers, each serving specific functions in the overall network architecture. The transport network must be designed to handle high volumes of traffic, provide low latency, and offer high reliability to support the diverse range of services offered by modern mobile networks.

Starting at the edge of the network, the access layer connects individual cell sites or base stations to the rest of the network. In traditional networks, this was often achieved using copper-based technologies like T1/E1 lines. However, with the increasing bandwidth demands of 4G and 5G networks, fiber optic connections have become the norm. These fiber connections provide the high capacity and low latency required to support advanced mobile services. In some cases, especially in rural or hard-to-reach areas, microwave links are used as a cost-effective alternative to fiber for backhaul connectivity.

Moving up the hierarchy, the aggregation layer collects traffic from multiple cell sites and consolidates it for transmission to the core network. This layer often employs Ethernet-based technologies, leveraging their cost-effectiveness and scalability. Carrier Ethernet services, such as **Ethernet over MPLS** (**EoMPLS**) or Ethernet VPNs, are commonly used to provide flexible and efficient transport of mobile traffic. The aggregation layer also plays a crucial role in traffic management, implementing QoS policies to ensure that different types of traffic (voice, data, and signaling) receive appropriate prioritization.

At the highest level of the transport hierarchy is the core layer, which interconnects major network nodes and provides connectivity to the mobile core network elements. This layer typically employs high-capacity optical transport technologies, such as **dense wavelength division multiplexing** (**DWDM**), to handle the enormous volumes of aggregated traffic. DWDM allows multiple optical carrier signals to be transmitted on a single fiber by using different wavelengths of laser light, greatly increasing the capacity of the fiber infrastructure.

Vulnerabilities in transport network

The transport network of a mobile communication service provider is susceptible to a wide range of vulnerabilities across multiple layers of the network stack and various operational aspects, as depicted in the mid-map (*Figure 10.13*). At the physical layer, risks include fiber optic cable cuts, power outages, hardware failures, and electromagnetic interference, which can disrupt network connectivity. Moving up to the data link layer, attackers might exploit vulnerabilities like MAC address spoofing, ARP poisoning, or VLAN hopping to gain unauthorized access or manipulate network traffic. Network layer threats encompass IP spoofing, routing table poisoning, DDoS attacks, and BGP hijacking, potentially leading to service disruptions or traffic redirection.

Transport layer vulnerabilities, such as TCP SYN flood attacks, SSL/TLS weaknesses, and session hijacking, can compromise data integrity and confidentiality. At the application layer, SQL injection, cross-site scripting, API vulnerabilities, and insecure authentication mechanisms pose risks to user data and service functionality. Mobile networks also face protocol-specific vulnerabilities in SS7, Diameter, and GTP, which can be exploited for location tracking, interception, or fraud.

Configuration and management issues, including misconfigured firewalls, weak passwords, unpatched systems, and inadequate access controls, create additional attack vectors. Encryption and security vulnerabilities, such as weak algorithms, improper key management, and susceptibility to man-in-the-middle attacks, can compromise data protection.

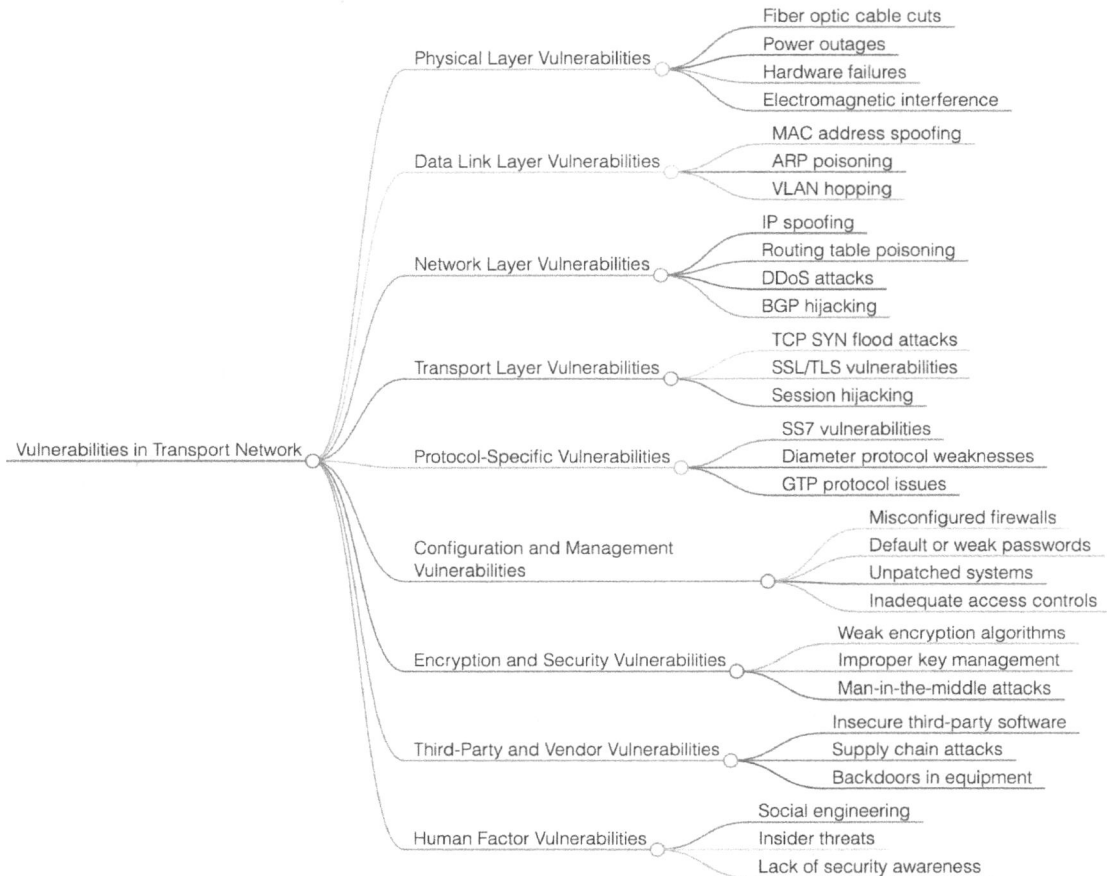

Figure 10.13: Vulnerabilities in transport network

Third-party and vendor vulnerabilities introduce risks through insecure software, supply chain attacks, or potential backdoors in equipment. Lastly, human factor vulnerabilities, including social engineering, insider threats, and lack of security awareness, remain significant challenges in maintaining the overall security posture of the transport network.

Securing transport network

Securing the transport network of a mobile communication service provider is a critical and multifaceted challenge in today's interconnected world. As the backbone of mobile communications, the transport network faces a wide array of threats ranging from physical attacks to sophisticated cyber intrusions. Effective security measures must address vulnerabilities at every layer of the network stack, from the physical infrastructure to the application layer.

A comprehensive approach to transport network security involves implementing robust physical safeguards, deploying advanced encryption technologies, establishing strict access controls, continuously monitoring for threats, and maintaining up-to-date security protocols. It also requires addressing human factors through regular training and fostering a security-conscious culture.

By adopting a holistic security strategy that combines technological solutions with operational best practices, mobile service providers can significantly enhance the resilience of their transport networks against evolving threats, ensuring the integrity, confidentiality, and availability of their services.

Physical security

As the transport network spreads across a specific geographic area, physical security is the foundation of a robust security strategy for the transport network of a mobile communication service provider. It involves protecting the tangible assets that make up the network infrastructure from unauthorized access, damage, and theft.

The first line of defense is the perimeter of the facilities housing critical network equipment. Robust access control systems are crucial for managing entry to sensitive areas. These can be achieved through the implementation of high-resolution cameras covering all critical areas, entrances, and exits, and AI-powered systems to detect unusual activities or unauthorized presence, among others.

The physical network infrastructure itself needs protection, due to this, it is recommended that the use of armored fiber optic cables for outdoor installations be adopted by the service provider. Pathways for cables within facilities must be protected and multiple physical routes for critical connections must be planned and implemented.

Device hardening

Device hardening is a critical component in securing the transport network of mobile communication service providers. In today's increasingly interconnected and complex telecommunications landscape, network devices serve as the backbone of data transmission, routing, and service delivery. These devices, including routers, switches, and various network appliances, are prime targets for cybercriminals due to their pivotal role in network operations. A single compromised device can potentially provide attackers with a foothold to infiltrate the entire network, leading to data breaches, service disruptions, or unauthorized access to sensitive information. Moreover, as threats evolve and become more sophisticated, the attack surface of these devices continually expands. Device hardening addresses these challenges by systematically reducing vulnerabilities, closing potential security gaps, and strengthening the overall security posture of the network. By implementing robust hardening measures, service providers can significantly enhance their network's resilience against both external threats and internal misconfigurations, ensuring the integrity, confidentiality, and availability of their critical infrastructure.

Secure device configuration

Replacing default passwords and managing default accounts is a crucial first step in securing network devices within a transport network. This process involves a comprehensive approach to credential management that goes beyond simple password changes. When implementing this security measure, network administrators must conduct a thorough inventory of all devices in the network, including routers, switches, firewalls, and any other network appliances. For each device, it is essential to identify all default accounts, including administrative accounts, service accounts, and any built-in user accounts that come preconfigured with the device.

Once identified, each default password should be replaced with a strong, unique password. These passwords should be complex, incorporating a mix of uppercase and lowercase letters, numbers, and special characters. It is crucial to avoid using easily guessable information such as device names, network details, or common words. Ideally, password generation should be automated using a secure password management system to ensure randomness and uniqueness across all devices. The length of these passwords should be substantial, typically at least 16 characters, to resist brute-force attacks effectively.

In addition to changing passwords, administrators should also modify default usernames wherever the device's firmware allows. This adds an extra layer of security by obscuring the identity of privileged accounts, making it more difficult for attackers to guess or socially engineer access to these accounts. When changing usernames, it is important to use naming conventions that do not reveal the account's purpose or privileges to potential attackers.

Disabling unnecessary services, protocols, and ports is another fundamental principle in network device hardening, crucial for reducing the attack surface of network equipment in transport networks. This process involves a meticulous review of each device's configuration to identify and remove any services that are not essential for its intended function. Common services that are often targeted for removal include *Telnet*, which transmits data in plain text and is vulnerable to eavesdropping; HTTP, which can expose device management interfaces to potential attacks; and older versions of SNMP (v1/v2), which lack strong authentication and encryption mechanisms. By disabling these services, network administrators significantly reduce the number of potential entry points for attackers.

Disabling unnecessary services requires a comprehensive audit of all active services on each device, including those that may be enabled by default but serve no purpose in the specific network environment. This might include services like **Cisco Discovery Protocol (CDP)** or **Link Layer Discovery Protocol (LLDP)** if they are not being used for network discovery, or auxiliary ports that are not connected to any equipment. Additionally, any unused network protocols, such as IPv6 if it is not being utilized, should be disabled to prevent potential abuse.

Firmware and OS updates

Regularly updating device firmware and operating systems involves more than simply applying the latest patches, it requires a systematic approach to ensure the updates enhance security without compromising network stability or introducing new vulnerabilities.

The first step in this process is staying informed about the latest stable versions released by device manufacturers. This involves subscribing to vendor security bulletins, participating in industry forums, and maintaining close relationships with vendor representatives. It is crucial to understand not only what updates are available but also what specific security issues or feature enhancements they address.

Once new updates are identified, they should not be immediately deployed across the entire network. Instead, a staged testing process should be implemented. This typically begins with testing in a lab environment that closely mimics the production network. During this phase, the updates are applied to test devices, and comprehensive functionality and security tests are conducted. These tests should cover all critical network functions, protocols, and integrations to ensure the update does not introduce unexpected behavior or conflicts with existing systems.

If the lab tests are successful, the next stage involves deploying the updates to a small subset of non-critical production devices. This pilot deployment allows for real-world testing without risking widespread network disruption. During this phase, network administrators should closely monitor device performance, log any anomalies, and be prepared to quickly roll back the updates if significant issues arise. Assuming the pilot deployment is successful, a phased rollout plan should be developed for the rest of the network. This plan should prioritize devices based on their criticality and potential impact on network operations. It is often advisable to update less critical devices first, gradually moving to more crucial network components. Throughout this process, each update should be followed by a period of intense monitoring and performance evaluation.

Access control

Implementing robust access control measures involves a comprehensive approach to **authentication, authorization, and accounting** (**AAA**), which forms the foundation of secure device access and management. Strong authentication mechanisms are the first line of defense against unauthorized access. Network administrators should implement centralized authentication services using protocols such as **Terminal Access Controller Access-Control System Plus** (**TACACS+**) or **Remote Authentication Dial-In User Service** (**RADIUS**). These protocols provide a centralized platform for managing user credentials and access policies across multiple devices, significantly enhancing security and simplifying administration. TACACS+ is often preferred in network device environments due to its ability to separate authentication, authorization, and accounting functions, providing more granular control. Where possible, MFA should be enabled for administrative access, adding an extra layer of security. MFA typically combines something the user knows, like a password, with something they have, such as a mobile device for generating one-time code, or something they are (biometric data), making it significantly more difficult for attackers to gain unauthorized access even if they manage to obtain user credentials.

Authorization controls should be implemented based on the principle of least privilege, which stipulates that users should be granted only the minimum level of access necessary to perform their job functions. This can be achieved through the implementation of RBAC policies. RBAC allows administrators to create predefined roles with specific sets of permissions and then assign users to these roles based on their job requirements.

Accounting, the final component of the AAA framework, involves logging and monitoring all access attempts to network devices, both successful and failed. This creates an audit trail that is invaluable for security monitoring, incident response, and compliance purposes. All authentication attempts, configuration changes, and significant system events should be logged. These logs should be sent to a centralized log management system, which aggregates data from multiple devices across the network. Centralized logging not only simplifies log analysis but also protects the integrity of the logs themselves, as they are stored away from the individual devices that might be compromised in a security incident. Advanced log management systems can provide real-time alerting for suspicious activities, such as multiple failed login attempts or unexpected configuration changes, allowing for rapid incident detection and response. Regular analysis of these logs can also reveal patterns of behavior that might indicate attempted breaches or insider threats, as well as opportunities for improving security policies and procedures.

Secure management protocols

Implementing secure management protocols is a crucial aspect of network device hardening in transport networks. **Secure Shell (SSH)** version 2 should be the primary method for remote management, replacing the outdated and insecure Telnet protocol. SSH2 provides robust encryption and improved security features compared to its predecessor, SSH1. When configuring SSH, it is essential to disable older, less secure versions to prevent potential downgrade attacks. Network administrators should also take care to configure SSH with strong ciphers (such as AES-256-GCM) and secure key exchange algorithms (like *Diffie-Hellman with 4096-bit keys* or *Elliptic Curve Diffie-Hellman*). These configurations ensure that the authentication process and subsequent communication sessions are well-protected against eavesdropping and man-in-the-middle attacks.

For web-based management interfaces, which are increasingly common in modern network devices, **HTTP Secure (HTTPS)** should be mandated, specifically using TLS version 1.2 or higher. TLS 1.2 and 1.3 offer significant security improvements over their predecessors, including stronger cryptographic algorithms and better protection against known vulnerabilities. It is crucial to disable older, insecure protocols such as SSL and early TLS versions (1.0 and 1.1), as these have known vulnerabilities that can be exploited by attackers. By enforcing the use of modern TLS versions, network administrators can ensure that web-based management sessions are encrypted and protected against various cyber threats.

For network monitoring and management, the **Simple Network Management Protocol** (**SNMP**) is often utilized. However, earlier versions of SNMP (v1 and v2c) lack strong security features. Therefore, if SNMP is required in the network, it is strongly recommended to use SNMPv3, which introduces robust authentication and encryption mechanisms. SNMPv3 supports user-based security models and view-based access control, allowing for fine-grained access management. If, due to legacy system requirements or other constraints, older versions of SNMP must be used, it is crucial to implement strict access controls. This includes restricting SNMP access to specific IP addresses or subnets, ideally from a dedicated management network. Additionally, when using SNMP v1 or v2c, strong community strings should be employed instead of the default *public* and *private* strings. These community strings should be treated like passwords, using complex, hard-to-guess combinations of characters. Regular rotation of these strings can provide an additional layer of security.

Control Plane Protection

Control Plane Protection (**CoPP**) is designed to safeguard the control plane of network devices from DoS attacks and other malicious traffic. The control plane, responsible for processing routing updates, management traffic, and other critical control packets, is vital for the overall stability and operation of the network.

Implementing CoPP involves carefully configuring rate limits for various types of control plane traffic, effectively creating a prioritized queue system. This allows essential traffic to be processed while potentially harmful or excessive traffic is rate-limited or dropped, preventing resource exhaustion on the device. For instance, ICMP traffic might be limited to a lower rate than routing protocol updates, which are typically given higher priority.

Securing routing protocols is equally crucial in the transport network of a service provider. Enabling authentication for routing protocols, such as using MD5 authentication for **Open Shortest Path First** (**OSPF**) and **Border Gateway Protocol** (**BGP**), ensures that routing updates are only accepted from trusted peers. This prevents malicious actors from injecting false routing information into the network, which could lead to traffic misdirection or network disruptions. Additionally, implementing route filters adds another layer of defense by allowing network administrators to explicitly define which routes should be advertised or accepted. This granular control helps prevent unauthorized route advertisements, whether they originate from configuration errors or malicious attempts to manipulate the network topology.

Access control lists and quality of service

ACLs and QoS policies are crucial components in securing and optimizing the transport network of mobile communication service providers. ACLs serve as a fundamental line of defense, acting as traffic filters that control data flow based on predefined security rules. In the context of network device hardening, two types of ACLs are particularly important: **infrastructure ACLs** (**iACLs**) and transit ACLs.

Infrastructure ACLs are deployed to protect the network devices themselves, creating a security perimeter around critical infrastructure components. These iACLs typically permit only necessary management and control plane traffic to reach the devices, effectively blocking potential attacks targeting the devices' own vulnerabilities. For instance, an iACL might allow SSH access from specific management IP addresses while denying all other incoming connections to the device's management interfaces.

Transit ACLs, on the other hand, are used to filter traffic passing through the network. These ACLs are applied to interfaces handling transit traffic, allowing fine-grained control over which packets are allowed to traverse the network. Transit ACLs can be used to implement security policies, such as blocking traffic from known malicious IP ranges, preventing spoofed packets, or restricting certain types of traffic based on protocol or port numbers. For example, a transit ACL might block incoming traffic on ports associated with vulnerable services or filter out packets with source IP addresses that should not appear on a particular network segment.

QoS mechanisms allow network administrators to prioritize critical traffic, ensuring that essential services receive the necessary bandwidth and processing resources even under high network load conditions. From a security perspective, QoS policies are instrumental in preventing resource exhaustion attacks, a type of DoS attack where an attacker floods the network with low-priority traffic to consume available resources and disrupt legitimate high-priority traffic. By implementing QoS policies, network devices can be configured to limit the bandwidth allocated to lower-priority traffic classes, preventing them from overwhelming the network during an attack.

QoS can be used in conjunction with ACLs to create more sophisticated traffic management schemes. For example, traffic identified and permitted by an ACL can be assigned to specific QoS classes, allowing for granular control over how different types of legitimate traffic are handled. This synergy between ACLs and QoS not only enhances security but also improves overall network performance and reliability.

Logging and monitoring

A cornerstone of logging and monitoring is the configuration of network devices to send detailed syslog messages to a centralized log management system. This centralization allows for comprehensive log collection, correlation, and analysis across the entire network infrastructure. When configuring Syslog, it is essential to ensure that the logs capture sufficient detail for both security analysis and potential forensic investigations. This includes information such as timestamps, source and destination IP addresses, port numbers, protocol information, and specific event details. The granularity of logging should be carefully balanced to provide necessary insights without overwhelming storage capacities or processing resources.

Complementing Syslog, the implementation of SNMP traps is vital for real-time alerting on critical events or when predefined thresholds are breached. These traps can be configured to notify network administrators immediately about issues such as interface status changes, CPU utilization spikes, or unusual traffic patterns, enabling rapid response to potential security incidents or performance issues.

Furthermore, enabling NetFlow or similar traffic analysis protocols adds another layer of visibility into network operations. NetFlow provides detailed insights into traffic patterns, including source and destination IP addresses, port numbers, protocol information, and traffic volume. This granular view of network traffic allows administrators to detect anomalies that might indicate security threats, such as data exfiltration attempts or distributed DDoS attacks. It also aids in capacity planning and troubleshooting by providing a clear picture of how bandwidth is being utilized across the network. When implementing these logging and monitoring solutions, it is crucial to consider factors such as log retention periods, secure transmission of log data, and regular review and analysis of collected information. Additionally, integrating these various data sources into a **security information and event management** (**SIEM**) system can provide holistic visibility and enable more sophisticated correlation and analysis of security events across the entire network infrastructure.

Vulnerability management

Regular vulnerability scanning is an essential practice that involves systematically examining network devices for known security weaknesses. These scans should be conducted using specialized tools designed specifically for probing network infrastructure. Unlike general-purpose vulnerability scanners, these specialized tools are aware of the unique characteristics and sensitivities of network devices, allowing them to safely probe without risking device stability or network disruption. The scanning process typically involves sending carefully crafted packets to devices and analyzing their responses to identify potential vulnerabilities. This can include checking for outdated software versions, misconfigurations, open ports, and known vulnerabilities specific to the device's make and model.

The frequency of these scans should be determined based on the criticality of the devices and the overall threat landscape. High-priority devices in critical network segments might require more frequent scans, potentially weekly or even daily, while less critical devices might be scanned monthly or quarterly. It is important to note that vulnerability scanning should be performed both from external network perspectives (simulating an outside attacker) and from within the network to identify internal vulnerabilities. The results of these scans should be carefully analyzed and prioritized based on the severity of the vulnerabilities discovered and the potential impact on the network's security posture.

Complementing the vulnerability scanning process and establishing a robust patch management system is equally critical. This involves creating a systematic approach for quickly deploying security patches to address newly discovered vulnerabilities. The process begins with maintaining an up-to-date inventory of all network devices, including their current software versions and patch levels. This inventory serves as the foundation for effective patch management, allowing network administrators to quickly identify which devices require updates when new vulnerabilities are discovered.

The patch management process should include several key steps. First, there needs to be a system in place for monitoring vendor announcements and security advisories to stay informed about new patches and vulnerabilities. When a new patch is released, it should be thoroughly tested in a controlled environment that mimics the production network. This testing phase is crucial to ensure that the patch does not introduce new issues or conflicts with existing configurations.

Once testing is complete, a rollout plan should be developed. This plan should prioritize critical vulnerabilities and high-risk devices while also considering network maintenance windows to minimize service disruption. The deployment itself should be automated where possible to ensure consistency and reduce the risk of human error. However, for critical devices or complex updates, a more hands-on approach might be necessary.

Post-deployment monitoring is also essential. After applying patches, network administrators should closely monitor device performance and network stability to quickly identify and address any unforeseen issues. Additionally, it is important to verify that the patches have been successfully applied and that the vulnerabilities have indeed been mitigated. This can be done through follow-up vulnerability scans or other verification methods.

Lastly, the entire vulnerability management process should be documented and regularly reviewed. This documentation should include scan results, patching decisions, deployment logs, and any issues encountered. Regular reviews of this process can help identify areas for improvement and ensure that the organization's approach to vulnerability management evolves alongside the changing threat landscape.

Out-of-band management

Implementing a separate out-of-band management network involves creating a dedicated network infrastructure that is physically or logically isolated from the primary production network. The out-of-band management network serves as a secure channel for administrators to access, configure, and monitor network devices without relying on the production network itself.

The primary purpose of an out-of-band management network is to enhance security and ensure continuous access to critical network devices, even in the event of a production network failure or security breach. By segregating management traffic from regular data traffic, organizations can significantly reduce the risk of unauthorized access to device administration interfaces. This separation also prevents potential attackers who may have gained access to the production network from easily pivoting to management interfaces.

Typically, an out-of-band management network is implemented using dedicated physical interfaces on network devices, connected to a separate switching infrastructure. This can involve the use of console servers, which provide centralized access to device console ports or dedicated management ports on devices that support them. In some cases, organizations may opt for a virtual out-of-band network using VLANs, though this approach may not offer the same level of isolation as a physically separate network.

The benefits of an out-of-band management network extend beyond security. It provides a reliable means of accessing devices during network outages, facilitating faster troubleshooting and recovery. This is particularly crucial in scenarios where in-band management access might be disrupted due to misconfigurations or routing issues. Additionally, by offloading management traffic from the production network, organizations can optimize bandwidth utilization and potentially improve overall network performance.

However, implementing an out-of-band management network also comes with its own set of challenges. It requires additional hardware, cabling, and potentially dedicated internet connections for remote access. There is also the added complexity of managing and securing this separate network infrastructure. Service providers must ensure that the out-of-band network itself is robustly secured, with strict access controls, encryption, and monitoring in place.

Configuration management

Configuration management and regular auditing are crucial aspects of maintaining a secure and well-functioning transport network. Regularly backing up device configurations is not merely a precautionary measure; it is a fundamental practice that ensures operational continuity and facilitates rapid recovery in case of device failures or security incidents. These backups should be stored securely, preferably in encrypted form and in multiple locations, to guard against both data loss and unauthorized access. Implementing version control for configurations goes beyond simple backups; it provides a historical record of changes, enabling network administrators to track modifications over time, identify when and by whom changes were made, and quickly roll back to a known good configuration if issues arise. This versioning system can be invaluable during troubleshooting or security investigations, offering insights into how configuration changes might have impacted network performance or security posture.

Conducting regular audits of device configurations is an equally critical practice. These audits serve multiple purposes: they ensure ongoing compliance with established security policies and industry best practices, detect unauthorized or potentially harmful changes, and identify configuration drift that could introduce vulnerabilities or performance issues. Audits should be systematic and comprehensive, covering all aspects of device configuration, from access controls and enabled services to routing protocols and security features. Automated tools can be employed to streamline this process, comparing current configurations against approved baselines and flagging discrepancies for review. However, human expertise remains crucial in interpreting audit results and understanding their implications for network security and performance.

Moreover, these audits should not occur in isolation but should be integrated into a broader governance framework. This framework should include processes for reviewing and updating security policies, incorporating lessons learned from audits into training programs, and continuously refining hardening practices based on audit findings and emerging threats. Regular reporting on audit results to management ensures visibility into the network's security status and helps justify investments in security measures. By maintaining this cycle of backup, versioning, auditing, and improvement, organizations can significantly enhance the resilience and security of their transport network infrastructure, staying ahead of potential threats and maintaining optimal network performance.

Encryption

Encryption-based security controls play a crucial role in protecting the confidentiality and integrity of data as it traverse the transport network of a mobile communication service provider. These controls are essential in safeguarding sensitive information from interception, tampering, and unauthorized access. In a transport network, encryption can be applied at various layers of the network stack, each offering different levels of protection and addressing specific security concerns.

At the network layer, IPsec is widely used to secure communications between network devices. IPsec provides a robust framework for encrypting and authenticating IP packets, ensuring the confidentiality and integrity of data as it travels across the network. It can be implemented in tunnel mode, which encapsulates the entire IP packet, or in transport mode, which only encrypts the payload. IPsec is particularly useful for securing inter-site communications, VPNs, and protecting routing protocol exchanges.

In a typical mobile network architecture, security gateways are strategically positioned at the boundaries between different network domains. For instance, they are commonly deployed at the edge of the RAN and the core network, or between the core network and external networks such as the internet. This placement allows them to secure traffic flows between these different domains effectively. Security gateways use IPsec to create encrypted tunnels, typically in tunnel mode, which encapsulates the entire original IP packet within a new IP packet. This approach not only encrypts the payload but also hides the original packet headers, providing an additional layer of privacy.

Moving up the stack, TLS and its predecessor, SSL, are commonly employed to secure higher-level protocols such as HTTP, SMTP, and FTP. In the context of a transport network, TLS is crucial for securing management interfaces, API communications, and any web-based services that the network might support. It provides end-to-end encryption between clients and servers, protecting against eavesdropping and man-in-the-middle attacks.

For voice and multimedia traffic, protocols like **Secure Real-time Transport Protocol (SRTP)** are essential. SRTP provides encryption, message authentication, and replay protection for RTP traffic, which is crucial for securing voice and video communications in mobile networks. It is often used in conjunction with **Session Description Protocol Security Descriptions (SDES)** or **Datagram TLS for SRTP (DTLS-SRTP)** for key exchange and management.

At the data link layer, **Media Access Control Security (MACSec)** has emerged as a powerful tool for securing Ethernet communications. MACSec, defined by the IEEE 802.1AE standard, provides point-to-point security on Ethernet links. It encrypts and authenticates nearly all information in Ethernet frames, excluding only the headers necessary for frame transmission. MACSec is designed to protect against a variety of threats, including eavesdropping, man-in-the-middle attacks, and unauthorized network access.

The use of MACSec in transport networks offers several significant advantages. Firstly, it provides comprehensive protection for all traffic on the Ethernet link, regardless of the higher-layer protocols in use. This makes it an excellent choice for securing the diverse traffic types typically found in mobile backhaul networks. Secondly, MACSec operates at wire speed, introducing minimal latency, which is crucial for maintaining network performance. Additionally, MACSec can work in conjunction with other security protocols like IPsec, providing layered security.

However, implementing MACSec in a transport network also presents several challenges. One of the primary challenges is key management. MACSec requires a robust key management system to distribute and rotate encryption keys securely. This can be complex in large, distributed networks typical of mobile operators. The IEEE 802.1X standard is often used for key management in MACSec deployments, but implementing this across a wide-area network can be operationally challenging.

Another challenge with MACSec is interoperability. While the standard is well-defined, not all network equipment vendors support MACSec, or they may support different versions or implementations. This can create difficulties when trying to implement MACSec across a heterogeneous network infrastructure, which is common in many mobile operator environments.

Performance considerations also come into play when implementing MACSec. While designed to operate at wire speed, enabling MACSec can still impact the throughput and latency of high-speed links, particularly on older hardware. Network operators must carefully evaluate the performance impact and ensure their equipment can handle the additional processing load, especially on critical high-bandwidth links.

Visibility can be another challenge when using MACSec. Since it encrypts nearly all of the Ethernet frame, it can interfere with certain network monitoring and troubleshooting tools that rely on deep packet inspection. This may require adjustments to network management practices and tools to maintain effective network visibility and troubleshooting capabilities.

Conclusion

In conclusion, this chapter has provided a comprehensive exploration of security challenges and solutions in **radio access network** (**RAN**) and transport networks. We began by examining various RAN deployment models and their unique security implications, particularly focusing on the trend of RAN decomposition that offers flexibility but introduces new vulnerabilities at interface points.

Our analysis covered the diverse threat landscape targeting RAN infrastructure, from physical attacks to sophisticated cyber intrusions, highlighting the necessity for multifaceted security strategies. We emphasized the critical importance of securing RAN interfaces and non-Service-Based Architecture reference points through robust authentication, encryption, and integrity protection mechanisms.

The emergence of Open RAN architectures has revolutionized the field while necessitating new security paradigms and standards. Our discussion then shifted to transport network vulnerabilities, examining threats at both physical and protocol levels. We explored effective security measures, including IPsec and MACsec encryption technologies, security gateway implementation, and comprehensive network hardening practices.

The chapter demonstrated that securing these networks requires a holistic approach combining technological solutions with operational best practices, continuous monitoring, and adaptive security policies. As 5G networks and beyond continue to evolve, maintaining strong security measures across both domains remains paramount for ensuring the reliability, privacy, and integrity of modern mobile communications.

The next chapter explores how container technologies are being embraced within 5G ecosystems, creating more agile, scalable, and efficient network infrastructures. The chapter alos analyzes how containers enable network function virtualization with unprecedented efficiency, allowing operators to deploy and scale services dynamically across diverse infrastructure environments.

Points to remember

- **Overview**: This chapter offers a thorough overview of the security challenges and solutions related to modern mobile networks, especially as they develop to support 5G and beyond. This chapter aims to provide network architects, security professionals, and decision-makers with the knowledge and insights needed to build and maintain secure, resilient, and high-performing mobile network infrastructures in an increasingly complex and threat-filled environment.

- **RAN deployment models and security implications:** The evolution from traditional macro cells to cloud RAN architectures has fundamentally transformed the security landscape. Cloud RAN, while offering unprecedented flexibility and resource optimization, introduces expanded attack surfaces that must be carefully managed. This includes securing virtualized network functions, containerized applications, and the underlying cloud infrastructure. Network operators must implement robust security controls that can adapt to these dynamic environments while maintaining performance requirements.

- **Interface security in disaggregated RAN:** RAN decomposition has revolutionized network architecture but introduces critical security considerations at interface boundaries. The disaggregation of RAN components requires robust protection mechanisms for both control and user plane traffic. Special attention must be given to securing interfaces like F1 (between CU and DU) and E1 (between CU-CP and CU-UP), as these represent potential attack vectors. Implementation of strong authentication protocols, encryption mechanisms, and continuous monitoring becomes essential to maintain the integrity of these critical communication paths.

- **Transport network security:** The transport network serves as the backbone connecting various RAN elements, making it a critical component requiring comprehensive security measures. Key considerations include:

- o Implementation of multiple security layers combining encryption protocols like IPsec and MACSec
- o Deployment of network segmentation strategies to isolate critical network components
- o Integration of security gateways at key network boundaries
- o Establishment of robust access control mechanisms to prevent unauthorized access. The security of the transport layer becomes increasingly crucial as networks become more distributed and complex, requiring careful attention to both physical and logical security controls.

- **O-RAN security framework**: The adoption of Open RAN brings both opportunities and challenges from a security perspective. The multi-vendor environment inherent in O-RAN deployments requires careful consideration of:
- o Standardized security protocols across different vendor implementations
- o Enhanced visibility into network operations through open interfaces
- o Rapid security update capabilities across the entire network
- o Comprehensive testing and validation procedures for multi-vendor integration. These considerations must be balanced against the potential increased complexity and attack surface that comes with open architectures.

Exercises

1. Compare and contrast the security implications of traditional macro cell deployments versus small cell configurations. What unique security challenges does each present?

2. In a cloud RAN architecture, what are the primary security concerns that differ from traditional RAN deployments?

3. How does the choice of RAN deployment model impact the overall security strategy for a mobile network operator?

4. Explain the concept of RAN decomposition and list the main functional splits defined by 3GPP.

5. How does RAN decomposition affect the security landscape of a mobile network? Provide specific examples of new security challenges introduced by disaggregation.

6. What security measures can be implemented to mitigate the risks associated with a disaggregated RAN architecture?

7. Identify and describe three potential physical threats to RAN infrastructure.

8. What are the most significant cyber threats facing modern RAN deployments? How have these evolved with the transition to 5G networks?

9. Propose a comprehensive threat model for a 5G RAN, considering both insider and external threats.

10. What are the key security considerations for the F1 interface in a disaggregated RAN scenario?

11. Describe the security mechanisms used to protect the X2 interface between eNodeBs in 4G networks. How do these evolve for the Xn interface in 5G?

12. Explain the importance of securing the fronthaul interface in a cloud RAN deployment. What methods can be used to ensure its security?

13. What are the primary security benefits and challenges introduced by the Open RAN concept?

14. How does the increased openness in ORAN impact the trust model for RAN components? Discuss potential mitigation strategies.

15. Describe the role of the RIC in ORAN and discuss its implications for network security.

16. Identify the main components of a typical mobile transport network and their functions.

17. What are the most critical vulnerabilities in mobile backhaul networks? How do these differ between fiber, microwave, and satellite backhaul?

18. Explain how network slicing in 5G impacts transport network security. What new security challenges does it introduce?

19. Describe the role of IPsec in securing mobile transport networks. What are its advantages and limitations?

20. How can network segmentation be implemented in a mobile transport network to enhance security? Provide specific examples.

21. Explain the function of security gateways in transport networks. Where are they typically deployed and what security features do they provide?

22. Compare and contrast layer 2 encryption (for example, MACSec) with layer 3 encryption (for example, IPsec) for securing transport networks. In what scenarios would you recommend each?

23. You are the chief security officer for a mobile network operator planning to deploy a 5G network with Open RAN architecture. Design a comprehensive security strategy that addresses:

    a. Secure RAN deployment and decomposition

    b. Threat mitigation for both RAN and transport network

    c. Securing critical interfaces and reference points

    d. Leveraging ORAN capabilities for enhanced security

    e. Implementing robust transport network security

    Present your strategy as a detailed plan, justifying your choices and addressing potential trade-offs between security, performance, and cost.

CHAPTER 11

Container Adoption in 5G Networks

Introduction

Container technology has transformed modern application deployment by offering enhanced flexibility, scalability, and efficiency. As containerization becomes increasingly prevalent in critical applications and services, understanding its security implications becomes essential. This chapter provides a comprehensive overview of container security fundamentals, examining both their powerful capabilities and inherent security challenges.

The discussion begins with container architecture fundamentals, focusing on Linux kernel features like namespaces and cgroups that enable containerization while establishing its security foundation. These core concepts are crucial for security professionals and developers to understand when building secure container environments.

The chapter explores specific security challenges in container environments, including image-based threats, runtime security issues, configuration vulnerabilities, and supply chain risks, particularly in large-scale deployments. It examines native security capabilities within container ecosystems, including features provided by container runtimes, orchestration platforms, and supporting tools, which are essential for implementing effective defense-in-depth strategies.

Special attention is given to securing the **continuous integration and continuous delivery** (**CI/CD**) process in container environments. This covers security throughout the container lifecycle, from development to deployment, emphasizing secure build processes, image scanning, and registry security. The chapter presents best practices and tools that help organizations implement security controls while maintaining the agility and efficiency that containers offer.

This comprehensive exploration equips security professionals, developers, and system administrators with essential knowledge for building and maintaining secure containerized applications in today's dynamic technology landscape.

Structure

This chapter will cover the following topics:

- Introducing the evolution of container security
- Inherent capabilities of containers
- Container vulnerabilities
- Inherent security capabilities
- Secure CI and CD process
- Securing coding and scanning

Objectives

The primary objective of this chapter is to provide readers with a comprehensive understanding of container security fundamentals, particularly focusing on both the inherent strengths and potential vulnerabilities within containerized environments. This chapter aims to explore the foundational capabilities of containers, including their architecture, isolation mechanisms, and resource management features, to establish a solid groundwork for understanding their security implications. Through detailed examination, readers will gain insights into how these inherent capabilities contribute to both security advantages and potential risk factors in container deployments.

A critical focus of this chapter is to thoroughly analyze and categorize the various vulnerabilities that exist within container environments. This includes exploring runtime security concerns, configuration weaknesses, network security risks, and supply chain vulnerabilities. Special attention is given to how these vulnerabilities manifest in modern deployment scenarios, particularly in complex environments like 5G networks, where container security becomes increasingly crucial for maintaining system integrity and protecting sensitive workloads.

The chapter further aims to demonstrate how the inherent security capabilities within container environments can be leveraged to create robust defense mechanisms. This includes detailed coverage of native security features such as namespace isolation, control groups (cgroups), mandatory access controls, and security contexts. Readers will learn how these built-in security capabilities can be effectively utilized to mitigate common vulnerabilities and establish strong security baselines for their container deployments.

Lastly, this chapter seeks to establish best practices for implementing secure CI/CD processes and the use of inherent security capabilities in Kubernetes environments. This encompasses the entire software development lifecycle, from secure image building and vulnerability scanning to secure deployment practices and runtime protection, and use of inherent network policies, namespaces, and secrets management. The objective is to provide readers with practical knowledge on implementing security controls throughout the container lifecycle, ensuring that security is embedded from the earliest stages of development through to production deployment.

Introducing the evolution of container security

The telecommunications industry has undergone a dramatic transformation in recent years, with service providers increasingly embracing cloud-native architectures and containerization to deliver agile, scalable, and efficient network services. This paradigm shift has fundamentally altered how network functions are deployed, managed, and secured, making container security a critical cornerstone of modern service provider infrastructure.

The advent of **network function virtualization** (**NFV**) and **software-defined networking** (**SDN**) marked the initial steps toward network modernization, but it was the emergence of containerization that truly revolutionized service provider architectures. Containers offer unprecedented flexibility, allowing network functions to be packaged as lightweight, portable units that can be deployed consistently across any environment. This capability has become particularly crucial for service providers who must manage complex, distributed networks spanning multiple data centers, edge locations, and cloud platforms.

Container platforms, led by technologies like Kubernetes, have become the de facto standard for orchestrating and managing these containerized workloads in service provider networks. These platforms provide the essential foundation for automating deployment, scaling, and management of network functions, enabling service providers to respond rapidly to changing demand patterns and introduce new services with unprecedented speed. However, this increased agility and flexibility have introduced new security challenges that traditional network security approaches are ill-equipped to address.

The integration of CI/CD pipelines has become instrumental in managing the security posture of containerized environments. Modern service providers must ensure security is embedded throughout the application lifecycle, from development to deployment and runtime. This *shift-left* approach to security has become particularly critical as the attack surface has expanded with the adoption of microservices architectures and container-based deployments. CI/CD pipelines now serve as the primary mechanism for implementing security controls, conducting vulnerability assessments, and enforcing compliance requirements across the container ecosystem.

The stakes for container security in service provider networks are particularly high given the critical nature of telecommunications infrastructure. A single security breach in a containerized network function could potentially impact thousands of customers and disrupt essential communications services. Moreover, service providers must comply with stringent regulatory requirements while maintaining the agility and efficiency promises of containerization. This delicate balance between security and operational efficiency has led to the emergence of specialized container security practices and tools designed specifically for telecommunications environments.

The convergence of container platforms with 5G network deployments has fundamentally transformed the telecommunications landscape. 5G networks represent a radical departure from traditional network architectures, requiring unprecedented levels of flexibility, scalability, and automation, characteristics that containers are uniquely positioned to deliver. In the 5G context, containers serve multiple critical functions: they enable the dynamic instantiation of network functions for network slicing, support the distributed nature of **Multi-access Edge Computing** (**MEC**), and facilitate the deployment of cloud-native 5G core components.

Network slicing, a key feature of 5G networks, relies heavily on containerization to create isolated, customized network instances for different use cases and customers. Each network slice may require specific security policies, resource allocations, and performance characteristics, requirements that containers can efficiently meet through their inherent isolation capabilities and resource management features. For instance, a network slice dedicated to emergency services requires different security controls and resource guarantees compared to a slice serving IoT devices, and containers provide the granular control needed to implement these varying requirements.

The deployment of 5G services at the network edge further emphasizes the importance of container security. Edge computing nodes, which bring computation and storage closer to the end users, typically operate in less controlled environments compared to centralized data centers. Containers running at these edge locations must be hardened against a broader range of threats while maintaining the ability to be rapidly deployed and updated. This distributed architecture introduces new security challenges, such as securing container registries across multiple edge locations, managing secrets in distributed environments, and ensuring consistent security policies across the entire edge-to-cloud continuum.

Moreover, the cloud-native 5G **Core Network Functions** (**CNFs**) are increasingly being deployed as containers, replacing traditional **virtual network functions** (**VNFs**). A depiction of how the CNFs are deployed in a compute node is shown in the following figure. These containerized network functions must process critical control plane and user plane traffic while maintaining strict security boundaries. The security of these containers directly impacts the integrity of the entire 5G network, making robust container security practices not just a technical requirement but a foundational element of 5G network reliability and trustworthiness.

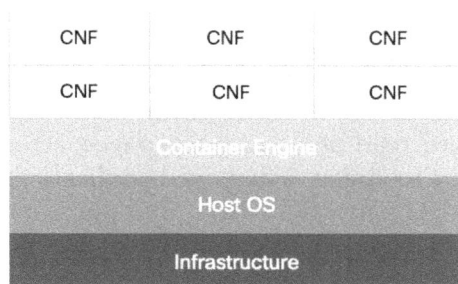

Figure 11.1: *Container network function deployment model*

The integration of containers in 5G networks also introduces new requirements for security automation and orchestration. Service providers must implement sophisticated security controls that can scale across thousands of containers, potentially distributed across hundreds of edge locations. This includes automated vulnerability scanning, runtime security monitoring, network policy enforcement, and secure communication between containerized microservices. The challenge is further complicated by the need to maintain continuous compliance with telecommunications regulations while operating at the speed and scale demanded by 5G services.

Inherent capabilities of containers

The adoption of container-based deployments in 5G networks is driven by several compelling technical and operational advantages that align perfectly with the demands of modern telecommunications infrastructure. The inherent capabilities of containers make them particularly well-suited for the dynamic, distributed nature of 5G and future deployments, offering benefits that traditional virtualization approaches cannot match.

Resource efficiency and density

The resource efficiency and density advantages of containers represent a fundamental shift in how telecommunications providers can optimize their infrastructure investments for 5G deployments. Unlike traditional virtualization approaches that require separate operating system instances for each virtual machine, containers share the host operating system kernel while maintaining process isolation through lightweight virtualization technologies such as Linux namespaces and cgroups. This architectural difference translates into significant resource savings that are particularly valuable in the context of 5G networks.

In a typical 5G deployment scenario, where numerous instances of similar network functions may be running across the infrastructure, this layered approach can reduce storage requirements by orders of magnitude compared to traditional virtual machine deployments. For instance, if a service provider deploys multiple instances of a UPF, each additional instance only needs to store its unique layers while sharing the base layers with other instances.

Memory utilization in container-based deployments shows equally impressive efficiency gains. Containers can share read-only memory pages across instances, significantly reducing the overall memory footprint of deployed applications. This sharing mechanism is particularly beneficial in 5G networks where multiple instances of the same network function might be running to handle different network slices or traffic types.

The startup efficiency of containers provides another crucial advantage for 5G networks. Container instantiation typically occurs in seconds or even milliseconds, as opposed to minutes for traditional virtual machines. This rapid startup capability becomes critical in scenarios requiring dynamic scaling of network functions, such as handling sudden traffic spikes or implementing network slicing. For example, when a mobile event causes a sudden increase in user density in a particular geographic area, container-based network functions can be instantiated almost instantly to handle the increased load, providing a level of responsiveness that would be impossible with traditional virtualization approaches.

CPU utilization in container environments also demonstrates superior efficiency through reduced overhead. Since containers do not require a separate operating system kernel for each instance, they eliminate the computational overhead associated with running multiple operating systems. This efficiency becomes particularly apparent in 5G core network functions, where processing requirements can be intense. A single physical server can host significantly more containerized network functions compared to virtualized ones, often showing improvements of 50% or more in CPU utilization efficiency.

In edge computing scenarios, where physical space and power consumption are often constrained, the ability to run more workloads on less hardware becomes crucial. Container-based deployments allow service providers to maximize the utility of edge locations without requiring additional physical infrastructure. This density optimization directly translates into cost savings through reduced power consumption, cooling requirements, and physical space needs.

Portability and consistency

The portability and consistency advantages offered by containers represent a transformative capability for 5G network deployments, fundamentally changing how service providers approach network function deployment and management. At its core, container technology achieves this through a sophisticated packaging mechanism that encapsulates not just the network function itself, but its entire runtime environment, including dependencies, libraries, and configuration files. This comprehensive packaging ensures that containerized 5G network functions maintain consistent behavior regardless of where they are deployed within the service provider's infrastructure.

The standardization of container images through technologies like the **Open Container Initiative** (**OCI**) has established a universal format that works consistently across different platforms and environments. This standardization is particularly crucial for 5G deployments, where network functions must operate seamlessly across a diverse landscape of infrastructure components. A containerized UPF, for instance, can be packaged once and deployed with identical functionality whether it is running in a centralized data center, a regional point of presence, or an edge computing facility. This consistency eliminates the traditional challenges of environment-specific configurations and dependency conflicts that often plague large-scale network deployments.

Service providers typically operate in multi-vendor environments, utilizing different hardware platforms and cloud providers across their network. Containers abstract away these underlying infrastructure differences through a standardized runtime environment. This abstraction allows network operators to move workloads freely between different environments without requiring significant modifications or reconfigurations. For example, a containerized 5G core network function can be seamlessly transferred from an on-premises deployment to a public cloud environment, or from one edge location to another, while maintaining its operational characteristics and performance parameters.

The container image serves as an immutable artifact that remains consistent from development through testing and into production. This immutability is particularly valuable in telecommunications environments, where rigorous testing and certification requirements must be met. When a network function passes certification tests in one environment, service providers can be confident that the same containerized function will behave identically when deployed across their network. This predictability significantly reduces deployment risks and simplifies compliance verification processes.

The portable nature of containers also facilitates more efficient disaster recovery and business continuity strategies. Service providers can maintain identical container images across geographically distributed locations, enabling rapid failover or workload migration when needed. If a network function needs to be relocated due to hardware failures, capacity issues, or maintenance requirements, the containerized approach ensures that the function can be instantiated at the new location with minimal disruption and without concerning variations in behavior or performance.

Rapid deployment and scalability

Traditional network function deployment processes, which often took hours or even days, have been transformed into automated operations that can be completed in seconds or minutes. This extraordinary improvement in deployment speed is achieved through containers' lightweight architecture and sophisticated orchestration mechanisms, which eliminate the need for full operating system initialization and complex hardware provisioning steps.

In the context of 5G networks, this rapid deployment capability becomes particularly crucial when managing dynamic network slices. Service providers can instantiate new network functions on demand to support emerging service requirements or unexpected traffic spikes. For instance, when a major event occurs in a specific geographic location, containers enable the rapid deployment of additional UPF at the network edge to handle the surge in data traffic. What once required extensive planning and manual effort can now be automated and completed within seconds using container orchestration platforms.

The scalability aspects of containerized deployments in 5G networks operate across multiple dimensions. Horizontal scalability allows service providers to spawn additional instances of network functions to handle increased load, while vertical scalability enables the dynamic adjustment of resource allocations to existing containers. This multi-dimensional scaling capability is particularly valuable in scenarios where different types of 5G services have varying resource requirements. For example, **enhanced Mobile Broadband (eMBB)** services might require horizontal scaling to handle more users, while **Ultra-Reliable Low-Latency Communication (URLLC)** services might need vertical scaling to ensure consistent performance.

Container orchestration platforms enhance these deployment and scaling capabilities by implementing sophisticated scheduling algorithms that optimize resource utilization across the infrastructure. When new containers need to be deployed or existing ones need to be scaled, the orchestrator can make intelligent decisions about placement based on factors such as current resource utilization, network latency requirements, and hardware capabilities. This intelligent scheduling ensures that 5G network functions are deployed in optimal locations while maintaining performance and reliability requirements.

The immutable nature of containers further accelerates deployment processes by eliminating configuration drift and ensuring consistency across all instances. When a network function needs to be updated or modified, rather than attempting to modify existing instances, new containers with the updated configuration are deployed and old ones are gracefully terminated. This approach is known as **immutable infrastructure**, it significantly reduces deployment-related errors and simplifies rollback procedures in case of issues. For service providers, this translates to higher reliability and reduced maintenance windows during network updates.

Auto-scaling capabilities in container environments provide another crucial advantage for 5G networks. By monitoring key performance indicators such as CPU utilization, memory usage, or network metrics, container platforms can automatically adjust the number of running instances to match current demand patterns. This automatic scaling ensures optimal resource utilization while maintaining service quality. For example, during peak hours, the system can automatically scale up control plane functions to handle increased signaling traffic and scale them down during off-peak hours to conserve resources.

Automated lifecycle management

Container orchestration platforms have revolutionized the way service providers manage network functions throughout their lifecycle in 5G deployments. These platforms provide a sophisticated automation framework that addresses the complex operational requirements of modern telecommunications infrastructure. At its core, the automated lifecycle management capabilities enabled by containers fundamentally transform how network functions are deployed, monitored, maintained, and retired within 5G networks.

The deployment phase of containerized network functions benefits significantly from automation through IaC practices. Service providers can define their entire network function deployment configurations, including resource requirements, networking policies, and security parameters, in declarative manifests. These manifests ensure consistent and repeatable deployments across different environments, from development to production. When a new network function needs to be deployed, the container orchestration platform automatically handles the intricacies of container scheduling, considering factors such as resource availability, hardware constraints, and affinity rules. This automated deployment process significantly reduces the potential for human error and ensures that network functions are deployed with their required configurations and security policies intact.

Health monitoring and self-healing capabilities represent another crucial aspect of automated lifecycle management in containerized 5G deployments. Container orchestration platforms continuously monitor the health of running containers through various mechanisms, including process health checks, application-level probes, and network connectivity tests. When issues are detected, the platform can automatically initiate corrective actions without human intervention. For instance, if a containerized network function becomes unresponsive, the platform can automatically restart the container or reschedule it to a different node. This self-healing capability ensures the high availability of network services and reduces the **mean time to recovery** (**MTTR**) for failed components.

Resource scaling and optimization in 5G networks benefit immensely from the automated lifecycle management capabilities of container platforms. The orchestration system can automatically adjust the resource allocation and number of container instances based on predefined metrics such as CPU utilization, memory usage, or custom performance indicators. This dynamic scaling ensures that network functions can handle varying loads efficiently while maintaining optimal resource utilization. For example, during peak usage periods, the platform can automatically scale out user plane functions to handle increased traffic and scale them back during off-peak hours to conserve resources.

Version management and rolling updates represent another critical aspect of automated lifecycle management that container platforms excel at handling. When new versions of network functions need to be deployed, container orchestration platforms can perform rolling updates that gradually replace old instances with new ones, ensuring zero downtime upgrades. The platform automatically manages the complex choreography of these updates, including traffic routing, health checking of new instances, and rollback procedures if issues are detected. This automated update process is particularly valuable in 5G networks, where different network functions may need to be updated at different times while maintaining service continuity.

Container platforms can automatically manage sensitive configuration data, such as certificates, credentials, and network policies, ensuring that containers always have access to the correct configuration values. This automated configuration management extends to service discovery and load balancing, where the platform automatically updates service endpoints and routing rules as containers are created, moved, or terminated.

Enhanced security isolation

Container technologies have revolutionized the approach to security isolation in 5G networks, offering a sophisticated multi-layered security architecture that addresses the unique challenges of modern telecommunications infrastructure. At its core, container security isolation leverages kernel-level features and security primitives to establish strong boundaries between different network functions and services, providing a level of protection that is both robust and flexible enough to meet the demanding requirements of 5G deployments.

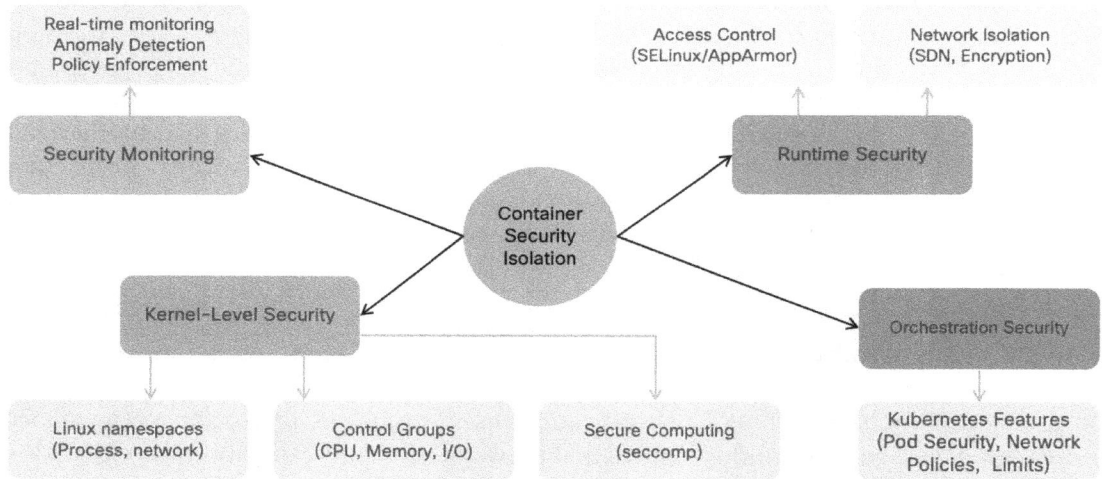

Figure 11.2: Container security isolations

Shown in *Figure 11.2* are the various tenants of container security isolation. The foundation of container security isolation rests on Linux kernel namespaces, which provide process-level isolation that effectively separates container workloads from each other and the underlying host system. In 5G networks, this capability is particularly crucial as it enables the secure coexistence of multiple network functions on the same physical infrastructure. For instance, UPF and control plane functions can run as separate containers on the same host while maintaining strict isolation of their processes, file systems, and network stacks. This isolation ensures that a security breach in one network function cannot easily propagate to others, maintaining the integrity of the overall network architecture.

Control groups (**cgroups**) complement namespace isolation by providing resource-level isolation and control. In 5G deployments, this capability allows service providers to enforce strict resource boundaries between different network functions and slices. For example, a container running a critical control plane function can be allocated guaranteed CPU and memory resources, preventing resource contention from affecting its performance or security posture. This resource isolation is particularly important in network slicing scenarios, where different virtual networks must maintain their performance characteristics without interfering with each other.

Modern container runtimes enhance security isolation through mandatory access control systems such as *SELinux* or *AppArmor*. These security frameworks enable fine-grained access control policies that can be tailored to the specific requirements of different 5G network functions. Service providers can define and enforce detailed security policies that restrict what actions containerized network functions can perform, which files they can access, and which system calls they can make. This level of control is essential for implementing the principle of least privilege and ensuring that network functions operate within well-defined security boundaries.

Network isolation in container deployments is achieved through sophisticated network namespaces and software-defined networking capabilities. Container networking solutions provide isolated network segments for different network functions, with support for encrypted communications and fine-grained network policies. In 5G networks, this enables the creation of secure communication channels between containerized network functions, ensuring that sensitive control plane traffic remains isolated from user plane traffic. Network policies can be implemented to control container-to-container communication, defining explicit rules for which network functions can communicate with each other and under what circumstances.

Secure computing mode (**seccomp**) profiles offer another layer of security isolation by restricting the system calls that containers can make to the kernel. This capability is particularly valuable in 5G networks, where different network functions may require different levels of system access. Service providers can create custom seccomp profiles that limit containers to only the system calls necessary for their operation, reducing the potential attack surface and minimizing the impact of potential security breaches.

Container orchestration platforms enhance these isolation capabilities by providing additional security features at the cluster level. For example, Kubernetes supports pod security standards and network policies that can be used to enforce consistent security standards across all containerized network functions. These policies can be automatically applied and enforced, ensuring that security isolation requirements are maintained even as the network scales and evolves.

Real-time monitoring and security enforcement capabilities are built into modern container platforms, allowing service providers to detect and respond to potential security breaches quickly. Container runtime security tools can monitor container behavior, detect anomalies, and enforce security policies in real-time. This dynamic security enforcement is essential in 5G networks, where the rapid detection and containment of security threats are crucial for maintaining network integrity and service availability.

Enabling multi-vendor 5G deployments

Infrastructure agnosticism stands as one of the most transformative capabilities that containers bring to 5G deployments, fundamentally changing how service providers architect and deploy their networks. This characteristic enables service providers to break free from traditional vendor lock-in constraints while maintaining operational consistency across their diverse infrastructure landscape. The ability to abstract away underlying infrastructure differences has become increasingly crucial as 5G networks continue to expand across heterogeneous environments, from centralized data centers to distributed edge locations.

The implementation of infrastructure agnosticism through containerization addresses several critical challenges that service providers face in their 5G deployments. Traditional network functions, whether physical or virtualized, often require specific hardware configurations or operating system versions, leading to complex qualification processes and restricted hardware choices. Containers eliminate these constraints by providing a consistent runtime environment that remains unchanged regardless of the underlying infrastructure. This abstraction layer ensures that containerized 5G network functions can be deployed seamlessly across different hardware platforms, cloud providers, and edge computing environments without modification or requalification.

In multi-vendor 5G environments, infrastructure agnosticism plays a crucial role in simplifying integration and operations. Service providers can deploy containerized network functions from different vendors on the same infrastructure, managing them through a unified orchestration platform. This capability dramatically reduces the operational complexity traditionally associated with multi-vendor deployments. For instance, a service provider can run containerized 5G core functions from one vendor alongside RAN functions from another vendor, while maintaining consistent deployment, monitoring, and management procedures across both.

By decoupling network functions from specific hardware requirements, providers can make infrastructure decisions based on cost-effectiveness and performance rather than vendor compatibility. This flexibility extends to cloud provider selection, allowing service providers to leverage multiple cloud platforms or shift workloads between private and public clouds based on operational requirements and cost considerations. The ability to avoid vendor lock-in and maintain negotiating power with infrastructure providers often results in substantial cost savings over the network's lifecycle.

Edge computing deployments in 5G networks particularly benefit from infrastructure agnosticism. Service providers must deploy network functions across numerous edge locations, each potentially having different hardware configurations or infrastructure constraints. Containerization ensures that these network functions can be deployed consistently across all edge locations, regardless of the underlying infrastructure differences. This consistency significantly simplifies edge deployment strategies and reduces the operational overhead associated with managing distributed network functions.

The standardization of container orchestration platforms, particularly Kubernetes, has further enhanced the value of infrastructure agnosticism in 5G networks. These platforms provide a uniform interface for deploying and managing containerized workloads across different infrastructure environments. Service providers can implement consistent automation, security policies, and operational procedures across their entire network, from core to edge, without worrying about infrastructure-specific modifications. This standardization has led to the emergence of a robust ecosystem of tools and solutions that work consistently across different infrastructure environments.

The security implications of infrastructure agnosticism also merit consideration. While containers provide consistent security capabilities across different infrastructures, service providers must implement comprehensive security strategies that account for the specific characteristics of each deployment environment. This includes adapting security controls and monitoring capabilities to address the unique threats and compliance requirements associated with different infrastructure environments while maintaining a consistent security posture across the entire network.

Container vulnerabilities

Radio container deployments in 5G environments face a complex web of interconnected security challenges that span multiple layers of the technology stack, creating a uniquely vulnerable landscape where traditional container security concerns intersect with emerging 5G-specific threats. At the foundation, container runtime security is threatened by vulnerable or malicious images, potential container escapes, and privilege escalation attacks, which can be particularly devastating in 5G environments where compromised containers might affect critical network functions or sensitive user data. These risks are amplified in 5G environments where network-specific vulnerabilities, particularly in network slicing and MEC, create additional attack surfaces. The distributed nature of 5G architecture, with its emphasis on edge computing and NFV, introduces new vectors for attacks that traditional container security measures might not adequately address.

Configuration weaknesses, ranging from excessive container permissions to misconfigured Kubernetes deployments, can provide adversaries with entry points into the system. In the context of 5G, these misconfigurations become more critical as they could potentially affect network slicing isolation or compromise the service-based architecture. The supply chain presents another critical vulnerability vector, where compromised CI/CD pipelines, insecure build processes, and inadequate registry security can introduce malicious code or unauthorized access points. This is particularly concerning in 5G deployments where rapid updates and continuous deployment are essential for maintaining network performance and functionality.

In the cloud-native context, these containers must contend with shared resource vulnerabilities, multi-tenancy risks, and microservice-specific threats such as API security gaps and service discovery issues. The integration with 5G infrastructure adds complexity through the need to secure containerized network functions while maintaining the ultra-low latency and high reliability requirements of 5G services. The security of container networking becomes even more crucial in 5G environments, where network slicing and service-based architecture require precise isolation and secure inter-container communication.

The convergence of traditional container security challenges with 5G-specific concerns creates a particularly complex security landscape, where vulnerabilities in one area can cascade across the entire infrastructure, potentially compromising both the container ecosystem and the underlying 5G network services. This is further complicated by the dynamic nature of containerized workloads and the high-performance, low-latency requirements of 5G applications, making security monitoring and response particularly challenging. The need to balance security measures with performance requirements adds another layer of complexity, as excessive security controls could potentially impact the ability to meet 5G SLAs and QoS requirements.

Additionally, the interaction between containerized applications and 5G network functions introduces unique challenges in terms of authentication, authorization, and access control. The potential for lateral movement between compromised containers and critical network functions requires sophisticated security measures that can maintain isolation while allowing necessary communication. The scale and speed of 5G networks also mean that security incidents can propagate rapidly, requiring advanced detection and response capabilities that can operate at 5G speeds while effectively protecting containerized workloads and network functions.

A mind map of the vulnerabilities in a container-based mobile network environment is shown in the following figure:

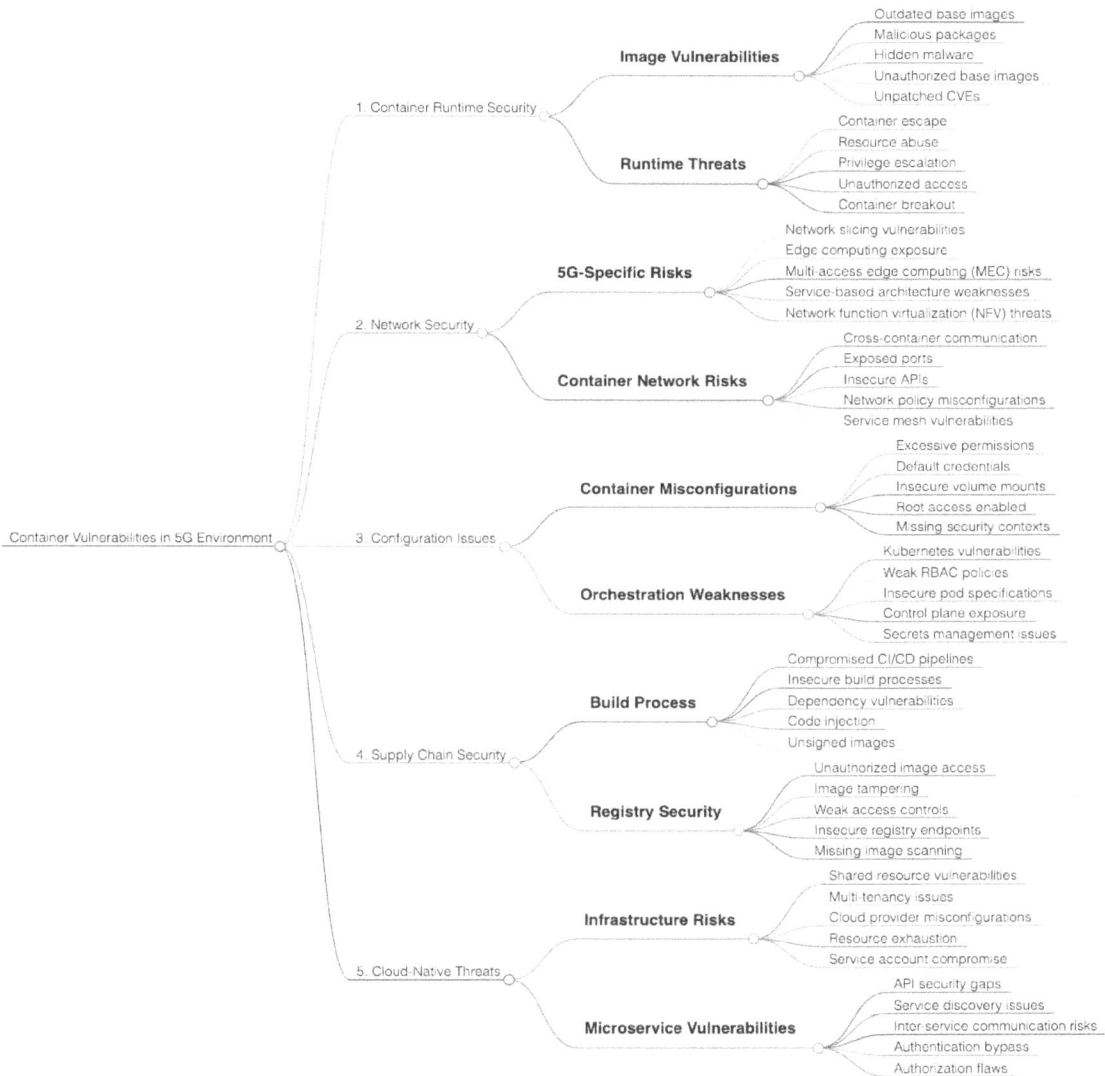

Figure 11.3: *Container vulnerabilities*

Inherent security capabilities

Container environments come equipped with inherent security capabilities that, when properly implemented, provide robust defense mechanisms against many common vulnerabilities. At their core, containers leverage Linux kernel security features such as namespaces and cgroups, which offer strong isolation boundaries and resource control mechanisms. Namespaces ensure process isolation by providing separate views of system resources, effectively containerizing processes and their children, while cgroups enable fine-grained control over resource allocation and usage limits, preventing resource exhaustion attacks and noisy neighbor issues.

Modern container platforms extend these foundational capabilities with additional security features such as MAC, seccomp profiles, and SELinux/AppArmor integration. These mechanisms allow for granular control over container privileges and system call access, significantly reducing the potential attack surface. Furthermore, container orchestration platforms like Kubernetes provide built-in security primitives including **Pod Security Policies (PSP)** or **Pod Security Standards (PSS)**, network policies for microsegmentation, and robust RBAC systems that help enforce least-privilege principles across the container ecosystem.

In the context of 5G environments, these native container security capabilities can be particularly effective when combined with 5G-specific security controls. The inherent support for image signing, vulnerability scanning, and runtime security monitoring helps ensure the integrity of containerized 5G network functions and applications. Additionally, the declarative nature of container configurations enables security-as-code practices, allowing organizations to implement and maintain consistent security policies across their 5G container infrastructure.

Isolation

Isolation is one of the fundamental security capabilities that containers provide. Through namespaces, containers create isolated workspaces for different network functions, ensuring that processes within one container cannot directly interact with or affect processes in other containers. This isolation extends to network interfaces, process trees, and file systems, which is particularly crucial for mobile network deployments where different network functions need to operate independently yet cohesively.

In the configuration shown in the following table, each 5G network function (like AMF and SMF) runs in its own network namespace. This ensures that each function has its own isolated network stack, including routing tables, firewall rules, and network interfaces. This isolation is crucial because it prevents network-level conflicts between different functions and provides an additional security boundary.

Access and Mobility Management Function (AMF) Pod Configuration	Network Policy for AMF isolation	Session Management Function (SMF) Pod Configuration
| ```
apiVersion: v1
kind: Pod
metadata:
  name: amf-function
  namespace: 5g-core
spec:
  containers:
  - name: amf-container
        image: 5gcore/
amf:latest
    securityContext:
      privileged: false
      capabilities:
        drop: ["ALL"]
          add: ["NET_
ADMIN", "NET_RAW"]
      resources:
      limits:
        memory: "4Gi"
        cpu: "2"
      requests:
        memory: "2Gi"
        cpu: "1"
    volumeMounts:
    - name: amf-config
        mountPath: /etc/
amf/config
        readOnly: true
  volumes:
  - name: amf-config
    configMap:
          name: amf-
configuration
``` | ```
apiVersion: networking.
k8s.io/v1
kind: NetworkPolicy
metadata:
    name: amf-network-
policy
    namespace: 5g-core
spec:
  podSelector:
    matchLabels:
      app: amf
  policyTypes:
  - Ingress
  - Egress
  ingress:
  - from:
    - podSelector:
        matchLabels:
          app: smf
    ports:
    - protocol: TCP
      port: 38412
  - from:
    - podSelector:
        matchLabels:
          app: nrf
    ports:
    - protocol: TCP
      port: 29518
  egress:
  - to:
    - podSelector:
        matchLabels:
          app: nrf
    ports:
    - protocol: TCP
      port: 29510
``` | ```
apiVersion: v1
kind: Pod
metadata:
  name: smf-function
  namespace: 5g-core
spec:
  containers:
  - name: smf-container
        image: 5gcore/
smf:latest
    securityContext:
      runAsUser: 1000
      runAsGroup: 3000
      fsGroup: 2000
      allowPrivilegeEs-
calation: false
      readOnlyRoot-
Filesystem: true
    resources:
      limits:
        memory: "3Gi"
        cpu: "1.5"
      requests:
        memory: "1.5Gi"
        cpu: "0.5"
``` |

Table 11.1: Sample configuration for CNF isolation
```

The security context configurations demonstrate how process-level isolation is implemented. For instance, the AMF container runs with dropped privileges, and only specific capabilities (**NET_ADMIN** and **NET_RAW**) are required for its operation. The SMF container runs as a non-root user (UID 1000) and has a read-only root filesystem, preventing any runtime modifications to the container's file system.

The resource specifications show how computing resources are isolated. The AMF is allocated up to 4GB of memory and two CPU cores, while the SMF has different resource constraints. This prevents resource contention and ensures predictable performance for each network function.

The **NetworkPolicy** example demonstrates how network traffic is isolated between different 5G network functions. The AMF is only allowed to communicate with specific functions (SMF and NRF) on specific ports, implementing the principle of least privilege at the network level.

To further enhance isolation in a 5G deployment, additional custom security policies and inter-function communication rules can be configured, as shown in the following table:

Custom Security Context Constraints for 5G core functions	Inter-function Communication Rules for 5G core

apiVersion: security.openshift.io/v1
kind: SecurityContextConstraints
metadata:
  name: 5g-core-scc
  annotations:
  kubernetes.io/description: "Custom SCC for 5G Core Network Functions"
allowPrivilegedContainer: false
runAsUser:
  type: MustRunAs
  uid: 1000
seLinuxContext:
  type: MustRunAs
  seLinuxOptions:
    level: "s0:c123,c456"
fsGroup:
  type: MustRunAs
  ranges:
  - min: 2000
  max: 2100
allowedCapabilities:
  - "NET_ADMIN"
	apiVersion: networking.k8s.io/v1
	kind: NetworkPolicy
	metadata:
	  name: cross-function-policy
	  namespace: 5g-core
	spec:
	  podSelector:
	    matchLabels:
	      app: upf
	  policyTypes:
	  - Ingress
	  - Egress
	  ingress:
	  - from:
	    - namespaceSelector:
	      matchLabels:
	        purpose: 5g-core
	      podSelector:
	        matchLabels:
	          type: control-plane
	    ports:
	    - protocol: UDP

Custom Security Context Constraints for 5G core functions	Inter-function Communication Rules for 5G core
| ```
  - "NET_RAW"
defaultAddCapabilities: []
requiredDropCapabilities:
  - "ALL"
volumes:
  - configMap
  - secret
  - emptyDir
  - persistentVolumeClaim
``` | ```
      port: 2152   # GPRS Tunneling
Protocol (GTP)
    - protocol: TCP
      port: 8805   # Packet Forwarding
Control Protocol
   egress:
   - to:
     - namespaceSelector:
         matchLabels:
           purpose: external-network
     ports:
     - protocol: TCP
       port: 80
     - protocol: TCP
       port: 443
     - protocol: UDP
       port: 53
``` |

Table 11.2: Sample configuration for security context and inter-function communication

Within the **Custom Security Context Constraints (SCC)**, the following are the listed parameters that need important considerations while formulating the configuration:

- User and group control is crucial for 5G functions like UPF that need specific file access permissions while maintaining security:
  - **runAsUser**: This forces containers to run as UID 1000, preventing root-level access.
  - **fsGroup**: This restricts file system group IDs to the range 2000-2100, controlling file permissions.
- SELinux integration is important for protecting sensitive subscriber data and network configuration:
  - **seLinuxContext**: This enforces mandatory access control.
  - **level: "s0:c123,c456"**: This defines specific SELinux categories for 5G workloads.
- Capability management is essential for network functions that need specific network operations while maintaining security.
  - **allowedCapabilities**: This only permits **NET_ADMIN** and **NET_RAW** capabilities.
  - **requiredDropCapabilities**: This drops all other capabilities by default.

- Volume access control provides granular control over container access to host system volumes by defining and enforcing specific permissions and mount options:
  - It restricts volume types to **configMap**, **secret**, **emptyDir**, and **persistentVolumeClaim**.
  - It prevents unauthorized storage access and data exposure.
  - This is critical for protecting subscriber data and network configurations.
- Inter-function communication rules target specific 5G network functions. The **podSelector** section, shown in the following code snippet, specifically targets UPF pod controls data plane traffic flow and is essential for maintaining network slice isolation.

```
podSelector:
  matchLabels:
    app: upf
```

- Ingress traffic control code restricts incoming connections to only 5G core components, allows only GTP (port 2152) and PFCP (port 8805) protocols, and is critical for maintaining secure control plane communication. Shown in the following is a code snippet depicting the same

```
ingress:
- from:
  - namespaceSelector:
      matchLabels:
        purpose: 5g-core
```

- Egress traffic management code, as shown in the following code snippet, controls outbound traffic to external networks, allows HTTP/HTTPS and DNS resolution, and is essential for managing user plane traffic securely.

```
egress:
- to:
  - namespaceSelector:
      matchLabels:
        purpose: external-network
```

Resource control and limitation

Resource control and limitation through cgroups serve as another critical security feature. Service providers can precisely allocate and limit CPU, memory, disk I/O, and network resources for each container. This prevents any single container from consuming excessive resources that could lead to DoS conditions, ensuring the stable operation of critical mobile network functions.

In a 5G network deployment, different network functions have varying resource requirements and priorities. For example, the UPF typically requires more CPU and memory resources due to its packet processing responsibilities, while the AMF needs guaranteed resources for session management but may not be as resource-intensive. The following configuration demonstrates how to implement cgroup controls in a containerized 5G environment using Kubernetes resource management:

Example Kubernetes resource limits for 5G network functions	Example Kubernetes resource limits for 5G network functions

<pre>apiVersion: v1
kind: Pod
metadata:
  name: amf-service
  labels:
    app: 5g-core
    function: amf
spec:
  containers:
  - name: amf-container
    image: 5gcore/amf:latest
    resources:
      requests:
        memory: "4Gi"
        cpu: "2"
      limits:
        memory: "8Gi"
        cpu: "4"
        hugepages-2Mi: "1Gi"
    volumeMounts:
    - mountPath: /dev/hugepages
      name: hugepage
  volumes:
  - name: hugepage
    emptyDir:
      medium: HugePages-2Mi</pre>
	<pre>apiVersion: v1
	kind: Pod
	metadata:
	  name: upf-service
	  labels:
	    app: 5g-core
	    function: upf
	spec:
	  containers:
	  - name: upf-container
	    image: 5gcore/upf:latest
	    resources:
	      requests:
	        memory: "16Gi"
	        cpu: "4"
	      limits:
	        memory: "32Gi"
	        cpu: "8"
	        hugepages-1Gi: "8Gi"
	    volumeMounts:
	    - mountPath: /dev/hugepages
	      name: hugepage
	    securityContext:
	      capabilities:
	            add: ["NET_ADMIN", "SYS_
	ADMIN"]
	    volumes:
	    - name: hugepage
	      emptyDir:
	        medium: HugePages-1Gi</pre>

Table 11.3: Sample configuration for cgroup controls

The following configuration demonstrates how to implement **cgroup** controls in a containerized 5G environment using **SystemD** slices:

```
# SystemD slice configuration for host-level control
[Slice]
# Slice for 5G network functions
CPUAccounting=yes
MemoryAccounting=yes
IOAccounting=yes

# CPU limits
CPUQuota=400%
CPUWeight=100

# Memory limits
MemoryMax=64G
MemoryHigh=48G

# I/O limits
IOWeight=100
IODeviceWeight=/dev/sda 100

# Network control
NetworkAccountingBytes=yes
```

For the AMF service, the code defines moderate resource limits since it handles control plane operations. The code snippet in the above table defines the following listed resource limits:

- Memory requests of 4GB with a limit of 8GB to handle session state.
- CPU requests of two cores with a limit of four cores.
- Allocation of 2MB huge pages for improved memory management.

While the UPF service has higher resource allocations due to its data plane responsibilities. The code snippet in the above table defines the following listed resource limits

- Memory requests of 16GB with a limit of 32GB for packet buffering.
- CPU requests of cores with a limit of eight cores.
- Larger 1GB huge page allocation (8GB total) for efficient packet processing.
- Additional network capabilities through security context settings.

At the system level, the code uses SystemD slices to provide an additional layer of resource control. The code snippet in the above SystemD code defines the following resource limits:

- CPU quota of 400% ensures the 5G services cannot consume more than four full CPU cores.

- Memory limits with a soft limit (`MemoryHigh`) of 48GB and a hard limit (`MemoryMax`) of 64 GB.

- I/O controls to ensure balanced disk access.

- Network accounting is enabled for monitoring data flow.

These configurations help prevent resource contention issues that could affect service quality. For example, if the UPF experiences a sudden spike in traffic, the `cgroup` limits ensure it does not starve other network functions of resources.

Network policy

Network security in containers is enforced through multiple mechanisms. **Container Networking Interfaces** (**CNIs**) enable fine-grained network policies, allowing service providers to control inter-container communication, implement network segmentation, and establish secure communication channels between different network functions. This capability is essential for implementing the complex network architectures required in mobile networks while maintaining security boundaries.

The following code depicts the network policy between AMF and SMF, URLLC-based slice policy, and security zone implementation:

```
# AMF based Network Policies
apiVersion: networking.k8s.io/v1
kind: NetworkPolicy
metadata:
  name: amf-network-policy
  namespace: 5gcore
spec:
  podSelector:
    matchLabels:
      app: amf
  policyTypes:
  - Ingress
  - Egress
  ingress:
  - from:
    - podSelector:
        matchLabels:
```

```
# SMF based Network Policies
apiVersion: networking.k8s.io/v1
kind: NetworkPolicy
metadata:
  name: smf-network-policy
  namespace: 5gcore
spec:
  podSelector:
    matchLabels:
      app: smf
  policyTypes:
  - Ingress
  - Egress
  ingress:
  - from:
    - podSelector:
        matchLabels:
```

```
        app: gnb  # Allow connections              app: amf
from gNodeB                                    ports:
    ports:                                     - protocol: TCP
    - protocol: SCTP                             port: 29502  # N11 interface
      port: 38412  # N2 interface          - from:
  - from:                                      - podSelector:
    - podSelector:                               matchLabels:
        matchLabels:                               app: upf
          app: smf  # Allow connections      ports:
from SMF                                      - protocol: TCP
    ports:                                      port: 29503  # N4 interface
    - protocol: TCP                          egress:
      port: 29502  # N11 interface          - to:
  egress:                                      - podSelector:
  - to:                                          matchLabels:
    - podSelector:                                 app: upf
        matchLabels:                           ports:
          app: smf                             - protocol: TCP
    ports:                                       port: 29503  # N4 interface
    - protocol: TCP
      port: 29502  # N11 interface
```

Table 11.4: Sample configuration of network policy between CNFs

The following table shows a sample code for URLLC-based slice policy:

```
# Network Slice Specific Policies        # Security Zone Policies
apiVersion: networking.k8s.io/v1         apiVersion: networking.k8s.io/v1
kind: NetworkPolicy                      kind: NetworkPolicy
metadata:                                metadata:
  name: urllc-slice-policy                 name: control-plane-zone-policy
  namespace: 5gcore-urllc                  namespace: 5gcore
spec:                                    spec:
  podSelector:                             podSelector:
    matchLabels:                             matchLabels:
      slice: urllc                             zone: control-plane
  policyTypes:                             policyTypes:
  - Ingress                                - Ingress
  - Egress                                 ingress:
  ingress:                                 - from:
  - from:                                    - podSelector:
    - namespaceSelector:                       matchLabels:
```

```
        matchLabels:                         zone: control-plane
            name: 5gcore               - namespaceSelector:
        podSelector:                       matchLabels:
          matchLabels:                         name: monitoring
            app: upf-urllc               podSelector:
      ports:                               matchLabels:
      - protocol: UDP                          app: prometheus
        port: 2152  # GTP-U port       ports:
    egress:                            - protocol: TCP
    - to:                                  port: 9090  # Metrics port
      - namespaceSelector:
          matchLabels:
            name: edge-compute
      ports:
      - protocol: TCP
        port: 443 # Secure communication
with edge applications
```

Table 11.5: *Sample configuration for URLLC based slice*

The core network policies establish strict communication boundaries between core network functions like AMF and SMF. The AMF policy specifically allows SCTP traffic on port 38412 for the N2 interface from gNodeBs and TCP traffic on port 29502 for the N11 interface with SMF. This ensures that core network components only communicate through designated interfaces and protocols.

The URLLC slice policy demonstrates how to isolate traffic for different network slices. It only allows specific UDP traffic on port 2152 for **GPRS Tunneling Protocol User Plane (GTP-U)** from designated UPF pods and restricts egress traffic to edge computing resources over secure HTTPS connections. This is crucial for maintaining the performance guarantees and security requirements of different network slices.

The control plane zone policy shows how to create security zones within the 5G core network. It restricts access to control plane components while allowing necessary monitoring access from Prometheus for metrics collection. This helps maintain the principle of least privilege and reduces the attack surface of critical control plane functions.

Secrets management

Secrets management is another inherent security capability of modern container platforms. Service providers can securely store and distribute sensitive information such as encryption keys, certificates, and credentials needed for mobile network operations. These secrets can be dynamically injected into containers at runtime while remaining encrypted at rest and in transit.

The following configuration establishes a secure secrets management system for various 5G network functions, particularly focusing on the AMF as an example. The setup uses HashiCorp Vault as the secrets management backend, integrated with Kubernetes through the **Container Storage Interface (CSI)** driver.

Vault configuration for 5G network components	Pod configuration using secrets	Network function authentication policy

apiVersion: v1
kind: Secret
metadata:
  name: amf-credentials
  namespace: 5g-core
type: Opaque
data:
  # Base64 encoded credentials for AMF authentication
  amf-id: YW1mLXJlZ2lvbjEtaWQ=
  amf-key: c2VjdXJlLWFtZi1rZXk=
  tls-cert: LS0tLS1CRUd-JTiBDRVJUSUZJQ-0FURS0t...
--- 	
apiVersion: secrets-store.csi.x-k8s.io/v1
kind: SecretProvider-Class
metadata:
  name: vault-5g-core
  namespace: 5g-core
spec:
  provider: vault
  parameters:
    vaultAddress: "https://vault.internal:8200"
    roleName: "5g-core-role"
    objects: |
      - objectName: "amf-cert"
	apiVersion: v1
	kind: Pod
	metadata:
	  name: amf-service
	  namespace: 5g-core
	spec:
	  containers:
	  - name: amf-container
	    image: 5g-amf:latest
	    volumeMounts:
	      - name: secrets-store-inline
	        mountPath: "/mnt/secrets-store"
	        readOnly: true
	    env:
	    - name: AMF_ID
	      valueFrom:
	        secretKeyRef:
	          name: amf-credentials
	          key: amf-id
	    - name: AMF_KEY
	      valueFrom:
	        secretKeyRef:
	          name: amf-credentials
	          key: amf-key
	  volumes:
	    - name: secrets-store-inline
	      csi:
	        driver: secrets-store.csi.k8s.io
	        readOnly: true
		apiVersion: authentication.k8s.io/v1
		kind: Policy
		metadata:
		  name: 5g-core-auth-policy
		  namespace: 5g-core
		spec:
		  rules:
		  - resources:
		    - secrets
		    operations:
		    - CREATE
		    - UPDATE
		    providers:
		    - name: vault-provider
		      vault:
		        roles:
		        - "5g-core-role"
		        policies:
		        - "5g-secrets-policy"

```
            secretPath:              volumeAttributes:
"s e c r e t / 5 g / a m f /            secretProvider-
certificates"                 Class: "vault-5g-core"
        secretKey: "tls.
crt"
     - objectName: "smf-
credentials"
            secretPath:
"secret/5g/smf/auth"
            secretKey:
"credentials.json"
---
```

Table 11.6: Sample configuration for secure secrets management

The first section in the above code defines basic credentials for the AMF, including its identifier and authentication key, stored as Kubernetes secrets. These are encoded in base64 format for security. The **SecretProviderClass** configuration establishes the connection between Kubernetes and Vault, defining how secrets should be retrieved and managed. It specifies paths for different types of secrets needed by 5G network functions. The pod configuration shows how a 5G network function (in this case, the AMF) can securely access these secrets. It mounts the secrets as a volume and uses environment variables for certain credentials. The authentication policy defines which network functions can access which secrets and what operations they can perform, implementing the principle of least privilege.

Secure CI and CD process

A secure CI/CD process serves as a critical foundation for container security in mobile networks, especially in 5G mobile deployments, acting as the first line of defense in ensuring that containerized network functions and applications are secure from development through deployment.

In the context of 5G deployments, containers house various network functions, including **virtualized Radio Access Network** (**vRAN**) components, core network functions, and edge computing applications. The CI/CD pipeline must incorporate security at every stage to protect these sensitive components that handle subscriber data and critical network operations.

Secure coding and scanning

The process begins at the development stage, where the CI/CD pipeline should enforce secure coding practices and automatically scan container images for vulnerabilities. For example, when a developer pushes code for a new 5G network function, the pipeline automatically triggers security scans using tools like *Anchore* or *Aqua Security* to identify known vulnerabilities in both the application code and the base container images. This helps catch issues like outdated software versions or known **Common Vulnerabilities and Exposures** (**CVEs**) in dependencies before they reach production.

The primary focus starts with writing secure code that follows industry best practices. This includes input validation, proper error handling, secure communication protocols, and proper access controls. For 5G applications, special attention must be paid to handling subscriber data and implementing proper network isolation. The code should be regularly analyzed using **Static Application Security Testing** (**SAST**) tools, as shown in the following CI/CD configuration table, where Semgrep is used to scan for OWASP Top 10 and CWE Top 25 vulnerabilities.

Container image scanning is implemented at multiple stages. The following pipeline configuration shows the use of **Trivy**, a comprehensive container scanner that checks for vulnerabilities in both the base image and added layers. For 5G applications, custom security policies are defined to check for specific requirements related to network function virtualization and container security.

Example GitLab CI/CD pipeline configuration for secure container builds	Secure Dockerfile example. Base image security—Pin a specific version and use minimal base
| ```
variables:
  DOCKER_CONTENT_TRUST: "1"
  DOCKER_TLS_CERTDIR: "/certs"
  SCANNER_VERSION: "latest"
  TRIVY_VERSION: "0.24.0"
  SECURE_LOG_LEVEL: "debug"

stages:
  - code-analysis
  - build
  - security-scan
  - sign
  - deploy

sast:
  stage: code-analysis
  script:
    - semgrep ci --config "p/owasp-top-ten" --config "p/cwe-top-25"
``` | ```
FROM    ubuntu:22.04@sha256:abc123...
AS build

# Set security-related build arguments
ARG USERNAME=appuser
ARG USER_UID=10001
ARG USER_GID=$USER_UID

# Install security updates and required packages
RUN apt-get update && apt-get upgrade -y && \
    apt-get install -y --no-install-recommends \
    ca-certificates \
    curl \
    && rm -rf /var/lib/apt/lists/*

# Create non-root user
``` |

```
  # Enable specific rules for 5G
components
  - semgrep ci --config "p/network-
security"
 artifacts:
   reports:
    sast: gl-sast-report.json

dependency-check:
  stage: code-analysis
  script:
     - dependency-check --project
"5g-container" --scan . --format JSON
   # Additional checks for known 5G
vulnerabilities
  - dependency-check --suppression
suppress-5g.xml
  artifacts:
   reports:
     dependency: dependency-report.
json

container-build:
  stage: build
  script:
     # Use multi-stage builds to
minimize attack surface
   - |
    cat > Dockerfile << EOF
      FROM golang:1.21-alpine AS
builder
     WORKDIR /app
     COPY . .
     RUN go mod verify
     RUN CGO_ENABLED=0 GOOS=linux go
build -a -installsuffix cgo -o main .

      FROM gcr.io/distroless/static-
debian11
    COPY --from=builder /app/main /
```

```
RUN groupadd --gid $USER_GID $USERNAME
\
    && useradd --uid $USER_UID --gid
$USER_GID -m $USERNAME \
    && chmod 755 /home/$USERNAME


# Set working directory and copy
application files
WORKDIR /app
COPY --chown=$USERNAME:$USERNAME . .

# Build application with security
flags
RUN go build -ldflags="-w -s" -o main

# Multi-stage build for minimal final
image
FROM        gcr.io/distroless/static-
debian11

# Copy only necessary files from
build stage
COPY --from=build /app/main /
COPY --from=build /etc/ssl/certs/ca-
certificates.crt /etc/ssl/certs/

# Use non-root user
USER nonroot:nonroot

# Define health check
HEALTHCHECK            --interval=30s
--timeout=3s \
    CMD ["/main", "health"]

# Use exec form of ENTRYPOINT
ENTRYPOINT ["/main"]
```

```
    USER nonroot:nonroot
    ENTRYPOINT ["/main"]
    EOF
  - docker build --no-cache -t ${CI_
REGISTRY_IMAGE}:${CI_COMMIT_SHA} .

trivy-scan:
  stage: security-scan
  script:
        - trivy  image  --severity
HIGH,CRITICAL            ${CI_REGISTRY_
IMAGE}:${CI_COMMIT_SHA}
    # Custom policies for 5G-specific
security requirements
        - trivy  conf  --policy
"./5g-policies/" .

cosign-sign:
  stage: sign
  script:
    - cosign sign --key ${COSIGN_KEY}
${CI_REGISTRY_IMAGE}:${CI_COMMIT_
SHA}
      - cosign verify --key ${COSIGN_
PUBLIC_KEY}              ${CI_REGISTRY_
IMAGE}:${CI_COMMIT_SHA}
```

Table 11.7: Sample pipeline configuration of Trivy

The Dockerfile itself implements several security best practices. It uses multi-stage builds to minimize the attack surface, employs specific version pinning with SHA256 digests to prevent supply chain attacks, and creates a non-root user for running the application. The final image is based on Google's distroless container, which contains only the application and its runtime dependencies, significantly reducing the attack surface. Runtime security is addressed through various mechanisms in the container configuration. The Dockerfile implements security-related build arguments, creates a non-privileged user, and sets appropriate file permissions. The container is configured to run with minimal capabilities and resources, following the principle of least privilege.

Image signing and verification

Image signing and verification are crucial in maintaining container integrity throughout the deployment process. Each container image in a 5G environment should be cryptographically signed using tools like *Notary* or *Cosign*. For instance, when deploying a container for a UPF, the CI/CD pipeline verifies the signature before allowing the deployment, ensuring that the container has not been tampered with between the build and deployment stages.

The signing process begins with establishing a robust key management system. Service providers typically use tools like *HashiCorp Vault* or *AWS KMS* to store and manage signing keys securely. These keys must be carefully protected as they form the root of trust for the entire container ecosystem. The **public key infrastructure** (**PKI**) established for signing container images should be separate from other PKI systems to maintain proper security boundaries.

Modern container signing commonly employs Cosign, a tool specifically designed for container and artifact signing. Cosign offers several advantages, including integration with cloud key management systems and support for keyless signing using OpenID Connect identities. In production environments, signing should be automated within the CI/CD pipeline, with keys securely injected during the build process.

The verification process must be enforced at multiple points in the deployment pipeline. First, verification occurs during the CI/CD process before containers are promoted to production repositories. Second, verification happens at runtime when containers are deployed to the Kubernetes cluster. This dual-verification approach ensures that even if the CI/CD pipeline is compromised, unsigned containers cannot reach production systems.

For 5G deployments, policy enforcement becomes particularly important. Kubernetes admission controllers can be configured to reject any container that lacks a valid signature from an authorized key. This ensures that even if an attacker gains access to the cluster, they cannot deploy unauthorized containers. The admission controller can also enforce additional policies, such as requiring specific signature annotations that indicate the container has passed security scans.

Docker Content Trust (**DCT**) provides an additional layer of signing capability that integrates directly with Docker registries. When enabled, DCT ensures that only signed images can be pulled from the registry. This is particularly useful in 5G environments where container registries might be distributed across edge locations, as it ensures consistency in signature verification regardless of where the container is deployed. An example of a container image signing and verification code is mentioned in the following:

```bash
#!/bin/bash
# Generate GPG keys for signing
gpg --gen-key
# Export the public key
gpg --armor --export "<your-email>" > public.key

# Sign container image using cosign
# First install cosign
```

```
curl  -O  -L  https://github.com/sigstore/cosign/releases/latest/download/
cosign-linux-amd64
sudo mv cosign-linux-amd64 /usr/local/bin/cosign
chmod +x /usr/local/bin/cosign

# Generate cosign key pair
cosign generate-key-pair

# Sign a container image
cosign sign --key cosign.key registry.example.com/myapp:1.0.0

# Verify a signed container image
cosign verify --key cosign.pub registry.example.com/myapp:1.0.0

# Using Docker Content Trust (Notary)
# Enable DCT
export DOCKER_CONTENT_TRUST=1

# Create a delegation key
docker trust key generate mykey
docker trust signer add --key mykey.pub mykey registry.example.com/myapp

# Sign and push image
docker trust sign registry.example.com/myapp:1.0.0

# Kubernetes manifest to enforce signing verification
apiVersion: admissionregistration.k8s.io/v1
kind: ValidatingAdmissionPolicy
metadata:
  name: image-signature-policy
spec:
  failurePolicy: Fail
  matchConstraints:
    resourceRules:
    - apiGroups: [""]
      apiVersions: ["v1"]
      operations: ["CREATE", "UPDATE"]
      resources: ["pods"]
  validations:
```

```
  - expression: "object.spec.containers.all(container,
      trusted.containsImage(container.image))"
    message: "All container images must be signed by trusted authorities"

# Example of integration with CI pipeline (GitLab CI)
sign_verify_job:
  script:
    - |
      # Import signing keys
      echo "$COSIGN_PRIVATE_KEY" > cosign.key
      echo "$COSIGN_PUBLIC_KEY" > cosign.pub

      # Build and sign image
      docker build -t $CI_REGISTRY_IMAGE:$CI_COMMIT_SHA .
      cosign sign --key cosign.key $CI_REGISTRY_IMAGE:$CI_COMMIT_SHA

      # Verify signature before deployment
      cosign verify --key cosign.pub $CI_REGISTRY_IMAGE:$CI_COMMIT_SHA
```

Configuration validation

Configuration validation is another critical aspect where the CI/CD pipeline ensures that container security policies are properly implemented. This includes validating network policies, resource limits, and security contexts. For example, when deploying containers for the 5G core network functions, the pipeline automatically checks that network policies are configured to allow only necessary communication between components, preventing unauthorized access between network slices.

At the fundamental level, configuration validation begins with Kubernetes manifests that define the security parameters for container deployments. These manifests must be validated against security best practices and organizational policies before deployment.

These configurations implement several critical security controls. The Pod specification demonstrates proper security context configuration, including running containers as non-root users, implementing read-only root filesystems, and dropping unnecessary capabilities. Resource limits are explicitly defined to prevent denial-of-service scenarios through resource exhaustion.

Service providers can use the network policy to implement network segmentation in a 5G environment, allowing only specific communication paths between network functions, like restricting communication to only allowed ports and specifically named components, which is crucial in a 5G core network where different network functions need to communicate in a controlled manner.

The OPA Gatekeeper, as shown in the following, can be used to implement policy-as-code, using Rego language to define and enforce security policies. These configurations should be regularly reviewed and updated to address new security requirements and threats.

```
# OPA Gatekeeper constraint template for validating security contexts
apiVersion: templates.gatekeeper.sh/v1beta1
kind: ConstraintTemplate
metadata:
  name: k8spspprivilegedcontainer
spec:
  crd:
    spec:
      names:
        kind: K8sPSPPrivilegedContainer
  targets:
    - target: admission.k8s.gatekeeper.sh
      rego: |
        package k8spspprivileged
        violation[{"msg": msg}] {
          c := input_containers[_]
          c.securityContext.privileged
         msg := sprintf("Privileged container is not allowed: %v", [c.name])
        }
        input_containers[c] {
          c := input.review.object.spec.containers[_]
        }
        input_containers[c] {
          c := input.review.object.spec.initContainers[_]
        }
```

The following Python validation script demonstrates how to implement custom validation logic that can be integrated into CI/CD pipelines. It checks for security context configurations and resource specifications, providing detailed feedback when violations are found. This type of validation can be expanded to include additional checks specific to 5G network function requirements.

```
# Example of a custom validation script using Python
import yaml
import sys

def validate_security_context(pod_spec):
```

```python
        containers = pod_spec.get('containers', [])
        for container in containers:
            security_context = container.get('securityContext', {})

            # Validate security settings
            if security_context.get('privileged', False):
                return False, "Privileged containers are not allowed"

            if security_context.get('allowPrivilegeEscalation', True):
                return False, "Privilege escalation must be disabled"

            if not security_context.get('readOnlyRootFilesystem', False):
                return False, "Root filesystem must be read-only"

        pod_security_context = pod_spec.get('securityContext', {})
        if not pod_security_context.get('runAsNonRoot', False):
            return False, "Pods must run as non-root"

        return True, "Security context validation passed"

def validate_resources(pod_spec):
    containers = pod_spec.get('containers', [])
    for container in containers:
        resources = container.get('resources', {})
        if not resources:
            return False, "Resource limits must be specified"

        limits = resources.get('limits', {})
        if not ('memory' in limits and 'cpu' in limits):
            return False, "Memory and CPU limits must be specified"

    return True, "Resource validation passed"

def main():
    with open(sys.argv[1], 'r') as f:
        pod_manifest = yaml.safe_load(f)

    # Run validations
```

```
        security_valid,   security_msg   =   validate_security_context(pod_
manifest['spec'])
    resources_valid, resources_msg = validate_resources(pod_manifest['spec'])

    if not all([security_valid, resources_valid]):
        print("Validation failed:")
        if not security_valid:
            print(f"Security context: {security_msg}")
        if not resources_valid:
            print(f"Resources: {resources_msg}")
        sys.exit(1)

    print("All validations passed")
    sys.exit(0)

if __name__ == "__main__":
    main()
```

To implement these configurations effectively, organizations should integrate these validation checks into their CI/CD pipelines. For example, the Python script can be executed as a pre-deployment check, while the OPA Gatekeeper constraints run continuously in the cluster to enforce policies at runtime.

Conclusion

Container security represents a critical balance between the transformative benefits of containerization and the complex security challenges it presents. While containers offer lightweight, rapid deployment and consistent environment management capabilities, they introduce a multifaceted vulnerability landscape that spans from image security to runtime threats, particularly pronounced in advanced deployments like 5G environments.

Containers provide robust inherent security features, including namespace isolation, cgroups resource controls, and mandatory access control systems. When combined with orchestration platform capabilities such as pod security policies, network policies, and RBAC systems, these features enable comprehensive security controls aligned with zero-trust principles.

A secure CI/CD process plays a vital role in maintaining container security throughout the application lifecycle. By implementing security controls at each pipeline stage, from code commit to production deployment, organizations can effectively **shift left** security practices. This includes robust image scanning, signing, and verification processes, secure registry maintenance, and immutable infrastructure practices.

As container technologies advance and new threats emerge, container security continues to evolve. Success in container security requires not only understanding and implementing current best practices but also maintaining adaptability and vigilance. Organizations must commit to continuous security improvement, regular control assessments, and adaptation to new vulnerabilities while preserving the agility and efficiency benefits that containerization provides.

In the next chapter, we focus on the critical boundaries where telecom networks interface with external systems and the internet. Perimeter and edge security represent the first line of defense for service provider networks, serving as crucial control points for traffic entering and exiting the network ecosystem. This chapter will explore the architectural considerations, threat models, and defense mechanisms specifically designed for telecom network perimeters. We will examine how traditional security concepts like defense-in-depth apply in modern telecom environments, the challenges of securing network edges in distributed cloud architectures, and the evolving role of edge computing in reshaping security paradigms.

Points to remember

- **Container isolation and resource management:** The foundation of container security lies in process-level isolation through Linux namespaces, which creates separate environments for processes, networks, and filesystems. This isolation is complemented by control groups (cgroups) that prevent resource exhaustion attacks by enforcing strict limits on CPU, memory, and I/O usage. Understanding these fundamental mechanisms is crucial for implementing effective security controls and preventing container escape vulnerabilities.

- **Multi-layered security approach:** Container security demands protection at multiple layers, from the base image to the runtime environment. This includes rigorous image scanning for known vulnerabilities, implementing secure base images with minimal attack surface, and maintaining strict access controls throughout the container lifecycle. Runtime security features such as seccomp profiles, SELinux/AppArmor policies, and capability restrictions work together to create a comprehensive security framework that protects against various attack vectors.

- **CI/CD pipeline security:** A secure continuous integration and deployment pipeline forms the backbone of container security. This encompasses automated security testing at every stage, including vulnerability scanning of dependencies, static code analysis for security flaws, and dynamic testing of running applications. Image signing and verification ensure the authenticity and integrity of container images, while secure registries with access controls prevent unauthorized modifications to container artifacts. The implementation of IaC security scanning helps identify misconfigurations before they reach production environments.

- **Network security and communication controls:** Network security in containerized environments requires careful attention to both internal and external communications. Network policies should enforce strict rules about which containers can communicate with each other, implementing the principle of least privilege at the network level. Service mesh implementations provide additional layers of security through mutual TLS authentication, traffic encryption, and fine-grained access controls, while also enabling detailed monitoring and logging of container communications.

Exercises

1. Explain how Linux namespaces contribute to container isolation and list at least three different types of namespaces.

2. What is the fundamental difference between containerization and virtualization in terms of isolation and resource sharing?

3. How do cgroups enhance container security? Provide two specific examples of their security benefits. Compare and contrast the security implications of traditional macro cell deployments versus small cell configurations. What unique security challenges does each present?

4. A container in your production environment is experiencing unexpected memory growth and affecting neighboring containers. Which inherent container security capabilities would you investigate, and what specific steps would you take to address this issue?

5. Your team has discovered a vulnerability in a production container image. Describe the complete process of:
   a. Assessing the vulnerability impact
   b. Implementing immediate mitigation
   c. Long-term remediation steps

6. Your organization is moving from traditional virtualization to containerization. Create a security migration plan those addresses:
   a. Network security considerations
   b. Storage security
   c. Access control mechanisms
   d. Monitoring and logging requirements

7. Write a sample Dockerfile that implements security best practices, including:
   a. Non-root user
   b. Minimal base image
   c. Multi-stage builds
   d. Security scanning

CHAPTER 12
Perimeter and Edge Security

Introduction

The telecommunications landscape is undergoing a fundamental transformation, characterized by the evolution from centralized network architectures to distributed computing models. This shift has elevated the critical importance of robust perimeter and edge security in protecting modern telecom infrastructure. As telecommunications networks expand beyond their traditional role of providing voice and data services, they now serve as essential infrastructure for diverse applications across healthcare, autonomous vehicles, and other critical sectors.

This chapter explores the comprehensive security frameworks necessary to protect these evolving networks, with a particular focus on the challenges and solutions at the network edge. We examine how security architectures have adapted to meet both regulatory requirements and emerging threats, while supporting the operational demands of modern telecommunications services. Special attention is given to the impact of **Multi-access Edge Computing** (MEC) and distributed edge infrastructure, which have fundamentally altered traditional security paradigms.

The discussion encompasses various crucial elements, from regulatory compliance with standards like GDPR and HIPAA to the technical implementation of security controls, including advanced firewalls, intrusion prevention systems, and encryption protocols. We explore how these components work together to create multi-layered defense strategies that protect both infrastructure and customer data. This comprehensive examination is essential for network architects, security professionals, and telecommunications engineers working to build and maintain secure, reliable network infrastructure in an increasingly complex digital landscape.

Structure

This chapter will cover the following topics:

- Need for perimeter and edge security
- Regulatory compliance and standards security
- Traditional infrastructure security
- MEC and edge infrastructure
- Perimeter and edge security controls
- Security architecture and design
- MEC security considerations and architecture

Objectives

This chapter examines the evolution and implementation of perimeter and edge security in modern telecommunications networks, with particular emphasis on the transition from traditional security models to those required by emerging edge computing architectures. The content progresses through several key areas, beginning with the fundamental principles of telecommunications security and its critical role in protecting infrastructure and ensuring service continuity.

We examine the regulatory landscape that shapes security implementations, including international standards and data protection laws that telecommunications providers must navigate. The chapter establishes a baseline understanding of traditional telecommunications infrastructure security before exploring how MEC and distributed edge infrastructure have transformed security requirements and architectures.

A comprehensive analysis of edge and perimeter controls details specific security mechanisms and technologies essential for protecting modern networks. This includes an examination of how traditional security controls are adapting to meet emerging requirements across distributed architectures. The discussion culminates in an in-depth exploration of MEC and perimeter security architectures, presenting contemporary approaches to securing edge computing environments while maintaining robust perimeter defenses.

The chapter aims to provide telecommunications professionals with both theoretical knowledge and practical insights necessary for developing and implementing effective security strategies. Through this progression, readers will understand how perimeter and edge security are evolving to address new challenges while ensuring the protection of critical infrastructure and services in an increasingly complex telecommunications landscape.

Need for perimeter and edge security

The telecommunications industry has undergone a dramatic transformation in recent decades, evolving from traditional circuit-switched networks to complex, distributed digital ecosystems, as we have seen in the initial chapters. This evolution has fundamentally changed how service providers must approach security, particularly in the context of perimeter and edge protection. As telecommunications service providers become increasingly central to global digital infrastructure, the importance of robust security measures cannot be overstated. Recent industry data reveals that telecommunications providers face an average of 1,500 cyberattacks per week, with the average cost of a data breach in the telecom sector exceeding $4.5 million in 2023. These statistics underscore the critical nature of securing modern telecom networks.

Modern telecom networks bear little resemblance to their predecessors. The traditional concept of clearly defined network boundaries has given way to a complex maze of interconnected systems and services. Today's networks are characterized by distributed architectures spanning multiple edge locations, seamlessly integrated cloud-native services, and dynamic resource allocation capabilities. This transformation has created what security experts refer to as a *disappearing perimeter*, where traditional security approaches no longer suffice to protect critical infrastructure and services. The integration of mobile edge computing and hybrid cloud-edge deployments has further complicated the security landscape, with recent studies indicating that 60% of telecom security incidents now originate at network edges rather than the core.

Telecom service providers handle vast amounts of sensitive information, from customer personal data and location information to communication metadata and payment details. The protection of this information at all network boundaries and edges is not just a security requirement but a legal and ethical obligation. Recent regulatory actions against telecom providers have demonstrated the severe consequences of data protection failures, with fines reaching millions of dollars and causing significant reputational damage. Adding on to these considerations, the proliferation of edge computing in telecommunications has introduced unprecedented security challenges. Processing data at the edge requires a fundamental rethinking of security architectures. Physical security limitations at edge locations, resource constraints affecting security implementations, and complex data flow patterns all contribute to an expanded attack surface. Security measures must evolve to address these challenges while maintaining the performance benefits that edge computing provides.

As telecommunications networks continue to evolve, several factors will further amplify the importance of perimeter and edge security. The rollout of 5G technologies introduces new requirements for network slicing security and ultra-low latency service protection. The emergence of quantum computing threats and AI-powered attacks necessitates forward-thinking security strategies. Additionally, the regulatory environment continues to evolve, with new compliance requirements and cross-border data protection rules shaping the security landscape.

Regulatory compliance and standards drivers

The telecommunications industry operates under a complex framework of regulations and standards designed to ensure network security, protect customer data, and maintain service reliability, as we saw in the initial chapter regarding compliance and standards. These requirements have become increasingly stringent as telecommunications infrastructure has become more critical to global operations and as cyber threats have evolved.

The **National Institute of Standards and Technology** (**NIST**) framework encompasses several key standards, particularly relevant to telecommunications security. *NIST Special Publication 800-53 Rev. 5* provides a comprehensive security and privacy controls framework, while NIST SP 800-207 defines the Zero Trust architecture as increasingly crucial for modern telecom networks. The NIST **Cybersecurity Framework** (**CSF**) 1.1 and its upcoming 2.0 version provide the core functions: *Identify, Protect, Detect, Respond,* and *Recover*. Telecom service providers often reference *NIST SP 800-160 Vol. 1* for system security engineering and *NIST SP 800-61 Rev. 2* for incident handling. For cryptographic standards, NIST FIPS 140-2 (and its successor FIPS 140-3) remain fundamental for validating security systems in telecom infrastructure. Similarly, the *ISO/IEC 27001:2013* (updated in 2022) serves as the primary standard for information security management systems. It works in conjunction with ISO/IEC 27011:2016 (updated in 2023), which provides specific guidelines for telecommunications organizations. For cloud security relevant to modern telecom infrastructure, ISO/IEC 27017:2015 provides additional controls, while ISO/IEC 27701:2019 addresses privacy information management, particularly relevant for telecom providers handling personal data.

The telecommunications industry has developed its own set of security standards through organizations such as GSMA and 3GPP. Current GSMA security guidelines provide detailed requirements for network edge protection, API security, and IoT service protection. The GSMA FS.13 through FS.18 series addresses network equipment security requirements. GSMA PRD FS.20 defines baseline security controls for IoT device connectivity. Current standards include GSMA FS.31 for 5G security assurance specifications and GSMA FS.40 for network slicing security. The recently superseded GSMA IR.88 (LTE and SAE roaming guidelines) remains relevant for many operators, while its successor IR.88 5G provides updated security requirements. 3GPP security specifications form the backbone of mobile network security. Core specifications include TS 33.501 (5G security architecture), which replaced TS 33.401 (4G security). Supplementary specifications include TS 33.51x series for security assurance, TS 33.535 for authentication and key management, and TS 33.503 for policy and charging control. The emerging TS 33.558 addresses security aspects of edge computing in 5G networks. Legacy specifications such as TS 33.102 (3G security) remain relevant for networks maintaining older infrastructure.

For perimeter and edge security, the **General Data Protection Regulation (GDPR) (EU)** *2016/679 Article 32* specifically addresses the security of processing, while *Articles 25* and *35* mandate privacy by design and data protection impact assessments. The **California Consumer Privacy Act (CCPA)** and its successor, the **California Privacy Rights Act (CPRA)**, require specific security measures for data protection at network edges. These regulations emphasize the need for encryption (both in transit and at rest), access controls, and continuous monitoring of data processing activities at edge locations.

The regulatory and standards landscape for telecom security continues to evolve as new technologies and threats emerge. Understanding and implementing these specific standards while preparing for emerging ones is crucial for maintaining effective security controls across both traditional and modern infrastructure.

Traditional infrastructure security

Radio Traditional infrastructure security in telecommunications remains foundational despite the rapid evolution of modern networks. While new technologies have transformed the industry, many core security principles and elements established in traditional infrastructure continue to serve as the backbone of telecom security. These fundamental security measures, when properly implemented and maintained, provide essential protection that complements modern security solutions. The protection of physical telecommunications infrastructure begins with robust site security measures. Central offices, data centers, and network facilities require multiple layers of physical protection. Access control systems serve as the first line of defense, utilizing a combination of security personnel, electronic access cards, and biometric authentication to ensure that only authorized personnel can enter sensitive areas. Environmental monitoring systems continuously track temperature, humidity, and power conditions, as their stability is crucial for equipment operation and security. These systems are supplemented by comprehensive video surveillance networks that provide continuous monitoring of both internal and external areas, with modern CCTV systems now incorporating AI-enabled motion detection and automated alert mechanisms.

Legacy network elements, while often considered outdated, continue to play a vital role in many telecom networks. Core network protection for these elements focuses on fundamental security controls such as robust authentication mechanisms, encrypted management interfaces, and carefully configured access control lists. However, these traditional security measures face significant limitations in today's threat landscape. Legacy systems often struggle with modern encryption standards, lack support for advanced security protocols, and may be vulnerable to contemporary attack vectors. Despite these limitations, many organizations must maintain these systems due to their critical role in supporting essential services. The traditional perimeter security model was built on the concept of a clear boundary between trusted internal networks and untrusted external networks. This approach utilized firewalls, intrusion detection systems, and **demilitarized zones** (**DMZs**) to create security boundaries. Network segmentation was implemented through VLANs and physical separation, while access controls were managed through static rules and policies. While these concepts have evolved significantly in modern networks, they established crucial principles that remain relevant: defense in depth, least privilege access, and the importance of network segregation.

Traditional infrastructure security approaches face several significant challenges in modern environments. The rigid nature of traditional perimeter security struggles to adapt to cloud services and mobile edge computing. Legacy authentication systems often lack support for modern multi-factor authentication standards. Additionally, traditional monitoring tools may not provide the granular visibility required for today's complex networks. These limitations highlight the need for evolution while underscoring the importance of maintaining and updating traditional security measures where they remain effective. The integration of traditional infrastructure security with modern approaches requires careful consideration. Service provider organizations must maintain essential physical security measures while adapting them to modern requirements. For example, traditional access control systems are being enhanced with mobile credentials and cloud-based management. Legacy network elements are being protected through additional security layers and modern monitoring tools. This hybrid approach ensures that fundamental security measures continue to provide value while addressing their inherent limitations.

MEC and edge infrastructure

The evolution towards edge computing in telecommunications networks has historically relied on centralized architectures, with data processing and application hosting concentrated in core data centers. However, the increasing demand for low-latency services and real-time applications has driven a fundamental shift towards edge computing. This evolution began with the need to reduce the physical distance between users and computing resources, as even the speed of light creates noticeable latency when data must travel hundreds or thousands of kilometers to centralized facilities. The transition to edge computing represents a paradigm shift in how telecommunications networks are architected, moving from a hierarchical, centralized model to a distributed computing framework that brings processing power closer to where data is generated and consumed.

MEC architecture in telecommunications networks creates a distributed cloud computing environment at the network edge, typically within or adjacent to mobile base stations, central offices, or aggregation points. This architecture requires careful integration with existing network elements, including **radio access network** (**RAN**) components, mobile core networks, and transport infrastructure. The integration challenges are multifaceted, involving both technical and operational aspects. Network operators implement sophisticated orchestration systems to manage distributed edge resources, ensure seamless connectivity between edge sites and core networks, and maintain consistent security policies across all edge locations. The integration also accounts for backward compatibility with existing services while enabling new edge-enabled capabilities.

The role of edge computing becomes particularly crucial in 5G networks and beyond. 5G's promise of **Ultra-Reliable Low-Latency Communications** (**URLLC**) and **massive Machine-Type Communications** (**mMTC**) is fundamentally dependent on edge computing capabilities. The 5G **service-based architecture** (**SBA**) inherently supports edge computing through network slicing and service function chaining, allowing operators to deploy customized network configurations for different use cases. Future network evolution will see even greater integration of edge computing, with 6G networks potentially incorporating AI and ML capabilities directly at the network edge for autonomous network operation and advanced service delivery. Edge computing enables a wide spectrum of applications across various industries. In industrial settings, edge computing supports real-time process control and automation, with local processing ensuring sub-millisecond response times critical for robotic systems and manufacturing processes. For autonomous vehicles, edge nodes process sensor data and make split-second decisions about vehicle operation, while also facilitating **vehicle-to-everything** (**V2X**) communications. Smart cities leverage edge computing for real-time video analytics, traffic management, and public safety applications. In the consumer space, edge computing enhances mobile gaming, augmented reality, and virtual reality experiences by reducing latency and improving application responsiveness.

Implementing edge computing infrastructure requires careful consideration of several technical aspects. Power efficiency becomes crucial as edge sites often have limited power availability compared to traditional data centers. Cooling solutions must be adapted for diverse deployment environments, from urban street cabinets to rural cell sites. The infrastructure must be highly resilient, with automated failover capabilities and self-healing mechanisms to maintain service continuity. Service providers must also implement sophisticated monitoring and management systems to maintain visibility and control over distributed edge resources. Edge computing introduces new security considerations in telecommunications networks. Each edge site becomes a potential attack surface that must be protected. This requires implementing robust physical and cybersecurity measures, including secure boot processes for edge servers, encrypted communications between edge sites and core networks, and sophisticated access control mechanisms. Data privacy considerations also become more complex with edge computing, as sensitive data may be processed across multiple edge locations. Operators must implement strong data governance frameworks and ensure compliance with regional data protection regulations.

Perimeter and edge security controls

Perimeter and edge security in telecom networks is particularly critical because these networks serve as the backbone of global communications. These security controls are applicable across the various touchpoints in the telecommunications network where there are interconnections with end users, other service provider partners, various service offerings, or even internet communication.

Physical security controls in mobile networks

The physical security for mobile networks encompasses multiple layers of protection at various infrastructure points. The RAN components, including base stations and cell towers, require specialized physical security measures. These sites typically employ reinforced enclosures with tamper-detection systems, environmental monitoring for temperature and humidity, and backup power systems. At larger facilities housing **Mobile Switching Centers** (**MSCs**) and gateway equipment, advanced access control systems utilize multi-factor authentication, often combining biometric verification with smart cards and PIN codes. Security personnel conduct regular patrols, and comprehensive video surveillance systems provide 24/7 monitoring with automated motion detection and alert capabilities. Environmental monitoring extends to include fire detection, water leakage sensors, and **Heating, Ventilation, and Air Conditioning** (**HVAC**) system monitoring to ensure optimal operating conditions for critical equipment.

Border gateway security implementation

Border gateway protocol security in mobile networks focuses on securing both the user and control plane traffic at network boundaries. The foundation of border gateway security in telecom networks centers on protecting **Border Gateway Protocol** (**BGP**) infrastructure, which handles critical routing decisions at network boundaries. This architecture implements multiple layers of security controls starting from the BGP speaker configuration itself. Each BGP router operates with hardened configurations that limit resource utilization, enforce strict session timeouts, and implement route dampening to prevent route flapping. The architecture incorporates redundant BGP speakers with separate physical and logical connectivity to ensure continued operation even if one path or device is compromised.

Resource Public Key Infrastructure (**RPKI**) forms a crucial component of BGP security by creating a trust hierarchy for route announcements. Telecom providers maintain RPKI repositories containing **Route Origin Authorizations** (**ROAs**) that cryptographically verify the ownership of IP address blocks and their authorized advertising autonomous systems. The validation process occurs in real-time as routes are received, with invalid routes being automatically rejected based on RPKI validation results. This system effectively prevents route hijacking attempts where malicious actors try to advertise address space; they do not legitimately own. The RPKI infrastructure requires regular maintenance, including certificate renewal and ROA updates, to maintain the security chain of trust.

Peer authentication and session security in a service provider BGP setup is provided by TCP-MD5 authentication, which enables basic protection against unauthorized BGP sessions, while newer implementations utilize **TCP-Authentication Option** (**AO**) for enhanced security. Each BGP peer relationship is explicitly configured with unique authentication keys, regularly rotated to maintain security. The implementation includes strict control over the maximum number of prefixes accepted from each peer, preventing resource exhaustion attacks. Session timers are carefully tuned to detect and recover from peer failures while avoiding unnecessary session resets that could impact routing stability. Route filtering in the border gateway implements multiple layers of prefix and AS-path filtering. Import and export policies control which routes are accepted from and advertised to each peer, based on prefix length, AS-path attributes, and community values. Maximum prefix limits are enforced per peer to prevent route table exhaustion attacks. The filtering framework includes specific controls for critical infrastructure prefixes, ensuring they can only be advertised by authorized autonomous systems. Real-time monitoring systems track prefix advertisements and withdrawals, alerting operators to suspicious routing changes that could indicate attempted attacks.

BGP FlowSpec provides dynamic traffic filtering capabilities at network edges. This implementation allows for rapid deployment of traffic filtering rules across the network in response to security incidents. FlowSpec rules can match multiple packet attributes, including source/destination addresses, port numbers, and protocol types, enabling precise control over traffic flows. The implementation includes safeguards to prevent abuse of FlowSpec capabilities, with strict controls over which systems can originate FlowSpec routes and what types of actions they can trigger.

Advanced firewall and access control mechanisms

The core of modern telecom network security relies on sophisticated **next-generation firewalls (NGFWs)** that go far beyond traditional packet filtering. These systems implement a multi-layered security approach that begins at the network layer and extends through the application layer. The firewall architecture is distributed across the network edge, with dedicated high-performance systems handling different types of traffic flows. These systems are designed for carrier-grade performance, capable of processing millions of concurrent sessions while maintaining strict security controls. The architecture includes dedicated management and control planes, ensuring that security policy enforcement does not impact traffic forwarding performance. **Deep packet inspection (DPI)** represents one of the most crucial capabilities in modern telecom firewalls. These systems examine not just packet headers but also the payload content, allowing them to identify and control specific applications and services. The DPI engines can recognize hundreds of protocols and applications, including encrypted traffic patterns. In telecom environments, this is particularly important for managing protocols such as **Session Initiation Protocol (SIP)**, **Real-time Transport Protocol (RTP)**, and various mobile networking protocols. The inspection engines maintain state information for all active sessions, allowing them to detect protocol violations and potential attacks that might span multiple packets or sessions. This capability extends to analyzing encrypted traffic patterns without necessarily decrypting the content, providing security while maintaining privacy.

Application Layer Gateways (ALGs) within the firewall infrastructure provide protocol-specific security for various services. These specialized components understand the intricacies of telecom protocols and can perform deep inspection and modification of traffic as needed. For example, SIP ALGs manage VoIP traffic, ensuring proper handling of signaling and media streams while preventing various forms of attacks specific to voice services. Similar specialized handling exists for other protocols such as H.323, RTSP, and various mobile network protocols. The ALGs maintain a protocol state and can detect and prevent protocol-specific attacks while ensuring the proper functionality of legitimate services. Some of the common firewall deployments include SGi and N6 firewalls securing the connectivity from the subscribers to the internet. The implementation of **access control lists (ACLs)** in telecom firewalls follows a hierarchical approach. At the highest level, network-wide policies control traffic flows between major security zones. These policies cascade down through various levels, with increasingly specific rules applied at each stage. The ACL infrastructure includes optimization mechanisms to ensure high-performance processing of large rule sets. Dynamic ACL updates allow for rapid response to security threats, with changes propagated across the firewall infrastructure in a controlled manner. The system includes conflict detection mechanisms to prevent policy contradictions that could create security vulnerabilities.

Carrier-grade NAT services form an integral part of the firewall infrastructure, managing address translation at a massive scale. These systems handle millions of concurrent translations while maintaining detailed logging for regulatory compliance. The NAT implementation includes sophisticated port allocation algorithms to ensure fair resource distribution among subscribers. Special consideration is given to protocols that embed IP addresses in their payload, with ALGs ensuring proper translation of these embedded addresses. The system includes mechanisms for handling NAT traversal protocols such as STUN and TURN, essential for services such as VoIP and video conferencing.

DDoS mitigation and IPS/IDS

Modern telecom networks implement a sophisticated multi-layered approach to intrusion detection and prevention. The foundation begins with distributed **intrusion detection systems (IDS)** sensors strategically positioned throughout the network, particularly at critical traffic aggregation points and network boundaries. These sensors employ both signature-based and anomaly-based detection methods, working in concert to identify potential security threats. The signature-based detection utilizes regularly updated threat intelligence feeds to identify known attack patterns, while anomaly-based detection establishes baseline behavior patterns for different types of network traffic and identifies deviations that could indicate security threats. The system incorporates ML algorithms that continuously refine detection capabilities by analyzing traffic patterns and attack indicators across the entire network.

Similarly, the DDoS protection infrastructure in telecom networks consists of multiple defensive layers designed to handle different types of attacks. At the network edge, dedicated scrubbing centers analyze incoming traffic using sophisticated behavioral analytics to distinguish between legitimate traffic spikes and attack traffic. These centers employ ML algorithms that continuously adapt to evolving attack patterns. The infrastructure includes specialized hardware accelerators for packet processing, allowing for real-time analysis of traffic at carrier-scale volumes. Traffic diversion mechanisms, such as BGP announcements and **Generic Routing Encapsulation** (**GRE**) tunneling, enable seamless redirection of suspicious traffic to scrubbing centers without impacting legitimate services. The framework implements intelligent traffic steering, ensuring that only suspicious traffic is diverted for inspection while allowing known good traffic to flow directly to its destination. The integration between IDS/IPS and DDoS protection systems creates a unified defense framework. When the IDS identifies potential attack patterns, this information is immediately shared with the DDoS protection infrastructure to enhance filtering capabilities. Conversely, the DDoS protection system feeds attack pattern information back to the **intrusion prevention systems** (**IPS**), allowing for more precise traffic filtering. This bidirectional information sharing enables rapid response to emerging threats and helps prevent false positives that could impact legitimate traffic. The integrated system maintains detailed traffic analytics and attack pattern databases, which are used to continuously refine detection and response mechanisms. For telecom-specific protocols such as SIP, diameter, and GTP, dedicated analysis engines can be used to examine signaling patterns to detect and prevent protocol-specific attacks. These systems can identify and mitigate various attack types, including volumetric attacks, protocol attacks, and application-layer attacks. Deep packet inspection capabilities allow for detailed analysis of traffic content while maintaining wire-speed performance through hardware acceleration and optimized processing algorithms. The infrastructure should include specific protection against DNS amplification attacks, TCP SYN floods, and other common DDoS attack vectors.

Security architecture and design

The establishment of robust security controls at the perimeter and edge of telecommunications service provider networks requires adherence to fundamental security principles that work in concert to create a comprehensive defense strategy. At the foundation lies the principle of zoning and segmentation, which involves the logical separation of network resources into distinct security zones based on their criticality, function, and access requirements. This segmentation creates clear boundaries between different network areas, allowing for the implementation of specific security policies and access controls tailored to each zone's unique requirements.

Security zones and trust boundaries are established to create clear demarcations between different network areas, with varying levels of security controls applied based on the sensitivity of data and systems within each zone. These zones typically progress from untrusted external networks through increasingly secure internal zones, with strict access controls and monitoring at each boundary. Traffic flow security is maintained through careful design of network paths and strict control over data movement between zones, often implementing one-way data flows where appropriate and monitoring all cross-boundary communications for potential security violations.

Defense in depth builds upon zoning by implementing multiple layers of security controls, where each layer provides distinct protective measures that complement and reinforce one another. This layered approach ensures that if one security control fails, other mechanisms continue to protect the network assets. In practice, this might manifest as a combination of perimeter firewalls, intrusion detection systems, access control lists, and protocol-specific security gateways, all working together to create a comprehensive security barrier. The defense-in-depth strategy extends beyond just technical controls to encompass physical security measures, administrative policies, and procedural controls, creating a holistic security framework.

The need for secure communication within the telecommunications network mandates the protection of all data traversing the network perimeter, whether it is customer traffic, management traffic, or inter-carrier communications. Encryption requirements are tailored to each security zone and data type, with stronger encryption protocols applied to sensitive data transit and storage. This typically includes end-to-end encryption for critical communications, transport layer security for data in transit between zones, and appropriate encryption for data at rest, with key management systems ensuring secure distribution and rotation of encryption keys across the network infrastructure. This involves implementing strong encryption protocols, secure tunneling mechanisms, and robust authentication methods for all communication channels. Particular attention is paid to securing signaling protocols specific to telecommunications networks, such as SS7, diameter, and SIP, which require specialized security controls due to their unique characteristics and potential vulnerabilities.

Defense in depth strategy

In telecommunications networks, defense in depth represents a multi-layered security approach that protects assets through multiple defensive mechanisms. At the physical layer, this starts with facility security, including biometric access controls, security personnel, and surveillance systems. The network layer implements multiple security controls, including firewalls, IDS, and IPS, at various points in the network. In modern telecom infrastructure, this extends to cloud and edge environments, where virtual firewalls, container security, and API gateways provide additional layers of protection.

Each defensive layer serves a specific purpose while complementing others. For instance, the perimeter defense includes NGFW for traffic filtering, while internal layers might employ network segmentation and access controls. In cloud and edge environments, this strategy incorporates cloud-native security controls such as **web application firewalls (WAF)**, container security, and API security gateways. The effectiveness of defense in depth is enhanced by security monitoring systems that provide visibility across all layers, enabling rapid detection and response to potential threats. Refer to the following figure to see a reference to the defense in depth design:

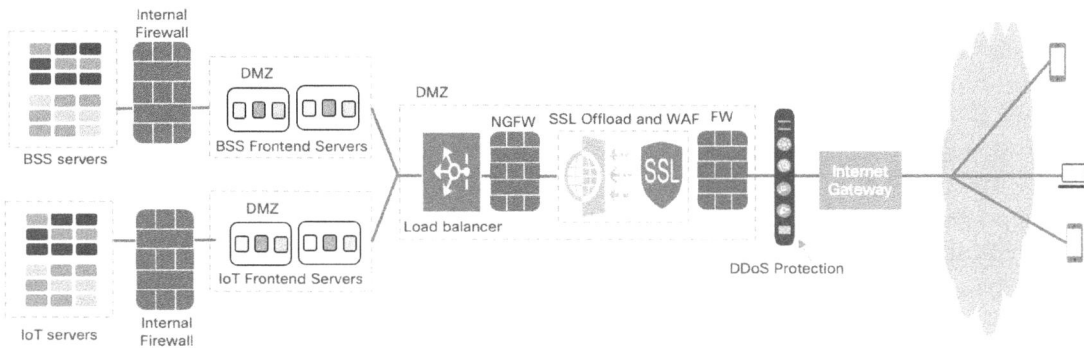

Figure 12.1: *Defense in depth design*

Figure 12.1 depicts the security controls that can be deployed in a DMZ to secure telecommunication-related services such as the **business support systems (BSS)** portals (mainly the portal used by subscribers to select and apply for a specific plan, ringtone, bill payment information, etc.) or the front-end portals for the IoT services that are offered by the service provider. Here, various security controls such as a DDoS protection device to secure denial of service attacks from the internet, a DMZ with controls such as firewalls, and an SSL offloading web application firewall help secure the front-end web applications, while the internal firewalls help to secure the back-end applications and database servers. This is the traditional setup that we normally see in a data center hosting a public-facing application.

Network segmentation

Network segmentation in telecommunications has evolved significantly from its origins in simple **Virtual Local Area Network (VLAN)**-based separation. Traditional approaches began with physical separation, where different network functions were isolated through dedicated hardware and cabling. As networks grew more complex, logical segmentation through VLANs provided a more flexible approach, allowing operators to create virtual boundaries within their physical infrastructure. Today's telecom networks incorporate sophisticated segmentation strategies that combine traditional methods with modern software-defined approaches, creating a comprehensive security framework that adapts to evolving threats and operational requirements. Effective network segmentation in telecommunications begins with the fundamental principle of isolation. Each network segment must operate independently while maintaining necessary interconnections through controlled interfaces. This approach extends beyond simple network isolation to encompass service isolation, where different telecommunications services are segregated based on their security requirements and operational characteristics. For instance, voice services might be isolated from data services, while signaling traffic is separated from user traffic. This granular approach to segmentation helps contain potential security breaches and prevents unauthorized access between service domains.

Mobile networks require specialized perimeter segmentation to protect both signaling and user traffic at network boundaries. The perimeter typically includes separate segments for different types of external interfaces. The S8 interface segment handles roaming traffic with specific security controls for inter-operator communications. A separate segment manages interconnection with **mobile virtual network operators** (**MVNOs**), implementing strict access controls and traffic monitoring. *Figure 12.2* depicts an example of an ideal security design consisting of SS77, **IP Multimedia Subsystem** (**IMS**), and diameter firewalls to secure connectivity from the roaming partners:

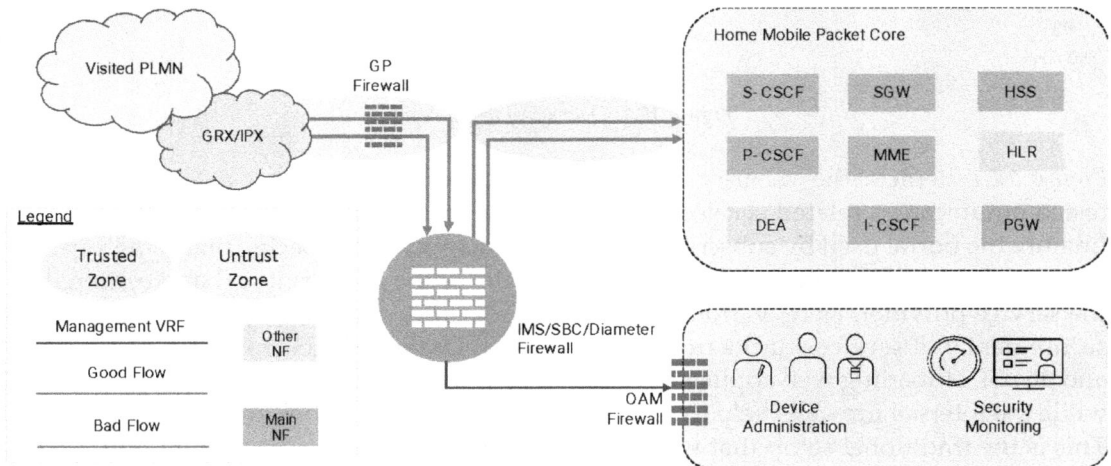

Figure 12.2: Roaming perimeter firewall

In addition, as telecommunications providers adopt cloud-native architectures, micro-segmentation becomes increasingly crucial. In these environments, traditional perimeter-based security proves insufficient, necessitating a more granular approach. Each network function, whether implemented as a virtual machine or container, receives its security perimeter, as detailed in the above section on defense in depth. This granular control extends to individual workloads and applications, with security policies defining allowed communications at the most detailed level. For instance, a virtual IMS function might be segmented into multiple microservices, each with specific communication patterns and security requirements.

Modern network segmentation in telecommunications aligns closely with zero-trust architecture principles. Every network segment, regardless of its location within the infrastructure, must validate all access attempts. This approach implements continuous authentication and authorization, ensuring that even trusted entities within a segment must prove their identity and rights before accessing resources. The integration of zero trust principles with network segmentation creates multiple security checkpoints throughout the network, significantly reducing the risk of lateral movement by potential attackers.

Special consideration must be given to operational technology networks within telecommunications infrastructure. These networks, which often control critical infrastructure elements such as power systems and cooling, require strict isolation from other network segments. The segmentation strategy must account for the unique requirements of OT systems, including their often legacy protocols and real-time operation requirements. Secure gateways and protocol converters provide controlled interfaces between OT segments and other network areas, ensuring operational integrity while maintaining security.

Security zones and trust boundaries

The 3GPP security architecture, primarily defined in TS 33.501, establishes a comprehensive framework for trust boundaries in modern telecommunications networks. This framework recognizes that security must be built on clearly defined trust relationships between network functions, domains, and operators. The architecture divides the network into distinct security domains, each with specific security requirements and trust levels.

The following are the security domains as defined in the TS 33.501:

- **Network access security (I)**: It is a set of security features that enable a UE to authenticate and access services via the network securely, including 3GPP access and non-3GPP access, and to protect against attacks on the (radio) interfaces. In addition, it includes security context delivery from SN to AN for access security.

- **Network domain security (II)**: It is a set of security features that enable network nodes to securely exchange signaling data and user plane data.

- **User domain security (III)**: It is a set of security features that secure the user's access to mobile equipment.

- **Application domain security (IV)**: It is a set of security features that enable applications in the user domain and in the provider domain to exchange messages securely. Application domain security is out of the scope of the present document.

- **SBA domain security (V)**: It is a set of security features that enable network functions of the SBA architecture to securely communicate within the serving network domain and with other network domains. Such features include network function registration, discovery, and authorization security aspects, as well as protection for the service-based interfaces. SBA domain security is a new security feature compared to TS 33.401.

- **Visibility and configurability of security (VI)**: It is a set of features that enable the user to be informed whether a security feature is in operation or not.

Figure 12.3 depicts the 3GPP overview of security zones:

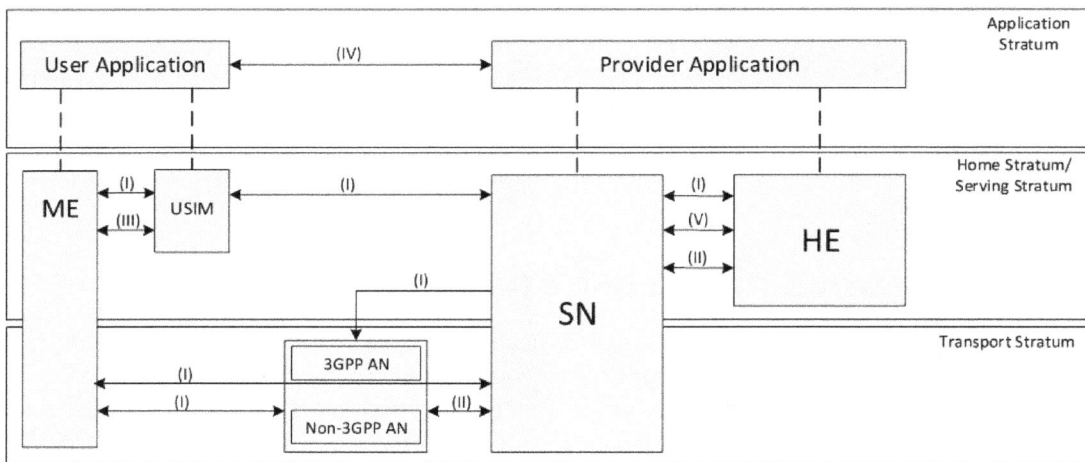

Figure 12.3: *3GPP overview of security zones/domains[1]*

In mobile networks, trust within the network decreases the further one moves away from the core. The idea is that at the center of the mobile core such as that of a 5G system, is where the crown jewel of the 5G system resides, which requires to be secured from any unwanted access, thus, making it the trust layer or zone that can be trusted due to the level of security controls that might be applied to secure the network functions within it. As depicted in *Figure 12.4*, the **Unified Data Management (UDM)** is at the heart of the 5G systems. UDM supports the **Authentication Credential Repository and Processing Function (ARPF)** and stores the long-term security credentials used in authentication for AKA. It also stores subscriber information.

Authentication Server Function (AUSF) supports authentication for 3GPP and non-3GPP access. AUSF also interacts with UDM and provides UE authentication service to the requester network function. As part of the innermost trust layer, we can consider UDM, AUSF network functions, or any other critical network function based on the type of data it handles:

---

1   Source: 3GPP TS-33.501

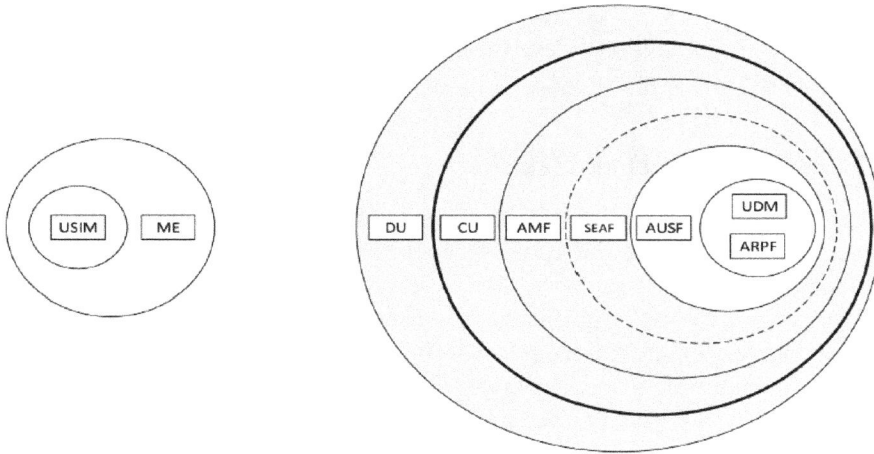

Figure 12.4: Trust model in a 5G system[2]

Understanding the roles of some of these network functions will help us create a trust boundary or a trust-based grouping, which can further be used to create a desired trust model, as per the communication service provider's process, policies, and regulatory requirements. Shown in *Figure 12.5* is a sample trust boundary that can be created for a 5G mobile core deployment:

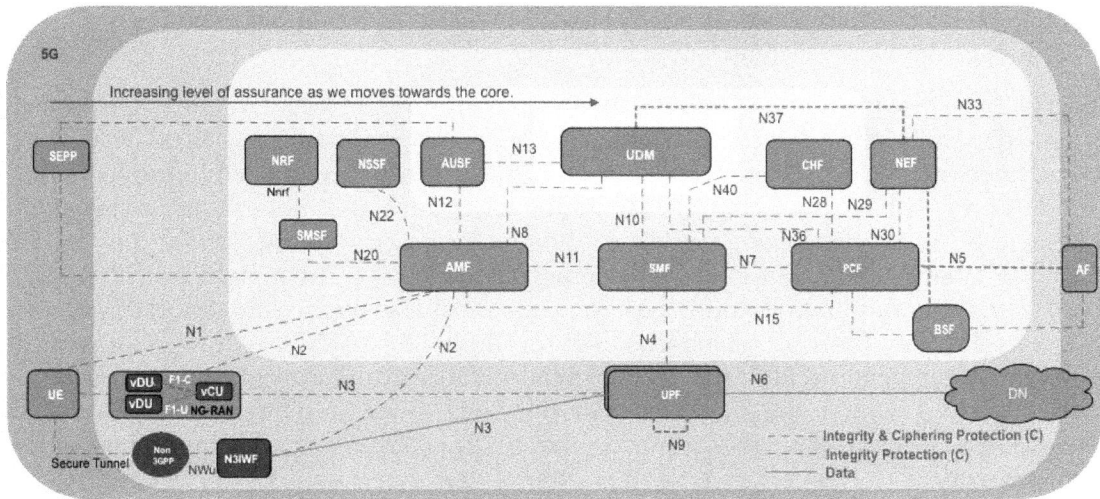

Figure 12.5: 5G trust layers

As shown in *Figure 12.5*, the main crown jewels of 5G components are the center of the trust layer. These components need to be well protected to ensure that critical and confidential customer data is not impacted for any reason. The trust level assurance increases as we

2   Source: 3GPP

move from the outer layers to the internal layers containing the crown jewels. These can be protected by deploying a layered, defense-in-depth-based security control. These controls have been discussed in the chapter for securing a 5G network.

Encryption requirements

The distributed nature of modern telecom infrastructure, combined with the processing of sensitive data at edge locations, requires a comprehensive approach to encryption that balances security requirements with performance needs and operational constraints. When data crosses network boundaries, whether at the perimeter or between different trust zones, strong encryption becomes essential. At these boundaries, telecom service providers must implement transport layer encryption using protocols, such as TLS 1.3, which provides perfect forward secrecy and protection against various cryptographic attacks. For control plane traffic crossing network boundaries, protocols such as IPSec with IKEv2 provide the necessary protection while ensuring interoperability with various network elements and peer providers.

Edge computing introduces unique encryption requirements due to the distributed nature of processing and storage. Data processed at edge locations must be protected both at rest and in transit. For data at rest, providers typically implement file system or volume-level encryption using standards such as AES-256 in appropriate modes of operation. The encryption mechanisms must be capable of rapid encryption and decryption to maintain the low-latency requirements of edge computing while ensuring data remains protected even if edge hardware is compromised.

Encryption implementations must balance security requirements with performance needs, particularly in edge computing environments where latency is critical. Hardware-accelerated encryption, when available, can help maintain performance while implementing strong encryption. The selection of encryption algorithms and modes must consider the processing capabilities of edge devices while maintaining required security levels. For example, ChaCha20-Poly1305 might be preferred over AES-GCM on devices without AES hardware acceleration. Encryption requirements must also align with various regulatory frameworks and industry standards. For example, the GDPR requires appropriate encryption for personal data protection, while PCI DSS mandates specific encryption requirements for payment data. Telecom providers must implement encryption that satisfies the strictest applicable requirements while maintaining interoperability across their network.

MEC security considerations and architecture

The security architecture for Edge/MEC infrastructure must address multiple layers of protection, starting from the physical security of edge sites through to application-level security controls. Each edge location represents a potential entry point into the network, requiring a comprehensive security framework that is both robust and flexible. The traditional security perimeter expands significantly with edge computing, as sensitive data and critical applications are now distributed across numerous edge sites. This distributed nature fundamentally changes how we must approach security, requiring a Zero Trust architecture where every access attempt is verified, regardless of its origin or previous authentication status.

Different edge applications demand distinct security approaches based on their specific requirements and risk profiles. For instance, industrial automation applications running at the edge require stringent access controls and real-time security monitoring to prevent any tampering that could affect production processes. These applications often need specialized protocols for industrial control systems, requiring security controls that understand and can protect these protocols while maintaining the ultra-low latency requirements critical for industrial operations.

In contrast, autonomous vehicle applications demand security controls optimized for mobility and rapid authentication, as vehicles move between different edge nodes. The security framework must support seamless handovers while maintaining continuous protection of vehicle control data. This includes specialized security measures for **vehicle-to-infrastructure** (**V2I**) communications and protection against potential spoofing or manipulation of navigation data.

Healthcare applications at the edge require security controls aligned with medical data protection regulations. This includes enhanced encryption for patient data, strict access controls based on medical staff roles, and detailed audit logging of all data access. The security controls must also ensure that emergency access to medical applications remains available even during security incidents.

Edge computing introduces complex data privacy challenges due to the distributed nature of data processing. The security framework must incorporate sophisticated data governance mechanisms that track and control where data is processed and stored. This becomes particularly crucial when edge nodes span different jurisdictions with varying data protection requirements. For instance, some regions may require certain types of personal data to be processed only within specific geographical boundaries. The security controls must support data anonymization and pseudonymization at the edge, reducing privacy risks before data is transmitted to central locations. This includes implementing privacy-preserving computation techniques that allow useful analytics while protecting individual privacy. The framework should also support dynamic data residency controls that can adapt to changing privacy regulations and user consent preferences.

Edge computing also requires sophisticated authentication mechanisms that can support various types of users and devices while maintaining strict security. This includes implementing context-aware access controls that consider factors such as location, device type, and application requirements when making authorization decisions. For example, **augmented reality** (**AR**) applications might require location-based authentication to ensure users can only access AR content appropriate for their physical location. The authentication framework must support different authentication methods based on use case requirements.

While some applications might require traditional username or password authentication, others might need biometric verification, hardware security tokens, or certificate-based authentication. The framework must be flexible enough to accommodate these varying requirements while maintaining consistent security standards.

There is no protection for anything that one cannot see. Thus, edge environments require distributed security monitoring capabilities that can detect and respond to threats in real-time. This includes implementing ML-based anomaly detection systems that understand normal behavior patterns for different types of edge applications. For example, an anomaly detection system for smart city applications would need to recognize normal patterns in traffic flow data, while one protecting industrial applications would focus on detecting unusual patterns in machine control commands. The monitoring infrastructure must support both local threat detection at each edge site and centralized security analytics that can identify distributed attack patterns across multiple edge locations. This dual-layer approach ensures both rapid local response to immediate threats and comprehensive protection against sophisticated, coordinated attacks.

Considering all these various security requirements, *Figure 12.6* shows the security design that can be applied to a general MEC design:

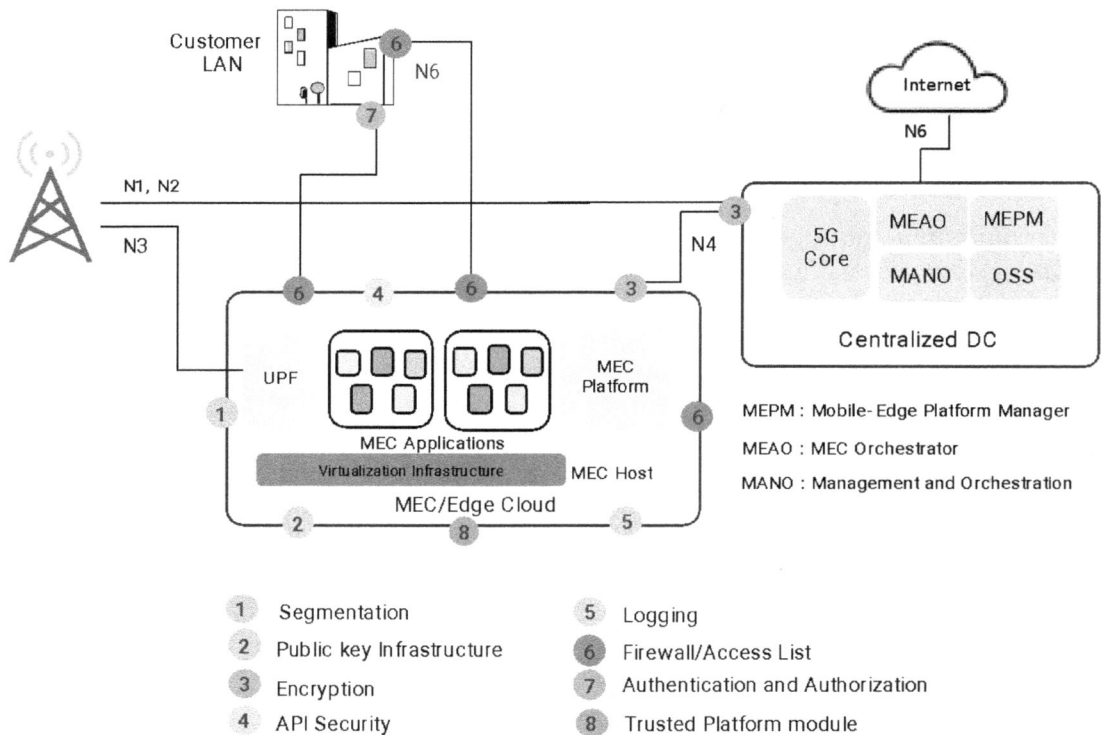

Figure 12.6: *MEC architecture and security controls*

Conclusion

As we conclude our examination of perimeter and edge security in telecommunications networks, we are witnessing a fundamental transformation in how networks are protected. The evolution from traditional perimeter defense to a sophisticated, multi-layered security framework reflects both technological advancement and the increasing complexity of security threats facing telecommunications providers.

The critical role of telecommunications networks in supporting global connectivity and essential services across healthcare, finance, and other sectors has driven the development of comprehensive security frameworks. These frameworks must now address both regulatory requirements and the technical challenges introduced by the shift toward virtualized environments and distributed architectures.

The emergence of MEC represents perhaps the most significant shift in network security architecture. This distributed computing model has necessitated a careful balance between maintaining robust security controls and meeting the demanding performance requirements of modern telecommunications services. The resulting security ecosystem combines traditional perimeter defenses with edge-specific controls, creating a flexible yet comprehensive protection strategy.

Looking ahead, the continued evolution of telecommunications technology, including 5G networks and the IoT, will drive further innovation in security architectures. Success in this dynamic landscape requires not just the implementation of individual security controls but the creation of an adaptive security ecosystem that enables innovation while maintaining protection. The principles and practices discussed in this chapter provide a foundation for building secure, resilient networks capable of meeting tomorrow's challenges.

In the next chapter, we discuss the critical domain where authentication, authorization, and accounting converge to protect network resources. In this chapter, we examine how modern telecom service providers implement robust IAM frameworks to govern who can access network elements, what privileges they possess, and how these activities are monitored and recorded. The complexity of telecom provider networks, with their vast array of interconnected systems spanning multiple technologies and vendors, presents unique IAM challenges that go beyond traditional enterprise environments. We'll explore how zero-trust principles are being adapted for telecom infrastructure, the role of privileged access management in protecting critical network functions, and how identity federation enables secure cross-domain operations in increasingly distributed network architectures.

Points to remember

- **Network evolution and security requirements**: Telecommunications networks have evolved from traditional centralized architectures to distributed edge computing environments, fundamentally changing security requirements. Modern networks must protect both conventional infrastructure and emerging edge computing platforms while maintaining service availability and performance. The increasing complexity of network architectures, combined with evolving threat landscapes, necessitates a comprehensive approach to security that addresses both traditional and emerging vulnerabilities.

- **Regulatory landscape and compliance**: Telecommunications providers must navigate a complex web of regulatory requirements across different jurisdictions. These regulations typically mandate specific security controls, data protection measures, and privacy safeguards. Organizations must demonstrate compliance with standards such as GDPR for data protection, telecommunications-specific regulations such as CPNI requirements, and industry standards such as ISO 27001. Security architectures must be designed with built-in compliance capabilities, including audit trails, data governance controls, and reporting mechanisms.

- **Traditional infrastructure protection**: The security of traditional telecommunications infrastructure remains crucial even as networks evolve. Core network elements, including switches, routers, and signaling systems, require robust protection against both conventional and emerging threats. Security controls must address physical security, logical access control, protocol-specific protection, and monitoring capabilities. The integration of legacy systems with modern security controls presents unique challenges that must be carefully managed to maintain security without disrupting essential services.

- **Edge computing and MEC security**: Multi-access edge computing introduces new security considerations by distributing computing resources closer to network edges. Each edge site becomes a potential attack surface requiring comprehensive protection. Security architecture must account for the distributed nature of edge computing while maintaining consistent security policies across all locations. The protection of edge infrastructure requires specialized controls that can operate effectively within the constraints of edge environments, including limited physical space and power availability.

- **Comprehensive security controls**: Effective perimeter and edge security requires multiple layers of controls working in concert. These include firewalls, intrusion detection and prevention systems, DDoS protection mechanisms, and access control systems. Security controls must be customized based on the specific requirements of different network segments and services. The implementation of security controls must balance protection requirements with performance needs, particularly for latency-sensitive edge applications.

- **Security architecture integration**: Security architecture must integrate protection for both traditional and edge infrastructure while maintaining operational efficiency. This requires careful consideration of how security controls interact across different network segments and computing environments. The architecture must support secure communication between edge sites and central locations while enabling local processing capabilities. Security policies must be consistently enforced across all environments while accommodating the unique requirements of different network segments and services.

- **Operational considerations**: Successful implementation of perimeter and edge security requires effective operational processes and procedures. This includes incident response capabilities, change management procedures, and regular security assessments. Organizations must maintain comprehensive monitoring and logging capabilities across all environments to enable effective security management. Regular testing and validation of security controls ensure continued effectiveness as networks evolve and new threats emerge.

- **Emerging technologies and future considerations**: Security architecture must be designed to accommodate emerging technologies and evolving network capabilities. This includes considerations for 5G networks, network function virtualization, and advanced edge computing applications. Security frameworks must be flexible enough to adapt to new requirements while maintaining robust protection for existing infrastructure and services. Organizations must stay informed about emerging threats and security capabilities to ensure their security architecture remains effective.

  Looking forward the future of telecommunications security will require continued evolution of security architectures and controls. Organizations must maintain a proactive approach to security, anticipating new requirements and threats before they impact network operations. Success requires ongoing investment in security capabilities, regular assessment of security effectiveness, and continuous improvement of security controls and processes.

Exercises

1. Which of the following best describes the primary reason for implementing perimeter security in telecom networks?

   a. To reduce operational costs

   b. To protect network boundaries from unauthorized access and threats

   c. To improve network performance

   d. To comply with a single regulatory requirement

2. In the context of MEC security architecture, what is the significance of Zero Trust?

   a. No security controls are required at the edge

   b. Trust is established once during initial authentication

   c. Every access request must be verified regardless of source

   d. Only internal users can be trusted

3. Which regulatory framework specifically addresses the protection of personal data in telecom networks within the European Union?

   a. HIPAA

   b. GDPR

   c. SOX

   d. PCI DSS

4. When implementing DDoS protection at the network edge, which capability is most crucial?

   a. Traffic encryption

   b. Traffic scrubbing and analysis

   c. User authentication

   d. Data backup

5. In a MEC environment, where should security controls ideally be implemented?

   a. Only at the central core

   b. Only at the network edge

   c. At both edge and core locations with coordinated policies

   d. Only at user access points

6. Explain three key differences between traditional centralized security architecture and MEC security architecture.

7. Describe how the principle of defense in depth applies to telecom network perimeter security.

8. What are the main challenges in implementing consistent security policies across distributed edge locations?

9. Scenario: A telecom provider is deploying a new edge computing service for autonomous vehicle support. Outline the key security considerations and controls that should be implemented.

10. Scenario: Your organization detects a DDoS attack targeting multiple edge locations. Describe the immediate response steps and long-term mitigation strategies.

11. Analyze the potential security implications of implementing network slicing in a 5G network with MEC capabilities.

12. Compare and contrast the security requirements for different types of edge applications (e.g., industrial automation vs. augmented reality).

13. Design a high-level security architecture for a telecom edge infrastructure that supports:

    a. IoT device connectivity

    b. Real-time video analytics

    c. Industrial automation includes key security controls and justifies their placement.

14. Create a security monitoring strategy for distributed edge locations that addresses:

    a. Real-time threat detection

    b. Incident response

    c. Compliance reporting

    d. Performance impact

15. True or false (Explain your answer): Edge computing reduces the overall attack surface of a telecom network.

16. True or false (Explain your answer): The same security controls can be uniformly applied across all edge locations regardless of the supported applications.

Join our book's Discord space

Join the book's Discord Workspace for Latest updates, Offers, Tech happenings around the world, New Release and Sessions with the Authors:

https://discord.bpbonline.com

Chapter 13

Identity and Access Management

Introduction

Identity and access management (IAM) stands as a cornerstone of security in modern telecommunications service providers, where the complexity of operations and the sensitivity of customer data demand robust access control mechanisms. In an industry that manages critical communications infrastructure, processes sensitive customer information, and handles vast amounts of billing data, the importance of a comprehensive IAM strategy cannot be overstated.

Telecommunications providers face unique challenges in implementing IAM solutions due to their hybrid operational environment, which encompasses traditional IT systems, **operational support systems (OSS)**, **business support systems (BSS)**, and network infrastructure. These diverse systems must seamlessly integrate while maintaining strict security controls and ensuring operational efficiency. The growing adoption of cloud services, 5G networks, and IoT devices has further complicated the IAM landscape, requiring more sophisticated and adaptable solutions.

This chapter explores the fundamental components of IAM within a telecommunications environment, focusing on four key areas. We begin by examining the enterprise-wide identity architecture, including its integration with critical operational systems and the role of directory services in managing identities across the organization. The discussion then moves to authentication infrastructure, where we explore modern authentication methods and the crucial role of public key infrastructure in securing access to sensitive systems.

Authorization frameworks form the third pillar of our discussion, where we discuss how telecommunications providers can implement effective access control mechanisms while maintaining operational agility. Finally, we address the full lifecycle of identity management, from creation to retirement, in the context of a dynamic telecommunications environment.

Structure

This chapter will cover the following topics:

- IAM for telecom infrastructure
- IAM architecture
- Authentication infrastructure
- Authorization framework
- Identity lifecycle management

Objectives

This chapter examines the fundamental components and considerations of implementing a robust IAM framework within a telecommunications environment, focusing on the unique challenges and requirements specific to telecom service providers.

The primary objective is to provide telecommunications security architects, engineers, and administrators with a comprehensive understanding of IAM architecture, authentication mechanisms, authorization frameworks, and identity lifecycle management. We will explore how these components must be designed and integrated to support both traditional telecom operations and emerging technologies while maintaining security, compliance, and operational efficiency.

Special attention will be given to the integration challenges between IAM systems and telecom-specific platforms such as OSS and BSS, which form the backbone of service provider operations. The chapter will demonstrate how to establish a cohesive identity architecture that spans across enterprise systems, customer-facing services, and network operations centers.

We will examine advanced authentication infrastructures essential for securing privileged access to critical telecommunications infrastructure, including the implementation of **multi-factor authentication (MFA)**, **public key infrastructure (PKI)**, and **Secure Shell (SSH)** key management systems. The chapter will also detail the development of authorization frameworks that support the dynamic nature of telecom operations while enforcing principles of least privilege and segregation of duties.

Through practical examples and industry best practices, readers will gain insights into managing identity lifecycles across diverse user populations, from field technicians to customer service representatives, and understand how to implement just-in-time access controls that balance security with operational agility in a telecommunications environment.

IAM for telecom infrastructure

IAM forms the cornerstone of security in modern telecommunication service provider environments. While telecom providers manage massive subscriber identity databases, this chapter focuses specifically on the critical domain of internal operational IAM, the systems, processes, and technologies that govern how employees, contractors, and automated services access and interact with telecom infrastructure.

The telecommunications industry presents unique challenges for operational IAM implementation. Telecom networks comprise a complex mesh of legacy systems, modern cloud-native infrastructure, and specialized network functions. This heterogeneous environment demands an IAM framework that can seamlessly bridge different technological eras while maintaining strict security controls. The introduction of 5G networks, with their containerized, cloud-native architecture, has further amplified this complexity.

Operational staff in telecom environments require access to a diverse array of systems, from physical network elements to virtualized network functions, OSS, and BSS. Each system may have its own authentication mechanisms, access control models, and security requirements. The IAM framework must unify these disparate systems under a coherent security model while ensuring operational efficiency.

The critical nature of telecom infrastructure adds another dimension to IAM requirements. Network downtime can have severe consequences, affecting emergency services, business operations, and daily communications for millions of users. Therefore, the IAM system must strike a delicate balance between rigorous security controls and operational flexibility. It must support emergency access procedures, break-glass mechanisms, and rapid response capabilities while maintaining security and audit trails.

Telecom operators must adhere to various national and international regulations governing critical infrastructure protection, data privacy, and communication security. The IAM framework serves as a crucial control point for demonstrating compliance with these regulations through access control, audit logging, and regular access reviews.

The convergence of IT and network technology in modern telecom networks has expanded the attack surface considerably. Adversaries targeting telecom infrastructure could potentially exploit IAM weaknesses to gain unauthorized access to critical systems. This risk is particularly acute in 5G networks, where the virtualized, software-defined nature of network functions requires robust identity verification and access control at both the infrastructure and application layers.

Similarly, automation and orchestration in modern telecom networks introduce additional IAM considerations. Service accounts, APIs, and automated processes require their identity management framework, complete with appropriate authentication mechanisms, access controls, and monitoring capabilities. These automated identities must be managed with the same rigor as human identities, if not more.

The following sections in this chapter will explore specific aspects of IAM implementation, from architectural considerations to practical guidance on authentication, authorization, and audit mechanisms. Each section addresses both traditional telecom infrastructure and modern cloud-native deployments, providing a comprehensive view of IAM requirements across the entire technological spectrum of telecom operations.

IAM architecture

The IAM architecture in telecommunications environments represents a complex orchestration of multiple systems, services, and security controls designed to manage access to critical network infrastructure. This architecture must seamlessly integrate traditional telecom systems with modern cloud-native network functions while maintaining stringent security controls and operational efficiency.

The IAM architecture follows a layered approach, with distinct tiers handling different aspects of identity and access management. At the top, the access control layer serves as the primary interface for various user types, from NOC teams and field engineers to network administrators and automated systems. This layer implements multiple access mechanisms, including enterprise **single sign-on** (**SSO**) portals for human users and **application programming interface** (**API**) gateways for automated systems and integrations.

At its core, the architecture centers around a robust IAM Core layer that houses the fundamental identity services. This includes the primary identity provider (typically Active Directory or LDAP), which serves as the source of truth for identity information. Supporting services such as OAuth/OIDC and SAML federation enable modern authentication patterns, while a **public key infrastructure** (**PKI**) infrastructure manages the critical certificate lifecycle for both traditional and cloud-native network functions. The privileged access management system within this core layer provides additional controls for high-risk, high-impact operations.

The Network Infrastructure layer represents the diverse landscape of systems requiring access control, spanning both traditional telecom systems (OSS, BSS, network management) and modern cloud-native network functions, particularly in 5G deployments. This hybrid environment necessitates flexible integration patterns that can accommodate both legacy authentication mechanisms and modern identity protocols.

The key architectural considerations should include:

- Centralized identity management with distributed authentication capabilities.

- High availability and fault tolerance at every layer.
- Scalability to handle large numbers of human and machine identities.
- Security controls appropriate for critical infrastructure protection.
- Audit and compliance capabilities built into every layer.
- Support for both traditional and modern authentication protocols.
- Integration capabilities with various telecom-specific systems and protocols.

A high-level architectural diagram depicting the various components of the IAM architecture, and its interconnections is shown in the following figure:

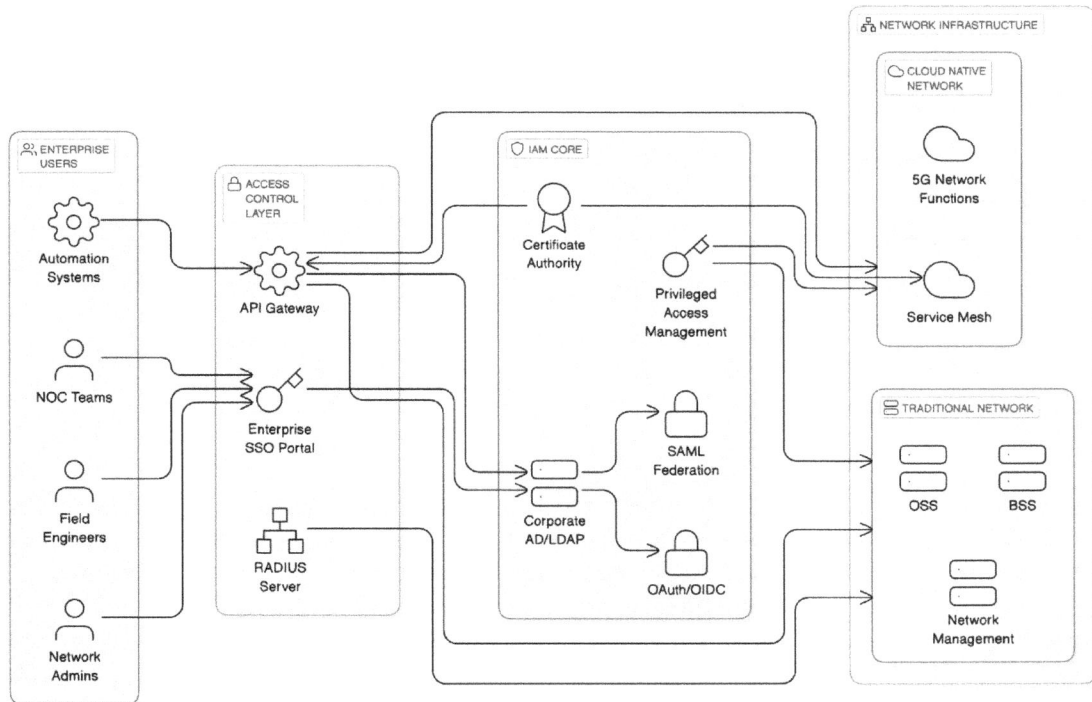

Figure 13.1: *IAM architecture*

Enterprise-wide identity architecture

The foundation of a telecom operator's identity architecture is built upon a hierarchical, multi-forest design that accommodates both traditional IT and telecom-specific requirements. This approach recognizes that telecom environments have unique operational demands that differ significantly from standard enterprise IT environments.

The architecture typically implements three distinct identity forests: corporate, operations, and network elements. This separation serves multiple purposes. The corporate forest manages standard enterprise identities and business function accounts, while the operations forest is dedicated to network operations teams and their specialized access requirements. The network elements forest specifically handles identities for network infrastructure components, including both physical and virtualized network functions.

An example of a typical operational and network element forest is shown in the following:

```
ops.telco.com
        ├── noc.ops.telco.com
        │    ├── noc-teams
        │    ├── field-engineers
        │    └── automation-accounts
        └── tools.ops.telco.com
             ├── monitoring-systems
             └── management-platforms
net.telco.com
        ├── ran.net.telco.com
        │    ├── base-stations
        │    └── controllers
        └── core.net.telco.com
             ├── switching
             └── transport
```

Trust relationships between these forests require careful consideration. Unlike traditional enterprise environments, where full forest trusts might be acceptable, telecom environments demand more granular control. Selective authentication is commonly implemented, allowing precise control over which security principals can access resources across forest boundaries. This is particularly crucial when managing access to critical network elements. Telecom environments must manage several distinct identity types, each with its lifecycle requirements, as mentioned in the following:

- **Human identities**: Including NOC operators, field engineers, and administrators. These identities require regular certification, skills-based access rights, and shift-based access patterns.

- **Service identities**: Used by automated systems, monitoring tools, and network management platforms. These require more stringent controls due to their potential broad access rights and automated nature.

- **Network element identities**: Representing both physical and virtual network components, these identities are crucial for secure inter-component communication, particularly in modern 5G networks.

- **Emergency identities**: Special-purpose accounts designed for crisis scenarios, requiring unique governance models and enhanced monitoring.

The access control strategy in telecom environments should extend beyond traditional RBAC.

While RBAC forms the foundation, it must be supplemented with the following context:

- **Attribute-based access control (ABAC)**: Incorporating factors such as time of day, location, network type, and emergency status into access decisions.
- **Time-bound access**: Particularly important for maintenance windows and emergency access scenarios.
- **Geographical controls**: Essential for managing access across different network regions and jurisdictions.
- **Risk-based access**: Incorporating real-time risk assessment into access decisions, particularly crucial for critical network elements.

This enterprise-wide identity architecture must remain flexible enough to accommodate evolving network technologies while maintaining strict security controls. Regular architectural reviews ensure it continues to meet both current operational needs and emerging requirements as networks evolve, particularly with the ongoing transition to 5G and cloud-native network functions.

Integration with OSS and BSS systems

The integration of IAM systems with OSS and BSS in telecommunications environments represents a complex challenge that spans both modern and legacy architectures. These integrations must bridge the gap between traditional telecom systems and contemporary cloud-native applications while maintaining robust security controls and operational efficiency.

Modern OSS/BSS systems increasingly adopt OAuth 2.0 and **OpenID Connect (OIDC)** as primary authentication mechanisms. This approach enables token-based authentication for APIs and web interfaces, providing fine-grained access control through scope definitions and supporting delegated authority for automated operations. The token-based approach particularly suits modern microservices architectures, where service-to-service authentication and authorization are crucial for maintaining security boundaries. For web-based interfaces, SAML-based federation has become a standard approach, enabling single sign-on capabilities across multiple OSS/BSS platforms. This federation model supports sophisticated attribute-based access control decisions and provides robust session management capabilities. It proves particularly valuable when integrating with third-party systems and managing contractor access to operational systems.

Legacy OSS/BSS systems, however, often require different integration approaches. RADIUS and TACACS+ protocols remain prevalent in network management systems, providing command-level authorization and detailed accounting of administrative actions. These protocols, while dated, offer robust integration capabilities with network elements and continue to play a crucial role in operational security. Additionally, many legacy systems rely on direct LDAP integration for authentication, leveraging existing directory services for basic authentication and group-based access control.

The authorization model for OSS/BSS integration must reflect the complex operational structure of telecom environments. Rather than simple RBA control, modern implementations require dynamic authorization decisions based on operational context. This includes considerations such as maintenance windows, emergencies, geographic location, and current network state. The authorization framework must support both predefined operational roles and dynamic, context-aware access decisions.

API Gateway patterns have emerged as a crucial integration point between IAM and OSS/BSS systems. These gateways serve as a central authentication and authorization enforcement point, handling token validation, credential management, and policy evaluation. They provide a consistent security boundary while supporting the diverse protocols and authentication mechanisms required in telecom environments. The gateway approach also enables centralized monitoring and policy enforcement, crucial for maintaining security compliance.

In cloud-native OSS/BSS deployments, service mesh architecture provides additional integration capabilities. Service meshes manage service-to-service authentication, certificate lifecycle management, and fine-grained traffic control. This pattern proves particularly valuable in modern 5G networks, where network functions are increasingly deployed as cloud-native applications requiring sophisticated IAM.

The future evolution of these integration patterns will likely be driven by the continued modernization of OSS/BSS systems and the adoption of cloud-native architectures. However, the need to support legacy systems will persist, requiring flexible integration approaches that bridge modern and traditional operational environments. Regular review and updates of integration patterns ensure they remain effective and aligned with evolving security requirements and operational needs of the telecommunication service provider.

Directory services and federation

Directory services in telecom environments serve as the foundational element of identity management, providing a centralized authentication and authorization information repository. These services must be designed to handle telecom operations' scale and complexity while supporting traditional and modern federation requirements.

The core directory infrastructure in telecom environments typically employs a distributed, multi-master architecture to ensure high availability and geographic redundancy. This architecture commonly utilizes Microsoft Active Directory or OpenLDAP as the primary directory service, supplemented by specialized directories for specific network functions.

The multi-master approach ensures that directory services remain available even during network partitions or regional outages, a critical requirement for maintaining operational capabilities.

Federation services in telecom environments bridge multiple identity domains, enabling seamless access across different operational systems. Modern federation implementations typically employ a hybrid approach, combining SAML 2.0 for web applications with OAuth 2.0 and OpenID Connect for API access and mobile applications. This hybrid model supports both traditional web-based operations tools and modern cloud-native applications.

Identity federation must accommodate various trust models, particularly when dealing with contractor access and third-party service providers. Claims-based identity becomes crucial in these scenarios, allowing fine-grained access control based on attributes such as certification levels, geographic permissions, and time-bound access rights. The federation service acts as a claim transformer, mapping internal directory attributes to standardized claims that can be consumed by various applications.

Time synchronization plays a critical role in federation services, particularly in geographically distributed environments. Federation protocols rely heavily on time-to-day validation for security, making accurate time synchronization essential across all participating systems. This often requires integration with telecom-grade timing sources and careful consideration of time zone handling in global operations.

The federation architecture must support selective authentication, allowing fine-grained control over which security principals can access specific resources across domain boundaries. This becomes particularly important when managing access to critical network elements and operational support systems. **Security Token Services** (**STS**) play a central role in managing cross-domain authentication. These services handle the transformation of security tokens between different protocols and formats, enabling interoperability between legacy systems and modern applications. The STS infrastructure must be highly available and geographically distributed to support global operations.

The PKI supporting federation services must handle certificate lifecycle management for both human and machine identities. This includes automated certificate renewal, revocation checking, and support for **Hardware Security Modules** (**HSMs**) for protecting critical signing keys.

Federation services generate significant audit data that must be captured and analyzed for security and compliance purposes. The monitoring infrastructure must track authentication patterns, token issuance, and federation protocol exchanges while supporting both real-time alerting and historical analysis. This data proves crucial for detecting potential security incidents and demonstrating compliance with regulatory requirements.

The evolution of directory services and federation in telecom environments continues to be driven by the adoption of cloud technologies and the need for more flexible identity solutions. While maintaining support for traditional systems, the federation architecture must adapt to support modern authentication patterns and emerging security requirements. This ongoing evolution requires regular review and updates to ensure the federation infrastructure continues to meet both security and operational needs.

Authentication infrastructure

The authentication infrastructure in telecom environments forms the backbone of secure access to network elements, operational systems, and management platforms. This infrastructure must support a diverse range of authentication mechanisms, from traditional password-based systems to modern biometric solutions, while maintaining the agility required for telecom operations. As networks evolve towards 5G and cloud-native architectures, the authentication infrastructure must bridge traditional telecom protocols with modern identity standards. This includes supporting various authentication methods across different security domains, managing machines and human identities, and ensuring the high availability of authentication services. A robust authentication infrastructure must also accommodate both routine operations and emergency scenarios, where rapid access to systems might be critical for service restoration.

Multi-factor authentication

Multi-factor authentication (**MFA**) in telecom environments will need to consider various telecommunication parameters like operational requirements, emergency access scenarios, and the diverse nature of systems requiring access. The implementation strategy must balance robust security with operational efficiency, particularly in critical network operations scenarios.

The primary MFA deployments in telecom environments typically include **Time-based One-Time Passwords (TOTP)**, hardware tokens, smart cards, and biometric authentication. TOTP applications prove particularly valuable for routine operations, offering a balance of security and convenience. Hardware tokens, while more cumbersome to manage, provide enhanced security for critical systems access and are often required for regulatory compliance.

Push notifications through mobile applications have gained prominence as an MFA method, particularly for routine operational access. These implementations must consider the security of the mobile devices themselves and provide fallback mechanisms when mobile networks are unavailable. The push notification infrastructure should be separated from the production network to ensure availability during network incidents.

Modern MFA implementations in telecom environments increasingly incorporate risk-based authentication. This approach considers factors such as access location, time of day, system criticality, and operation type when determining authentication requirements. During normal operations, standard MFA protocols apply, but during emergency scenarios, risk-based systems can adapt authentication requirements while maintaining appropriate audits.

Automated systems and scripts require programmatic MFA solutions that can operate without human intervention while maintaining security. This often involves certificate-based authentication combined with API keys or tokens, with regular rotation schedules and comprehensive monitoring.

Legacy systems in telecom environments often lack native support for modern MFA protocols. Integration strategies might include implementing MFA at the access gateway level, using jump hosts with MFA enforcement, or deploying specialized proxy solutions. These integration points must be carefully designed to prevent circumvention while maintaining operational efficiency. The MFA infrastructure must be deployed in a highly available, geographically distributed architecture. Authentication services should be positioned close to major operational centers to minimize latency, with local caching mechanisms to handle temporary connectivity issues. The architecture must include redundant authentication servers, synchronized token databases, and reliable backup communication channels.

PKI infrastructure for network elements

PKI in telecom environments serves as a critical foundation for securing network element communications, authenticating components, and establishing trust relationships across the network. The evolution towards 5G networks and cloud-native network functions has significantly expanded the scope and complexity of PKI requirements in telecom operations.

The PKI architecture for network elements must support both traditional hardware-based network functions and modern cloud-native deployments. This hybrid environment requires a hierarchical **certificate authority** (**CA**) structure that separates different trust domains while maintaining interoperability. Root CAs are typically maintained offline for maximum security, while multiple subordinate CAs handle day-to-day certificate issuance for different network domains such as RAN, core network, and operations support systems. Shown in *Figure 13.2* is a high-level architectural diagram of a PKI infrastructure.

Network Function Virtualization (**NFV**) and **Cloud-native Network Functions** (**CNFs**) introduce new requirements for PKI automation. Certificate lifecycle management must be integrated with container orchestration platforms and service mesh implementations to support dynamic workload scaling. Automated certificate provisioning and rotation become essential for maintaining security in these ephemeral environments.

Network elements use certificates for multiple purposes, including mutual TLS authentication, secure management access, and establishing secure communication channels. The PKI infrastructure must support different certificate profiles and key usage patterns based on the specific requirements of each network element type. This includes supporting both traditional RSA certificates and modern **elliptic curve cryptography (ECC)** implementations. 5G network functions require additional certificate-based security mechanisms to support network slicing and secure SBA. The PKI infrastructure must provide certificates that include specific extensions and attributes to support these features while maintaining compatibility with existing network elements.

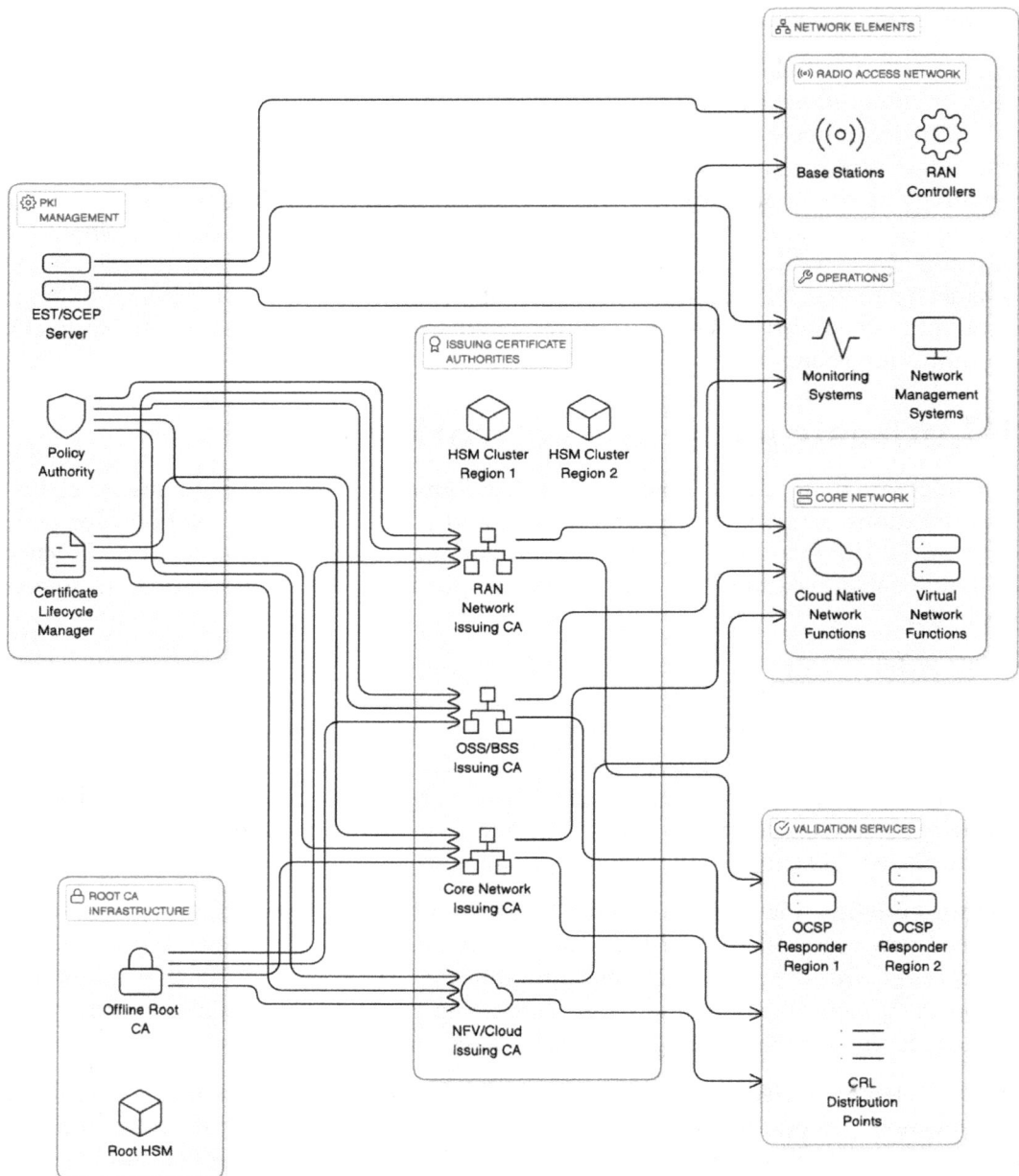

Figure 13.2: PKI infrastructure

The PKI infrastructure must maintain high availability across geographically distributed locations. This typically involves deploying certificate authority services in multiple regions with automated failover capabilities. The design must ensure that certificate services remain available even during significant network disruptions, particularly for critical network elements.

HSMs play a crucial role in protecting CA private keys and providing cryptographic operations for certificate signing. These HSMs must be deployed in a redundant configuration across geographic locations while maintaining strict security controls and audit capabilities.

Zero Trust security models in modern telecom networks rely heavily on certificate-based authentication. The PKI infrastructure must support rapid certificate issuance and validation to enable a zero-trust architecture while maintaining performance requirements. This includes supporting short-lived certificates for ephemeral workloads and implementing efficient validation mechanisms. Integration with modern identity and access management systems allows for unified governance of human and machine identities. The PKI infrastructure must support federation with enterprise identity systems while maintaining separate trust domains for network elements.

SSH key management and rotation

SSH key management in telecom environments presents unique challenges due to the scale of operations, diversity of network elements, and critical nature of services. Effective key management must balance security requirements with operational efficiency while maintaining strict access controls across the infrastructure. Telecom operators must implement a centralized SSH key management system that provides visibility and control over all SSH keys across the infrastructure. This system serves as the single source of truth for authorized keys and manages the complete lifecycle of SSH credentials. The centralized approach ensures consistent policy enforcement and simplifies audit processes.

Integration with existing identity and access management systems is crucial for maintaining synchronized access rights. When staff members are onboarded, transferred, or offboarded, their SSH access rights must be automatically updated across all relevant systems. This integration helps prevent access control gaps and reduces the risk of unauthorized access through outdated SSH keys.

The key management system should enforce strong key generation policies, including appropriate key lengths, algorithms, and passphrase requirements. Modern telecom environments typically standardize ED25519 or RSA keys with a minimum 4096-bit length, with clear policies on acceptable algorithms and parameters.

Key distribution must be secured through encrypted channels and integrated with change management processes. When new network elements are deployed or existing systems are updated, the key management system should automatically provide appropriate SSH keys while maintaining detailed records of all distributions.

Regular key rotation is crucial for maintaining security, but it must be implemented carefully to avoid operational disruptions. The rotation schedule should be risk-based, with more frequent rotation for high-privilege accounts and critical systems. Automated rotation processes should include:

- Pre-rotation testing to verify system accessibility.
- Parallel deployment of new keys before old key removal.
- Automatic rollback capabilities if issues are detected.
- Verification of successful rotation.
- Comprehensive audit logging of all rotation activities.

The following figure shows the relationships between different components of SSH key management:

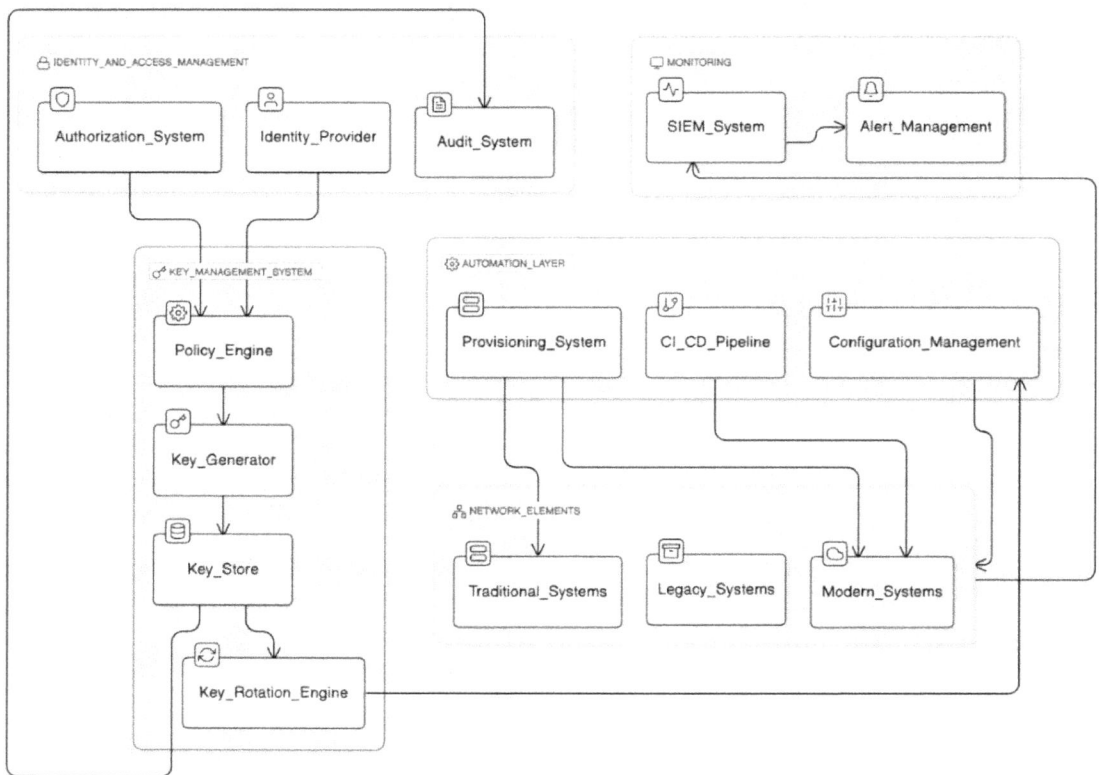

Figure 13.3: SSH key management and rotation workflow

The adoption of comprehensive identity and access management infrastructure-based best practices is no longer optional for modern telecom service providers. As networks evolve toward 5G, cloud-native architectures, and increasingly complex hybrid environments, the attack surface expands dramatically. Telecom operators must implement robust IAM infrastructure practices not only to comply with regulatory requirements but to protect critical infrastructure that underpins essential communications services. Telecom operators must consider a hybrid authentication architecture that bridges traditional telecom protocols with modern identity standards while deploying geographically distributed authentication services to minimize latency and ensure high availability. Operators should balance security requirements with operational efficiency by selecting appropriate MFA methods for different access scenarios within the telecom environment. Implementation of risk-based authentication that adapts requirements based on context factors such as location, time, system criticality, and operation type should be part of the infrastructure best practices. Establishing a hierarchical Certificate Authority structure with offline root CAs and separate trust domains for different network segments including RAN, core network, and operations support systems, along with centralize SSH key management to provide comprehensive visibility and control across the infrastructure while serving as the single source of truth for authorized keys, is must have in an operator's authentication infrastructure.

Failure to adopt these practices can result in security breaches with far-reaching consequences, including service disruptions, data exfiltration, and compromise of customer privacy.

Authorization framework

The authorization framework in telecom environments serves as the cornerstone for controlling access to network resources, operational systems, and management platforms. In an industry where unauthorized access or misconfigured permissions can impact critical communications infrastructure, a robust authorization framework is essential. This framework must support various control mechanisms, from role-based access to dynamic, context-aware authorization decisions while maintaining operational efficiency and compliance requirements. The implementation must be flexible enough to accommodate both traditional network elements and modern cloud-native functions while providing comprehensive audit trails of all authorization decisions.

RBAC implementation for network operations

RBAC in telecom network operations demands a sophisticated approach that reflects the complex hierarchy and specialized nature of telecom operations. The implementation extends beyond traditional IT roles to encompass specialized network operations functions, emergency procedures, and regulatory requirements. This comprehensive approach ensures that access controls align with operational responsibilities while maintaining security and compliance.

The role hierarchy in network operations mirrors the organizational structure and expertise levels found in telecom environments. At the core of operations, **network operations center (NOC)** teams are typically structured in tiers, each with increasing levels of responsibility and access rights. NOC Tier 1 personnel focus on basic monitoring and initial incident response, requiring limited access to system configurations. Tier 2 and 3 personnel progressively receive broader access rights to support advanced troubleshooting and complex problem resolution. NOC supervisors maintain oversight capabilities and manage escalation procedures, requiring additional administrative access.

Field operations present unique challenges for RBAC implementation. Field technicians require specific access rights that align with their physical maintenance responsibilities, while network engineers need broader configuration and optimization capabilities. Senior engineers and regional managers require access rights that span multiple systems and domains to support their architectural and coordination responsibilities. These roles must be carefully defined to ensure appropriate access while maintaining security boundaries.

Permission mapping in telecom RBAC implementations must consider the diverse range of operational activities. Access rights span multiple domains, including network element configuration, performance monitoring, fault management, and service provisioning. Each domain requires careful consideration of access levels, from read-only monitoring capabilities to full administrative control. The granularity of these permissions must support operational efficiency while preventing unauthorized access or changes.

Modern telecom operations require dynamic role assignment capabilities that adapt to changing operational needs. Maintenance windows, emergencies, and shift schedules all influence access requirements. The RBAC system must support temporary role assignments and emergency access procedures while maintaining security controls and audit capabilities. Geographic considerations also play a crucial role, as access rights often need to align with regional responsibilities and regulatory jurisdictions.

Integration with OSS and BSS is fundamental to effective RBAC implementation. The authorization framework must seamlessly integrate with network management platforms, monitoring systems, trouble ticketing, and change management processes. This integration ensures consistent access control across all operational systems while supporting automated workflows and processes.

Automation plays an increasingly important role in network operations, requiring the RBAC implementation to support automated processes while maintaining security controls. Configuration management, network provisioning, and performance optimization workflows must operate within the defined role boundaries. The authorization framework must validate automated actions against role permissions while maintaining comprehensive audit trails.

The effectiveness of RBAC in telecom environments depends heavily on regular review and updates of role definitions and permissions. As network technologies evolve and operational requirements change, the RBAC implementation must adapt while maintaining security controls and compliance requirements. This ongoing maintenance ensures that the authorization framework continues to support both operational efficiency and security objectives effectively.

Segregation of duties in telecom operations

Segregation of duties (SoD) in telecom environments represents a critical security control that prevents any single individual or role from having excessive control over critical network operations. In an industry where configuration changes can impact services for millions of users, proper SoD implementation becomes crucial for both security and operational integrity.

The implementation of SoD in telecom operations requires careful consideration of operational workflows and potential risks. Critical network changes, such as core network configurations or security parameter modifications, typically require involvement from multiple teams. For instance, while network engineers may design and propose changes, separate validation teams must review these changes, and different administrative teams must implement them. This multi-stage approach ensures that no single person can implement unauthorized or potentially harmful changes to critical infrastructure.

Configuration management in telecom environments demonstrates the practical application of SoD principles. The process typically separates configuration design, review, and implementation roles. Engineers who design network changes should not have direct implementation access, while those implementing changes should not have the authority to approve them. This separation extends to the tools and systems used, with distinct access credentials and audit trails for each role in the process.

Emergency scenarios present unique challenges for SoD implementation. While maintaining strict separation is crucial, the system must also support rapid response to critical incidents. This often involves implementing *break-glass* procedures where normal SoD rules can be suspended but with enhanced monitoring and post-event review requirements. Such exceptions must be carefully documented and require senior management approval.

Automation and orchestration systems require special consideration in SoD implementation. While automated processes can help enforce the separation of duties, they must themselves be subject to appropriate controls. Development teams creating automation scripts should not have direct access to production systems, and changes to automation workflows should require separate review and approval processes.

Security operations in telecom environments benefit from clear SoD implementation. Security monitoring teams typically operate independently from network operations teams, ensuring objective oversight of network activities. Similarly, security incident response teams maintain separation from routine operations, allowing them to investigate and respond to security events without potential conflicts of interest.

Figure 13.4 shows a workflow diagram that illustrates the key relationships and controls:

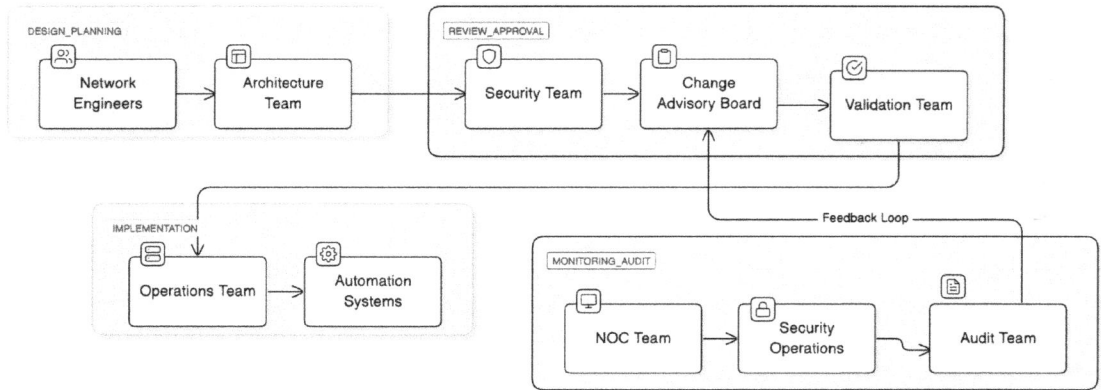

Figure 13.4: SoD workflow

Change management processes in telecom environments must embed SoD principles throughout their workflow. Changes to critical systems require multiple levels of review and approval from different organizational units. This might include technical review by architecture teams, security validation by security teams, and final approval by change advisory boards, each operating independently to ensure comprehensive oversight.

The ongoing evolution of telecom networks, particularly with the adoption of cloud-native technologies and 5G infrastructure, requires regular review and updates to SoD policies. As new technologies and operational models emerge, organizations must reassess and adjust their separation of duties framework to ensure it remains effective while supporting operational efficiency.

JIT access for maintenance windows

Just-in-time (**JIT**) access management in telecom environments provides a sophisticated approach to controlling privileged access during maintenance windows. This model ensures that elevated privileges are granted only when needed and automatically revoked when the maintenance window closes, significantly reducing the attack surface while maintaining operational efficiency.

The implementation of JIT access begins with the maintenance window planning process. When maintenance activities are scheduled, the system automatically creates time-bound access policies aligned with the approved maintenance window. These policies define not only the duration of access but also the specific systems, commands, and operations that will be permitted during the maintenance period. Integration with the change management system ensures that access rights precisely match the approved change scope.

Automated workflows manage the entire JIT access lifecycle. When a maintenance window approaches, eligible personnel receive access credentials or elevation of privileges automatically. This automation extends to multi-factor authentication requirements, where additional verification might be required before elevated access is granted. The system maintains strict time synchronization across all components to ensure accurate access window enforcement.

All activities performed using elevated privileges must undergo enhanced logging and monitoring. Security teams should receive immediate notifications of any actions that deviate from the approved maintenance plan, allowing for rapid response to potential security incidents. The monitoring system should also track the completion of maintenance tasks to ensure that access is revoked precisely when no longer needed. While standard maintenance windows follow predetermined schedules, emergency maintenance might require immediate privileged access. The JIT system includes expedited approval workflows for emergency scenarios, but with additional monitoring and post-event review requirements. These emergency procedures maintain security controls while supporting rapid response capabilities.

Integration with existing operational tools ensures seamless implementation of JIT access. The system interfaces with trouble ticketing systems, change management platforms, and network management tools. When maintenance tickets are approved, the JIT system automatically schedules the necessary access rights. This integration should extend to automated configuration management tools, ensuring they receive appropriate elevated privileges during maintenance windows.

Post-maintenance processes form an integral part of the JIT framework. Once the maintenance window closes, the system should automatically revoke elevated privileges and generate detailed activity reports. These reports should undergo automatic analysis to identify any anomalies or policy violations that might require investigation. The system should also capture metrics about maintenance efficiency and access usage patterns to inform future improvements. The following JIT figure illustrates the process:

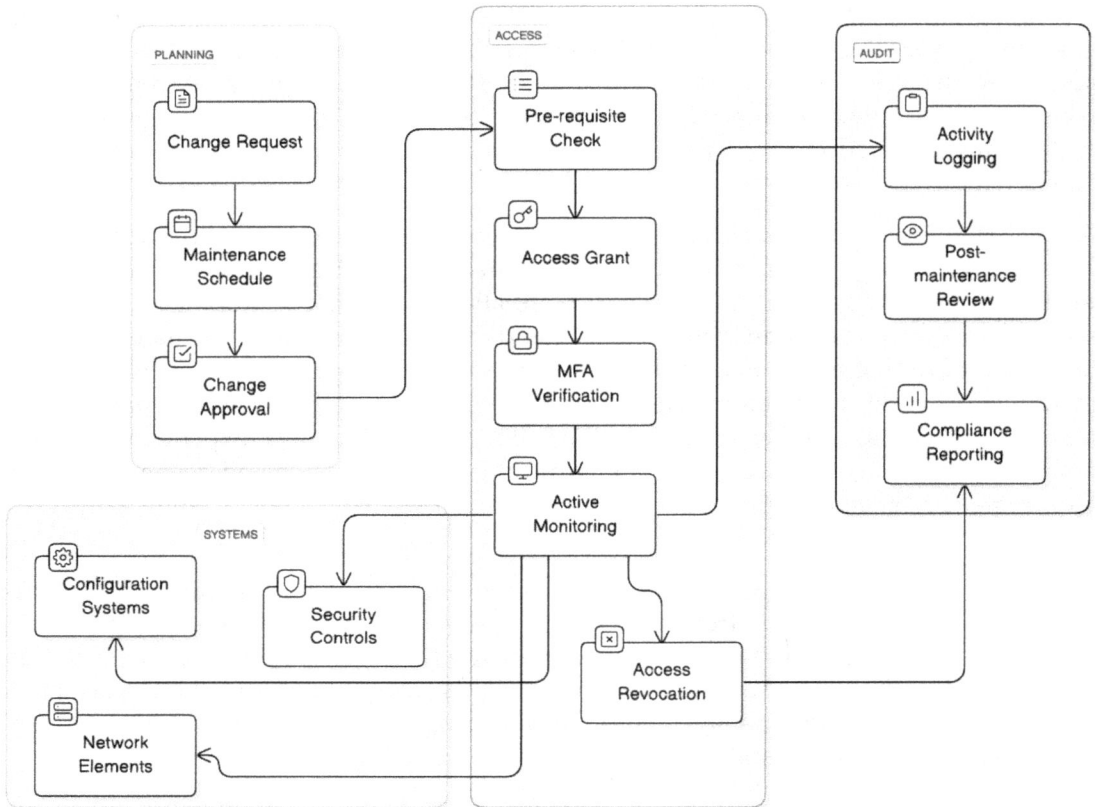

Figure 13.5: JIT workflow

Adhering to authorization best practices in telecom environments is imperative for safeguarding critical telecom infrastructure while maintaining operational efficiency. As telecom networks become increasingly complex with the integration of traditional elements and cloud-native functions, a robust authorization framework becomes the cornerstone of comprehensive security. For RBAC, role engineering is the need of the hour. It should begin with a thorough analysis of operational workflows and responsibilities rather than organizational structures alone. A detailed responsibility matrices that map specific operations to required access levels across different systems must be created. Developing role templates for common job functions while allowing for customization based on regional requirements or specialized expertise should be considered as part of this engagement. Aligning these with the role review process ensures that roles remain aligned with operational needs while preventing permission creep and unauthorized access.

It is recommended that telecom operators move beyond static role-based authorization by implementing context-aware access controls that consider factors such as time of day, location, device security posture, and current network status. All access must be continuously validated, and zero trust principles must be applied across the environment.

Identity lifecycle management

Identity lifecycle management in telecom environments encompasses the complete journey of managing identities from creation through retirement, ensuring secure and efficient access to network resources throughout their lifecycle. This process is particularly critical in telecom operations where staff members require access to sensitive infrastructure components and operational systems. The lifecycle management framework must accommodate various identity types, from operations staff and contractors to service accounts and emergency access credentials, while maintaining strict security controls and compliance requirements.

Onboarding and offboarding workflow

The onboarding process for telecom operations staff begins with a comprehensive workflow that aligns access rights with operational responsibilities. Initial access provisioning follows a template-based approach, where predefined role templates establish baseline access rights based on job functions. These templates consider both the immediate needs of new staff members and the progressive access rights they may require during their tenure.

Security clearance and background checks form an integral part of the onboarding process, particularly for roles involving critical infrastructure access. The workflow integrates with HR systems to ensure all necessary verifications are completed before granting system access. This includes validation of professional certifications, regulatory compliance requirements, and any specialized training needed for specific network domains.

Access provisioning during onboarding follows a staged approach, with initial access limited to essential systems and expanded based on demonstrated competency and operational requirements. The process includes mandatory security training, familiarization with emergency procedures, and verification of understanding of operational policies. Each stage of access expansion requires appropriate approval and documentation.

System access setup incorporates multiple authentication mechanisms appropriate to the role. This includes provisioning of standard credentials, configuration of multi-factor authentication, and, where applicable, distribution of hardware security tokens or smart cards. The process ensures that all access methods align with the organization's security policies and operational requirements.

The offboarding workflow is equally critical, requiring careful coordination to maintain security while ensuring operational continuity. When staff members depart or change roles, the system initiates an automated revocation process that identifies and removes all access rights across network systems. This includes deactivation of user accounts, removal of SSH keys, revocation of certificates, and updates to relevant access control lists.

Knowledge transfer becomes a crucial component of the offboarding process, particularly for specialized operational roles. The workflow includes checkpoints to ensure critical operational knowledge is documented and transferred to appropriate team members before access revocation. This helps maintain operational continuity while ensuring security controls remain intact.

The offboarding process includes a comprehensive audit to verify the complete removal of access rights across all systems. This audit examines direct access rights, group memberships, delegated permissions, and any specialized access credentials. The results are documented and retained for compliance purposes, providing a clear record of access termination.

A post-offboarding review ensures that all system dependencies and access remnants are identified and addressed. This includes reviewing shared accounts, service accounts, or automated processes that might have been created or managed by the departed staff member. The review helps prevent any potential security gaps that could arise from overlooked access points.

All lifecycle events, from initial onboarding through final offboarding, are logged with detailed metadata including timestamps, approvers, and justifications. This audit trail supports both internal security reviews and external compliance requirements, providing clear documentation of all identity management actions throughout the staff member's tenure.

Service account lifecycle management

Service accounts in telecom environments represent a critical component of network operations, enabling automated processes, system-to-system communications, and scheduled maintenance activities. These non-human identities require specialized lifecycle management approaches that differ significantly from standard user accounts, particularly given their elevated privileges and continuous operational requirements.

The creation of service accounts should begin with a rigorous request and approval process. Each request must document the account's purpose, required access levels, systems it will interact with, and expected lifetime. Network architects and security teams review these requests to ensure the principle of least privilege is maintained and that appropriate security controls are implemented from the outset.

Credentials management for service accounts follows strict security protocols. Initial credentials are generated using automated systems that ensure complex passwords or certificates meet security requirements. These credentials are then securely distributed to authorized systems and stored in **privileged access management** (**PAM**) solutions. Modern implementations often utilize dynamic secrets management, where credentials are automatically rotated on predetermined schedules.

Monitoring service account activity forms a crucial part of their lifecycle management. Automated systems continuously track usage patterns, authentication attempts, and executed commands. Any deviation from established patterns triggers immediate alerts for security review. This monitoring extends to tracking dependencies between service accounts and operational systems to prevent unintended service disruptions during maintenance or changes. Regular validation of service account permissions helps prevent privilege creep and ensures ongoing alignment with operational needs. Automated scanning tools identify unused permissions, excessive rights, or access to systems no longer required for the account's primary function. This validation process includes reviewing integration points, API access, and system dependencies.

Certificate management plays a vital role in service accounts used in automated processes and system integrations. The lifecycle management system tracks certificate expiration dates, initiates automated renewal processes, and ensures proper distribution of updated certificates to relevant systems. This process includes maintaining backup authentication methods to prevent service disruptions during certificate rotations.

The decommissioning service accounts process begins with a comprehensive dependency analysis to identify all systems and processes relying on the account. A phased decommissioning approach allows for the gradual removal of dependencies while maintaining service continuity. This includes updating configuration files, modifying automation scripts, and adjusting integration points. Integration with change management systems ensures that service account modifications align with broader operational changes. Any modifications to service account permissions, credentials, or configurations must go through appropriate change control processes. This integration helps prevent unauthorized changes while maintaining clear audit trails of all modifications.

Contractor and vendor access management

Managing access for contractors and vendors in telecom environments presents unique challenges due to the temporary nature of engagements and the potential sensitivity of network infrastructure access. Organizations must maintain strict security controls while enabling efficient access for third parties who play crucial roles in network operations, maintenance, and support activities.

The contractor onboarding process begins with a comprehensive vendor risk assessment and security validation. This includes reviewing the vendor's security practices, conducting background checks on individual contractors, and validating professional certifications. Legal agreements establish clear security requirements, confidentiality obligations, and compliance responsibilities before any access is granted.

Unlike regular employees, contractor access rights are automatically tied to project timelines or contract durations. The identity management system maintains detailed records of contract start and end dates, automatically triggering access reviews and revocation processes as these dates approach.

Vendor access requirements vary significantly based on their role in network operations. Equipment vendors might need direct access to specific network elements, while software providers require access to management platforms or development environments. The access management system supports these diverse requirements through granular permission controls and role-based access templates specifically designed for different vendor categories.

Remote access for contractors undergoes additional security controls. Dedicated VPN profiles, jump hosts, and secure access gateways ensure that contractor connections are properly segregated and monitored. Multi-factor authentication is mandatory for all remote access, with hardware tokens often required for access to critical systems.

All contractor activities must undergo enhanced logging and real-time monitoring, with automated systems detecting and alerting any unusual patterns. Regular activity reports are shared with both internal stakeholders and vendor management teams to ensure compliance with operational procedures.

The offboarding process for contractors requires careful coordination between multiple stakeholders. When engagements end, automated workflows ensure comprehensive access removal across all systems. This includes revoking VPN access, disabling accounts, removing certificates, and updating relevant access control lists. A final audit verifies the complete removal of all access rights.

Future access considerations are documented during the offboarding process. For vendors with recurring engagements, the system maintains records of previous access patterns, security clearances, and any issues encountered. This information streamlines future access provisioning while ensuring security lessons learned are applied to subsequent engagements.

Conclusion

IAM forms the foundation of security in modern telecommunications environments, where complex infrastructure demands sophisticated access control solutions. The integration of IAM with OSS/BSS systems demonstrates the intricate relationship between operational efficiency and security requirements, while federation services enable secure access across organizational boundaries.

A multi-layered authentication infrastructure, anchored by MFA, PKI, and SSH key management, creates a robust defense against unauthorized access. These components form an adaptive authentication framework that serves both traditional and emerging telecom technologies.

Authorization frameworks implement granular access control through RBAC and least privilege principles. Modern telecom providers balance security with operational demands through SoD and JIT access, effectively reducing risk while maintaining service quality. Comprehensive identity lifecycle management ensures access rights align with organizational roles throughout the employee journey, from onboarding to retirement.

This foundation of IAM controls supports broader security initiatives, particularly in security monitoring across telecom infrastructure. Through tools like network traffic analysis, SIEM systems, and advanced threat detection, which is discussed in the next chapter, providers can verify IAM control effectiveness and identify potential security incidents before they impact service delivery.

Points to remember

- IAM architecture in telecommunications requires a holistic approach that spans both IT and network domains. The enterprise-wide identity architecture must seamlessly integrate with both OSS and BSS, ensuring unified identity management across customer-facing services and internal operations. Directory services, particularly Active Directory and LDAP implementations, serve as the foundation for identity storage and management, while federation enables secure cross-domain authentication with partners and third-party service providers.

- Authentication infrastructure in telecom environments demands robust security measures due to the critical nature of network operations. MFA implementation should consider both technical and operational staff requirements, with special attention to emergency access procedures. PKI Infrastructure must be designed to handle both human and machine identities, supporting secure communication across network elements. SSH key management requires particular attention due to the prevalence of remote access to network devices and systems.

- The authorization framework must balance security with operational efficiency. RBAC should align with organizational structure while considering the specific requirements of network operations teams. SoD is crucial in preventing unauthorized configuration changes and fraud, particularly in billing and customer data access. JIT access mechanisms help minimize standing privileges while ensuring rapid response capabilities for network incidents.

- Identity lifecycle management in telecom environments presents unique challenges due to the diverse workforce and complex contractor ecosystem. The provisioning and de-provisioning processes must be tightly integrated with HR systems and contractor management platforms. Regular access reviews are essential, particularly for privileged accounts with access to critical network infrastructure. Automated workflows should handle routine identity management tasks while maintaining proper approval chains for sensitive access requests.

- Security monitoring and audit trails take on additional importance in telecom environments due to regulatory requirements and the critical nature of services. All identity-related events, particularly those involving privileged access to network elements and customer data, must be logged and monitored. Regular compliance assessments should verify the effectiveness of IAM controls, with particular attention to privacy regulations and telecommunications-specific requirements.

Exercises

1. In a telecom environment, which component typically serves as the authoritative source for subscriber identity information?

   a. Enterprise Active Directory

   b. Home Subscriber Server

   c. LDAP Directory

   d. Identity provider

2. When implementing federation between OSS/BSS systems and enterprise IAM, which protocol is most commonly used?

   a. OAuth 2.0

   b. RADIUS

   c. SAML 2.0

   d. Kerberos

3. A telecom provider wants to implement MFA for network engineers accessing critical infrastructure. Which combination would provide the strongest security?

   a. Password + SMS OTP

   b. Password + Hardware token + Biometric

   c. Password + Email OTP + Security questions

   d. Password + Mobile authenticator app

4. In the context of segregation of duties for a billing system administrator, which combination of access rights would violate SoD principles?

   a. View customer records + Generate bills

   b. Create billing plans + Apply customer discounts

   c. Modify billing rates + Approve billing adjustments

   d. View billing reports + Process payments

5. Which approach best describes JIT access in a telecom environment?

    a. Granting permanent access based on role

    b. Providing temporary elevated access with automatic revocation

    c. Implementing time-based access controls

    d. Creating emergency access procedures

6. Explain how PKI infrastructure in a telecom environment differs from traditional enterprise PKI implementations. Include considerations for scale and distribution.

7. Describe three key challenges in implementing a unified identity architecture that spans both IT and NetOps environments in a telecom organization.

8. Design a high-level SSH key management workflow for network administrators who need to access multiple geographic regions' network infrastructure. Include considerations for key rotation and emergency access.

9. Your telecom organization is implementing RBAC for OSS/BSS systems. Outline the key roles and their corresponding access levels you would recommend, considering both business and technical users.

10. Explain how identity lifecycle management in a telecom environment needs to handle both employee and subscriber identities. What are the key differences in requirements and processes?

Join our book's Discord space

Join the book's Discord Workspace for Latest updates, Offers, Tech happenings around the world, New Release and Sessions with the Authors:

https://discord.bpbonline.com

CHAPTER 14

Security Monitoring

Introduction

In today's telecommunications landscape, the complexity and sophistication of network infrastructure have reached unprecedented levels. With the convergence of traditional telecommunications services and modern cloud-native applications, securing these environments has become both critical and challenging. This chapter explores the fundamental aspects of security monitoring in telecommunications environments, with a particular focus on network functions and applications that form the backbone of modern communication services.

As telecommunications providers continue to evolve their networks to support 5G, network slicing, and edge computing, the traditional security monitoring approaches must adapt to address new threats and vulnerabilities. The integration of **security operations centers (SOC)** and **security information and event management (SIEM)** systems with telecom devices requires a carefully planned strategy that considers multiple dimensions from business imperatives and regulatory compliance to operational efficiency and data management.

This chapter begins by examining various approaches to SOC and SIEM integration, considering crucial factors such as business use cases that drive security requirements, regulatory frameworks that govern telecommunications security, industry best practices, and the growing importance of advanced data analytics. Special attention is given to storage considerations, given the massive volume of security events generated in modern telecom networks.

The chapter then introduces the principles of log integration from telecom devices, providing a structured approach to log categorization and establishing integration priorities. Understanding the different types of logs and their significance in security monitoring is crucial for building an effective security monitoring framework.

Finally, it explores domain-specific integration strategies across various telecommunications technologies, including 5G, LTE, MPLS, and transport networks. This section provides practical insights into applying the previously discussed approaches and principles in real-world scenarios, helping readers understand how security monitoring requirements vary across different domains of the telecommunications infrastructure.

Through this comprehensive examination, readers will gain a thorough understanding of how to design and implement effective security monitoring solutions for modern telecommunications environments.

Structure

This chapter will cover the following topics:

- Need for security monitoring
- SOC in telecommunications
- Approach for SOC integrations
- Cybersecurity framework alignment
- Log integration principles
- Domain based integration guidelines

Objectives

This chapter explores the critical aspects of security monitoring within telecommunications service provider environments, focusing on the integration of network functions and applications into security operations. As telecommunications infrastructure becomes increasingly complex and virtualized, establishing robust security monitoring frameworks is paramount for maintaining service integrity and regulatory compliance.

We examine three fundamental areas: First, we will explore SOC/SIEM integration approaches, analyzing how business requirements, regulatory mandates, and industry standards shape monitoring strategies. This section also addresses the challenges of data analytics and storage optimization in high-volume telecommunications environments.

The second section establishes principles for telco device log integration, providing a structured framework for log categorization and prioritization. We present methodologies for determining which logs are essential for security monitoring, considering factors such as operational impact, security relevance, and resource utilization.

Finally, we explore domain-specific integration patterns across various telecommunications technologies, including 5G, LTE, MPLS, and transport networks. This section demonstrates how the previously established approaches and principles can be applied to different network domains while addressing their unique security monitoring requirements and challenges.

Through this comprehensive examination, readers will gain practical insights into designing and implementing effective security monitoring solutions for modern telecommunications environments.

Need for security monitoring

Today, telecommunications service providers form the very backbone of our digital society. They facilitate everything from simple phone calls and text messages to complex data transfers, internet access, and critical infrastructure communication. This central role makes them a prime target for malicious actors. A successful attack on a telco can have devastating consequences, ranging from service disruption and financial losses to the compromise of sensitive personal data and even national security implications. Therefore, robust security measures are not merely a best practice for telcos; they are an absolute necessity.

At the heart of any effective security posture lies continuous security monitoring. The need for security monitoring in a telco environment arises from several interconnected factors. The sheer complexity of telco networks, encompassing a vast array of interconnected systems, devices, and protocols, creates a sprawling attack surface. This complexity offers numerous potential entry points for attackers, from legacy systems to cutting-edge 5G infrastructure, each presenting unique vulnerabilities. Without comprehensive monitoring, identifying and addressing these vulnerabilities before exploitation becomes a near-impossible task. Compounding this challenge is the constantly evolving threat landscape. Cyber threats, too, are not static; attackers continuously develop increasingly sophisticated techniques to bypass traditional security defenses. New malware, phishing campaigns, denial-of-service attacks, and **advanced persistent threats** (APTs) emerge regularly. Effective monitoring provides the crucial ability to detect these evolving threats in real-time, enabling swift response and mitigation.

Furthermore, regulatory compliance and adherence to industry standards play a significant role in ensuring adequate monitoring mechanisms. Numerous regulations and industry standards, such as the **General Data Protection Regulation** (GDPR), the **Payment Card Industry Data Security Standard** (PCI DSS), and the NIST Cybersecurity Framework, mandate robust security practices, including continuous monitoring. Compliance is not only often a legal requirement but also serves as a public demonstration of a telco's commitment to security, fostering customer trust. The need for business continuity and uninterrupted service availability also drives the imperative for monitoring. Service disruptions can have severe financial and reputational repercussions for telcos. Security monitoring plays a vital role in ensuring business continuity by detecting and preventing attacks and fraudulent activities that could lead to outages or service degradation.

Telcos handle vast amounts of sensitive customer data, including personal information, call records, **International Mobile Subscriber Identity** (**IMSI**) details, and browsing history. Safeguarding this data from unauthorized access and breaches is paramount. Monitoring helps detect suspicious activity that could indicate a data breach, enabling timely intervention and minimizing the impact on affected individuals. While external threats often dominate headlines, internal threats, whether malicious or accidental, can also pose a significant risk. Monitoring can help detect insider activity that deviates from established baselines, potentially uncovering malicious intent or unintentional errors that could compromise security.

These, along with the evolution of telecommunications infrastructure from hardware-centric systems to **Software-Defined Networks** (**SDN**) and **Network Functions Virtualization** (**NFV**), have fundamentally changed the security monitoring paradigm. Traditional perimeter-based security approaches are no longer sufficient; instead, providers must implement comprehensive monitoring solutions that provide visibility across virtualized network functions, cloud-native applications, and traditional network elements. This hybrid environment requires advanced SIEM capabilities, real-time threat detection, and automated response mechanisms to effectively identify and mitigate security incidents. Real-time monitoring allows for the immediate identification of suspicious activity, enabling rapid response and preventing attacks from escalating into major incidents.

The integration of diverse network elements into an SIEM system and SOC presents significant challenges for telecommunications service providers due to the scale, complexity, and heterogeneous nature of their infrastructure. Service providers must adopt a structured approach to SIEM integration that considers both legacy network elements and modern cloud-native infrastructure components. The complexity is further amplified by the need to monitor and correlate events across multiple technology generations from legacy 2G or 3G networks to advanced 5G infrastructure while maintaining comprehensive visibility across the entire service delivery chain. This integration challenge is compounded by the diverse vendor ecosystem typical in telecommunications environments, where equipment from multiple manufacturers must coexist and interoperate. Each vendor often implements proprietary logging mechanisms, event formats, and security controls, creating a complex tapestry of security data that must be unified within the SIEM platform. Additionally, the real-time nature of telecommunications services demands that SIEM integration be accomplished without impacting service performance or availability, requiring careful consideration of bandwidth utilization, processing overhead, and storage requirements. A systematic approach to SIEM integration is therefore essential, encompassing everything from business requirement gathering, initial planning, use case definition, KPI creation, and architecture design to ongoing optimization and maintenance of the security monitoring infrastructure.

SOC in telecommunications

The SOC represents the central nervous system of a telecommunications provider's cybersecurity infrastructure, serving as the primary command post for monitoring, detecting, analyzing, and responding to security threats across the extensive network ecosystem. Unlike SOCs in other industries, a telecommunications SOC must maintain continuous visibility across an extraordinarily complex technology landscape that spans from traditional IT infrastructure to specialized telecommunications equipment, subscriber-facing services, and interconnection points with other carriers. This complexity necessitates a tailored approach to security monitoring that addresses the unique challenges and requirements of telecommunications environments.

In the telecommunications sector, the SOC assumes responsibility for protecting both the provider's infrastructure and the communications services delivered to millions of subscribers. This dual mandate requires the SOC to monitor not only traditional security events but also service-affecting security incidents that could impact network availability or subscriber communications. The telecommunications SOC monitors critical network elements, including radio access networks, core switching infrastructure, signaling systems, subscriber databases, and interconnection points with other providers. This extensive monitoring scope generates massive volumes of security event data that must be effectively collected, normalized, analyzed, and correlated to identify genuine security threats.

Beyond traditional security monitoring, a telecommunications SOC plays a crucial role in regulatory compliance, working closely with legal and regulatory teams to ensure adherence to telecommunications-specific requirements. These requirements often include specialized provisions for communications privacy, lawful interception capabilities, and critical infrastructure protection. The SOC maintains detailed documentation of security controls, monitoring coverage, and incident response activities to demonstrate compliance during regulatory audits and assessments. This compliance function extends to supporting privacy requirements, as telecommunications providers handle vast amounts of sensitive subscriber data that must be protected according to increasingly stringent privacy regulations.

The telecommunications SOC operates across multiple technology domains, each with distinct security requirements and threat landscapes. In the network infrastructure domain, the SOC monitors for attacks targeting core network elements, signaling protocols, and routing infrastructure. For subscriber-facing services, the SOC focuses on detecting fraudulent activities, unauthorized access attempts, and potential privacy violations. In the interconnection domain, the SOC monitors peering points and interconnection interfaces for signs of attacks originating from partner networks or attempts to exploit interconnection protocols. This domain-specific monitoring approach requires specialized expertise and tools tailored to telecommunications technologies.

Incident response represents another critical function of the telecommunications SOC, with response procedures carefully designed to address security incidents while minimizing service disruption. When security incidents occur, the SOC must coordinate response activities across multiple technical teams, including network operations, engineering, and customer support. This coordination becomes particularly important during major security incidents that could affect service delivery, requiring careful balancing of security measures against operational impact. The telecommunications SOC typically maintains specialized response playbooks for different types of incidents, from signaling protocol exploits to subscriber authentication attacks, ensuring consistent and effective response regardless of incident type.

As telecommunications networks evolve toward software-defined and virtualized architectures, the SOC must adapt its monitoring capabilities to address new security challenges. Modern telecommunications SOCs increasingly implement advanced security analytics, leveraging machine learning and behavioural analysis to detect sophisticated threats that traditional signature-based approaches might miss. These analytics capabilities help the SOC identify anomalous patterns in network traffic, signaling messages, and subscriber activities that could indicate security compromises. The growing adoption of these advanced capabilities transforms the telecommunications SOC from a reactive security function into a proactive threat hunting operation that can identify emerging threats before they impact critical services.

Approach to SOC integration

In the dynamic landscape of telecommunications, the integration of network devices with SIEM systems and SOC requires a carefully orchestrated approach that balances multiple organizational imperatives. Telecom service providers must begin by establishing clear business use cases that align security monitoring with their operational objectives, ensuring that the integration delivers tangible value beyond basic security compliance. The regulatory landscape shapes the foundation of this integration strategy, as telecommunications providers operate under stringent oversight that demands comprehensive monitoring and reporting capabilities. In most cases, the potential for transforming security data into actionable business intelligence presents opportunities for value-added services, making it crucial to design the integration with future analytics capabilities in mind. In the overall service provider network, the challenge from the sheer volume of log data generated by telecommunications network devices from core network elements to customer-facing systems necessitates a thoughtful consideration of storage infrastructure that can scale with the organization's growing needs. This abundance of log data also underscores the critical importance of optimization strategies, as unrefined log collection can quickly overwhelm even the most robust security monitoring systems, making it essential to implement intelligent log management practices that balance comprehensive security visibility with operational efficiency.

Business use cases

The integration of network devices with security monitoring infrastructure serves multiple business objectives that extend beyond traditional security concerns. Understanding these use cases and developing the SIEM platform accordingly helps telecommunications providers justify the investment and design an integration strategy that delivers maximum value to the organization.

Fraud detection and prevention

Telecommunications providers face unique fraud challenges that can significantly impact revenue and reputation. By integrating network devices with SIEM systems, providers can detect and respond to various fraud scenarios in real-time. For instance, when a sudden spike in international calls occurs from multiple subscribers to a specific destination, the SIEM can correlate this pattern with historical baseline data to identify potential **Private Branch Exchange** (**PBX**) hacking attempts. Similarly, monitoring signaling traffic from SS7 networks helps identify subscription fraud, where criminals attempt to exploit roaming services or bypass billing systems.

Regulatory compliance monitoring

While specific regulations vary by jurisdiction, telecommunications providers must demonstrate continuous compliance monitoring capabilities. Integrating network devices with SIEM or SOC infrastructure creates an auditable trail of security events and configuration changes. For example, when an engineer modifies access control lists on core routers, the SIEM captures these changes, their authentication context, and maintains chain of custody documentation that proves compliance with change management requirements.

Infrastructure protection and availability

Telecommunications infrastructure represents critical national assets that require sophisticated protection mechanisms. SIEM integration enables providers to detect and respond to threats targeting core network components. For instance, monitoring BGP routing updates across border routers helps identify potential route hijacking attempts that could disrupt internet connectivity for entire regions. Similarly, correlating authentication failures across network management interfaces helps detect coordinated attempts to compromise network infrastructure.

Network performance and security correlation

The convergence of security and network operations provides valuable insights into service delivery. When network devices feed performance metrics into the SIEM alongside security events, service providers can identify security incidents that manifest as performance issues. Consider a scenario where a distributed DDoS attack targets the provider's DNS infrastructure. The correlation between increased DNS query volumes, network utilization metrics, and security events enables faster detection and response, ultimately protecting service availability for legitimate customers.

Incident response and service level agreements

The integration supports incident response processes and helps maintain service-level agreements. When security events from network devices flow into the SIEM in real-time, security teams can rapidly assess incident scope and impact. Consider a scenario where a zero-day vulnerability affects specific router models. Integrated monitoring helps identify all affected devices, prioritize patches based on exposure, and demonstrate compliance with contractual response time obligations.

Customer experience impact analysis

Security events often have direct implications for customer experience. By correlating security monitoring data with customer-facing services, providers can proactively address security issues before they affect subscribers. Consider a scenario where a malware infection causes a customer's device to generate excessive signaling traffic. Integrated security monitoring can identify this behavior, enabling the provider to notify the customer and prevent service degradation for other subscribers sharing the same network resources.

Regulatory requirements

Telecommunications service providers operate under a complex web of regulatory requirements that directly influence their security monitoring practices. The integration of network devices with SIEM and SOC infrastructure must be carefully considered to ensure continuous compliance while protecting critical communications infrastructure.

Data protection and privacy

Telecommunications providers handle vast amounts of sensitive customer data, including call records, location information, and personal identifiers. Privacy regulations require providers to implement robust monitoring controls that can detect and prevent unauthorized access to this information. When integrating network devices with security monitoring systems, providers must ensure that the monitoring itself does not violate privacy mandates. This means implementing strict access controls on monitoring data, masking sensitive information in log files, and maintaining detailed audit trails of who accesses what information and when.

For telecommunications providers operating in or serving customers in the European Union, GDPR establishes strict requirements for protecting personal data. The NIST framework provides a comprehensive approach to security monitoring through its core functions: identify, protect, detect, respond, and recover. NERC CIP Standards like CIP-007-6, CIP-008-5, and CIP-010-2 dictate monitoring guidelines for telecommunications providers supporting critical infrastructure. Similarly, various controls (A.12.4, A.12.7, A.16.1, and A.18.2) in the ISO 27001 Information Security Management standard provide a framework for security monitoring.

Critical infrastructure protection

As essential service providers, telecommunications companies must comply with critical infrastructure protection regulations. These regulations typically require continuous monitoring of network infrastructure for security threats and operational anomalies. The monitoring system must be capable of detecting and alerting to potential compromises quickly enough to prevent service disruptions. For instance, when a core router experiences multiple failed authentication attempts followed by configuration changes, the security monitoring infrastructure must correlate these events and trigger appropriate response protocols within mandated timeframes.

Lawful interception requirements

Many jurisdictions require telecommunications providers to maintain capabilities for lawful interception of communications when presented with proper legal authorization. This creates unique challenges for security monitoring integration, as providers must ensure their monitoring systems can distinguish between authorized interception activities and potential security incidents. The monitoring infrastructure needs to maintain detailed records of all interception activities while protecting this sensitive information from unauthorized access.

Communication service continuity

Regulatory frameworks often specify minimum service availability requirements for telecommunications providers. Security monitoring plays a crucial role in meeting these obligations by detecting and responding to events that could impact service delivery. The integration must support real-time monitoring of service-affecting security incidents and provide adequate visibility into the security posture of critical network components.

Incident reporting obligations

Telecommunications regulators typically require prompt reporting of security incidents that meet certain threshold criteria. The security monitoring infrastructure must support this requirement by collecting and correlating relevant event data that helps determine when an incident meets reporting thresholds. This includes maintaining accurate timestamp information, preserving event context, and supporting the generation of regulatory reports in required formats.

Records retention and auditability

Regulations specify varying retention periods for different types of security event data. When integrating network devices with security monitoring systems, providers must implement retention policies that satisfy the longest applicable retention period while managing storage costs effectively. The system must maintain the integrity and authenticity of retained data, ensuring it remains admissible for regulatory investigations or legal proceedings.

Cross-border data handling

Many telecommunications providers operate across multiple jurisdictions, each with its own regulatory requirements. Security monitoring systems must accommodate these varying requirements, particularly regarding data localization and cross-border data transfers. This might necessitate implementing monitoring architectures that can segregate data based on jurisdiction while maintaining comprehensive security visibility.

Cybersecurity framework alignment

While specific frameworks vary by region, most telecommunications regulators require providers to align their security practices with recognized cybersecurity frameworks. Security monitoring integration must support the controls and metrics defined in these frameworks, enabling providers to demonstrate continuous compliance through automated monitoring and reporting capabilities.

Industry alignment

The telecommunications industry's unique security challenges and interconnected nature necessitate a standardized approach to threat intelligence and security monitoring. The **Groupe Speciale Mobile Association (GSMA) Mobile Threat Intelligence Framework (MoTIF)** represents a collaborative industry effort to establish a common foundation for security monitoring and threat intelligence sharing among telecommunications providers. This framework becomes particularly crucial when designing the integration approach for security monitoring infrastructure, as it ensures that the collected data can contribute to and benefit from industry-wide threat intelligence initiatives.

The GSMA MoTIF framework changes how telecommunications providers approach security monitoring by establishing standardized taxonomies for mobile threats and security events. When integrating network devices with SIEM and SOC infrastructure, providers must consider how their monitoring architecture will align with these standardized classifications. This alignment enables providers to contribute meaningful threat intelligence to the broader telecommunications community while simultaneously enriching their security monitoring capabilities with industry-wide insights. The framework's emphasis on mobile network infrastructure, signaling protocols, and subscriber security provides a comprehensive lens through which providers can evaluate their monitoring requirements.

The following two figures show the MoTIF matrix referenced from the public GSMA FS.57 document:

Reconnaissance	Resource Development	Initial Access	Execution	Persistence	Privilege Escalation	Defence Evasion
Monitor Radio Interface	Acquire Infrastructure	Exploit Interconnection Link		Adversary-in-the-Middle		Masquerading
Broadcast Channel	Core Signalling Infrastructure Access	International Direct Signalling Link		Radio Interface Authentication Relay*		Originating Entity Spoofing
Gather Victim Identity Information	Radio Interface Access	National Direct Signalling Link				Disguise Signalling Messages
Phone and Subscription Information	Develop Capabilities	Exploit via Core Signalling Interface				Unexpected Encoding
Search Closed Sources	Mobile Network Tool	SS7 Protocol				
Mobile Network Operator Sources		Diameter Protocol				
Search Open Websites/Domains		HTTPS/2 Protocol				
Social Media		Exploit via Radio Interface				
		AS Signalling				
		NAS Signalling				
		Radio Broadcast Channel				
		Trusted Relationship				
		Exploit Interconnection Agreements				
		Supply Chain Compromise				
		Compromise Software Supply Chain				

Figure 14.1 (a): GSMA MoTIF Matrix-1

Credential Access	Discovery	Lateral Movement	Collection	Command and Control	Exfiltration	Impact
Access Subscriber Data	Network Service Scanning		Identify Subscriber			Data Manipulation
Subscriber Authentication Data	Scan Signalling Addresses		Retrieve Subscriber Identity Information			Stored Data Manipulation
Exploitation for Credential Access	Exploit via Radio Interface		Retrieve Subscriber Network Information			
	NAS Signalling		Access Subscriber Data			
	Identify Subscriber		Subscriber Authentication Data			
	Trigger Subscriber Terminated Activity		Network Sniffing			
	Retrieve Subscriber Identity Information		Radio Interface			
	Retrieve Subscriber Network Information		Locate Subscriber			
	Network Function Service Discovery		Core Network Function Signalling			

Figure 14.1 (b): GSMA MoTIF Matrix-2
(Source: GSMA FS.57 MoTIF principles)

Data analytics

Security monitoring infrastructure in telecommunications networks serves as a rich source of data that, when properly analyzed, can provide profound insights beyond traditional security use cases. Understanding how to harness this data effectively transforms security monitoring from a cost center into a strategic asset that drives business value.

Network behaviour analytics

The extensive data collected from network devices enables sophisticated behavioral analysis that can enhance both security and service delivery. By applying advanced analytics to this data, telecommunications providers can develop a deep understanding of normal network behavior patterns. When analyzing network traffic patterns, providers can identify subtle anomalies that might indicate security threats or service issues before they impact customers. For instance, ML algorithms processing historical traffic data can establish baseline behaviors for different times of day, days of the week, and seasonal variations. This behavioral baseline becomes invaluable for detecting anomalous patterns that traditional threshold-based monitoring might miss.

Customer experience analytics

Security monitoring data contains valuable insights into customer experience metrics. By analyzing authentication patterns, session data, and service access logs, providers can understand how customers interact with their services. This analysis helps identify friction points in service delivery, such as repeated authentication failures that might indicate usability issues rather than security threats. Furthermore, analyzing security event data alongside customer support tickets can reveal correlations between security controls and customer satisfaction, enabling providers to optimize security measures without compromising user experience.

Threat intelligence generation

The vast amount of security monitoring data collected across a telecommunications network can be transformed into actionable threat intelligence. By analyzing attack patterns, malicious behavior indicators, and security incidents across their infrastructure, providers can develop proprietary threat intelligence that benefits both their security operations and their customers. This analysis might reveal emerging attack trends specific to telecommunications infrastructure, enabling providers to enhance their security controls proactively and share insights with their enterprise customers.

Service development insights

Analytics performed on security monitoring data can inform service development decisions. By analyzing how customers interact with security controls, providers can identify opportunities for new service offerings or improvements to existing services. For instance, analysis of VPN usage patterns might reveal demand for advanced security services among specific customer segments, guiding the development of new secure communication offerings.

Cross-domain analysis

Security monitoring data becomes particularly valuable when analyzed alongside data from other business domains. By correlating security events with customer relationship management data, network operations data, and business performance metrics, providers can develop a more comprehensive understanding of their operations. This cross-domain analysis might reveal, for example, how security incidents impact customer churn rates or how security investments correlate with customer retention.

Storage considerations

The massive scale of telecommunications networks generates an unprecedented volume of security monitoring data, making storage architecture one of the most critical aspects of SIEM and SOC integration. Understanding and implementing appropriate storage strategies ensures both operational efficiency and regulatory compliance while managing costs effectively.

Storage volume planning

Telecommunications service providers must carefully consider the exponential growth of security monitoring data. A typical provider's network generates security events from multiple layers of infrastructure, from radio access networks to core switching systems, each producing thousands of events per second. When we examine a medium-sized provider's daily log generation, we might see upwards of 10 terabytes of raw security event data. This volume multiplies when we consider the need to store enriched data with additional context and correlation information.

The planning process must account for various factors that influence storage requirements. Network growth projections play a crucial role as providers expand their 5G infrastructure, for instance, the number of connected devices and network elements increases dramatically, leading to corresponding growth in security event data. Similarly, the introduction of new services or security controls often results in additional logging requirements that impact storage needs.

Data lifecycle management

Effective storage management requires comprehensive data lifecycle policies. The lifecycle begins when security events are first captured and includes several crucial phases:

- **Initial processing and enrichment**: Raw security events undergo enrichment with additional context, potentially increasing their storage footprint. The storage architecture must accommodate both the original events and their enriched versions while maintaining data integrity and relationships.
- **Retention period management**: Different types of security events require varying retention periods based on operational and regulatory requirements. For instance,

authentication events might need longer retention than routine network health checks. The storage system must support flexible retention policies while ensuring no premature data deletion occurs.

- **Regulatory requirements management**: Telecommunications providers must navigate a complex landscape of regulatory requirements that directly influence how security monitoring data is stored, managed, and eventually disposed of throughout its lifecycle. Under EU regulations, providers must classify data into distinct categories that determine their lifecycle requirements:

- **Traffic data**: Information about call routing, duration, and network usage patterns must be retained for 6 to 24 months, depending on the member state's implementation of the data retention directive.

- **Location data**: Geographic information about mobile device connections requires special handling, with retention periods typically limited to twelve months.

- **Subscriber data**: Basic account and identity information may be retained for the duration of the service relationship plus an additional period specified by national regulations.

Data compression and optimization

Storage optimization techniques play a vital role in managing large-scale security monitoring data:

- **Real-time compression**: Implementing efficient compression algorithms reduces storage requirements while maintaining quick access to recent events. The compression strategy must balance storage savings against processing overhead, particularly for high-volume event sources.

- **Deduplication**: Telecommunications networks often generate redundant security events across different monitoring points. Intelligent deduplication strategies can significantly reduce storage requirements while preserving essential security context. For example, multiple failed authentication attempts from the same source might be consolidated without losing critical security information.

Log integration principles

Telecommunications service providers must adopt a systematic approach to log collection and integration that encompasses both traditional network elements and modern virtualized network functions across their infrastructure. This integration strategy needs to account for the diverse array of network segments, including **radio access network** (**RAN**) components like base stations and radio controllers, **Multi-access Edge Computing** (**MEC**) nodes that process data at the network edge, transport network elements handling data transmission, core network components managing subscriber and service data, and interconnection points for peering and roaming services. Each network segment generates distinct log types, from signaling protocol messages like Diameter and SS7 to application-level logs from virtualized network functions. These logs serve multiple SOC use cases, including threat detection, service availability monitoring, fraud prevention, and security compliance verification. The horizontal nature of telecommunications infrastructure necessitates careful consideration of log sources from various categories of devices, including physical network elements, **virtualized network functions (VNFs)**, **cloud-native network functions (CNFs)**, security appliances, and operational support systems. Network operators must particularly focus on monitoring critical interfaces and protocols unique to telecommunications, such as the S1 interface in LTE networks, Diameter signaling in the core network, and GTP tunneling protocols, as these represent potential attack vectors that could compromise network integrity and service availability.

Categorization of devices

The effectiveness of security monitoring in telecommunications networks heavily depends on proper categorization of devices and systems, which determines logging priorities, retention policies, and integration approaches. Understanding these categories helps security teams implement appropriate monitoring strategies that align with both operational requirements and security objectives.

Critical security and core network devices

At the heart of telecommunications infrastructure lie the critical, category 1, security devices and core network elements that form the foundation of service delivery. These devices require the most comprehensive and granular logging configuration due to their central role in network operations. The main routing and switching infrastructure in this category handles the bulk of network traffic, making their logs invaluable for detecting network-based attacks, traffic anomalies, and potential service disruptions. Authentication servers, including **Home Subscriber Servers (HSS)** and **authentication, authorization, and accounting (AAA)** systems, process sensitive subscriber credentials and generate crucial security events that must be monitored in real-time. Security appliances such as firewalls, intrusion prevention systems, and DDoS mitigation platforms generate high-priority security alerts that demand immediate attention from SOC teams.

Supporting systems and service platforms

The second category encompasses systems that, while not directly involved in network operations, handle sensitive customer and operational data that requires careful monitoring. Billing platforms generate logs that are critical for detecting fraud attempts and revenue assurance. Customer databases, including **customer relationship management (CRM)** systems and subscriber databases, require monitoring to ensure data privacy and detect unauthorized access attempts. Service delivery platforms, which manage value-added services and content delivery, generate application-level logs that provide insights into service usage patterns and potential security violations. The logging requirements for these systems focus on data access patterns, authentication events, and transaction logs that could indicate fraudulent activities or data breaches.

Edge and access network systems

The third category includes edge devices, access networks, and auxiliary systems that form the outer layer of the telecommunications infrastructure. RAN components like base stations and small cells generate logs related to subscriber connectivity and signal quality. Edge routers and access switches produce logs that help monitor the network perimeter and detect unauthorized access attempts. Auxiliary systems, including monitoring platforms and testing equipment, generate operational logs that, while less critical, still contribute to the overall security posture. The logging strategy for these devices typically focuses on volumetric anomalies, access control violations, and operational status changes.

Integration priorities and considerations

In telecommunications networks, the strategic integration of network devices into a **security operations center** (**SOC**) infrastructure requires a carefully planned approach that balances security requirements with operational efficiency. This prioritization framework ensures that the most critical security monitoring capabilities are established first, followed by progressive integration of supporting systems.

Critical security and core network integration

The integration of *Category 1* devices represents the foundation of telecommunications security monitoring. These devices generate security-critical logs that serve as the primary data source for detecting and responding to security threats. Core network elements like **Mobile Switching Centers** (**MSC**), **Mobility Management Entities** (**MME**), and **Session Border Controllers** (**SBC**) process millions of subscriber sessions daily, making their logs invaluable for security analysis. The authentication servers, including HSS and **Authentication Centers** (**AuC**), handle sensitive subscriber credentials and generate authentication logs that must be monitored in real-time to detect potential compromise attempts. Similarly, billing mediation platforms process **charging data records** (**CDRs**) that are crucial for detecting fraud attempts and revenue leakage.

The integration of these devices demands immediate attention for several compelling reasons. First, these systems process and transmit sensitive subscriber data, including location information, call metadata, and authentication credentials. Any compromise of these systems could lead to severe privacy breaches and regulatory violations. Second, these devices form the backbone of service delivery, making their security logs essential for maintaining service continuity and detecting potential service-affecting security incidents. Third, the logs from these devices provide visibility into critical network protocols like Diameter and SS7, enabling the detection of protocol-specific attacks that could compromise network integrity.

Supporting systems integration

Once *Category 1* devices are successfully integrated, telecommunications providers should proceed with the integration of *Category 2* systems. These supporting platforms, while not directly involved in network operations, handle significant amounts of sensitive customer and operational data. Customer databases store personal information, service preferences, and account details, making their access logs valuable for detecting unauthorized data access or potential insider threats. Service delivery platforms managing value-added services generate application-level logs that can reveal attempts to exploit service vulnerabilities or conduct fraud.

The integration of Category 2 devices follows a *should* priority level because while they handle sensitive information, their logs are typically less time-critical for incident detection and response compared to Category 1 devices. However, their integration remains important for maintaining a comprehensive security monitoring posture and supporting forensic investigations when needed.

Selective edge and access network integration

The integration of *Category 3* devices requires careful consideration of specific use cases beyond routine security monitoring. These devices, including radio access network elements and auxiliary systems, generate enormous volumes of operational logs that can quickly overwhelm storage systems and consume SIEM licensing capacity if not properly filtered. The decision to integrate these devices should be driven by specific business requirements or security use cases that justify the additional resource consumption.

For instance, if a telecommunication provider needs to analyze subscriber usage patterns for security anomaly detection or requires detailed visibility into edge network behavior for specific threat-hunting scenarios, the integration of relevant *Category 3* devices becomes warranted. However, this integration should be preceded by careful planning to implement appropriate log filtering and aggregation mechanisms that ensure only relevant security events are forwarded to the SOC infrastructure.

Types of logs for integration

In telecommunications environments, effective security monitoring relies on the collection and analysis of diverse log types generated by various network elements, services, and applications. Understanding these different log types, their formats, and their security implications is crucial for implementing comprehensive security monitoring. To generate the best result from a SIEM tool, the following types of device logs should be fed into the monitoring tool:

- **Authentication and access control logs**: Authentication logs form a critical component of security monitoring in telecommunications networks. These logs are generated when users, systems, or subscribers attempt to access network resources or services. In traditional network elements, authentication logs often come from RADIUS or TACACS+ servers, providing detailed information about administrator user access attempts, privilege levels, and command execution. In virtualized environments, authentication logs might originate from **identity and access management** (**IAM**) systems or Kubernetes cluster authentication events. The correlation of these logs helps security teams detect unauthorized access attempts, privilege escalation activities, and potential credential compromise scenarios. For instance, multiple failed authentication attempts across different network elements might indicate a systematic attempt to breach network security.

Integration priority of these authentication and access controls logs with SIEM is a MUST for service provider SOC deployments.

- **Security event logs**: Security event logs are generated by dedicated security devices and security modules within network elements. These logs often follow structured formats and contain specific security-related events like firewall policy violations, intrusion detection alerts, and malware detection events. Traditional network elements typically generate these logs through SNMP traps or syslog messages, while cloud-native environments might use container security logs or security event feeds from **cloud security posture management** (**CSPM**) tools. Security event logs are crucial for detecting and investigating potential security incidents, such as unauthorized access attempts, policy violations, or malicious activities within the network. Their integration is non-negotiable due to their direct security relevance and the potential impact of missing critical security events.

Integration priority of these security event logs with SIEM is a MUST for service provider SOC deployments.

- **Audit logs:** Audit logs provide a detailed record of system and user activities, making them invaluable for security monitoring and compliance purposes. In telecommunications environments, audit logs capture configuration changes, system modifications, and administrative actions across both traditional and virtualized network functions. These logs often maintain structured formats that include timestamps, user identities, actions performed, and the outcome of those actions. The correlation of audit logs across different systems helps security teams track unauthorized system changes, detect potential insider threats, and maintain compliance with security policies. Logs recording administrative actions and configuration changes **MUST** be integrated due to their security significance and potential insider threat indicators. System-generated audit events **SHOULD** be integrated after careful filtering to focus on security-relevant information. This tiered approach ensures critical security visibility while managing log volumes effectively.

Integration priority of these audit logs, which contain administrative action, with SIEM is a MUST, and logs for system-generated events SHOULD be integrated with SIEM, for service provider SOC deployments.

- **Operational logs:** Operational logs provide insights into the functioning of network elements and services. While primarily used for performance monitoring, these logs can also indicate security-relevant events. Traditional network elements generate operational logs through syslog or SNMP, while virtualized functions might use container logs or cloud platform logging services. The security significance of operational logs becomes apparent when analyzing service disruptions that might indicate denial-of-service attacks or when investigating performance anomalies that could signal security incidents. Operational logs **SHOULD** be integrated with appropriate filtering mechanisms in place. While these logs can indicate security-relevant events, their high volume requires careful selection of which events to forward to the SIEM. Service providers should establish clear criteria for identifying security-relevant operational events and implement filtering at the source to prevent SIEM overload.

  Service providers SHOULD consider integrating these operational logs with selective filtering while setting up SIEM for telco SOC deployments.

- **Protocol-specific logs:** Integration priority, MUST for security-relevant protocols, MAY for others. Protocol logs that require a differentiated approach:

  o **MUST integrate**: Signaling protocol logs (SS7, Diameter) due to their security implications, and Authentication protocol logs (RADIUS, Diameter)

  o **SHOULD integrate**: GTP protocol logs for roaming and interconnect interfaces

  o **MAY integrate**: Other protocol logs based on specific security use cases

Telecommunications networks generate extensive protocol-specific logs that require special attention in security monitoring. These include logs from signaling protocols like diameter and SS7, which can reveal attempts to exploit protocol vulnerabilities or conduct fraud. The logs often contain structured information about protocol transactions, including source and destination addresses, message types, and transaction results. Security teams correlate these logs to detect protocol-specific attacks, such as SS7 map scanning or diameter-based location tracking attempts.

Log severity levels and their security implications

Telecommunications logs typically follow standardized severity levels, ranging from emergency (level 0) to debug (level 7). Understanding these severity levels is crucial for proper security monitoring:

- **Emergency (0) and Alert (1)**: Indicate critical security events requiring immediate attention

- **Critical (2) and Error (3)**: Often signal security-relevant system failures or policy violations

- **Warning (4)**: May indicate potential security issues requiring investigation

- **Notice (5) and Informational (6)**: Provide context for security investigations
- **Debug (7)**: Useful for detailed forensic analysis during security incidents

Priority recommendations based on severity:

- **MUST integrate**: Emergency (0), Alert (1), Critical (2)
- **MUST integrate**: Error (3) events related to security controls
- **SHOULD integrate**: Warning (4) events with security implications
- **MAY integrate**: Notice (5) and Informational (6) based on specific use cases
- **SHOULD NOT integrate**: Debug (7) unless needed for specific investigations.

Domain based integration guidelines

The telecommunications infrastructure comprises multiple specialized domains and services, each presenting unique security challenges and monitoring requirements. As providers evolve their networks to support advanced services like 5G, IMS, and various transport technologies, the complexity of security monitoring increases exponentially. Understanding how to effectively integrate these diverse domains with security monitoring infrastructure requires a systematic approach that considers the unique characteristics and security requirements of each service domain. From the radio access network to the core infrastructure, each domain contains specialized network functions that generate distinct security events and face unique threats. For instance, the security monitoring requirements for a 5G core network function differ significantly from those of traditional transport network elements, necessitating tailored integration approaches. Similarly, IMS services present their own set of security challenges, particularly in the context of SIP-based communications and real-time multimedia sessions.

Thus, it is important to examine these domains through three critical lenses: the inherent security threats they face, the specific SIEM use cases that address these threats, and the practical logging considerations for various network functions. This structured approach helps security architects and engineers understand not only what to monitor but also why and how to monitor it effectively. By understanding these domain-specific requirements, telecommunications providers can develop comprehensive security monitoring strategies that address both domain-specific and cross-domain security challenges while maintaining operational efficiency.

LTE

The **Evolved Packet Core (EPC)** in LTE networks represents a critical telecommunications infrastructure that demands comprehensive security monitoring. Understanding the threats, risks, and appropriate monitoring approaches helps telecommunications providers implement effective security controls and detection mechanisms. Refer to the following figure:

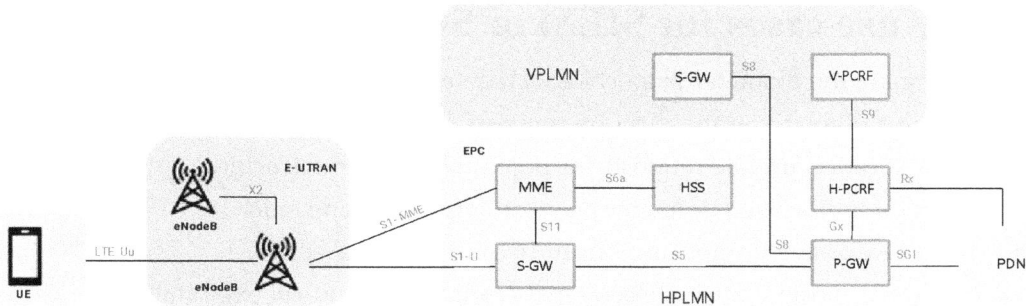

Figure 14.2: *LTE architecture*

Threats and risks in the EPC and LTE environment

The EPC and LTE infrastructure face sophisticated threats that can compromise both network security and subscriber privacy. Attackers frequently target the diameter signaling interfaces between network elements, attempting to exploit vulnerabilities that could lead to unauthorized access to subscriber information, service disruption, or fraudulent usage of network resources. The exposure of EPC components like the MME, SGW, and PGW to various interconnection points creates potential attack surfaces that malicious actors can exploit. The following are two important factors that are the main contributors to the threats to the LTE environment:

- **Infrastructure-level threats and risks**: The core network infrastructure faces sophisticated attacks that can compromise service delivery and subscriber privacy. Attackers often exploit vulnerabilities in signaling protocols, particularly diameter and GTP, to breach network security. Malicious actors might attempt to compromise network elements through unauthorized access, often targeting management interfaces or misconfigured network services. Configuration tampering on core network elements can lead to service disruption or unauthorized traffic routing. Additionally, DDoS attacks targeting core network components can cause widespread service outages.

- **Subscriber-related threats**: Subscribers face various risks from attacks targeting their service usage and privacy. Location tracking attempts through signaling protocol exploitation can compromise subscriber privacy. Authentication bypass attacks might allow unauthorized access to network services. Subscription fraud through compromised subscriber credentials or SIM cloning affects both subscribers and operators. Man-in-the-middle attacks at the radio interface or core network can intercept subscriber traffic.

Security use cases for SIEM or SOC implementation

The following are the diameter protocol attack detection:

- Monitor diameter authentication requests for unusual patterns.
- Track location update requests for potential subscriber tracking.
- Detect unauthorized diameter peers attempting connection.
- Detect excessive retransmissions or invalid response codes.
- Identify abnormal message sequences indicating protocol exploitation.

The following are SS7 attack detection:

- SS7 Unauthorized Message type detection.
- Subscriber tracking.
- Fraud and DDoS detection.

The following are the subscriber authentication anomalies:

- Monitor authentication failures across MME/HSS interfaces.
- Track simultaneous authentications from different locations.
- Detect unusual roaming patterns indicating potential fraud.
- Identify multiple authentication attempts within short timeframes.

The following are the core network access controls:

- Monitor administrative access to core network elements.
- Track configuration changes on critical network functions.
- Detect unauthorized access attempts to management interfaces.
- Identify privilege escalation attempts on network elements.

The following are the traffic pattern anomalies:

- Monitor unusual traffic patterns through PGW or SGW.
- Track sudden spikes in signaling traffic.
- Detect abnormal roaming traffic patterns.
- Identify unusual subscriber behavior patterns.

The following are the system integrity monitoring:

- Track system file changes on core network elements.
- Monitor process creation and termination.
- Detect unauthorized software installation.
- Identify system resource exhaustion attempts.

EPC or LTE network elements and logging requirements

The following table details the logging considerations for various network functions in an LTE network:

Device detail	Device category	Log type
EMS for eNodeB	Category 1	Authentication logs, audit logs
MME, HSS	Category 1	Authentication logs, security event logs, audit logs, protocol-specific logs (diameter)
PGW, SGW	Category 1	Security event logs, protocol-specific logs (GTP), operational logs
EMS for MME, SGW, PGW	Category 1	Authentication logs, audit logs
EMS for PCRF	Category 2	Authentication logs, audit logs
GMLC/SMLC/EIR	Category 3	Authentication logs, audit logs
SGi FW	Category 3	Authentication logs, security event logs, and audit logs
SCTP/GTP/Diameter FW	Category 1	Authentication logs, security event logs, audit logs, and protocol-specific logs
Peering Router	Category 2	Authentication logs, audit logs
DRA/DEA	Category 1	Protocol-specific logs (diameter), security event logs
Roaming Firewall	Category 2	Authentication logs, security event logs, audit logs, protocol-specific logs
eNodeBs	Category 3	Authentication logs, audit log

Table 14.1: Logging considerations for LTE

5G

The transition to 5G represents a fundamental shift in telecommunications architecture, introducing a cloud-native, service-based approach that differs significantly from traditional mobile networks. Unlike previous generations that relied on point-to-point interfaces between network functions, 5G adopts a flexible, software-defined architecture where network functions communicate through **Service-Based Interfaces** (**SBI**), as shown in the following figure. This architectural evolution, combined with technologies like network slicing, edge computing, and virtualization, enables unprecedented service capabilities but also introduces new security challenges that require sophisticated monitoring approaches.

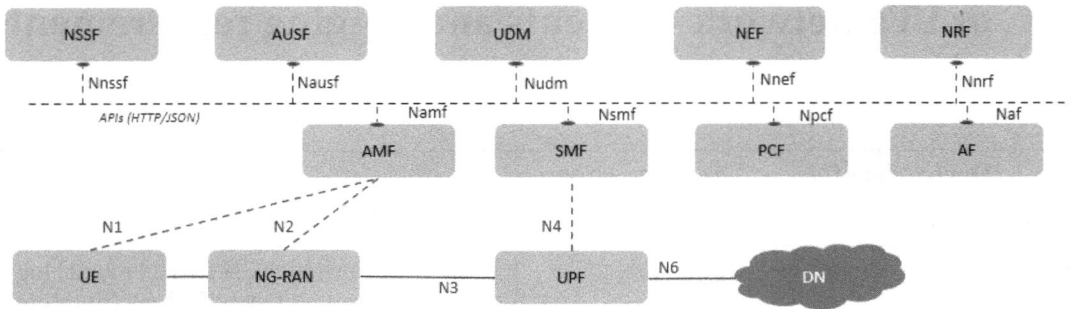

Figure 14.3: 5G architecture

Threats and risks in 5G environment

The 5G network architecture introduces new security challenges due to its service-based architecture, network slicing capabilities, and integration with edge computing. The virtualization of network functions and the adoption of cloud-native principles create an expanded attack surface where traditional perimeter-based security approaches are insufficient. Attackers can potentially exploit the service-based interfaces between network functions to gain unauthorized access or disrupt services. The distributed nature of 5G networks, with their emphasis on edge computing and low-latency services, means that security breaches can have localized yet severe impacts on critical services. Network slicing, while providing isolation between different service types, introduces risks related to slice security policy enforcement and cross-slice isolation breaches. The increased reliance on software-defined networking and network function virtualization exposes the infrastructure to software-based attacks, including container escape vulnerabilities and orchestration system compromises.

From a subscriber perspective, while 5G introduces enhanced security features compared to previous generations, risks still exist. The integration with non-3GPP access networks creates potential vulnerabilities in authentication and authorization mechanisms. The support for massive IoT deployments introduces risks related to device authentication and management at scale. **Enhanced Mobile Broadband (eMBB)** services, with their high bandwidth capabilities, can be targeted for data interception or service theft. **Ultra-Reliable Low-Latency Communication (URLLC)** services, critical for industrial applications and autonomous systems, face risks from timing attacks and service disruption attempts that could have severe real-world consequences.

Security use cases for SIEM or SOC implementation

The following are the SBI monitoring:

- Detect unauthorized NF (network function) registration attempts.
- Monitor NF service discovery patterns.

- Track abnormal service access patterns.
- Identify suspicious inter-NF communications

The following are the network slice security monitoring:

- Track slice creation and modification events.
- Monitor slice resource allocation.
- Detect cross-slice interference attempts.
- Identify slice policy violations.

The following are the edge computing security:

- Monitor MEC platform access.
- Track application deployment changes.
- Detect resource utilization anomalies.
- Identify unauthorized edge service access.

The following are the container and orchestration security:

- Monitor container runtime activities.
- Track orchestration platform events.
- Detect unauthorized container access.
- Identify suspicious container behavior.

The following are the authentication and access monitoring:

- Track UE authentication events.
- Monitor non-3GPP access attempts.
- Detect anomalous registration patterns.
- Identify subscriber profile modifications.

5G network elements and logging requirements

The following table details the logging considerations for various network functions in a 5G network:

Device detail	Device category	Log type
AMF	Category 1	Authentication logs, security event logs, protocol-specific logs (HTTP/2)
SMF	Category 1	Security event logs, protocol-specific logs, and audit logs
UPF	Category 1	Security event logs, protocol-specific logs, and operational logs

Device detail	Device category	Log type
AUSF, PCF	Category 1	Authentication logs, security event logs, and audit logs
NRF	Category 1	Security event logs, audit logs, protocol-specific logs
NEF	Category 1	Security event logs, API logs, and authentication logs
N6 FW	Category 3	Authentication logs, security event logs, and audit logs
NSSF	Category 1	Security event logs, audit logs, protocol-specific logs
Peering Router	Category 2	Authentication logs, audit logs
SEPP (Security Edge Protection Proxy)	Category 1	Security event logs, protocol-specific logs, and authentication logs
UDM	Category 1	Authentication logs, security event logs, and audit logs
MEC Platform	Category 2	Security event logs, authentication logs, and operational logs
gNB	Category 3	Authentication logs, and audit log

Table 14.2: Logging considerations for 5G

IP Multimedia Subsystem

The **IP Multimedia Subsystem (IMS)**, shown in the following figure, serves as the control layer for delivering multimedia services over IP networks, acting as a crucial bridge between traditional telephony and modern IP-based communications. As the foundation for **Voice over LTE (VoLTE)**, **Voice over WiFi (VoWiFi)**, and **Rich Communication Services (RCS)**, IMS integrates various protocols including SIP, Diameter, and H.248/Megaco to enable seamless service delivery. This complex protocol interaction, combined with the need to maintain high availability for critical voice and messaging services, creates unique security monitoring requirements. The interconnection of IMS with both legacy networks and modern IP services further emphasizes the importance of comprehensive security visibility across all communication layers.

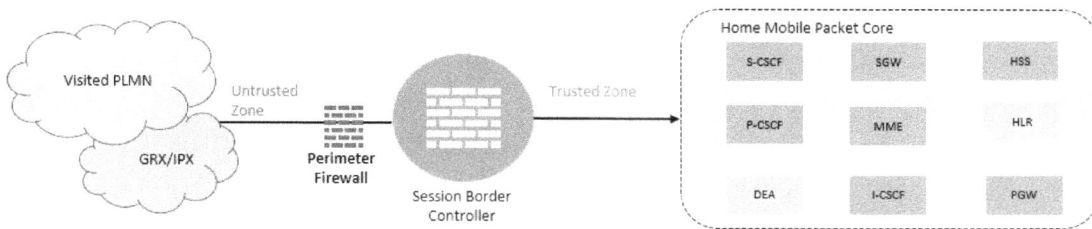

Figure 14.4: *IMS architecture*

Threats and risks in IMS environment

The IMS infrastructure faces multifaceted security challenges due to its position as a convergence point for various communication services. SIP-based attacks targeting the IMS core components can lead to service disruption or unauthorized access to voice and multimedia services. The exposure of SIP interfaces to external networks, particularly through interconnects and roaming partnerships, creates opportunities for toll fraud, service theft, and signaling-based attacks. Registration hijacking and identity spoofing attempts can compromise subscriber services and privacy, while malformed SIP messages can potentially crash critical IMS components or cause service degradation. The integration with legacy networks through media gateways introduces risks associated with protocol translation and interworking functions, potentially exposing both domains to cross-protocol attacks. Additionally, the dependency on DNS for service routing creates vulnerabilities where DNS poisoning or hijacking could redirect traffic to malicious endpoints or cause service outages.

Security use cases for SIEM or SOC implementation

The following are the SIP signaling monitoring:
- Detect unauthorized SIP registration attempts.
- Monitor for SIP flooding attacks.
- Track abnormal call patterns indicating fraud.
- Identify malformed SIP message attacks.

The following are the SBC security monitoring:
- Blacklisted phone number or IP address with successful registration detection.
- Detection of multiple successful and failed registration attempts.
- Fraudulent user-based activity detection.
- Detection of misconfigured or incorrectly provisioned profiles.
- Tracking IP address associated with multiple user profiles.
- Monitor high volumes of failed registrations for brute force indicators.

The following are the VoIP security detection:

- Detect unauthorized IP activity targeting VoIP devices.
- Identify malicious code delivered via phishing or watering hole attacks.
- Monitor binary files used to deploy malicious scripts.
- Detect anomalous device behavior indicating compromise.

The following are the media gateway security:

- Monitor media gateway access attempts.
- Track unusual traffic patterns through gateways.
- Detect unauthorized protocol translations.
- Identify resource exhaustion attempts.

The following are the service authentication and authorization:

- Track IMS registration events.
- Monitor service profile modifications.
- Detect multiple registration attempts.
- Identify unauthorized feature access.

The following are the interconnect security:

- Monitor interconnect signaling patterns.
- Track border element security events.
- Detect unusual traffic volumes.
- Identify protocol misuse attempts.

The following are the DNS security monitoring:

- Track DNS query patterns.
- Monitor DNS response validity.
- Detect cache poisoning attempts.
- Identify unusual DNS traffic patterns.

IMS network elements and logging requirements

The following table details the logging considerations for various network functions in the IMS network:

Device detail	Device category	Log type
P-CSCF	Category 1	Security event logs, protocol-specific logs (SIP), and authentication logs
S-CSCF, HSS	Category 1	Authentication logs, security event logs, protocol-specific logs (SIP, diameter)

Device detail	Device category	Log type
I-CSCF, IBCF	Category 1	Security event logs, protocol-specific logs (SIP), operational logs
TAS	Category 2	Security event logs, authentication logs, protocol-specific logs
MGW	Category 2	Operational logs, security event logs, protocol-specific logs
MGCF	Category 2	Security event logs, protocol-specific logs (H.248), operational logs
SGi FW	Category 3	Authentication logs, security event logs, and audit logs
SBC	Category 1	Security event logs, protocol-specific logs (SIP), and authentication logs
DNS servers	Category 1	Security event logs, authentication logs, and operational logs

Table 14.3: Logging considerations for IMS

Transport and MPLS network

The transport network, as shown in the high-level figure following, serves as the telecommunications infrastructure's backbone, providing critical connectivity between various network domains through **multiprotocol label switching** (**MPLS**) technology. Unlike access or core networks that focus on subscriber services, transport networks prioritize high-speed, reliable data transmission between network segments, making their security requirements unique. MPLS networks create virtual paths through the infrastructure using **label-switched paths** (**LSPs**), enabling traffic engineering and service separation. This sophisticated traffic management, combined with the network's role in carrying multiple traffic types (user data, signaling, management) across different network segments (RAN, Core, IMS), makes security monitoring particularly crucial, as any compromise could affect multiple services and domains simultaneously.

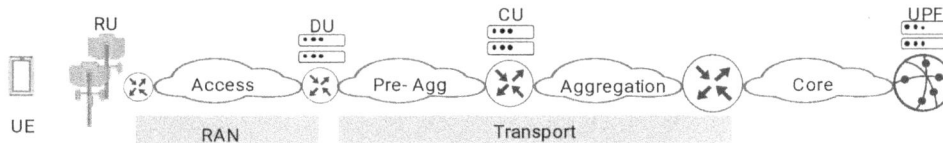

Figure 14.5: Transport network

Threats and risks in the transport or MPLS environment

The transport infrastructure's critical nature makes it an attractive target for sophisticated attacks aimed at disrupting network connectivity or intercepting traffic. MPLS label spoofing attacks can redirect traffic flows, potentially exposing sensitive data or causing service disruption across multiple network segments. The distributed nature of transport networks, often spanning large geographical areas, creates numerous points of potential compromise through unauthorized physical or logical access to network elements. BGP-based attacks targeting the control plane can manipulate routing tables and traffic paths, leading to traffic blackholing or unauthorized traffic redirection. The integration of legacy TDM services with packet-based transport introduces complexity around protocol conversion points, creating potential vulnerabilities in hybrid networks. Additionally, the reliance on network management systems for configuration and monitoring creates risks where compromised management access could lead to widespread network disruption.

Security use cases for SIEM or SOC implementation

The following are the MPLS control plane monitoring:

- Track LSP establishment and teardown events.
- Monitor label distribution protocol messages.
- Detect unauthorized label advertisements.
- Identify abnormal path changes.
- Manipulation of labels.

The following are the BGP security monitoring:

- Monitor BGP session states.
- Track routing table modifications.
- Detect unauthorized peer announcements.
- Identify route hijacking attempts.

The following are the network element access controls:

- Monitor management interface access.
- Track configuration changes.
- Detect unauthorized access attempts.
- Identify privilege escalation events.
- Password brute force attempts.
- Reconnaissance attempts.

The following are the traffic engineering security:

- Monitor bandwidth reservation patterns.
- Track QoS policy changes.
- Detect unauthorized traffic prioritization.
- Identify resource allocation anomalies.

The following are the physical infrastructure security:

- Monitor environmental alarms.
- Track physical access events.
- Detect fiber cuts or tampering.
- Identify power system anomalies.

Transport network elements logging requirements

The following table details the logging considerations for various network functions in MPLS or transport networks:

Device detail	Device category	Log type
P, PE router	Category 1	Security event logs, protocol-specific logs (MPLS, BGP), and authentication logs
Route reflectors	Category 1	Protocol-specific logs (BGP), security event logs, and operational logs
SDH/DWDM equipment	Category 2	Operational logs, audit logs, and authentication logs
Aggregation routers, CSR	Category 3	Operational logs, audit logs, and authentication logs
AAA server	Category 1	Security event logs, audit logs, and authentication logs
Security gateways	Category 1	Security event logs, audit logs, and authentication logs

Table 14.4: Logging considerations for transport and MPLS

Value-added services

Value-added services represent the diverse portfolio of enhanced telecommunications offerings that differentiate service providers and generate additional revenue streams. These services, including VoLTE, Broadband, IPTV, **video on demand** (**VoD**), and Wi-Fi, share common infrastructure elements but maintain unique service delivery requirements. The integration of these services with core network components, coupled with their direct interaction with end-users and content providers, creates a complex security landscape. The convergence of different technologies, protocols, and content delivery mechanisms requires a sophisticated security monitoring approach that can protect both the service infrastructure and the subscriber experience while ensuring content security and service continuity.

Threats and risks in the VAS environment

The multi-faceted nature of value-added services creates a diverse threat landscape that spans both infrastructure and content security domains. Service theft and unauthorized access attempts are common across all VAS platforms, with attackers attempting to bypass authentication mechanisms or exploit misconfigured service policies. Content piracy and unauthorized redistribution pose significant risks for IPTV and VoD services, where premium content could be intercepted and illegally shared. In broadband services, subscriber line exploitation could lead to unauthorized network access or service theft through techniques like MAC address spoofing or DHCP starvation attacks. VoLTE services face risks from signaling exploitation and voice fraud attempts, while Wi-Fi services are vulnerable to rogue access points and man-in-the-middle attacks. The integration with billing systems creates additional risks where service usage could be manipulated to avoid charges or fraud. Additionally, the reliance on **content delivery networks** (**CDN**) and caching systems introduces risks related to content integrity and unauthorized access to cached content.

Security use cases for SIEM or SOC implementation

The following are the service access monitoring:

- Track service authentication events.
- Monitor service activation patterns.
- Detect unauthorized service access.
- Identify service usage anomalies.

The following are the content security monitoring:

- Monitor content access patterns.
- Track content distribution events.
- Detect unauthorized content access.
- Identify content manipulation attempts.

The following are the subscriber authentication:

- Monitor authentication methods.
- Track failed authentication attempts.
- Detect credential abuse patterns.
- Identify unusual access patterns.

The following are the qualities of service security:

- Monitor service degradation events.
- Track resource utilization patterns.

- Detect service disruption attempts.
- Identify QoS policy violations.

The following are the Wi-Fi security monitoring:
- Track access point associations.
- Monitor authentication methods.
- Detect rogue access points.
- Identify wireless attacks.

VAS network elements and logging requirements

The following table details the logging considerations for various network functions in the value-added application's network:

Device detail	Device category	Log type
VoLTE application server	Category 1	Authentication logs, security event logs, protocol-specific logs (SIP)
IPTV head-end	Category 1	Security event logs, authentication logs, and content access logs
VoD servers	Category 2	Content access logs, security event logs, and authentication logs
CDN nodes	Category 2	Content access logs, security event logs, and operational logs
DRM servers	Category 1	Authentication logs, security event logs, and content access logs
BRAS	Category 1	Authentication logs, security event logs, and protocol-specific logs
DSLAM/OLT	Category 2	Operational logs, security event logs, and authentication logs
Wi-Fi controllers	Category 1	Security event logs, authentication logs, protocol-specific logs
Access points/ ONT	Category 3	Security event logs, authentication logs, and operational logs
BNG	Category 1	Security event logs, authentication logs, and audit logs
IDAM (subscriber auth)	Category 1	Security event logs, authentication logs, and audit logs

Table 14.5: Logging considerations for VAS

Conclusion

This chapter has presented a comprehensive framework for implementing security monitoring across the telecommunications landscape, addressing the complexity of modern network infrastructures while providing practical implementation guidelines. At its core, our framework introduces a strategic device categorization system that classifies network elements into three tiers: critical security devices (*Category 1*), supporting systems (*Category 2*), and edge devices (*Category 3*). This classification enables telecommunications providers to prioritize their monitoring efforts effectively and allocate resources efficiently.

We have established detailed guidelines for log management and analysis, examining various log types and their security significance. Through clear MUST, SHOULD, and MAY recommendations, organizations can make informed decisions about log collection and integration priorities. Our domain-specific analysis spans crucial areas including EPC/LTE, 5G, IMS, transport/MPLS, and value-added services, demonstrating the framework's adaptability while maintaining consistent monitoring principles.

The framework's strength lies in its structured approach to device categorization and log type prioritization, creating a practical reference for security teams implementing SIEM solutions. This methodology facilitates effective cross-domain security monitoring and correlation, essential for detecting sophisticated attacks across multiple network segments. As telecommunications networks continue to evolve, these foundational principles remain relevant, adapting to new technologies while ensuring robust security monitoring.

In the next chapter, we will explore the critical domain of telecommunications application testing within service provider environments. Modern telecommunications services rely heavily on complex applications that manage everything from subscriber authentication to service delivery. We will explore comprehensive testing methodologies that address both security and functionality, examining how to validate applications across different network domains and services.

Points to remember

- Network security monitoring in telecommunications requires a comprehensive understanding of both traditional IT security approaches and telco-specific requirements. When implementing security monitoring solutions, remember that telecom environments demand real-time visibility across multiple technology domains, from radio access networks to core services.

- Integration with SOC and SIEM systems must be approached strategically, considering both business and regulatory perspectives. Regulatory compliance, particularly around data privacy and critical infrastructure protection, should drive the scope and depth of monitoring. The integration strategy should also align with industry standards and best practices while accommodating future scalability requirements for data analytics and storage.

- Log management forms the foundation of effective security monitoring in telecom environments. The categorization of logs should follow a risk-based approach, prioritizing critical network functions and services. Consider both security-specific logs and operational logs that may indicate security incidents. Remember that log retention policies must balance regulatory requirements, storage costs, and analytical needs.

- Domain-specific integration requires understanding the unique characteristics and security requirements of each network segment. For 5G networks, focus on monitoring containerized network functions and securing service-based interfaces. In LTE environments, prioritize monitoring of control plane elements and interfaces between different network domains. MPLS and transport network monitoring should emphasize configuration changes and routing protocol security.

- Storage and performance considerations are crucial for successful implementation. Remember that telecom networks generate massive volumes of log data, requiring efficient storage solutions and careful consideration of retention periods. Consider implementing log aggregation and filtering mechanisms at the source to reduce storage and processing overhead while maintaining visibility into security-relevant events.

- Integration priorities should be established based on threat modeling and risk assessment results. Remember to consider both external threats and insider risks when defining monitoring requirements. The monitoring solution should provide visibility into both north-south and east-west traffic patterns, particularly important in modern telecom architectures that leverage network function virtualization and software-defined networking.

- Analytics capabilities should be designed to support both real-time detection and historical analysis. Remember that telecom security monitoring requires correlation across multiple domains and the ability to detect complex attack patterns that may span different network segments. Consider implementing machine learning capabilities to improve detection accuracy and reduce false positives while handling the scale of telecom operations.

- The success of security monitoring implementation depends heavily on proper planning and stakeholder alignment. Remember to involve both security and network operations teams in the design phase, ensuring that monitoring solutions meet both security and operational requirements. Regular review and updates of monitoring policies and procedures are essential to maintain effectiveness as the threat landscape evolves.

Exercises

1. Which of the following considerations is MOST critical when determining log storage requirements for 5G network functions?

   a. The total number of subscribers in the network

   b. Regulatory retention requirements and compliance standards

   c. Available storage capacity in existing systems

   d. Current SOC team size

2. When prioritizing log integration from telecom devices, which factor should be evaluated first?

   a. Volume of logs generated

   b. Business impact of the service

   c. Ease of integration

   d. Storage costs

3. In the context of SIEM integration for an MPLS network, what is the primary reason for implementing log categorization?

   a. To reduce storage costs

   b. To simplify reporting structures

   c. To enable effective correlation and analysis

   d. To meet vendor requirements

4. Which type of logs should be prioritized for integration in a 5G Core deployment?

   a. Debug logs from all network functions

   b. Security logs from user plane functions only

   c. Critical security events from all network functions

   d. Performance metrics from control plane functions

5. For transport network security monitoring, which approach best aligns with industry standards?

   a. Collecting all available logs without filtering

   b. Implementing selective logging based on risk assessment

   c. Logging only critical failures

   d. Recording user activities only

6. Scenario: A large telecom provider is implementing security monitoring for their newly deployed 5G network. They need to integrate security logs from various network functions while considering their existing SOC capabilities.

   a. Describe the key considerations for log categorization in this scenario

   b. Propose a phased approach for log integration, explaining your prioritization criteria.

   c. Identify potential challenges in correlating events across different network functions and suggest solutions.

7. Scenario: A telecommunications company is upgrading their security monitoring capabilities to meet new regulatory requirements. They need to implement comprehensive logging for their LTE and MPLS networks while ensuring efficient storage utilization.

   a. Develop a framework for determining log retention periods across different network domains.

   b. Explain how you would implement log aggregation while maintaining data segregation requirements.

   c. Describe the KPIs you would establish to monitor the effectiveness of the logging solution.

Join our book's Discord space

Join the book's Discord Workspace for Latest updates, Offers, Tech happenings around the world, New Release and Sessions with the Authors:

https://discord.bpbonline.com

Network Security Testing

Introduction

Security testing in telecommunications has evolved from simple network perimeter checks to the comprehensive evaluation of complex, interconnected systems. Modern telecom environments present unique challenges due to their multi-tenant nature, virtualized infrastructure, and integration of various services across different domains. This chapter explores the essential security testing strategies that telecommunications service providers must employ to protect their network functions and applications while ensuring service reliability and regulatory compliance.

The transformation of telecom networks from hardware-centric systems to software-defined architectures has expanded the attack surface significantly. **Network function virtualization** (**NFV**) and **software-defined networking** (**SDN**) have introduced new security considerations that traditional testing approaches cannot fully address. Furthermore, the adoption of cloud-native principles and microservices architecture in 5G networks demands a fundamental shift in how we approach security testing.

This chapter provides telecommunications professionals with a structured framework for implementing comprehensive security testing programs that address both traditional and emerging security challenges in modern telecom environments.

Structure

This chapter will cover the following topics.

- Core security testing
- Integration testing
- Automation and CI/CD testing
- Threat modeling

Objectives

Security testing in telecommunications has undergone a dramatic transformation, paralleling the industry's technological advancement. From its origins in testing physical infrastructure and basic perimeter security, the field has evolved to address the complexities of modern virtualized networks and cloud-native architectures.

The shift began with 4G networks, as telecommunications infrastructure became increasingly software-oriented. However, the true paradigm shift occurred with the widespread adoption of virtualization. Security testing expanded to encompass VNFs, requiring new methodologies to verify resource isolation, workload security, and infrastructure integrity across virtualized environments.

The emergence of 5G technology has further revolutionized testing requirements. Network slicing, edge computing, and cloud-native architectures demand continuous security testing throughout the development lifecycle. Modern testing must address containerized applications, API security, and complex interactions between network functions. This includes rigorous verification of network segmentation, particularly crucial in 5G networks where network slicing introduces additional complexity.

Testing methodologies have evolved from periodic manual assessments to automated, continuous security testing integrated into CI/CD pipelines. The adoption of DevSecOps practices has made security testing an integral part of development rather than a separate phase. This comprehensive approach addresses multiple dimensions: infrastructure security (virtualized environments and container platforms), application security (APIs and microservices), and data protection (encryption and privacy controls).

The criticality of telecommunications infrastructure, handling of sensitive customer data, and interconnected nature of modern telecom services make this evolution in security testing essential for protecting against cyber threats while ensuring regulatory compliance.

Core security testing

Security testing in telecom environments represents a complex piece of the puzzle where each thread must be carefully examined and tested to ensure the overall fabric remains secure. Unlike traditional IT environments, telecom networks operate with unique constraints and requirements that demand specialized testing approaches. This section explores the fundamental security testing domains that form the cornerstone of a comprehensive telecom security testing strategy.

Infrastructure security testing

The infrastructure security testing serves as the bedrock upon which all other security measures are built. In modern telecom networks, this infrastructure has evolved from physical hardware to a complex mesh of virtualized components, each requiring specific security considerations. Think of it as testing the foundation and structural integrity of a skyscraper; if the foundation is compromised, every floor above becomes vulnerable.

Virtualization layer security

In today's telecom networks, virtualization technology creates multiple isolated environments from shared physical resources. Imagine a single large office building subdivided into multiple secure zones, each operating independently yet sharing the same physical structure. When testing virtualization security, many critical areas like the ones mentioned in the following need to be paid special attention to:

- **Resource isolation testing**: Consider two major corporations sharing the same office building. Just as each corporation needs guaranteed access to its allocated space and resources, VNFs require strict resource isolation. The testing should verify that when one VNF, such as a **virtual Evolved Packet Core** (**vEPC**), experiences a high load or a security incident, it cannot impact other VNFs running on the same hardware.

- **CPU pinning and NUMA testing**: Modern telecom VNFs often require deterministic performance, like how a heart surgeon needs guaranteed access to an operating room. The resource isolation test should include ways to test CPU pinning configurations to ensure that critical VNFs have dedicated CPU resources. For example, when testing a virtual IMS system, we might configure it as follows:

The IMS core processes are pinned to specific CPU cores 0-7, while the media handling components are pinned to cores 8-15. The testing, under high load conditions, should be able to verify the following scenarios:

- The pinned CPUs remain exclusively dedicated to their assigned VNF processes.

- Other VNFs cannot pre-empt or interfere with these dedicated resources.

- CPU cache coherency is maintained within the NUMA node.

- Memory access patterns remain local to the assigned NUMA node.

A practical test scenario involves generating a high CPU load on adjacent cores and verifying that the IMS's performance metrics remain within acceptable bounds. Tools like stress-ng can be used to create intensive workloads on nearby cores while monitoring the

IMS's signal processing latency and call setup times. Along with resource isolation and CPU-related tests, memory protection and network interface-based testing, listed in the following are crucial for virtualization layer security:

- **Memory protection verification**: Memory isolation in virtualized environments is like ensuring that secure document storage areas in different office suites remain separate. Scenarios where malicious code might attempt to access memory spaces of other VNFs or the hypervisor itself must be tested. This includes testing for vulnerabilities like cross-VM memory access or hypervisor escape attempts.

    Just as a busy highway needs dedicated lanes for emergency vehicles, critical VNFs need guaranteed memory bandwidth, and that is where memory bandwidth isolation and its related testing come in. This can be tested by:

    o Configuring huge pages for critical VNFs to reduce TLB misses.

    o Verifying memory bandwidth QoS settings using Intel's **Cache Allocation Technology** (**CAT**).

    o Testing memory bandwidth isolation under various load conditions.

    o Monitoring for any unauthorized access to reserved memory bandwidth

- **Network interface testing**: Modern telecom VNFs often use **single root I/O virtualization** (**SR-IOV**) for direct hardware access to network interfaces. Security testing should validate the following factors:

    o **Virtual functions** (**VFs**) remain properly isolated from each other.

    o Performance remains consistent even when some VFs experience high traffic.

    o Hardware queues are correctly assigned and maintained.

    o NIC interrupt handling does not create CPU contention.

Network segmentation security

Border network segmentation in 5G networks introduces new complexities that require sophisticated testing approaches. Consider it similar to managing multiple independent transportation systems that share the same physical infrastructure but must never interfere with each other. The following are the ways in which control plane and user plane separation can be tested, along with slice-based testing:

- **Control and user plane separation testing**: Modern telecom networks separate control signals, the traffic lights and railway signals, from user data, the cars and trains themselves. Testing should ensure this separation remains absolute under all conditions. For instance, verify that a compromise in the user plane cannot lead to unauthorized access to control plane functions.

    In a typical 5G core deployment, verify the physical separation of control and user plane functions through detailed configuration testing. Consider this example configuration for a 5G **User Plane Function** (**UPF**):

The UPF's N4 interface (control plane) is configured on a dedicated network segment, as shown in the following:

```
interface N4-Control
  vlan 100
  ip address 10.10.1.0/24
  access-list N4-ACL in
  qos-policy control-plane
```

N4-ACL configuration:

```
  permit tcp host 10.10.1.1 host 10.10.1.2 eq 8805
  permit udp host 10.10.1.1 host 10.10.1.2 eq 8805
  deny ip any any log
```

While the N3 interface (user plane) operates on a separate segment, as shown in the following:

```
interface N3-User
  vlan 200
  ip address 10.20.1.0/24
  access-list N3-ACL in
  qos-policy user-plane
```

N3-ACL configuration:

```
  permit udp any any eq 2152
  deny ip any any log
```

- **Network slice testing**: Network slicing creates multiple virtual networks that share physical infrastructure while maintaining complete isolation. Testing network slice security involves verifying both the configuration and runtime behavior of slice isolation.
- **Slice configuration example**: Consider three network slices: emergency services (eMBB-priority), mobile broadband (eMBB-standard), and IoT (mMTC). Each slice requires a specific security configuration, as mentioned in the following:

Shown in the following is a sample configuration of the emergency services slice:

```
slice-config eMBB-priority
  slice-id 1
  isolation-level strict
  qos-profile ultra-reliable
  security-policy {
```

```
    encryption aes-256-gcm
    integrity-protection required
    replay-protection window 32
  }
  resource-reservation {
    cpu-quota 40%
    memory-guaranteed true
    bandwidth-minimum 1Gbps
  }
```

Shown in the following is a sample configuration of Mobile Broadband Slice:

```
slice-config eMBB-standard
  slice-id 2
  isolation-level standard
  qos-profile balanced
  security-policy {
    encryption aes-128-gcm
    integrity-protection optional
    replay-protection window 64
  }
  resource-reservation {
    cpu-quota 30%
    memory-guaranteed false
    bandwidth-minimum 100Mbps
  }
```

Security testing should ensure that slice isolation remains intact under various conditions, some of which are mentioned in the following:

- Generating high-volume traffic in one slice and verifying that it does not impact other slices.
- Attempting cross-slice communication and ensuring it is blocked.
- Verifying that slice-specific security policies are enforced.
- Testing resource allocation guarantees under network congestion.

Runtime security testing for slices can be done dynamically to verify slice isolation during operation, which includes:

- Simulating slice resource exhaustion attacks.

- Testing slice-specific security policy enforcement.
- Verifying slice monitoring and logging capabilities.
- Validating slice-specific access control mechanisms.

Security testing tools

The complexity of modern telecom infrastructure requires a sophisticated toolkit. Various testing tools that are normally deployed in real-world scenarios are mentioned in the following:

- **OpenVAS in virtualized environments**: When deploying OpenVAS for vulnerability scanning in telecom networks, configure it to understand the dynamic nature of virtualized infrastructure. This includes setting up custom scan profiles that account for the unique characteristics of telecom VNFs. For example, when scanning a virtual IMS, OpenVAS must be configured to recognize legitimate service-to-service communications while identifying potential security vulnerabilities.

- **Nessus professional for compliance verification**: In telecom environments, Nessus plays a crucial role in verifying compliance with industry standards. Security testers must customize Nessus policies to check for telecom-specific security requirements, such as the proper implementation of 3GPP security specifications. For instance, when testing a virtualized EPC, Nessus verifies that all interfaces implement the required security controls as specified in 3GPP standards.

- **Container security assessment**: For containerized network functions, employ specialized tools like *Docker Bench* to verify security configurations. This includes checking container isolation, resource limits, and security policies. When testing a containerized 5G core function, verify that containers cannot escalate privileges or access unauthorized resources, even under stressful conditions.

- **System hardening verification**: Tools like *Lynis* help ensure that the underlying systems maintain a strong security posture. Customize these tools to account for telecom-specific requirements, such as verifying that management interfaces are properly secured and that system hardening aligns with telecom industry best practices.

Integration testing

The telecommunications ecosystem represents a complex web of interconnected services, where applications must seamlessly and securely interact with numerous provider-specific systems. Integration testing in this context goes beyond traditional application testing, as it must account for the unique characteristics of telecom environments, including high availability requirements, real-time processing demands, and stringent security protocols.

Authentication and identity management services

Authentication and identity management services represent one of the most critical integration points in telecom environments. These services operate on two distinct but equally important levels: subscriber authentication and network device administration. Each level requires specialized security testing approaches to ensure comprehensive protection of the telecommunications infrastructure.

Subscriber authentication integration testing focuses on how applications interact with the provider's identity management systems for end-user authentication. When applications integrate with a provider's identity management system, they must handle multiple authentication scenarios, from basic subscriber authentication to complex roaming situations. For instance, when a mobile application authenticates a user, it typically interfaces with the **Home Subscriber Server (HSS)** or **Unified Data Management (UDM)** in 5G networks. The security testing of this integration must verify not only the authentication logic but also the handling of security contexts across different network domains. Consider a **Voice over LTE (VoLTE)** service integration scenario. The application must interface with the **IP Multimedia Subsystem (IMS)** while maintaining security throughout the session establishment process. Security testing in this context must verify the proper handling of authentication vectors, the secure negotiation of media parameters, and the maintenance of security contexts throughout the call duration. This includes testing scenarios such as mid-call authentication refresh, roaming conditions, and handling of authentication failures.

Network device administrator **authentication, authorization, and accounting (AAA)** testing represents another crucial aspect of security testing in telecom environments. Modern telecommunications networks comprise numerous network elements, each requiring secure administrative access. Testing must verify the proper integration between network devices and centralized AAA servers, such as RADIUS or TACACS+. Security testing must verify that network devices properly integrate with centralized authentication systems for administrative access. This includes testing scenarios such as authentication failover, multiple authentication attempts, and session timeout handling. For example, when a primary AAA server becomes unavailable, testing must verify that authentication requests properly fail over to backup servers while maintaining security controls.

Role-based access control (RBAC) integration testing should ensure that network devices properly enforce role-based access controls based on administrator privileges defined in the centralized AAA system. Testing scenarios should verify that:

- The correct application of privilege levels across different administrative interfaces.
- Proper enforcement of command authorization based on administrator roles.
- Accurate implementation of read-only versus read-write access permissions.
- Correct handling of privilege escalation requests.
- Proper integration between local and remote RBAC configurations.

For instance, when testing RBAC integration for a core router, security testing must verify that an NOC operator with read-only privileges cannot execute configuration commands, even if they attempt to bypass restrictions through different access methods such as console, SSH, or NETCONF interfaces.

Accounting and audit trail integration must also be ensured during the testing process. Security testing must verify that administrative actions are properly logged and transmitted to centralized accounting servers. This includes testing the accurate recording of the following listed audit and accounting events:

- Administrator login and logout events
- Configuration changes with before and after states
- Privilege level changes and escalation attempts
- Failed authentication and authorization attempts
- System-level command execution

Consider a scenario where an administrator attempts to modify routing policies on a provider edge router. Testing must verify that all actions, whether successful or failed, are properly recorded and transmitted to the accounting server with accurate timestamps, administrator identities, and command details.

With the increasing adoption of automation in network management, security testing must also verify that automated systems properly integrate with AAA services. This includes testing the following listed AAA integrations:

- API-based authentication for automation tools
- Service account privilege enforcement
- Automated configuration change accounting
- Integration with privileged access management systems

For example, when an automation platform deploys configuration changes across multiple network devices, testing must verify that it properly authenticates with each device, operates within its assigned privilege levels, and generates appropriate accounting records for all actions performed.

API integration testing

Modern telecom networks rely heavily on APIs for service interaction, management, and orchestration. These APIs serve as the communication highways between different network functions, management systems, and external services. The security of these interfaces becomes paramount as they often represent critical access points into the network infrastructure. Consider the case of a 5G core network's **service-based architecture** (**SBA**), where network functions communicate through RESTful APIs. The security testing framework for these APIs must address multiple layers of protection, starting with API authentication.

The **Network Repository Function** (**NRF**) in a 5G core handles service registration and discovery through APIs. A robust security testing approach for NRF APIs should include an authentication test, as mentioned in the following:

```python
# Example API security test case for NRF authentication
def test_nrf_authentication():
    # Test case: Unauthorized NF registration attempt
    test_payload = {
        "nfInstanceId": "b9e6e2cb-5ce8-4cb6-9173-a266dd9a2f0c",
        "nfType": "AMF",
        "nfStatus": "REGISTERED"
    }

    response = send_registration_request(
        endpoint="/nrf-nfm/v1/nf-instances",
        payload=test_payload,
        auth_token=None  # Attempting without authentication
    )

    assert response.status_code == 401
    assert verify_error_headers(response.headers)
    assert verify_audit_log_entry(
        "Unauthorized NF registration attempt detected"
    )
```

API authorization in telecom environments must enforce strict access controls based on network function types and security policies. Security testing must validate these controls through scenarios such as the example shown in the following:

```python
# Authorization test for network function API access
def test_nf_authorization():
    # Configure test case parameters
    test_cases = [
        {
            "nf_type": "AMF",
            "target_api": "subscriber_data",
            "expected_access": False
        },
```

```
        {
            "nf_type": "UDM",
            "target_api": "subscriber_data",
            "expected_access": True
        }
    ]


    for test_case in test_cases:
        response = request_api_access(
            nf_type=test_case["nf_type"],
            api=test_case["target_api"]
        )


        if test_case["expected_access"]:
            assert response.status_code == 200
        else:
            assert response.status_code == 403
```

Input validation is another critical API-based testing that service providers need to conduct. Management APIs must properly validate and sanitize all input to prevent injection attacks and malformed requests. Security testing includes verification of input handling, as shown in the following example:

```
def test_input_validation():
    test_payloads = [
        {
            "name": "SQL Injection Test",
            "payload": "'; DROP TABLE users; --",
            "expected_status": 400
        },
        {
            "name": "Command Injection Test",
            "payload": "$(rm -rf /)",
            "expected_status": 400
        }
    ]
```

```
for test in test_payloads:
    response = send_management_request(
        payload=test["payload"]
    )
    assert response.status_code == test["expected_status"]
    assert verify_error_handling(response)
```

These test cases represent foundational elements of API security testing in telecom environments. There can be more similar API tests that can be incorporated, like rate limits, monitoring, and logging. The testing framework should be continuously updated to address new threats and vulnerabilities as they emerge in the telecommunications landscape.

Advanced integration testing scenarios

Policy control system integration testing has become increasingly important with the evolution of telecom networks. Applications must interact with the **Policy and Charging Rules Function** (**PCRF**) or **Policy Control Function** (**PCF**) in 5G networks to ensure appropriate service quality and charging enforcement. Security testing must verify that policy decisions are properly enforced and that the integrity of policy rules cannot be compromised. For example, when testing a video streaming application's integration with policy systems, scenarios must verify that QoS parameters cannot be manipulated by unauthorized parties.

Billing and charging system integration presents another critical area where security testing becomes paramount. Modern telecom services often implement real-time charging, requiring secure and accurate integration with **Online Charging Systems** (**OCS**) and **Charging Data Function** (**CDF**). Security testing must verify that charging events are generated accurately, transmitted securely, and properly recorded for both real-time and offline charging scenarios. This includes testing the handling of various charging models, from simple duration-based charging to complex event-based charging scenarios.

Similarly, location service integration presents unique security challenges, particularly concerning privacy and data protection. Applications accessing location information must undergo rigorous security testing to ensure compliance with privacy regulations and proper handling of location data. This includes testing scenarios such as location data accuracy throttling, privacy filters, and secure transmission of location information to authorized applications only.

Integration resilience testing

Resilience testing forms a crucial aspect of integration security testing in telecom environments. Applications must maintain security even when provider services experience degraded performance or partial failures. This involves testing scenarios such as:

- Service timeout scenario testing must verify that applications handle service timeouts gracefully while maintaining security. For instance, when an authentication service experiences high latency, the application should maintain session security without compromising the authentication process.

- In partial system failure testing, applications must handle scenarios where some provider services are unavailable while others continue to function. Security testing must verify that such partial failures do not create security vulnerabilities. For example, if a charging system becomes unavailable, the application should implement appropriate fallback mechanisms without exposing sensitive charging data.

- Network degradation testing is another important integration testing that needs to be considered by service providers. Security testing must verify that applications maintain security controls even under poor network conditions. This includes testing the handling of packet loss, network latency, and out-of-order message delivery while maintaining security protocols.

Regulatory and compliance integration testing

Telecommunications providers must navigate a complex landscape of regulatory requirements that vary by region, service type, and customer base. Integration testing plays a crucial role in ensuring compliance with these regulations while maintaining service functionality and security.

The European Union's **General Data Protection Regulation** (**GDPR**) has set a global benchmark for data protection requirements. In telecom environments, this translates into specific integration testing scenarios. Consider a European mobile operator providing roaming services: When a subscriber roams into a partner network, their location data, calling patterns, and service preferences must be shared between operators while maintaining GDPR compliance. Integration testing for this scenario must verify several aspects, one of which is data minimization. This testing process verifies that only essential subscriber data is transmitted between home and visited networks. For example, when a subscriber activates roaming services, the home network should share only the minimum subscriber profile information necessary for service provision, such as allowed services and quality of service parameters, while excluding unnecessary personal data like billing history or demographic information. Similarly, purpose limitation testing must confirm that shared data is used only for its intended purpose. For instance, when location data is shared for emergency services (E112 in Europe), integration testing verifies that this data cannot be accessed or used for marketing or analytics purposes without explicit consent.

For telecom providers offering mobile payment or banking services, compliance with financial regulations becomes crucial. Consider a mobile money service operating in multiple African countries; which needs to conduct the following testing like payment services testing where the testing must verify compliance with various financial regulations:

- **Know Your Customer** (**KYC**) requirements during user registration.
- Transaction monitoring for **anti-money laundering** (**AML**) compliance.
- Integration with national payment systems.
- Cross-border transaction controls and reporting.

Industry standards and security frameworks-based testing is another critical testing that service provider needs to conduct. 3GPP security specifications provide detailed security requirements for mobile networks. Integration testing must verify compliance with these specifications across network elements. For example, when testing the integration between a 5G core network and radio access network, service providers should test for compliance with various frameworks like the security features as defined in 3GPP TS 33.501, which include compliance with the following points:

- Proper implementation of security contexts and key hierarchies.
- Correct execution of security procedures during handovers.
- Accurate implementation of subscriber privacy features.
- Proper handling of security algorithm negotiation.

GSMA Security Guidelines influence how roaming and interconnection services are implemented. Integration testing must verify compliance with GSMA IR.88 (LTE and SAE Roaming Guidelines) and IR.77 (Inter-Operator IP Backbone Security Requirements). For instance, when testing roaming interface security, the following are the mentioned points that need to be considered:

- IPsec implementation for roaming interfaces
- Certificate management for secure interconnection
- Proper implementation of signaling screening
- Accurate filtering of GTP traffic

Automation and CI/CD testing

In the dynamic landscape of telecommunications, where service reliability and security are paramount, automated security testing integrated into the **continuous integration and continuous deployment** (**CI/CD**) pipeline becomes essential. Telecommunications networks present unique challenges for security testing automation. Unlike traditional enterprise applications, telecom services often involve complex interactions between multiple network functions, real-time processing requirements, and stringent reliability standards. Each code change or configuration update could potentially impact critical services, from voice calls to emergency services. This complexity necessitates a comprehensive automated testing approach that can validate security at multiple levels while maintaining service continuity.

The integration of security testing into the CI/CD pipeline for telecom applications requires careful consideration of both the testing sequence and the potential impact on production systems. The pipeline must be designed to catch security issues early while ensuring that testing does not impact service availability. For instance, when deploying updates to a VNF, the pipeline must verify security controls without disrupting existing sessions or compromising network stability.

Early-stage security testing should focus on code quality and known vulnerabilities. This includes scanning both custom code and dependencies for security issues before they enter the build process. As artifacts progress through the pipeline, testing becomes more comprehensive, including dynamic analysis and security configuration verification. The final stages must validate security in an environment that closely mirrors production, including interactions with other network functions and services.

Figure 15.1 represents a comprehensive security-focused CI/CD pipeline specifically designed for containerized applications in 5G network environments. This pipeline integrates security at every stage of the software delivery process, from initial code development through to production deployment, ensuring that security is not merely an afterthought but a foundational element throughout the application lifecycle.

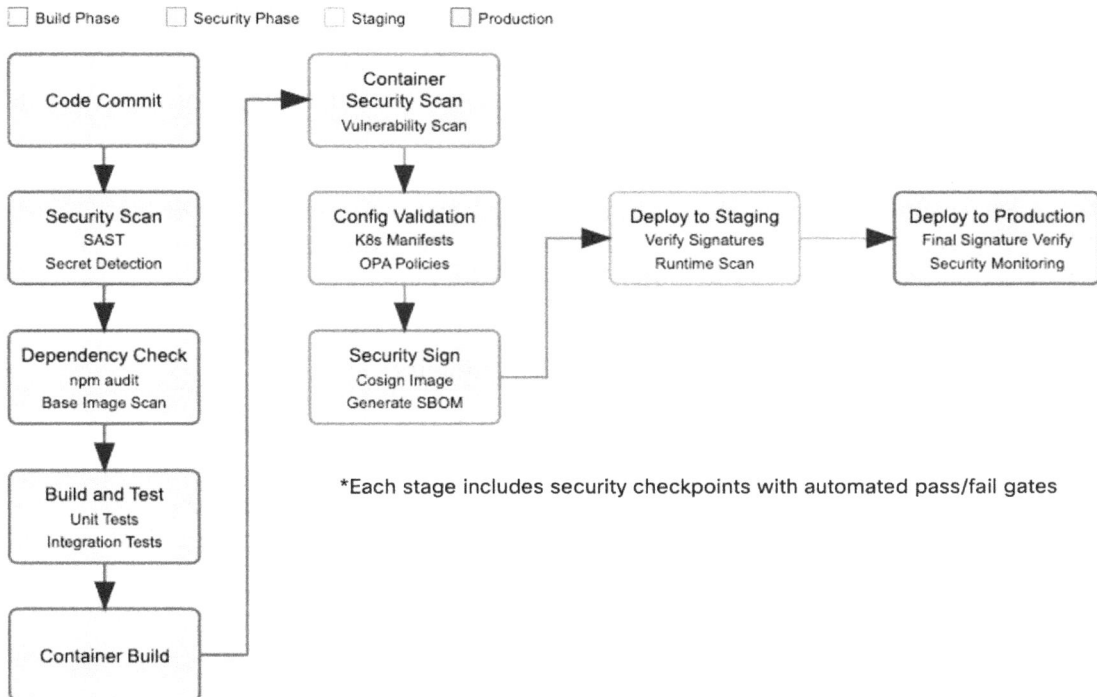

Figure 15.1: CI CD workflow in a 5G container deployment

The figure visualizes a mature DevSecOps approach where development, security, and operations converge to create a seamless, automated workflow with clearly defined security checkpoints. Each stage is designed with security gates that must be passed before progressing to the next phase, creating multiple layers of protection against vulnerabilities, misconfigurations, and malicious code.

This workflow combines automated security tooling with well-defined processes to continuously evaluate, validate, and secure containerized applications before they reach production environments. The color-coded stages highlight the progression from build activities (blue) through security-specific processes (green), staging verification (orange), and finally to production deployment (red), where the highest security standards are enforced.

The pipeline architecture follows a shift-left security paradigm, where security testing begins in the earliest development stages and continues throughout the entire delivery process. This approach is particularly crucial for 5G networks, where the implications of security breaches extend beyond data theft to potential service disruption of critical communications infrastructure.

Building a security-focused CI/CD pipeline

A security-focused CI/CD pipeline for telecom applications must address both application security and network function security requirements. Consider the following example pipeline structure for a 5G network function:

- **Early-stage security validation**: The pipeline begins with code-level security checks integrated directly into the development environment. For instance, when a developer commits changes to a **Session Border Controller** (**SBC**) configuration, automated checks should verify the following items:
  - Security parameter validation in configuration files.
  - Compliance with security hardening guidelines.
  - Presence of required security controls.
  - Known vulnerability detection in dependencies.
- **Build stage security testing**: As the code moves through the build process, more comprehensive security testing needs to be conducted, like the ones mentioned in the following:
  - Static analysis of custom protocols and interfaces.
  - Security validation of containerized components.
  - Verification of security-critical configurations.
  - Automated security documentation generation.
- **Integration testing stage**: This stage validates security in a more complete environment with the following tests:

- o   Automated penetration testing of exposed interfaces.
- o   Security testing of service chaining.
- o   Validation of security policy enforcement.
- o   Testing of security monitoring integration.
- **Pre-production security validation**: The final testing stage occurs in an environment that mirrors production and can include the following tests:
  - o   End-to-end security testing of service flows.
  - o   Load testing with security validation.
  - o   Failover and recovery testing with security checks.
  - o   Compliance verification with audit trail generation.

Automation compliance verification

Network automated compliance testing in telecom environments must address multiple regulatory frameworks simultaneously. Consider a mobile network operator providing services in the European Union. These telecom service providers need to undergo compliance-specific tests like the ones mentioned in the following:

- **Data protection compliance**: The automation framework testing that continuously verifies GDPR compliance is mentioned in the following:
  - o   Automated scanning for personal data handling.
  - o   Verification of data protection mechanisms.
  - o   Testing of data subject rights implementation.
  - o   Validation of consent management systems.
- **Industry-specific compliance**: Simultaneously, the testing should check telecom-specific requirements, some are mentioned in the following:
  - o   3GPP security specifications compliance.
  - o   GSMA security guidelines adherence.
  - o   National regulatory requirements.
  - o   Emergency services compliance.

For example, when testing a new subscriber management function, automated tests verify:

- o   Proper encryption of subscriber data.
- o   Accurate implementation of data retention policies.
- o   Correct handling of lawful intercept requirements.
- o   Appropriate access controls and audit logging.

Continuous security monitoring

The continuous monitoring extends the CI/CD pipeline into production, providing ongoing security validation. Consider a mobile network operator's security monitoring framework that will need to incorporate the following testing:

- **Real-time security validation**: The monitoring system should continuously verify the following validations:
  - o Security control effectiveness
  - o Configuration drift detection
  - o Anomaly detection and analysis
  - o Compliance status monitoring

  For example, when monitoring a running IMS system, the testing should cover the following aspects:
  - o Real-time analysis of SIP signaling patterns
  - o Continuous verification of security certificates
  - o Automated detection of unauthorized access attempts
  - o Regular validation of security policy enforcement

Tool integration

The implementation of automated security testing in telecom environments requires a carefully orchestrated combination of specialized tools. Each tool category addresses specific aspects of security testing, from code analysis to runtime validation. The integration of these tools into the CI/CD pipeline must account for the unique characteristics of telecom applications, including protocol-specific vulnerabilities, real-time processing requirements, and complex service interactions.

Static Application Security Testing (**SAST**) tools analyze source code and binaries for security vulnerabilities before deployment. In telecom environments, these tools must be configured to understand industry-specific protocols, architectures, and security requirements. For example, when analyzing code for an SBC, SAST tools need to identify vulnerabilities specific to SIP processing, media handling, and signaling security.

Key capabilities for SAST in telecom environments are as mentioned in the following:

- Protocol-specific vulnerability detection (SIP, Diameter, GTP, etc.)
- Security policy compliance verification
- Identification of hardcoded credentials and security parameters
- Analysis of access control implementations
- Validation of cryptographic implementations

Recommended SAST Tools for relevant testing are as mentioned in the following:

- **SonarQube with custom telecom security rules**: Particularly effective for analyzing protocol implementations and detecting telecom-specific security issues
- **Fortify static code analyzer**: Provides comprehensive analysis with support for telecom protocols and frameworks.
- **Checkmarx CxSAST**: Offers strong support for distributed applications and microservices architectures
- **Coverity scan**: Excels at identifying complex security vulnerabilities in protocol implementations.

Dynamic Application Security Testing (**DAST**) tools test running applications and services, identifying security vulnerabilities that may only become apparent during execution. In telecom environments, DAST tools must be capable of testing complex protocols, handling stateful communications, and validating security controls across distributed systems.

Key capabilities for DAST in telecom environments must include the following points:

- Protocol fuzzing for telecom-specific interfaces
- Security testing of API endpoints and service interfaces
- Validation of authentication and authorization mechanisms
- Testing of session management and state handling
- Verification of encryption and security control effectiveness

Recommended DAST tools for testing in a telco environment include the ones that are listed in the following:

- **OWASP ZAP with custom telecom plugins**: Highly customizable for testing telecom protocols and APIs
- **Burp Suite enterprise**: Provides comprehensive security testing with support for custom protocols
- **Acunetix**: Offers strong API security testing capabilities
- **Qualys web application scanning**: Features robust compliance checking and vulnerability detection

Threat modeling

In the complex world of telecommunications, where networks carry sensitive data and support critical communications, understanding potential security threats becomes important. Threat modeling serves as a systematic approach to identifying security risks and developing appropriate protections. This section walks through a practical threat modeling exercise, focusing on one of the most significant vulnerabilities in traditional telecommunications networks: the **Signaling System 7** (**SS7**) protocol.

Understanding the modeling use case

Before diving into threat modeling, we need to understand why SS7 presents such an interesting case study. SS7 was developed in an era when telecommunications networks operated as closed systems, trusted by all participants. Picture a small club where everyone knows and trusts each other. This was the telecommunications landscape of the 1970s, with a limited number of national operators all working together in a spirit of mutual trust.

Today's reality is vastly different. The telecommunications landscape now resembles a bustling marketplace rather than an exclusive club. Hundreds of operators, **Mobile Virtual Network Operators** (**MVNOs**), and service providers all need access to SS7 networks. This transformation from a trusted, closed network to an open, diverse ecosystem creates numerous security challenges.

Building the threat model

Think of threat modeling as creating a security map for your system. Just as a city planner needs to understand traffic flows to design safe roads, we need to understand how data flows through our network to identify potential security risks. This process can be broken down into the following steps:

1. **System decomposition**: Imagine SS7 as a city's transportation system. Different components serve different purposes, as mentioned in the following:

   a. **Signal Transfer Points** (**STPs**) act like traffic routing centers, directing signaling messages to their correct destinations.

   b. The **Home Location Register** (**HLR**) serves as a central database, similar to a city's resident registry.

   c. **Mobile Switching Centers** (**MSCs**) function like major intersections, handling call routing and mobility management.

   d. The **Visitor Location Register** (**VLR**) works like a temporary resident registry for roaming subscribers.

2. **Understanding data flows**: Just as a city has different types of traffic (emergency vehicles, public transport, private cars), SS7 networks handle various types of signaling messages, as mentioned in the following:

   a. Location updates when subscribers move between different areas

   b. Authentication messages to verify subscriber identity

   c. Call setup signals to establish connections

   d. **Short Message Service** (**SMS**) routing information

Real-world threat scenario, location privacy breach

Let us examine a specific threat scenario that has been observed in real telecom networks. Imagine a situation where an attacker wants to track someone's location by exploiting SS7 vulnerabilities. This scenario is particularly relevant because it has been demonstrated in real-world situations and highlights the inherent trust issues in SS7 networks.

Attack pathway

The attack takes advantage of a legitimate SS7 message type called **SendRoutingInfoForSM (SRI-SM)**. In normal operations, this message helps route SMS messages to subscribers. However, in the threat scenario, an attacker can misuse this message to track a subscriber's location. The following is a sample of a scenario of how the attack is done.

- First, the attacker needs access to the SS7 network. This might be achieved through a compromised or malicious operator connection. Think of it as getting access to a restricted area by using a stolen security badge.

- Next, the attacker identifies their target by their phone number (MSISDN). The attacker can then send repeated SRI-SM queries to the target's home network, each query revealing which MSC is currently serving the subscriber. By tracking changes in the serving MSC, the attacker can monitor the target's movement between different network areas.

Analyzing the threat using STRIDE

The STRIDE methodology helps one understand different aspects of this threat, as mentioned in the following:

- **Spoofing**: The attacker can pretend to be a legitimate network element because SS7 lacks strong authentication mechanisms. It is similar to using a fake ID to gain access to restricted areas.

- **Tampering**: While this attack does not modify messages, the ability to inject unauthorized queries represents a form of system tampering. It is like inserting unauthorized transactions into a banking system.

- **Repudiation**: Because SS7 does not provide strong audit trails, the attacker can deny sending these tracking messages. This is similar to committing a crime in an area without security cameras.

- **Information disclosure**: This is the primary threat in our scenario. The attacker gains unauthorized access to location information, similar to someone illicitly accessing confidential records.

- **Denial of service**: Repeated queries could overwhelm network elements, potentially affecting service for legitimate users. This is like flooding a highway with fake traffic, preventing normal travel.

- **Elevation of privilege**: The attacker gains access to location information that should only be available to authorized network operations.

Implementing security controls

Understanding these threats leads us to develop specific security measures, some are mentioned in the following:

- SS7 firewalls filter suspicious queries, acting like security checkpoints.
- Rate limiting prevents excessive queries from single sources.
- Message screening blocks suspicious patterns of behavior.

For the location tracking scenario, these controls might work together as the firewall would monitor SRI-SM messages, flagging unusual patterns such as repeated queries for the same subscriber. Rate limiting would prevent rapid-fire queries that might indicate tracking attempts. Category-based blocking would restrict messages from networks with suspicious behavior patterns.

Continuous validation and improvement

Security is not a one-time achievement but an ongoing process. Regular testing helps ensure controls remain effective. Security teams should conduct regular tests to verify protection mechanisms, some of these tests are mentioned in the following:

- Simulating tracking attempts to test detection systems.
- Verifying that filtering rules properly block unauthorized queries.
- Ensuring monitoring systems accurately identify suspicious patterns.

Future considerations

As telecommunications networks evolve, new security challenges emerge. The lessons learned from SS7 vulnerabilities help inform security designs for newer protocols and systems. For instance, 5G networks incorporate security by design, learning from the vulnerabilities discovered in legacy systems like SS7. This practical example of threat modeling demonstrates how systematic analysis can help identify and address security vulnerabilities in telecommunications systems. By understanding these processes, security professionals can better protect their networks and subscribers from evolving threats.

Conclusion

The testing framework presented in this chapter demonstrates the vital importance of comprehensive security testing in modern telecom environments. As telecommunications networks grow more complex, a multi-faceted approach combining core security, integration testing, automation, and threat modeling has become essential. Core security testing establishes the foundation for infrastructure integrity and network segmentation, while integration security testing ensures secure interoperability between system components, particularly in authentication, API integration, and compliance. The framework emphasizes resiliency testing, which is crucial for maintaining critical communication infrastructure.

The integration of security testing into CI/CD pipelines marks a significant advancement in telecom security practices. By embedding security controls throughout the development lifecycle, organizations can identify and address vulnerabilities earlier, reducing risks and costs. Continuous security monitoring, enhanced by automation, enables swift threat detection and response. Threat modeling serves as the strategic framework that unifies these components, providing context for prioritizing testing efforts and resources.

In the next chapter, we explore the revolutionary technologies shaping telecommunications beyond 5G. As we venture into the realm of 6G architecture, we will examine how digital twins are enabling unprecedented network simulation and optimization. The chapter delves into AI-driven networks that adapt and self-heal in real-time, the groundbreaking potential of quantum communications for unbreakable security, and the expanding frontier of space-based communications. These emerging technologies are not just evolutionary steps but represent a fundamental transformation in how we conceive, build, and secure telecommunications networks of the future.

Points to remember

- **Core security testing**: Telecom service providers must maintain robust security testing procedures for their infrastructure and network components. Infrastructure security testing involves a comprehensive assessment of physical data centers, network elements, and virtualized assets that form the backbone of telecom operations. Regular vulnerability scanning and penetration testing help identify potential weaknesses before they can be exploited.

- **Network segmentation testing**: It ensures proper isolation between different network zones, particularly between subscriber traffic, control plane signaling, and management networks. This separation is crucial for preventing unauthorized access and containing potential security breaches. Security tools used in testing must be specifically configured to handle telecom protocols and services, including specialized tools for SS7, Diameter, and other telecom-specific protocols.

- **Integration security testing**: Authentication and identity management testing verifies that access controls work correctly across the complex hierarchy of users in a telecom environment. This includes testing subscriber authentication, roaming partner integration, and administrative access to the controls. The testing must verify that identity federation works securely with multiple partners while maintaining proper access boundaries.

- **API integration testing**: This focuses on the security of interfaces exposed to partners, third-party services, and internal systems. This includes verification of input validation, rate limiting, and proper implementation of security controls. Resiliency testing examines the system's ability to maintain security during high load, network congestion, and various failure scenarios.

- **Regulatory compliance testing**: This ensures that security controls meet requirements from multiple jurisdictions. This includes data privacy regulations, lawful intercept requirements, and industry-specific security standards.

- **Automation and CI/CD testing**: Security-focused CI/CD processes integrate security testing at every stage of development and deployment. This includes automated vulnerability scanning, configuration validation, and compliance checking. The automation framework must be scalable to handle the large number of network elements and services in a telecom environment.

- **Continuous security monitoring**: It provides real-time visibility into potential security incidents. This includes automated detection of anomalies, policy violations, and potential attacks. Integration with **security information and event management** (**SIEM**) systems ensures proper tracking and response to security events.

- **Threat modeling**: For telecom providers, it must consider both traditional IT security threats and telecom-specific attack vectors. This includes analyzing potential attacks on signaling protocols, roaming interfaces, and subscriber services. Risk assessments should account for the critical nature of telecom infrastructure and its potential impact on emergency services.

- **Regular updates to threat models**: This ensures they remain relevant as new technologies and threats emerge. This includes consideration of 5G security features, network virtualization risks, and emerging attack techniques targeting telecom infrastructure.

Exercises

1. Which of the following best describes the primary purpose of network segmentation testing in a telecom environment?

   a. Testing network speed and latency

   b. Verifying proper isolation between different network zones and preventing unauthorized access

   c. Monitoring bandwidth usage

   d. Testing backup systems

2. In the context of API integration testing, which security control is MOST critical for protecting sensitive subscriber data?

   a. Rate limiting

   b. Input validation

   c. OAuth 2.0 implementation

   d. SSL/TLS encryption

3. When implementing security testing in a CI/CD pipeline, at which stage should vulnerability scanning be performed?

   a. Only in production

   b. Only in development

   c. At every stage of the pipeline

   d. Only during user acceptance testing

4. Which threat modeling methodology is most suitable for analyzing telecom applications with multiple third-party integrations?

   a. STRIDE

   b. Attack trees

   c. PASTA

   d. DREAD

5. During infrastructure security testing, what is the most effective approach to identify potential DNS-related vulnerabilities?

   a. Manual DNS record verification

   b. Automated DNS enumeration tools

   c. Passive DNS monitoring

   d. Both b and c

6. In resiliency testing, which scenario should be prioritized for a telecom service provider?

   a. Natural disaster recovery

   b. DDoS attack mitigation

   c. Hardware failure

   d. Data center power outage

7. Describe three key components that should be included in a comprehensive security-focused CI/CD process for a telecom service provider's application deployment. Explain how each component contributes to the overall security posture.

8. Your team has discovered that third-party API integration is storing unencrypted authentication tokens. Design a threat modeling exercise that would help identify similar vulnerabilities across other integrations. Include specific steps and stakeholders that should be involved.

9. Compare and contrast the approaches to security testing in traditional waterfall development versus modern CI/CD pipelines in a telecom environment. What are the key differences in terms of:

   a. Test frequency and automation

   b. Security tool integration

   c. Risk management

   d. Compliance verification

10. A telecom provider is planning to implement continuous security monitoring. Create a detailed framework that addresses:

    a. Essential metrics to monitor

    b. Alert thresholds and response procedures

    c. Integration with existing security tools

    d. Compliance reporting requirements

Join our book's Discord space

Join the book's Discord Workspace for Latest updates, Offers, Tech happenings around the world, New Release and Sessions with the Authors:

https://discord.bpbonline.com

CHAPTER 16
Beyond 5G

Introduction

The telecommunications landscape stands at the cusp of a transformative era that extends far beyond the current capabilities of 5G networks. As we look toward the horizon of telecommunications evolution, the convergence of revolutionary technologies is reshaping not just how we communicate but how we secure these communications in an increasingly connected world.

This chapter explores the critical developments that will define the future of telecommunications security, focusing on four key areas that are fundamentally changing the industry landscape. First, we examine the evolution beyond 5G networks and the emergence of 6G technologies, where new network architectures and capabilities bring both unprecedented opportunities and security challenges. The integration of terahertz communications, cell-free massive **Multiple-Input Multiple-Output** (**MIMO**) systems, and advanced security protocols will form the foundation of future telecommunications infrastructure.

The rise of intelligent network infrastructure represents another crucial dimension, where artificial intelligence, network virtualization, and edge computing converge to create more adaptive and resilient networks. These intelligent systems not only enhance network performance but also introduce new paradigms in security management and threat response.

Quantum communications and security emerge as a critical component of future telecommunications systems, offering new methods for securing information in an era where traditional cryptographic approaches may become vulnerable to quantum computing threats. The development of quantum key distribution, post-quantum cryptography, and quantum-safe protocols will be essential for maintaining security in this new landscape.

Finally, the chapter explores the expanding frontier of space-based communications, where satellite constellations and integrated space-ground-air networks are creating new possibilities for global connectivity while presenting unique security challenges that must be addressed.

Together, these developments represent not just an evolution in telecommunications technology but a fundamental reimagining of how we approach security in an increasingly complex and interconnected world.

Structure

This chapter will cover the following topics.

- Overview
- Evolution beyond 5G network and 6G
- Intelligent network infrastructure
- Quantum communications and security
- Space based communications

Objectives

This chapter aims to provide telecommunications professionals, security architects, and network engineers with a comprehensive understanding of the emerging technologies that will shape the future of service provider networks beyond 5G, along with their associated security implications. As the telecommunications industry undergoes a transformative evolution, it becomes crucial to understand not just the technological advancements but also the new security challenges and opportunities they present.

The primary objective of this chapter is to explore the fundamental shifts in network architecture, from the evolution of 6G networks to the integration of quantum communications and space-based systems. By examining these technologies in detail, readers will gain insights into how these advancements will impact service provider security strategies and operational frameworks. The chapter seeks to bridge the gap between theoretical concepts and practical implementation considerations, providing a balanced perspective on both opportunities and challenges.

A key focus is placed on understanding the convergence of multiple technologies, including AI, edge computing, quantum communications, and space-based networks. Through this lens, the chapter aims to demonstrate how these technologies interact and influence each other, creating both synergies and potential vulnerabilities that security professionals must address. Special attention is given to emerging security paradigms and protocols that will be essential for protecting next-generation telecommunications infrastructure.

The chapter also aims to prepare telecommunications professionals for the challenges of securing hybrid networks that incorporate both traditional and emerging technologies. By examining real-world implications and potential implementation scenarios, readers will better understand how to approach security architecture design for future networks. This understanding is crucial for developing robust security strategies that can adapt to evolving threats while maintaining the performance and reliability requirements of advanced telecommunications systems.

Overview

The telecommunications industry stands at the cusp of a revolutionary transformation that extends far beyond the current 5G infrastructure. As we peer into the future, a convergence of groundbreaking technologies promises to reshape how we communicate, connect, and process information. This chapter explores the key technological advances that will define the next generation of telecommunications services.

The evolution towards 6G networks represents more than just an incremental improvement in speed and connectivity. It signifies a fundamental shift in network architecture, introducing terahertz communications, cell-free massive MIMO systems, and sub-millimeter wave technologies. These advances will enable unprecedented data rates, near-zero latency, and ubiquitous connectivity, opening doors to applications that seem like science fiction today.

Intelligent network infrastructure will form the backbone of future telecommunications systems. Through extensive virtualization, cloud integration, and AI-driven management, networks will become more adaptive, efficient, and resilient than ever before. Digital twins will enable precise modelling and optimization of network behavior, while edge computing will bring processing power closer to where it is needed most.

The user experience in telecommunications is poised for dramatic enhancement through technologies that blur the line between physical and digital realms. Holographic communications, brain-computer interfaces, and tactile internet applications will transform how we interact with each other and our environment. These technologies will enable new forms of presence and interaction, making distance increasingly irrelevant in human communication.

Space-based communications will play a crucial role in achieving truly global connectivity. The integration of non-terrestrial networks, particularly through vast constellations of low

Earth orbit satellites, will extend high-speed communications to every corner of the globe. This space-ground-air integrated network architecture will ensure seamless connectivity across all environments and scenarios.

As sustainability becomes increasingly critical, the telecommunications industry is embracing green technologies and energy-efficient solutions. Future networks will incorporate renewable energy sources, smart power management systems, and environmentally conscious architectures, ensuring that the expansion of telecommunications capabilities does not come at the cost of environmental degradation.

Perhaps most intriguingly, quantum technologies are set to revolutionize both communications and security. Quantum key distribution, post-quantum cryptography, and the emerging quantum internet will provide unprecedented levels of security while enabling entirely new forms of communication and computation. These advances will be crucial in an era where traditional cryptographic methods may become vulnerable to quantum computing attacks.

Together, these technological advances represent not just an evolution but a revolution in telecommunications. As we explore each area in detail throughout this chapter, we will examine how these technologies interact and complement each other, creating a communications infrastructure that will support the next generation of human innovation and connectivity.

Evolution beyond 5G networks and 6G

The telecommunications industry is witnessing an unprecedented transformation as we move beyond the **fifth generation (5G)** of wireless communications. While 5G deployment continues to expand globally, researchers, industry leaders, and standardization bodies are already laying the groundwork for the next generation of wireless technology-6G. This evolution is driven not just by the natural progression of technology but by the emerging needs of a society increasingly dependent on seamless, instantaneous, and ubiquitous connectivity.

The journey beyond 5G represents more than just an incremental improvement in network capabilities. It embodies a fundamental shift in how we perceive and implement telecommunications infrastructure. This transition is necessitated by several key factors that current 5G networks, despite their advanced capabilities, may not fully address in the coming decades. These factors include the exponential growth in connected devices, the emergence of new immersive applications, the increasing role of artificial intelligence, and the growing demand for sustainable technology solutions.

As we look toward the 2030s, when 6G is expected to be commercially deployed, the telecommunications landscape will be characterized by a convergence of multiple technologies and paradigms. The integration of terrestrial, aerial, and space networks will create a three-dimensional communication fabric that envelops our planet. This evolution will be marked by the emergence of new frequency bands, novel network architectures, and revolutionary applications that will reshape how humans and machines interact with their environment.

The driving forces behind this evolution encompass several critical dimensions. Societal needs play a fundamental role in shaping the future of telecommunications. There is an ever-growing demand for immersive experiences that blur the lines between physical and digital realms. Industries across the spectrum are moving toward increased automation, requiring more sophisticated and reliable communication networks. The imperative for sustainable technologies has become more pressing than ever, while the vision of universal connectivity remains a crucial goal for bridging the digital divide and ensuring equal access to digital resources.

Technological advancement continues to push the boundaries of what is possible in telecommunications. Significant progress in materials science and semiconductor technology is enabling the development of more efficient and capable communication systems. The rapid evolution of artificial intelligence and machine learning is revolutionizing network management and optimization. Parallel developments in quantum computing and communications are opening new frontiers in secure and ultra-fast data transmission. Moreover, innovations in energy harvesting and storage are paving the way for more sustainable network operations.

Market demands are equally influential in driving this evolution. There is a relentless push for higher data rates and lower latency to support emerging applications and services. Energy efficiency has become a critical requirement, not just for environmental reasons but also for operational sustainability. Enhanced security and privacy features are non-negotiable in an era of increasing cyber threats. Additionally, there is a strong industry push for reduced network complexity to make deployment and maintenance more manageable and cost-effective.

Environmental considerations have emerged as a crucial factor in shaping the future of telecommunications. Network design must now prioritize sustainability from the ground up. There is an increasing emphasis on energy-efficient communications to reduce the carbon footprint of global telecommunications infrastructure. Hardware manufacturers are being challenged to develop recyclable and eco-friendly components. The overall reduction of carbon footprint has become a key metric in evaluating new telecommunications technologies and solutions.

This evolution beyond 5G will enable a world where the physical and digital realms converge seamlessly, creating new possibilities for human interaction, industrial automation, and technological innovation. The next generation of wireless networks will not only connect people and things but will also sense, compute, and control the physical world in real-time, leading to what many researchers call the *Internet of Everything*.

As we delve deeper into the capabilities and architecture of 6G networks in the following sections, it becomes clear that this evolution represents a transformative leap forward in telecommunications technology. The integration of artificial intelligence, quantum communications, and advanced materials science will create a network infrastructure that is more intelligent, efficient, and capable than anything we have seen before.

6G network architecture and capabilities

The architecture of 6G networks represents a paradigm shift from traditional telecommunications infrastructure, introducing revolutionary concepts that extend far beyond current 5G capabilities. While formal standardization efforts are in their early stages, organizations like ITU-T's Network 2030 Focus Group, as shown in the following figure, and the Next G Alliance have begun outlining foundational frameworks for 6G architecture. These early frameworks emphasize a three-dimensional integrated network that seamlessly unifies terrestrial, aerial, and satellite communications.

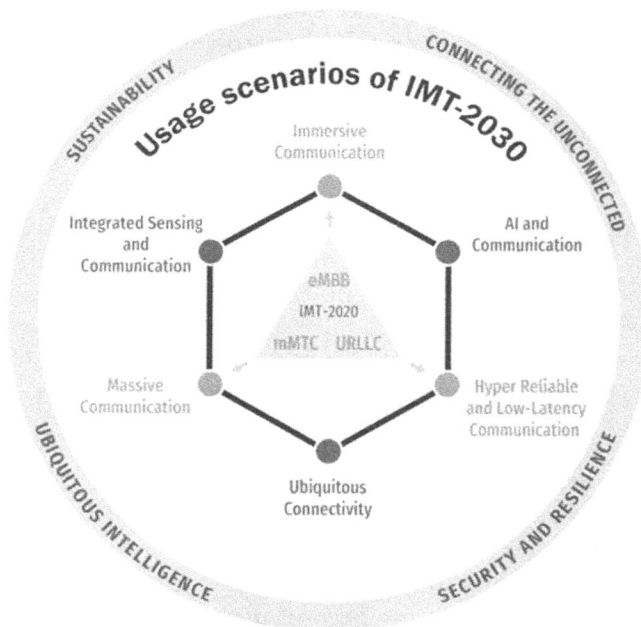

Figure 16.1: IMT-2023 6G Usage Scenarios
(*Source: https://www.3gpp.org/news-events/3gpp-news/sa1-6g*)

At the heart of 6G architecture lies native AI integration, a fundamental departure from current approaches where AI is typically an overlay service. In 6G, artificial intelligence is deeply embedded within every network layer, from physical infrastructure to application services. This native integration enables real-time network optimization, predictive maintenance, and autonomous network management. The network can dynamically allocate resources, self-heal, and adapt to changing conditions without human intervention, representing a level of intelligence far beyond current capabilities.

Distributed intelligence forms another cornerstone of 6G architecture. The network implements a cloud-native core with computing capabilities distributed across multiple layers. This distribution extends from centralized data centers to intelligent edge nodes and even to smart surfaces capable of actively shaping electromagnetic waves. This approach enables more efficient resource utilization and reduces latency by bringing processing power closer to where it is needed. The **European Telecommunications Standards Institute** (ETSI) has already begun exploring frameworks for distributed intelligence in future networks.

Perhaps the most revolutionary aspect of 6G architecture is its move toward a cell-less paradigm. Unlike traditional cellular networks, where users connect to specific base stations, 6G implements a user-centric approach where devices can simultaneously connect to multiple access points. This cell-less architecture, sometimes referred to as network virtualization, enables truly seamless connectivity and uniform service quality across the coverage area.

The integration of quantum technologies represents another architectural innovation in 6G networks. A dedicated quantum integration layer enables secure communications through quantum key distribution, enhanced sensing capabilities, and integration with quantum computing resources. This layer also facilitates quantum-enhanced network optimization, potentially revolutionizing how networks handle complex resource allocation problems.

Network disaggregation in 6G architecture allows for unprecedented flexibility in network deployment and management. By separating different network functions and components, operators can independently scale various parts of the network, implement redundancy where needed, and perform upgrades without disrupting the entire system. The O-RAN Alliance has already begun developing specifications for open and disaggregated network architectures that will likely influence 6G standards.

The capabilities enabled by this revolutionary architecture are equally impressive. 6G networks are expected to achieve peak data rates of up to 1 Terabit per second, with user-experienced rates reaching 100 Gigabits per second. This massive increase in data throughput will enable new applications like holographic communications and immersive extended reality experiences. End-to-end latency is expected to drop below 100 microseconds, enabling truly real-time applications and services.

Coverage in 6G networks extends beyond traditional two-dimensional thinking to encompass three-dimensional space. The integration of terrestrial, aerial, and satellite networks creates a seamless coverage bubble that extends from deep indoors to outer space. This comprehensive coverage supports up to 10 million connected devices per square kilometer, enabling massive **Internet of Everything** (IoE) deployments while maintaining energy efficiency through intelligent power management and energy harvesting capabilities.

Precision networking capabilities in 6G enable sub-centimeter positioning accuracy and integrated sensing and communication functions. This precision, combined with enhanced spatial awareness and context sensitivity, opens new possibilities for applications in autonomous systems, precision healthcare, and smart city infrastructure. The network can not only communicate but also sense and interact with its environment in real-time.

Energy efficiency takes center stage in 6G capabilities through the implementation of smart power management systems and energy harvesting technologies. These features ensure sustainable network operations while maintaining the high-performance requirements of next-generation applications. The incorporation of AI-driven power management and renewable energy sources helps optimize energy consumption across the network.

This combination of revolutionary architecture and advanced capabilities positions 6G as more than just a new generation of wireless technology. It represents a fundamental reimagining of how telecommunications networks are built and operated, creating a foundation for applications and services that will define the digital landscape of the 2030s and beyond.

Expected 6G performance metrics and use cases

The anticipated performance metrics of 6G networks represent a quantum leap over current telecommunications capabilities, setting new benchmarks that will enable revolutionary applications and use cases. These metrics are being shaped by both technological advancements and emerging application requirements that are expected to materialize in the 2030s timeframe.

*Figure 16.*2 provides a summary of the capabilities of IMT-2030, including nine enhanced capabilities viz. peak data rate, user experienced data rate, spectrum efficiency, area traffic capacity, connection density, mobility, latency, reliability, and security/privacy/resilience; and six new capabilities namely, coverage, positioning, sensing-related capabilities, AI-related capabilities, sustainability, and interoperability. The figure displays estimated target values for these capabilities, intended for IMT-2030 research and investigation.

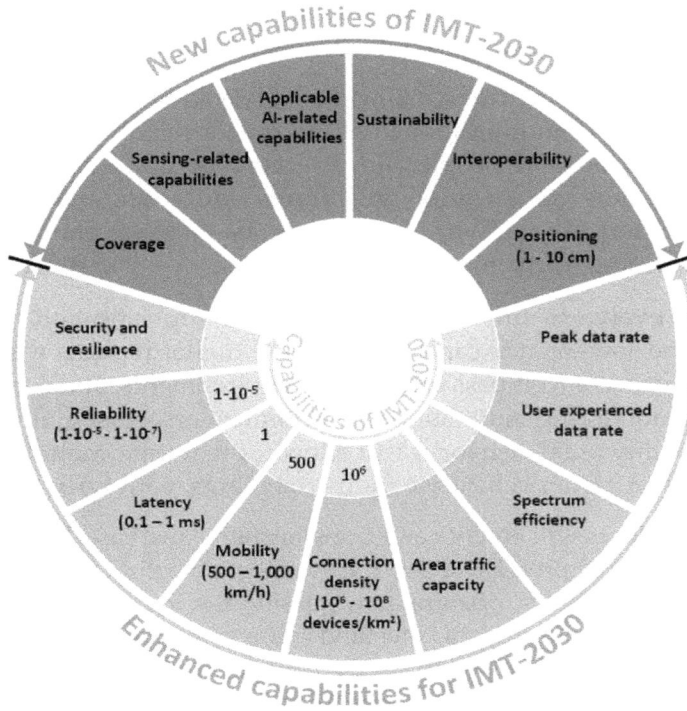

Figure 16.2: *Capabilities of IMT-2030*
(**Source**: *ITU-R, DRAFT NEW RECOMMENDATION. Framework and overall objectives of the future development of IMT for 2030 and beyond*)

Refer to the link: **https://www.itu.int/en/ITU-R/study-groups/rsg5/rwp5d/imt-2030/Pages/default.aspx**

Note: The range of values given for capabilities is estimated targets for research and investigation of IMT-2030.

Performance metrics for 6G networks are projected to push the boundaries of what is possible in wireless communications. Peak data rates are expected to reach one Terabit per second, representing a 100-fold increase over 5G capabilities. User-experienced data rates are anticipated to consistently deliver 100 Gigabits per second, enabling seamless transmission of massive amounts of data in real-time. Latency requirements are becoming increasingly stringent, with end-to-end latency targets below 100 microseconds and jitter reduced to microsecond levels, essential for supporting time-critical applications.

Network reliability in 6G systems is expected to achieve a remarkable 99.99999% availability, making it suitable for mission-critical applications. Coverage metrics extend beyond traditional ground-based measurements to include three-dimensional space, with altitude coverage reaching up to 10 kilometers through integrated ground-air-space networks. The connection density is projected to support up to 10 million devices per square kilometer while maintaining energy efficiency at the nanojoule-per-bit level.

The enhanced performance metrics of 6G will enable a wide array of transformative use cases. True holographic communications will become a reality, enabling realistic three-dimensional representations of people and objects to be transmitted in real-time. This will revolutionize remote collaboration, healthcare, education, and entertainment. The technology will support not just visual and auditory information, but also tactile and haptic sensations, creating truly immersive experiences.

Digital twins will evolve to unprecedented levels of sophistication, enabled by 6G's high-bandwidth and low-latency capabilities. These digital replicas will extend beyond industrial applications to encompass entire cities, environments, and even human bodies, enabling real-time monitoring, simulation, and optimization across multiple domains. The precision and reliability of 6G networks will allow for real-time control and coordination of autonomous systems, from vehicles to industrial robots, with zero perceived delay.

Brain-computer interfaces will emerge as a transformative use case, leveraging 6G's ultra-low latency and high reliability. These interfaces will enable direct neural communication between humans and machines, opening new possibilities in healthcare, accessibility, and human augmentation. The high data rates and massive connectivity of 6G will support widespread deployment of sensing networks, creating an Internet of Senses that can detect and respond to environmental changes in real-time.

In the industrial sector, 6G will enable synchronized control of thousands of robots and machines with microsecond precision. This capability will revolutionize manufacturing, logistics, and automation across industries. The technology will also support advanced emergency and disaster response systems, using its high-precision positioning and sensing capabilities to coordinate complex rescue operations and maintain communications in challenging conditions.

Extended reality (XR) applications will evolve to new levels of sophistication, combining augmented, virtual, and mixed reality with haptic feedback and neural interfaces. These applications will transform how we work, learn, and interact, creating seamless bridges between physical and digital realms. The high bandwidth and low latency of 6G will enable real-time rendering of complex virtual environments and instantaneous response to user interactions.

Healthcare applications will benefit significantly from 6G capabilities, enabling remote surgery with haptic feedback, real-time health monitoring through implanted sensors, and AI-driven diagnostic systems. The combination of high reliability, low latency, and massive connection density will support continuous health monitoring and immediate intervention when needed.

Space-based applications will emerge as a crucial use case, with 6G networks extending into low Earth orbit and beyond. These networks will support space tourism, satellite communications, and deep space exploration while also enabling global coverage for terrestrial applications. The integration of ground, air, and space networks will create new possibilities for global connectivity and communication.

These performance metrics and use cases represent not just technological achievements but stepping stones toward a more connected and capable society. As 6G networks mature and deploy, they will enable applications and services that we can only begin to imagine today, fundamentally transforming how we live, work, and interact with our environment.

Advanced radio technologies in 6G

The evolution of radio technologies in 6G networks introduces three revolutionary approaches that will fundamentally transform wireless communications: cell-free massive MIMO systems, terahertz communications, and sub-millimeter wave technologies. These technologies work in concert to deliver unprecedented capacity, coverage, and efficiency in next-generation networks.

Cell-free massive MIMO represents a paradigm shift from traditional cellular architecture. In this approach, many distributed access points simultaneously serve multiple users through precise beamforming and coordination. Unlike conventional cellular networks, where users connect to specific base stations, cell-free massive MIMO creates a distributed array of antennas that cooperatively serve all users in the coverage area. This architecture eliminates cell boundaries and significantly reduces interference, providing uniform quality of service throughout the network. The system employs advanced signal processing techniques to coordinate transmissions from multiple access points, maximizing spectral efficiency and minimizing power consumption.

Terahertz communication capabilities open entirely new possibilities by utilizing frequencies between 100 GHz and 10 THz. This vast spectrum availability enables data rates to reach multiple terabits per second, which is essential for future applications like holographic communications and high-precision digital twins. The following figure shows a diagrammatic representation of the position of the THz band in the radio spectrum:

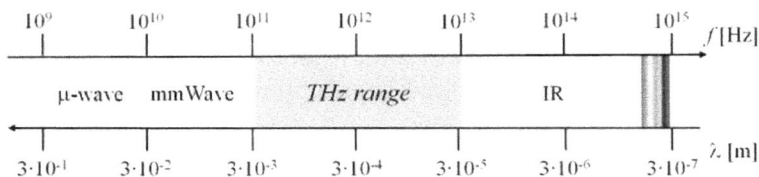

Figure 16.3: ETSI-Position of the THz band in the radio spectrum
(*Source: https://www.etsi.org/deliver/etsi_gr/THz/001_099/002/01.01.01_60/gr_THz002v010101p.pdf*)

Operating in the terahertz band presents unique challenges, including high path loss and atmospheric absorption. However, these limitations are being addressed through innovative solutions such as ultra-massive MIMO arrays, intelligent reflecting surfaces, and adaptive beamforming techniques. The development of new materials and components capable of efficiently generating and detecting terahertz signals is rapidly advancing, making these frequencies increasingly viable for commercial applications.

Sub-millimeter wave technology bridges the gap between traditional millimeter-wave and terahertz communications. Operating in frequencies typically ranging from 100 GHz to 300 GHz, sub-millimeter wave systems provide a crucial stepping stone toward full terahertz implementation. These frequencies offer significant advantages in terms of available bandwidth while presenting fewer technical challenges than higher terahertz bands. Sub-millimeter wave systems employ advanced antenna designs and signal processing techniques to overcome propagation limitations and deliver reliable high-speed communications over practical distances.

The integration of these three technologies creates a synergistic effect that enhances overall network performance. Cell-free massive MIMO provides the architectural framework for efficient spectrum utilization, while terahertz and sub-millimeter wave technologies supply the raw bandwidth needed for extreme data rates. Together, they enable:

- Advanced imaging and sensing capabilities that can detect and track objects with unprecedented precision.
- High-resolution positioning services are accurate to within millimeters.
- Ultra-high-speed backhaul links that can support the massive data requirements of distributed networks.
- Real-time environmental mapping and adaptation that enables intelligent network optimization.

The practical implementation of these technologies requires significant advances in several areas. New materials and components capable of efficiently operating at terahertz frequencies are being developed. Advanced signal processing algorithms are being created to manage the complexity of cell-free massive MIMO systems. Novel antenna designs are being engineered to support efficient beam steering and formation at sub-millimeter wavelengths. These developments are supported by ongoing research in areas such as metamaterials, artificial intelligence, and quantum communications.

While these technologies present considerable technical challenges, their potential benefits make them central to the 6G vision. The combination of cell-free architecture with extremely high-frequency communications will enable applications that are simply not possible with current technology. As research continues and manufacturing capabilities advance, these technologies will mature into practical solutions that form the foundation of 6G networks.

Success in implementing these advanced radio technologies will require close collaboration between industry stakeholders, research institutions, and standardization bodies. Organizations like 3GPP, IEEE, and ITU-R are already beginning to explore frameworks and standards for these technologies, ensuring that their development aligns with broader

6G objectives and requirements. This collaborative approach will be crucial in overcoming technical challenges and creating commercially viable solutions that can be deployed at scale.

6G, key security considerations

As telecommunications networks evolve beyond 5G and into the 6G era, the security landscape becomes increasingly complex and multifaceted. The integration of new technologies, architectures, and use cases introduces novel security challenges that must be addressed comprehensively to ensure the integrity, confidentiality, and availability of future communications systems.

The distributed nature of 6G networks, with their cell-less architecture and multiple access points, creates new attack surfaces that must be protected. Traditional perimeter-based security approaches become insufficient in this environment, necessitating a zero-trust architecture where every network component and communication session must be continuously authenticated and verified. The massive increase in connected devices and network endpoints also amplifies the potential for DDoS attacks and requires sophisticated traffic monitoring and anomaly detection systems.

Artificial Intelligence integration in 6G networks presents both opportunities and challenges from a security perspective. While AI can enhance threat detection and response capabilities, it also introduces vulnerabilities related to adversarial attacks on AI systems themselves. The security of AI models and their training data becomes crucial, as compromised AI systems could lead to network-wide vulnerabilities. Additionally, the use of AI for network optimization and management requires robust safeguards to prevent the manipulation of these automated systems.

The emergence of quantum computing poses a significant threat to current cryptographic methods, necessitating the development and implementation of quantum-safe security protocols. Post-quantum cryptography must be integrated into the fabric of 6G networks from the ground up, rather than as an afterthought. The challenge lies in developing cryptographic solutions that are both quantum-resistant and efficient enough to maintain the ultra-low latency requirements of 6G applications.

Privacy considerations become increasingly critical with the advent of new 6G applications such as holographic communications and brain-computer interfaces. These technologies collect and transmit highly sensitive personal and biometric data, requiring robust privacy-preserving mechanisms. The implementation of **privacy-enhancing technologies (PETs)** must be balanced with the performance requirements of real-time applications, necessitating innovative approaches to data protection.

Physical layer security takes on new importance in 6G networks, particularly with the use of terahertz and sub-millimeter wave frequencies. These high-frequency communications are potentially more vulnerable to interception and jamming attacks, requiring novel approaches to secure the physical transmission of signals. The use of intelligent reflecting surfaces and beamforming technologies must incorporate security considerations to prevent unauthorized signal manipulation.

The integration of terrestrial, aerial, and satellite networks in 6G creates unique security challenges related to handovers and inter-network communications. Securing communications across different network domains while maintaining seamless connectivity requires sophisticated key management and authentication mechanisms. The potential for satellite-based attacks and space-based threats must also be addressed through specialized security protocols.

Energy-efficient security becomes a crucial consideration in 6G networks, as the massive scale of connected devices requires security mechanisms that minimize power consumption. Lightweight cryptography and energy-aware security protocols must be developed to protect resource-constrained devices while maintaining robust security levels. The challenge lies in finding the right balance between security strength and energy efficiency.

Trust and identity management in 6G networks must evolve to handle the complexity of device-to-device, human-to-machine, and machine-to-machine communications. Distributed ledger technologies and blockchain-based solutions may play a crucial role in maintaining secure and verifiable identity management across the network. The implementation of secure credential management systems must account for the dynamic nature of 6G networks and the diverse range of connected entities.

Standardization of security protocols and interoperability requirements becomes essential as 6G networks evolve. Industry collaboration and international cooperation will be crucial in developing and implementing consistent security standards that can be applied across different network implementations while maintaining the flexibility to adapt to emerging threats.

These security considerations must be addressed proactively during the development and deployment of 6G networks to ensure that the promise of advanced communications capabilities can be realized without compromising the security and privacy of users and systems.

Intelligent network infrastructure

The concept of intelligent network infrastructure represents a fundamental transformation in how telecommunications networks are designed, deployed, and managed. As we move beyond traditional networking paradigms, the integration of advanced technologies such as artificial intelligence, cloud computing, and automation is reshaping the very foundation of telecommunications infrastructure. This evolution marks a shift from static, hardware-centric networks to dynamic, software-defined systems that can adapt and respond to changing demands in real-time.

In this new era, network intelligence is not merely an add-on feature but a core characteristic that permeates every layer of the infrastructure. The convergence of virtualization, cloud technologies, digital twins, artificial intelligence, and edge computing creates a synergistic ecosystem that enables unprecedented levels of network automation, optimization, and resilience. This intelligent infrastructure forms the backbone of next-generation telecommunications services, supporting everything from enhanced mobile broadband to mission-critical communications.

The transformation toward intelligent infrastructure is driven by several key factors. First, the exponential growth in network complexity and scale has made traditional manual management approaches unsustainable. Second, the diverse and dynamic nature of modern network services requires infrastructure that can rapidly adapt to changing requirements. Third, the need for improved efficiency and reduced operational costs demands more automated and intelligent network management solutions.

This intelligent infrastructure is characterized by its ability to self-organize, self-optimize, and self-heal. Networks can automatically detect and resolve issues, optimize resource allocation based on real-time demands, and even predict and prevent potential problems before they impact services. The integration of digital twins provides unprecedented visibility into network operations, while edge computing brings intelligence closer to where it is needed most.

As we explore the components of intelligent network infrastructure in detail, we will examine how these technologies work together to create more efficient, reliable, and capable telecommunications networks. From network virtualization and cloudification to AI-driven optimization and edge computing, each element plays a crucial role in realizing the vision of truly intelligent infrastructure that can meet the demanding requirements of future communications systems.

Network virtualization and cloudification

Network virtualization and cloudification represent cornerstone technologies in the evolution of intelligent telecommunications infrastructure. This transformation is guided by several industry frameworks and standards, including **European Telecommunications Standards Institute (ETSI) Network Functions Virtualization (NFV)**, **Open Network Automation Platform (ONAP)**, and TMForum's **Open Digital Architecture (ODA)**, which collectively define the blueprint for modern virtualized network infrastructures.

The virtualization journey in telecommunications has evolved from basic NFV concepts to full cloud-native implementations. Following the cloud-native principles established by the **Cloud Native Computing Foundation (CNCF)**, modern telecom networks are increasingly adopting containerized architectures using technologies like Kubernetes. The 3GPP's specifications for 5G **Service Based Architecture (SBA)** have further accelerated this transformation, laying the groundwork for even more advanced virtualization in future networks.

Network virtualization decouples network functions from proprietary hardware, enabling them to run as software instances on standard computing platforms. This separation is guided by the ETSI NFV architectural framework, which defines standard interfaces and reference points for virtualizing various network components. The **Open Radio Access Network (ORAN)** Alliance has extended these concepts to radio access networks, promoting open interfaces and virtualization of RAN functions.

Cloudification goes beyond simple virtualization, embracing cloud-native principles such as microservices architecture, containerization, and DevOps methodologies. The Linux Foundation's LF Networking projects, including ONAP and **Open Platform for NFV (OPNFV)**, provide open-source implementations of these concepts, enabling operators to build and manage cloud-native network infrastructure. TMForum's ODA framework complements these efforts by defining standard approaches for implementing digital services in a cloud-native environment.

Key aspects of network virtualization and cloudification include:

- The implementation of network slicing, supported by 3GPP specifications, enables the creation of multiple virtual networks on shared physical infrastructure. Each slice can be optimized for specific service requirements, from ultra-reliable low-latency communications to massive IoT deployments. The GSMA's Network Slicing Taskforce provides additional guidelines for implementing and managing network slices effectively.

- Service orchestration and management in virtualized networks follow the ETSI **Open Source MANO (OSM)** framework, which defines standard approaches for managing virtualized network functions and services. This is complemented by the MEF **Lifecycle Service Orchestration (LSO)** framework, which addresses service orchestration across multiple network domains and providers.

- Infrastructure abstraction plays a crucial role, with frameworks like OpenStack and Kubernetes providing standardized approaches for managing virtualized infrastructure resources. The **Telecom Infra Project (TIP)** has further contributed to this space by developing open specifications for disaggregated network components and virtualized infrastructure management.

- Looking toward future developments, the **Next Generation Mobile Networks (NGMN)** Alliance has outlined requirements for cloud-native architectures in 6G networks, emphasizing the need for even greater flexibility and automation. The ITU-T's Focus Group on cloud computing has also provided recommendations for cloud-native telecommunications infrastructure, addressing aspects such as inter-cloud connectivity and edge computing integration.

- The economic benefits of network virtualization and cloudification are substantial, with operators reporting significant reductions in operational costs and improved service agility. According to TM Forum's research, operators implementing these technologies have seen up to 40% reduction in network operation costs and up to 70% improvement in time-to-market for new services.

However, challenges remain in areas such as interoperability between different vendors' virtual network functions, performance optimization of virtualized networks, and security in multi-tenant environments. Industry bodies like 3GPP, ETSI, and the Linux Foundation continue to work on addressing these challenges through enhanced specifications and reference implementations.

This transformation toward virtualized, cloud-native network infrastructure represents not just a technological evolution but a fundamental shift in how telecommunications networks are built and operated. As these technologies mature and new standards emerge, they will continue to shape the future of intelligent network infrastructure.

Digital twin implementation in telecommunications

Digital twins represent a revolutionary approach to network management and optimization in telecommunications, creating virtual replicas of physical networks and infrastructure components that enable real-time monitoring, simulation, and predictive analysis. This implementation marks a significant shift from traditional network management approaches to a more dynamic and proactive methodology.

In telecommunications, digital twins operate at multiple levels of abstraction, from individual network elements to entire network ecosystems. At the infrastructure level, digital twins create precise virtual representations of physical network components such as base stations, routers, switches, and data centers. These virtual models continuously sync with their physical counterparts through real-time data streams, providing operators with unprecedented visibility into network operations.

The architecture of telecommunications digital twins typically consists of three primary layers. The physical layer encompasses the actual network infrastructure and its associated sensors and monitoring systems. The data layer handles the continuous flow of information between physical assets and their digital counterparts, including performance metrics, configuration data, and environmental parameters. The analytics layer processes this information using advanced algorithms and AI models to generate insights, predictions, and recommendations.

Shown in *Figure 16.4* is the recommendation from ITU-T Y.3090, which describes the requirements and architecture of a **digital twin network (DTN)**:

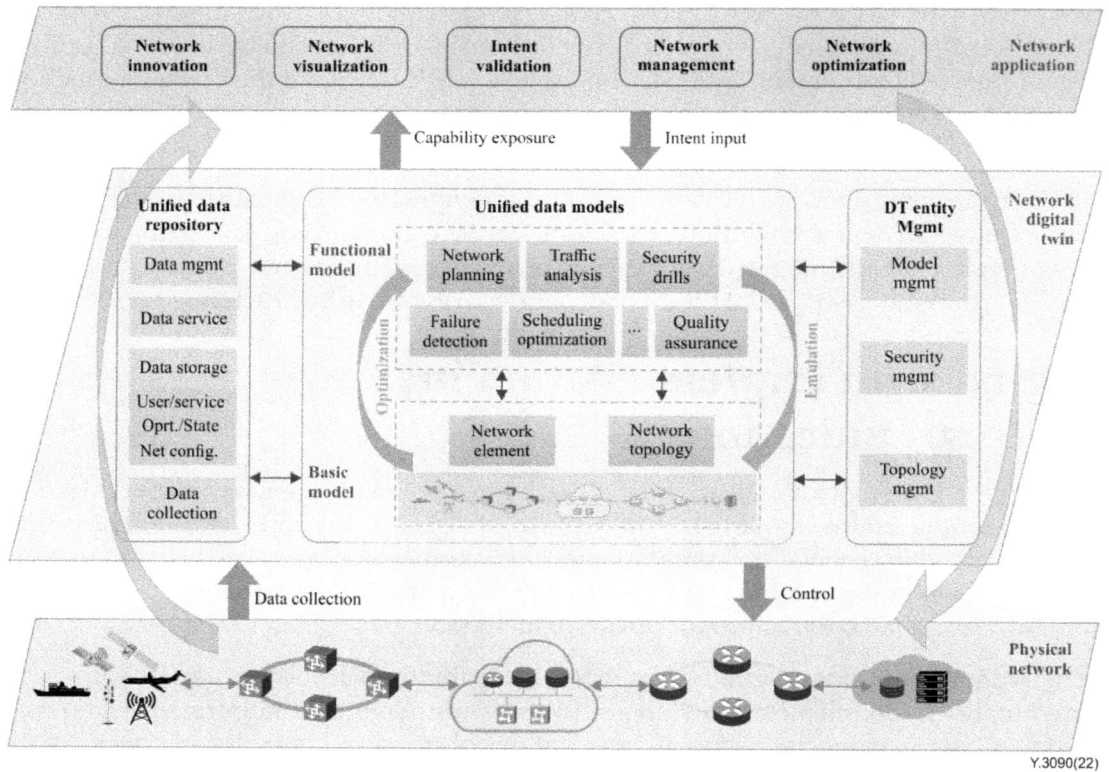

Figure 16.4*: ITU-T Y.3090, reference architecture of a digital twin network*
*(**Source:** https://www.itu.int/itu-t/recommendations/rec.aspx?rec=14852)*

One of the most powerful aspects of digital twin implementation is its ability to support scenario planning and testing. Network operators can use these virtual environments to simulate various network conditions, test new configurations, and evaluate the impact of proposed changes before implementing them in the physical network. This capability significantly reduces the risk associated with network modifications and helps optimize network performance without disrupting live services.

Real-time monitoring and predictive maintenance represent another crucial application of digital twins in telecommunications. By analyzing patterns in network behavior and performance metrics, digital twins can predict potential failures or performance degradation before they occur. This predictive capability enables proactive maintenance scheduling and reduces network downtime, ultimately improving service reliability and customer satisfaction.

The implementation of digital twins also facilitates network optimization through continuous analysis of network performance and resource utilization. By creating detailed models of network behavior under various conditions, operators can identify opportunities for optimization and automatically adjust network parameters to maintain optimal performance. This level of automation and intelligence is particularly valuable in managing complex 5G and future 6G networks.

Security and compliance monitoring benefit significantly from digital twin implementation. Virtual models can simulate security threats and test defense mechanisms without risking actual network infrastructure. Additionally, digital twins can monitor compliance with regulatory requirements and industry standards in real-time, helping operators maintain regulatory compliance while identifying potential violations before they become critical issues.

The integration of digital twins with other intelligent network technologies creates powerful synergies. When combined with AI and ML systems, digital twins can provide more accurate predictions and better optimization recommendations. Integration with edge computing enables faster response times and more efficient processing of the massive amounts of data generated by network monitoring systems.

However, implementing digital twins in telecommunications networks also presents several challenges. These include managing the vast amounts of data required for accurate modeling, ensuring real-time synchronization between physical and virtual environments, and maintaining the security of the digital twin infrastructure itself. Industry standards and best practices are still evolving to address these challenges.

Looking toward the future, digital twins will play an increasingly important role in telecommunications network management and optimization. As networks become more complex and dynamic, the ability to simulate, predict, and optimize network behavior in a virtual environment will become essential for maintaining network performance and reliability. The continued evolution of digital twin technology, coupled with advances in AI and edge computing, will enable even more sophisticated applications in network management and optimization.

This transformation in network management through digital twin technology represents a fundamental shift in how telecommunications networks are operated and maintained, paving the way for more efficient, reliable, and intelligent network infrastructure.

AI-driven network optimization and management

Artificial intelligence has emerged as a transformative force in telecommunications network management, fundamentally changing how networks are optimized, maintained, and operated. This evolution represents a shift from reactive, rule-based management systems to proactive, intelligent networks that can predict, adapt, and self-optimize in real-time.

The implementation of AI in network management encompasses multiple dimensions of network operations. At its core, AI-driven systems continuously analyze vast amounts of network data to identify patterns, anomalies, and optimization opportunities. Machine learning algorithms process data from various network elements, user devices, and environmental sensors to build comprehensive models of network behavior and performance.

Network resource allocation has been revolutionized through AI-driven approaches. Dynamic resource management systems use deep learning algorithms to predict network demands and automatically adjust network resources accordingly. This includes spectrum allocation, computing resources, and network slicing configurations. These systems can anticipate peak usage periods and proactively reallocate resources to prevent congestion and maintain service quality.

Predictive maintenance represents another crucial application of AI in network management. By analyzing historical performance data and real-time metrics, AI systems can identify potential equipment failures or performance degradation before they impact service. This predictive capability enables operators to schedule maintenance activities more effectively, reducing network downtime and maintenance costs while improving overall network reliability.

Traffic management and quality of service optimization have been significantly enhanced through AI implementation. Advanced algorithms analyze traffic patterns and user behavior to optimize routing decisions and quality of service parameters in real-time. These systems can automatically detect and mitigate network congestion, prioritize critical services, and ensure optimal user experience across different types of applications and services.

Self-healing networks have become a reality through AI-driven fault management systems. These systems can automatically detect network anomalies, diagnose root causes, and implement corrective actions without human intervention. In cases where human intervention is required, AI systems can provide detailed diagnostics and recommended actions, significantly reducing the time required to resolve network issues. Energy efficiency in network operations has been substantially improved through AI optimization. Smart power management systems use machine learning to predict network load and adjust power consumption accordingly. This includes optimizing the operation of network equipment, managing cooling systems in data centers, and implementing intelligent sleep modes for network elements during low-usage periods.

Security and threat detection have been enhanced through the implementation of AI-based systems. ML algorithms can detect and respond to security threats in real-time by analyzing network traffic patterns and identifying anomalous behavior. These systems can automatically implement security measures to protect network infrastructure and services from various types of attacks.

The integration of AI with other network management technologies creates powerful synergies. When combined with digital twins, AI systems can perform more accurate simulations and predictions. Integration with edge computing enables faster response times and more efficient processing of network data. These combinations enhance the overall effectiveness of network management systems.

However, implementing AI-driven network management also presents challenges. These include ensuring the accuracy and reliability of AI models, managing the computational resources required for AI processing, and maintaining transparency in AI decision-making processes. Industry standards and best practices continue to evolve to address these challenges. Looking forward, the role of AI in network management will continue to expand. As networks become more complex and dynamic, particularly with the advent of 6G technologies, AI-driven systems will become increasingly essential for maintaining network performance and reliability. The continued evolution of AI technologies, coupled with advances in computing capabilities and automation, will enable even more sophisticated applications in network management and optimization.

This transformation in network management through AI represents a fundamental shift in how telecommunications networks are operated and maintained, paving the way for more efficient, reliable, and intelligent network infrastructure that can meet the growing demands of future communications systems.

Edge computing evolution and distributed intelligence

The evolution of edge computing and distributed intelligence represents a fundamental shift in how telecommunications networks process and manage data, moving from centralized cloud architectures to a more distributed model that brings computing resources closer to where data is generated and consumed. This transformation is reshaping network architectures and enabling new classes of applications that require ultra-low latency and high reliability.

Edge computing has evolved through several distinct phases, beginning with basic content delivery networks and progressing to today's sophisticated **Multi-access Edge Computing (MEC)** platforms. The ETSI MEC framework, shown in the following figure, provides standardized approaches for implementing edge computing in telecommunications networks, while initiatives from the **Linux Foundation's (LF)** Edge project offer open-source solutions for edge computing deployment:

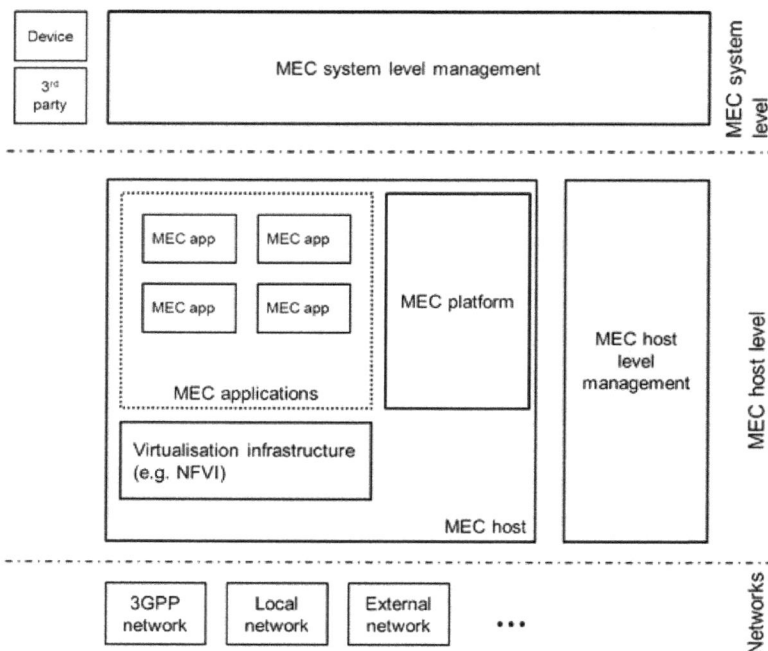

***Figure 16.5**: ETSI Multi-access Edge Computing framework*
(Source: *https://www.etsi.org/deliver/etsi_gs/MEC/001_099/003/02.01.01_60/gs_MEC003v020101p.pdf)*

The distributed intelligence architecture in modern telecommunications networks operates across multiple tiers. At the device edge, intelligent endpoints perform local processing and decision-making. The network edge hosts more substantial computing resources, enabling complex applications and services. Regional edge nodes provide additional processing capabilities, while centralized cloud resources handle tasks requiring massive computing power or global coordination.

Real-time processing capabilities have become a defining characteristic of edge computing evolution. Modern edge platforms can process data streams in real-time, enabling applications such as augmented reality, autonomous vehicles, and industrial automation. This capability is particularly crucial for applications that require immediate response times and cannot tolerate the latency associated with cloud processing. Network optimization through distributed intelligence has reached new levels of sophistication. Edge nodes can autonomously make decisions about traffic routing, resource allocation, and service delivery based on local conditions and requirements. This distributed decision-making capability improves network efficiency and reduces the load on centralized systems while enabling more responsive and reliable services.

The integration of artificial intelligence at the edge represents a significant advancement in distributed intelligence. Edge AI systems can perform complex analytics and decision-making tasks locally, reducing the need for constant communication with centralized cloud resources. This local processing capability is particularly valuable for applications requiring real-time analysis of large data streams, such as video analytics and industrial monitoring.

Security and privacy considerations have evolved alongside edge computing capabilities. Edge nodes now incorporate advanced security features, including hardware-based security elements and AI-powered threat detection systems. The distributed nature of edge computing also enhances privacy by enabling data to be processed locally rather than being transmitted to centralized locations.

Resource management in distributed edge environments has become increasingly sophisticated. Intelligent workload distribution systems can dynamically allocate processing tasks across edge nodes based on available resources, network conditions, and application requirements. This dynamic resource management capability ensures optimal utilization of edge computing resources while maintaining service quality.

The emergence of edge-native applications represents another significant development. These applications are specifically designed to leverage the capabilities of distributed edge computing environments, taking advantage of local processing, reduced latency, and improved reliability. The development of edge-native applications is driving innovation in areas such as smart cities, industrial IoT, and immersive media experiences.

Looking toward the future, edge computing and distributed intelligence will play an increasingly crucial role in telecommunications networks. The advent of 6G technologies will further accelerate this evolution, enabling new classes of applications that require even more sophisticated edge computing capabilities. The continued development of standards and best practices will help ensure interoperability and consistency across different edge computing implementations.

This transformation in network architecture through edge computing and distributed intelligence represents a fundamental shift in how telecommunications networks are designed and operated, creating new opportunities for innovation while addressing the growing demands for low-latency, high-reliability services.

The convergence of edge computing with other emerging technologies such as AI, 5G, and beyond will continue to drive innovation in telecommunications, enabling new services and applications that were previously impossible. This evolution represents not just a technological advancement but a fundamental reimagining of how networks process and manage data in an increasingly connected world.

Security implications of intelligent infrastructure

The emergence of intelligent infrastructure in telecommunications brings forth a new paradigm in network security, introducing both enhanced capabilities and novel challenges. The complex interplay of virtualization, AI-driven systems, edge computing, and distributed intelligence creates a multifaceted security landscape that requires innovative approaches to protect network assets and user data. The virtualization of network functions, while providing greater flexibility and efficiency, expands the potential attack surface of telecommunications infrastructure. Virtual network elements can be compromised through software vulnerabilities, misconfiguration, or malicious code injection. The dynamic nature of virtualized environments requires continuous security monitoring and automated response mechanisms to detect and mitigate threats in real-time.

Artificial intelligence in network infrastructure presents a dual-edged security scenario. While AI systems enhance threat detection and response capabilities, they also become potential targets for adversarial attacks. Malicious actors may attempt to manipulate AI models through data poisoning or exploit biases in ML algorithms. Protecting AI systems themselves becomes crucial for maintaining the integrity of network operations.

Edge computing introduces new security considerations by distributing processing capabilities across multiple locations. Each edge node becomes a potential entry point for attacks, requiring robust security measures at every level of the network. The distributed nature of edge computing also complicates security management, necessitating automated security orchestration and consistent policy enforcement across all edge locations.

Data privacy in intelligent infrastructure requires particular attention due to the vast amount of sensitive information collected and processed across the network. The implementation of privacy-preserving technologies must be balanced with the need for network optimization and service delivery. Edge computing can enhance privacy by enabling local data processing, but it also requires careful management of data access and storage practices.

Security automation becomes essential in intelligent infrastructure due to the speed and complexity of potential threats. AI-driven security systems must be capable of detecting and responding to threats in real-time, often without human intervention. However, this automation must be carefully designed to prevent false positives and ensure that automated responses do not inadvertently disrupt legitimate network operations.

Identity and access management in intelligent infrastructure requires sophisticated approaches to handle the complex interactions between various network elements, services, and users. Zero Trust security principles have become crucial, requiring continuous verification of every network interaction. The implementation of robust authentication and authorization mechanisms must span across virtual and physical network components.

Supply chain security emerges as a critical concern in intelligent infrastructure, particularly regarding the integrity of software components and virtual network functions. The use of trusted platform modules, secure boot processes, and continuous integrity verification becomes essential for maintaining the security of network elements and preventing supply chain attacks.

Regulatory compliance in intelligent infrastructure presents unique challenges due to the dynamic nature of virtualized environments and distributed processing. Security systems must be capable of demonstrating compliance with various regulatory requirements while maintaining the flexibility needed for efficient network operation. This includes implementing appropriate data protection measures and maintaining detailed audit trails of network activities. The convergence of multiple technologies in intelligent infrastructure necessitates a holistic approach to security. Security measures must be integrated across all layers of the network, from physical infrastructure to virtual network functions and application services. This integration must support rapid detection and response to security incidents while maintaining network performance and reliability.

As intelligent infrastructure continues to evolve, security strategies must adapt to address emerging threats and vulnerabilities. The development of new security standards and best practices will be crucial for ensuring the resilient operation of telecommunications networks in an increasingly complex and challenging security environment.

Quantum communications and security

The emergence of quantum technologies represents a transformative shift in telecommunications security and communications capabilities. As classical computing approaches its physical limits and quantum computers threaten current cryptographic systems, quantum communications offers new paradigms for securing information and enabling novel forms of data transmission. This convergence of quantum physics and telecommunications infrastructure promises to revolutionize how we protect and transmit sensitive information in the digital age.

The field of quantum communications leverages fundamental principles of quantum mechanics, such as superposition, entanglement, and the no-cloning theorem, to create theoretically unbreakable communication channels and develop new methods of secure information exchange. As quantum computing capabilities advance, the need for quantum-safe communications becomes increasingly critical for protecting sensitive data and maintaining the integrity of telecommunications infrastructure.

QKD and PQC

Quantum key distribution (**QKD**) and **post-quantum cryptography** (**PQC**) represent two complementary approaches to addressing the security challenges posed by quantum computing. QKD harnesses the principles of quantum mechanics to generate and distribute cryptographic keys with unconditional security, while PQC focuses on developing mathematical algorithms that remain secure against both quantum and classical computing attacks.

QKD systems utilize quantum states, typically encoded in photons, to establish secure cryptographic keys between communicating parties. The fundamental security of QKD stems from the quantum mechanical principle that any attempt to measure or copy quantum states inevitably disturbs them, making eavesdropping detectable. Modern QKD implementations employ various protocols, such as BB84 and E91, each offering different advantages in terms of security, distance, and key generation rates. Post-quantum cryptography, on the other hand, develops classical cryptographic algorithms that are resistant to attacks from both quantum and classical computers. These algorithms are based on mathematical problems that remain computationally difficult even with access to quantum computing resources. Major categories include lattice-based cryptography, hash-based signatures, and multivariate cryptography, each offering different trade-offs between security, key size, and computational efficiency.

The integration of QKD and PQC creates a comprehensive quantum-safe security framework. While QKD provides information-theoretic security for key distribution, PQC ensures that the actual data encryption remains secure against quantum attacks. This hybrid approach addresses both the immediate need for quantum-resistant cryptography and the long-term goal of unconditionally secure communications. Recent advancements in both fields have led to significant improvements in practical implementations. QKD systems have achieved increased transmission distances and key generation rates, while PQC algorithms have become more efficient and practical for real-world deployment. International standardization efforts, led by organizations like NIST and ETSI, are working to establish standards for both technologies to ensure interoperability and security.

The commercial adoption of these technologies is already underway, with several telecommunications providers implementing QKD networks and organizations beginning to transition to post-quantum cryptographic algorithms. This early adoption is particularly crucial for protecting sensitive data with long-term security requirements, as encrypted data collected today could be stored and later decrypted when sufficiently powerful quantum computers become available.

However, challenges remain in both QKD and PQC implementations. QKD systems must overcome practical limitations such as distance constraints, hardware requirements, and integration with existing network infrastructure. PQC algorithms must balance security requirements with performance considerations and compatibility with current systems. Addressing these challenges requires continued research and development in both fields.

Quantum network and sensing technologies

The convergence of quantum internet architecture and quantum sensing capabilities represents a revolutionary advancement in telecommunications infrastructure, creating new possibilities for both communication and measurement. This integration enables not just the transmission of quantum information but also precise sensing and measurement capabilities that enhance network performance and reliability.

Quantum internet architecture is built upon a hierarchical structure that combines quantum and classical communication elements. At its foundation lie quantum repeaters, which enable the extension of quantum entanglement over long distances through quantum state teleportation and entanglement swapping. These repeaters form the backbone of quantum networks, creating entanglement distribution networks that can support various quantum communication protocols and applications.

The architecture incorporates quantum memory elements, which serve as temporary storage for quantum states and are crucial for implementing quantum repeater protocols. These memories must maintain quantum coherence for sufficient durations to enable the successful transmission of quantum information across network nodes. Current implementations utilize various physical systems, including trapped ions, atomic ensembles, and solid-state quantum devices.

Quantum sensing and metrology bring unprecedented precision to telecommunications infrastructure monitoring and optimization. These technologies leverage quantum effects to achieve measurements with accuracy far beyond classical limits. In telecommunications, quantum sensors can detect minute variations in electromagnetic fields, precisely measure timing signals, and monitor physical parameters critical for network operation.

The integration of quantum sensing with network architecture enables real-time monitoring of network performance at the quantum level. Quantum magnetometers and atomic clocks provide ultra-precise measurements for network synchronization and timing. These capabilities are particularly crucial for maintaining the coherence and synchronization required in quantum networks and improving the performance of classical networks.

Time-frequency transfer in telecommunications networks benefits significantly from quantum sensing technologies. Quantum clocks and frequency standards provide unprecedented accuracy for network synchronization, essential for both quantum and classical communication protocols. This precise timing enables better coordination between network nodes and improves overall network efficiency.

Quantum-enhanced phase estimation and frequency measurements enable more precise control of telecommunications signals. These capabilities are particularly valuable in fiber-optic networks, where precise control of signal phase and frequency is crucial for maintaining high data transmission rates and minimizing errors.

Environmental monitoring through quantum sensors provides detailed information about physical conditions affecting network performance. These sensors can detect variations in temperature, strain, and electromagnetic fields that might impact quantum and classical communication channels. This information enables proactive network optimization and maintenance.

The convergence of these technologies creates a feedback loop where quantum sensing capabilities inform and optimize network architecture. Real-time sensor data enables dynamic adjustment of network parameters, routing decisions, and resource allocation, leading to more efficient and reliable network operation.

However, implementing these advanced capabilities presents significant challenges. The integration of quantum sensors with existing network infrastructure requires careful consideration of compatibility and interference issues. Additionally, maintaining the stability and reliability of quantum sensing systems in real-world telecommunications environments remains an ongoing challenge. Looking forward, the continued development of quantum network architecture and sensing technologies will enable new applications in telecommunications. From secure quantum communication networks to ultra-precise timing and measurement systems, these technologies will play a crucial role in shaping the future of telecommunications infrastructure.

Quantum-safe protocols and network integration

The implementation of quantum-safe security protocols and their integration with classical networks represents one of the most crucial challenges in modern telecommunications. As quantum computing capabilities advance, the need for protocols that can resist both quantum and classical attacks becomes increasingly urgent, while maintaining compatibility with existing network infrastructure.

Quantum-safe security protocols encompass a range of cryptographic mechanisms designed to withstand attacks from both quantum and classical computers. These protocols must address various security requirements, including key exchange, digital signatures, and encryption, while maintaining acceptable performance levels for real-world applications. The **National Institute of Standards and Technology** (**NIST**) has played a crucial role in standardizing these protocols through its Post-Quantum Cryptography standardization process.

As of August 2024, NIST has approved several quantum-safe algorithms for standardization. The CRYSTALS-Kyber algorithm has been selected as the primary **key-encapsulation mechanism** (**KEM**), offering a balanced approach to security and efficiency. For digital signatures, CRYSTALS-Dilithium serves as the primary algorithm, while FALCON provides an alternative for applications requiring smaller signatures. Additionally, SPHINCS+ has been approved as a stateless hash-based signature scheme, offering security based on different mathematical assumptions.

The integration of these NIST-approved algorithms into existing cryptographic protocols presents several challenges. Current protocols like TLS, SSH, and IPsec must be modified to support quantum-safe algorithms while maintaining backward compatibility. This hybrid approach, combining both classical and quantum-safe algorithms, ensures security against both current and future threats while allowing for a gradual transition in existing networks.

Integration challenges with classical networks extend beyond protocol modifications. The higher computational requirements and larger key sizes of quantum-safe algorithms can impact network performance and resource utilization. Network equipment must be upgraded or replaced to support these new algorithms, requiring significant investment in infrastructure modernization.

Interoperability between quantum and classical systems presents another significant challenge. The transition to quantum-safe protocols must be managed carefully to ensure the continuous operation of existing services while new security measures are implemented. This requires careful planning and coordination across different network segments and service providers.

Performance optimization in hybrid quantum-classical networks requires sophisticated approaches to resource management. Load balancing between quantum and classical processing elements, managing key distribution across different types of networks, and optimizing protocol overhead all present significant technical challenges that must be addressed for successful integration.

Certificate management and **public key infrastructure** (**PKI**) must evolve to support quantum-safe algorithms. This evolution includes updates to certificate formats, validation procedures, and key management systems. The transition period requires careful handling of both classical and quantum-safe certificates to ensure continuous security coverage.

Security assurance in hybrid environments requires new approaches to testing and validation. Security protocols must be verified for both quantum and classical resistance, while ensuring that the integration itself does not introduce new vulnerabilities. This includes developing new security metrics and testing methodologies specific to quantum-safe implementations.

Standards development continues to evolve as new quantum-safe protocols are developed and implemented. Organizations like ETSI, ISO, and IETF are working to create comprehensive standards for quantum-safe cryptography and its integration with classical networks. These standards must address both technical requirements and operational considerations for successful deployment.

The successful integration of quantum-safe security protocols with classical networks requires a coordinated effort across the telecommunications industry. This includes hardware manufacturers, software developers, network operators, and standards organizations working together to ensure smooth transition and effective implementation of quantum-safe security measures.

Looking ahead, the continued evolution of quantum computing capabilities will drive further developments in quantum-safe security protocols and integration techniques. The telecommunications industry must remain agile in adapting to these changes while maintaining the security and reliability of existing network infrastructure.

Space-based communications

The evolution of space-based communications represents a paradigm shift in global connectivity, extending telecommunications infrastructure beyond terrestrial boundaries to create a truly ubiquitous communication network. This transformation is driven by technological advancements in satellite systems, launch capabilities, and communication technologies, enabling new possibilities for global coverage, high-speed connectivity, and resilient communications infrastructure.

Space-based communications are becoming increasingly crucial in addressing connectivity challenges, particularly in remote and underserved regions. The integration of space, air, and ground networks creates a three-dimensional communication fabric that promises to deliver high-speed, low-latency connectivity anywhere on Earth. This new era of space-based telecommunications is characterized by advanced satellite technologies, innovative network architectures, and sophisticated integration mechanisms that enable seamless communication across different network domains.

NTN and LEO constellation integration

The convergence of **Non-Terrestrial Networks** (**NTN**) and **Low Earth Orbit** (**LEO**) satellite constellations is revolutionizing the telecommunications landscape. These systems operate in closer proximity to Earth compared to traditional geostationary satellites, offering significantly reduced latency and increased coverage capacity. The integration of these technologies creates a dynamic network architecture that can provide high-speed, low-latency communications to previously underserved regions.

LEO satellite constellations, operating at altitudes between 500 to 2000 kilometers, are being deployed in unprecedented numbers. Major initiatives like Starlink, OneWeb, and Project Kuiper are launching thousands of satellites to create massive constellations that provide global internet coverage. These constellations utilize inter-satellite links and advanced phased array antennas to create a mesh network in space, enabling efficient data routing and reduced ground infrastructure requirements.

The integration of NTN with terrestrial networks presents unique opportunities and challenges. 3GPP standards have evolved to support NTN integration, defining specifications for satellite access in 5G networks and beyond. This integration enables seamless handover between terrestrial and satellite networks, allowing devices to maintain connectivity regardless of their location or movement.

Network orchestration in this integrated environment requires sophisticated management systems. **Software-defined networking** (**SDN**) and **network function virtualization** (**NFV**) technologies are being adapted for space-based systems, enabling flexible resource allocation and dynamic network configuration. These capabilities are crucial for managing the complex interactions between satellite constellations and terrestrial networks.

Frequency coordination and spectrum management become critical in LEO constellation deployments. The large number of satellites and their dynamic nature require careful coordination to prevent interference and ensure efficient spectrum utilization. International regulatory frameworks are evolving to address these challenges while promoting sustainable space operations.

The economic implications of LEO constellation deployment are significant. While the initial investment in satellite manufacturing and launch is substantial, the potential for global coverage and high-speed connectivity creates new business opportunities. The competition among multiple constellation operators is driving innovation and cost reduction in satellite technology and launch services.

The integration of these systems with emerging technologies like edge computing and AI creates new possibilities for advanced services. LEO satellites can serve as edge nodes in space, providing computing capabilities closer to users and enabling new applications in areas such as the **Internet of Things (IoT)**, autonomous vehicles, and remote sensing.

Space-ground-air and optical communications

The convergence of space, ground, and air networks, combined with advanced optical communication technologies, represents a new frontier in telecommunications infrastructure. This integrated approach creates a seamless, three-dimensional communication fabric that leverages the unique advantages of each domain while overcoming their individual limitations.

Space-ground-air integrated networks (**SGAIN**) employ a layered architecture that combines satellites, **high-altitude platforms** (**HAPs**), **unmanned aerial vehicles** (**UAVs**), and terrestrial infrastructure. Each layer serves specific functions while maintaining interconnectivity with other layers. Satellites provide broad coverage and global connectivity, HAPs offer regional coverage with lower latency, and UAVs provide flexible, on-demand coverage for specific areas or events.

Optical wireless communications (**OWC**) play a crucial role in this integrated architecture, offering unprecedented data rates and security advantages. **Free-space optical** (**FSO**) communication systems use laser technology to achieve data rates in the terabits-per-second range, far exceeding traditional **radio frequency** (**RF**) capabilities. These systems are particularly effective for satellite-to-satellite links and high-bandwidth connections between space and ground segments.

The integration of these technologies enables new networking paradigms. SDN and NFV are being adapted to manage the complex interactions between different network segments. Dynamic routing algorithms optimize data paths across the integrated network, considering factors such as weather conditions, network load, and service requirements.

Atmospheric challenges present unique considerations for optical communications. Laser beams can be affected by atmospheric turbulence, clouds, and other weather phenomena.

Advanced adaptive optics systems and sophisticated error correction mechanisms are employed to maintain reliable communications under varying atmospheric conditions. MIMO techniques in optical systems further enhance reliability and throughput.

Inter-layer handover mechanisms ensure seamless connectivity as users or devices move between different network segments. These mechanisms must account for the dynamic nature of satellite orbits, platform movement, and changing atmospheric conditions. ML algorithms are increasingly used to predict and optimize handover decisions, reducing latency and improving service quality.

The implementation of QKD over optical links adds another dimension to secure communications. Space-based QKD systems can distribute encryption keys over global distances, providing quantum-safe security for sensitive communications. The integration of quantum and classical optical communications creates new possibilities for secure, high-speed data transmission.

Energy efficiency and sustainability considerations are crucial in the design of integrated networks. Solar-powered HAPs and energy-efficient optical terminals help reduce the environmental impact of network operations. The use of optical communications also reduces power consumption compared to traditional RF systems, particularly for long-distance links.

Standardization efforts are ongoing to ensure interoperability between different segments of the integrated network. Organizations like the **International Telecommunication Union** (**ITU**) and the **Consultative Committee for Space Data Systems** (**CCSDS**) are developing standards for optical communications and network integration. These standards address aspects such as link protocols, quality of service, and network management.

The future evolution of space-ground-air integration and optical communications will likely see increased automation and intelligence in network operations. AI-driven network management systems will optimize resource allocation, predict and mitigate potential disruptions, and ensure efficient operation of the integrated network infrastructure.

These advancements in integrated networks and optical communications are paving the way for new applications and services that require global coverage, high bandwidth, and low latency. From supporting IoT deployments to enabling advanced scientific research, these technologies are fundamental to the future of global telecommunications infrastructure.

Security of space-based communication systems

Space-based communication systems present unique security challenges that span both traditional cybersecurity concerns and space-specific vulnerabilities. The distributed nature of space-based infrastructure, combined with its critical role in global communications, makes security a paramount consideration in system design and operation.

Physical security in space-based communications extends beyond traditional concepts. Satellites and space-based assets face threats from space debris, solar events, and potentially hostile actions from other space-based systems. The protection of ground stations and uplink/downlink facilities requires comprehensive security measures that address both physical and cyber threats. Additionally, the growing concern about anti-satellite weapons (ASAT) and space-based interference systems necessitates new approaches to ensuring communication resilience.

Cybersecurity in space-based systems must address multiple attack vectors. The command and control channels for satellites are particularly critical, as unauthorized access could lead to catastrophic consequences. Encryption of both telemetry and payload data is essential, with special consideration given to the unique constraints of space-based platforms, including power limitations, radiation effects, and communication delays. The implementation of quantum-safe cryptography becomes increasingly important as quantum computing capabilities advance.

Signal interference and jamming present significant security challenges. Space-based communications are vulnerable to both intentional jamming and unintentional interference. Advanced anti-jamming techniques, including frequency hopping, spread spectrum technologies, and adaptive beamforming, are crucial for maintaining reliable communications. The detection and mitigation of spoofing attacks, particularly in navigation and timing signals, requires sophisticated authentication mechanisms.

Supply chain security is particularly critical for space-based systems. The complex international nature of satellite manufacturing and launch services requires careful verification of components and systems. Hardware trojans, backdoors, and compromised software could have devastating effects on space-based communication networks. Rigorous supply chain validation procedures and secure hardware designs are essential for maintaining system integrity.

Authentication and access control in integrated space-ground networks require sophisticated approaches. The dynamic nature of satellite constellations and their interaction with ground systems necessitates flexible yet secure authentication mechanisms. Zero Trust architectures are being adapted for space-based systems, ensuring that every interaction between network components is properly authenticated and authorized.

Privacy considerations in satellite communications have become increasingly important. The global coverage of satellite systems raises concerns about data privacy and sovereignty. Encryption and data protection measures must comply with various international regulations while maintaining operational efficiency. The implementation of privacy-preserving technologies must account for the unique characteristics of space-based communications.

Resilience and redundancy are crucial security aspects. Space-based communication systems must maintain operational capability even when individual components are compromised or fail. This includes redundant communication paths, backup systems, and the ability to rapidly reconfigure network resources in response to security incidents. The development of autonomous security response capabilities is particularly important given the remote nature of space-based assets.

International cooperation and regulation play vital roles in space-based security. The development of international standards and protocols for secure space communications requires collaboration between multiple stakeholders. Organizations like the **International Telecommunication Union (ITU)** and the **Committee on the Peaceful Uses of Outer Space (COPUOS)** are working to establish frameworks for secure and responsible use of space-based communication systems.

Looking toward the future, the security of space-based communications will continue to evolve. The integration of artificial intelligence for threat detection and response, the implementation of quantum-safe security measures, and the development of new protective technologies will be crucial for maintaining the integrity and reliability of space-based communication systems. This comprehensive approach to security ensures that space-based communication systems can continue to provide critical services while maintaining resilience against both current and emerging threats. The ongoing development of security technologies and protocols will be essential for protecting these vital infrastructure components in an increasingly complex threat landscape.

Conclusion

The evolution of telecommunications beyond 5G marks a pivotal transformation in network security and infrastructure management. This chapter has explored how the convergence of 6G networks, quantum communications, intelligent infrastructure, and space-based systems creates both groundbreaking opportunities and complex security challenges for service providers. The transition to 6G networks necessitates a complete redesign of security frameworks to accommodate enhanced capabilities and complex architectures. The integration of AI, edge computing, and distributed intelligence demands adaptive security measures that can respond to dynamic threats while maintaining optimal network performance. Quantum technologies offer revolutionary tools for data security but challenge existing protocols, while space-based communications expand the threat landscape beyond terrestrial boundaries, introducing new attack vectors at the intersection of satellite and ground infrastructure. The chapter emphasizes the critical importance of proactive security planning, highlighting how service providers must develop security frameworks that are both robust and flexible. Success in this evolving landscape requires sustained collaboration between industry stakeholders, standards organizations, and regulatory bodies to ensure the resilient operation of next-generation telecommunications networks.

As we move into our final chapter, we will examine the broader implications of these technological advances through the lens of real-world implementations and incidents. The chapter will explore current trends in telecom service adoption and analyze significant security incidents that have shaped the industry's approach to protection. By examining cases such as major network breaches, infrastructure compromises, and successful defense strategies, we will extract valuable lessons that can guide future security implementations. This analysis will provide practical insights for service providers navigating the complex landscape of telecommunications security, helping them build more resilient networks while avoiding proven pitfalls in their security architecture.

Points to remember

- 6G network advancements represent a quantum leap in telecommunications capabilities, introducing terahertz communications and cell-free massive MIMO systems. These technologies deliver unprecedented data rates and near-zero latency while requiring enhanced security protocols to protect against new categories of threats and vulnerabilities.

- Intelligent infrastructure development relies heavily on virtualization, cloud technologies, and AI-driven management systems. While enabling autonomous network operations, these systems demand sophisticated security frameworks that can protect against both conventional cyber threats and emerging AI-specific vulnerabilities.

- Quantum communications technology emerges as a crucial security component, with quantum key distribution and post-quantum cryptography serving as primary defenses against quantum computing threats. The implementation of NIST-approved quantum-safe algorithms, particularly CRYSTALS-Kyber and CRYSTALS-Dilithium, provides essential protection for future telecommunications systems.

- Space-based communications systems extend network coverage globally through LEO satellite constellations and integrated space-ground-air networks. These systems require specialized security measures to address unique challenges, including protection against signal interference, management of supply chain vulnerabilities, and securing space-based assets.

- Convergence security requirements necessitate an integrated security approach that can effectively protect interconnected systems while supporting advanced telecommunications capabilities. This holistic strategy must address the complexities of securing multiple technologies working in concert while maintaining operational efficiency.

Exercises

1. Which of the following is a key characteristic of 6G network architecture?

   a. Centralized processing only

   b. Native AI integration

   c. Single-layer security

   d. Fixed resource allocation

2. In quantum communications, which mechanism provides unconditional security for key distribution?

   a. RSA encryption

   b. Quantum key distribution

   c. Traditional public key infrastructure

   d. Symmetric encryption

3. What is the primary advantage of LEO satellite constellations over traditional geostationary satellites?

   a. Higher orbit altitude

   b. Lower manufacturing cost

   c. Reduced latency

   d. Simpler ground infrastructure

4. Which technology is crucial for implementing digital twins in telecommunications networks?

   a. Only physical sensors

   b. Manual data collection

   c. Real-time data synchronization

   d. Periodic updates

5. How does native AI integration in 6G networks differ from AI implementation in previous generations?

6. Explain the significance of quantum-safe security protocols in telecommunications.

7. Describe the challenges in implementing digital twins for telecommunications networks.

8. What are the primary security considerations for space-based communication systems?

9. How does edge computing evolution impact intelligent network infrastructure?

CHAPTER 17
Securing Future Networks

Introduction

As we conclude our comprehensive exploration of telecommunications service provider security, we stand at a crucial intersection of technological advancement and security imperatives. The telecommunications landscape has undergone a remarkable transformation over the past decade, with 5G networks reaching over 70% of the global population and cloud-native network functions becoming the norm rather than the exception. This rapid evolution, while enabling unprecedented connectivity and services, has also expanded the attack surface for malicious actors.

In this final chapter, we will examine the global statistical perspective of various telecom service deployments and their adoption rates, providing insight into both the scale of our security challenges and the opportunities that lie ahead. We will also delve into critical lessons learned from significant security breaches that have shaped the industry's approach to cybersecurity. From the 2021 mobile network operator breaches in Southeast Asia to the recent supply chain compromises affecting European carriers, these incidents have provided valuable insights into the industry's vulnerabilities and resilience.

By analyzing these elements collectively, we aim to chart a path forward that balances innovation with security, ensuring that telecommunications providers can continue to drive digital transformation while maintaining the trust of their billions of users worldwide.

Structure

This chapter will cover the following topics.

- Global statistics perspective
- Lessons learnt from security breaches
- Path forward

Objectives

Network security in telecommunications has evolved from securing traditional voice services to protecting a complex ecosystem of interconnected digital services that form the backbone of modern communication. This chapter examines the global landscape of telecommunications security through empirical data on service adoption rates, deployment patterns, and their corresponding security implications. By analyzing historical breach incidents across major service providers and evaluating their impact on industry security practices, we will identify recurring patterns and extract valuable insights for future security architectures.

Our objective is to synthesize the key themes presented throughout this book through the lens of real-world implementation data and incident analysis. We will explore how varying rates of technology adoption across different regions have created unique security challenges, examine how major security incidents have shaped industry best practices, and outline a framework for building more resilient telecommunications infrastructure. This analysis will help security architects and telecommunications professionals better understand the relationship between service evolution, threat landscapes, and security control effectiveness in an increasingly interconnected world.

Global statistical perspective

The telecommunications landscape has undergone a remarkable transformation since its inception, with each generation marking significant milestones in connectivity and service delivery. The **first generation (1G)** analog networks, pioneered by **Nippon Telegraph and Telephone Corporation (NTT)** in 1979 in Japan, followed by Nordic Mobile Telephone in 1981, and AMPS in the United States in 1983, revolutionized mobile communications. By their peak in the early 1990s, 1G networks served approximately 20 million subscribers globally. The complete phase-out of 1G occurred between 2002 and 2008, with Japan's NTT being the last major operator to sunset these services, marking the end of the analog era in mobile communications.

2G networks, introduced in 1991 with GSM in Finland, achieved unprecedented global penetration, connecting over 5 billion devices at their peak in 2012. The technology saw particularly strong adoption in developing regions, with India and China accounting for over 45% of global 2G connections. As of 2024, while 2G still serves approximately 750 million devices globally, primarily in developing regions, major operators have accelerated their sunset plans. AT&T completed its 2G shutdown in 2017, Verizon in 2019, and most European operators, including Vodafone, Deutsche Telekom, and Orange, have announced complete shutdowns by 2025. In Asia, countries like Japan, South Korea, and Singapore have already completed their 2G sunsets, while others like India plan completion by 2025.

3G networks, which introduced mobile data services and peaked at over 3 billion connections in 2015, are experiencing rapid decline. Major U.S. carriers completed their 3G shutdowns between 2022 and 2023, with AT&T, T-Mobile, and Verizon redirecting spectrum resources to 4G and 5G services. In Europe, approximately 65% of operators have either completed or announced 3G shutdowns by 2025 while maintaining 2G for legacy IoT services. The Asia-Pacific region shows varying approaches, with developed nations like Japan and South Korea having completed 3G shutdowns while others maintain hybrid operations.

4G/LTE will remain the backbone of global mobile communications in 2024, serving approximately 4.7 billion connections worldwide. The technology accounts for 58% of all mobile connections globally, with particularly high penetration in developed markets (over 80% in North America, Europe, and developed Asia). LTE-Advanced and LTE-Advanced Pro networks, offering theoretical speeds of up to 3Gbps, are deployed by 420 operators across 180 countries. The rise of VoLTE is notable, now supported by 262 operators globally, carrying over 60% of global mobile voice traffic.

5G has exceeded early adoption projections, reaching 1.8 billion connections globally by 2024. The Asia-Pacific region leads with 1.1 billion connections, followed by North America (235 million) and Europe (290 million). China alone accounts for 745 million 5G connections, supported by over 2.3 million 5G base stations. Standalone 5G networks are operational in 35 countries, with 120 operators having launched commercial 5G SA services.

Fixed network services have shown equally impressive growth. FTTH/B subscriptions have reached 850 million globally, with China leading at 627 million connections, followed by the European Union (88 million) and the United States (54 million). The technology shows a global compound annual growth rate of 15% over the past five years. VoWiFi services are now supported by over 200 operators across 100 countries, handling approximately 25% of mobile voice traffic in developed markets. VoBB serves approximately 1.2 billion subscribers, with significant growth in emerging markets where it often complements or replaces traditional fixed-line services.

IPTV has grown to 350 million subscribers globally, showing a compound annual growth rate of 7.5% over the past five years. China leads with 180 million subscribers, followed by the European Union (62 million) and Southeast Asia (45 million). The service has achieved particularly high household penetration in countries like South Korea (over 50%), Hong Kong (over 60%), and France (over 45%).

IMS core networks, the foundation of modern IP-based services, are now deployed by over 85% of tier-1 operators globally. These networks support various services, from VoLTE (serving 3.2 billion subscribers) to Rich Communication Services (2.5 billion users). The technology has been crucial in enabling service convergence, with 178 operators having deployed VoLTE roaming and 165 offering VoWiFi services through IMS cores.

This comprehensive statistical overview demonstrates the scale and complexity of modern telecommunications networks, setting the stage for our concluding discussion on the critical security implications and challenges faced across these technological generations and services. The data underscores not just the technical evolution but also the increasing importance of robust security frameworks to protect these vast and interconnected networks.

Lessons from major breaches

In the complex landscape of telecommunications security, major incidents have served as pivotal moments that shaped industry practices and regulatory frameworks. These incidents, occurring across different generations of network technologies, have exposed vulnerabilities in what were considered robust security architectures. Their impacts extend far beyond immediate financial losses, affecting subscriber trust, regulatory compliance, and industry-wide security practices. The following cases represent some of the most significant security breaches in telecommunications history, each demonstrating unique attack vectors and resulting in transformative changes to security approaches. These incidents have not only highlighted the critical importance of proactive security measures but have also led to fundamental shifts in how service providers approach network security, customer data protection, and incident response.

The series of major security incidents discussed in the following section represents more than isolated breaches. They collectively illustrate the evolving threat landscape in telecommunications security and provide crucial insights for future network architectures and security frameworks. These incidents, spanning different technologies and network generations, offer valuable lessons that continue to shape the industry's approach to security.

A critical pattern emerging from the following incidents is the exploitation of trust relationships within telecommunications networks. From the SS7 vulnerabilities to Open Radio Access Network interface compromises, attackers have consistently targeted areas where systems implicitly trust each other. This has led to a fundamental shift towards zero-trust architectures across the industry, where every interaction, whether internal or external, requires explicit verification.

The incidents also highlight the increasing complexity of telecommunications networks and the security challenges this presents. As networks evolve from monolithic architectures to disaggregated, software-defined systems, the attack surface has expanded dramatically. The VoLTE and Open RAN breaches particularly demonstrate how modern networks' programmability and openness, while offering significant operational benefits, can also create new vulnerabilities if not properly secured.

One significant recurring theme is the impact of legacy systems and protocols. The SS7 vulnerabilities and roaming fraud incidents show how older protocols, designed in an era of trusted relationships between operators, can become significant liabilities in today's threat landscape. This has accelerated the industry's move towards modern, security-first protocols and architectures.

The financial implications of these breaches extend far beyond immediate losses. The cumulative cost across these incidents, including direct losses, remediation costs, and regulatory fines, exceeds €1 billion. However, the long-term impact on customer trust and brand reputation has proven even more significant, forcing operators to prioritize security investments and enhance transparency in their security practices.

The path forward requires a delicate balance between innovation and security. As telecommunications networks continue to evolve towards 6G and beyond, the lessons learned from these incidents provide crucial guidance. The future of telecommunications security lies not just in stronger technical controls but in creating resilient ecosystems that can adapt to emerging threats while maintaining the essential services that modern society depends upon.

These incidents have demonstrated that security in telecommunications is not a destination but a journey of continuous improvement and adaptation. As we move forward, the industry must maintain this vigilance while embracing new technologies and architectures that will define the next generation of telecommunications services.

Greek Vodafone wiretapping scandal

The Vodafone Greece incident (2004-2005) stands as one of the most sophisticated telecommunications security breaches in history. The attack exploited legitimate lawful intercept functionality within Ericsson's AXE telephone exchanges, specifically targeting the **Remote Exchange Surveillance** (**RES**) subsystem. The attackers, who were never officially identified, demonstrated an intimate knowledge of both the AXE architecture and Vodafone's network topology.

The breach involved the installation of rogue software on four of Vodafone's **Mobile Switching Centers** (**MSCs**). This software created additional shadow copies of lawful intercept channels, effectively allowing the attackers to monitor conversations without triggering standard surveillance alerts. The modified system intercepted calls to and from approximately 100 high-profile individuals, including then Prime Minister Costas Karamanlis, senior military officers, civil rights activists, and journalists.

The exploitation method was particularly sophisticated in its utilization of legitimate lawful intercept interfaces without triggering monitoring systems. The attackers implemented complex call routing to conceal surveillance activities while maintaining normal operations. Through advanced techniques, they avoided detection in system logs and modified core switch software without disrupting services. What made this attack particularly concerning was its ability to operate within the legitimate lawful intercept framework while completely bypassing all standard security controls and audit mechanisms.

The incident remained undetected for ten months until a system update failed due to the presence of the rogue software. The subsequent investigation revealed that standard security audit procedures had been bypassed, and monitoring systems had been compromised. This prolonged period of undetected surveillance highlighted significant gaps in the operator's security monitoring capabilities.

Vodafone's response was comprehensive, though initially controversial. Their immediate removal of the rogue software, while intended to protect customer privacy, was later criticized as it destroyed potential evidence that might have helped identify the perpetrators. The operator subsequently implemented enhanced security monitoring systems across all exchanges and conducted a complete overhaul of lawful intercept procedures and access controls. A dedicated security operations center was established to provide 24/7 monitoring of network operations, with particular focus on lawful intercept systems.

The financial implications were substantial, with compensation payments exceeding €76 million to affected individuals. Beyond direct costs, Vodafone introduced mandatory security audits by external firms and developed new incident response procedures that became a model for other operators globally. The company also invested heavily in employee training and awareness programs, particularly focusing on the handling of lawful intercept systems and sensitive network operations.

The regulatory impact reshaped the telecommunications security landscape across Europe. New telecommunications security legislation was introduced in Greece, leading to enhanced oversight of lawful intercept systems across the European Union. The incident prompted the implementation of stricter auditing requirements for telecom operators and the development of new security standards for lawful intercept systems. Perhaps most significantly, it led to the creation of mandatory incident reporting frameworks that have since become standard practice globally.

SS7 global banking fraud

The **Signaling System 7 (SS7)** banking fraud of 2016 represents a watershed moment in telecommunications security, exposing fundamental vulnerabilities in the global signaling infrastructure that had existed since its inception. The incident particularly affected German banking customers, but its implications resonated throughout the global telecommunications and banking industries. The attack demonstrated how legacy protocols designed in an era of implicit trust could be weaponized in modern digital banking scenarios.

The attackers exploited inherent vulnerabilities in the SS7 protocol's location updating and SMS interception capabilities. By manipulating the location update request messages within the SS7 network, the attackers could effectively redirect SMS messages containing two-factor authentication codes to their own devices. The exploitation process involved multiple steps; first, the attackers would obtain banking credentials through conventional phishing methods. Then, using compromised SS7 access points, they would initiate location update procedures that would redirect the victim's SMS messages to networks under their control.

The technical sophistication of the attack lay in its ability to manipulate core network signaling without raising immediate alarms. The attackers utilized legitimate SS7 messages and procedures, making the malicious traffic indistinguishable from normal roaming operations. They specifically targeted the **Mobile Application Part (MAP)** of

SS7, exploiting functions typically used for legitimate subscriber location tracking and SMS delivery.

The fraud resulted in significant financial losses, with German banks reporting unauthorized transactions exceeding €40 million. However, the true impact extended far beyond immediate financial damages. The incident exposed how vulnerabilities in telecommunications infrastructure could undermine security measures in other sectors, particularly banking and financial services. Many banks had relied heavily on SMS-based two-factor authentication, considering it a secure channel for delivering one-time passwords.

In response to the attack, German telecom operators implemented extensive security measures. Deutsche Telekom and other carriers deployed SS7 firewalls with advanced filtering capabilities and established dedicated security monitoring teams for their signaling networks. They also implemented real-time analytics to detect and block suspicious SS7 messages, particularly those attempting to manipulate subscriber location or intercept messages.

The banking sector's response was equally comprehensive. Major banks accelerated their transition away from SMS-based authentication toward app-based solutions and hardware tokens. Some institutions implemented additional verification steps for high-value transactions, including callback verification for suspicious activities. The incident also led to closer cooperation between telecommunications providers and financial institutions, resulting in the establishment of joint security working groups and threat intelligence sharing mechanisms.

The GSMA responded by developing new SS7 security guidelines and establishing a Fraud and Security Group focused on signaling security. These guidelines mandated stricter access controls for SS7 connections, regular security audits, and the implementation of monitoring systems. The incident also accelerated the industry's move toward more secure signaling protocols like Diameter and APIs secured by modern cryptographic methods.

Regulatory bodies across Europe used this incident to strengthen telecommunications security requirements. The **European Union Banking Authority (EBA)** revised its guidelines on payment security, specifically addressing the risks of SMS-based authentication. Telecommunications regulators mandated enhanced security measures for signaling networks and required regular security assessments of critical infrastructure.

China mobile database breach

The China mobile database breach of 2019 stands as one of the most extensive data compromises in telecommunications history, affecting 142 million subscribers and exposing critical customer information. The incident highlighted the vulnerabilities inherent in managing massive customer databases and the cascading effects of improper data access controls in large telecommunications infrastructure.

The breach originated from an improperly secured MongoDB database containing customer records that were accidentally exposed to the internet. The attack vector was particularly concerning as it exploited fundamental misconfigurations in database access controls rather than sophisticated cyberattacks. Investigators discovered that the database had been running with default credentials and was accessible through multiple unauthorized entry points. The exposed data included not just basic subscriber information but detailed call records, location data, billing information, and, in some cases, detailed web browsing histories.

What made this breach particularly severe was the real-time nature of the exposed data. The compromised database was not just a static backup but an active system handling current subscriber information. The attackers maintained access to the system for approximately six weeks before detection, during, which they could monitor and extract real-time customer data. This included the ability to track the location information of subscribers through cell tower connection data, effectively creating a massive surveillance capability.

China mobile's initial response faced criticism for its lack of transparency and delayed notification to affected customers. However, the subsequent remediation efforts were comprehensive. The company established a dedicated incident response team comprising over 500 security experts and engineers. They conducted a complete audit of all database systems, implementing new access control protocols and encryption standards. The company also rebuilt its database architecture, moving to a zero-trust security model with segregated access levels and continuous monitoring.

The financial impact was substantial, with direct costs exceeding $125 million in technical remediation alone. Regulatory fines amounted to $7.5 million, but the longer-term impact on customer trust and market reputation proved far more significant. The company implemented a comprehensive customer compensation program, offering affected subscribers free identity protection services and credit monitoring for three years.

The incident prompted China's Ministry of Industry and Information Technology to implement stricter data protection regulations for telecommunications providers. These new regulations mandated annual security audits, encryption of all customer data, and implementation of advanced threat detection systems. The requirements extended to third-party vendors and contractors, creating a more comprehensive security ecosystem.

Global SIM swap attacks

The coordinated SIM swap attacks of 2020 represented one of the most sophisticated and financially damaging campaigns in telecommunications history. Unlike previous isolated incidents, these attacks demonstrated a complex interplay of social engineering, insider threats, and technical exploits, affecting over 400,000 customers across twelve major operators globally, with financial losses exceeding $200 million. The scope and complexity of these attacks marked a significant evolution in telecommunications fraud, combining traditional social engineering with advanced technical exploitation of operating systems.

The attackers employed a multi-staged approach that began months before the actual SIM swaps, with an initial phase involving extensive reconnaissance of target operators' procedures and systems. They specifically identified operators using legacy subscriber management systems that lacked modern authentication protocols and those with decentralized customer service operations. This meticulous planning phase allowed the attackers to map out vulnerabilities across multiple operators and create a coordinated attack strategy that would prove devastating in its execution.

The technical exploitation involved multiple sophisticated attack vectors targeting various aspects of the operating systems. The primary attack vector focused on the operators' subscriber management systems through compromised customer service credentials. The attackers exploited vulnerabilities in the password reset mechanisms of these systems, using social engineering to obtain emergency access codes. They specifically targeted systems using the older MAP protocols that lacked strong authentication mechanisms for SIM changes. A secondary vector involved compromising the **customer operations and revenue systems** (**CORS**) platforms, where attackers exploited vulnerabilities in the API interfaces between customer service applications and core network elements.

The human element of the attack demonstrated unprecedented sophistication in its approach to social engineering and insider recruitment. The attackers created elaborate fake personas, complete with forged corporate emails and LinkedIn profiles, to target customer service representatives. These personas were used in spear-phishing attacks and to establish long-term relationships with key personnel in customer service operations. The insider threat component expanded through the dark web recruitment of customer service agents, offering substantial payments for access to subscriber management systems. Subsequent investigations revealed a complex network of compromised employees across different organizational levels, from front-line customer service to IT support staff.

The attacks unfolded in three distinct waves, beginning with operators in Southeast Asia in March 2020, followed by European operators in June 2020, and culminating with North American carriers in September 2020. Each wave demonstrated increasing sophistication, with the attackers learning from and adapting to the security measures implemented after each phase. This progressive evolution made the attacks particularly difficult to defend against, as the attackers constantly modified their techniques to bypass new security measures.

The financial impact was most severe in cryptocurrency theft, with attackers specifically targeting known cryptocurrency investors and exchange operators. By gaining control of victims' phone numbers, the attackers could bypass SMS-based two-factor authentication on cryptocurrency exchanges and wallet services. The largest single theft amounted to $18 million in Bitcoin from a Hong Kong-based cryptocurrency trader, but the cumulative losses across all affected users far exceeded this figure. The targeting of cryptocurrency holders demonstrated the attackers' strategic approach to maximizing financial gains from their operations.

The response from affected operators was comprehensive and far-reaching. Immediate measures included the implementation of biometric verification for all SIM swap requests, mandatory cooling-off periods between requests, enhanced monitoring of subscriber management system access, and the implementation of blockchain-based SIM activation verification. Long-term measures involved a complete overhaul of SIM replacement procedures, the implementation of AI-based fraud detection systems, the introduction of hardware security keys for customer service system access, and the development of secure API gateways for all subscriber management operations.

Customer protection measures were equally extensive, including the provision of free credit monitoring services for affected customers, the establishment of dedicated fraud response teams, the implementation of customer notification systems for any account changes, and the creation of compensation funds for affected customers. These measures were designed not only to address immediate concerns but also to rebuild customer trust in operator security systems.

The regulatory impact of these attacks led to significant changes in the telecommunications security landscape. New requirements were implemented for mandatory waiting periods for SIM swaps, multi-factor authentication in subscriber management systems, regular auditing of customer service operations, and mandatory reporting of all SIM swap attempts. Perhaps most significantly, the attacks led to the formation of the **Global Telco Security Alliance (GTSA)**, a consortium of operators sharing threat intelligence and best practices for preventing SIM swap attacks. The GSMA also developed new security guidelines specifically addressing SIM swap vulnerabilities, making them part of the GSMA Security Accreditation Scheme.

European roaming fraud incident

The European Roaming Fraud Incident of 2021 exposed critical vulnerabilities in international roaming architectures and wholesale billing systems, resulting in fraudulent calls worth €145 million and affecting 23 operators across Europe. This sophisticated attack exploited the complex nature of inter-operator roaming agreements and the inherent trust relationships between telecommunications providers, demonstrating how legacy wholesale billing systems could be manipulated at scale.

The attack's sophistication lay in its exploitation of the **General Packet Radio Service roaming exchange (GRX)** infrastructure. The perpetrators established legitimate **mobile virtual network operator (MVNO)** operations in multiple small European countries, gaining access to the GRX network and roaming agreements. They then exploited vulnerabilities in the **Transferred Account Procedure (TAP)** files used for wholesale billing between operators. By manipulating these files and exploiting delays in the clearing process, they could generate massive volumes of fraudulent traffic while avoiding detection by traditional fraud management systems.

The technical execution involved compromising the SS7 network to manipulate **Mobile Station Roaming Numbers (MSRNs)** and route calls through specific networks where they had established control. The attackers created a complex web of traffic routing that made it extremely difficult to trace the origin of fraudulent calls. They specifically targeted weekend periods when fraud detection teams typically operated with reduced staffing, allowing them to generate significant traffic volumes before detection.

The financial impact extended beyond the immediate €145 million in fraudulent calls. Operators faced additional costs in investigating and remedying the vulnerabilities, implementing new security measures, and managing customer complaints. The incident severely disrupted the inter-operator trust framework that had been the foundation of international roaming services. Several smaller operators faced significant financial strain due to the delayed recognition of fraudulent charges in their wholesale billing systems.

The response from the European telecommunications community was unprecedented in its scale and coordination. The GSMA established an emergency response team to coordinate actions across affected operators. This led to the development of the **Real-time Roaming Data Exchange** (**RUDE**) system, implementing blockchain technology to provide immediate visibility of roaming activities across networks. The incident also accelerated the adoption of **Billing and Charging Evolution** (**BCE**) standards, moving away from the traditional TAP files to more secure, real-time billing mechanisms.

VoLTE protocol exploitation

The VoLTE Protocol Exploitation of 2022 represented a significant escalation in attacks targeting **IP Multimedia Subsystem** (**IMS**) infrastructures. The incident affected multiple tier-1 operators globally, causing service disruption for 18 million subscribers and demonstrating critical vulnerabilities in VoLTE implementations. The attack was particularly significant as it compromised both service availability and call privacy, leading to potential surveillance capabilities.

The technical exploitation centered on vulnerabilities in the **Session Initiation Protocol** (**SIP**) implementation within IMS cores. The attackers discovered ways to manipulate SIP headers and **Session Description Protocol** (**SDP**) parameters to bypass authentication mechanisms and inject malicious traffic into the VoLTE service plane. They specifically targeted the interface between **Proxy-Call Session Control Function** (**P-CSCF**) and **Serving-Call Session Control Function** (**S-CSCF**), exploiting weaknesses in the security association establishment process.

What made this attack particularly devastating was its ability to leverage legitimate-looking SIP messages to create a cascade of service failures. The attackers implemented a sophisticated traffic amplification technique that could trigger resource exhaustion in the IMS core components. This led to widespread service degradation, affecting not just voice services but also emergency calling capabilities in several regions.

The response required unprecedented cooperation between operators, vendors, and security researchers. A major technical overhaul of VoLTE implementations was undertaken, including the implementation of enhanced SIP message validation, stronger authentication mechanisms for IMS registration, and the development of new anomaly detection systems specifically designed for VoLTE traffic patterns. The incident led to the creation of the VoLTE Security Alliance, a collaborative effort between operators and vendors to develop more secure VoLTE implementations.

Path forward

As we conclude our comprehensive examination of telecommunications security evolution, from the first analog networks to today's sophisticated 5G ecosystems, the criticality of robust security frameworks has never been more apparent. The transformation of telecommunications from simple voice services handling 20 million subscribers in the 1G era to today's complex networks supporting over 4.7 billion 4G and 1.8 billion 5G connections underscores the massive scale at which security must operate.

The transition from hardware-centric networks to software-defined infrastructure has fundamentally reshaped the security landscape. Our analysis of major security incidents, from the sophisticated Vodafone Greece wiretapping scandal to the recent Open RAN breaches, demonstrates how this evolution has introduced new vulnerabilities while also providing tools for enhanced security controls. The financial impact of these breaches, exceeding billions in cumulative losses, emphasizes that security can no longer be an afterthought but must be embedded in the network's fundamental architecture.

The convergence of IT and telecommunications, evidenced by the widespread adoption of **software-defined networking (SDN)**, **network functions virtualization (NFV)**, and cloud-native technologies, has erased traditional security boundaries. Modern service providers must defend against threats spanning multiple domains, from legacy SS7 vulnerabilities exploited in banking frauds to sophisticated API attacks in Open RAN deployments. This convergence is further complicated by the massive scale of operations, with services like FTTH reaching 850 million subscribers globally and VoWiFi supported by over 200 operators across 100 countries.

The series of major security incidents we have examined, from the €145 million European roaming fraud to the VoLTE protocol exploitation affecting 18 million subscribers, highlights how security breaches can impact both operator finances and customer trust. These incidents have driven fundamental changes in how the industry approaches security, leading to the formation of global security alliances and the development of new security frameworks.

Looking ahead, several critical challenges and opportunities demand attention:

- The rise of Open RAN and disaggregated networks requires new security paradigms. While these technologies offer greater flexibility and vendor choice, the 2023 Open RAN security breach affecting 24 million subscribers demonstrates the critical need for robust security controls at previously unexposed interface points.

- The increasing role of edge computing in 5G and future 6G networks pushes security requirements closer to the network edge. With over 2.3 million 5G base stations in China alone, securing the edge infrastructure becomes paramount for protecting the entire network ecosystem.

- Quantum computing's emergence poses both threats and opportunities. While it threatens current cryptographic systems, it also offers new tools for secure communication through quantum key distribution, particularly crucial for protecting the massive volume of sensitive data traversing modern networks.

- AI and ML have become essential tools for security operations, enabling real-time threat detection and automated response across networks serving billions of connections. However, as demonstrated by recent incidents, these technologies must be implemented thoughtfully to avoid creating new vulnerabilities.

- Advanced security monitoring must evolve beyond traditional perimeter-based approaches. As networks become increasingly distributed, monitoring strategies need to incorporate Zero Trust principles and continuous validation across all network segments. The integration of behavioral analytics capable of detecting anomalies across billions of daily connection events will be crucial for identifying sophisticated threats that evade signature-based detection.

- Security testing methodologies require fundamental transformation in the era of network slicing and dynamic service provisioning. Automated, continuous testing that can validate security controls across virtualized network functions serving hundreds of millions of subscribers will replace traditional point-in-time assessments. The industry must develop standardized testing frameworks specifically designed for the unique characteristics of telecommunications infrastructure.

- SIEM and SOC capabilities face unprecedented scale challenges as they integrate with network operations centers. Modern telecommunications SOCs must process and correlate events from diverse sources spanning physical infrastructure, virtualized network functions, and cloud environments. The convergence of security and network operations will drive the evolution of integrated platforms capable of providing unified visibility across domains serving billions of connections.

- CI/CD pipeline security becomes critical as telecommunications infrastructure adopts DevOps methodologies. With the average tier-1 operator managing thousands of software releases annually across their virtualized infrastructure, securing the development pipeline against supply chain attacks and ensuring proper security validation before deployment becomes essential for maintaining network integrity and service availability.

- AI-driven security automation will evolve from reactive to predictive capabilities. Next-generation security systems will anticipate threats based on subtle pattern recognition across vast datasets of network behavior. However, the telecommunications industry must address the unique challenges of implementing AI in critical infrastructure, including explainability requirements, model bias, and the potential for adversarial manipulation of AI security systems.

Perhaps the most important lesson from our analysis is that successful security implementations require a balance between theory and practice. The real-world security breaches we have studied demonstrate that while perfect security might be unattainable, practical, risk-based approaches can provide effective protection while enabling business objectives.

As we move forward, security will continue to be a critical enabler of telecommunications innovation. Service providers must remain vigilant, adaptive, and proactive in their security approach. The frameworks, architectures, and recommendations presented in this book, built upon lessons learned from major security incidents and evolving network technologies, provide a roadmap for this journey. However, the specific path will depend on each organization's unique circumstances, scale of operations, and security requirements.

In this era of unprecedented connectivity, where telecommunications form the backbone of global digital infrastructure, security is not just about protecting networks and services; it is about maintaining the trust that underlies all digital communications. As we have seen through our analysis of major security incidents and global deployment statistics, this trust, once broken, has far-reaching implications for both operators and subscribers. The future of telecommunications security will be shaped by how well we learn from these experiences while adapting to new challenges in an ever-evolving threat landscape.

Conclusion

As we reach the end of our journey through telecommunication service provider security, the global landscape reveals both promise and peril. With mobile penetration exceeding 7.3 billion connections worldwide and fixed broadband serving over 1.2 billion households, the scale of telecommunication infrastructure represents both a remarkable achievement and a significant security challenge. The rapid adoption of 5G networks is projected to serve 25% of global connections by 2025, further expanding the attack surface in unprecedented ways.

The major breaches we have examined from the 2016 SS7 protocol exploitation that exposed cellular communications to the 2021 roaming fraud incident affecting multiple tier-1 carriers share common threads: insufficient security-by-design principles, delayed patch management, and inadequate threat monitoring. These incidents have collectively affected hundreds of millions of subscribers and damaged consumer trust in telecommunications security.

The path forward demands a fundamental shift in approach. First, security must migrate from perimeter-based models to Zero Trust architectures that verify every access request regardless of origin. Second, telecom providers must embrace continuous security validation through automated testing and threat hunting. Third, international cooperation on security standards must evolve beyond recommendations to enforceable frameworks with meaningful accountability.

As telecommunications increasingly underpins critical infrastructure from smart grids to healthcare delivery networks, the stakes of security failures multiply beyond privacy concerns to potential threats to human safety. The industry stands at an inflection point: either proactively address systemic vulnerabilities through transformative security practices or face increasingly consequential breaches as adversaries continue their relentless evolution.

Index

www.ingramcontent.com/pod-product-compliance
Lightning Source LLC
Chambersburg PA
CBHW061737210326
41599CB00034B/6712

* 9 7 8 9 3 6 5 8 9 7 7 4 6 *